GAMES FOR BUSINESS
AND ECONOMICS

GAMES FOR BUSINESS AND ECONOMICS

ROY GARDNER
Indiana University

John Wiley & Sons, Inc.
New York · Chichester · Brisbane · Toronto · Singapore

Acquisitions Editor	Whitney Blake
Marketing Manager	Debra Riegert
Senior Production Editor	Jennifer Knapp
Design	Initial Graphics Systems, Inc.
Manufacturing Manager	Susan Stetzer
Illustration Coordinator	Rosa Bryant

This book was set in 10/12 New Baskerville by J.M. Post Graphics, a division of Cardinal Communications Group, Inc. and printed and bound by Malloy Lithographing. The cover was printed by NEBC.

Library of Congress Cataloging in Publication Data:
Gardner, Roy, 1947–
    Games for business and economics / Roy Gardner
        p.   cm.
    Includes bibliographical references
    ISBN 0-471-31150-2 (paper)
    1. Managerial economics.   2. Game theory   3. Economics,
Mathematical.   I. Title.
    HD30.22.G37   1995
    658.4'0353–dc20
                                                    94-22110
                                                        CIP

Printed in the United States of America

10   9   8   7

To Carla, Sara, and James

Preface

This book is based on the economics, managerial economics, and game theory courses I have taught over the last dozen years at Iowa State University, the J.L. Kellogg Graduate School of Management, Northwestern University, and Indiana University. I have taught the ideas of game theory at every level: advanced undergraduate, M.B.A., and Ph.D. For Ph.D. students, I have used Friedman's admirable *Game Theory with Applications to Economics*. For advanced undergraduates—both business majors and economics majors—and for M.B.A. students, however, I was never satisfied with the textbooks available. The feeling was widespread that this was a market terribly underserved by both publishers and game theorists. My desire for a better resource—together with the interest on the part of several publishers all at once—led to this book.

The chief purpose of this book is to enable the student to set up and solve games, especially games that arise in business and economics. Setting up a game requires considerable modeling skills, as well as the ability to implement a certain format, the form of the game. I try to develop both sets of skills with frequent applications and examples of setups that have proved their value in my own research and in the research of others. Solving a game requires some mathematical performance on the part of the student, rather like that involved in calculus. I use an analogous framework of necessary condition (equilibrium) and sufficient conditions (e.g., undominated strategies, symmetry, subgame perfection) to motivate solutions. The biggest difference from calculus is that a game may have more than one solution, and these solutions may differ in value from one another. This situation, which does not arise in 1-person maximization problems, is rather endemic to n-person problems. Although this multiplicity may create consternation in a beginner, it is unavoidable.

The advanced undergraduates in my classes have come from a variety of backgrounds, as have the M.B.A. students. All have either had some economics background, or acquired some right away. A year of introductory economics at the level of, say, Dornbusch, Fischer, and Schmalensee's *Introduction to Economics,* should suffice for the economics background. All users of this text, of whatever background, should have completed a year of college mathematics. At Indiana, this prerequisite is satisfied by a two-course sequence in finite mathematics (with an emphasis on probability) and calculus, required of all arts and sciences majors and business majors for graduation. Students need to know how to differentiate the common functions, compute the expected value of a random variable, and solve small systems of linear equations. I have made every effort to keep the mathematical load at precisely this level. In this respect I follow Max Black, who once told me "You mustn't hide behind your equations."

The target audience for this book includes any student who is serious about strategy. This covers a lot of interests—from students who want to take on the casinos, to students who want to be lawyers, to students who want to earn Ph.D.'s in economics, to students who want an M.B.A. and a business career. For this reason, the book has to do a lot of things for a lot of different people. Thus it draws on very different strands of literature and walks of life. As a student, I learned game theory the theorem–proof way, but as a teacher I prefer to liven things up with examples. The examples range from the Bible to Wall Street. I especially like to bring in current events—President Clinton getting American Airlines and its flight attendants to go to arbitration, OPEC dropping its quotas, and the proposal to expand the UN Security Council, to name just three. These are events that shed some light on game theory, but they are also events on which game theory sheds light. Naturally, each instructor is free to supply his or her own favorite examples, or to skip the examples entirely, depending on teaching style.

Unfortunately, given the mathematical prerequisites, this book is somewhat above the level of the general reader. Heaven knows that some parts of the Beltway, for instance, could use sounder strategic analysis than is to be found nowadays. My conscience in this regard is cleared by that fact that the general reader is already well-served by Dixit and Nalebuff's *Thinking Strategically* and McMillan's *Strategy for Managers.*

I have accumulated a mountain of debts in the writing of this book, which I can hardly repay here. I thank my coauthors of long standing, Molly Morris, Elinor Ostrom, Roger Stover and James Walker, with whom working with has been so fruitful and has had a positive influence on this book. I thank the following for research support: Dean, College of Arts and Sciences, Dean of Faculties, and Vice President for Research, Indiana University; National Science Foundation, grant SES 8921884; and United States Department of Agriculture, cooperative agreement 43-3AEM-1-80078. I thank the Department of Economics, University of Mannheim, Germany, and in particular Professor Juergen von Hagen. It was during a very fruitful stay in his department that I was able to finish the first draft of the book, free from all distractions. The seminar that he organized, focusing on the book, provided excellent feedback at a very crucial moment. I thank the participants of this seminar—Majdid Amir, Boris Maurer,

Tone Dieckman, Mr. von Kalkreuth, Juergen Stanovsky, Stephan Monissen, Ulrich Schwalbe, Professor Roland Vaubel, Professor Siegfried Berninghaus, Professor Volker Boehm, and Professor Juergen von Hagen—for their many improvements to the first draft. I thank the Special Research Project 303 of the University of Bonn, and especially Professor Reinhard Selten. My stay in Bonn enabled me to finish the final draft of the book in a very short span of time. In addition, my intellectual debt to Professor Selten should be clear to all. I thank my colleagues—Robert Becker, for useful discussions and for testing the book in class, and Fred Witney, for generously allowing me time for an interview. I thank Friedrich Breyer, Sara Gardner, Rob Robbins, and Kristin Youngquist for comments on individual chapters, and Claudia Keser, who pointed out a major error. I thank audiences at the Universities of Constance, Dortmund, and Bonn, for their suggestions to improve chapters presented there. I thank Patty Dalecki, for showing me how to print the various drafts and allowing me to do so on her machine.

A number of colleagues have reviewed drafts of the manuscript, and their comments have resulted in a substantially improved book. I thank all of these reviewers for their helpful comments:

Michael Baye
Pennsylvania State University

Jeffrey Banks
University of Rochester

Andreas Blume
University of Iowa

Peter Coughlin
University of Maryland

Andrew Daughety
University of Iowa

Nicholas Feltovich
University of Pittsburgh

James Hartigan
University of Oklahoma

Sumit Joshi
George Washington University

Ehud Kalai
Northwestern University

Andrew McLennan
University of Minnesota

Stephen Morris
University of Pennsylvania

Larry Samuelson
University of Wisconsin

Dale Stahl
University of Texas

M.A. Vigneault
Bishops University

Henry Wan
Cornell University

Inigo Zapater
Brown University

I thank the entire team at John Wiley & Sons, Inc., for their tireless efforts on behalf of this project, from acquisition to production to marketing. I especially thank my Acquiring editor at Wiley, Whitney Blake. Without her enthusiastic support and incredible energy, this book would not exist. The other Wiley professionals with whom I have worked, including Kevin O'Brien, Paul Constantine, Ellen Ford, Sigmund Malinowski, Karen Allman, Jennifer Knapp, and Jenifer Cooke, have been extremely helpful.

Finally, I thank my family, who had to endure more than the usual unpleasantness, as I became increasingly obsessed with writing this book. I hope to have written a good book, and I apologize in advance to all if I have not.

Guide for the Reader

Although it is a lot easier to learn game theory in class, with a professor, it is possible to learn the theory by reading on your own. Here are some tips for those readers who are doing just that.

The material in Chapters 1 and 2, up to section 2.9, is crucial to all that follows. Do not venture into later chapters until you have understood this basic material. From section 2.9 onward, there are plenty of choices. I have intentionally put more material in the book than will interest every reader, so that you can pick and choose. The appendixes provide a good example of this flexibility. If you are interested in Blackjack and Poker, then you should definitely read the appendixes to Chapters 2 and 3; if not, then you can safely skip them. If you are interested in game experiments, you should definitely read the appendixes to Chapters 4, 6, 8, 11, and 12; if not, again, you can skip these. Finally, if you are a devoted reader of a newspaper such as *The Wall Street Journal,* the *Washington Post,* or *The New York Times,* many of the business and economics events covered in this book will be familiar to you and you need only skim this material. This category includes the current events material presented in section 5.8 (cigarette prices), section 7.4 (OPEC drops quotas), sections 9.7 and 15.5 (RJR/Nabisco takeover), section 12.8 (United States–Japan trade talks), and section 14.8 (Bosnian peace plans).

Some parts of the book are rather more mathematical than average, and can safely be skipped by a reader who doesn't have to study for an examination. These include section 2.9 (fixed points), the appendix to Chapter 5 (contraction mappings), sections 8.2 and 8.4 (simple differential equations), section 9.6 (Bayes's rule), section 14.1 (Lagrange multiplier), section 14.6 (set functions), and section 16.8 (the combinations function).

Given these basic guidelines, two tracks are available. In both tracks, you read Chapters 1 through 7. In the first track, the one that emphasizes cooperation, you then read Chapters 12 through 15 and sections 16.6 through 16.8. This track essentially covers all the games whose solutions are efficient. In the second track, which emphasizes noncooperation, you read Chapters 8 through

11 and Chapter 16 up to section 16.6. This track essentially covers all the games whose solutions are inefficient. This track is a little bit tougher going, reflecting the fact that building efficiency into the solution of a game makes that solution easier to find. Of course, there are many other possibilities, depending on your interests. Whatever your choice, I hope you enjoy reading about game theory.

Contents

PART ONE

Basic Game Theory

CHAPTER 1

❌❌❌

An Introduction to Games and Their Theory

❌ 1.1 What Is a Game? ■ ■ ■ ■ ■ ■ ■ ■ ■ ■ ■ ■ ■ ■ ■ ■ ■ ■

In ordinary English, a **game** is any pastime or diversion. This definition covers a lot of terrain. Let's try to organize it somewhat. We can start by identifying different varieties of games. First, there are games played on a board, *board games*. These include Chess, Checkers, and Monopoly.[1] Chess and Checkers have exactly two players, whereas Monopoly can have anywhere from two to eight players. In Chess and Checkers, the outcome of the game is win, lose, or draw: either one player wins and the other loses, or both players draw. In Monopoly, the player with the most assets at the end of the game is the winner; all the rest are losers. Second, there are games played with cards, *card games*. These include Solitaire, Poker, and Blackjack. Solitaire is special, since it has

---

[1] Games have proper names, just as people do, so we capitalize them in this book.

only one player. Poker and Blackjack can have two to seven players—you study them in the next two chapters. Third, there are games played on a video screen against a computer, *video games*. These games are rather like Solitaire, in that they have only one human player. Computers can play many games; later in this chapter we see how and why. Finally, there are games played on a field or a court, *field games*. These include baseball, football, basketball, and hockey, the major professional sports in the United States. Field games are played by two aggregate players, the opposing teams, which are composed of individuals, the members of each team.

All these things are called games, so, according to Aristotle's theory of categories, they must have some feature in common that brings them all under the same name.[2] Let's look for what this feature, or set of features, might be. First, all games have *rules*. The rules specify what a player can and cannot do. A player who breaks the rules is penalized—again, according to the rules—and in extreme cases can be removed from the game altogether. Second, in every game *strategy matters*. There are good and bad strategies, and players can be and are criticized for choosing bad strategies. One of the tasks of game theory is to tell the difference between good and bad strategies. Third, there is an *outcome* to the game, for example, one player wins and the other loses. Fourth, this outcome depends on the strategies chosen by each of the players, a phenomenon we call **strategic interdependence.** Even a bad strategy can win if the opponent chooses a worse one. We combine these features to define a game as *any rule-governed situation with a well-defined outcome, characterized by strategic interdependence.* This describes the Aristotelian category to which games belong.

A lot of things that aren't called games in ordinary English satisfy this definition. Consider firms competing in the same business. There are rules governing their competition, including the law of contracts and property and government regulations, which specify what a firm can and cannot do. A firm that breaks the rules can be penalized, and in extreme cases, such as bankruptcy, can even be removed from the game. The outcome of firms' competition is typically something observable, such as the amount of money each firm makes or the amount of market share each firm has. These outcomes are often reported in a firm's financial statements. As we will see, a firm's strategies can include price, quantity, advertising, which markets it operates in, what kinds of contracts it offers its employees—a host of things. Finally—and this is the most important truth in this book—*the outcome for a given firm depends not just on what strategy it chooses, but also on what strategies its competitors choose.* A firm can have the greatest product line in the world and still get clobbered by the competition if its strategies are no good. When firms compete in a market, they operate in a rule-governed situation, with well-defined outcomes, characterized by strategic interdependence. We have a word for this: it's a *game,* in this case a

---

[2] See Aristotle, *Categories and De Interpretatione* (J. L. Ackrill, ed.) (Oxford: Oxford University Press, 1963).

business game. Firms competing in a market are just as much players in a game as are Poker players seated around a poker table. Indeed, the stakes in a business are almost always a lot higher. What began as a metaphor at the beginning of this century has become literally and categorically true.

Let's take an example that works on both sides of the literal and metaphorical aspect of *game*: a professional sports franchise, the Chicago Bulls.[3] The Bulls play professional basketball in the National Basketball Association, and play it very well, having won the championship for 3 straight years. The Bulls are also a corporation, owned by private investors, mostly from the Chicago area, which is in business to make money each year. The more games the Bulls win on the basketball court, the more money the owners of the Bulls make from ticket sales, broadcasting rights, and concessions. Although winning at basketball isn't the same thing as winning in business, the two are closely related in this case.

Another example, not at all sports related, is the cola industry. Cola was invented in Atlanta in 1886. The inventor later went on to found Coca-Cola Corporation. Other cola drinks entered the market soon thereafter. Since the 1920s, Coke and Pepsi, with the largest market shares and highest profits, have dominated the U.S. market and have battled head-to-head for cola business. Their competition, commonly known as the cola wars,[4] has included price wars, new product competition (Pepsi Clear is the latest entry), new packaging (the 2-liter plastic bottle), and advertising campaigns (Coke Is It! The Pepsi Generation). How much money Pepsi makes from its cola operations depends on what Coke does, and vice versa. This is strategic interdependence manifested in the market.

Business isn't the only arena in which we see games in the extended sense—they are at the very heart of economics, too. Think of domestic economic negotiations, such as those between the White House and Congress on domestic economic policy issues, for example, the budget, or between the White House and the Fed on monetary policy. Think of international economic negotiations, such as those among the G-7 countries, involving international trade and finance.[5] **Economic negotiations** such as these have all the makings of a game. There are rules (domestic and international law) governing what each party to the negotiations can do. Strategy matters—if you are absent from the negotiations, you should not be surprised if your interests are not represented. There is a clearly defined outcome—the status quo if negotiations break down, some sort of agreement if negotiations are brought to a successful conclusion. Finally, the outcome of negotiations depends not only on what your side does, but on what the other side does, too. Various forms of bargaining, negotiation,

---

[3] All the examples in this book are drawn from real life. You will never encounter the word *widget*, to say nothing of the markets in which these mythological objects are bought and sold.

[4] The title is from J. C. Louis, *The Cola Wars* (New York: Everest House, 1980).

[5] The G-7 countries are the world's seven largest economies (United States, Japan, Germany, France, United Kingdom, Italy, Canada); their representatives meet frequently to negotiate issues that involve economic relations among them.

and arbitration—all games with at least an element of cooperation—are studied in the last third of this book.

▚ 1.2 What Is Game Theory, and Why? ■ ■ ■ ■ ■ ■ ■ ■ ■

Game theory is the science that studies games and takes games seriously enough to solve them. Game theory is a product of the twentieth century, the brainchild of one of the century's greatest minds, John von Neumann.[6] Von Neumann discovered one of the central regularities of games, the solution for 2-person, zero-sum games, which is covered in Chapter 2. He provided the framework that this book uses to study games in general. Together with Oskar Morgenstern, his fellow refugee from fascism, Von Neumann was the first to solve games in business and economics.[7]

Game theory is a lot like calculus. We use calculus to solve maximum and minimum problems. We use game theory to solve games. A solution of a game should tell each player what outcome to expect and how to achieve that outcome, just as the solution to a maximum problem should tell what the maximum value is and how to achieve it. Game theory began as applied mathematics, which this book attempts to make as user-friendly as possible, using the adage that you should tell beginners the truth, but not the whole truth. If you are a beginner and you master this book, then you are ready to go on to more advanced texts, such as those listed in the suggestions for further reading at the end. At the beginning, you are spared the theoretical niceties and the jargon you don't yet need or can't yet appreciate. Game theory is a subject that gets deep fast enough as it is. Think of it as a swimming pool in which even the shallow end can be over your head.

Not only is game theory a lot like calculus, it actually uses calculus as part of the process of solving a game. This should come as no surprise. Players in a game are trying to do the best they can, to get the best possible outcome; that is a maximization problem, one for each player. A game with three players is like three maximization problems in calculus all going on at the same time. This means that solving a game is harder than solving a maximization problem—a lot harder, which is why it has its own theory.

---

[6]Besides creating game theory, von Neumann also provided the mathematical foundation for quantum mechanics, designed the implosion lens for the atomic bomb, and created the architecture of the computer. An excellent biography is Norman McRae, *John von Neumann* (New York: Pantheon Books, 1992.)

[7]The title of their magnum opus, John von Neumann and Oskar Morgenstern, *The Theory of Games and Economic Behavior* (Princeton: Princeton University Press, 1944), shows how much their work was driven by the possibility of economic applications. Later on, after the creation of game theory, it became apparent that earlier economists, among them Cournot, Bertrand, Edgeworth, and Stackelberg, had found solutions to games also.

Although game theory began as applied mathematics, it has become a dominant mode of reasoning in business and economics. The well-known macroeconomist Robert Lucas argues that the most important contributions to macroeconomics since Keynes have been the result of formulating macroeconomic problems as games and then solving those games.[8] It is easy to see why this is true. In the heyday of Keynesian economics, economists designed policies for the government to use assuming that the public's expectations, government policies of other countries, and the like would not be affected. This assumption is tantamount to assuming that the public and other governments are not players in a game. We know better now. Expectations held by the public, which show up, for instance, in the investment and portfolio decisions taken in the private sector, make an enormous difference to the outcome of economic policy. When something is a game—and the entire economy surely is one—you have to treat it as a game if you are going to understand it at all well.

Another example, which arises both in business and in economics, is called *mechanism design*. Suppose you have a certain goal in mind, for example, collecting $1.5 trillion in taxes, and you want to achieve that goal as inexpensively as possible. You need to design a mechanism—here, the tax system—to achieve the goal. This process involves a game, since taxpayers have strategies that respond to various kinds of taxation. If you don't include taxpayer strategies in your mechanism, you can be sure that it will fail miserably—just as if the Chicago Transit Authority thought it could double revenue by doubling fares. We study one particular kind of mechanism design, incentive-based contracts, in Chapter 10.

There are several purely selfish reasons for studying game theory, above and beyond the desire to know the truth that this science has to offer. These reasons might apply to your job or your career someday—even if you aren't going to be the next Robert Lucas. First and foremost, game theory can improve your strategic decision making. It makes you more aware of when you are in a situation in which strategy matters, to say nothing of making you aware of strategic nuance on the part of your competitors or opponents. Second, it can improve your ability to run a business and to evaluate changes in policy. The phrases "competitive advantage," "everyday low pricing," and "winner's curse" will make a lot more sense to you after they have been strategically explicated (in Chapters 2, 3, and 11, respectively). Finally, game theory can help you become a better economist or a better manager. Game theory is the central paradigm of economics and finance. It contains or informs all the current buzzwords, such as market failure, credibility, incentive contracts, hostile takeovers, and coalition building, to name just a few. And—if you are into that sort of thing—game theory might even make you a better Poker player. Of course, if none of these things appeals to you, then studying game theory is probably not for you.

[8]Lucas is one of the principal architects of the rational expectations revolution in macroeconomics. See his *Models of Business Cycles* (Oxford: Basil Blackwell, 1987).

Like any theory that involves mathematics, there is no royal road to understanding game theory. You have to follow the arguments, understand the proofs, work the problems (there are problems at the end of each chapter), study the examples, and think about it all in terms of your own life and your own work. If you do the work, then you will complete this book knowing how to set up and solve a whole arsenal of games—and even more important, knowing how to think about games in an intelligent way. You won't easily fall prey to strategically unsound thinking; instead, you'll know what embarrassing questions to ask, and when to ask them, when you hear strategic nonsense on stilts.

The book is organized as follows. Part I covers the fundamentals, ideas and techniques that are used throughout game theory. Part II looks at games within games (subgames), repeated games, and games that are out of equilibrium. Part III is especially concerned with games of imperfect information. Part IV focuses on games in which cooperation pays off—negotiation, bargaining, and arbitration. Part V deals with the interaction between games, markets, and politics and introduces the link with micro- and macroeconomics.

This is a lot of material to cover, so let's get started. Theory is something you do, not something you talk about doing. We begin with the simplest possible games, those with a single player and perfect information.

1.3 One-Person Games with Perfect Information ■ ■ ■ ■ ■ ■ ■ ■ ■ ■ ■ ■ ■ ■ ■ ■ ■ ■ ■

Games with a single player are as simple as games get. Such games are *degenerate* in the sense that, even though strategic decisions have to be made, there is no strategic interaction among players. Solitaire provides the clearest example— it's you, the player, against the deck of cards. In any science, it makes sense to start with really simple problems, real morale boosters. Solving these prepares you for tackling tougher problems later on. That's precisely why we start with 1-player games.

The information available to the players in a game makes a big difference to what they can or should do. A player has **perfect information** if he or she knows exactly what has happened every time a decision needs to be made. A game has perfect information if every player in it has perfect information. Chess is a game with perfect information. As long as both players can see the board, they can see exactly what has happened every time they have to make a move.[9] If some player does not have perfect information, then the game is one of **imperfect information.** Poker is a game with imperfect information. One player does not know—unless he or she is cheating—what cards have been dealt to another player. Games with imperfect information are very important, but they

---

[9]There is a version of Chess, called Kriegspiel, in which players do not see the board; Kriegspiel thus has imperfect information.

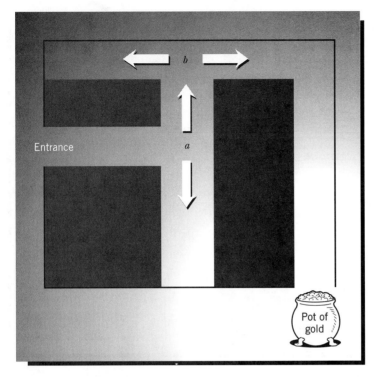

Figure 1.1. The maze.

are more difficult to solve than games with perfect information. In this section we study games with perfect information; later, we tackle games with imperfect information.

As a paradigm for a 1-player game with perfect information, consider a player about to enter the maze in Figure 1.1. Give this player a number, say, 1. Although a number isn't needed to identify a single player, numbers do become useful to identify the players once there are several of them. Action begins when player 1 enters the maze. Player 1's goal is to get to the pot of gold at the end of the maze without running into a wall first. The minute the player runs into a wall, the call is over. The pot of gold is worth M (for money) dollars, and if the player reaches it, the outcome is M. Player 1 gets paid the amount M, which we write

$$u_1(\text{pot of gold}) = M$$

If player 1 runs into a wall, the game ends and the outcome is 0. We write this as

$$u_1(\text{wall}) = 0$$

In this book, and for the vast majority of time in real life, a player prefers more money to less:

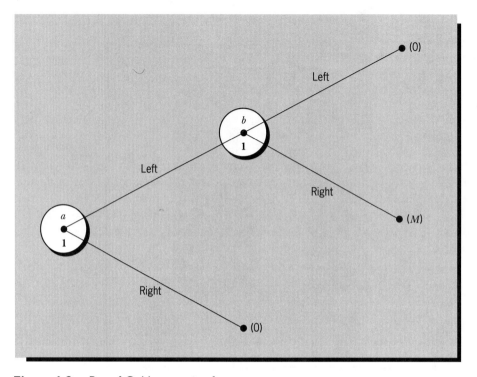

Figure 1.2.   Pot of Gold, extensive form.

$$u_1(\text{pot of gold}) = M > 0 = u_1(\text{wall})$$

These are the two possible outcomes when the player enters the maze shown in Figure 1.1.

Now we are going to walk with player 1 through the maze. Player 1 reaches a *decision point,* marked *a,* soon after entering the maze. At this decision point, player 1 has two choices: go left or go right. If player 1 goes right, he or she runs into a wall and the game ends. If player 1 goes left, a second decision point, marked *b,* is encountered. At this decision point, player 1 can go either left or right. If player 1 goes left, he or she runs into a wall and the game ends. If player 1 goes right, he or she eventually reaches the pot of gold.

Now let's see how game theory looks at this maze. Game theory has a precise way of describing any game, a description called the **extensive form** of the game. Figure 1.2 shows the extensive form of the maze in Figure 1.1. The game is dubbed Pot of Gold. We will walk you through the extensive form of Pot of Gold, and then look at some definitions.

Playing a game is all about the decisions the player makes, so the description of Pot of Gold begins with the first decision point, *a,* shown as the circled *a* and 1 at the left of Figure 1.2. A circle means that some player must make a decision at that point. The number of the player whose decision it is, here, player 1, is included inside the circle. Coming out of this decision point are two straight lines. These straight lines represent the two choices player 1 can make at decision point *a:* left or right. The line labeled Right runs into a wall, causing the game to end. The end of the game is represented by an *endpoint.* An outcome is attached to each endpoint. Since running into a wall means getting $0, the outcome 0 is attached to this endpoint. If player 1 goes left, then he or reaches another decision point, *b.* At this decision point, player 1 has two choices, left or right. These choices (also called moves) are again represented by lines coming out of decision point *b,* labeled Left and Right. If player 1 goes left, he or she again runs into a wall (an endpoint) and the outcome is 0. If player 1 goes right, he or she exits from the maze and reaches the pot of gold, the outcome *M.*

The extensive form shown in Figure 1.2 contains all the information about Pot of Gold that is needed to solve it. Mathematically speaking, the extensive form is a *tree diagram,* so-called because it looks like a tree if you are at the starting point, facing right. There are fancy names for the elements of the extensive form. Points in the tree are called *nodes.* Every game begins with an *initial node.* In Pot of Gold, this is the node *a.* A node with a circle around it and a player number inside is called an **information set.** An information set shows which player has to move and what the player knows when making the move. The lines coming out from a node are called *branches,* again in keeping with the tree metaphor. The outcomes attached to endpoints are called *payoffs.* Pot of Gold has perfect information: whenever a decision has to be made, that is, at nodes *a* and *b,* player 1 knows exactly where he or she is in the maze. Later we will see what imperfect information looks like in a tree diagram.

There is a way to solve Pot of Gold and games like it that always works: start from the pot of gold and work backward until the entrance is reached. Working from the end of a game back to the beginning in order to solve it is called **backward induction** and is the procedure used to solve every 1-person game with perfect information. Here's how backward induction is used to solve Pot of Gold (see Figure 1.3).

Start at the least decision point of the game, node *b.* At node *b,* player 1 reaches the pot of gold by going right. We denote this by an arrow on the branch labeled Right coming out of node *b.* Now it is up to player 1 to reach node *b,* since this puts the player in position to get the gold. The only way to reach node *b* is by going left at node *a.* We denote this by an arrow on the branch labeled Left coming out of node *a.* We now have a complete path from the initial node *a* to the endpoint where the pot of gold is:

go left at *a,* go right at *b*

This plan of play solves Pot of Gold and gets the payoff *M,* the pot of gold. We have just solved your first game.

It is possible to get the payoff 0 in Pot of Gold. All it takes is a bad strategy. A **strategy** is a complete plan of play for a game. The good strategy in Pot of Gold leads to the pot of gold. There are three other strategies for Pot of Gold, all of

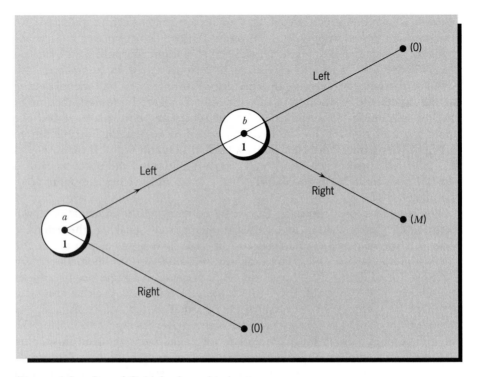

Figure 1.3.   Pot of Gold, backward induction.

which are bad because they run into a wall and get payoff 0. To construct a strategy, you first identify every decision that a player might make. Here, player 1 has to make a decision at node *a* and again at node *b*. At node *a*, player 1 has two choices; at node *b*, two choices. A strategy for Pot of Gold fills in the following blanks:

_____ at *a*, _____ at *b*

Since there are two possible ways to fill in the blank at *a* and two possible ways to fill in the blank at *b*, there are (2)(2) = 4 strategies for Pot of Gold. We have already identified the good strategy. Here are the three bad strategies:

right at *a*, right at *b*
left at *a*, left at *b*
right at *a*, left at *b*

Good play avoids these three strategies.

We have seen that the extensive form of Pot of Gold consists of nodes, branches, endpoints, and payoffs. Game theory has another way to describe Pot of Gold. This description, based only on strategies, is called the **normal form.** The normal form of a 1-player game lists each of the player's strategies and the payoff alongside each. Figure 1.4 shows Pot of Gold in normal form. It lists

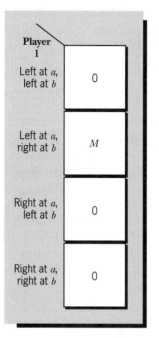

Figure 1.4. Pot of Gold, normal form.

player 1's four strategies and the payoff, 0 or M, alongside each. The normal form codes all the information of the extensive form into a matrix, here a matrix with four rows and one column. In this code, it is easy to spot the solution to Pot of Gold: pick the strategy (left at a, right at b) that pays M.

You ought to be wondering why there are two representations, normal form and extensive form, of the same game. Some purists think that we should study games only in extensive form. Von Neumann and Morgenstern, the originators of the distinction, thought studying games in normal form led to more general insights. This book takes a pragmatic approach: pick the form that is easier to write down and solve. This is usually the normal form. However, if the game is already written down in extensive form, you can solve it in that form without bothering with the normal form. In 1-player games of perfect information, the same solution is derived from both the extensive form and the normal form.[10]

♟ 1.4 Utility ■

Before we launch into 1-player games with imperfect information, we need a new concept. This concept has an old name, utility, which in its original sense

---

[10] Chapter 6 shows to what extent this is true for more complicated games.

tells how to compare apples and oranges. "If the utility of five apples is greater than that of five oranges, then a consumer prefers five apples to five oranges when they are priced the same"—statements like that. With imperfect information, however, a player has to compare more than apples and oranges; he or she has to compare probability distributions. This is not an easy thing to do—members of our species have trouble making such comparisons even today.

To see why comparisons of probability distributions are unavoidable when information is imperfect, consider the problem of picking a stock. You don't know whether the stock price will go up, stay the same, or go down. You do know, however, that there are probabilities attached to these three events. There is a probability that a given stock will go up ($\frac{1}{4}$, say), a probability that it will stay the same ($\frac{3}{20}$), and a probability that it will go down ($\frac{3}{5}$). The big question is which stock to buy. If each stock is identified by its own probability distribution, then the answer is, "Buy the stock with the highest utility, if all stocks are selling at the same price." Instead of comparing apples and oranges, you are comparing the probability distribution of stock X with the probability distribution of stock Y. In order to make this stock-buying recommendation operational, however, we must first attach meaning to the phrase "utility of a probability distribution."

The way to attach utility to probability distributions in game theory, proposed by von Neumann and Morgenstern, is called **expected utility.**[11] To motivate expected utility, let's consider the problem of picking a stock in more detail. Suppose that all the stocks being ranked sell for $1/share and that there are three possible events: the stock rises to $2/share, the stock stays at $1/share, or the stock falls to $0/share. We denote the probabilities of each of these three events by $p(\$2)$, $p(\$1)$, and $p(\$0)$. For instance, the stock that rises to $2 with probability $\frac{1}{4}$, stays the same with probability $\frac{3}{20}$, and falls to $0 with probability $\frac{3}{5}$ is identified by the probability distribution $\mathbf{p} = [p(\$2),p(\$1),p(\$0)]$, where

$$\mathbf{p} = \left(\frac{1}{4}, \frac{3}{20}, \frac{3}{5}\right)$$

Any vector $\mathbf{p}$ whose components are nonnegative and sum to 1 is a probability distribution and can represent a stock.

The set of all possible stocks, as identified by their probability distributions, is shown by the equilateral triangle in Figure 1.5. At the three vertices of the equilateral triangle, we locate the three sure-thing stocks:

(1,0,0): the stock goes up to $2 with probability 1

(0,1,0): the stock stays at $1 with probability 1

(0,0,1): the stock drops to $0 with probability 1

[11] The idea of expected utility goes back to the mathematician Bernoulli, who wrote an article on gambling, in Latin, in 1738.

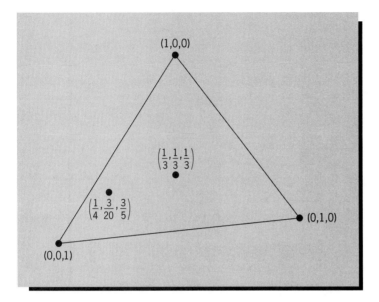

Figure 1.5. Equilateral triangle of probability distributions.

The center of gravity of the equilateral triangle is the stock that is equally likely to have any value:

$$\mathbf{p} = \left(\frac{1}{3}, \frac{1}{3}, \frac{1}{3} \right)$$

We also plot the nearby stock ($\frac{1}{4}$, $\frac{3}{20}$, $\frac{3}{5}$). Every point in the equilateral triangle corresponds to a probability distribution, and we want to attach a utility to each and every one of these probability distributions.

We attach utility to the sure things first. For any utility,

$$u(2) > u(1) > u(0)$$

Expected utility extends this ordering to all probability distributions in the following way. Write $Eu(\mathbf{p})$ for the expected utility of the probability distribution $\mathbf{p}$. We have

$$Eu(\mathbf{p}) = p(\$2)\,u(2) + p(\$1)\,u(1) + p(\$0)\,u(0)$$

Note first of all that expected utility extends the ordering of the sure things:

$$Eu(1,0,0) = 1u(2) + 0 + 0 > Eu(0,1,0) = 0 + 1u(1) + 0 > 0 + 0 + 1u(0)$$

What expected utility says in addition is that indifference curves drawn through probability distributions are parallel straight lines. To illustrate, suppose that

$$u(2) = 2, \ u(1) = 1, \text{ and } u(0) = 0$$

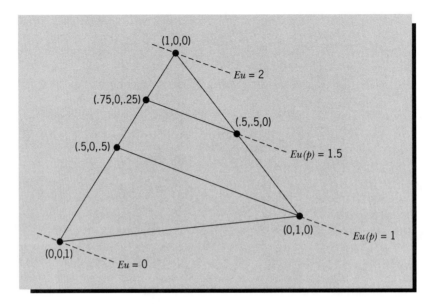

Figure 1.6.   Expected utility, indifference lines.

All the stocks with $Eu(\mathbf{p}) = 1$ lie on the straight line connecting the probability distributions $(0,1,0)$, $(\frac{1}{3},\frac{1}{3},\frac{1}{3})$, and $(\frac{1}{2},0,\frac{1}{2})$, as in Figure 1.6. All the stocks with $Eu(\mathbf{p}) = 1.5$ lie on the straight line connecting the probability distributions $(\frac{1}{2},\frac{1}{2},0)$ and $(\frac{3}{4},0,\frac{1}{4})$. These two straight lines are parallel.

There are several attractive properties of expected utility as a ranking of probability distributions. First, the indifference curves never cross, so the ranking is rational. Second, the indifference curves increase in the right direction. The closer a probability distribution is to the best sure thing, $(1,0,0)$, the higher its utility. Third, the indifference curves and the rankings they represent are invariant to positive linear transformations of sure-thing utility. That is, if we add a constant to the sure-thing utilities or multiply them by the same positive constant, the indifference lines stay put. If

$$u(1) = .5u(2) + .5u(0)$$

as in Figure 1.6, then we also have

$$u(1) + 1 = .5[u(2) + 1] + .5[u(0) + 1] = .5u(2) + .5u(0) + 1$$

transforming sure-thing utility by adding 1, and

$$2u(1) = .5[2u(2)] + .5[2u(0)] = 2[.5u(2) + .5u(0)]$$

transforming sure-thing utility by multiplying by 2. Thus expected utilities are *measurable utilities* in exactly the same sense that temperature is measurable. Fix the zero point and the unit on the utility scale:

$$u(0) = 0; \ u(1) = 1$$

Then, to measure $u(2)$, find the probability distribution $\mathbf{p} = [p(\$2),0,p(\$0)]$ such that

$$p(\$2)\,u(2) + p(\$0)\,u(0) = u(1)$$

Substituting the zero point and unit on the utility scale, we get

$$p(\$2)\,u(2) = u(1) = 1$$

The desired measure of utility is

$$u(2) = \frac{1}{p(\$2)}$$

If a player is indifferent about having \$1 for sure versus having \$2 with probability $p(2)$ and \$0 otherwise, then the ratio $\frac{1}{p}(\$2)$ measures the utility of having \$2 for this player.

These three properties of indifference curves—they never cross, they increase in the right direction, and they lead to measurable utility—are very appealing. In particular, they allow us to tackle 1-person games with imperfect information.

1.5 One-Person Games with Imperfect Information ■■■■■■■■■■■■■■■■■■

Information in a 1-person game is imperfect if the player does not know where he or she is in the game when a decision must be made. Uncertainty is the cause of this imperfection. Because of forces beyond the control of the player—we call such forces chance—the player is in the dark. To include imperfect information in the extensive form requires two additional devices, one to represent chance, another to exhibit the effects of chance on the game.

Figure 1.7 shows how these two devices look. At the beginning of the game, initial node a, you see the number 0 circled. The player numbered 0 always represents chance. An information set with chance attached means that a chance move takes place there. For instance, the deal at the start of a card game is a chance move, as is the coin toss at the start of a football game. The branches coming out of node a represent the two different directions chance can take. These branches have special labels, $p(good)$ and $p(bad)$, representing probabilities. What chance does is create a probability distribution. With probability $p(good)$, something good happens; with probability $p(bad)$, something bad happens. In this case, good and bad refer to conditions good for business and bad for business.

Once chance has moved, it is player 1's turn to move. Unfortunately for player 1, he or she does not know what chance did. Player 1's information is imperfect. Chance may have moved to the good node g or to the bad node b in player 1's information set. Any information set that contains more than one

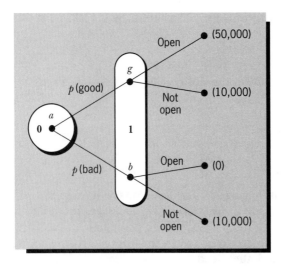

Figure I.7. Small Business, imperfect information.

node reflects imperfect information on the part of the player who must make a decision there. Visually, you can tell that a game has imperfect information if it has at least one information set with two or more nodes. Thus, the game shown in Figure 1.7, called Small Business, has imperfect information. In particular, player 1 does not know whether he or she is at node *g* or node *b* of the information set when it is time to move. All player 1 knows are the probabilities with which each of these nodes is reached, namely, p(good) and p(bad).

Despite this imperfect information, player 1 has to make a decision, whether to open a small business or not. This decision is represented by the branches labeled Open and Not open coming out of nodes *b* and *g*. Opening a small business is always risky. When the climate for business is good, then a small business will thrive. The chance that the climate for business is good is measured by the probability p(good). When the climate for business is bad, then a small business will fail. The chance that the climate for business is bad is measured by the probability p(bad). Player 1 does not know what the climate for business is when he or she has to decide whether to open a small business or not. Payoffs are as follows. Player 1 has $10,000 to invest. If player 1 does not open a small business, he or she keeps the $10,000. If player 1 opens a small business and the climate for business is good, then the business thrives and it is worth $50,000. If player 1 opens a small business and the climate for business is bad, the business fails and it is worth $0. The branch labeled Open leading from node *g* reaches the very best payoff, $50,000. However, the branch labeled Open leading from node *b* reaches the very worst payoff, $0. The reason these two branches have the same label is that they are consequences of the same decision by player 1, to open a small business. On the other hand, the two branches labeled Not open both lead to the payoff $10,000. If player 1 does not open a small business, then player 1's payoff is not affected by chance.

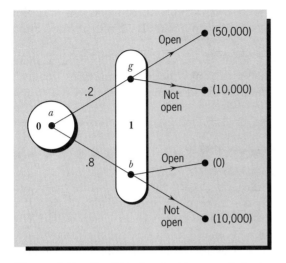

Figure 1.8. Small Business, risk-neutral player.

Suppose that $p(\text{good}) = .2$ and $p(\text{bad}) = .8$, as in Figure 1.8. These probabilities are actually in the ballpark for the success and failure rates of small business in the United States. To solve Small Business, player 1 has to ask whether a sure \$10,000 is preferable to the probability distribution

\$50,000 with probability .2
\$0 with probability .8

This is a comparison of a probability distribution and a sure thing, a comparison that expected utility is designed to handle. How any specific player ranks opening a small business against not opening one depends on player's utilities for the sure-thing payoffs \$0, \$10,000, and \$50,000. Let's consider first a person for whom the utility of money is money:

$$u_1(m_1) = m_1$$

Here, u_1 is player 1's utility function, and m_1 is the amount of money player 1 gets paid. For this person, $u_1(10,000) = \$10,000$; this is the utility of not opening a small business. Now let's compare this to the expected utility of opening a small business, written $Eu_1(\text{open})$, which is shorthand for the expected utility of the probability distribution faced by opening a small business. Substituting, we get

$$\begin{aligned} Eu_1(\text{open}) &= p(\text{good})\,u_1(50,000) + p(\text{bad})\,u_1(0) \\ &= (.2)(50,000) + (.8)(0) \\ &= 10,000 \end{aligned}$$

For this player, it's a tie: opening a small business and not opening a small business are on the same indifference curve, with utility equal to 10,000 each.

This result is reflected by attaching arrows to both branches, Open and Not open, in Figure 1.8. This is the solution to Small Business, at the stated probabilities, when utility equals money.

Not all players rank opening a small business and not opening a small business the same. Indeed, how a player ranks these two strategies depends crucially on the player's attitude toward risk—a connection spelled out in the next section.

◼ 1.6 The Three Attitudes toward Risk ◼ ◼ ◼ ◼ ◼ ◼ ◼ ◼ ◼

Players with different attitudes toward risk look at the world differently and often react to it differently. There are three main attitudes toward risk. If a player is **risk neutral,** then a sure dollar is the same as an expected dollar. The player in the last section, for whom money is utility, is risk neutral. A sure $10,000 for such a player is worth just as much as a probability distribution whose expected value is $10,000. Risk doesn't affect such a decision maker as long as it doesn't affect expected value, hence the name *risk neutral.* There are two kinds of nonneutral attitudes toward risk as well. If a player is **risk averse,** then a sure dollar is better than an expected dollar. Risk-averse players avoid risks unless the odds are sufficiently in their favor. If a player is **risk seeking,** then an expected dollar is better than a sure dollar. Risk seekers take risks unless the odds are sufficiently against them.

These three attitudes toward risk can be identified by the shape of the sure-thing utility function of a player, $u_1(m_1)$. Risk-neutral players have the linear utility function

$$u_1(m_1) = m_1$$

or any positive linear transformation thereof. Only risk-neutral players represent dollar payoffs directly as utilities when they evaluate the outcomes in a decision tree. All other players transform dollars into a different measure, and these transformations are nonlinear. Recall that a concave function is one whose second derivative is nonpositive, whereas a convex function is one whose second derivative is nonnegative. A risk-averse player has a concave utility function, and a risk-seeking player has a convex utility function.

This book uses the following family of utility functions, which contains all three attitudes toward risk as special cases:

$$u_1(m_1) = \frac{m_1^a}{a} \qquad \text{when } a \neq 0$$
$$= \log(m_1) \qquad \text{when } a = 0$$

When $a = 1$, player 1 is risk neutral; when $a > 1$, player 1 is risk seeking. For example, with $a = 2$, $u_1(m_1) = m^2/2$, a convex function. When $a < 1$, player 1 is risk averse. For example, with $a = 0.5$, $u_1(m_1) = m_1^{0.5}/0.5 = 2\ m_1^{0.5}$, a concave function. The parameter a reflects a player's attitude toward risk. The bigger a is, the less averse to risk a player is.

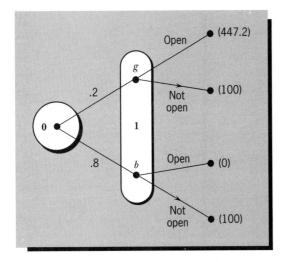

Figure 1.9. Small Business, risk-averse player.

We have already seen that a risk-neutral player is indifferent about opening or not opening a small business. Next we will see that a risk-seeking player definitely prefers opening a small business and that a risk-averse player definitely prefers not opening a small business.

Figure 1.9 shows the game Small Business as a risk-averse player with $a = 0.5$ sees it. The payoffs have been transformed from dollars to utility. For instance, $u(50,000) = 2(50,000)^{0.5} = 447.2$. Computing the expected utility of the strategy Open for player 1, written $Eu_1(\text{open})$, we get

$$Eu_1 \text{ (open)} = .2(447.2) + .8(0) = 89.4$$

The expected utility of the strategy Not open for this player is

$$Eu_1 \text{ (not open)} = 2(10,000)^{0.5} = 200$$

Since $200 > 89.4$, the strategy Not open is clearly better than the strategy Open. This result is indicated by attaching arrows to the branches labeled Not open leading from player 1's information set. This result makes sense, intuitively. If you were risk averse, why on earth would you open a small business when the chance of failure is so high?

Figure 1.10 shows the game Small Business as a risk seeker with $a = 2$ sees it. The payoffs have again been transformed from dollars to utility. For instance, $u(10,000) = (10,000)^2/2 = 10^8/2 = 50$ million. Computing the expected utility of the strategy Open for player 1, we get

$$Eu_1 \text{ (open)} = .2(1.25 \text{ billion}) + .8(0) = 250 \text{ million}$$

The expected utility of the strategy Not open is only 50 million. For this risk seeker, the strategy Open is clearly better than the strategy Not open. This conclusion is denoted by attaching arrows to the branches labeled Open leading from player 1's information set in Figure 1.10. Again this result makes

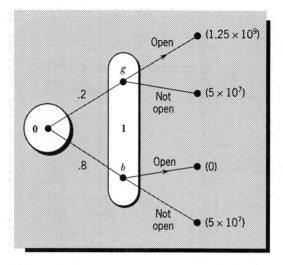

Figure 1.10.   Small Business, risk-seeking player.

sense intuitively. If you are risk seeking, opening a small business offers you plenty of what you seek.

Most of the time this book assumes that agents are risk neutral and see the game exactly as it is drawn when the payoffs are in dollars. When attitudes to risk are crucial to the solution of a game, as they are with Small Business, then you are so warned, and the extra transformation steps needed to solve the game are performed.

Sometimes all three attitudes agree that one decision is better than another. Consider the game in Figure 1.11, called Subsidized Small Business. If the climate for business is bad, then an agency of the federal government steps in, compensating small business failure in full; otherwise the game is the same as Small Business. Notice that the strategy Not open cannot possibly be better than the strategy Open. If the climate for business is bad, then both strategies pay the same. If the climate for business is good, the strategy Open pays much more than the strategy Not open does. In equation form,

$$Eu_1(\text{open}) = p(\text{good})\,u(50{,}000) + p(\text{bad})\,u(10{,}000)$$

compared to

$$Eu_1(\text{not open}) = u(10{,}000)$$

For all utility functions and probabilities we have

$$Eu_1(\text{open}) \geq Eu_1(\text{not open})$$

and the only time there is a tie is when $p(\text{bad}) = 1$. If there is even a tiny possibility that a small business will succeed, then the solution for anybody playing Subsidized Small Business is to open a small business.

Ranking probability distributions is a controversial area, and there are many other ways of ranking in addition to expected utility. One very influential

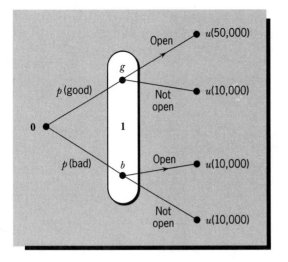

Figure 1.11. Subsidized Small Business.

alternative, derived by the psychologists Kahneman and Tversky, is called prospect theory.[12] All reasonable ways of ranking probability distributions do agree on one point, however. One probability distribution has **stochastic dominance** over another if it never pays less and sometimes pays more. More generally, if one probability distribution attaches higher probability to high payoffs and lower probability to low payoffs than another probability distribution does, the former stochastically dominates the latter. For instance, in Subsidized Small Business, the probability distribution associated with opening a small business stochastically dominates the (sure-thing) probability distribution associated with not opening a small business. It never pays less than $10,000, and with probability p(good) it pays more. Any reasonable ranking of probability distributions agrees with stochastic dominance. One of the chief attractions of expected utility theory, an attraction it shares with prospect theory and a number of other nonexpected utility theories, is that it agrees with stochastic dominance.

1.7 Two-Person Games with Perfect Information ■

All the games studied so far have been degenerate, in the sense that they had only one player. The rest of this chapter and the next two chapters are devoted to games with two players. For now, we restrict our attention to 2-person games

---

[12]We won't go into this theory here. See Daniel Kahneman and Amos Tversky, "Prospect Theory," *Econometrica* 47 (1979):263–91.

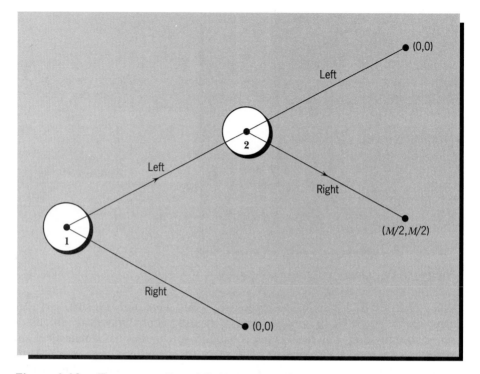

Figure 1.12.   Two-person Pot of Gold, extensive form.

with perfect information, a simple example of which is shown in Figure 1.12, 2-person Pot of Gold.

Player 1 moves first, and can go either left or right. If player 1 goes right, the game ends. At the endpoint is attached the payoff vector **u,** given by

$$\mathbf{u} = (u_1, u_2) = (0,0)$$

Each player gets 0 at this endpoint. If player 1 goes left, then it is player 2's turn to move. Player 2 can go either left or right. If player 2 goes left, then the game ends with the payoff vector

$$\mathbf{u} = (0,0)$$

If player 2 goes right, then the game ends as well. In this event, the players have found the pot of gold, whose value they divide evenly:

$$\mathbf{u} = \left(\frac{M}{2}, \frac{M}{2}\right)$$

Solving Pot of Gold with two players is no different from solving Pot of Gold with one player. We use backward induction, starting with player 2, the last player to move. Player 2, who prefers half the pot of gold to none, moves right. This brings us to player 1's move. Player 1, who also prefers half the pot of gold

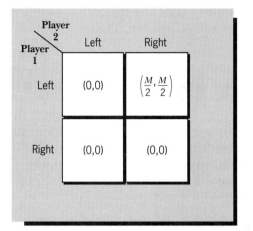

Figure 1.13. Two-person Pot of Gold, normal form.

to none, moves left. This solution is denoted by the arrows through Figure 1.12. We have just solved our first 2-person game.

Pot of Gold with two players is a parable—it tells a large story in a small space. Consider any business deal that has profit potential for both parties. The pot of gold valued M represents the deal. What the two sides have to do is find their way to the deal. The path "1 goes left, 2 goes right" represents how the two sides find their way to the deal. This path is called the *solution path*. In 2-person Pot of Gold, there is only one solution path, the path that gets to the pot of gold. All the other paths get zeros instead. Of course, most business deals are a lot more complicated than 2-person Pot of Gold; this complexity is addressed in later chapters.

Although the extensive form of 2-person Pot of Gold closely resembles the extensive form of the 1-person version (compare Figures 1.2 and 1.12), its normal form looks a lot different (compare Figures 1.4 and 1.13). To construct its normal form, we list the strategies for each player. Player 1 has a single information set, with two choices at that set, so player 1 has $(1)(2) = 2$ strategies. These are Left or Right. Similarly, player 2 has a single information set, with two choices at that set, so player 2 also has two strategies, Left or Right. We array these strategies in a 2×2 matrix (that is, a matrix with two rows and two columns). The rows correspond to player 1's two strategies; the columns, to player 2's two strategies. We move the payoff vectors from the endpoints of the extensive form into the appropriate cell of the normal form matrix. For instance, the pair of strategies

1 goes left, 2 goes right

leads to the payoff vector $(M/2, M/2)$, which appears in row 1 (player 1 goes left) and column 2 (player 2 goes right) in the matrix. Throughout game theory, 2×2 games prove useful as parables of larger questions, a good reason to avail ourselves of them as often as possible. Let's now turn to a class of very special 2-person games with perfect information, games like Chess.

❖ 1.8 Games like Chess ■

A 2-person game with perfect information is like Chess if is satisfies the following requirements. First, the players alternate turns. Second, each player has at most a finite number of strategies. Third, the outcomes are limited to win, lose, or draw. Either player 1 wins and player 2 loses (w,l) or both players get a draw (d,d) or player 1 loses and player 2 wins (l,w). These are all features of Chess. The first theorem ever proved about games says:

■ ■

Theorem on Games like Chess. In **games like Chess,** exactly one of the following is true: player 1 can guarantee a win, player 2 can guarantee a win, or each player can guarantee a draw.[13]

We will prove this theorem for the class of extensive form games like Chess shown in Figure 1.14, all of whose normal forms are 2 × 2. Player 1 moves first and can move either left or right. If player 1 moves right, the game ends with the payoff vector *x*. If player 1 moves left, then it is player 2's turn. Player 2 can move either left or right. If player 2 moves left, the payoff vector is **u;** if player 2 moves right, the payoff vector is **v.** The payoff vectors **u, v,** and **x** can take any of the following forms:

(w,l) (d,d) (l,w)

Since each possible payoff vector can take any of three forms and there are three payoff vectors, there are $3^3 = 27$ possible games represented in Figure 1.14. The following proof applies to each of these 27 games.

The proof works via backward induction. Start with player 2, at the end of the game. Player 2 maximizes utility, given the payoff vectors **u** and **v.** There are three possible cases facing player 2.

Case 1. Player 2 can reach a win in at least one of the payoff vectors **u** or **v.** Then player 2 so moves. In this case, if the play reaches player 2, player 2 can guarantee a win.

Case 2. Player 2 cannot reach a win with either move, but can reach a draw from at least one of the payoff vectors **u** or **v.** Then player 2 so moves. In this case, if the play reaches player 2, player 2 can guarantee a draw.

Case 3. Player 2 faces a loss no matter what move is made: **u** = **v** = (w,l). In this case, player 1 can guarantee a win by moving left. The play reaches player 2, who is sure to lose.

---

[13]This theorem was first stated and proved by the mathematician Zermelo in 1911.

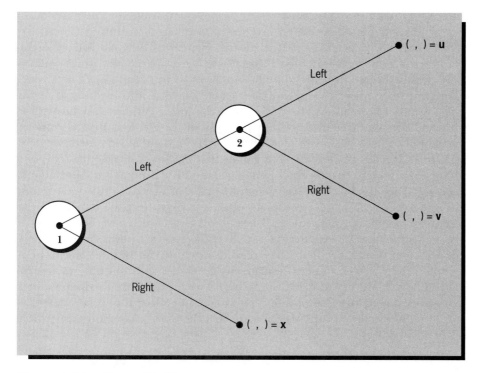

Figure 1.14. Games like Chess.

Now we come back to the start of the game, and player 1's move. If case 2 holds, then the worst player 1 can do is get a draw. If the payoff vector $\mathbf{x} = (w,l)$, then player 1 moves right and guarantees a win. Otherwise, player 1 moves left and guarantees a draw. Finally, suppose that case 1 holds. If $\mathbf{x} = (l,w)$, then player 1 loses no matter what he or she chooses, left or right. In this case, player 2 guarantees a win. If $\mathbf{x} = (d,d)$, then player 1 guarantees a draw by moving right. Finally, if $\mathbf{x} = (w,l)$, player 1 guarantees a win. This completes the proof.

There are a lot of games like Chess. Tic-Tac-Toe is one example. For Tic-Tac-Toe, the theorem can be sharpened to the following: each player in Tic-Tac-Toe can guarantee a draw. Chess is a lot more complicated than Tic-Tac-Toe. For instance, in Chess, player 1 (white) has 20 possible opening moves, and player 2 (black) has 20 possible responses to each opening move by white. Already the extensive form is beyond the capabilities of conventional human graphics. It is estimated that the extensive form of Chess would require something on the order of 10^{30} nodes to write down. Chess is so complicated that it is still not known whether in fact white can guarantee a win, although the empirical evidence certainly suggests that moving first is an advantage.

Games like Chess are important, and not just as amusements. Chapter 6 shows that, with only a slight alteration of the payoffs in Figure 1.14, we get one of the most important games played in business, involving possible entry into a market and attempts by established firms to deter that entry.[14] Games like Chess show with crystalline clarity that strategy matters. Suppose you are player 1 in such a game, and it is known that player 1 can guarantee a win. Somehow you manage to lose instead. You have no excuses. You can't blame luck, since there are no chance moves. You can't blame missing information, since you have perfect information. The only reason you lost is because you chose a bad strategy. You snatched defeat from the jaws of victory. You have no one to blame but yourself when you play a bad strategy and get a bad outcome.

Games like Chess were the first games that machines could play. The only thing a machine needs to play a game like Chess is a program to determine its strategy. Once the machine has a complete plan of play, or a rule for computing the various pieces of a complete plan, it is ready to play. In a game like Chess, strategy is all that matters. Chess-playing machines have been rising in the world rankings steadily for the past 20 years. They are now ranked in the 60 to 70 range, that is, the best Chess-playing machine can beat all but 60 or so people. The world champion human has never lost to a machine in tournament Chess; however, in Speed Chess, where each player has a strict time limit per move, the picture is a lot different. Fritz2, one of the top three Chess-playing machines in the world,[15] can already beat the world champion Kasparov, as Figure 1.15 shows.[16]

1.9 Extensive Form, Normal Form, and Coalition Function Form ■■■■■■■■■■■■■■■■■■■■■■■■■■

Sometimes the line between a game like Chess and a game that is not like Chess can be very fine indeed. Consider the two extensive form games in Figures 1.16. The game in Figure 1.16*a* is like Chess, and player 1 can guarantee a draw by going left. The game in Figure 1.16*b* is not like Chess, since it has imperfect information. However, if we look at the normal forms of these two games, we see that they are exactly the same! The normal form of both is shown in Figure 1.17. Each player has one information set, with two choices at that information set, so each player has two strategies. That makes the normal form a 2 × 2 matrix in each case. When both players go left, the outcome is a draw (d,d), and so on, so that the payoffs match up. Even though

---

[14] This game is called Telex versus IBM, for reasons that will become clear in Chapter 6.

[15] The other two top-ranked Chess-playing machines are called Deep Thought and Deep Blue, both at Carnegie Mellon University. Fritz2 is a German machine.

[16] This story is drawn from Shelby Lyman, "Chess," *Chicago Tribune*, April 18, 1993, sec. 13, p. 35.

Chicago Tribune, Sunday, April 18, 1993   Section 13   Page 35   Arts

Chess

By Shelby Lyman

If you have trouble beating your dedicated chess computer or your personal computer armed with chess-playing software, you are in good company.

At the end of December, Garri Kasparov played an impromptu session of blitz games in Cologne, Germany, against the chess program Fritz2. The surprising result, as reported by chess computer specialist Frederick Friedel: the microcomputer program won nine and drew four of the 37 games they played!

Afterwards the world champion, himself an exceptional speed player, offered an evaluation of Fritz:

"It does not play the opening especially well. It is strategically weak but tactically very dangerous. And rather than giving up, it always finds a way to create difficulties."

Of course, the outcome of Kasparov vs. Fritz is misleading. Playing at a standard and much slower time control, Kasparov would probably not have lost a single game to the program.

But computers are notoriously difficult opponents in fast chess. Humans need a certain minimum time per move before their ability to judge and intuit kicks in at an effective level. Unlike machines, humans—even champions—frequently "blunder" when they have little time to think over moves.

The true test of "man vs. machine" will take place sometime next year when Kasparov plays a match at a conventional time limit against Deep Blue— an updated, 1,000-times-faster version of Deep Thought, which for several years has been the most powerful chess-playing machine on the planet.

Below is a win by Fritz2 from Cologne.

Fritz2	Kasparov
1. Nf3	d5
2. d4	e6
3. c4	c6
4. e3	f5
5. Bd3	Bd6
6. c5	Bc7
7. Nc3	Qf6
8. h3	Nh6
9. Bd2	Nd7
10. 0-0	g5
11. b3	g4
12. hxg4	Nxg4
13. Qc2	Rg8
14. Bc1	Nf8
15. Bb2	Qg6
16. g3	Qh6
17. Ne2	Ng6
18. Kg2	Qg7
19. Rh1	e5
20. dxe5	N(6)xe5
21. Bxf5	Qf7
22. Bxg4	Bxg4
23. N(f)d4	h5
24. Nf4	0-0-0
25. f3	Bd7
26. Nxh5	R(d)f8
27. Nf4	Nxf3!?
28. Kxf3	Rxg3ch
29. Kxg3	Bxf4ch
30. Kf2	Bc5ch
31. Ke1	Bg4
32. Qg2	Rg8
33. Nb5!	Qe7
34. Nxa7ch	Kb8
35. Bxe5ch	Qxe5
36. Nxc6ch	bxc6
37. Qh2	Qxh2

and Black resigns.

Figure 1.15. Fritz2 beats Kasparov.

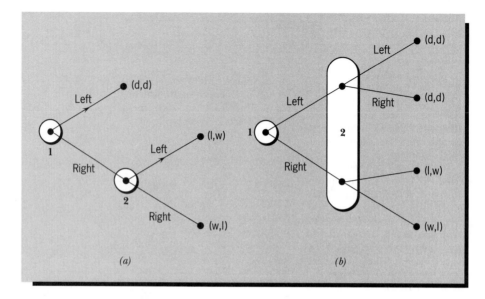

Figure 1.16.   Games nearly like Chess.

the game in Figure 1.16*b* is not like Chess, it is close enough that it has the same normal form as a game that is like Chess.

It often happens that games with different extensive forms have the same normal form, because the normal form suppresses some information that is available in the extensive form. For instance, you can see at once that the game in Figure 1.16*a* has perfect information, but this inference is no longer available in the normal form. Every extensive form has a unique normal form

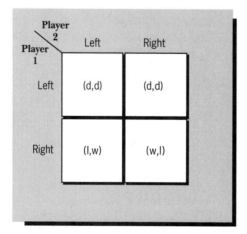

Figure 1.17.   Games in normal form.

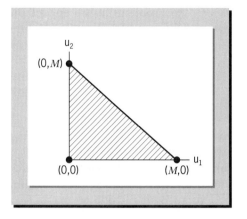

Figure 1.18. Two-person Pot of Gold, coalition function form.

representation. However, for every game in normal form there are usually several possible games in extensive form that could give rise to it. Thus things that are true for games like Chess may also be true for games nearly like Chess.

In Figure 1.16*b*, just as in Figure 1.16*a*, player 1 can guarantee a draw by moving left. In the extensive form, we find this out by backward induction. In normal form, we see this in another way. If player 1 chooses the strategy Left, then he or she gets a draw in every cell of the corresponding row of the matrix. If player 1 chooses the strategy Right, and if player 2 chooses Left (which would make sense), then player 1 loses. Since a draw is better than losing, player 1 goes left. Thus, we get the same answer in normal form as in extensive form, although the reasoning is slightly different.

In addition to the extensive and normal forms, there is a third form of games, especially useful for games with a largely cooperative character, called the **coalition function form.** This form requires the answers to only two questions: what can each player guarantee for himself or herself, and what can the two players acting together guarantee for themselves? For the win, lose, or draw game, such as that shown in Figure 1.16*a*, the coalition function form simply says that player 1 can guarantee a draw, as can player 2. The players acting together cannot guarantee anything more. For 2-person Pot of Gold, the coalition function form says that player 1 can guarantee 0 (because player 2 goes left), player 2 can guarantee 0 (because player 1 goes left), but together they can guarantee M (because player 1 goes right and player 2 goes left). This coalition function form is depicted in Figure 1.18. The coalition function form is used primarily when studying how the gains of cooperation are divided up among those involved in a deal—a question focused on in Chapter 12.

Most of the time, if a game has imperfect information, it will not be anything at all like Chess. Relaxing any of the hypotheses of the theorem for games like Chess makes it possible to construct counterexamples to the theorem. Chapter 4 shows that a game like Chess with three players no longer obeys the theorem.

You can construct other counterexamples in the problems at the end of this chapter. Problem solving is an essential part of game theory. You exhibit mastery of the theory through the games you solve—and only through the games you solve.

:: SUMMARY

1. A game is any rule-governed strategic situation with a well-defined outcome, characterized by strategic interdependence among the players.

2. There is a great variety of games in the literal sense: board games, card games, video games, and field games. Business and economics exhibit games in the extended sense. The Chicago Bulls provide an example of both senses.

3. Game theory is the science that studies games and takes them seriously enough to solve them. Game theory began as applied mathematics, but is now central to the way we think about business and economics.

4. Games serve as models for business interactions and economic negotiations. The cola wars between Coke and Pepsi are an example of a game in business; negotiations among the G-7 countries, of a game in economics.

5. The extensive form is the basic description of a game. An extensive form is a tree diagram, with nodes, branches, an initial node, information sets, and endpoints.

6. A 1-player game with perfect information can be solved by backward induction, starting at the end and working back to the beginning.

7. A game has perfect information if every information set contains a single node. A game with imperfect information requires a player to rank probability distributions, which requires an extended notion of utility.

8. Expected utility ranks probability distributions. In this theory, indifference curves are parallel straight lines and there are three main attitudes toward risk: risk neutral, risk averse, and risk seeking. Each attitude has a systematic way of viewing the world and a systematic way of playing, as shown in the game Small Business.

9. One probability distribution stochastically dominates another when it never pays less and sometimes pays more. In this case its expected utility is higher, regardless of attitude toward risk.

10. Two-person games with perfect information can be solved by backward induction, just like 1-person games with perfect information.

11. For a game like Chess, exactly one of the following is true: player 1 can guarantee a win, player 2 can guarantee a win, or each player can guarantee a draw.

12. A computer can now beat the world Chess champion at Speed Chess.

13. There are three representations of games: extensive form, normal form, and coalition function form. The normal form looks at the implications of strategies, while suppressing some of the detail contained in the extensive

form. The coalition function form suppresses even more detail than the normal form and is used mainly for studying cooperation among players.

▞ KEY TERMS

game	backward induction
strategic interdependence	strategy
business game	normal form
economic negotiation	expected utility
game theory	risk neutral/averse/seeking
perfect/imperfect information	stochastic dominance
extensive form	games like Chess
information set	coalition function form

▞ PROBLEMS

1. Give examples of strategic interaction in each of the following industries: entertainment, beer, automobile, and financial services.

2. Draw the extensive form of the maze in Figure 1.19 (page 34), then solve it.

3. You are thinking about opening a cinema complex. You have $100,000 to invest. If you open the complex, the probability is .35 that you will make $300,000 (including your investment) and .65 that you will lose all your money. If you don't open the cinema complex, then you keep your $100,000 for sure. Chance moves before you do. Draw the game tree. What should you do if you are risk neutral? Would your strategy change if the probability of success was .3 instead of .35?

4. Redo problem 3 in the following two ways: (a) you are risk averse and your utility function is $u = m^{1/3}$; (b) you are risk seeking and your utility function is $u = m^3$. Explain the difference, if any, between the risk-averse, risk-seeking, and risk-neutral players.

5. Show in detail that all three risk types rate Open a small business above Do not open a small business in Subsidized Small Business.

6. In a casino, the expected value of all the games is negative. Which of the risk types, if any, will definitely play? Which definitely won't?

7. Consider the schema of Figure 1.14. Find payoff vectors **u, v,** and **x** such that (a) player 1 can guarantee a win; (b) player 2 can guarantee a win; and (c) either player can guarantee a draw.

8. Suppose you play Tic-Tac-Toe on a 2 × 2 board, as shown in Figure 1.20. The usual rules apply. Player 1, who goes first, puts an X in any one of the cells. Player 2, who goes second, puts an O in one of the remaining cells. The first player to fill a row, column, or diagonal with his or her marks

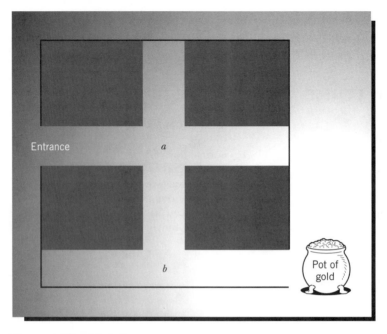

Figure 1.19.   Maze II.

wins. Show that this game is like Chess. Draw its extensive form. Which player can guarantee a win?

Violate any one of the conditions that make a game like Chess and the game may no longer satisfy the conclusion of the theorem for games like Chess. This is the theme of the next two questions.

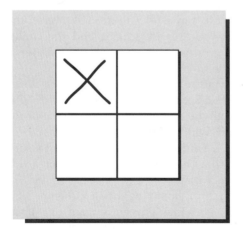

Figure 1.20.   Tic-Tac-Toe on a 2 × 2 board. Player 1 has just moved.

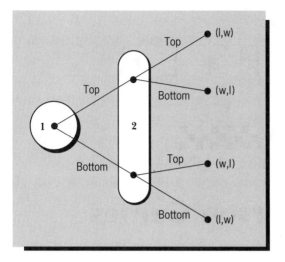

Figure 1.21. Escape and Evasion.

9. The game Pick the Largest Number is a 2-player, win, lose, or draw game with perfect information. Player 1 picks any number. Player 2 hears player 1's number, then picks any number he or she wants. If player 1's number is bigger than player 2's, the game ends in a win for player 1. If player 1's number equals player 2's number, the game ends in a draw. If player 1's number is smaller than player 2's number, then player 1 gets to choose again. If player 1 picks a larger number than player 2's, the game goes on. Show that Pick the Largest Number is not like Chess in one crucial respect. Then show that it never comes to an end.

10. The game Escape and Evasion shown in Figure 1.21 is a 2-person, win, lose, or draw finite game. Player 1, the escapee, has just escaped from jail, and can go either top or bottom. Player 2, the jailer, can also go either top or bottom, but does not know which way the escapee has gone. If the jailer goes the same way as the escapee, the jailer catches the escapee—a win for the jailer. If the jailer goes a different way from the escapee, the escapee gets away—a win for the escapee. Show that Escape and Evasion has imperfect information. Then show that neither player can guarantee a win.

11. According to expected utility theory, the same principles apply to the game Pot of Gold whether M is $1 or $1 million. Do you agree or disagree? Why?

CHAPTER 2

Two-Person Games

This chapter focuses on games with exactly two players, 2-person games. *Player* can be interpreted quite broadly. As indicated in Chapter 1, machines can be players. Chapter 8 shows that animals can be players, too. When game theory was invented, however, these possibilities were in the future, reason enough to stick with the traditional phrase "2-person games." Two-person games are the simplest, and therefore the most suitable for beginners. The more players in a game, the more complicated the game gets. The study of *n*-person games is deferred to Chapter 4.

Games where the players' interests are completely opposed are called *zero-sum* and *constant-sum* games. This chapter shows the relationship between these two types of games, introduces a technique (the arrow diagram) to solve them, and proves that all solutions to such games have the same payoffs. The chapter then presents the phenomenon of competitive advantage in business and shows why firms are driven by strategic forces to adopt new technologies. The same phenomenon arises, albeit in a different guise, in Poker. Games where the players' interests are not completely opposed are called *variable-sum* games.

Such games arise in business on an everyday basis, and solving them is not an easy task. This chapter examines several types of variable-sum games, all of which are played in business, and then proves an existence theorem for a solution for 2-person, variable-sum games. Not all solutions for such games are the same. Finally, cigarette advertising on television is discussed. When such advertising was banned in 1971, cigarette companies' profits actually went up. Game theory, in particular the prisoner's dilemma, explains why. The chapter appendix shows how it is possible to beat the dealer at the casino game Blackjack.

2.1 Zero-Sum Games and Constant-Sum Games ■

Let's start with a 2-person game. Suppose that for every possible outcome of the game, the utility of player 1, u_1, plus the utility of player 2, u_2, adds to zero. In an equation,

$$u_1 + u_2 = 0$$

One example is provided by a game like Chess, with win, lose, or draw outcomes. If the utility of a win to a player is +1, the utility of a draw is 0, and the utility of a loss is –1, the game is a **zero-sum game.** There are three possible outcomes:

1 wins: payoff vector (+1,–1), sum = +1 + (–1) = 0

a draw: payoff vector (0,0), sum = 0 + 0 = 0

2 wins: payoff vector (–1,+1), sum = –1 + (+1) = 0

In every case, the sum of utilities is zero. This is the zero-sum condition. Poker is another example of a zero-sum game as long as the players are risk neutral and utility equals dollars. Both players put the same amount of money in the pot (the center of the table where all bets are placed). The winner takes all the money in the pot—the winner's gain is the loser's loss.

The former dean of the Sloan School at MIT, Lester Thurow, wrote an influential book, *The Zero-Sum Society,* describing in bleak terms how our economy would look, and how bad it would be for business, if the entire economy were structured on the principle of "If I win, you have to lose." No value can be created in a zero-sum game: the players are forever at each other's throats. In such a society, economic change is nearly impossible, and when it is possible, it comes only at a very high cost.[1]

Zero-sum games are a special instance of constant-sum games. In a **constant-sum game,** whatever the outcome, the player's utilities add up to a constant k. If

---

[1]For the complete argument, read Lester C. Thurow, *The Zero-Sum Society: Distribution and the Possibilities for Economic Change* (New York: Basic Books, 1980).

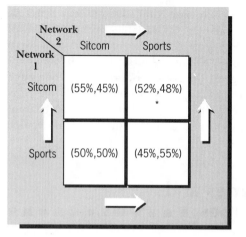

Figure 2.1. Battle of the Networks, normal form.

k happens to equal 0, then you have a zero-sum game. It often happens in business that $k = 1$. When firms are competing on the basis of market shares, then the market shares add up to 100%. Consider the game **Battle of the Networks,** the normal form of which is shown in Figure 2.1. Two television networks, which we will call 1 and 2, are battling for shares of total viewers. Viewer shares are important because the higher the viewer share, the more money the network can make from selling advertising time on that program. Each network can show either a sitcom or a sports event, and the networks make their programming decisions independently and simultaneously. Network 1 has a programming advantage in sitcoms. If both networks show sitcoms, then network 1 gets a 55% viewer share. Network 2 has a programming advantage in sports; if both networks show sports, then network 2 gets a 55% viewer share.

We can solve Battle of the Networks by attaching arrows to the normal form of this game in Figure 2.1. The arrow on the left pointing up shows that network 1 prefers showing a sitcom and getting a viewer share of 55% to showing sports and getting a viewer share of 50% when network 2 is showing a sitcom. Similarly, the arrow at the bottom pointing to the right indicates that network 2 prefers showing sports and getting a viewer share of 55% to showing a sitcom and getting a viewer share of 50% when network 1 is showing a sitcom. There is a single situation in which arrows point in from both directions: network 1 is showing a sitcom and network 2 is showing sports, with network 1 getting 52% of the viewers. This situation is denoted by an asterisk (*).

A situation in which arrows point in from both directions is called an **equilibrium.**[2] At the equilibrium of Battle of the Networks, it would be a mistake for either network to adopt a different strategy from its equilibrium

---

[2]The terms *game equilibrium, strategic equilibrium,* and *Nash equilibrium* are used synonymously. I prefer the term *equilibrium,* if only because it is shorter.

strategy. If network 1 were to switch from its sitcom to a sports show, its viewer share would drop 7%, from 52% to 45%. If network 2 were to switch from its sports show to a sitcom, its viewer share would drop 3%, from 48% to 45%. Each network is getting the best ratings it can, given the competition it is up against. This is the sense of equilibrium: each player is doing the best possible given the competition. The equilibrium of Battle of the Networks, which is the pair of strategies (network 1 shows a sitcom, network 2 shows sports), is the solution of the game. Arrow diagrams are used throughout the book to solve games, so be sure you understand this one before going any further.

There is an easy way to relate constant-sum and zero-sum 2-person games. Let u_1 and u_2 be the payoffs in a k-sum game. Now consider a new set of payoffs of the form

$$v_1 = u_1 - u_2$$
$$v_2 = u_2 - u_1$$

Clearly, $v_1 + v_2 = 0$, so we now have a zero-sum game. Substituting the constant-sum condition

$$u_1 + u_2 = k$$

We have

$$v_1 = 2u_1 - k$$
$$v_2 = 2u_2 - k$$

These are positive, linear transformations of utility, and so, according to the expected utility theorem, they have no effect on decisions. What these transformations do is measure utility in terms of viewer share advantage. If v_1 is positive, network 1 has a larger viewer share than network 2 and v_1 measures how large network 1's advantage is.

Figure 2.2 shows Battle of the Networks as a zero-sum game. To see how the payoffs from Figure 2.2 follow from Figure 2.1, take the case where both networks show a sitcom. Network 1 gets a 55% viewer share in this case. Using the previous transformation with $k = 1$, we get

$$v_1 = 2(0.55) - 1 = 0.1$$

or 10%. This is the entry for network 1's utility in the cell (sitcom, sitcom). Network 1 has a 10% advantage in viewer share in this case. Similarly, for network 2,

$$v_2 = 2(0.45) - 1 = -0.1$$

or −10%. This is the entry for network 2's utility in the cell (sitcom, sitcom). Notice that these two entries do indeed add up to zero. You can work out all the other payoffs in Figure 2.2 in this way.

Notice that the arrow diagram of Figure 2.2 is exactly the same as the arrow diagram of Figure 2.1. This is no coincidence, but reflects the fact that strategic

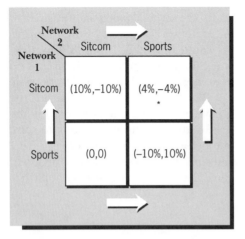

Figure 2.2. Battle of the Networks, zero-sum version.

reasoning remains the same for any positive linear transformation of players' utilities. Whether these networks reason in terms of total viewer share, in which case the game is one sum, or in terms of viewer advantage, in which case the game is zero sum, the solution is the same. Network 1 shows a sitcom; network 2, sports. The dollar reality behind these utilities is the same in either case. No matter how you look at them, higher ratings mean more advertising dollars.

2.2 Competitive Advantage ■ ■ ■ ■ ■ ■ ■ ■ ■ ■ ■ ■ ■ ■ ■ ■

In a technologically advanced economy like that of the United States, firms constantly encounter the following situation. A new technological advance becomes available. If one firm adopts the new technology, it gains an advantage over its competitors, a **competitive advantage.** If all firms adopt the new technology, then the advantage vanishes. The game these firms are in is called Competitive Advantage. To take just one of many possible examples, consider the hospital industry. Magnetic resonance imaging (MRI) is a new technology that enhances conventional X rays with the assistance of computers. It allows doctors to see body damage in ways that were not previously possible. Once MRI became available, any hospital that installed an MRI unit gained a competitive advantage over other hospitals in its area. It got more referrals and could offer a wider range of services.

Figure 2.3 shows Competitive Advantage in normal form. The payoff parameter a measures the size of the competitive advantage conferred by the new technology. Each firm has two strategies, either Stay put or Adopt the new technology. Firm 1 has an incentive to adopt the new technology. In the event that firm 2 stays put, then firm 1 gets the competitive advantage a by adopting the new technology. This situation is represented by the arrow on the right,

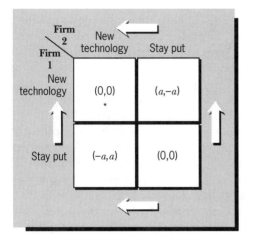

Figure 2.3. Competitive Advantage.

pointing up. In the event that firm 2 adopts the new technology, then firm 1 erases its competitive disadvantage $-a$ by adopting the new technology. This situation is represented by the arrow on the left, pointing up. The arrows on the top and bottom pointing to the left reflect similar incentives for firm 2.

The equilibrium of Competitive Advantage, where arrows point in from both directions, is when each firm adopts the new technology. At equilibrium, the competitive advantage vanishes. No firm has a competitive advantage over the other, but no firm can afford to stay put, either. The firms in this game are driven to adopt any technology that comes along. The force behind this drive is the solution to Competitive Advantage. To return to the MRI example, it may not make much sense from a public policy standpoint for every hospital to have its own MRI unit. These units are expensive to buy and to operate—they can eat up millions of dollars. Also, one MRI unit can sometimes handle the traffic of several hospitals. At the same time, an individual hospital would be at a competitive disadvantage if it didn't have its own MRI. As long as hospitals play Competitive Advantage, they are going to adopt every new technology that comes along.

In the Battle of the Networks and Competitive Advantage, strategy is all-important and luck plays no role. Let's now turn to a zero-sum game, Poker, where strategy is important, and so is luck. Poker is all about being lucky *and* playing your cards right. We will study a simple version of Poker—so simple, in fact, that it has the same normal form that Competitive Advantage has.

◆ 2.3 One-Card Stud Poker ■ ■ ■ ■ ■ ■ ■ ■ ■ ■ ■ ■ ■ ■ ■ ■ ■

This section looks at a version of Poker that, although very simple, exhibits many of the principles of good Poker play. Poker is a complicated game, the more so, the more cards a player holds. We will keep things simple by studying a version of Poker in which each player is dealt exactly one card, hence the name **1-card Stud Poker.**[3] We will also keep things simple by having only two players, although this game can easily be played by more than two players, as shown in Chapter 4.

Call the two players 1 and 2. The deck of cards consists of 50% aces and 50% kings. (You can create such a deck and play this game yourself). Prior to the deal, each player puts an amount of money a, called the *ante*, into the center of the table, called the *pot*. Each player is dealt one card face down, which neither the player nor the opponent sees.[4] At this point, a player can either bet an amount b (also placed in the pot) or pass. The players make this decision simultaneously.[5] Once the betting round has concluded, the game is over. If one player bet and the other passed, the player who bet takes the pot. If both players bet or both players passed, both turn over their card (the showdown). The player with the highest card wins the pot, with an ace beating a king. If both players in a showdown have equal cards, they split the pot.

Figure 2.4 shows 1-card Stud Poker in extensive form. The game begins with a chance move, the deal. A deal consists of a pair (card to player 1, card to player 2). For instance, the deal where player 1 gets an ace and player 2 gets a king is represented (A, K). There are four possible deals, each with probability $1/4$. Player 1 is the next to move. Player 1 does not know which deal has occurred, and so player 1's information set contains four nodes corresponding to the four possible deals. Player 1 either bets or passes. Player 2 is the last to move. Player 2 does not know which deal has occurred or what player 1 has done, and so player 2's information set contains eight nodes corresponding to the four possible deals times the two possible moves by player 1. Player 2 bets or passes. At this point the game ends.

There are 16 endpoints to 1-card Stud Poker in extensive form. These are shown in Figure 2.4, and we will walk through some of them. Suppose the deal is (A, A) and both players bet. The pot contains $2(a + b)$ dollars. At the showdown, the hands are equal, so the players split the pot. Each player breaks even—the outcome $(0,0)$. The same outcome occurs when the deal is (K, K) and both players bet, when the deal is (A, A) and both players pass, and when the deal is (K, K) and both players pass. Next, suppose that player 1 bets and player 2 passes. Then, regardless of the cards, player 1 wins player 2's ante—the outcome $(a, -a)$. Player 2 may have the better card, or a card of equal value, but by folding hands the ante over to player 1. There are 4 endpoints with the outcome $(a, -a)$. By reversing the strategies, with player 1 passing and player 2

[3]In Draw Poker, as opposed to Stud Poker, players can discard some cards and replace them with new ones, a move called drawing cards. In Stud Poker, players have to play with the cards dealt them.

[4]This is another simplification, since in real-life Poker players have the option of seeing their own cards, but not those of their opponents. This assumption is relaxed in Chapter 3.

[5]In most Poker games, the players bet in sequence rather than simultaneously, which introduces an element of signaling into the game. Signaling is studied in Chapters 9, 12, and 13.

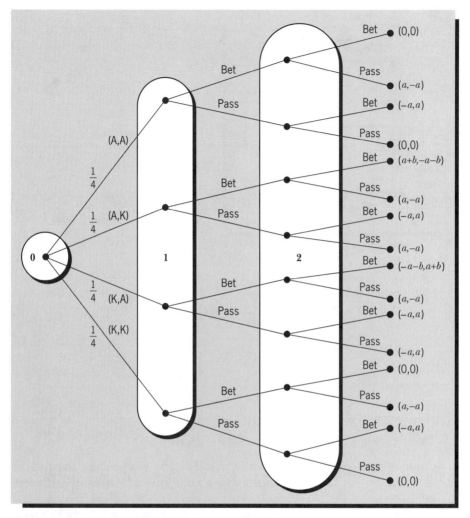

Figure 2.4. One-Card Stud Poker, extensive form.

betting, we get 4 endpoints of the form $(-a,a)$. Finally, suppose the deal is (AK) and both players bet. The pot contains $2(a + b)$ dollars. At the showdown, player 1 beats player 2 and collects the entire pot. Player 1's gain, $a + b$, is what player 2 anted and bet. This is the outcome $(a + b, -a - b)$.

As is usually the case, it is pretty hard to see from the extensive form what each player should do. Fortunately, the extensive form of Figure 2.4 boils down to a much simpler normal form—Figure 2.5. Note first of all that each player has a single information set, at which there are two possible moves, bet or pass. Thus the strategy set for each player is {bet, pass}. These are the rows and columns of Figure 2.5. Now we need to fill in the cells. Start with the pair of strategies (bet, bet). This pair of strategies leads to the following probability distribution over endpoints of the game:

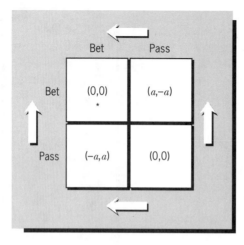

Figure 2.5. One-Card Stud Poker, normal form.

(0,0) with probability $\frac{1}{4}$; deal (A, A)

$(a + b, -a - b)$ with probability $\frac{1}{4}$; deal (A, K)

$(-a - b, a + b)$ with probability $\frac{1}{4}$; deal (K, A)

(0,0) with probability $\frac{1}{4}$; deal (K, K)

Taking expected values, we get for player 1

$$EV_1 = .25(0) + .25(a + b) + .25(-a - b) + .25(0) = 0$$

and similarly for player 2. This is the payoff vector (0,0) in the cell for (bet, bet) in Figure 2.5. Carrying out the exact same calculation for the strategies (pass, pass) yields the payoff vector for that cell. Finally, for the strategy vector (bet, pass), player 1 wins and player 2 loses regardless of the cards, the payoff vector $(a, -a)$.

Following the arrows, the solution of 1-card Stud Poker is for each player to bet. With this solution, both players break even.[6] A player who does not bet is beaten by a player who does bet. This result, players breaking even, reflects the fact that the deal is *fair:* each player has the same chance of getting a good hand. If the deal were unfair, then the solution to Poker would favor the player getting good cards more of the time (end-of-chapter problem). Unfair deals are generated by cheating. With a fair deal, when both players adopt the same strategy, the cards even out and the payoff vector (0,0) results. Even though (pass, pass) is not a solution, if both players use this strategy, then they both break even. If you persistently lose at Poker and the deal is fair, you have only yourself to blame. You are not playing the best available strategy. If you were,

[6]This holds true for more general forms of Poker.

you would at least break even. A loser fails to follow the strategic principles that could improve play. A loser who doesn't learn from his or her losses remains just that—a loser.

Now compare Figures 2.3 and 2.5. Except for the names of the games and the names of the strategies, they are exactly the same. 1-card Stud Poker and Competitive Advantage have the same strategic content. Just as adopting a new technology gives a business a competitive advantage, betting in Poker gives a Poker player a playing advantage over a player who passes. Nothing ventured, nothing gained—and in the case of Poker, Nothing bet, the ante lost. At first sight, it may seem rather remarkable that MRIs and Poker could have anything in common. However, this happens all the time in game theory, so you might as well get used to it. The same game can show up all over the economy, and even in the games we play at home.

We can say something even stronger about Competitive Advantage and 1-card Stud Poker, namely, that there is only one good way to play these games. More precisely, a strategy is a **strictly dominant strategy** if it pays more than another in every contingency. A strategy is a **dominant strategy** if it pays at least as much as another in every contingency and more in some contingency. In Competitive Advantage, the strategy that adopts the new technology strictly dominates the strategy that stays put:

$a > 0$ when the opponent stays put

$0 > -a$ when the opponent adopts the new technology

Similarly, the strategy Bet strictly dominates the strategy Pass in 1-card Stud Poker. Not only is adopting the new technology the solution to Competitive Advantage, it also strictly dominates the alternative strategy Stay put. If I have a strictly dominant strategy, then no matter what my opponent does, I do best by playing my strictly dominant strategy. It is a serious and costly mistake in a game to play a strategy that is strictly dominated. No such strategy can be played as part of an equilibrium. An arrow would point away from such a strategy toward the strictly dominant strategy instead. In Competitive Advantage and 1-card Stud Poker, the parameter a measures just how costly a mistake it is to play the strictly dominated strategy.

▚ 2.4 Solutions of Two-Person, Zero-Sum Games ■■■■■■■■■■■■■■■■■■■■■■

Two-person, zero-sum games were the first to be solved.[7] All such games we have encountered so far have had unique equilibria, and so we did not have to

---

[7] This feat was accomplished by the father of game theory, John von Neumann, in an article in German entitled "Zur Theorie der Gesellschaftsspiele" (Toward a theory of social games), *Mathematische Annalen* 100 (1928):295–320. This article is available in both English and German in von Neumann's *Collected Papers*.

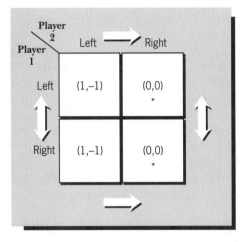

Figure 2.6.   Two-person, zero-sum game with two solutions.

worry about the solution. If a game has a unique equilibrium, that is its solution. However, a 2-person, zero-sum game may have multiple equilibria. Consider the game in Figure 2.6. Both players can move either left or right simultaneously. If player 2 moves left, he or she automatically loses regardless of what player 1 does; therefore, player 2 moves right. If player 1 moves left, the result is a draw; if player 1 moves right, likewise a draw. These two equilibria (left, right) and (right, right) lead to the same payoffs, zero utility for each player. Either equilibrium counts as a solution.

Figure 2.7 gives an even more complicated example, a 2-person, zero-sum game with four equilibria. Both players can move left, center, or right simultaneously. The only way player 2 can lose is by getting caught in the center when player 1 isn't in the center. The only way player 1 can lose is by getting caught in the center when player 2 isn't in the center. All other strategy combinations lead to a draw. Note the four equilibria: (left, left), (left, right), (right, left), and (right, right). All have the same payoffs, corresponding to a draw.

In both examples of multiple equilibria, we see that payoffs to each player are the same at every equilibrium. This is no coincidence; rather, it is a mathematical necessity that every equilibrium of a 2-person, zero-sum game have the same payoffs. We shall now prove that this must be the case.

■ ■

Solution Theorem for 2-Person, Zero-Sum Games. Every equilibrium of a 2-person, zero-sum game has the same value.

We will prove the **solution theorem** for the case of 2×2 games, although it holds true in general. Consider the game in Figure 2.8. The proof is by contradiction. By hypothesis, the payoff vectors $(a, -a)$ and $(b, -b)$ are equilibria, and a is not equal to b. These two different solutions cannot lie on the same row or column, which would be an immediate contradiction. We lose no generality by locating these two

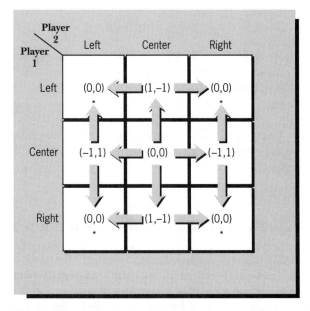

Figure 2.7. Two-person, zero-sum game with four solutions.

different equilibria at the corners. From the arrow diagram, we have the following system of inequalities:

$$a > d$$
$$b > c$$
$$-a > -c$$
$$-b > -d$$

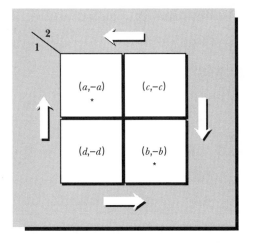

Figure 2.8. Proof of the solution theorem.

Solving this set of inequalities, we get

$$a > d > b > c > a$$

a contradiction. If we make any or all of the arrows two-headed, and thus replace an inequality with an equality, you still get a contradiction. Thus the two equilibria must have the same value. This completes the proof.

Since all equilibria of a 2-person, zero-sum game have the same value, we can identify the solution payoffs with any of them. As we will soon see, this is not true for general variable-sum games. Once a game has variable-sum payoffs, it may have equilibria with very different payoff values. In such a case, we have to think harder about what a solution is.

2.5 Two-Person Variable-Sum Games ■ ■ ■ ■ ■ ■ ■ ■ ■ ■

Most of the games that occur in business are not constant sum. If the sum of players' utilities in a game varies at a single outcome, that game is a **variable-sum game.** Variable-sum games are more complex than constant-sum games, and the solution theory for them is much more involved. Here is an example, inspired by Hollywood, called **Let's Make a Deal.** Player 1, a movie star, and player 2, a director, are trying to put together a movie deal. They estimate that the movie is capable of making $30 million in profits. There is an offer on the table—to split the profits evenly. If both the movie star and the director say yes to the deal, it's a deal. If either one rejects the deal, the game is over and no movie gets made. The normal form for this game is shown in Figure 2.9.

As you can see from the arrow diagram, Let's Make a Deal has two equilibria. One equilibrium, (yes, yes), means there is a $30 million deal, from which both

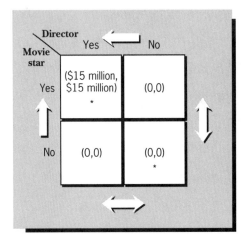

Figure 2.9. Let's Make a Deal.

sides get $15 million. The second equilibrium, (no, no), means there is no deal, and both sides get $0. If you are the movie star and you know the studio is going to reject the deal, you lose nothing by rejecting it either. These two equilibria have dramatically different payoffs, reflecting the variable-sum nature of the game. This phenomenon forces us to distinguish between equilibrium and solution. Again, an equilibrium is any pair of strategies with arrows pointing to it from both directions. At an equilibrium, every player has maximized utility and no player has an incentive to change strategy. Not all equilibria have the same payoffs once a game is variable sum.

Solving a game is a lot like solving a calculus problem. Let's say you want to minimize the function $f(x) = x^2$. The necessary condition for the minimization is that the derivative of the function, df/dx, vanishes: $df/dx = 2x = 0$. A **necessary condition** is a condition that needs to be satisfied by any candidate for a solution. Since $x = 0$ satisfies the necessary condition, It becomes a candidate for solving the minimization problem. Now we check part of the **sufficient condition,** that the second derivative of the function, $d^2f/dx^2 > 0$. We have $d^2f/dx^2 = 2 > 0$, so this part of the sufficient condition is satisfied. The entire sufficient condition for a maximum is that the second derivative be negative and the first derivative be positive. Satisfying both necessary and sufficient conditions clinches a solution: $x = 0$ solves the minimization problem, and the minimum value of the function is $f(0) = 0$.

In just the same way, *an outcome needs to be an equilibrium (necessary condition) before it can be a candidate for a solution.* If an outcome is not an equilibrium, then some player gains by a change of strategy, and behavior cannot be at rest—which is what an equilibrium is supposed to be. However, just because an outcome is an equilibrium does not mean it is a solution. To be a solution requires that an equilibrium also satisfy sufficient conditions. We now turn to our first sufficient condition.

■■ 2.6 A Sufficient Condition for Solving Variable-Sum Games ■■■■■■■■■■■■■■■■■■■■■■■■■

Let's introduce a sufficient condition that will choose between the high-value equilibrium and the low-value equilibrium in Let's Make a Deal. Notice that as far as the movie star is concerned, the strategy Yes pays as least as much as the strategy No for every possible strategy chosen by the director. For instance, if the director says yes, then the movie star gets $15 million for saying yes and $0 for saying no. Saying yes dominates saying no, although the domination is not strict. If the director says no, then the movie star gets $0 for saying yes and $0 for saying no. It's a toss-up in this case. You can check that the strategy Yes dominates the strategy No for the director as well. Neither player has any reason to say no, because saying yes dominates saying no. This is enough to make us suspicious of the equilibrium (no, no) as a solution. This suspicion is borne out by the following sufficient condition:

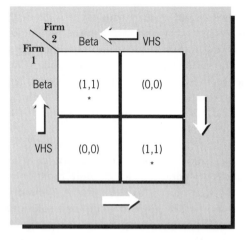

Figure 2.10.   Video System Coordination.

■ ■

Undominated Strategies. Suppose that (s,t) is an equilibrium. Suppose further that some other strategy s^* dominates s for player 1, and that the strategy t^* dominates t for player 2. Then the equilibrium (s,t) is not a solution.

Applying the sufficient condition of **undominated strategies** to Let's Make a Deal, we see that (no, no) cannot be a solution, since Yes dominates No for both players. Just like sufficient conditions in calculus, sufficient conditions in game theory tell you that something can't be a solution, even though it is an equilibrium. They are meant to rule out certain equilibria as possible solutions. Let's Make a Deal does have another equilibrium, (yes, yes), and this equilibrium does pass the test posed by the sufficient condition of undominated strategies. Therefore, the solution to Let's Make a Deal is for both the movie star and the director to say yes to the deal. We have just solved our first variable-sum game.

Here is another example, inspired by the video market, called **Video System Coordination.** There are two kinds of video systems, VHS and Beta. Both work equally well. A firm can adopt either VHS or Beta technology. However, once a firm adopts one of these technologies, it cannot successfully interact with a firm using the other. This is called a **coordination problem:** the problem is to get everybody to coordinate on a single strategy. Video System Coordination is shown in Figure 2.10. This coordination game has two equilibria.[8] It doesn't really matter whether firms choose Beta or VHS, as long as they both choose the same system. Since neither system dominates the other, both satisfy the sufficient condition of undominated strategies. Either Beta or VHS solves Video System Coordination. This shows that satisfying sufficient conditions does not guarantee uniqueness of a solution.

[8]Chapter 3 exhibits a third equilibrium, which you can't see from the arrow diagram here.

A useful way to think of 2-person games like Let's Make a Deal and Video System Coordination is as parables. They boil down to the bare essentials the strategic aspects of a given situation, such as making a deal or setting up a network. The way parables work is by showing us how to apply what we have learned in a bare-bones situation to the richer situations that we encounter in real life. Of course, a really good parable will also apply immediately to real life, as the following surprise from the 1970s shows.

⊞ 2.7 Cigarette Advertising on Television[9] ■ ■ ■ ■ ■ ■ ■ ■ ■ ■

In the years before 1964, all tobacco companies in the United States advertised heavily on television. You could see actors, celebrities, and ex-athletes lighting up all the time. In 1964 the surgeon general issued the first official warning that cigarette smoking might be hazardous to public health. At first, the cigarette companies were loath to carry the now-familiar warning label on their product. They feared, and rightly so, that carrying the warning would open them up to devastating liability lawsuits. After protracted negotiations, the industry and the U.S. government reached an agreement in 1970. According to the agreement, the companies would carry the warning label and would cease advertising on television in exchange for immunity from lawsuits based on federal law.[10]

The agreement went into effect on January 1, 1971. To see the effect of this agreement, we need to work out the strategic interaction in the industry before and after the agreement went into effect. Although there were four large tobacco companies involved, American Brands, Reynolds, Philip Morris, and Liggett & Myers, and the same considerations operated for all firms in the industry, for simplicity let's consider the strategic interaction between only two of them. Then, for the sake of anonymity, let's call the two companies company 1 and company 2. Assume that when the companies adopt comparable strategies, they enjoy comparable market share and profits as well.

The strategies of each firm are to advertise on television or not. The entries of the payoff matrix are each company's profits in 1970 dollars. To convert these profits to current dollars, you should multiply by a factor of about 3.5. The 2-firm variable-sum game that results is shown in Figure 2.11. You can see from the matrix that advertising on television is a powerful marketing tool. If company 1 advertises on television and company 2 doesn't, then company 1's profits go up 20%; the same is true with the roles reversed. Each company has an incentive to advertise its cigarettes on television. Indeed, this is a strictly dominant strategy for

---

[9] Material in this section is drawn from Frederick M. Scherer, *Industrial Market Structure and Economic Performance,* 2d ed. (Boston: Houghton Mifflin, 1980), especially p. 389 and the references listed therein.

[10] The cigarette companies continue to be potentially liable under state law, since the states were not part of this agreement. All cigarette lawsuits now pending are being handled in state courts.

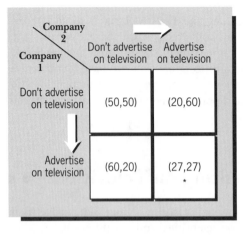

Figure 2.11. Cigarette Television Advertising. All payoffs in millions of dollars.

each of the companies. There is a single equilibrium—hence the solution—with both companies advertising on television.

Notice, however, what happens to earnings when both companies advertise on television at the same time. Earnings are only $27 million each, $23 million less than if the companies refrained from advertising on television. The reason for this result is that all advertisements tend to cancel each other out, leaving industry sales about the same but costs much higher.

We say that an outcome is **efficient** if there is no other outcome that pays all players more. An important feature of *Cigarette Television Advertising* is that the solution of the game turns out to be very inefficient in this sense. The payoffs earned by the companies are much less than they might otherwise be, in particular if they did not play the equilibrium solution. There is a whiff of paradox here: why would solving something make you worse off? If the companies are at any of the disequilibrium outcomes, one or both of them can make a lot more money by changing the strategy. These are not places where the players can rest. The paradox only arises when you try to compare something that cannot persist—a disequilibrium—with something that can persist—an equilibrium. In a strategic sense, the might-have-been payoffs are ephemeral, and nothing more.

Any game in which every player has a strictly dominant strategy has a unique solution, which is to play the strictly dominant strategy. When that solution is bad for the players, the phenomenon is called the prisoner's dilemma. The players are prisoners of their own strategies, unless something changes the game for them. In the case of the tobacco companies, that something was the U.S. government. By agreeing with the government to carry the warning label and stop advertising on television, the cigarette companies gave up the strategy of advertising on television. They were left with only the strategy Don't advertise on television. Cigarette companies are heavy advertisers at all times. The big four companies spent $315 million advertising their products in 1970, but only $252 million on advertising in 1971. This $63 million decrease came right out of the television advertising accounts. At the same time, it came as something of a surprise to the industry, and a welcome one at that, that profits rose by $91 million.

It often happens in variable-sum games that the solution is not efficient. Note, however, that the solution is efficient in Let's Make a Deal and Video System Coordination. From time to time, we encounter such games. One of the biggest differences between constant- and variable-sum games is that solutions to the former are always efficient, whereas solutions to the latter are rarely efficient. Since economists are paid to worry about efficiency and efficiency means money in business, too, you should always be on the lookout for games whose solutions are efficient. An artful change in the rules of the game—such as in cigarette advertising on television—which makes an inefficient solution efficient, can make all the difference to profits.

2.8 Two-Person Games with Many Strategies ■■■■■■■■■■■■■■■■■■■■■■■

This chapter has presented normal form games with at most three rows and three columns. As you might suspect, there is nothing sacred about the number 3. A player could have billions of strategies—and we could still analyze the game. To do so requires some notation. This book never introduces more notation than is needed, and this particular piece is indispensable.

Let x_1 denote the strategy chosen by player 1 and x_2 denote the strategy chosen by player 2. Player 1's utility function, $u_1(x_1,x_2)$, depends on both strategies. Player 2's utility function, $u_2(x_1,x_2)$, also depends on both strategies. This is strategic interaction in a nutshell. Suppose that x_1 could take on 100 different values, and so could x_2. You need a 100×100 matrix to write down the game. Nobody wants to write down a matrix that big. It gets worse. Suppose that x_1 and x_2 could be any number between 0 and 1. There are uncountably many numbers to choose from—writing down that matrix would take longer than eternity. Nevertheless, we can still solve games with lots of strategies, even if we can't, or don't want to, write out their normal form as a matrix.

The key to unlocking games with lots of strategies is calculus. As long as the utility functions are differentiable, we can find game equilibria by using calculus techniques. First, we maximize each player's utility, a standard calculus problem. Then we solve the two equations in two unknowns, x_1 and x_2. When we are finished, the solution $\mathbf{x}^* = (x_1^*, x_2^*)$ is an equilibrium. If there is only one solution to the calculus part of the problem, then it is also the solution to the game. If there is more than one solution, then we appeal to sufficient conditions for game solutions, too.

Here is an example to show how all this works. Suppose that x_1 and x_2 represent the advertising budgets of firms 1 and 2. An advertising budget can be any number between \$0 and \$1000. Firm 1's profits, $u_1(x_1,x_2)$, are represented by the function

$$u_1(x_1,x_2) = 1000x_1 - x_1^2 - x_2^2$$

Firm 1's profits are increasing with respect to its own advertising budget up to a certain level ($x_1 = \$500$), after which they are decreasing. Firm 1's profits are also decreasing with respect to firm 2's advertising budget. Maximizing firm 1's profits with respect to firm 1's advertising budget, we have

$$0 = \frac{\partial u_1}{\partial x_1} = 1000 - 2x_1$$

Note in this maximization that firm 1 treats firm 2's advertising budget, x_2, as if it were a constant. This assumption only holds true at equilibrium. Firm 2's profits, $u_2(x_1,x_2)$, are given by the function

$$u_2(x_1,x_2) = 1000x_2 - x_1x_2 - x_2^2$$

Maximizing firm 2's profits with respect to firm 2's advertising budget, we have

$$0 = \frac{\partial u_2}{\partial x_2} = 1000 - x_1 - 2x_2$$

We now have to solve simultaneously the two equations

$$0 = 1000 - 2x_1$$
$$0 = 1000 \, (-x_1) - 2x_2$$

From the first equation, we have $x_1^* = 500$. Substituting this into the second equation, we get $x_2^* = 250$. The vector $\mathbf{x}^* = (x_1^*,x_2^*) = (500,250)$ is the equilibrium of this advertising game with many strategies. The corresponding profits are $u_1(\mathbf{x}^*) = \$187,500$ and $u_2(\mathbf{x}^*) = \$62,500$.

It is worth noting that the game equilibrium we have found still involves too much advertising. These firms could each make more money if they advertised less. Solving the calculus problem, to maximize $u_1 + u_2$, we have

$$0 = \frac{\partial(u_1 + u_2)}{\partial(x_1)} = 1000 - 2x_1 - x_2$$

and

$$0 = \frac{\partial(u_1 + u_2)}{\partial(x_2)} = 1000 - x_1 - 2x_2 - 2x_2$$

The advertising budgets that maximize industry profits are the solution of this pair of equations. Solving, we get $x_1 = 428.6$ and $x_2 = 142.9$. Firm profits in this case are $u_1 = \$224,482$ and $u_2 = \$81,423$. The moral of Cigarette Television Advertising continues to hold when firms can choose the size of their advertising budget and not just whether to advertise or not. Firms competing with one another through their advertising tend to advertise too much.

▓ 2.9 Existence of Equilibrium[11] ■ ■ ■ ■ ■ ■ ■ ■ ■ ■ ■ ■ ■ ■ ■ ■

It is worth knowing when the calculus-based technique we just used for finding an equilibrium will work. We can actually show when a solution will exist to the equations that define an equilibrium. The following theorem guarantees that there is an equilibrium, if only we can find it.

First, some setup is needed. Each player has the strategy space [0,1].[12] Player 1 picks strategy x_1 from this interval; player 2, strategy x_2. Player 1 has the utility function $u_1(x_1,x_2)$; player 2 has the utility function $u_2(x_1,x_2)$. These utility functions are twice continuously differentiable. Moreover, utility is strictly concave in a player's own strategy. This is the case, for instance, if the players are profit-maximizing firms, whose revenue and cost functions are twice continuously differentiable and whose profit functions are strictly concave in their own strategy.

Define player 1's best-response function $f_1(x_2)$ to be the value of x_1 that maximizes $u_1(x_1,x_2)$, for any fixed x_2. That is, $f_1(x_2)$ solves the equation[13]

$$0 = \frac{\partial u_1}{\partial x_1}$$

Given our assumptions on utility, $f_1(x_2)$ is a continuous function of x_2. Similarly, define player 2's best-response function $f_2(x_1)$ as the value of x_2 that maximizes $u_2(x_1,x_2)$ for any fixed x_1. That is, $f_2(x_1)$ solves the equation

$$0 = \frac{\partial u_2}{\partial x_2}$$

Given our assumptions on utility, $f_2(x_1)$ is a continuous function of x_1.

Let $\mathbf{f} = [f_1(x_2), f_2(x_1)]$ be the vector function of these best-response functions. Since the component functions of $\mathbf{f}$ are continuous, $\mathbf{f}$ is continuous. The function $\mathbf{f}$ is called the best-response function for the entire game. Start out with a pair of strategies (x_1,x_2). Player 1 makes his or her best response to x_2, $f_1(x_2)$. At the same time, player 2 makes his or her best response to x_1, $f_2(x_1)$. The best-response function for the game records these responses. Play has gone from (x_1,x_2) to $[f_1(x_2), f_2(x_1)]$. Figure 2.12 illustrates the best-response functions

$$f_1(x_2) = 500; f_2(x_1) = 500 - \frac{x_1}{2}$$

[11] The material in this section is harder than in the rest of the chapter, and may be omitted upon first reading.

[12] Any bounded interval, and not just [0,1], will do.

[13] Best-response functions are also known as reaction functions. In the event of a corner maximum, we take the appropriate value of x_1, either 0 or 1, instead. A sign that we need to inspect the corners is that the solution to this first-order condition does not lie within bounds.

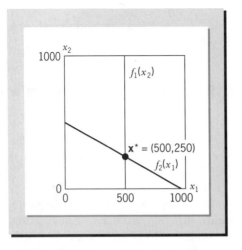

Figure 2.12.   Advertising, many strategies, best-response functions.

These are the best-response functions for the advertising game we just solved.

A vector **x*** that satisfies both best-response conditions is an equilibrium. Graphically, this means that the two best-response functions cross at **x***. For instance, in Figure 2.12, the two best-response functions cross at (500,250), which is the equilibrium.

Another way to describe a solution to this pair of equations is the following. Write down the system

$$x_1^* = f_1(x_2^*)$$

and

$$x_2^* = f_2(x_1^*)$$

Using vector notation, we can rewrite these equations more compactly as

$$(\mathbf{x}^*) = \mathbf{f}(\mathbf{x}^*) = [f_1(x_2^*), f_2(x_1^*)]$$

A point at which function **f** maps into itself is called a *fixed point*. A game equilibrium is a fixed point of the best-response mapping. At equilibrium, neither player has an incentive to make a response other than the one he or she is currently making. To guarantee that a game has an equilibrium, we have to guarantee that the equation involving the best-response function for the game has a fixed point **x***. Fortunately, there is a mathematical answer to this question, contained in the following fixed-point theorem:

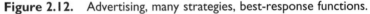

Fixed-Point Theorem. If *f* is a continuous function from the unit square to the unit square, then *f* has a fixed point, namely, *x*, where *x* = *f(x)*.

Figure 2.13 illustrates the fixed-point property for the advertising game we just solved. Moreover, since the best-response function of the game under our assump-

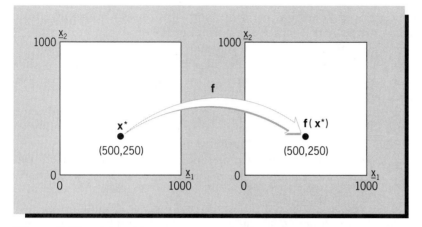

Figure 2.13. Advertising, many strategies, best-response mapping.

tions is continuous, it must have a fixed point according to the fixed-point theorem. Any such fixed point is an equilibrium.

We can now collect our argument in the form of a theorem:

■ ■

Existence of Equilibrium. Suppose that for each player *i*, u_i is twice continuously differentiable and strictly concave in x_i. Then there exists a game equilibrium vector ***x****.

It is important to appreciate that the existence argument guarantees that there will be an equilibrium when strategy sets are well behaved (bounded intervals), and utility functions are well behaved (twice continuously differentiable, strictly concave in a player's own strategy). At the same time, the existence theorem is silent when strategy sets or utility functions are nasty. In those cases, a game might have an equilibrium, and it might not. This topic is pursued relentlessly in advanced texts.

▞ SUMMARY

1. A game is zero sum when the sum of the players' utilities is zero regardless of the outcome. Zero-sum games are a special case of constant-sum games. Every constant-sum game can be converted to a zero-sum game.
2. Two-person, zero-sum games can be solved using an arrow diagram. Arrows point toward an equilibrium. At an equilibrium, each player has maximized utility, given what the opposing player has done.
3. A firm can achieve a competitive advantage by adopting a new technology if its competitors stay put. In a game equilibrium, however, each firm adopts a new technology and no firm gains a competitive advantage.

4. One-card Stud Poker has the same normal form as Competitive Advantage, but strategy and luck are important in Poker.

5. Every equilibrium of a 2-person, zero-sum game has the same value.

6. When the sum of players' utilities in a game varies, the game is called variable sum. Variable-sum games are more complicated than zero-sum games, and they have different characteristics.

7. Being an equilibrium is a necessary condition for a strategy combination to be a solution to a game. If a strategy combination is not an equilibrium, then at least one player has an incentive to change play.

8. Variable-sum games usually have multiple equilibria (Let's Make a Deal, Video System Coordination). These equilibria may have very different values, as in Let's Make a Deal.

9. Undominated strategies is a sufficient condition for a solution to a game. An equilibrium in dominated strategies cannot be a solution according to this sufficient condition.

10. Cigarette Television Advertising shows that the solution to a game may involve seriously eroded profits. Changing the rules of the game can lead to large profit increases in such a case.

KEY TERMS

zero-sum game
constant-sum games
Battle of the Networks
equilibrium
competitive advantage
1-card Stud Poker
strictly dominant/dominant strategy
solution theorem
variable-sum game

Let's Make a Deal
necessary condition
sufficient condition
undominated strategies
Video System Coordination
coordination problem
Cigarette Television Advertising
efficiency

PROBLEMS

1. Suppose that in Battle of the Networks, if each network plays a sitcom, network 1 gets a market share of 66%. There are no other changes in the normal form. What is the solution of the game? Does this change make a difference? Why?

2. Convert the version of Battle of the Networks in problem 1 into a zero-sum game, then solve. Explain why the solution to the game in problems 1 and 2 are really the same.

3. Show that a win, lose, or draw game is not zero sum if each player has utility = 1 for a win, utility = 0.5 for a draw, and utility = –1 for a loss. What does this result imply about the generality of zero-sum games?

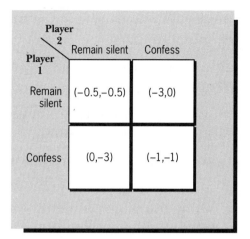

Figure 2.14. Prisoner's Dilemma. All numbers are years of time served.

4. Give examples of competitive advantages in the following industries: personal computers, automobiles, pharmaceuticals.

5. In 1-card Stud Poker, suppose the ante is $2 and the bet is $1. Draw the normal form of the game and solve.

6. Unfair 1-card Stud Poker I. Suppose that player 1 always gets an ace, and player 2 always gets a king. Draw the normal form and solve. (This is called cheating on the part of player 1.) Does player 2 break even?

7. Solve Let's Make a Deal when there is only $35,000 to be split evenly. Draw the normal form and spell out all the steps of your reasoning.

8. Suppose that in Video System Coordination the payoff if both firms are on the VHS system is 2 instead of 1. How does this affect the solution? Why might firms prefer one equilibrium to another?

9. Solve the game in Figure 2.14. Show in addition that each player has a dominant strategy. Relate your solution to advertising.

10. In a market economy where all goods are private and competition is perfect, an equilibrium is an optimum. However, in many 2-person games, equilibria are not optima. Why?

11. You are hired by a large U.S. beer company as a strategic consultant. You are asked to appraise their heavy television advertising activity. Outline your presentation and your advice.

■■ APPENDIX. WINNING AT BLACKJACK.[14]

In the fall of 1961, a young mathematician, Edward O. Thorp, astounded the gambling world by enumerating a strategy to beat the dealer in the casino game

[14]This material is based on Edwin O. Thorp, *Beat the Dealer* (New York: Random House, 1961, 1966).

Blackjack. Previously, casinos had thought they had the advantage at every game they played, including Blackjack. Indeed, it is true that for every casino game except Blackjack, the casinos have a positive expected value. Thorp's shocking discovery was based on millions of computer simulations, backed up by extensive play in the casinos. To present the complete strategy, together with a summary of the argument behind it for the casino version of Blackjack, requires an entire book. The two principles underlying it are fairly easy to understand, however. This appendix presents a simpler game, called Ten, which models Blackjack. Ten shares all the important strategic features of Blackjack, but can be solved without resort to heavy-duty computing. Once you have mastered Ten, if you are still interested in beating the dealer at Blackjack, read Thorp's book.[15]

The rules of Ten are as follows:

■ ■

Players. There are two players. Player 1 is you or me. Player 2 is the dealer, who represents the casino. From now on, we will call player 1 the player and player 2 the dealer.[16]

The pack. The pack consists of 11 cards, four 10s and seven 5s. You can construct such a pack and play the game yourself.

The deal. Before play begins, the cards are shuffled by the dealer and cut by the player. Then two cards are removed by the dealer and shown to the player. These cards are said to have been burned. The dealer then deals one card face down to the player and one card face up to himself or herself.

Betting. Player 1 bets before his or her card is dealt, but after the two cards have been burned. The minimum bet is $1; the maximum bet is $5. The minimum and maximum bet can be varied to suit the action.

Value of the cards. A 10 is worth 10 points; a 5, 5 points. If a player draws a second card, its value is added to that of the first to obtain the total value of the hand.

Object of the player. The player tries to obtain a total value that is greater than that of the dealer, but does not exceed 10—hence the name Ten.

The draw. The player looks at his or her card. If it is a 5, the player may elect either to draw a second card or to stand pat. If the player draws a second card and it is a 10, the total value of the hand is 15, which exceeds 10, and the player immediately loses to the dealer. This is called going bust. If the player draws a second card and it is a 5, the player has a total value of 10 and stands pat. Once the player has either drawn a card or stood pat, it is then the dealer's turn to draw. If the dealer has a 10, the dealer stands pat. If the dealer has a 5, he or she *must* draw. If the dealer draws a 10, the total is 15 and the dealer loses. If the dealer draws a 5, the total value is 10 and the dealer stands pat.

The settlement. If the player has not gone bust and the dealer has, then the player wins an amount equal to the bet. If neither the player nor the dealer has gone bust, the person with the higher total wins an amount equal to the bet of the player. If the

---

[15] Let the reader beware. Applying Thorp's system under casino conditions requires unflinching concentration and extraordinary devotion to detail for long periods of time. It is not meant for casual players.

[16] Actually, Ten can be played with a dealer and two other players, as shown in the next chapter.

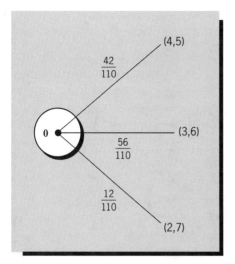

Figure 2.15. The burn in Ten.

player and the dealer both have the same total, not exceeding 10, no money changes hands.

This completes the set of rules for Ten. The biggest simplifications from Blackjack are the smaller deck (11 cards instead of 52) and the smaller number of different card values (2 different values instead of 11). It is not at all obvious from reading the rules of Ten that if the player bets $1 every hand, he or she can expect to lose on average 2 cents for every dollar bet. This is a losing experience consistent with that for average casino play. Now let's turn to the proof—not just for curiosity's sake, but because the proof will reveal a strategy for beating the dealer.

Let's begin our analysis with the burning of two cards, as shown in Figure 2.15. The original pack consists of four 10s and seven 5s, hereafter denoted (number of 10s, number of 5s) = (4,7). After burning two cards, there are three possible packs: (4,5), (3,6), and (2,7). The probabilities of each of these burns is given in the figure. The most likely burn is one card of each type, which happens a little more than 50% of the time (56/110), to be precise).

It is important to understand that the strategic situations represented by the different packs are different. The situation (4,5) is favorable to the player, whereas the situations (3,6) and (2,7) are favorable to the dealer. Note that the latter two situations are rich in 5s. In general (and this is true of casino Blackjack, too), the more 5s, the more likely a situation is to be unfavorable to the player.

Case 1. The pack is (4,5). The extensive form for this part of the game is shown in Figure 2.16. At this point, there are four possible deals: (player, dealer) = (10,10),

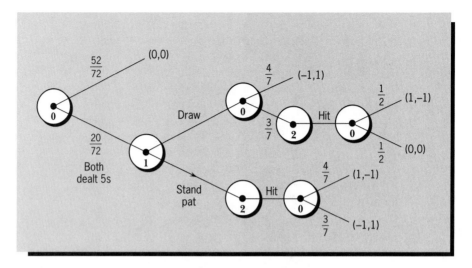

Figure 2.16.   Ten after the pack (4,5).

(10,5), (5,10), or (5,5). The deal (10,10) is easy—an automatic tie, with payoffs (0,0). Now consider the deals (10,5) and (5,10). The dealer has to hit when the deal is (10,5), whereas the player wants to hit when the deal is (5,10). Since both face the same pack, at this point (3,4), they both face the same odds. So these two deals average out to a draw also. This situation is reflected by the payoff (0,0) reached with probability 52/72, the probability that at least one 10 has been dealt.

The only deal left to consider is (5,5). The player can either draw a card or stand pat. If the player draws a card, he or she gets a 10 with probability 4/7 and goes bust, payoff (−1,1). If the player draws a 5, a probability 3/7 event, then it is the dealer's turn. The dealer must draw a card. With probability 3/6, that card is a 10 and the dealer has gone bust—the player wins, payoff (1,−1). With probability 3/6, that card is a 5 and the dealer and the player tie at 10 apiece, payoff (0,0). The expected value to the player of drawing a card is the following:

$$1 \text{ with probability } \frac{3}{14}$$
$$0 \text{ with probability } \frac{3}{14}$$
$$-1 \text{ with probability } \frac{8}{14}, EV = -\frac{5}{14}$$

This is not promising. Now consider what happens if the player stands pat. The dealer must draw a card. With probability 4/7, that card is a 10 and the dealer has gone bust—the player wins, payoff (1,−1). With probability 3/7, that card is a 5 and the dealer wins, 10 to 5—payoff (−1,1). The expected value to the player of standing pat is

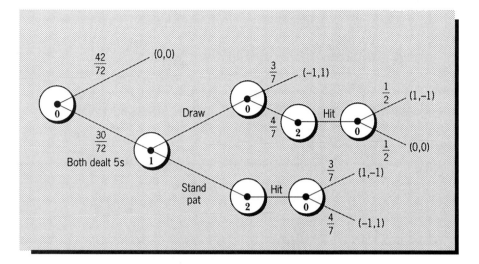

Figure 2.17. Ten after the pack (3,6).

1 with probability $\frac{4}{7}$

−1 with probability $\frac{3}{7}$, $EV = \frac{1}{7}$

That's much better. The player stands on 5 when the dealer has a 5 and beats the dealer. The overall expected value to the player from the pack (4,5) is

0 with probability $\frac{52}{72}$

$\frac{1}{7}$ with probability $\frac{20}{72}$, $EV = \frac{20}{504}$

It's not big, but it's positive.

Case 2. The pack is (3,6). The game tree for this case is shown in Figure 2.17. As in case 1, play is even except when two 5s are dealt, a 30/72 probability event. In this case, if the player takes a card, he or she has the following expected value:

1 with probability $\frac{4}{14}$

0 with probability $\frac{4}{14}$

−1 with probability, $EV = -\frac{1}{7}$

Not good. If the player stands pat and forces the dealer to take a card, the player's expected value is the following:

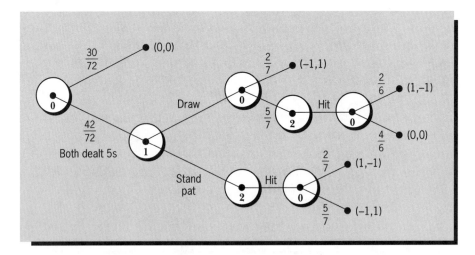

Figure 2.18.   Ten after the pack (2,7).

1 with probability $\dfrac{3}{7}$

−1 with probability $\dfrac{4}{7}$, $EV = -\dfrac{1}{7}$

Not good either. This case is a loser for the player, with an overall expected value

0 with probability $\dfrac{42}{72}$

$-\dfrac{1}{7}$ with probability $\dfrac{30}{72}$, $EV = -\dfrac{30}{504}$

Case 3. The pack is (2,7). It is up to you to show that this case is also a loser for the player—you get a big hint in the form of Figure 2.18. You can show that the expected value to the player of play from a (2,7) pack is

0   with probability $\dfrac{30}{72}$

$-\dfrac{1}{21}$ with probability $\dfrac{42}{72}$, $EV = -\dfrac{14}{504}$

Again, not good.

We have exhausted the three cases and can now compute the expected value of betting the minimum, \$1, each and every time, no matter what the pack is. We have

$\dfrac{20}{504}$ with probability $\dfrac{42}{110}$ the pack (4,5)

$-\dfrac{30}{504}$ with probability $\dfrac{56}{110}$ the pack (3,6)

$-\dfrac{14}{504}$ with probability $\dfrac{12}{110}$ the pack (2,7)

so the expected value is

$$EV = -\frac{1008}{55,440}$$

The player can expect to lose about 2 cents of every dollar bet, as indicated.

You were promised a payoff for going to all this trouble and here it is. We have just uncovered a valuable distinction for the player:

■ ■

Principle of Ten 1. Some situations are favorable to the player, others are not. The player, as long as he or she can recognize the difference, can vary bets to exploit situations in his or her favor.

This leads to:

■ ■

Principle of Ten 2. Bet the minimum in unfavorable situations; bet the maximum in favorable situations. These two principles imply the following strategy. Bet $5 when the burn leads to the situation (4,5); otherwise, bet the minimum, $1.

This strategy has the following expected value:

$\dfrac{100}{504}$ with probability $\dfrac{42}{110}$ the pack (4,5) with $5 bet

$-\dfrac{30}{504}$ with probability $\dfrac{56}{110}$ the pack (3,6) with $1 bet

$-\dfrac{14}{504}$ with probability $\dfrac{12}{110}$ the pack (2,7) with $1 bet

$$EV = \frac{2352}{55,440}$$

The player can expect to earn about 4 cents for every dollar bet using these two principles. These principles turn the player from a loser into a winner. *The player beats the dealer with this improved strategy.* And there is nothing the dealer can do about it—short of changing the rules or outright cheating.

Even though Blackjack is more complicated than Ten, the strategic principles just enunciated for Ten apply to it with a vengeance. The biggest challenge in using a strategy like that of Thorp is to identify the situations favorable to you under casino conditions. Naturally, the casinos take game theory seriously enough to have introduced various countermeasures to prevent the identification of favorable situations. These include increasing the number of decks (making it harder for the player to count), having the dealer count and reshuffle the deck whenever it is favorable to the player, and, as a last resort, banning players like Thorp who consistently win.[17]

PROBLEMS

1. Suppose that after the burn in Ten, the pack is (3,6). Verify the assertion in the text that the player breaks even over the deals where either the dealer or the player is dealt a 10.
2. Using Figure 2.18 as a big hint, show that the deck (2,7) is unfavorable to the player. Verify that the player stands to lose $-14/504$ when facing this deck.

---

[17] Courts have upheld the constitutionality of this exclusion, which extends to Thorp himself (at least in Nevada).

CHAPTER 3

Mixed Strategies
and Mixed Strategy
Equilibrium

All the strategies considered so far have been completely deterministic: they have involved definite plans of play, with everything that a player has to do specified in advance. Any strategy that is completely deterministic is a **pure strategy.** An equilibrium in which every player plays a pure strategy is called a **pure strategy equilibrium.** All the games we have solved so far have had pure strategy equilibria as solutions. Sometimes, however, an equilibrium involves players' using strategies that are not completely deterministic. Any strategy that is not completely deterministic, but instead involves chance, is called a **mixed strategy.** When a player uses a mixed strategy, it is as if he or she becomes a special kind of slot machine. An equilibrium in which at least one player plays a mixed strategy is called a **mixed strategy equilibrium.** This chapter will show why a player might play a mixed strategy and so act randomly, just as if he or she were a slot machine with probabilities set in advance.

The first section defines mixed strategies and shows that the right way to play the game Matching Pennies is to employ a mixed strategy. Discussion then turns to how mixed strategies can be used in a game involving entry into a market niche, where there is only room for one firm. In the context of such market niche games, a contradiction between efficiency and fairness of equilibria can be seen. Section 3.3 defines bluffing and shows how bluffing naturally arises in Liar's Poker. Coordination games are then introduced. These games always have mixed strategy equilibria. When firms playing Market Niche are asymmetrical, these equilibria are asymmetrical, too. Finally, this chapter reveals how sales involve mixed strategies. The strategy behind sales has a real-world analogue, Everyday Low Pricing. Sears's attempt in 1989–90 to charge everyday low prices proved to be a fiasco, which can best be appreciated from the cold glare of game theory. The appendix examines in detail the mixed strategy bluffing that arises in a more complicated version of 1-card Stud Poker.

◼ 3.1 Mixed Strategies ◼ ◼ ◼ ◼ ◼ ◼ ◼ ◼ ◼ ◼ ◼ ◼ ◼ ◼ ◼ ◼ ◼ ◼ ◼

A pure strategy is a strategy that does not involve chance. All the strategies we have looked at so far have been pure. A player using a pure strategy is completely predictable—just like clockwork. A mixed strategy involves chance. A player uses a mixed strategy when he or she does not want to be completely predictable. Mathematically, a mixed strategy is a **probability distribution** over pure strategies. Some pure strategies may not be used at all, but at least two pure strategies are used with some positive probability. A player playing a mixed strategy has in effect replaced himself or herself with a random device set and has set the probabilities governing that random device in an attempt to maximize expected utility.[1]

The simplest game in which mixed strategies are important is quite familiar: **Matching Pennies.** The normal form for Matching Pennies is shown in Figure 3.1. There are two players, and the game is zero sum. Each player has two pure strategies, Heads (H) and Tails (T). Each player bets a fixed amount, a penny. If both players choose heads or if both players choose tails—this is called a match—then player 1 wins player 2's bet. If there is no match, then player 2 wins player 1's bet.

Notice from the arrow diagram in Figure 3.1 that Matching Pennies has no pure strategy equilibrium. Take (H,H). Player 2 has an incentive to switch to tails, T, thereby turning a 1-cent loss into a 1-cent gain. The same thing happens at each of the four pure strategy combinations. One of the players wants to switch strategy. Thus, none of the pure strategy combinations is a rest point. Matching Pennies cannot be solved by playing pure strategies.

Nevertheless, Matching Pennies does have a solution—you just can't see it

---

[1]This is not the only possible interpretation of mixed strategies. For an alternative interpretation in terms of players' beliefs, see John Harsanyi, "Games with Randomly Disturbed Payoffs: A New Rationale for Mixed Strategy Equilibrium Points," *International Journal of Game Theory* 2 (1973):1–23.

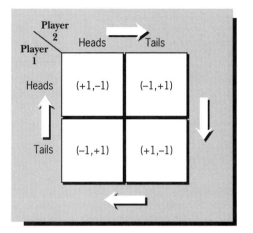

Figure 3.1. Matching Pennies. All payoffs in cents.

from the arrow diagram. To find this solution, we resort to mixed strategies. This should not come as a complete surprise. The way people usually play Matching Pennies is by tossing a coin. The act of tossing a coin is a random device for picking between heads and tails. As we shall soon see, the solution to Matching Pennies requires that each player toss a coin whose probability of coming up heads is exactly .5. The way people play this game in real life thus makes sense from the standpoint of game theory.

There is another example, called **Market Niche,** where the importance of mixed strategies is not so apparent. There are two firms, 1 and 2, and a single market niche that either of them could occupy. If one firm occupies the market niche, it gets a return of 100. If both firms occupy the market niche, each loses 50. If a firm stays out of this market, it breaks even. The firms decide whether to enter the market niche or not simultaneously. Figure 3.2 shows the normal form of Market Niche.

You can see from the arrow diagram that Market Niche has two pure strategy equilibria, (enter, stay out) and (stay out, enter). These involve exactly one firm occupying the market niche. The firm entering the market niche enjoys a much greater payoff than the firm staying out of the market niche. Also notice that this game is symmetrical: both firms get the same payoff when they choose the same strategy. When the firms switch strategies, they switch payoffs. The two pure strategy equilibria, where the players use different strategies and get different payoffs, are asymmetrical: the firms get very different payoffs. Market Niche also has a symmetrical equilibrium, which you cannot see from the arrow diagram. This equilibrium is in mixed strategies and pays each player the same. We now turn to the task of describing mixed strategies and solving for a mixed strategy equilibrium. Then we will solve for the mixed strategy equilibria of Matching Pennies and Market Niche.

69

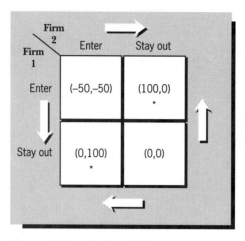

Figure 3.2.   Market Niche.

3.2 Computing Mixed Strategy Equilibria in 2 × 2 Games ■

Let's begin our computations with Matching Pennies (recall figure 3.1). We know that Matching Pennies does not have a pure strategy equilibrium, which forces us to look for a mixed strategy equilibrium. The key insight to a mixed strategy equilibrium is the following. *Every pure strategy that is played as part of a mixed strategy equilibrium has the same expected value.* If one strategy pays less than another, then you should play only the strategy that pays more to the exclusion of the strategy that pays less. The only strategies that are not excluded pay the same. We will apply this principle over and over again to find mixed strategy equilibria.[2]

Before proceeding, we need a little more notation. Let $p_1(H)$ equal the probability that player 1 plays heads and $p_1(T)$ equal the probability that player 1 plays tails. Similarly, let $p_2(H)$ be the probability that player 2 plays heads and $p_2(T)$ be the probability that player 2 plays tails. Now take player 1's payoffs. Suppose that player 1 uses the pure strategy Heads and player 2 uses some mixed strategy $p_2 = [p_2(H), p_2(T)]$. Since player 2 is using a mixed strategy, player 1 faces an expected value, $EV_1(H)$, from playing heads:

$$EV_1(H) = p_2(H)(+1) + p_2(T)(-1)$$

When player 2 picks heads, the result is a match and player 1 gains, +1; when player 2 picks tails, the result is a mismatch and player 1 loses, −1. Now suppose

---

[2]The existence proof given in Chapter 2 for pure strategy equilibria can be adapted to guarantee the existence of mixed strategy equilibria as well. In particular, for a game with a finite number of pure strategies, the operation of mixing strategies supplies the needed continuity. See J. Nash, "Noncooperative Games," *Annuals of Mathematics* 54 (1951):289–95, for details.

that player 1 is using the other pure strategy, Tails. Since player 2 is using a mixed strategy, player 1 faces an expected value, $EV_1(T)$, from playing tails:

$$EV_1(T) = p_2(H)(-1) + p_2(T)(+1)$$

When player 2 picks heads, the result is a mismatch and player 1 loses, -1; when player 2 picks tails, the result is a match and player 1 gains, $+1$.

All we have to do now is set the payoffs of player 1's two strategies equal to each other:

$$EV_1(H) = EV_1(T)$$

Substituting, we have

$$p_2(H)(+1) + p_2(T)(-1) = p_2(H)(-1) + p_2(T)(+1)$$

To this condition we add the requirement that player 2's mixed strategy be a probability distribution, the probabilities of whose events add up to 1:

$$p_2(H) + p_2(T) = 1$$

At this point we have two equations to solve in two unknowns, $p_2(H)$ and $p_2(T)$. A little algebra will show that the solution to these two equations is

$$p_2(H)^* = p_2(T)^* = .5$$

Use of * here indicates that these are mixed strategy equilibrium values for player 2.

There is an odd thing about mixed strategies that you have to get used to. The value of a player's own pure strategy depends on the opponent's mixed strategy. The condition that the player's pure strategies pay the same implies something about the opponent's mixed strategy, and vice versa. At a mixed strategy equilibrium, the opponent has made the player indifferent about his or her pure strategies, just as the player has made the opponent indifferent about his or her pure strategies.

We are now in a position to compute player 1's expected value from either pure strategy in his or her mixed strategy:

$$EV_1(H) = (.5)(+1) + (.5)(-1) = 0 = EV_1(T)$$

Player 1 breaks even by using either of the pure strategies as long as he or she uses them in a mixed strategy. At this point we also know what probabilities player 2 must use in a mixed strategy to keep player 1 honest. If player 2 chose heads more than tails, then player 1 could guarantee a winning percentage by always choosing heads. For instance, if player 2 used Heads 60% of the time, then player 1, by using Heads also, would match 60% of the time for a gain of 1 and would mismatch 40% of the time for a loss of 1, a net gain of 20%.

We can go through the same process for player 2. When we do so, we find that player 1 plays heads with probability $p_1(H)^* = .5 = p_1(T)^*$, the probability with which he or she plays tails. This situation leads to an expected value to player 2 from using either of the pure strategies of:

$$EV_2(H) = p_1(H)*(-1) + p_1(T)*(+1)$$
$$= (.5)(-1) + (.5)(+1)$$
$$= 0$$
$$= EV_2(T)$$

Even though Matching Pennies is not a symmetrical game, it has a symmetrical equilibrium. At this symmetrical equilibrium, each player plays heads with probability .5 and tails with probability .5. In the process, each player can expect to break even in dollar terms. This mixed strategy equilibrium explains why people, when they play Matching Pennies (for whatever stakes), toss their coins. The coin toss is an effort to implement 50–50 odds of heads and tails that break even at the mixed strategy equilibrium.

Since our linear equations had a unique solution, we are also assured that this mixed strategy equilibrium is the only equilibrium. The only way for people to play Matching Pennies is to replace themselves with random devices.

Let's now turn to Market Niche (recall Figure 3.2). As you can see from the arrow diagram, Market Niche has two pure strategy equilibria, (enter, stay out) and (stay out, enter). At these pure strategy equilibria, the firm that enters the market niche gets a much higher payoff than the firm that stays out of the market niche. Market Niche also has a mixed strategy equilibrium. This mixed strategy equilibrium is symmetrical: both firms adopt the same mixed strategy and get the same payoff.

To find this mixed strategy equilibrium, we can employ the same argument used for Matching Pennies. Let $p_1(enter)$ equal the probability that firm 1 enters the market niche and $p_1(stay\ out)$, equal the probability that firm 1 stays out of the market niche. Similarly, let $p_2(enter)$ equal the probability that firm 2 enters the market niche and $p_2(stay\ out)$ equal the probability that firm 2 stays out of the market niche. Now compute firm 1's payoffs. Suppose that firm 1 chooses the pure strategy Enter, whereas firm 2 uses some mixed strategy $p_2 = [p_2(enter), p_2(stay\ out)]$. Since firm 2 is using a mixed strategy, firm 1 faces an expected value, $EV_1(enter)$, from entering the market niche:

$$EV_1(enter) = p_2(enter)(-50) + p_2(stay\ out)(100)$$

This equation results because when firm 2 enters the market niche as well, both firms lose 50. When firm 2 stays out of the market niche, then firm 1 gets the market niche all to itself, a payoff of 100.

Now suppose that firm 1 uses its other pure strategy, Stay out of the market niche. Regardless of what firm 2 does, this strategy pays 0. All we have to do now is set the payoffs of player 1's two pure strategies equal to each other:

$$EV_1(enter) = EV_1(stay\ out) = 0$$

Substituting, we have

$$p_2(enter)(-50) + p_2(stay\ out)(100) = 0$$

To this condition we add the requirement that player 2's mixed strategy be a probability distribution, the probabilities of whose events add up to 1:

$p_2(\text{enter}) + p_2(\text{stay out}) = 1$

At this point we have two equations to solve in two unknowns, $p_2(\text{enter})$ and $p_2(\text{stay out})$. A little algebra will show that the solution to these two equations is

$$p_2^*(\text{enter}) = \frac{2}{3}; \ p_2^* (\text{stay out}) = \frac{1}{3}$$

Use of * here indicates the mixed strategy equilibrium values for firm 2.

We are now in a position to compute firm 1's expected value from either pure strategy:

$$EV_1(\text{enter}) = \left(\frac{2}{3}\right)(-50) + \left(\frac{1}{3}\right)(100) = 0 = EV_1(\text{stay out})$$

Firm 1 breaks even when firm 2 uses the equilibrium mixed strategy, which puts a 2/3 probability on entering the market niche. You can show that the same probabilities apply to firm 1:

$$p_1^*(\text{enter}) = \frac{2}{3}; \ p_1^* (\text{stay out}) = \frac{1}{3}$$

with an expected value to either pure strategy of 0.

As you can see, the payoffs from this symmetrical mixed strategy equilibrium, (0,0), are inefficient. One of these firms could make a lot of money by entering the market niche, if it was sure that the other firm would not enter that same niche. This assurance is precisely what is missing. It's a free country and a free market: each firm has exactly the same right to enter the market niche. The only way for *both* firms to exercise their right to enter the market niche is to play the inefficient, but symmetrical, mixed strategy equilibrium.

You can think of Market Niche as a **parable**. In most industrial markets there is only room for a few firms—a situation called *natural oligopoly*. Chance plays a major role in the identity of the firms that ultimately enter such markets. If too many firms enter, then there are losses all around and in the long run some firms must exit. If we know the mixed strategy equilibrium, we can actually predict how often there will be too many entrants. Since the probability of entry by either firm is 2/3, the probability that both firms enter is $(2/3)^2 = 4/9$. A little over 44% of the time, two firms enter the market niche when there is only room for one firm. In the long run, one of these firms must leave the market. This is a process we observe all the time—as illustrated by the several hundred now-defunct U.S. automobile companies.

It is hard to keep firms from adopting the same strategy in Market Niche. Here we confront a clash of important principles, efficiency and fairness. Efficiency says to play an equilibrium with the highest total payoffs, here, 100. Fairness says to play an equilibrium that pays each player the same, which in this case has total payoffs of 0, drastically lower. The two principles cannot be reconciled in a game like Market Niche. The clash between efficiency and equal rights occurs a great deal in economics and business, so it is no wonder that it shows up in games for economics and business.[3]

There is a fancy name for efficiency as it applies to game equilibria:

■ ■

Payoff Dominance. If everyone is better off at one game equilibrium than at another game equilibrium, then the latter equilibrium is not the solution.

Payoff dominance is in many respects an attractive contender for a sufficient condition. Unfortunately, if we try to make both payoff dominance and symmetry sufficient conditions for a solution, we run into a nasty contradiction. No solution can satisfy both payoff dominance and symmetry at the same time. The game Market Niche provides a ready-made counterexample: its one and only symmetrical equilibrium is payoff dominated by either of its asymmetrical equilibria. We can only ask for so much in the way of a solution to a game. Nevertheless, efficiency is desirable, so we should try whenever possible to build into a solution all the efficiency we can. This issue is further elaborated in section 3.4.[4]

▞ 3.3 Mixed Strategies and Bluffing: Liar's Poker ■ ■ ■ ■

Whenever a player uses a mixed strategy, he or she is trying to be unpredictable—just like the weather. "The probability of rain today is 30%" and "The probability that I will go to the hot fishing spot today is 30%" are statements on the same logical footing. Many times in a game with imperfect information a player has information that might be valuable to an opponent and detrimental to the player were it to be revealed. In such cases the player has a strong incentive to keep this information secret. The trouble is, strategic behavior might give the information away. This situation gives rise to bluffing.[5]

Bluffing is any attempt to mislead or deceive. The purpose of the deception is to prevent the opponent from being able to infer what the player knows, what information he or she is privy to. Bluffing all the time just doesn't pay: a bluff is too often called and the bluffer pays a heavy price. A player wants to

---

[3]One rubric under which this clash appears is the liberal paradox. The original presentation is by A. K. Sen, *Social Choice and Welfare* (San Francisco: Norton, 1970), chap. 9. There is a vast literature on the subject.

[4]For a careful argument of why rights-based notions such as symmetry might have priority over the notion of efficiency, see John Rawls, *A Theory of Justice* (Cambridge: Harvard University Press, 1971).

[5]An entire chapter is devoted to this issue (Chapter 9). The idea of a strategy's revealing private information is central to modern theories of finance.

bluff just enough to keep the opponent honest—to keep the opponent from being able to read what the player knows by observing how he or she plays. Mixed strategies are the vehicle for bluffing, and a mixed strategy equilibrium tells just how much a player needs to bluff to protect the value of his or her information.

Here is a simple example of how protecting information can be valuable. The game is called **Liar's Poker,** because it resembles Poker and lying plays a large part in its solution.[6] There are two players, 1 and 2, and two cards in the pack, an ace and a king. An ace ranks higher than a king. Player 1 is dealt a card, face down, which he or she can look at but which player 2 never sees. All player 2 knows is that with probability .5 the card is an ace; with probability .5, a king. Now player 1 says something. Player 1 can say what the card is or lie about it and say that he or she has a higher-ranking card. If the card is an ace, player 1 can't lie about having a better card and must say that it is an ace. If the card is a king, player 1 can say "ace" or "king." Player 2 hears what player 1 says. If player 1 says "ace," then player 2 can either call or fold. If player 2 calls and player 1's card is not an ace, then player 1 loses and pays $1 to player 2. If player 2 calls and player 1's card is an ace, then player 2 loses and pays $1 to player 1. If player 2 folds, then player 1 automatically wins $0.50 from player 2. Finally, if player 1 says "king," then the game ends and both players break even.[7]

The extensive form of this game is shown in Figure 3.3a. Notice that player 1 has two strategies in this game based on the one information set at which he or she has a choice, namely when dealt a king:

A: say "ace" when the card is a king

K: say "king" when the card is a king

At player 1's other information set, he or she does not have a choice. Player 1's strategy A is bluffing. If player 2 believes player 1 when he or she says the card is an ace, then player 1 wins $0.50 even though he or she has a bad hand. By contrast, player 1's strategy K is not bluffing—rather, it is entirely honest, without a trace of deception. Unfortunately for player 1, this strategy also doesn't make any money. Similarly, player 2 has two strategies in this game, Call and Fold, based on the one information set he or she has. We now show that Liar's Poker has a unique equilibrium, which is in mixed strategies. In particular, the solution to Liar's Poker involves quite a bit of lying.

The best way to see all this is in the normal form, which is shown in Figure 3.3b. Here is the story behind the payoffs. Take (A, fold): player 1 always says

[6]The form of Liar's Poker analyzed here is the simplest possible. To see what a real-life game of Liar's Poker looks like, read the first chapter of Michael Lewis's best-seller, *Liar's Poker* (New York: Norton, 1989).

[7]In real-life versions of Liar's Poker, the possible hands are ranked as in 5-card Stud Poker (straight flush beats four of a kind beats a full house, etc.), and player 1 loses whenever he or she is caught lying, that is, when he or she says the hand is better than it really is and is called. If player 1 claims to have the lowest possible hand (no pair), then he or she can't be lying about its strength and the outcome is a tie.

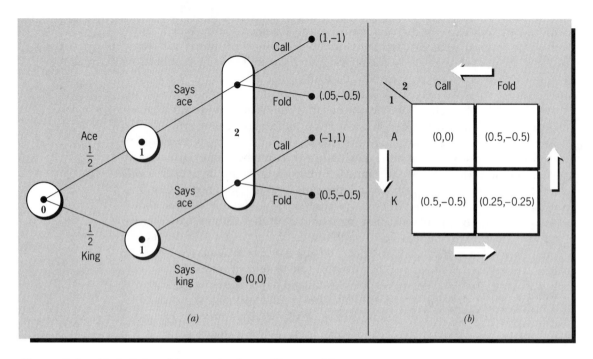

Figure 3.3.   Liar's Poker: (*a*) extensive form; (*b*) normal form.

the card is an ace, and player 2 always folds. With probability .5, player 1 is dealt an ace. Player 1 says the card is an ace, and player 2 folds, so player 1 wins $0.50. With probability .5, player 1 is dealt a king, in which case player 1 again says the card is an ace, and player 2 again folds, so player 1 again wins $0.50. These are the payoffs in the cell (A, fold). Now suppose that player 1 always says the card is an ace, but player 2 calls instead of folding. With probability .5, player 1 is dealt an ace. Player 1 says the card is an ace, and player 2 calls, so player 1 wins $1. With probability .5, player 1 is dealt a king, in which case player 1 again says the card is an ace. Player 2 calls, so player 1 loses $1. The expected value to player 1 is

$$EV_1 = (.5)(+1) + (.5)(-1) = 0$$

Both players expect to break even in the cell (A, call). Next, suppose that player 1 says the card is a king when a king is dealt, and player 2 calls. With probability .5, player 1 is dealt an ace and says so. Player 2 calls, so player 1 wins $1. With probability .5, player 1 is dealt a king and says so. The payoff to player 1 in this case is $0. Player 1's expected value is

$$EV_1 = (.5)(1) + (.5)(0) = 0.5$$

The payoffs to the cell (K, call) are (0.5,–0.5). Finally, suppose that player 1 says the card is a king when a king is dealt, and player 2 folds. With probability .5, player 1 is dealt an ace and says so. Player 2 folds, so player 1 wins \$0.50. With probability .5, player 1 is dealt a king and says so. The payoff to player 1 in this case is \$0. Player 1's expected value is

$$EV_1 = (.5)(0.5) + (.5)(0) = 0.25$$

The payoffs to the cell (K, fold) are (0.25,−0.25). This completes the setup of the normal form.

As you can see from the arrow diagram of Figure 3.3b, Liar's Poker does not have a pure strategy equilibrium. This means we have to look for a mixed strategy equilibrium, at which neither player is completely predictable. Denote by p_2(call) the probability that player 2 calls; by p_2(fold), the probability that player 2 folds. Player 1's strategies A and K pay the same when

$$0.5p_2(\text{fold}) = 0.5p_2(\text{call}) + 0.25p_2(\text{fold})$$

From this we infer that

$$0.25p_2(\text{fold}) = 0.5p_2(\text{call})$$

that is, player 2 should fold twice as much as he or she calls. By the laws of probability, this means that

$$p_2^*(\text{fold}) = .67; \; p_2^* \, (\text{call}) = .33$$

We now turn to player 2. Denote by p_1(A) the probability that player 1 says the card is an ace when it is a king; by p_1(K), the probability that player 1 says the card is a king when it is a king. Player 2's strategies Call and Fold pay the same when

$$p_1(\text{K})(-0.5) = p_1(\text{A})(-0.5) + p_1(\text{K})(-0.25)$$

From this we infer that

$$0.25p_1(\text{K}) = 0.5p_1(\text{A})$$

that is, player 1 should tell the truth twice as often as he or she lies. By the laws of probability, this means that

$$p_1^*(\text{K}) = .67; \; p_1^*(\text{A}) = .33$$

This pair of probability distributions is the solution to Liar's Poker.

Notice that the solution of Liar's Poker requires that player 1 lie a lot. In fact, the probability is .17 that player 1 is lying. When player 1 gets an ace (probability .5), he or she says so. That's telling the truth. When player 1 gets a king (probability .5), two-thirds of the time he or she says so, but the rest of the time he or she lies. So the probability that player 1 is lying is (.5)(.33) = .17. At the same time, all this lying pays off for player 1. To see this, substitute the mixed strategy equilibrium values p_2*(call) and p_2*(fold) into player 1's expected value from saying the card is an ace when it is a king. You get

$$EV_1^* = (.33)(0) + (.67)(.5) = \$0.33.$$

You would get the same answer if you substituted into player 1's expected value from saying the card is a king when it is a king also. No matter how you look at it, for every \$1 bet, player 1 expects to make \$0.33, for a handsome rate of return of 33%. Since Liar's Poker is zero sum, player 2 expects to lose that \$0.33. Indeed, the only fair way to play Liar's Poker in real life is via a rotation: each player gets the same chance of going first.[8]

3.4 Mixed Strategy Equilibria of Coordination Games and Coordination Problems ■ ■ ■ ■ ■ ■ ■ ■ ■ ■ ■ ■ ■ ■ ■ ■

You were warned that some of the games studied in Chapter 2 had equilibria you could not see from an arrow diagram. Now that you know how to compute mixed strategy equilibria, we can go back and find these equilibria. Let's begin with Video System Coordination (Figure 2.10). This game has two pure strategy equilibria, both of which are symmetrical. There is nothing to suggest that there are any other equilibria. One diagnostic, however, follows. Neither Beta nor VHS dominates the other, and the two pure strategy equilibria are at opposite corners of the game matrix. When this happens, it is usually the case that the equations governing a mixed strategy solution have a solution.

Let $p_1(\text{Beta})$ be the probability that firm 1 chooses Beta and $p_1(\text{VHS})$ be the probability that firm 1 chooses VHS. Similarly, let $p_2(\text{Beta})$ be the probability that firm 2 chooses Beta and $p_2(\text{VHS})$ be the probability that firm 2 chooses VHS. Now take firm 1's payoffs. Suppose that firm 1 chooses Beta and firm 2 uses some mixed strategy, $p_2 = [p_2(\text{Beta}), p_2(\text{VHS})]$. Since firm 2 is using a mixed strategy, firm 1 faces an expected value, $EV_1(\text{Beta})$, from choosing Beta:

$$EV_1(\text{Beta}) = p_2(\text{Beta})(+1) + p_2(\text{VHS})(0)$$

This equation is obtained because when firm 2 chooses Beta, the result is a match and firm 1 gains, +1, and when firm 2 chooses VHS, the result is a mismatch and firm 1 gets 0.

Now suppose that firm 1 is using its other pure strategy, VHS. Since firm 2 is using a mixed strategy, firm 1 faces an expected value, $EV_1(\text{VHS})$, from choosing VHS:

$$EV_1(\text{VHS}) = p_2(\text{Beta})(0) + p_2(\text{VHS})(+1)$$

This equation is derived because when firm 2 chooses Beta, the result is a mismatch and firm 1 gets 0, and when firm 2 chooses VHS, the result is a match and firm 1 gains, +1.

All we have to do now is set the payoffs of firm 1's two pure strategies equal to each other:

[8]The players can use a 50–50 random device to determine who goes first. Alternatively, they can use a deterministic rotation, with each player going first half of all rounds.

$$EV_1(\text{Beta}) = EV_2(\text{VHS})$$

Substituting, we have

$$p_2(\text{Beta})(+1) + p_2(\text{VHS})(0) = p_2(\text{Beta})(0) + p_2(\text{VHS})(+1)$$

To this condition we add the requirement that firm 2's mixed strategy be a probability distribution, the probabilities of whose events add up to 1:

$$p_2(\text{Beta}) + p_2(\text{VHS}) = 1$$

At this point we have two equations to solve in two unknowns, $p_2(\text{Beta})$ and $p_2(\text{VHS})$. A little algebra will show that the solution to these two equations is

$$p_2^*(\text{Beta}) = p_2^*(\text{VHS}) = 0.5$$

Use of the * indicates that these are mixed strategy equilibrium values for player 2. An appeal to symmetry shows that the same mixed strategy is an equilibrium for firm 1. At the mixed strategy equilibrium for Video System Coordination, each firm has an expected value of 0.5. This low payoff arises because half the time, the two firms are not on the same system. Even though this payoff satisfies symmetry (it has the same payoff for both firms), it pales in comparison to either of the symmetrical pure strategy equilibria, both of which pay twice as much. Here is an instance in which we can use payoff dominance to throw out a low-paying symmetrical equilibrium to a symmetrical game. In this case, there is no conflict between payoff dominance and symmetry: both point toward a solution that is efficient.

3.5 Asymmetrical Mixed Strategy Equilibria ■ ■ ■ ■ ■

So far all our mixed strategy equilibria have been symmetrical. Mixed strategy equilibria can also be asymmetrical. Go back to the game Market Niche (Figure 3.2). When we make things ever so slightly asymmetrical, then we get an asymmetrical mixed strategy equilibrium. Now consider the following slightly asymmetrical version of Market Niche (see Figure 3.4). In this version, firm 1 gets a payoff of 150 if it gets the market niche to itself. Otherwise, the game is precisely the same as shown in Figure 3.2. The change reflects the competitive advantage firm 1 has over firm 2 in the event that it is the sole entrant. This competitive advantage could be due to lower costs, better marketing, or many other factors. **Asymmetrical Market Niche** has pure strategy equilibrium payoffs of (150,0) and (0,100). It also has an asymmetrical mixed strategy equilibrium, which we now compute.

Let $p_1(\text{enter})$ equal the probability that firm 1 enters the market niche; $p_1(\text{stay out})$ equal the probability that firm 1 stays out; $p_2(\text{enter})$ equal the probability that firm 2 enters the market niche; and $p_2(\text{stay out})$ equal the probability that firm 2 stays out. Now compute firm 1's payoffs. Suppose that

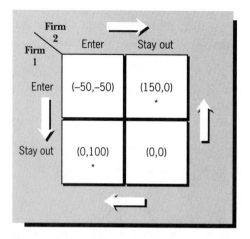

Figure 3.4. Asymmetrical Market Niche.

firm 1 enters while firm 2 is using the mixed strategy p_2 = [p_2(enter),p_2(stay out)]. Since firm 2 is using a mixed strategy, firm 1 faces an expected value, EV_1(enter), from entering the market niche:

$$EV_1(\text{enter}) = p_2(\text{enter})(-50) + p_2(\text{stay out})(150)$$

Next, suppose that firm 1 uses its other pure strategy, Stay out. In this case, firm 1 is guaranteed the payoff 0 regardless of what firm 2 does. Setting these two expected values equal to each other, we get

$$p_2(\text{enter})(-50) + p_2(\text{stay out})(150) = 0$$

To this condition we add the requirement that firm 2's mixed strategy be a probability distribution, the probabilities of whose events add up to 1:

$$p_2(\text{enter}) + p_2(\text{stay out}) = 1$$

At this point we have two equations to solve in two unknowns, p_2(enter) and p_2(stay out). Again, a little algebra will show that the solution to these two equations is

$$p_2^*(\text{enter}) = \frac{3}{4}; \ p_2^*(\text{stay out}) = \frac{1}{4}$$

Compared to the symmetrical version of Market Niche, the less efficient firm enters the market niche with a somewhat higher probability (3/4 versus 2/3). As before, firm 1 breaks even at the mixed strategy equilibrium:

$$EV_1(\text{enter}) = \left(\frac{3}{4}\right)(-50) + \left(\frac{1}{4}\right)(150) = 0 = EV_2(\text{stay out})$$

Since firm 2's payoffs have not changed, player 1's mixture probabilities do not change:

$$p_1(\text{enter})^* = \frac{2}{3}; \ p_1(\text{stay out})^* = \frac{1}{3}$$

Firm 1 still expects to break even at the mixed strategy equilibrium:

$$EV_2(\text{enter}) = \left(\frac{2}{3}\right)(-50) + \left(\frac{1}{3}\right)(100) = 0 = EV_2(\text{stay out})$$

Since this version of Market Niche is asymmetrical, considerations of symmetry no longer apply. Since symmetry was the only thing the mixed strategy equilibrium had going for it, it is really tempting to somehow exclude that equilibrium from further attention as the solution. Moreover, the asymmetrical pure strategy equilibrium outcomes are no longer mirror images of each other. The equilibrium (enter, stay out), which assigns the more efficient firm to the market niche, yields the largest total payoff, and the weaker payoff equilibrium also dominates the mixed strategy equilibrium.[9] All this makes (stay out, enter) an attractive candidate for a solution to the game.

Retailers are involved in a coordination problem rather like Asymmetrical Market Niche, only they are already in the market. A sale won't work if all retailers run one at the same time. The only way a sale will work is if it comes as a surprise. The very logic of sales cries out for a mixed strategy solution. This is the subject of Everyday Low Prices.

◼◻ 3.6 Everyday Low Prices[10] ◼◼◼◼◼◼◼◼◼◼◼◼◼◼◼◼

In the spring of 1989, retailing giant Sears announced with great fanfare a new pricing policy, everyday low prices. Sears argued that it was running too many sales and that its sales were not generating enough volume. Therefore, it was going to run low prices, but not quite as low as sale prices, every day from then on. Unfortunately for Sears, the policy of everyday low prices did not reverse its troubled retailing fortunes. The policy may have even exacerbated the situation. Game theory in general, and mixed strategy solutions in particular, will clue us in as to why this could happen. Sometimes the last thing you want to do is give up your mixed strategy.

When firms like Sears use price as a strategic variable, they try hard to keep price above marginal cost. As Chapter 5 will show, as long as their products are differentiated, they are able to do this at a pure strategy equilibrium. Giant retailers like Sears, Wal-Mart, and KMart are household names—a definite sign of differentiation. Still, there are competitive pressures driving price toward

[9]The tie in payoff to firm 2 prevents this dominance from being strict.
[10]This material is inspired in part by Hal Varian, "A Model of Sales," *American Economic Review* 70 (1980):651–59.

marginal cost. A simple model of **sales** that captures these features is presented here. For a much more general kind of model, the reader should consult the Varian article.

There are two differentiated firms, called 1 and 2, locked in price competition. Each firm has a choice between two different prices for a large appliance, a normal price, NP, and a sale price, SP, with NP higher than SP. Even the sale price is above cost. To keep things as simple as possible, unit cost is constant. For purposes of a concrete example, take the following numbers: NP = $600, SP = $500, unit cost = $450. This is the supply side of the model.

On the demand side of the model, there are two kinds of buyers. First, there are buyers who are in the market for the appliance no matter what the price is, as long as it does not exceed the normal price, NP. These buyers also don't shop around for the lowest price: they simply take the first price they see. Such buyers are often called u-buyers (u for uninformed). Suppose there are 100 such u-buyers in the market, and they show up randomly at either firm, so each firm can expect to make 100/2 = 50 sales to u-buyers regardless of price. Second, there are buyers who are in the market for the appliance only if it is on sale, and then only if they find it at the sale price. These buyers shop around for the lowest price, and if they don't find that price they don't buy. Such buyers are often called i-buyers (i for informed). Suppose there are 120 such i-buyers in the market. These are the buyers that a sale price might attract.

We now have enough data to construct a game matrix. First, suppose that both firms charge a normal price. In this case, each firm sells only to u-buyers (50 units) at a profit margin of $150/unit (NP − unit cost = $600 − $450) for a profit of $7500. This is not an equilibrium. Suppose that firm 1 decides to run a sale. By cutting its price to the sale price of $500, it reduces its profit margin to $50/unit, but it increases its sales from 50 units (to the u-buyers, who don't even notice there is a sale going on) to 170 units (adding all 120 i-buyers). Firm 1's profits are now $50/unit times 170 units = $8500. Firm 1 raises profits by lowering its price, so it is not an equilibrium for all firms to charge a normal price.

What if both firms charge the sale price? That isn't an equilibrium either. In this case, each firm sells to 50 u-buyers plus 60 i-buyers (the i-buyers get distributed randomly in the market, too). The profit margin for each firm is $50 at the sale price, and so profits for each are $50/unit times 110 units, or $5500. This is not an equilibrium. Take firm 2 this time, and suppose that it raises its price back up to the normal level. It triples its profit margin, from $50 to $150, and it still keeps its customer base of 50 u-buyers. The profit from this price increase is $150/unit times 50 units, or $7500. So when all firms charge the sale price it is not an equilibrium either.

The normal form of the game Everyday Low Pricing is shown in Figure 3.5. **Given symmetry, neither firm is going to give in and let the other make more money.** Instead, the firms use mixed strategies. Mixed strategies lead to a **pricing cycle,** with firms' prices constantly fluctuating between normal and sale prices as they employ their mixed strategies. At a mixed strategy, a firm charges

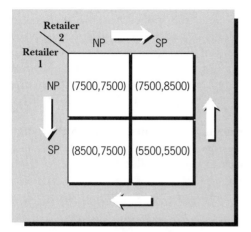

Figure 3.5. Everyday Low Pricing.

the normal price some of the time and the sale price the rest of the time. Whatever firms do contains an element of surprise.

To wrap up, let's find this mixed strategy. Let $p(NP)$ be the probability of charging the normal price and $p(SP)$, the probability of charging the sale price.[11] At a mixed strategy equilibrium, the expected profit from charging the normal price, $EV(NP)$, and the expected profit from charging the sale price, $EV(SP)$, are equal. By charging the normal price, a firm locks in a profit of \$7500. At a sale price, it expects a profit of

$$EV(SP) = \$8500p(NP) + \$5500p(SP)$$

At a mixed strategy equilibrium, the profits from normal pricing, \$7500, have to equal the profits from sale pricing, $EV(SP)$. The probabilities that do this are the following:

$$p(NP)* = \frac{2}{3}; \ p(SP)* = \frac{1}{3}$$

At this mixed strategy equilibrium, each firm expects to earn \$7500, just as if it were normal pricing.

If a firm runs sales one-third of the time, then it will defend its profits against its competitor. Its sales will be effective, because they will come as a surprise. Running sales at the right frequency will defend profits at the same level as at normal prices. Sale pricing is just like bluffing in Poker: good players do it, but they don't do it more often than necessary. Finding the mixed strategy equilibrium answers just how much surprise is needed.

We can criticize Sears's policy of everyday low pricing from the standpoint of

[11]The game looks the same to both firms, so we don't need to know the firms' identities in this calculation.

mixed strategies. What Sears gave up with this policy was the element of surprise. What it got in return was the low rates of profit associated with prices near cost. If the basic problem at the end of 1988 was running too many sales, then the solution was to run fewer sales, not to run nothing but sales. Mistakes in game theory class only cost you points on an exam, but strategic pricing mistakes in the real world can cost a lot of people (read "shareholders") real money.

After 18 months of everyday low pricing, Sears quietly gave up the policy. Sears's everyday low pricing continues to be widely regarded by retailing industry analysts as a fiasco. Sears is back to running sales once more.

◨ SUMMARY

1. A pure strategy does not involve chance; a mixed strategy does. Players use a mixed strategy when they do not want their behavior to be predictable.

2. A mixed strategy equilibrium is an equilibrium where players use mixed strategies. The solution to Matching Pennies is a mixed strategy equilibrium. One way to realize the equilibrium is for each player to toss a fair coin.

3. The game Market Niche is a parable for natural oligopoly, where there is only room for a limited number of firms in the market. It has both pure strategy and mixed strategy equilibria.

4. Every pure strategy that is part of a mixed strategy must pay the same expected value. A mixed strategy must also obey the laws of probability. Finding a mixed strategy equilibrium in a 2×2 game requires solving two systems of two linear equations in two unknowns, one such system for each player.

5. The conditions of payoff dominance and symmetry are incompatible, as the game Market Niche shows. This clash of principles is related to the trade-off between efficiency and equity.

6. Bluffing is any attempt to mislead or deceive. The purpose of bluffing is to protect the value of information that only you hold. Mixed strategies, as in Liar's Poker, are a practical way to bluff.

7. Coordination games, such as Video System Coordination, have mixed strategy equilibria that are payoff dominated by the pure strategy equilibria of such games.

8. Asymmetrical Market Niche has asymmetrical pure strategy equilibria and an asymmetrical mixed strategy equilibrium. The most efficient of these equilibria is the pure strategy equilibrium that has the most efficient firm enter the market niche.

9. Sales involve a mixed strategy. A strategy involving sales only part of the time may be better than charging everyday low prices, as Sears's experience in 1989–90 showed.

10. When a mixed strategy equilibrium is played in price competition, the observed prices form a pricing cycle.

KEY TERMS

pure strategy
pure strategy equilibrium
mixed strategy
mixed strategy equilibrium
probability distribution
Matching Pennies
Market Niche

payoff dominance
bluffing
Liar's Poker
Asymmetrical Market Niche
coordination problem
sales
pricing cycle

PROBLEMS

1. **Asymmetrical Matching Pennies.** Suppose that player 1 wins +2 in the event of a match on heads; otherwise the game is the same as in Figure 3.1. Find the mixed strategy equilibrium.

2. Suppose that in Market Niche, only firm 1 is aware of the fact that a market niche has opened up. What equilibrium would you predict in this case? Should firm 2 enter the market niche if firm 1 is already there?

3. Suppose that in Liar's Poker, player 1 wins $0.60 if player 2 folds. The rest of the payoffs are the same. How does this affect the solution? Does player 1 lie more or less often with this rule change?

4. In a variant of Video System Coordination, suppose that it matters whether players coordinate on Beta or VHS in the sense that coordinating on Beta pays 2, while coordinating on VHS pays 1. Find the three equilibria for this game (two pure, one mixed), and then solve, using payoff dominance and symmetry.

5. Make symmetrical Market Niche (Figure 3.4) asymmetrical in the following way. The market niche is worth 90 to firm 2. Nothing else about the game changes. Find the three equilibria (two pure, one mixed) for this game.

6. Give three examples of bluffing in business. For each example, what happens to the bluffer if he or she is found out?

7. Here is a game that arises in resource economics. There are two fishing spots, one hot and one cold. The hot spot has 20 fish, whereas the cold spot has only 12 fish. There two fishers, 1 and 2. A fisher can go to either spot to fish, but only to a single spot. If two fishers go to the same spot, they divide the catch equally. Find three equilibria for this game.

8. In fishing games such as that of problem 7, conflicts often break out over the fishing grounds. How might an asymmetrical equilibrium, such as that

provided by the 200-mile fishing limit among nations, lead to a more efficient outcome?

9. Work out the mixed strategy equilibrium to Everyday Low Pricing when there are 90 u-buyers in the market instead of 100. What is the intuition behind your result?

10. In Everyday Low Pricing, suppose there are only 20 i-buyers in the market instead of 120. How does this affect the solution? Might there be times when firms would never want to run sales?

▚ APPENDIX. BLUFFING IN ONE-CARD STUD POKER

Now that we have studied the basics of bluffing in Liar's Poker, we're ready to tackle a version of 1-card Stud Poker that has plenty of bluffing. To get bluffing as part of equilibrium behavior, two complications are essential. First, the deck for 1-card Stud Poker now consists of three kinds of cards, aces (A), kings (K), and queens (Q), each appearing with frequency 1/3. The game begins with an ante of size a. Each player is dealt one card face down. The players see their own card—this is the second complication—but not that of their opponent. Each player either bets an amount of size b or passes; this decision is taken simultaneously. From here on the rules are the same as before, with an ace beating a king beating a queen.

There are nine possible deals in this version of 1-card Stud Poker. In our notation for hands, (1's hand, 2's hand) = (A,K) when 1 is dealt an ace and 2 is dealt a king. Since the deal is fair and each card is equally likely, each of these nine deals is equally likely and has probability 1/9. Since a player sees his or her own card (three possibilities) and can either bet or pass after seeing that card (two possibilities), $2^3 = 8$ pure strategies are available to the player. They are:

I: Bet an ace, bet a king, bet a queen
II: Bet an ace, bet a king, pass a queen
III: Bet an ace, pass a king, bet a queen
IV: Bet an ace, pass a king, pass a queen
V: Pass an ace, bet a king, bet a queen
VI: Pass an ace, bet a king, pass a queen
VII: Pass an ace, pass a king, bet a queen
VIII: Pass an ace, pass a king, pass a queen

The following discussion refers to these strategies by their roman numerals.

Strategy I bets everything—a very aggressive strategy, designed especially for defending one's ante. Strategies I, III, V, and VII all bet a queen. Since a queen can never win a showdown, all these strategies contain an element of bluffing. Strategy IV only bets when a player can't lose—a very conservative strategy, and the very opposite of bluffing. The minute you see a player using strategy IV bet, you know he or she has an ace. This strategy alerts a player's opponent to the fact that he or she is up against an ace. Strategy VIII is the ultimate in timidity—it never bets. Strategy VII is obviously perverse—it only bets a card that can't win (a queen). This strategy is just as informative as strategy IV—only it lets the opponent know that a player can't beat him or her.[12]

Not all these strategies deserve our attention. For instance, you can show that strategies V, VI, VII, and VIII, all of which share the feature that they pass an ace, a card that can't lose, are all bad. Every one of them is strategically dominated by the strategy that bets the ace instead (I dominates V, II dominates VI, and so on). The only strategies that really deserve our attention are I, II, III, and IV, all of which share the feature that they bet an ace. Next, the game is symmetrical: both players have the same strategies and get on average the same quality of cards. Therefore, if we solve the game for player 1, say, then that solution also works for player 2. Next, again because of symmetry, if the same strategy is played against itself, I against I for instance, then the strategy breaks even. Finally, and again because of symmetry plus the fact that Poker is zero sum, the payoff for I versus II when player 1 uses strategy I is minus the payoff of II versus I when player 1 uses strategy II. All of this means we only have to compute six pairs of strategies (I vs. II, I vs. III, I vs. IV, II vs. III, II vs. IV, and III vs. IV).

The results of this computation are shown in Figure 3.6. We will walk through one of the entries, I versus II, step-by-step; the rest is left as an end-of-appendix problem. Strategy I bets everything its gets, and strategy II bets everything except a queen. Here is what happens on the nine possible deals to player 1, who is using strategy I, when facing an opponent who is using strategy II:

(A,A): Both bet, there is a showdown, a tie; payoff = 0
(A,K): Both bet, there is a showdown, 1 wins; payoff = $a + b$
(A,Q): A bets, Q passes, 1 wins; payoff = a
(K,A): Both bet, there is a showdown, 2 wins; payoff = $-a - b$
(K,K): Both bet, there is a showdown, a tie; payoff = 0
(K,Q): K bets, Q passes, 1 wins; payoff = a
(Q,A): Both bet, there is a showdown, 2 wins; payoff = $-a - b$
(Q,K): Both bet, there is a showdown, 2 wins; payoff = $-a - b$
(Q,Q): 1 bets Q, 2 passes Q, 1 wins; payoff = a

Adding up these outcomes and multiplying by the probability $1/9$ yields $(a - 2b)/9$, the result given in Figure 3.6 for player 1 for the entry (I,II). Minus this number, $(-a + 2b)/9$, is the result given for player 1 for the entry (II,I).

Notice that there are only two unequivocal cases in which one strategy beats another, regardless of the size of the ante and the size of the bet. These are I

---

[12]Of course, since the players are moving simultaneously, this information is not immediately available.

Player 1 \ Player 2	I	II	III	IV
I	$(0,0)$	$\left(\dfrac{a-2b}{9}, \dfrac{2b-a}{9}\right)$	$\left(\dfrac{2a}{9}, \dfrac{-2a}{9}\right)$	$\left(\dfrac{4a-2b}{9}, \dfrac{2b-4a}{9}\right)$
II	$\left(\dfrac{2b-a}{9}, \dfrac{a-2b}{9}\right)$	$(0,0)$	$\left(\dfrac{b}{9}, \dfrac{-b}{9}\right)$	$\left(\dfrac{a-b}{9}, \dfrac{b-a}{9}\right)$
III	$\left(\dfrac{-2a}{9}, \dfrac{2a}{9}\right)$	$\left(\dfrac{-b}{9}, \dfrac{b}{9}\right)$	$(0,0)$	$\left(\dfrac{2a-b}{9}, \dfrac{b-2a}{9}\right)$
IV	$\left(\dfrac{2b-4a}{9}, \dfrac{4a-2b}{9}\right)$	$\left(\dfrac{b-a}{9}, \dfrac{a-b}{9}\right)$	$\left(\dfrac{b-2a}{9}, \dfrac{2a-b}{9}\right)$	$(0,0)$

Figure 3.6.   One-card Stud Poker. Payoff matrix, player I.

versus III, which pays $2a/9$, and II versus III, which pays $b/9$. Every other pairing could go either way, depending on the size of the ante relative to the bet. This situation has implications for the solution. Let's fix the ante ($a = \$1$) and vary the bet b. Suppose the bet is \$2. Substituting into Figure 3.6 yields Figure 3.7. There is a pure strategy equilibrium at (IV,IV); indeed, this is the only equilibrium. Thus the solution to 1-card Stud Poker (with queens) when the ante is \$1 and the bet is \$2 is to bet only an ace. The bet is too large relative to the ante to risk losing it on hands that can be beaten. Each player breaks even at this solution, which is to be expected from symmetry.

Now suppose that the bet is the same size as the ante, \$1. The resulting payoff matrix is given in Figure 3.8. The unique pure strategy equilibrium occurs at (II,II). Each player bets both an ace and a king, but passes a queen. Again, no bluffing is present, and both players break even. Somewhere between a bet size of \$1 and \$2, the solution of the game jumps from strategy II to strategy IV. It is in this zone, where the solution jumps, that mixed strategy equilibria and bluffing are found.

Set the bet at $b = \$1.50$. Figure 3.9 shows the payoffs that result. Notice that neither II nor IV is an equilibrium. Indeed, there is no pure strategy equilibrium, so this size bet lies in the zone we just talked about. Now we have to look for a mixed strategy solution to Poker. Since the undominated strategies are I,

Player 1 \ Player 2	I	II	III	IV
I	(0,0)	$\left(\frac{-3}{9}, \frac{3}{9}\right)$	$\left(\frac{2}{9}, \frac{-2}{9}\right)$	(0,0)
II	$\left(\frac{3}{9}, \frac{-3}{9}\right)$	(0,0)	$\left(\frac{2}{9}, \frac{-2}{9}\right)$	$\left(\frac{-1}{9}, \frac{1}{9}\right)$
III	$\left(\frac{-2}{9}, \frac{2}{9}\right)$	$\left(\frac{-2}{9}, \frac{2}{9}\right)$	(0,0)	(0,0)
IV	(0,0)	$\left(\frac{1}{9}, \frac{-1}{9}\right)$	(0,0)	(0,0) *

Figure 3.7. One-card Stud Poker. Payoff matrix, player I, $a = \$1$, $b = \$2$.

II, III, and IV, you might think that there is a mixed strategy equilibrium consisting of all four of these. Let $p(\text{I})$, $p(\text{II})$, $p(\text{III})$, and $p(\text{IV})$ be the respective probabilities of these four pure strategies in a mixed strategy. We need all these strategies to pay the same:

$$
\begin{aligned}
EV(\text{I}) &= 0p(\text{I}) - \frac{2}{9}\,p(\text{II}) + \frac{2}{9}\,p(\text{III}) + \frac{1}{9}\,p(\text{IV}) \\
&= EV(\text{II}) = \frac{2}{9}\,p(\text{I}) + 0p(\text{II}) + \frac{1}{6}\,p(\text{III}) - \frac{1}{18}\,p(\text{IV}) \\
&= EV(\text{III}) = -\frac{2}{9}\,p(\text{I}) - \frac{1}{6}\,p(\text{II}) + 0p(\text{III}) + \frac{1}{18}\,p(\text{IV}) \\
&= EV(\text{IV}) = -\frac{1}{9}\,p(\text{I}) + \frac{1}{18}\,p(\text{II}) - \frac{1}{18}\,p(\text{III}) + 0p(\text{IV})
\end{aligned}
$$

We also need the strategies to add up to 1:

$$p(\text{I}) + p(\text{II}) + p(\text{III}) + p(\text{IV}) = 1$$

Unfortunately, these equations have no solution. Every attempt to solve them leads to a contradiction. This situation tells us that there is no mixed strategy solution consisting of all four of these strategies.

Player 1 \ Player 2	I	II	III	IV
I	(0,0)	$\left(\frac{-1}{9}, \frac{1}{9}\right)$	$\left(\frac{2}{9}, \frac{-2}{9}\right)$	$\left(\frac{2}{9}, \frac{-2}{9}\right)$
II	$\left(\frac{1}{9}, \frac{-1}{9}\right)$	(0,0) *	$\left(\frac{1}{9}, \frac{-1}{9}\right)$	(0,0)
III	$\left(\frac{-2}{9}, \frac{2}{9}\right)$	$\left(\frac{-1}{9}, \frac{1}{9}\right)$	(0,0)	$\left(\frac{1}{9}, \frac{-1}{9}\right)$
IV	$\left(\frac{-2}{9}, \frac{2}{9}\right)$	(0,0)	$\left(\frac{-1}{9}, \frac{1}{9}\right)$	(0,0)

Figure 3.8. One-card Stud Poker. Payoff matrix, player 1, $a = b = \$1$.

Brute force can only carry an argument so far. At this point, it's time to stop and think. The most suspect strategy in the set under consideration is III: it bets aces and queens (even though queens can't win a showdown), while passing kings (even though kings win as many showdowns on average as they lose). Strategy III also has the biggest negatives in Figure 3.8. Let's exclude it by setting $p(\text{III}) = 0$. We next look for a mixed strategy consisting only of I, II, and IV. We now need to solve the equations:

$$EV(\text{I}) = 0p(\text{I}) - \frac{2}{9}\,p(\text{II}) + \frac{2}{9}\,(0) + \frac{1}{9}\,p(\text{IV})$$

$$= EV(\text{II}) = \left(\frac{2}{9}\right)p(\text{I}) + (0)\,p(\text{II}) + \frac{1}{6}\,(0) - \frac{1}{18}\,p(\text{IV})$$

$$= EV(\text{IV}) = -\frac{1}{9}\,p(\text{I}) + \frac{1}{18}\,p(\text{II}) - \frac{1}{18}(0) + (0)\,p(\text{IV})$$

We also need the strategies to add up to 1:

$$p(\text{I}) + p(\text{II}) + 0 + p(\text{IV}) = 1$$

These equations actually do have a solution, which you can check:

$$p(\text{I})^* = \frac{1}{7};\ p(\text{II})^* = \frac{2}{7};\ \text{and}\ p(\text{IV})^* = \frac{4}{7}$$

Player 1 \ Player 2	I	II	III	IV
I	(0,0)	$\left(\frac{-2}{9}, \frac{2}{9}\right)$	$\left(\frac{2}{9}, \frac{-2}{9}\right)$	$\left(\frac{1}{9}, \frac{-1}{9}\right)$
II	$\left(\frac{2}{9}, \frac{-2}{9}\right)$	(0,0)	$\left(\frac{1.5}{9}, \frac{-1.5}{9}\right)$	$\left(\frac{-0.5}{9}, \frac{0.5}{9}\right)$
III	$\left(\frac{-2}{9}, \frac{2}{9}\right)$	$\left(\frac{-1.5}{9}, \frac{1.5}{9}\right)$	(0,0)	$\left(\frac{0.5}{9}, \frac{-0.5}{9}\right)$
IV	$\left(\frac{-1}{9}, \frac{1}{9}\right)$	$\left(\frac{0.5}{9}, \frac{-0.5}{9}\right)$	$\left(\frac{-0.5}{9}, \frac{0.5}{9}\right)$	(0,0)

Figure 3.9. One-card Stud Poker. Payoff matrix, player 1, a = \$1, b = \$1.50.

This mixed strategy equilibrium is the only solution to the set of linear equations, so it must be the solution to 1-card Stud Poker (with queens).

There is a considerable amount of bluffing going on according to this mixed strategy. To see this, let's consider what this mixed strategy does on the basis of 21 deals. In 7 of 21 deals, a player is dealt an ace. Since strategies I, II, and IV all bet an ace, in these 7 deals the player always bets an ace. In another 7 of 21 deals, a player is dealt a king. Strategies I and II bet a king, which happens 3 of 7 times (1/7 + 2/7), whereas III passes a king, which happens 4 of 7 times. This strategy is already deceptive: sometimes this player bets a king, sometimes he or she doesn't. In yet another 7 of 21 times, a player is dealt a queen. Strategy I bets this queen, which happens 1 of 7 times, whereas II and III pass the queen, which happens 6 of 7 times. In 21 deals, the player using this strategy bluffs in the purest form (betting a card that cannot win, a queen) once, a bluffing rate of 1/21 (5%) on hands that cannot win. This level of bluffing is on the order of magnitude of what you observe in real-world Poker games involving good players. The whole point of this mixed strategy is to throw the opponent off, to prevent the opponent from drawing any information from the fact that a player bet—and it does this admirably. Play this strategy and no one will know what your cards are. This strategy also breaks even:

$$EV(\text{I}) = EV(\text{II}) = EV(\text{IV}) = 0$$

As usual in Poker, you go to an awful lot of work just so you won't lose money. In order to make money, you still have to find a sucker who doesn't play the right strategy. Then your strategy *will* make money.

PROBLEMS

1. Verify the entry in Figure 3.6 for strategy II versus strategy III.
2. Suppose that the bet in 1-card Stud Poker is only $0.25 and the ante is still $1. What is the solution? What about when the bet is $1.60? What does this tell about the relationship between the solution to 1-card Stud Poker and the size of the bet?

CHAPTER 4

n-Person Games in Normal Form

Every game that we have studied so far, such as Battle of the Networks, Let's Make a Deal, Video System Coordination, Cigarette Television Advertising, Competitive Advantage, and Market Niche, had exactly two players. All these games, however, can be played by more than two players. There is nothing sacred about the number 2. For instance, there are more than two television networks, more than two cigarette companies, and more than two principals usually involved in putting together a movie deal. Sometimes it makes a big difference whether there are exactly two players in a game or more than two. Since we want to apply game theory to the real world, we need to be able to write down and solve games that have more than two players. The goal of this chapter is to meet that need.

This chapter begins with two main results for 2-person games, the determination theorem for games like Chess and the solution theorem for 2-person, zero-sum games, and shows that these results no longer hold when there are three players, one of whom plays the role of a spoiler. Next, 3-person versions of Competitive Advantage and Market Niche are introduced to show what difference a third player makes, and the method for writing down and solving Video System Coordination and Let's Make a Deal with three players is explained. Cigarette Television Advertising with four players—the big four tobacco companies in 1971—is described. A famous episode in U.S. history, Stonewalling at Watergate, is a 3-person Prisoner's Dilemma that brought down the Nixon presidency. For games with more than three players, the concept of symmetry provides a useful shortcut, both for modeling the game and for solving it. A symmetrical game looks the same to every player. The sufficient condition of payoff symmetry holds that the solution of a symmetrical game should pay each player the same amount. The chapter then presents a phenomenon known as the tragedy of the commons, which occurs when a resource, such as rangeland, is used in common by a large number of players. The game Tragedy of the Commons is a parable for negative aspects of global environmental change. It is also bad for business, as the game Geothermal Tragedy of the Commons shows. The appendix describes how the Tragedy of the Commons can be recreated in the laboratory. Laboratory experiments in game theory are an exciting way to enhance understanding of strategic behavior, and they lead to some surprises, too.

4.1 Fundamental Differences with Three Players: The Spoiler ■■■■■■■■■■■■■■■■■■■■■■■■■

When there are three players in a game instead of two, fundamental differences arise. It is as if there were a continental divide between the cases $n = 2$, and $n = 3$ (the parameter n refers to the number of players from now on); sometimes a result gets across the divide and sometimes it doesn't. One result that definitely doesn't hold for $n = 3$ is the determination theorem for games like Chess (section 1.8). The easiest way to show that a result is not general is to provide a **counterexample,** an example that runs counter to the generalization.

Figure 4.1 shows an extensive form game called Spoiler, for reasons that will soon become apparent. Spoiler has perfect information, the players move in sequence, it is win, lose, or draw, and it is finite. Unlike the determinate games of Chapter 1, it has three players. Players 1 and 2 get payoffs but do not actually have any choices to make. A player who gets a payoff but does not have any choices to make is called a **strategic dummy.** In this game, only player 3 has any choices to make. Player 3 chooses either top or bottom. Payoff vectors **u** are of the form $\mathbf{u} = (u_1, u_2, u_3)$. Player 3 is indifferent about top and bottom—he or she loses no matter what—therefore, both get arrows. Then player 1 could win—player 3 chooses top and the payoff vector is (w,l,l)—or player 2 could win—player 3 chooses bottom and the payoff vector is (l,w,l). The game is indeterminate.

The counterexample of Figure 4.1 could be much more complicated, for instance by having lots of moves for players 1 and 2. As long as at the end of the

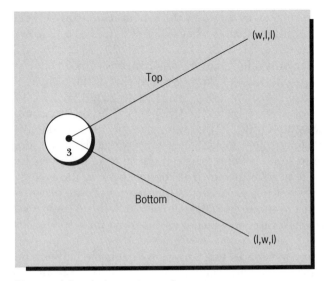

Figure 4.1. Indeterminate three-person game.

game the determination boils down to a move by player 3 and the payoffs attached to that move are (w,l,l) and (l,w,l), the game is indeterminate.

Another result that cannot be generalized to three players is the solution theorem for 2-person, zero-sum games (section 2.4). Once there are more than two players, a zero-sum game in normal form can have solutions that do not have the same value. To follow the counterexample for this case, one more introductory remark is needed. As usual, player 1 controls the rows of the matrix and player 2 controls the columns. Now, the additional player, player 3, controls the matrix. The counterexample given, now in normal form, shows that the solution theorem is not true for $n = 3$ (see Figure 4.2). Let the utility of winning $= 1$ and the utility of losing $= -1/2$. Since players 1 and 2 are strategic dummies, the matrix they play on is 1×1. Player 3 picks either the matrix on the left, corresponding to the move Top in Figure 4.1, or the matrix on the right, corresponding to the move Bottom in Figure 4.1. Player 3 is

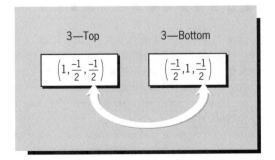

Figure 4.2. Multiple solutions, 3-person, zero-sum game.

indifferent about these two choices, as shown by the two-headed arrow between the two matrices. Player 3 loses no matter what he or she does. We have two solutions with very different values $(1,-1/2,-1/2)$ and $(-1/2,1,-1/2)$. Player 3, while maximizing his or her own utility, can be simultaneously maximizing or minimizing player 1's utility—all because player 2 is also part of the picture.

There is an explanation for what is going on in these games, at least for politics or sports. In politics, a player is called a **spoiler** if he or she cannot win but can determine who does win. For example, take the 1992 presidential election: 1 = Bush, 2 = Clinton, 3 = Perot. Perot can't win, at least not after dropping out of the race in June. If Perot stays out of the race, Bush gets just enough of the voters in the middle to win. If Perot gets back in the race, he pulls just enough votes away from Bush that Clinton wins. Perot plays the spoiler in this campaign, just as shown in Figures 4.1 and 4.2. In a two-way race, no one can play a spoiler; in a three-way race, there is room for a spoiler like Perot.

You can have spoilers in team sports, too. Any individual game between two teams is win, lose, or draw. However, when an entire league of teams are fighting for a championship, then a team that is out of the running could play the spoiler. For all of you USA ice hockey fans, 1980 was a magic year—the last time the United States won the gold medal in the Olympics. You could win a bar bet with the statement, "I'll bet you think that when the USA beat the USSR 4 to 3, they won the gold medal." The problem with this statement is that the Olympics weren't over yet, and the United States still had to play Finland, a tough team. Finland was out of the medal race, but it could have played the spoiler. If Finland had beaten the United States, the USSR would have won the gold medal. As it turned out, the United States beat Finland 4 to 1. That's when the United States clinched its gold medal.

When spoilers don't occur, then the results for 2-player games work for 3-player games as well. The next section shows that this is true for Competitive Advantage and Market Niche.

4.2 Competitive Advantage and Market Niche with Three Players ■■■■■■■■■■■■■■■■■■■■■■■■■■■

Recall the game Competitive Advantage from Chapter 2. This game can actually be played by more than two firms. Let's consider what Competitive Advantage looks like with three firms, labeled 1, 2, and 3. As before, each firm has a choice between staying put or adopting the new technology. If no firm adopts the new technology, then there is no competitive advantage and the payoff vector is $(0,0,0)$. If exactly one firm adopts the new technology, then that firm gets the competitive advantage a, while each firm at a competitive disadvantage loses $a/2$. Thus if only firm 1 adopts the new technology, then the payoff vector is $(a,-a/2,-a/2)$. You can think of this as firm 1 taking market share away from

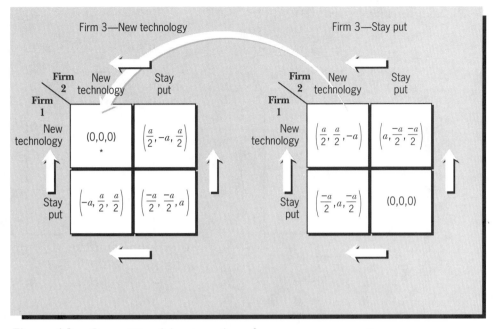

Figure 4.3. Competitive Advantage, three firms.

both firm 2 and firm 3. If exactly two firms adopt the new technology, then these two firms split the competitive advantage and the firm at a disadvantage loses a. Thus, if firms 1 and 2 adopt the new technology, the payoff vector is $(a/2, a/2, -a)$. The firm that lags behind loses big. Finally, if all three firms adopt the new technology, there is again no competitive advantage and the payoff vector is $(0,0,0)$. Figure 4.3 shows the normal form of Competitive Advantage with three players.

As you can see from the arrow diagram, the unique equilibrium occurs when each firm adopts the new technology. This is precisely what happens when there are only two firms. No firm can afford to be left behind in the race to adopt the new technology—this is just as true for n players as it is for two or three players. This is our first example of a result that extends from two players to more than two players. It is quite rare, although not impossible, for firms to play the role of spoilers.

Let's turn to Market Niche with three firms (recall Figure 3.2), firms 1, 2, and 3. As before, each firm has to choose between entering the market niche or staying out, and there is only room in the market niche for a single firm. Any firm that stays out breaks even. If exactly one firm enters the market niche, it gains 100. If more than one firm enters the market niche, each firm that does so loses 50. The normal form of Market Niche with three players is shown in Figure 4.4.

As you can see from the arrow diagram, Market Niche has three pure strategy equilibria: (stay out, stay out, enter), (enter, stay out, stay out), and

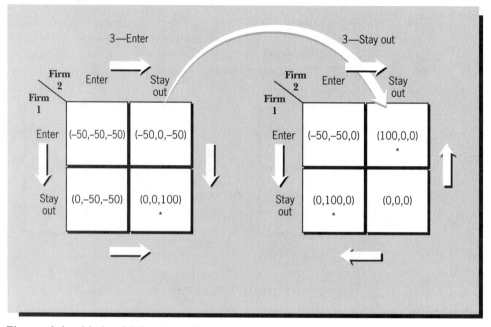

Figure 4.4.   Market Niche, three firms.

(stay out, enter, stay out). At each of these pure strategy equilibria, exactly one firm occupies the market niche and the other two firms stay out. Each equilibrium is efficient. However, their payoff consequences are very different: each firm would like to be the one that enters the market niche. These outcomes are lopsided.

In addition to the three asymmetrical pure strategy equilibria, there is a symmetrical mixed strategy equilibrium. At this symmetrical mixed strategy equilibrium, each firm gets the same payoff. To compute the mixed strategy equilibrium, let p(enter) be the probability that a firm enters the market niche and p(stay out) be the probability that a firm stays out of the market niche. Consider the choice facing firm 1. If firm 1 enters the market, it encounters the following probability distribution:

with probability p(enter)^2, two other firms are present

with probability $2p$(enter)p(stay out), one other firm is present

with probability p(stay out)^2, no other firm is present[1]

Thus, the expected value to firm 1 of entering the market niche, EV_1(enter), given the mixed strategies played by its competitors, is

$$EV_1(\text{enter}) = (-50)[1 - p(\text{stay out})^2] + (100)p(\text{stay out})^2$$

---

[1]These probabilities are derived from the binomial probability distribution. You can also generate them from a tree diagram, with random devices in the role of players 2 and 3.

because if one or both other firms are present, firm 1 loses 50. Firm 1's alternative is to stay out, and that pays a sure 0, hence an expected 0, EV_1(stay out) = 0. Setting these two expected values equal to each other, we get

$$0 = (-50)[1 - p(\text{stay out})^2] + (100)p(\text{stay out})^2$$

which is one equation in one unknown, p(stay out). Solving this equation, we arrive at

$$p(\text{stay out})^* = .58$$

At the mixed strategy equilibrium, the probability that an individual firm will stay out of the market is .58; the probability that it will enter the market, .42. At this symmetrical equilibrium, each firm expects to break even.

From the standpoint of the market, the distribution of number of firms in the market niche, according to the mixed strategy equilibriums is as follows:

with probability $p(\text{enter})^{*3} = .08$, three firms enter

with probability $3p(\text{enter})^{*2}p(\text{stay out})^* = .31$, two firms enter

with probability $3p(\text{enter})^*p(\text{stay out})^{*2} = .42$, one firm enters

with probability $p(\text{stay out})^{*3} = .19$, no firm enters

It is very likely (probability .81) that the market will be served, but also rather likely (probability .39) that the market will be overserved. This high probability of overserving the market is the price the firms will pay if they are all to get the same payoffs. Although in one respect—namely, the firms all break even—this outcome is like perfect competition, in another respect it is not. The only outcomes that guarantee that the market niche will be filled, the pure strategy equilibria, must be upheld by some form of limitation on free entry. Only in that way does exactly one firm know that, at equilibrium, it is safe to enter the market niche.

4.3 Three-Player Versions of Video System Coordination, Let's Make a Deal, and Cigarette Television Advertising ■

This section reviews three more games that occur in business, in which spoilers play no role; consequently, the outcomes are fairly close to those of the two-player versions. Consider first Video System Coordination, shown in Figure 4.5. As in the 2-player version, in the 3-player version every firm has to be on the same system in order for networking to take place. You can think of these players as three firms under the same corporate umbrella—unless they are on the same system, they can't make anything. Either system, Beta or VHS, does equally well. As you can see from the arrow diagram, there are two pure strategy equilibria, one with all firms on the Beta system and another with all

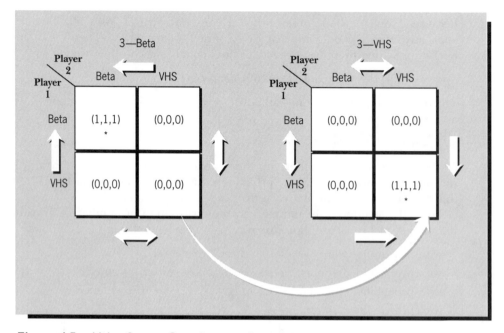

Figure 4.5.   Video System Coordination, three firms.

firms on the VHS system. The payoffs associated with these outcomes are the same, so we can't say that one is better than the other.

Just as in the 2-player version of Video System Coordination, in the 3-player game there is an additional equilibrium in mixed strategies. At this mixed strategy equilibrium, it is easy to show that each firm is on either system with equal probability:

$$p(\text{Beta})^* = p(\text{VHS})^* = .5$$

With probability $.5^3 = .125$, all firms are on the Beta system; with probability .125, on the VHS system. Thus, the chance that firms coordinate on some system is only 25%. This result implies a large failure to coordinate rate of 75%. Things only get worse as the number, *n*, of firms grows. You can show that the chances of coordinating in the *n*-player version of Video System Coordination at the mixed strategy equilibrium go to zero as *n* gets large. The moral of all this is that coordination is too important to be left to chance. Firms must somehow solve the game they are in for one of its pure strategy equilibria or pay the consequences.

Next let's look at Let's Make a Deal, now with 3 players. The three players are 1, the movie star; 2, the director; and 3, the producer. The producer is important because he or she usually provides the financing for the movie. As before, there is $15 million at stake. If all three players say yes, they split the $15 million equally. If one of them says no, then it's no deal and each player gets $0. The normal form of this game is shown in Figure 4.6.

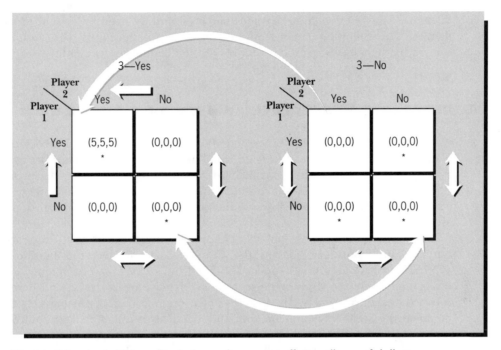

Figure 4.6. Let's Make a Deal, three players, payoffs in millions of dollars.

As you can see from the arrow diagram, Let's Make a Deal with three players has five pure strategy equilibria. One of these pays well—everybody says yes. All the rest pay poorly—nobody gets anything. Any strategy vector where at least two people say no is an equilibrium. This situation explains why there are so many bad equilibria. However, saying no is dominated by saying yes. If everyone else says yes, then saying yes pays $5 million while saying no pays $0. In every other case, saying either yes or no pays $0. That's enough for dominance. Hence, using the sufficient condition of undominated strategies, the solution to Let's Make a Deal is the Yes vector—(yes, yes, yes).

As the final multiplayer game from the business world in this section, consider Cigarette Television Advertising. The cigarette companies are labeled companies 1, 2, 3, and 4 to protect their anonymity. When we looked at two cigarette companies in the case in Chapter 2, each company had a dominant strategy to advertise on television. This situation holds true for four companies as well. The solution of the game is for each company to advertise on television. In the 2-player version, when both companies advertised on television their profits were less than when both refrained from advertising on television. Again, this holds true with four cigarette companies. All four cigarette manufacturers made more money when the government banned television advertising.

The phenomenon where every player has a strictly dominant strategy that leads to a very bad outcome for all players has a special name: the **prisoner's**

dilemma. This phenomenon pervades our lives, and we need to be alert to its danger. The following famous episode from twentieth-century U.S. history shows what happens when the incentives of the dilemma are present.

⁘ 4.4 Stonewalling Watergate[2] ■ ■ ■ ■ ■ ■ ■ ■ ■ ■ ■ ■ ■ ■ ■

On June 17, 1972, burglars broke into the headquarters of the Democratic National Committee in the Watergate Hotel in Washington, D.C. Thus began a strategic odyssey that ended with Richard Nixon's resignation from the presidency 2 years later. This section considers one of many aspects of the Watergate affair, namely, the way those closest to the president dealt with the investigating authorities.

White House spokesmen publicly denounced the break-in as a third-rate burglary and continued to run the Committee to Reelect the President (CREEP) as if nothing had happened. Behind the scenes, however, plenty was happening. In White House tape recordings, dated June 21, 1972, and newly released by the National Archives, we can hear the president discussing what to do about the break-in. Nowadays, this kind of activity is called damage control. According to the Associated Press report of the tape, Nixon said, in a mocking tone, "It's a horrible thing to bug.... Most people around the country think it's probably routine, everybody's trying to bug everybody else, it's politics. That's my view." Then he added, "I don't think you're going to see a great, great uproar in the country about the Republican Committee trying to bug the Democratic headquarters."[3]

The Nixon administration decided to control the damage by a combination of denial and cover-up. In the weeks that followed, three members of the Nixon team—in alphabetical order, John W. Dean III, counsel to the president; John D. Ehrlichman, assistant to the president for domestic affairs; and H. R. Haldeman, White House chief of staff—took full charge of the Watergate damage control plan. The primary objective of the plan was to reelect the president. If it could be proved that the White House was involved in the break-in, the president's overwhelming lead in the polls would be jeopardized. The secondary objective of the plan was to keep the cover-up itself covered up. Obstruction of justice and conspiracy were just two of the felony charges available to federal prosecutors in the event that the cover-up failed. The White House even coined a new word to describe this aspect of the plan: **stonewalling.** Just as Union troops ran into a stone wall whenever they attacked the Confederate general Thomas (Stonewall) Jackson, so federal investigators would run

---

[2]This material is inspired in part by Carl Bernstein and Robert Woodward, *All the President's Men* (New York: Simon & Schuster, 1974).
[3]See the Bloomington *Herald Telephone*, May 15, 1993.

into a stone wall whenever they tried to cut through the White House cloak of silence.

In the 1972 election, Nixon won a landslide victory against McGovern, carrying 49 of 50 states. CREEP had done its job, but the stonewalling had only just begun. The plan at this stage was given a code name: Operation Candor. The three players in the game were the three White House insiders entrusted with carrying out Operation Candor: Dean, Ehrlichman, and Haldeman. Boiled down to its simplest terms, each had a pair of strategies. A player could stonewall or talk. Stonewalling meant refusing to cooperate with federal prosecutors, making reporters' lives as difficult as possible, and keeping up the pressure on all lower-ranked personnel involved. Given the speedy apprehension and conviction of the Watergate burglars, even this strategy invited some loss—and the prospect of loss grew, the closer the investigation got to the White House. Talking meant either talking to the federal prosecutors, talking to reporters, such as Woodward and Bernstein, or talking to the player's own lawyer. Talking would begin to rip apart the cloak of secrecy and would leave coconspirators "to twist in the wind," as the White House tapes put it. Again, keeping things simple, there were four possible outcomes to the game. Once reporters and federal investigators got sufficiently close to White House involvement in the break-in—in March, 1974, when indictments were handed down—the payoff to stonewalling looked pretty bad. Even if all three players toughed it out, there was still a good chance that they would get felony convictions and do some hard time. Call the utility of this outcome –3. The least undesirable outcome was to talk, especially if the player talked to federal authorities and copped his own plea. We won't distinguish here between talking to the federal authorities and other forms of talking. For instance, a player could accomplish much the same thing by talking to his own lawyers and instructing them to start negotiations with the federal prosecutor in the hope of leniency. In any event, if a player talked, the payoff was –2, rather better than –3. Also, if a player talked, he left his coconspirators to twist in the wind, a payoff of –5. Finally, if all players talked, the prosecutors had an open-and-shut case, but would ask for slightly less than maximum penalties. Call the utility of this outcome –4. The game that results is shown in Figure 4.7.

As you can see from the arrow diagram, there is a unique pure strategy equilibrium. At this equilibrium, Dean, Ehrlichman, and Haldeman all talk. The temptation to give up on stonewalling and seek a better deal from the prosecutors was too much to resist. The outcome for each player is worse than if he had been the only one to quit stonewalling. Indeed—and this is what makes the Prisoner's Dilemma so fiendish—the outcome is worse than if they had all stuck to stonewalling in the first place. The payoff to stonewalling is (–3,–3,–3), hardly great, but better than the (–4,–4,–4) at equilibrium. The moral of the story is, as long as there is a more attractive option available than staying inside a conspiracy, someone is going to take it. There is a good strategic reason why cover-ups uncover themselves.

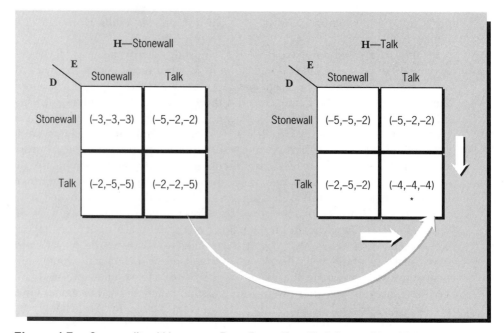

Figure 4.7.   Stonewalling Watergate. D = Dean; E = Ehrlichman; H = Halderman.

▓ 4.5 Symmetry and Games with Many Players ▪ ▪ ▪ ▪ ▪

Once a game has more than three players or each player has more than eight strategies or so, writing down the entire game in extensive or normal form becomes rather impractical. We need a notation that allows us to study more involved games. Just as utility functions of many variables came to the rescue in Chapter 2, so they will come in handy here.

Suppose that there are *n* players, indexed by the letter $i = 1, 2,\ldots,n$. Each player *i* has a set of available strategies, $X(i)$. The strategy that player *i* actually chooses, x_i, must belong to the set of strategies $X(i)$. Finally, each player *i* has a utility function of the form $u_i(x)$, where $\mathbf{x} = (x_1, x_2,\ldots,x_n)$ is a vector of the strategies chosen by all the players individually. This compact notation covers every *n*-person game studied so far, including 2-person games.

To see how this notation works in an example, consider Video System Coordination with three firms. First we need to code the strategies. For each firm *i*, let $X(i) = \{0, 1\}$, where $x_i = 1$ means that firm *i* is on the Beta system, and $x_i = 0$ means that firm *i* is on the VHS system. Then we can write the utility function for firm *i* succinctly as

$u_i(x) = 1$ if $\Sigma x_i = 3$ or 0

$u_i(x) = 0$ otherwise

This functional notation contains all the information in Figure 4.5. See if you can write down Competitive Advantage, Market Niche, or Let's Make a Deal in this notation.

This notation enables us to write down games with many players, each with many strategies. All we need to do is specify the utility function of each player as a function of n variables, one variable for each player's strategy. We will put this notation to work in solving games shortly.

First, however, we need a new concept, *symmetry*. Intuitively, a game is a **symmetrical game** when it looks the same to each player. "Looks the same" boils down to two major considerations. First, each player i has the same set of strategies $X(i)$; one player does not have more strategies than, or different strategies from, another. Second, every pair of players i and j have the same utility function in the sense that, given the strategies of all the other players, interchanging the strategies of players interchanges their payoffs:

$$u_i(x_i, x_j, \text{rest of strategies}) = u_j(x_j, x_i, \text{rest of strategies})$$

In particular, when two players choose the same strategy $x_i = x_j$, then

$$u_i(x_i, x_i, \text{rest of strategies}) = u_j(x_i, x_i, \text{rest of strategies})$$

In a symmetrical game, when players choose the same strategy, they get the same payoffs.

As an example of a symmetrical game, consider Let's Make a Deal. To check the first condition, note that the strategies Yes and No are available to each player. To check the second condition, note that when they all say yes, they get the same payoff ($5 million) and when they all say no, they get the same payoff ($0). Finally, to check the rest of the payoff **interchange condition,** taking $1 = i$ and $2 = j$ and letting Yes = 1 and No = 0,

$$u_1(1,0,0) = u_2(0,1,0) = 0$$
$$u_1(0,1,0) = u_2(1,0,0) = 0$$
$$u_1(1,0,1) = u_2(0,1,1) = 0$$
$$u_1(0,1,1) = u_2(1,0,1) = 0$$

You can check the interchange condition for every other pair of players; the result is exactly the same as the one shown here. The game Let's Make a Deal looks just the same to the movie star as to the director as to the producer.

Symmetrical games are important for two reasons. First, they provide good approximations to complicated games when the players are not very different, and they are easier to solve. Second, symmetrical games inspire a sufficient condition for a solution. Since a symmetrical game looks the same to every player, there is no reason to believe that one player has an advantage over another. All players have equal opportunity. The solution to a symmetrical game ought to reflect this equality of opportunity.[4] This notion is the content of the following sufficient condition:

[4]Recall, however, the conflict raised in the last chapter between symmetry and payoff dominance. The reader may well prefer payoff dominance to symmetry as a sufficient condition. This subject remains controversial.

■ ■

Payoff Symmetry. The solution of a symmetrical game has the same payoff for all players.

The sufficient condition of **payoff symmetry** would not make much sense unless there were equilibria that could satisfy it. An equilibrium is a **symmetrical equilibrium** if all players use the same strategy and receive the same payoff. It is possible to show that every symmetrical game that has an equilibrium has a symmetrical equilibrium.[5]

To see the power of symmetry as a sufficient condition, consider 3-player Let's Make a Deal, which has five equilibria. Two of these, the Yes vector and the No vector, are symmetrical. The three other equilibria are asymmetrical: two players do different things. Even these three asymmetrical equilibria satisfy payoff symmetry however, since every player gets paid $0. This situation shows that a symmetrical game can have asymmetrical equilibria. Thus, the condition of payoff symmetry has some teeth in it—it rules out all these bad equilibria in Let's Make a Deal as solutions. Then, if we apply payoff dominance, we can rule out all equilibria except (yes, yes, yes). This book applies symmetry prior to payoff dominance—although such a procedure remains somewhat arbitrary.[6]

Market Niche (with two or three players) provides an example of a symmetrical game whose asymmetrical equilibria do not satisfy payoff symmetry. Recall Figures 3.2 and 4.4. Market Niche satisfies the interchange and diagonal conditions: the asymmetrical equilibria are (enter, stay out) and (stay out, enter), and the firm that enters gets a much higher payoff. The only symmetrical equilibrium of Market Niche is in mixed strategies.

4.6 Solving Symmetrical Games with Many Strategies ■

When the players in a game have a lot of strategies, we use calculus to find the game's equilibria. When the players in a symmetrical game have a lot of strategies, we again use calculus to find the game's symmetrical equilibrium. Calculus becomes especially useful when a symmetrical game has a lot of players (big *n*), each with a lot of strategies. What follows is an example of how the technique works, first with two players, then with *n* players. You can think of the players as firms in a market game, where they compete in terms of

---

[5]The proof is tricky and requires some abstract algebra, which you are spared! See J. Nash, "Noncooperative Games," *Annals of Mathematics* 54(1951):289–295, for details.

[6]For an extensive argument for applying symmetry prior to payoff dominance, see John Harsanyi and Reinhard Selten, *A General Theory of Equilibrium Selection in Games* (Cambridge: MIT Press, 1988).

advertising, quantity, price, or some other dimension. Chapter 5 develops various interpretations.

Each player has the strategy set [0,10]—any number between 0 and 10. Player 1 has the utility function $u_1(x) = x_1(20 - \Sigma x_1)$. For $n = 2$, this becomes

$$u_1(x) = x_1(20 - x_1 - x_2)$$

A generic player i has the utility function $u_i(x) = x_i(20 - \Sigma x_i)$. We can check that these utility functions satisfy the payoff interchange condition when $n = 2$:

$$u_1(x_1, x_2) = x_1(20 - x_1 - x_2) = u_2(x_2, x_1)$$

Any time a player's utility function can be written in the form $u_i(x_i, \Sigma x_i)$ and the form of the function u is the same for all players, then the payoff interchange condition is satisfied. There is a reason for this. Each player's payoff depends only on his or her own action and on the aggregate action of all the players. In the aggregate, each player is the same as every other player. That is where the symmetry lies.

Now let's solve the game when there are two players. In Chapter 3 we solved the game by maximizing utility for each player and then solving the resulting two equations. There is a shortcut, however. First, we maximize utility for one player, say, player 1. Then, we exploit symmetry—the fact that at a symmetrical equilibrium, each player does the same thing. Finally, we solve the single equation that results. Here goes. Maximizing player 1's utility means setting marginal utility equal to zero:

$$0 = \frac{[\delta] u_1}{[\delta] x_1} = 20 - 2x_1 - x_2$$

Now, set $x_1 = x_2$, since at equilibrium both players will be doing the same thing:

$$0 = 20 - 3x_1$$

Now solve the equation to get $x_1 = 20/3$. This gives the equilibrium of the game:

$$(x_1^*, x_2^*) = \left(\frac{20}{3}, \frac{20}{3}\right)$$

You can better appreciate the power of this technique by seeing how it solves this game with 100 players. Instead of solving a system of equations with 100 players and 100 unknowns, we simply perform these three steps, where the sum of strategies is $(x_1 + x_2 + \cdots + x_{100})$. The $\cdots$ notation says that you can fill in the dots easily. Maximizing player 1's utility means setting marginal utility equal to zero:

$$0 = \frac{\partial u_1}{\partial x_1} = 20 - 2x_1 - x_2 - \cdots - x_{100}$$

Now set $x_1 = x_2 = \cdots = x_{100}$ and substitute:

$$0 = 20 - 101x_1$$

Now solve the equation to get $x_1 = 20/101$. This gives us the equilibrium of the game:

$$\left(x_1^*, x_2^*, \ldots, x_{100}^* \right) = \left(\frac{20}{101}, \frac{20}{101}, \ldots, \frac{20}{101} \right)$$

Games with many players can get pretty crowded. Think of perfect competition, where there are many, many firms, each with a tiny market share. There are so many firms that market price is driven down to cost, and none of the firms makes very much money. Of course, consumers make out like bandits. Something similar occurs when too many companies exploit the same resource in common, only in this case consumers aren't any better off, either. Everybody is a loser in the tragedy of the commons.

4.7 The Tragedy of the Commons[7] ■ ■ ■ ■ ■ ■ ■ ■ ■ ■ ■ ■

The following scenario is played out the world over. A group of individual producers or businesses access a resource that no one of them owns. The resource is a *commons,* freely available to all. One example of a commons is an underground aquifer, such as the Ogallala aquifer, which extends under the Great Plains from the Dakotas to Texas. No one owns the aquifer, and anyone who wants to pump its water up to the surface, usually for agricultural production, can do so. When such underground water sources are hot, such as in geysers, they offer a valuable source of energy. Another example of a commons is a species of whale, such as the minke whale, swimming the high seas. No one owns the whales, and any nation that wants to hunt them is free to do so.[8] Yet another example of a commons is the atmosphere. Any business can store its waste in the atmosphere at essentially no cost.[9]

A **tragedy of the commons** occurs when too many players exploit the resource. This practice leads to a double-edged disaster. First, the resource is either degraded or destroyed. Second, rates of return of all the producers involved are lower than they could be. In its most virulent form, the tragedy plays out as destruction of the resource and a zero rate of return to the firms involved. We will see this both in a simple game model and in real life.

---

[7]Material for this section has been drawn from Richard A. Ken, "Geothermal Tragedy of the Commons," *Science* 253 (1991):134–35.

[8]The hunting of whales is currently subject to an international agreement. This agreement is a direct result of the tragedy of the commons.

[9]As in the case of the whales, the commons tragedy of the atmosphere, manifested as degraded air quality, had led to a change in the rules of the game.

Let i be an index of potential users of the commons. We will call all potential users companies. Let x_i represent company i's strategy: $x_i = 1$ means that company i uses the commons; $x_i = 0$ means that company i does not use the commons. If company i does not use the commons, it gets a normal rate of return on its assets in another sector of the economy equal to 10%, or 0.1. If company i uses the commons, then the rate of return depends on how many other companies use the commons as well. The production function for the entire commons, $F(\Sigma x_i)$, measures how much is produced in total, depending on how many companies are using the commons (Σx_i).

To keep things symmetrical, assume that all companies that use the commons get an equal share of the commons production. If there are m companies using the commons, then an individual company using the commons gets $F(m)/m$ as its payoff.[10] The utility function for company i, $u_i(x)$, is given as follows:

$$u_i(x) = 0.1 \text{ if } x_i = 0$$
$$= \frac{F(m)}{(m)} \text{ if } x_i = 1$$

where $m = \Sigma x_i$. This utility function can be written a bit more compactly as

$$u_i(x) = 0.1(1 - x_i) + x_i \frac{F(m)}{m}$$

The utility of a company measures its rate of return—what makes the stockholders happy. A company faces a trade-off between the sure return of 10% and a strategically risky return from the commons, $F(m)/m$. Each company has the same set of strategies and the same form of utility function, and utility depends only on what the company itself does and the aggregate strategy of all the companies. Hence the game is symmetrical.

We will first solve the case with two companies, $n = 2$. To fix ideas, let's take a specific commons production function, $F(m)$, namely,

$$F(m) = 1.1m - .1m^2$$

This production function exhibits diminishing returns. When a single company is using the commons, the rate of return is fantastic, 100% [$F(1) = 1$], but as the number of companies using the commons increases, the returns drop off dramatically. By the time there are 11 companies using the commons, returns are down to zero [$F(11) = 0$]. Figure 4.8 shows the game played by two companies on this commons. When a company does not use the commons, it gets a return of 10%. This is way below what it can get if it uses the commons by itself (100%) and also below what it can get even if it has to share the commons (90%). The unique equilibrium where both companies use the common is the

---

[10]The tragedy of the commons does not depend on symmetry. It takes place in asymmetrical situations as well as in symmetrical ones.

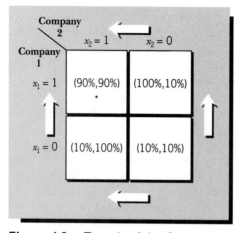

Figure 4.8. Tragedy of the Commons, two firms.

solution—and a very attractive solution it is. Two companies earning a 90% rate of return in an economy is a whole lot better than two companies earning a 10% rate of return. This is hardly a tragedy.

The tragedy arises when there are a lot more than two companies using the commons. The magic number of companies for the tragedy is 10. The reason lies in the entry mechanism. The whole point of a commons is that anyone can enter it and exploit it. When another company sees the first two companies earning super rates of return, it is going to want to get in on the action, too. The criterion for entry is that the company earns more from entering the commons than the 10% it earns from staying out. This is precisely the criterion for equilibrium in the game as well. Suppose that there are 10 companies, $n = 10$. You can check that $F(m)/m$ for $m = 1, 2, \ldots, 9$ exceeds 10%, so they all enter. For instance, $F(9)/9 = 20\%$, still well above 10%. Now look at the situation facing the 10th company. If it enters the commons, it gets $F(10)/10 = 10\%$, precisely the same as if it stays out. This firm is on the margin. Since the game is symmetrical, at equilibrium each firm does the same thing, in this case, it enters the commons. This makes sense: the companies are moving simultaneously, so a company cannot know whether it is 10th or not. This outcome is tragic. Rates of return well above 10% have been irretrievably lost because the commons has been overused. Since every company in the commons is getting the return it would get if it weren't using the resource, the resource isn't adding any value to the economy. It has been totally wasted.

One way to measure the waste is to compare the efficient solution of the same problem to the game solution. To get the most return from the commons, you would seek the number m that maximizes

$$\max F(m) - 0.1m$$

If the commons were private property, then the owners would want to maximize its return in just this fashion, by leasing the rights to use it to just the right number of companies, no more, no less. The way to maximize that return is to maximize gross return less cost, where it costs a 10% rate of return to hire a company to work the resource. The maximum occurs at

$$0 = 1.1 - 0.2m - 0.1$$

Solving, we get $m^* = 5$. The right number of companies to exploit the commons is five. Any number of companies beyond that launches on the inexorable path to tragedy. And since anyone can use the commons, there is no way to keep the number of companies at just five.

The Geysers of northern California is the nation's largest geothermal energy field, producing more than 6% of California's energy and 75% of the nation's geothermal energy. When the field was first developed in 1960, rates of return were very high, and Pacific Gas and Electric (PG&E), the principal developer, was earning a hefty rate of return. By California law, the field was a commons, open to all. Attracted by high rates of return and unrestricted entry, many companies entered the area. By 1990, there was more than 2000 megawatts of installed energy capacity at the surface.

Unfortunately, 25% of this capacity is currently idle, and even worse, the underground steam capacity is steadily falling. Quite simply, the geysers for which the field was named are drying up. Without sufficient water underground, they cannot produce steam to drive the turbines at the surface. The culprit in all of this is clear. As one developer put it, "Put simply, there are too many straws in the teapot."

The future of the Geysers is bleak. Energy production is projected to fall another 50% by the end of this decade. This is not just a tragedy for fans of alternative energy sources or for the companies and their shareholders—it's a tragedy for the geysers, too.

▚ SUMMARY

1. When there are three players in a game instead of two, fundamental differences arise. The determination theorem for games like Chess and the solution theorem for 2-person, zero-sum games no longer hold, because a third player can play the spoiler.

2. Spoilers are a lot less frequent in business than they are in politics and sports. Most of the time, when there is a third or fourth firm in a market, the impact on profits or market shares is not that dramatic.

3. When each player has a strictly dominant strategy, a game has a unique equilibrium. The unique equilibrium for Cigarette Television Advertising, taking into account all four firms, is for each cigarette company to advertise on television.

4. The phenomenon where every player has a strictly dominant strategy that leads to a very bad outcome for all players is called the prisoner's

    dilemma. This phenomenon pervades our lives, and we need to be alert to its danger. The game Stonewalling Watergate exemplifies the prisoner's dilemma in real life.

5.   Once a game has more than three players or each player has more than eight strategies, writing it down in its entirety becomes impractical. A more compact mathematical notation is used to study such games.

6.   A game is symmetrical when it looks the same to each player. Each player has the same set of strategies, and utility functions satisfy the interchange property.

7.   The sufficient condition of payoff symmetry requires that solution of a symmetrical game have the same payoff for all the players. This sufficient condition is meaningful, since every symmetrical game has a symmetrical equilibrium.

8.   When each player's payoff depends only on that player's own action and on the aggregate action of all the players, and when all utility functions have the same form, a game is symmetrical. We can use calculus to find the symmetrical equilibrium of such a game.

9.   A commons is a resource that is freely available to all. A tragedy of the commons occurs when too many players exploit the resource.

10.   One way to measure the tragedy of the commons is by the ratio of equilibrium payoffs to optimal payoffs. The closer this ratio is to zero, the worse the tragedy is.

11.   The tragedy of the commons is observed in the drying up of the Geysers of California and also in laboratory experiments (see chapter appendix).

KEY TERMS

counterexample	interchange condition
strategic dummy	payoff symmetry
spoiler	symmetrical equilibrium
prisoner's dilemma	asymmetric game
stonewalling	tragedy of the commons
symmetrical game	

PROBLEMS

1.   Suppose that there are now three networks in Battle of the Networks. The market shares of the existing two networks have fallen by 10% each to make room for the new network. Redraw the normal form and find the solution. Interpret your new result in terms of network programming strategy.

2. Show that talking is a strictly dominant strategy in Stonewalling Watergate. Why is the equilibrium of a game where every player has a strictly dominant strategy unique?

3. Suppose that in Stonewalling Watergate, only Dean and Ehrlichman get to make choices. Haldeman is under the complete control of the president and must stonewall until the bitter end. Redraw the normal form and find the solution. (*Hint:* Haldeman is a strategic dummy in this version of the game.)

4. Find the mixed strategy equilibrium of Video System Coordination with three firms.

5. Write down the 3-player versions of Market Niche, Competitive Advantage, and Let's Make a Deal in the $u_i(x)$ notation. Show that each of these is symmetrical.

6. In 3-player Let's Make a Deal, there is $40 million on the table. Player 1 gets paid twice as much as either player 2 or player 3 in the event there is a deal. Find all the equilibria you can, then solve.

7. Show that Let's Make a Deal with two or three players does not have a mixed strategy equilibrium. (*Hint:* Suppose that it does, and show that the resulting equations have no solution.)

8. In Tragedy of the Commons, the commons production function $F(m) = 1.6m - 0.2m^2$. The rate of return outside the commons remains 0.1. Solve the game when there are five players. Is your solution tragic?

9. Suppose that in Tragedy of the Commons all you know is that $F(m)/m$ is decreasing, and that this ratio eventually gets close to zero. You know nothing else about the production function F. Show that the solution is tragic as the number of companies gets large.

10. You run a large energy company that is considering diversifying into thermal energy. Your company is being offered a 30-year lease on a Siberian geyser field, the second largest in the world after Yellowstone. Your Russian consultants assure you that Russia will be politically stable during the life of the lease. What sorts of questions do you still need answered before proceeding with this project? You have access to all data publicly available on the California Geysers.

■ APPENDIX. TRAGEDY OF THE COMMONS IN THE LABORATORY[11]

The goal of any scientific theory is to explain and to predict. In this respect, game theory is no different from any other theory. Most of the applications of game theory to real life are explanatory. Occasionally, there is enough informa-

---

[11]Material in this appendix is based on E. Ostrom, R. Gardner, and J. Walker, *Rules, Games, and Common-Pool Resources* (Ann Arbor: University of Michigan Press, 1993).

tion to make a sound prediction as well. One of the exciting developments in game theory in recent years has been the application of controlled laboratory experiments to games. Although *experimental games* are reported already in Luce and Raiffa (1957), this activity has really taken off lately.[12] This section reports on the results of games played in an experimental commons. Some results are not surprising—the tragedy of the commons appears in the laboratory just as it does in the field. Some results are surprising—a change in the game that should not affect the solution (making the players richer), does. This is why we run experiments: not just to tell us what we already know, but also to tell us what we don't suspect, but should.

The experiments described here are run as follows. Volunteers are recruited from undergraduate classes at Indiana University. Recruits are told that they will be making decisions in an economic choice situation and that they will be paid in person, in private, at the end of the experiment, based on the decisions they and others in the experiment have made. They are told that they will be paid $3 for showing up for the experiment and that they can make substantially more than that in the experiment proper. *The experimenter never lies to the subjects.* The experiment begins with subjects' signing a federally mandated release form, in accordance with federal regulations on the treatment of human subjects in treatments. Subjects then go through a set of instructions to teach them the game they are about to play. Subjects have to pass a quiz on their understanding of the game before they go on to actual play. Finally, subjects play the game three times for practice before they begin to play for real money. Since the average subject makes about $15 for a 90-minute experimental session, in addition to the show-up bonus, there is no difficulty recruiting volunteer subjects.

Eight subjects played the following Commons game.[13] Each player *i* picks a number x_i between 0 and *w*. The parameter *w* is the number of tokens a player has—10 or 25, depending on the experimental design. A player can put as many tokens as he or she wants into the bank for 5 cents each. Tokens not put into the bank go into the commons, where the rate of return depends on the number of tokens invested in the commons. Player *i*'s payoffs, in cents, is given by

$$u_i(\mathbf{x}) = 5(w - x_i) + x_i F(m)/m$$

where *m* is the number of tokens invested in the commons. Note the similarity with the utility function in the Tragedy of the Commons game of section 4.7.

---

[12]The earliest experiments are reported in R. Duncan Luce and Howard Raiffa, *Games and Decisions*, (New York: Wiley & Sons, 1957). An excellent overview of what has been done with experimental games is given in John Kagel and Alvin E. Roth, eds., *Handbook of Experimental Economics* (Princeton, N.J.: Princeton University Press, 1994).

[13]Ten subjects were recruited for each experiment. If more than eight showed up, the surplus subjects were paid $5 for showing up and a place was reserved for them in the next experiment.

The only differences are an outside opportunity worth 5% per unit of asset instead of 10%; $w = 10$ or 25 instead of 1; and m equal to the number of tokens in the commons instead of the number of companies in the commons. The production function in these experiments is given by

$$F(m) = 23m - 0.25m^2$$

Substituting, we have the utility function

$$u_i(\mathbf{x}) = 5(w - x_i) + x_i(23 - 0.25m)$$

Note that this utility function depends on player i's decision as well as on the aggregate decision, so the game is symmetrical.

This symmetrical experimental game has a unique symmetrical equilibrium, which, according to the sufficient condition of payoff symmetry, is the solution. We can find this symmetrical equilibrium using the technique employed earlier. First, we maximize player 1's utility:

$$0 = \frac{\partial u_1}{\partial x_1} = -5 + (23 - 0.25m) + x_1(-0.25)$$

using the rule for the derivative of a product. Now we exploit symmetry. Since there are eight players, each choosing the same decision as player 1, $m = 8x_1$. Substituting into the first-order condition, we get

$$0 = -5 + 23 - 2x_1 - 0.25x_1$$

Solving, we get

$$x_1 = 8$$

At the symmetrical equilibrium, each player invests eight tokens. This is pretty close to the tragedy of the commons. The standard way to measure the severity of the tragedy of the commons is to compare players' payoffs to those that could be achieved by an efficient allocation of resources. An efficient allocation of resources maximizes

$$F(m) - 5m$$

since the value of the resource in cents is $F(m)$ and the cost of each input is 5 cents. Substituting, we get

$$\max 23m - 0.25m^2 - 5m$$

The maximum occurs at

$$0 = 23 - 0.5m - 5$$

Solving, we get $m = 32$. Exactly 32 tokens should be invested in the commons, not the 64 tokens invested by the eight players at the symmetrical equilibrium. The maximum total return from the resource is $F(32) - 5(32) = 18(32) - 8(32) = 320$ cents. The total return from the resource at equilibrium is $F(64) -$

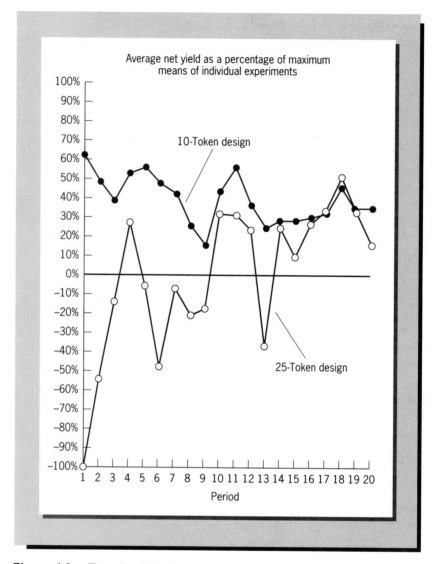

Figure 4.9.   Tragedy of the Commons in the laboratory.

$5(64) = 18(64) - 16(64) = 128$ cents. The *relative efficiency* of the equilibrium is its payoff divided by the maximum payoff, here 128 cents/320 cents = 40%.

Figure 4.9 shows the relative efficiency observed in the experiment when the Commons game is played for money 20 straight times. When players have 10 tokens each, the outcome fluctuates around the symmetrical equilibrium. The average relative efficiency over the 20 periods is 43%, quite close to the game equilibrium prediction. The fluctuations,[14] have yet to be explained, but the fact that the average behavior is close to game equilibrium is reassuring. That is the good news. The bad news is what happens when subjects have 25 tokens to invest instead of 10. The effect of this alteration is to make the subjects 150% richer as far as money in the bank is concerned. The first-order condition for the equilibrium does not depend on the number of tokens at all, so this makes no difference to the equilibrium. According to the equilibrium, subjects should simply put the extra 15 tokens in the bank and play the same as before. However, this is not what they do. They invest way too many tokens into the commons, making returns negative. After about a dozen repetitions, they finally get into the positive return zone, but even then they are still below the symmetrical equilibrium earnings. On average over all 20 repetitions, these subjects earn slightly negative earnings (–4%). They are doing *worse* than the tragedy of the commons, which predicts that earnings go to zero, but not below. This experimental result is also yet to be explained.

The tragedy of the commons is real, both in the field and in the laboratory. We as individuals and as businesses ignore it at our own peril.

✦ PROBLEMS

1. How does the game equilibrium change if the value of a token is 10 cents instead of 5 cents in this experiment?
2. Suppose that you run this Tragedy of the Commons experiment, but it comes out very differently. In particular, you observe relative efficiencies of 95%. Can you reconcile this observation with the game theory of this chapter?

---

[14]There are two competing explanations. One is that behavior is noisy in a statistical sense; the other, that behavior is chaotic in a deterministic sense.

CHAPTER 5

✖✖✖✖✖✖

Noncooperative
Market Games
in Normal Form

The previous chapters have reviewed games that arise in business: Competitive Advantage, Market Niche, Let's Make a Deal, Cigarette Television Advertising, and Tragedy of the Commons. However, the economic structure available when a game is played in a market has not yet been fully exploited. Now that you have experience with solving games, you are in a position to exploit the structure that a market gives to a game.

This chapter looks at **noncooperative market games in normal form.**[1] In such games, each firm in the market picks its strategy—here, quantity or price—at the same time as its competitors. Each firm gets a payoff, in terms of profit or loss, after the market has processed all the strategic information submitted to it. Since each firm is acting alone, the game is noncooperative. As such, there is no presumption that the outcome will be efficient. Quantity competition between two firms selling products that are perfect substitutes is presented first.

[1]Chapters 6 and 7 present market games in extensive form. Chapter 15 presents market games in coalition function form.

Then the chapter describes what happens when the number of firms grows large. In this case, quantity competition approaches as a limit perfect competition, a result known as the Cournot limit theorem. The first example, Are Coffee Prices Going Up?, analyzes recent developments in the world coffee market on the basis of Cournot competition between countries. Then price competition—also known as Bertrand competition—is studied, first between two firms, and then among many firms, each selling perfect substitutes. Competing on price does not lead to the same equilibrium as does competing on quantity. In particular, price competition can lead to perfectly competitive equilibrium with as few as two firms. Then the chapter considers the impact of product differentiation on both quantity and price competition. Product differentiation acts to mute the strategic difference between quantity and price competition. The second example, Price War in the Cigarette Industry, looks at recent pricing developments in the cigarette industry from the standpoint of Bertrand competition and product differentiation. In most of the games of this chapter, the equilibrium is unique. The appendix gives a useful condition that suffices for a game equilibrium to be unique.

✠ 5.1 Quantity Competition between Two Firms ■ ■ ■ ■

In some markets, firms compete in terms of quantity. Each cereal company, for example, tries to get as much shelf space in the grocery store as possible. In other markets, firms compete in terms of price. The number of seats offered by the airlines is roughly constant, but they are continually offering all kinds of deals on fares. The first market games we consider involve markets where firms compete in terms of quantity. This type of game was the first studied by a French economist, Augustin Cournot, a century and a half ago. His model of competition is now called Cournot competition, and the equilibrium of his market game, Cournot equilibrium, in his honor.[2] We will study Cournot competition as a noncooperative game in normal form and show that the equilibrium of this game leads to a market outcome where price is above marginal cost, and it is therefore inefficient.

In **Cournot competition,** each firm i brings a quantity x_i to market. For the moment, we keep things simple by having only two firms in the market. Each firm has constant returns to scale, hence constant average variable costs, denoted by c. The products of the two firms, numbered 1 and 2, are perfect substitutes, and so must sell at the same market price. Market price, P, is determined by market demand:

---

[2]Cournot's remarkable work appeared in the last chapter of his book, *Researches into the Mathematical Principles of the Theory of Wealth* (New York: Macmillan, 1897). Originally published in 1838. Cournot's solution thus predates von Neumann's famous paper by 90 years.

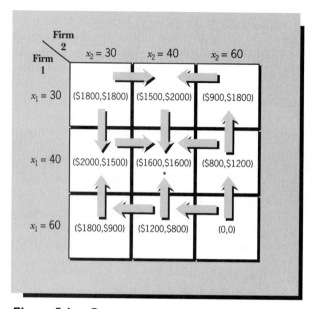

Figure 5.1.   Cournot competition, two firms.

$$P = 130 - Q \quad \text{if } Q \text{ does not exceed } 130$$
$$= 0 \quad\quad\quad \text{otherwise}$$

where Q = market quantity = Σx_i. We assume that each firm i wants to maximize profits. Let $\mathbf{x} = (x_1, x_2)$ be the vector of each firm's quantity delivered to the market. Firm's 1's profits, written $u_1(\mathbf{x})$, are determined by firm 1's revenue minus cost:

$$u_1(\mathbf{x}) = \text{revenue} - \text{cost}$$
$$= Px_i - cx_i$$
$$= (P - c)x_1$$

The term $P - c$ represents the profit margin on each unit firm 1 sells. Firm 2's profits have the same look:

$$u_2(\mathbf{x}) = (P - c)x_2$$

The strategic interaction between the two firms comes about because the market price, P, is determined by how much *both* firms produce and sell.

For purposes of this example, set $c = \$10$ for both firms. Let's first work out the case where each firm has three strategies: produce and sell 30, 40, or 60 units. The normal form game that results is shown in Figure 5.1. The entries of the matrix can be computed as follows. Take $x_1 = x_2 = 30$. Sixty units are shipped to market. The price at which these 60 units sell is

$$P = 130 - Q = 130 - 60 = \$70$$

Since average cost = $\$10$, the profit margin is $P - c = \$70 - \$10 = \$60$/unit. Finally, since each firm i is selling 30 units, it earns a profit

$$u_i(\mathbf{x}) = (P - c)x_i = \$60/\text{unit} \ (30 \text{ units}) = \$1800$$

These are the entries corresponding to the quantities ($x_1 = 30$, $x_2 = 30$). You can work out the other entries of the matrix in a similar fashion.

Restricted to only these three strategies, the market game has a single equilibrium: each firm produces 40 units. Arrows point in to this outcome from both directions, whereas arrows point away from every other outcome in at least one direction. This is the **Cournot equilibrium: $\mathbf{x}^* = (40,40)$.** At this equilibrium, the market price is $\$130 - \$80 = \$50$, which is substantially above marginal cost, $\$10$. The firms involved are making considerable profits, with a profit margin of $\$40$ on each of the 40 units they sell, for total profits of $\$1600$.

5.2 Cournot Competition, Two Firms, Many Strategies ■

The restriction to three strategies each might somehow influence the earlier result, where quantity competition led to a unique equilibrium with price well above cost. This section relaxes this restriction and shows that this result is perfectly general: *Cournot competition between two firms leads to an outcome between monopoly and perfect competition.* We now allow each firm to ship any number of units on the interval [0,130]. If a firm ships 0 units, this is tantamount to its leaving the market. It is totally inactive. If a firm ships 130 units, it drives the price down to zero all by itself. This is no way to make money—a sure sign of a bad strategy. As we shall see, in a Cournot equilibrium, firms avoid both these extremes.

The firms face the same market and cost conditions as before, so they have the same utility functions as before:

$$u_i = (P - c)x_i$$

Each firm has the same set of strategies and the same form of utility function, which depends only on what a firm itself does and on aggregate firm behavior. Thus we have all the ingredients for a symmetrical game. This makes intuitive sense: the firms produce under the same cost conditions and sell products that are perfect substitutes for one another. We will now find a symmetrical equilibrium of the market game with many strategies.

Consider firm 1. This firm maximizes its profit by producing up to the point where marginal profit equals zero:

$$0 = \frac{\partial u_1}{\partial x_1} = (P - c) + x_1 \frac{\partial P}{\partial x_1}$$

using the product rule from calculus.

Substituting in the market demand function and its slope, we get

$$0 = (120 - x_1 - x_2) + x_1(-1)$$

which simplifies to

$$0 = 120 - 2x_1 - x_2$$

At this point we exploit symmetry, setting $x_1 = x_2$. We have

$$0 = 120 - 3x_1$$

or

$$x_1^* = 40 = x_2^*$$

The vector $\mathbf{x} = (40,40)$ is the Cournot equilibrium. Notice that this is the same equilibrium we got in the last section, even though now firms can choose any quantity they want.

We can now compare Cournot equilibrium with other kinds of market outcomes. In *perfect competitive equilibrium,* market price equals marginal cost. If this market were perfectly competitive, the price would be $10, since marginal cost is $10. In *monopoly equilibrium,* market profits are as large as possible. A monopoly[3] in this market would maximize total market profits, u, where u is given by

$$u = u_1 + u_2 = (P - c)Q$$

We find this maximum by ordinary calculus. Substituting in the market demand curve and average cost, we seek the maximum of

$$u = (120 - Q)Q$$

with respect to Q. A necessary condition[4] for a maximum is

$$0 = \frac{\partial u}{\partial Q} = 120 - 2Q$$

or

$$60 = Q^*$$

A monopoly will produce and sell 60 units, with a corresponding price of $70, a profit margin of $60, and total profits of ($60)(60) = $3600. The monopoly equilibrium, Cournot equilibrium, and perfectly competitive equilibrium are shown in Figure 5.2. Monopoly is associated with the highest price, lowest quantity, and highest profits. Perfect competition is associated with the lowest price, highest quantity, and lowest profits ($0). Cournot equilibrium lies in between on all three dimensions.

We can also find the Cournot equilibrium graphically. This method is based on the best-response functions of the two firms. The best-response functions

---

[3]One way to create such a monopoly is to have all the firms in the market form one gigantic merger. The Federal Trade Commission, which has the responsibility for keeping markets competitive, typically disallows such mergers.

[4]Notice that this condition is also sufficient. Applying the second derivative test for a maximum, we find that $du^2/dQ^2 = -2 < 0$. Hence, the sufficient condition for a maximum is also satisfied.

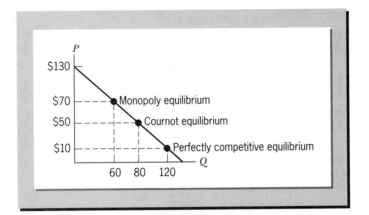

Figure 5.2. Cournot equilibrium in the market.

are found by rearranging the first-order conditions for profit maximization. Firm 1's first-order condition is

$$2x_1 + x_2 = 120$$

Solving for x_1 as a function of x_2 yields firm 1's best-response function,

$$x_1 = f_1(x_2) = 60 - \frac{x_2}{2}$$

Notice that if $x_2 = 0$, firm 1's best response is the monopoly response. Similarly, firm 2's best-response function is

$$x_2 = f_2(x_1) = 60 - \frac{x_1}{2}$$

Since the Cournot market game is symmetrical, so are the best-response functions. Now plot these best-response functions on the square of strategies (see Figure 5.3). The Cournot equilibrium is found where the best-response functions cross, with each firm selling 40 units of its product in the market. This technique also works when the two firms are asymmetrical, as we see later.

We can prove directly that the monopoly and perfect competition outcomes are *not* game equilibria. This argument actually generalizes the arrow diagram of Figure 5.1. First, suppose that firm 1 monopolizes the market, $x_1 = 60$. Firm 2's best response is not to let firm 1 monopolize the market unmolested. Firm 2's best response is

$$f_2(60) = 60 - \frac{60}{2} = 30$$

Firm 2 sells 30 units, rather than letting firm 1 monopolize the market. This shows that the monopoly outcome is not a game equilibrium for this 2-firm industry. Next, suppose that the firms together are selling 120 units, for instance, 60 units apiece. Then firm 1 would want to cut back its sales to

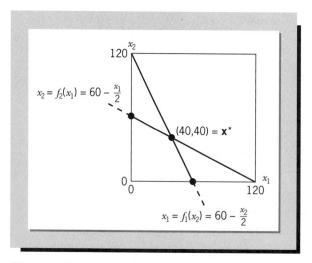

Figure 5.3. Cournot best responses, $\mathbf{x}^* =$ Cournot equilibrium.

$$f_1(60) = 60 - \frac{60}{2} = 30 \text{ units}$$

Firm 2 would want to cut its sales, too. These cutbacks in production show that the perfectly competitive outcome is also not a game equilibrium. The only equilibrium for these two firms competing in terms of quantity produced and sold is the Cournot equilibrium.

5.3 Cournot Variations, Including Many Firms ■ ■ ■ ■

A Cournot equilibrium has some of the same properties as a perfectly competitive equilibrium. In particular, it obeys a form of the law of supply: if costs increase, Cournot equilibrium quantity falls and price rises. We will now verify this result. We retain the market demand structure of the previous two sections. We can show that the only change in the first-order conditions for profit maximization is that the average cost, c, is deducted from the demand reservation price 130 in all expressions:

$$2x_1 + x_2 \;\; = 130 - c \qquad \text{(first-order condition, firm 1)}$$
$$x_1 + 2x_2 = 130 - c \qquad \text{(first-order condition, firm 2)}$$

From this pair of first-order conditions, it is easy to get the Cournot equilibrium:

$$x_1^* = x_2^* = \frac{(130 - c)}{3} \text{ units}$$

Cournot market supply therefore is

$$Q^* = \frac{2(130 - c)}{3} \text{ units}$$

As cost c increases, Cournot market supply falls, just as predicted. For instance, we saw that when unit costs were = \$10, Cournot market supply was 80 units. When unit costs rise to \$40, Cournot market supply falls to

$$Q^* = \frac{2(130 - 40)}{3} = 60 \text{ units}$$

At the same time, Cournot market price rises from \$50 to \$70, so a large part (\$20 of \$30) of the cost increase is passed on to consumers. In this respect, firms in Cournot competition react to cost increases in much the same way that firms in perfect competition do.

Another variation that is important in practice involves cost advantages. Now not all firms have the same costs. Firm 1 has a **cost advantage** over firm 2 when firm 1's average costs are lower than firm 2's at any level of output. In the model we are studying, we can represent a cost advantage by firm 1 over firm 2 as follows:

$$C_1(x_1) = c_1 x_1$$
$$C_2(x_2) = c_2 x_2$$

and $c_1 < c_2$. You can show (see problem 2) that a firm with a cost advantage over its rival sells more at a Cournot equilibrium. A cost advantage gets translated into a market share advantage, and the market share advantage is bigger, the bigger the cost advantage. This is an example in which an asymmetrical game leads to an asymmetrical outcome.

A third variation involves changes in the demand side of the market. Everything that we have done so far with the demand curve $P = 130 - Q$ can be done for general linear demand $P = a - bQ$, with positive a and b. Things get more complicated for nonlinear demand (see problem 3). As long as demand is downward sloping, however, the qualitative relationship between monopoly, Cournot equilibrium, and perfectly competitive equilibrium of Figure 5.2 still holds.

A fourth variation involves the number of firms in Cournot competition. Everything that we have done for $n = 2$ firms can be done for a larger number n. All we have to do is note the fact that a lot of firms are selling in the market:

$$Q = x_1 + x_2 + \cdots + x_n = \Sigma x_i$$

Let's return to the basic model with constant unit costs = \$10 and demand given by $P = 130 - Q$. With more firms you might expect more intense competition, and this is exactly what happens. As the number of firms in Cournot competition gets large, the Cournot equilibrium gets closer to perfect competition. In the limit as the number of firms goes to infinity, Cournot equilibrium goes to perfect competition. This remarkable result, first noted by Cournot, is called the **Cournot limit theorem.** Now we'll work out the details.

Let's focus on firm 1. Since all firms face the same costs and sell identical products, the game is symmetrical and every firm faces the same problem that firm 1 faces. Firm 1 wants to maximize profits,

$$u_1(\mathbf{x}) = (P - 10)x_1$$

where $\mathbf{x} = (x_1, x_2, \ldots, x_n)$ is the vector of firms' sales. Firm 1 maximizes profit when

$$0 = \frac{\partial u_1}{\partial x_1} = (P - 10) + x_1 \left(\frac{\partial P}{\partial x_1}\right)$$
$$= 120 - \Sigma x_1 - x_1$$

At this point, we invoke symmetry: $\Sigma x_1 = n x_1$, since all n firms act alike. Substituting, we have

$$0 = 120 - (n + 1)x_1$$

or

$$\frac{120}{(n + 1)} = x_1^*$$

This holds true for each firm i. As the number of firms n goes to infinity, each firm's individual quantity goes to zero. This reflects the fact that, as competition becomes more nearly perfect, each individual firm has a very small (here, $1/n$) market share. Cournot market quantity therefore is

$$Q^* = \frac{120n}{(n + 1)}$$

We can verify this result. For $n = 1$ (monopoly), we get $Q^* = 60$, which corresponds with the result obtained before. For $n = 2$, we get $Q^* = 80$, which again corresponds. The larger n gets, the closer Q^* gets to 120, which is the perfect competitive outcome. On the price side, as the number of firms grows, the price facing buyers drops:

$$P^* = 130 - Q^* = 130 - \left[\frac{120n}{(n + 1)}\right]$$

In the limit as n goes to infinity, $P^* = 130 - 120 = 10$, the perfectly competitive price. The market price approaches marginal cost as the number of firms gets large and competition among them intensifies. This is the Cournot limit theorem in action.

In Chapter 4, when we took the limit as the number of energy firms using the commons grew large, we called the outcome tragic: the resource was wasted, and there was no offsetting gain for anyone else involved. No one stands to gain from the destruction of a commons. The situation here is different. In a market, there are buyers involved as well as sellers. Rather than being a tragedy, from the standpoint of the buyers, prices near marginal cost are a really good deal. When we consider both buyers' and sellers' gains from

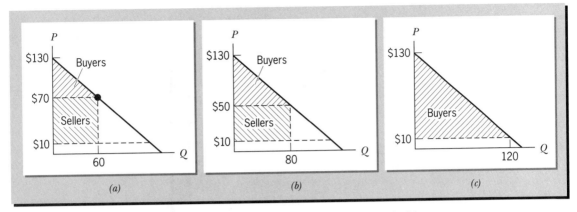

Figure 5.4. Cournot limit theorem, surplus analysis: (a) $n = 1$; (b) $n = 2$; (c) $n = \infty$.

trade in a market, we will see that the limit of Cournot equilibrium as the number of firms grows large is a good thing.

We can use market surplus analysis to show why the Cournot outcome with many firms is no tragedy. Every market generates a surplus, reflecting **market gains from trade.** The surplus to buyers is the area between the demand curve and the market price; the surplus to sellers is the area between market price and marginal cost. Figure 5.4 shows the gains to buyers, sellers, and the total gain for increasing n in the Cournot limit. For $n = 1$ (Figure 5.4a), the sellers' surplus is the area $60 \times 60 = 3600$; the buyers' surplus is the area $60 \times 60/2 = 1800$; and the total gain from trade is $3600 + 1800 = 5400$. For $n = 2$, (Figure 5.4b) the sellers' surplus is $40 \times 80 = 3200$; the buyers' surplus, $80 \times 80/2 = 3200$; and the total gain from trade is $3200 + 3200 = 6400$. Sellers lose as their numbers grow, but buyers gain, and the gains of the buyers more than make up for the reduced gains of the sellers. For infinitely large n, (Figure 5.4c) sellers' surplus $= 0$; buyers' surplus $= 120 \times 120/2 = 7200$. The total gain from trade is $0 + 7200 = 7200$. As expected, perfect competition maximizes the total gain from trade; unfortunately for the sellers, all that gain goes to the buyers. In contrast, monopoly maximizes gain to the seller, but it does this at the expense of total gains from trade.

▨ 5.4 Are Coffee Prices Going Up?[5] ■ ■ ■ ■ ■ ■ ■ ■ ■ ■ ■ ■ ■

Coffee is grown in over 30 countries on four continents. At a meeting in Kampala, Uganda, on August 16, 1993, the major coffee-producing countries of

---

[5]Some material in this example is drawn from *Mannheimer Morgen*, "Kaffee teurer" (Coffee more expensive), August 19, 1993.

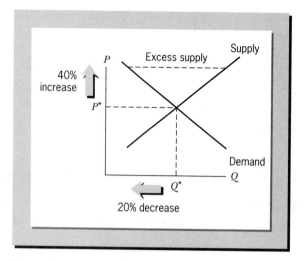

Figure 5.5.   World coffee market.

Africa, Asia, and Latin America agreed to reduce by 20% their shipments to the world coffee market. The effective date for this action was October 1, 1993.

Figure 5.5 shows the world coffee market prior to the Kampala agreement. Market quantity is Q^*; market price, P^*. Since the Kampala agreement calls for quantity restrictions, we can infer that competition in this market is in terms of quantities, hence Cournot competition. The role of a firm in this market is played by the national marketing board of each individual country. With over 30 countries playing, we have a large n, large enough for the Cournot limit theorem to be working. Thus, we can infer that the current market equilibrium quantity Q^* is approximately a Cournot equilibrium and that the current market price equilibrium P^* ($0.60/pound) is near marginal cost.

Coffee demand is price inelastic, with a price elasticity of demand of about −0.5. Using the formula for price elasticity, namely,

$$\text{Price elasticity} = \frac{\% \text{ change in quantity}}{\% \text{ change in price}}$$

we get for the coffee market

$-0.5 = -20\% / \% \text{ change in price}$

or

$\% \text{ change in price} = 40\%$

This price increase of 40% would be a real boon to coffee-producing countries and is the reason behind the Kampala agreement.

The question that comes up immediately is, will the quantity reduction hold? There are reasons to doubt that it will. First, consider the market as a whole. With a 40% increase in price, producing countries must withhold a large excess supply from the market. If they do not, then this excess supply will find its way to the market, driving the price back down to P^* in the process. The Kampala agreement creates a potential disequilibrium in the market. Second, at the individual country level, the Kampala agreement creates a strategic disequilibrium. The easiest way to see this is to consider what happens if every country but one holds to the agreement. Price has risen 40% above costs. The country we are considering can now make a killing by selling *all* its coffee at a 40% higher price than before. But what one country can do, they all can do. Once countries stop withholding supplies, the excess coffee gets back on the market and down goes the price.

This is not the first time in this century that coffee-producing countries have tried to raise coffee prices by voluntarily restricting supplies, only the latest. Every other attempt has failed, and this attempt looks to share the same fate. As long as supply restrictions are voluntary, each and every country has an incentive to cheat on the restriction—an incentive that only disappears at Cournot equilibrium.

♦ 5.5 Price Competition between Two Firms ■ ■ ■ ■ ■ ■

The next market games we will consider involve markets where firms compete in terms of price. This market game was first studied a century ago by a French critic of Cournot, J. Bertrand. Bertrand's model of competition is now called **Bertrand competition,** and the equilibrium of his market game, **Bertrand equilibrium,** in his honor. This section presents Bertrand competition as a noncooperative game in normal form, and shows that the equilibrium of this market game, Bertrand equilibrium, is different from Cournot equilibrium.[6]

Intuitively, using the experience of monopoly as a guide, you might think that it doesn't matter whether firms use price or quantity as a strategic variable. It certainly doesn't matter for a monopoly. But then a monopoly doesn't have competitors. In both Cournot and Bertrand competition, competitors are present, and the way their presence is felt depends on how the market aggregates their behavior. In a market where quantity is the strategic variable, market price depends on market quantity, which is *the sum of firm's quantities.* In a market where price is the strategic variable, it is *the minimum of all the firms' prices* that determines market price. Informed buyers will not pay more than they have to, and they don't have to pay more than the lowest price being offered. This in a nutshell is why Bertrand competition and Cournot competition differ.

To elaborate on this difference, start with the same market demand used before, only inverting price and quantity:

[6]The reference is J. Bertrand, "Review of 'Théorie mathématique de la richesse sociale,' by A. Cournot," *Journal des Savants* 68(1883):499–508. This was the first published review of Cournot's book, 45 years after it was written. The pace of science in the nineteenth century was a lot more relaxed than it is today.

$$Q = 130 - P$$

Firm 1's profits are revenue minus cost, here

$$u_1(\mathbf{p}) = (p_1 - c)x_1(\mathbf{p})$$

where $\mathbf{p} = (p_1, p_2)$ is the vector of firms' prices, and $x_1(\mathbf{p})$ is the demand facing firm 1. Firm 2's profits are given analogously:

$$u_2(\mathbf{p}) = (p_2 - c)x_2(\mathbf{p})$$

We retain the cost structure of section 5.1, with unit cost $c = \$10$; the firms are selling products that are perfect substitutes.

A problem we immediately encounter is how to define firm 1's quantity demanded, $x_1(\mathbf{p})$. The quantity firm 1 sells depends both on its price and on the price of its competitor, firm 2. There are three cases to consider. First, firm 1 is asking the lowest price, $p_1 < p_2$. In this case, firm 1 gets the entire market, since consumers maximize their utility by buying at the lowest available price. We have $x_1(\mathbf{p}) = 130 - p_1$. Second, firm 2 is asking the lowest price, $p_2 < p_1$. In this case, firm 2 gets the entire market and firm 1 sells nothing. Firm 1 has been *undersold* by firm 2. We have $x_1(\mathbf{p}) = 0$. Third, suppose that both firms ask the same price, $p_1 = p_2$. In this case they somehow share the market. For the sake of symmetry, let's assume that the firms share the market equally.[7] We summarize this discussion succinctly by the following demand curve for firm 1:

$$
\begin{aligned}
x_1(\mathbf{p}) &= 130 - p_1 && \text{when } p_1 < p_2 \\
&= \frac{(130 - p_1)}{2} && \text{when } p_1 = p_2 \\
&= 0 && \text{when } p_1 > p_2
\end{aligned}
$$

This is the demand curve for firm 1 in Bertrand competition. The strategic interaction in this form of competition shows up solely through the demand curve. The demand curve for firm 2 is similar:

$$
\begin{aligned}
x_2(\mathbf{p}) &= 130 - p_2 && \text{when } p_2 < p_1 \\
&= \frac{(130 - p_1)}{2} && \text{when } p_1 = p_2 \\
&= 0 && \text{when } p_1 < p_2
\end{aligned}
$$

Notice that demand is discontinuous at the point where prices are equal (see Figure 5.6).

We now go about finding a Bertrand equilibrium. We first consider a matrix version as we did for Cournot equilibrium, with prices corresponding to the quantities in Figure 5.1. Each firm can charge one of three possible prices, \$70, \$50, and \$10. The matrix game to which this leads is shown in Figure 5.7. We will walk through two of the profit entries. If both firms charge price $= \$70$, then both sell $(130 - 70)/2 = 30$ units. The profit margin is $\$70 - \$10 =$

---

[7]The Bertrand equilibrium has the same form, regardless of the exact market sharing rule used.

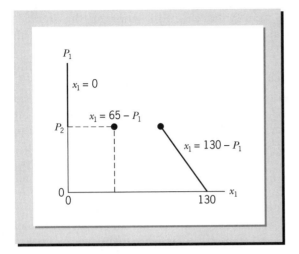

Figure 5.6. Bertrand demand, firm 1.

$60/unit, so profits are $60(30) = $1800, as shown by the outcome for $p_1 = p_2 = 70. If one firm charges a rock-bottom price equal to cost, then nobody in the market will make any money. This accounts for all the zeros along the bottom and the right side of the matrix.

There are two Bertrand equilibria. The first is right in the middle of the matrix, just as the Cournot equilibrium was, at price $p_1^* = p_2^* = 50. The other is at the rock-bottom price $p_1^* = p_2^* = 10. This second equilibrium is in dominated strategies, however—notice that the strategy Price = $50 dominates

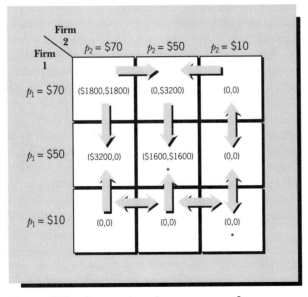

Figure 5.7. Bertrand market game, two firms.

(although not strictly so) the strategy Price = $10. Applying the sufficient condition of undominated strategies, the equilibrium $\mathbf{p}^* = (\$50,\$50)$ is the solution.

Unfortunately for the firms involved, if they aren't restricted to just three prices and can charge any price they want, only the zero-profit equilibrium, price = $10, is left to them. Let each firm's set of strategies be the price interval [0,130]. A firm charging a price above $130 has *priced itself out of the market* and guarantees that it will sell nothing. A price just below $130 may actually sell something, and so has a chance of actually making a profit. A firm charging $0 *is giving its product away*. Again, this is no way to make money. We don't expect to see firms charging extreme prices, such as $130 or $0, in equilibrium, and we won't.

Since the two firms have the same costs and sell perfect substitutes, they are economically symmetrical. Since they have the same strategy sets and same-shaped profit functions, the market game they are in is symmetrical. To solve the game, we look for a symmetrical equilibrium, where $p_1 = p_2$. Unfortunately, since the utility functions aren't continuous, much less differentiable, we have to look at cases instead of derivatives. There are two different cases to consider:

Case 1. $p_1 = p_2 > 10$. Let p denote the price common to both firms. The payoff to firm 1 is the following:

$$u_1 = (p - 10)\, \frac{(130 - p)}{2}$$

This is not an equilibrium for firm 1. If firm 1 raises its price above p, it loses all sales, so this is not the right way to go. If firm 1 lowers its price ever so slightly, then it doubles its sales, while only reducing its profit margin by a tiny amount. For all practical purposes, it doubles its profits. For example, let the common price $p = \$50$, which was an equilibrium in Figure 5.7. Then profits at a price of $50 are $(50 - 10)(40) = \$1600$, whereas profits at a price of $49.99 are $(49.99 - 10)(130 - 49.99) = \$3200$, to the nearest dollar. The same argument shows that this is also not an equilibrium for firm 2. Any price above cost gets undercut.

Case 2. $p_1 = p_2 = 10$. Prices are now down to unit cost, so both firms break even. If a firm cuts the price any further, it cuts its own throat—and goes into the red. Moreover, if a firm raises its price above $10, it gets no sales, and so continues to break even. This is the only symmetrical equilibrium left to the firms.[8] *The Bertrand solution in this case is precisely the perfectly competitive outcome, price = marginal cost.* Although it takes a lot more than two firms in Cournot

[8]This equilibrium remains suspect however, since it is in dominated strategies. If there is a minimum monetary unit, such as $0.01, then there is an equilibrium $p^* = (\$10.01, \$10.01)$, which is not in dominated strategies. This result shows the mathematical problems that can arise when utility is not continuously differentiable.

competition to get perfect competition, in Bertrand competition with perfect substitutes and lots of prices possible, two firms constitute just enough competition to yield perfect competition. This result is the conclusion of the Bertrand limit theorem, that the limit of Bertrand competition is perfectly competitive equilibrium, already with $n = 2$.

Although two firms in Cournot competition would be a tight oligopoly with outcomes not too far from monopoly, two firms in Bertrand competition essentially cut each other's throats. Price competition, even among a few firms, tends to be much more intense, and much more corrosive of profits, than quantity competition. For this reason, such competition is often called **ruinous competition.** If carried to extremes, it can ruin profits.

⚏ 5.6 Bertrand Variations ■

This section looks at several variations on the Bertrand model of the previous section. These include a cost advantage for one of the firms, a more complicated demand specification, and more than two firms. Let's begin with a cost advantage for one of the firms. Suppose that firm 1 has a cost advantage over its rival. The cost advantage takes the form we have seen before:

$$c_1 < c_2$$

where c_1 denotes the constant average cost of each firm i. The game is now asymmetrical, and we expect an asymmetrical equilibrium. The arguments we have rehearsed so far rule out all alternatives as equilibria except price vectors near the following:

$$(p_1, p_2) = (c_1, c_2)$$

This is not quite an equilibrium, although it is close. This is precisely what marginal cost pricing would endorse in this case, although cost-disadvantaged firm 2 would sell nothing for its trouble. The reason this is not an equilibrium is that firm 1 can raise its price—to a certain extent—with impunity. Indeed, firm 1 can raise its price really close to $p_1 = c_2$, just as long as it stays below its rival's marginal cost, c_2. If we introduce a minimum monetary unit, such as the penny, then $p_1 = c_2 - 0.01$ is a better response for firm 1 than $p_1 = c_1$.

However, we are still not done. At any price below c_2, firm 1 in effect enjoys a monopoly. Hence, it checks whether the pure monopoly price—here, $(130 + c_1)/2$—is lower than just undercutting its opponent. If it is, then firm 1 lowers its price even further to the monopoly level (see problem 7 for a detailed example).

Another variation to consider is a market demand curve that is nonlinear. In this case, individual firm demand curves inherit the nonlinearity, again with discontinuity at $p_1 = p_2$. The only difference is that the downward-sloping segment in Figure 5.6 is now curved instead of straight. If both firms have the same constant marginal cost, c, we still get the Bertrand equilibrium $\mathbf{p}^* = (c, c)$

The final variation to consider is a variation in the number of firms, n. If every firm has the same constant average cost, c, then once $n = 2$, game equilibrium implies marginal cost pricing in the market. A larger number of firms certainly doesn't raise prices, and since prices are already rock-bottom, it can't lower them any further. So the analogue of the Cournot limit theorem, which we can call the **Bertrand limit theorem,** is:

■ ■

Bertrand Limit Theorem. When n is greater than or equal to 2, all products are perfect substitutes, and no firm has a cost advantage, then the Bertrand game equilibrium implies that price equals marginal cost.[9]

This excursion through Bertrand variations makes one thing quite clear. It is very hard to keep price above cost when price is the strategic variable and goods are perfect substitutes. As we see next, a very different picture emerges when goods are imperfect substitutes. The surest way to prevent your product from having a perfect substitute is to differentiate it.

⬛ 5.7 Market Games with Differentiated Products ■ ■ ■

Firms differentiate their products in order to avoid the ravages of Cournot and Bertrand competition on their demand and their profits. Commonly used differentiation techniques include quality, labels and brand names, advertisements, warranties and guarantees, and promotions. All **differentiated products** have one thing in common: if the price is slightly above the average price in the market, a firm doesn't lose all its sales.

Consider two firms locked in Bertrand competition. Firm 1 faces the following demand for its product:

$$x_1(\mathbf{p}) = 180 - p_1 - (p_1 - \text{average price})$$

where average price is the average price in the market. The idea behind this demand curve is that if a firm's price is higher than the market average, then some previously loyal customers will desert it for a cheaper alternative, but not all the firm's customers will do so. Since there are just two firms in the market, this average price is $(p_1 + p_2)/2$. Firm 1 does not lose all its sales if it is undersold. Suppose that firm 1 charges \$25 and its opponent, firm 2, charges \$15. The market average price is $(\$15 + \$25)/2 = \$20$, and firm 1's sales are

---

[9]A variation we do not pursue is when firms have nonlinear costs. In this case, there may fail to exist a Bertrand equilibrium in pure strategies, and mixed strategy equilibria are hard to compute.

$$x_1(25,15) = 180 - 25 - (25 - 20) = 150$$

which is a lot more than zero. Thanks to product differentiation, some of firm 1's customers are still willing to pay $10 more for this product. Suppose that firm 2 faces the same shape of demand:

$$x_2(\mathbf{p}) = 180 - p_2 - (p_2 - \text{average price})$$

When both firms have the same slope of demand with respect to their own price and with respect to the market average price, then the demand side of the model is still symmetrical—just not so extreme as with perfect substitutes. The two goods here are imperfect substitutes and so can sell at different prices.

To complete the description of Bertrand competition, suppose that both firms have the same constant average (and marginal cost), $20. We can now define profits for each firm and start solving the Bertrand game between them. Firm 1 has profits

$$
\begin{aligned}
u_1(p_1, p_2) &= (p_1 - 20) x_1 \\
&= (p_1 - 20)(180 - 2p_1 + \text{average price}) \\
&= (p_1 - 20)(180 - 1.5p_1 + 0.5p_2)
\end{aligned}
$$

We have substituted the demand curve into the profit function to get profits as a function of the vector of price strategies. Firm 2 faces the same sort of profit function:

$$u_2(p_1, p_2) = (p_2 - 20)(180 + 0.5p_1 - 1.5p_2)$$

These profit functions are differentiable, so we can find a Bertrand equilibrium by taking derivatives.

Firm 1 maximizes its profits when its marginal profit is zero. This happens when

$$0 = \frac{\partial u_1}{\partial p_1} = (p_1 - 20)(-1.5) + (180 - 1.5p_1 + 0.5p_2)$$

using the rule for the derivative of a product from calculus. Let's rewrite this as a best-response function by solving for firm 1's price (doing this also helps solve the game). Rearranging the first-order condition for profit maximization,

$$0 = 210 - 3p_1 + 0.5p_2$$

Solving for p_1, we get firm 1's best-response function $f_1(p_2)$:

$$p_1 = f_1(p_2) = 70 + \frac{p_2}{6}$$

This best-response function is shown in Figure 5.8. Notice that the best response is upward sloping. When a competitor raises its price, a firm's demand shifts out, so even if it doesn't change its own price its profits go up. But now the firm can also afford to raise its price slightly, by $1/6$ dollar for every $1 price increase by its opponent.

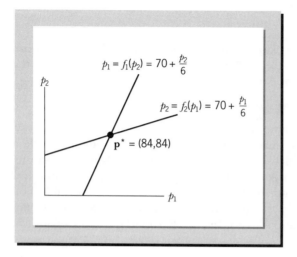

Figure 5.8. Bertrand best responses, two firms, differentiated products.

Going through the same argument for firm 2, we find its maximum profits where

$$0 = \frac{\partial u_2}{\partial p_2} = (p_2 - 20)(-1.5) + (180 + 0.5p_1 - 1.5p_2)$$

Firm 2's best-response function has a similar shape to that of firm 1:

$$p_2 = f_2(p_1) = 70 + \frac{p_1}{6}$$

This best-response function is also shown in Figure 5.8. The Bertrand equilibrium of the market game is located where the two best-response functions cross: $p_1^* = 84 = p_2^*$. The most important thing about this price, $84, is that it is way above marginal cost, $20. It can really pay to differentiate your product. At this Bertrand equilibrium, each firm sells

$$x_1 = 180 - 84 = 116 \text{ units}$$

and earns a profit of

$$(p_1^* - 20)x_1^* = (84 - 20)116 = \$7424$$

Each firm could spend over $7000 on differentiating its product and still come out ahead.[10]

We can also show that, as the number of firms bringing their own differentiated products to the market grows, making competition ever more intense,

---

[10]As we have already seen (Cigarette Television Advertising), if firms differentiate their products through advertising, and if they make their advertising decision *after* they make their pricing decision, they may spend too much on advertising. In game theory, it can matter a lot *when* a player makes a decision.

Bertrand equilibrium will converge toward a zero-profit equilibrium. This situation, where products are differentiated but profits are driven down to zero, is called **monopolistic competition.** Here is how it works. Firm 1's market demand is given by

$$x_1 = 180 - p_1 - \left(\frac{n}{2}\right)(p_1 - \text{average price})$$

only now the average price is $(p_1 + p_2 + \cdots + p_n)/n$. The term $n/2$ in front of the price differential reflects increasingly intense competition. The more firms that occupy niches in the market, the closer a firm's price has to be to the market average if it wants to maintain its sales. Firm 1 has a profit function of the form

$$u_1(\mathbf{p}) = (p_1 - 20)x_1$$

where $\mathbf{p} = (p_1, p_2, \ldots, p_n)$ is the vector of all firms' prices. Setting marginal profit for firm 1 equal to zero, we get

$$0 = \frac{\partial u_1}{\partial p_1} = (p_1 - 20) - \frac{(n+1)}{2} + x_1$$

It will simplify our notation if we set

$$K = \frac{n+1}{2}$$

At this point in the argument, it is time to exploit the symmetry inherent in the problem. Each firm faces the same costs and the same demand structure. In particular, demand is a function of a firm's own price and of the sum of all the firm's prices. Thus, we satisfy all the requirements for a symmetrical game. A Bertrand equilibrium with n firms will have all firms charging the same price; hence, none of them will charge above the market average. Substituting demand into the marginal profit condition when $p_1 = $ average price, then rearranging, yields

$$K(p_1 - 20) = 180 - p_1$$

Solving, we get

$$p_1^* = \frac{180}{(K+1)} + \frac{20K}{(K+1)}$$

When $n = 2$, $K = 1.5$, and this formula checks with our previous result.

Now we take the limit of p_1^* as n goes to infinity. Since K goes to infinity with n, the term involving the reservation price 180 goes to zero. We are left with a term whose numerator and denominator both involve K. Dividing both the numerator and the denominator by K, we get

$$\lim p_1^* = \lim \frac{20}{(1 + 1/K)} = 20$$

as n and K go to infinity. In the limit, price equals marginal cost, and profits have vanished. This limit is monopolistic competition. The analysis of differentiated products that we have just carried out for Bertrand equilibrium can also be carried out for Cournot equilibrium. The main mathematical step is to rewrite a firm's demand so that quantity appears on the right-hand side. To illustrate for the case of two firms, we want to write the firm's demands with prices on the left and quantities on the right.

$$x_1 = 180 - 1.5p_1 + 0.5p_2$$
$$x_2 = 180 + 0.5p_1 - 1.5p_2$$

This means solving two linear equations in two unknowns. The solution is

$$p_1 = 180 - 0.75x_1 - 0.25x_2$$
$$p_2 = 180 - 0.25x_1 - 0.75x_2$$

You can now proceed to define profits for each firm, and then maximize profits for each firm simultaneously. The result is the Cournot equilibrium (see problem 9). If you do problem 9, you will see that the Cournot equilibrium is not so very different from the Bertrand equilibrium. Differentiated products tend to mute the difference between these two forms of competition.

❌ 5.8 Bertrand Competition among Differentiated Products in the Cigarette Industry[11] ■ ■ ■ ■ ■ ■ ■ ■ ■ ■ ■

In 1981, discount cigarettes had a 0% share of the U.S. cigarette market. The big-name, high-priced brands, led by number 1–ranked Philip Morris (Marlboro) with a 43% market share and number 2–ranked RJR Nabisco[12] (Winston, Camel) with a 30% market share, dominated the market. Large market shares, together with high profit margins ($0.55/pack of Marlboros at the beginning of 1993), led to fabulous profits throughout the decade. Philip Morris alone was making over $5 billion annually, pretax, from its cigarette operations. Times couldn't have been better for cigarette company stockholders.

Also in 1981, discount brands started making inroads into the market. These brands, usually priced under $1/pack, have a low profit margin, around $0.05/pack, but they also require almost no advertising to sell. By 1987, discount brands had 10% of the U.S. market. As of April 1993, their market share was 36%. Consumers of these brands are smokers who don't appreciate the difference, when it costs over $1/pack, between Marlboro and West.

The spectacular market penetration of the discount brands has forced the major brands to cut prices to around $2/pack, already hurting profits. Even worse, Philip Morris and RJR have begun to produce their own discount

---

[11]Material for this example has been drawn from the *Wall Street Journal,* April 5, 1993.

[12]This was Reynolds in our case from Chapter 2, Cigarette Television Advertising.

brands. With these discount brands, Philip Morris and RJR are cannibalizing their own major brand sales. Right now, RJR controls one-third of the discount brands market, with Monarch its big seller. RJR also sells house brands for Kmart, Circle K, and BP Oil. Philip Morris controls one-quarter of all discount brand sales (Cambridge, Bronson). "They are in a mutual dance of death that is strangling their full-price business," said a tobacco industry consultant of the situation Philip Morris and RJR are in.

Given their growing dominance of the discount brands—now over 60%—Philip Morris and RJR have a strong mutual interest in stopping the further market penetration by discount brands and returning to the good old days of high prices on all brands in the market. To this end, both companies have pushed up wholesale prices on their discount brands by 40% since August 1992. The chain stores—convenience stores, retailers, grocers, gasoline stations—have balked at the wholesale price increases and sought other suppliers for discount brands at $1/pack. As a result, the wholesale price increases have not stuck.

On April 4, 1993, Philip Morris cut the price of Marlboros by as much as 20%. Philip Morris also projected a $2 billion drop in profits as a result of the latest cigarette pricing developments. Wall Street took this announcement to heart: the value of Philip Morris stock dropped $13 billion in one day. Tobacco experts are not bullish on this stock even at its new low price. Says one, "It is risky. It may create permanent and insidious downward pricing pressuring on their most profitable brands."

Bertrand competition, even with differentiated products, can really hurt profits as the market gets crowded. But as far as Marlboro smokers are concerned, times couldn't be better.

◼◼ SUMMARY

1. In a normal form market game, firms pick their strategies simultaneously and earn profits according to the market outcome. At the equilibrium of such a market game, each firm has maximized its profits, given the strategy of its competitors.

2. In Cournot competition, firms use quantity shipped to market as their strategic variable. The equilibrium of a Cournot market game is called a Cournot equilibrium.

3. In a Cournot equilibrium, when firms' products are perfect substitutes, price lies below monopoly levels but above marginal cost. Neither monopoly nor perfect competition is a Cournot equilibrium.

4. As the number of firms selling perfect substitutes in Cournot competition grows large, the Cournot equilibrium price approaches marginal cost. This phenomenon is called the Cournot limit theorem.

5. In a market game, the closer price is to marginal cost, the better the

outcome is from the standpoint of efficiency. Efficiency is maximal when price equals marginal cost.

6. In Bertrand competition, firms use price called out in the market as their strategic variable. The equilibrium of a Bertrand market game is called a Bertrand equilibrium.

7. In a Bertrand equilibrium, when firms' products are perfect substitutes and firms' costs are the same, price equals marginal cost.

8. When firms' products are not perfect substitutes, they are said to be differentiated. Bertrand and Cournot equilibria are still different when products are differentiated, but the differences are muted.

9. The limit of Bertrand or Cournot competition with differentiated products when the number of firms grows large is monopolistic competition. In monopolistic competition, profits are driven to zero.

10. The cigarette price war of 1993 shows how devastating Bertrand competition can be to firms' profits as the number of brands grows, even when products are differentiated.

▞ KEY TERMS

noncooperative market games in
   normal form
Cournot competition
Cournot equilibrium
cost advantage
Cournot limit theorem
market gains from trade

Bertrand competition
Bertrand equilibrium
ruinous competition
Bertrand limit theorem
differentiated products
monopolistic competition

▞ PROBLEMS

1. Market demand is given by $P = 140 - Q$. There are two firms, each with unit costs = \$20. Firms can choose any quantity. Find the Cournot equilibrium and compare it to the monopoly outcome and to the perfectly competitive outcome. Why aren't the latter equilibria of the market game?

2. Suppose that in problem 1, firm 1's unit costs fall to \$10, while firm 2's unit costs don't change. This gives firm 1 a cost advantage. How much does firm 1 sell at a Cournot equilibrium? Is it more or less than firm 2? Why?

3. Suppose that market demand is nonlinear, taking the form $P = 100 - Q^2$. Suppose that firms' unit costs are \$5. Find the Cournot equilibrium. What does this suggest about the properties of Cournot competition in general?

4. Prove the Cournot limit theorem for the following markets: (a) market

demand is given by $80 - 4Q$, and each firm has unit cost = \$10; (b) the market in problem 3.

5. Look up the price of coffee on the world market (cash and futures). Has the price risen since the Kampala accord of October 1, 1993?

6. Suppose that two firms both have average variable cost = \$50. Market demand is given by $Q = 100 - P$. Find the Bertrand equilibrium. Would your answer change if there were three firms?

7. Same demand as in problem 6. Find the Bertrand equilibrium if firm 1 has average variable cost = \$40 and firm 2 has average variable cost = \$60. Show that the Bertrand equilibrium changes when firm 2 has average variable cost = \$90. Explain.

8. Same demand as in problem 6, only now there are two firms with average variable cost = \$50 and two firms with average variable cost = \$60. Find the Bertrand equilibrium. Is it the same as the perfectly competitive equilibrium?

9. Solve for the Cournot equilibrium of the market game given at the end of section 5.7. Compare your result (output, price, profits) to the Bertrand equilibrium. How different are they?

10. Here is a model of cigarette product differentiation. There are n brands of cigarettes. Each brand of cigarette i has the demand curve:

$$x_i = 15{,}000 - 1000p_i - (1000n)(p_i - \text{average price})$$

where p_i is brand i's price in dollars. Average cost is \$1/pack throughout the industry. What happens to industry profits at Bertrand equilibrium when the number of firms rises from $n = 2$ to $n = 3$? How does this relate to the price of Marlboros?

◼ APPENDIX. UNIQUENESS OF EQUILIBRIUM

Many of the market games in this chapter have had unique equilibria. This appendix provides a condition that guarantees that the equilibrium of a game must be unique. This condition, called the contraction mapping condition, applies, for instance, to the equilibrium of a 2-firm Cournot market with linear demand and constant returns to scale. It also applies to both kinds of competition when products are differentiated.

The idea of contraction mapping is used throughout mathematics to prove that something is unique. Here we will use it to prove that the equilibrium of a game is unique. Let $f(x)$ be a function of x. Let $d(x,y)$, "the distance between x and y," measure the distance between two points x and y in the domain of f. If x and y are scalars, then $d(x,y) = |x - y|$, the absolute value of the difference between the points x and y. Likewise, the distance $d[f(x),f(y)]$, measures the distance between two points in the range of f. If $f(x)$ and $f(y)$ are scalar functions, then $d[f(x),f(y)] = |f(x) - f(y)|$, the absolute value of the difference between $f(x)$ and $f(y)$. If $\mathbf{x}$ and $\mathbf{y}$ are two-dimensional vectors instead of scalars, $\mathbf{x} = (x_1, x_2)$ and $\mathbf{y} = (y_1, y_2)$, then $d(\mathbf{x}, \mathbf{y})$ is the sum of the absolute values of the differences in each dimension:

$$d(\mathbf{x}, \mathbf{y}) = |x_1 - y_1| + |x_2 - y_2|$$

The function f *is a contraction* if there is a constant $k < 1$, such that for any two distinct points in the domain of f,

$$d[f(x), f(y)] \leq k\, d(x, y)$$

In this definition, k is a contraction factor. What contraction mapping does is to bring two points closer together than they were before the mapping. If you think about the shrinkage function on a copy machine, you have a real-life model of contraction mapping. The closer the contraction factor is to zero, the more the mapping contracts.

Here are two simple examples of contraction mapping. Let $f(x) = c$, the constant function. The constant function is a contraction mapping. To see this, let's perform the contraction test. Take two distinct points x and y in the domain of f:

$$d[f(x), f(y)] = d(c, c) = |c - c| = 0 < k\, d(x, y)$$

for any positive k less than 1. The constant function is the ultimate in contraction: it makes everything the same size. Next, consider the linear function $f(x) = x/2$. This, too, is a contraction. Take two points in the domain, x and y. Performing the contraction test, we get

$$d[f(x), f(y)] = d\left(\frac{x}{2}, \frac{y}{2}\right) = \left|\frac{x}{2} - \frac{y}{2}\right| = \frac{1}{2}|x - y| = \frac{1}{2}\, d(x, y)$$

So, $k = 1/2$ is a contraction factor.

It is important to note that each contraction mapping has a unique fixed-point solution:

$$f(c) = c$$

where c is the fixed point, and

$$f(0) = \frac{1}{2}(0) = 0$$

where 0 is the fixed point. This is no accident. *Every contraction mapping has a unique fixed point.* Recall that fixed-point solutions to equations of the form $\mathbf{f(x)} = \mathbf{x}$, where $\mathbf{x}$ is a strategy vector and $\mathbf{f}$ is the best-response mapping, are equilibria. So if we can show that the best-response function is a contraction mapping, we know that there is a unique equilibrium for that game.

We can see how to use the contraction mapping test to show when a game equilibrium is unique, based on the two-dimensional versions of the functions we have just seen to be contractions. First, write the best-response function $\mathbf{f} = [f_1(x_2), f_2(x_1)]$, where $f_1(x_2)$ is player 1's best-response function and $f_2(x_1)$ is player 2's best-response function. Suppose that both f_1 and f_2 are constant mappings. This happens when each player has a strictly dominant strategy. Let $x_1^* = f(x_2)$ and $x_2^* = g(x_1)$ be these strictly dominant strategies. Consider a pair of distinct strategy vectors $\mathbf{x} = (x_1, x_2)$ and $\mathbf{y} = (y_1, y_2)$. The distance between $\mathbf{f}(\mathbf{x})$ and $\mathbf{f}(\mathbf{y})$ is zero, since each maps to the same point $\mathbf{x}^* = (x_1^*, x_2^*)$. The distance between $\mathbf{x}$ and $\mathbf{y}$ is positive, since they are distinct. Therefore we have, for any contraction factor k,

$$d[\mathbf{f}(\mathbf{x}), \mathbf{f}(\mathbf{y})] = |\mathbf{x}^* - \mathbf{x}^*| = 0 < k\, d(\mathbf{x}, \mathbf{y})$$

We have just shown that if each player has a strictly dominant strategy, then the best-response mapping is a contraction, which in turn implies that the equilibrium of any such game is unique.

Next, take the Cournot best-response functions from section 5.2:

$$x_1 = f_1(x_2) = 60 - \frac{x_2}{2}$$

$$x_2 = f_2(x_1) = 60 - \frac{x_1}{2}$$

Let $\mathbf{x}$ be a quantity vector for each firm and let $\mathbf{y}$ be a different quantity vector for each firm. To measure distance between best responses, we work dimension by dimension. First consider the difference in firm 1's quantity dimension. This is given by

$$d[f_1(x_2), f_1(y_2)] = d\left(\frac{60 - x_2}{2}, \frac{60 - y_2}{2}\right) = \left|\frac{60 - x_2}{2} - \frac{60 + y_2}{2}\right|$$

$$= \frac{1}{2}|y_2 - x_2| = \frac{1}{2}\, d(x_2, y_2)$$

We get a contraction factor of $1/2$ in firm 1's quantity dimension. Exactly the same thing happens when we measure the distance in firm 2's quantity dimension. Putting it all together, we have

$$d[\mathbf{f}(\mathbf{x}), \mathbf{f}(\mathbf{y})] = \frac{1}{2}\, d(\mathbf{x}, \mathbf{y})$$

for the basic Cournot model. The contraction factor of $1/2$ for this game guarantees that its equilibrium is unique.

This argument may be a little intense. Here's a numerical example to see what is going on. Let $\mathbf{x} = (60, 60)$ be the outcome of perfect competition and $\mathbf{y} = (60, 0)$ be the outcome of monopoly. The best response to $\mathbf{x}$ is $(30, 30)$; the best response to $\mathbf{y}$ is $(60, 30)$. The distance between the best responses is $|60 - 30| = 30$ in firm 1's dimension and $|30 - 30| = 0$ in firm 2's dimension, for an overall distance in the two dimensions of $|30 + 0| = 30$. The distance between x and y themselves is $|60 - 60| = 0$ in firm 1's dimension and $|60 - 0| = 60$ in firm 2's dimension. The overall distance between the starting points is $|0 + 60| = 60$. The distance between ending points, 30, is exactly half the distance between starting points, 60. This calculation is portrayed in Figure 5.9.

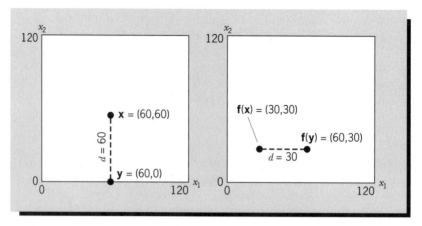

Figure 5.9. Cournot best-response mapping contracts.

Two cautions are in order. First, a game may have a unique equilibrium despite failing the contraction mapping test. The result here is silent about what happens when the contraction mapping test fails. Again, it may be too difficult to apply the contraction mapping test. This is the reason other tests for uniqueness of equilibrium have been developed as well.

◼ PROBLEMS

1. Show that the best-response mapping for the 2-firm Bertrand market game of section 5.7 is a contraction mapping. What does this say about the number of Bertrand equilibria of this game?

2. Here is a 2-player game. Player 1 chooses the strategy x_1 from $[-1,1]$. Player 1's utility function is

$$u_1(\mathbf{x}) = \frac{x_1^2}{2} - x_1 x_2$$

Player 2 chooses the strategy x_2 from $[-1,1]$. Player 2's utility function is

$$u_2(\mathbf{x}) = \frac{x_2^2}{2} + x_1 x_2$$

Find the best-response mapping for this game. Show that the equilibrium of this game is unique. Then show that the best-response function is not a contraction. Explain your result.

PART TWO

Games with Sequential Structure

C H A P T E R 6

Credibility and Subgame Perfect Equilibrium

Threats and promises are a major part of everyday life and a major part of doing business. When to believe someone's threat or promise and when not to is a key part of decision making. As long as we stick to games in normal form, the question whether a strategy containing a threat or a promise is credible or not doesn't come up. Threats and promises are tied to the future, whereas all strategic choices in normal form games are made simultaneously in the present. However, in games in extensive form, the issue of credibility comes up in a big way. Making a threat or making a promise becomes a move in the game, and it may have an impact on players who have to move later in the game. For this reason, all the games studied in this chapter are in extensive form.

The chapter begins by introducing the crucial notion of a **subgame.** A subgame is a part of an entire game that, when detached from its parent game, can stand alone as a game. Normal form games cannot have subgames, but extensive form games can. Then the related concept of *subgame perfection,* which is how credibility is expressed in game theory, is discussed. A strategy is subgame perfect when it plays an equilibrium on every subgame. This chapter shows how subgame perfection relates to dominated strategies and why subgame perfection enshrines a notion of credibility. When every strategy in an equilibrium is subgame perfect, the equilibrium itself is subgame perfect. Subgame perfection is a sufficient condition for solving a game in extensive form. Next subgame perfection is applied to two episodes a century apart in U.S. history, both of which raise interesting credibility issues. The first of these deals with conscription during the American Civil War (1861–65); the second involves the Cuban missile crisis (1962). Discussion then returns to noncooperative market games, only now in extensive form. *Stackelberg competition* refers to such a market game in which one firm must move first. Sections 6.6 and 6.7 show how Stackelberg competition affects Cournot and Bertrand equilibria. In Cournot competition, the firm that moves first has the advantage; in Bertrand competition, the firm that moves second has the advantage. As a final example of credibility, the strategic detail of the often heard marketing claim This Offer Is Good for a Limited Time Only is presented. As you will see, it takes powerful precommitment devices to make this claim credible. The appendix looks at some experiments involving ultimatums.

6.1 Subgames and Their Equilibria ■ ■ ■ ■ ■ ■ ■ ■ ■ ■ ■

A subgame is any part of a game that can itself be played as a game. A subgame has an initial node, and all the information sets that players need to play the subgame are present. Consider the game in Figure 6.1*a*. It has a subgame, starting with player 2's move. This subgame is surrounded by a dashed square. We will discuss this subgame shortly. Next, consider the game in Figure 6.1*b*. This game does not have a subgame. Player 2 has imperfect information and does not know whether player 1 has gone left or right. When it is player 2's turn to move, there is no way to start a game there.

The difference between these two games comes down to one of timing and information. In the game in Figure 6.1*a*, each player has perfect information. Player 1 moves first, and player 2 knows what player 1 has done when he or she has to move. *Every game with perfect information has subgames.* A complicated game with perfect information has many subgames. In the game in Figure 6.1*b*, both players move simultaneously. Player 2 does not see what player 1 has done. This makes the game one of imperfect information. This game does not have a subgame. *No game in which the players move simultaneously once and for all has subgames other than itself.* In particular, this statement applies to games in normal form. The difference between the two games in Figure 6.1 is sufficiently subtle that they have the same normal form (see Figure 6.2).

The game in Figure 6.1*a* is called Telex versus IBM.[1] These two computer firms, one a giant (IBM), the other an upstart (Telex), were battling for market

---

[1]This game was invented by Reinhard Selten, "The Chain Store Paradox," *Theory and Decision* 9 (1977):127–59. Another name for it is Entry.

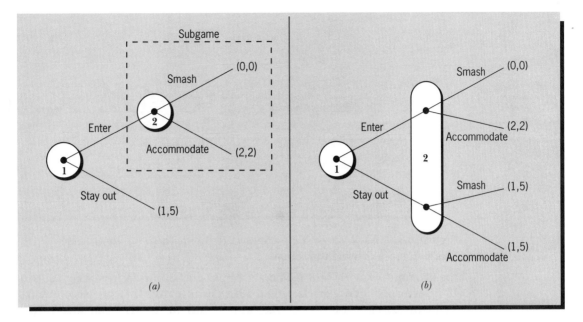

Figure 6.1. Telex versus IBM, extensive form: (*a*) subgame, perfect information; (*b*) no subgame, imperfect information.

share and profits in the late 1960s. Telex was making inroads into IBM's market share by creating almost perfect substitutes for IBM's hardware. Telex products, such as computer printers and memories, were plug compatible, which meant they could be plugged right into an IBM machine and work fine. Call player 1 Telex, and player 2, IBM. Telex moves first. Telex can either enter IBM's market or stay out. If Telex stays out, it earns a normal profit somewhere else in

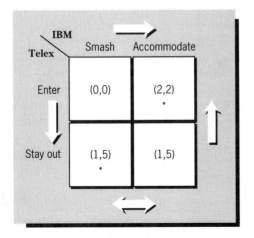

Figure 6.2. Telex versus IBM, normal form.

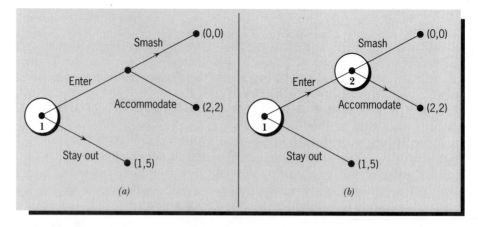

Figure 6.3. Telex versus IBM, extensive form equilibria: (*a*) noncredible equilibrium; (*b*) credible equilibrium.

the economy ($u_1 = 1$) and IBM makes monopoly profits in its market ($u_2 = 5$). If Telex enters IBM's market, then IBM has to move. IBM can accommodate Telex by letting it into the market without a fight. Or IBM can smash Telex, slashing prices to the bone so that both companies are making no profit. The term *smash* for this strategy comes from an internal IBM memorandum of the period, entitled Operation Smash, which outlined precisely this response to Telex's entry attempt.[2] If IBM accommodates Telex's entry, then they each get the payoff 2. If IBM smashes Telex, then they each get the payoff 0. After either of these moves by IBM, the subgame ends and the overall game ends.

As you can see from the arrow diagram of Figure 6.2, Telex versus IBM has two pure strategy equilibria. Figure 6.3 shows the same equilibria via labels on the game tree: (stay out, smash) is an equilibrium; so is (enter, accommodate). The former equilibrium presents a **credibility problem.** A credibility problem is present if, at the moment when a threat must actually be carried out, a player does not maximize utility by carrying out the threat. Smash is a threat designed to discourage Telex from entering. It is as if IBM said to Telex, "If you enter my market, I will smash you." Suppose Telex stands up to the threat by entering IBM's market. Now it's time for IBM to make good its threat to smash Telex. The trouble with carrying out the threat is that it minimizes IBM's payoff ($u_2 = 0$) instead of maximizing that payoff ($u_2 = 2$). There is a further problem with the strategy Smash: it is dominated by the strategy Accommodate. Arrows point in toward Accommodate along both rows of the payoff matrix. As we shall soon see, this is no coincidence. Where there is a credibility problem, strategic domination is usually a problem, too.

---

[2]This memorandum became a key piece of evidence in the court case involving Telex and IBM. See Gerald W. Brock, *The U.S. Computer Industry* (Cambridge, Mass.: Ballinger, 1975), especially pages 114–24, for further details. It should be noted that strategies that smash a business competitor are sometimes illegal in the United States.

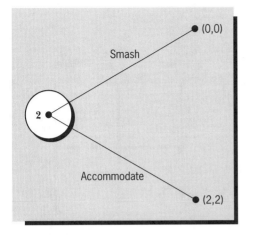

Figure 6.4. Telex versus IBM, subgame equilibrium.

No credibility problem attends the strategy Accommodate. It maximizes utility on the subgame that begins with player 2's decision. Indeed, it represents the unique equilibrium on that subgame (Figure 6.4). The equilibrium (enter, accommodate), which does not have a credibility problem, turns out to be the solution of Telex versus IBM with perfect information.

Here is a second example, called Centipede, which contains a promise that is not credible.[3] In Centipede, there are two players. Player 1 moves first, player 2 moves second. After at most two moves, the game ends. The game begins with $1 sitting on the table. Player 1 can either take the dollar or wait. If player 1 takes the dollar, the game is over, and player 1 gets to keep the dollar. If player 1 waits, the dollar on the table quadruples to $4. Now it is player 2's turn. Player 2 can either take the entire $4 on the table or split the $4 evenly with player 1. Figure 6.5a shows Centipede in extensive form.

Player 2's strategy to split the money with player 1 implicitly contains the following promise addressed to player 1: "If you wait, then I will split the $4 with you." The trouble is, this promise has a credibility problem. Suppose player 1 does wait. Now it is player 2's turn to make good on the promise to player 1 to split the money on the table. If player 2 makes good on the promise, player 2 minimizes his or her utility ($u_2 = 2$) instead of maximizing it ($u_2 = 4$). Player 2 has every reason in the world to break the promise and take all the money instead.

The credibility problem posed by the promise to split the money is apparent in the fact that the only equilibrium on the subgame beginning with player 2's move is for player 2 to take all the money. There is an even bigger problem with player 2's promise to split the money: it is not part of *any* equilibrium. You can see this in Figure 6.5b, which shows Centipede in normal form. The only

---

[3]This game was introduced by Robert Rosenthal, "Games of Perfect Information, Predatory Pricing, and the Chain Store Paradox." *Journal of Economic Theory* 25 (1982):92–100.

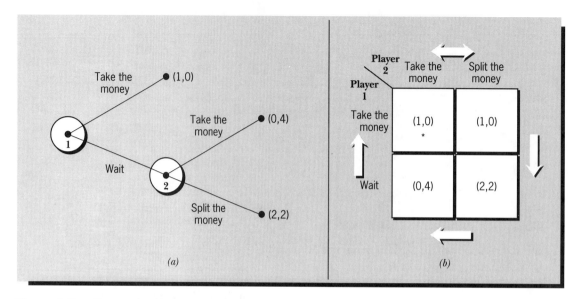

Figure 6.5.   Centipede: (*a*) extensive form; (*b*) normal form.

equilibrium for Centipede is (take the money, take the money). Each player takes the money if the opportunity ever presents itself. Indeed, the strategy Take the money dominates the strategy Split the money for player 2. Again, this strategic domination is due to the credibility problem adhering to the strategy Split the money.

A credibility problem attends any strategy containing a threat or promise, the carrying out of which is costly to the player making it. Players who make such threats or promises and then do not carry them out are said to lose their credibility, a phenomenon familiar in business and more so in politics. Here are two examples. Suppose that during the campaign a presidential candidate promises to balance the federal budget, and that candidate wins.[4] Now it is time for the newly elected president to keep the promise to balance the budget. Unfortunately, keeping the promise will throw the country into a deep recession. In such a case, it is better for the president to lose a little credibility, rather than wreak havoc on the whole economy.[5] As another example, suppose that the prime minister of a large European country promises that that country will never devalue its currency, even if it means keeping unemployment in double digits.[6] Again, this is a promise that the citizens, especially those

---

[4]Even though federal budgets have rarely been balanced since 1932, candidates for president routinely promise to balance them.

[5]Thus it was much better for President Reagan to run budget deficits than to keep the promise of candidate Reagan to balance the budget.

[6]The latest example of this situation occurred on August 2, 1993: the European Monetary System was altered so that the French franc could fall 2 days after Prime Minister Balladur promised to defend the franc at all costs.

unemployed, would rather see broken. In cases such as these, politicians are notorious for trading off their credibility for other goods, such as the good of their nation's economy. The moral here is that you should not make a threat or a promise unless you are prepared to carry it out. Otherwise, your threat or promise has ritual, rather than strategic, value. It is a ritual for politicians to say certain things—and later retract them if they become an embarrassment to policy. Business leaders have to be rather more careful with what they say, since money takes priority over ritual in business. If a CEO promises the stockholders record earnings, and those earnings don't materialize, the CEO has a lot to answer for to those same stockholders. In such a case, losing credibility may mean losing corporate control in a nasty proxy fight or takeover battle.

There is one intrinsic asymmetry between threats and promises that games don't always capture, but that is a part of our moral norms. We have a moral norm saying, "You should keep your promises," but we don't have a moral norm saying, "You should carry out your threats." In this sense, breaking a promise is worse than not carrying out a threat—regardless of credibility. Even this moral norm has its limits, though. A person who never breaks a promise can just as easily be a monster as a hero. Take the story of Jephthah from the Bible (Judges 11:29–31). Jephthah commands the Israelites in battle against the Moabites. He promises God that if he prevails in battle, he will sacrifice the first living thing he sees in the wake of victory. Jephthah does prevail in battle, and the first living thing he sees in the wake of victory is his daughter. Jephthah keeps his promise, promptly turning his live daughter into a dead sacrifice. In so doing, Jephthah commits a terrible crime. It is not good to make a promise whose consequences might be dire, especially if you are someone who keeps promises at all costs.

▨ 6.2 Maintaining Credibility via Subgame Perfection ▪

The advice game theory gives on the credibility problem is simple: never make a threat or promise unless you are prepared to carry it out. To make your threat or promise credible to others, it must pay you to make good on your threat or promise if the time comes to do so. There is a sufficient condition for the solution of a game in extensive form that captures this notion. A game equilibrium is a **subgame perfect equilibrium** if every player plays an equilibrium on every subgame. The sufficient condition is the following:

■ ■

Subgame Perfection. The solution of a game in extensive form is subgame perfect.

Notice that this sufficient condition is restricted to games in extensive form, since it has no force for games in normal form, which lack subgames. All strategies and equilibria that fail the test of subgame perfection are called *imperfect*. The imperfection of a strategy consists in the fact that at some point in the game, it has an unavoidable credibility problem.

The sufficient condition just given would be no good if a game in extensive form had no subgame perfect equilibrium. This is another example of an existence problem. Fortunately, if a game is finite, it has equilibria, and we can construct a subgame perfect equilibrium for it by **backward induction,** the same reasoning we used to determine the outcome of games like Chess in Chapter 1. To construct a subgame perfect equilibrium, start at the final subgame of the game. When the game is finite, it has one or more final subgames. Find a subgame equilibrium for each of those subgames. Now work back through the game tree from each final subgame to the next subgame that strictly contains it. Find a subgame equilibrium for this larger subgame. Now work back through the game tree once more from this subgame and so on until you reach the start of the game. Following the equilibrium path you have just taken through the game tree yields a subgame perfect equilibrium. We have constructed an equilibrium on every subgame.

We are now in a position to solve, via backward induction, the games we looked at in the last section. Consider first the perfect information version of Telex versus IBM (see Figure 6.3*b*). The final subgame (the only subgame) has a single equilibrium, with IBM choosing Accommodate. Working back to the next subgame, we reach the start of the game. Telex has the choice between staying out and getting $u_1 = 1$ or entering and getting $u_2 = 2$. The subgame perfect equilibrium path has Telex entering and IBM accommodating. This is the only subgame perfect equilibrium of Telex versus IBM with perfect information. Hence, by the solution postulate, it is the solution to Telex versus IBM. When we turn to the imperfect information and normal form versions of Telex versus IBM, we get the same solution, but for a different reason. Subgame perfection has no bite here, since the games are in normal form. In both these games, however, IBM's strategy Accommodate dominates Smash. Hence, by applying the sufficient condition of undominated strategies, we arrive at the solution (enter, accommodate)—the same as before.

Next consider Centipede, which has a unique equilibrium (Figure 6.5). On the final subgame, player 2 takes all the money. At the start, player 1 takes all the money, rather than waiting for player 2 to take it. This is the subgame perfect equilibrium path, indeed, the only equilibrium path.

▞ 6.3 Credible Threats and Promises ■ ■ ■ ■ ■ ■ ■ ■ ■ ■ ■

So far we have looked at threats and promises with a credibility problem. There are plenty of threats and promises that you had better believe. Depending on the **type of opponent** you are playing against, a strategy that had a credibility problem might instead be credible. We turn to some of these now. Consider

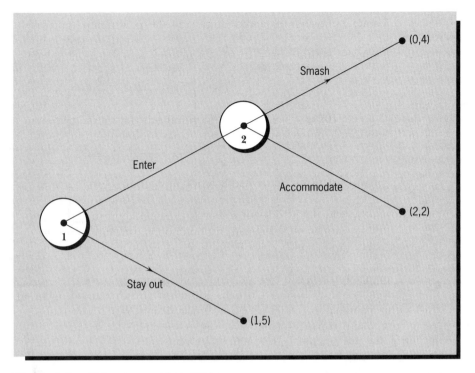

Figure 6.6. Telex versus Mean IBM.

the game in Figure 6.6, Telex versus Mean IBM. The only difference between this perfect information version of Telex versus IBM and the version we solved previously is that the payoff to IBM when it smashes Telex is $u_2 = 4$. Mean IBM is so called because it gets more utility from driving rivals out of business than from making profits.[7] Mean IBM has a perfectly credible threat to smash— smash is the only equilibrium on this player's final subgame. The only equilibrium, hence the solution, for Telex versus Mean IBM is (don't enter, smash). A firm would be foolhardy to enter a market against such a rival—the rival wants the other firm to enter, it so enjoys smashing others.

An example of a game with a credible promise is Centipede with a Nice Opponent (Figure 6.7). The only difference between this version of Centipede and the version we reviewed earlier is in the payoff to player 2 when he or she takes all the money. Player 2 gets called "nice" because he or she would much rather divide the money evenly ($u_2 = 2$) than take it all ($u_2 = 0$). We could explain this by appealing to player 2's sense of fairness, perhaps. Games can model emotions, such as meanness, kindness, or fairness, but they have to stray from monetary payoffs to do so. Now player 2's promise to split the money evenly is perfectly credible. Indeed, player 1's strategy Take the money, which

[7]Of course, running a business like this has fairly serious implications for stockholders' profits, a theme pursued in Chapter 10.

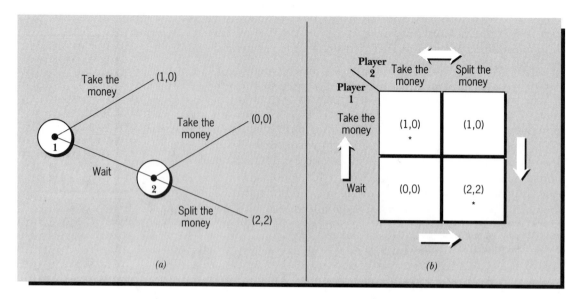

Figure 6.7.   Centipede with a Nice Opponent: (*a*) extensive form; (*b*) normal form.

before was the only sensible one, now is dominated by the strategy Wait. Curiously enough, Centipede with a Nice Opponent has a second, imperfect equilibrium, (take the money, take the money) (see Figure 6.7*b*). At this equilibrium, player 2 noncredibly threatens to take all the money, and player 1, believing this threat, takes the money first. In the extensive form version of Centipede with a Nice Opponent, this noncredible equilibrium is ruled out by subgame perfection. In the normal form version of the game, this equilibrium is ruled out by undominated strategies. For player 2, the strategy Split the money dominates the strategy Take the money. Thus, in either form, the solution to Centipede with a Nice Opponent is (wait, split the money), and the players split the $4 evenly.

If you compare the outcome of Telex versus IBM to that of Telex versus Mean IBM, it is clear that it would pay IBM to pretend to be mean, even if it weren't, if information was less than perfect. Again, if you compare the outcome of Centipede to Centipede with a Nice Opponent, it would pay player 2 to pretend to be nice, even it he or she weren't, if information was less than perfect. In the case of Telex versus IBM, IBM would be bluffing Telex out; in the case of Centipede, player 2 would be misleading player 1 to make it easier to betray him or her. These kinds of behavior, called Machiavellian after the notorious political philosopher of Renaissance Italy who first advocated them, are rife in games of imperfect information.[8] If you don't know who you are playing against, you really have to be on your guard against deception. Chapter

[8]See Niccolò Machiavelli, *The Prince*, trans. Peter Bondanella and Mark Musa (Oxford: Oxford University Press, 1984).

9 returns to this important topic. For now, we look at two episodes in U.S. history instead—important episodes, full of strategic content and credibility issues. The first of these comes from the American Civil War.

▞ 6.4 Reluctant Volunteers: Conscription in the American Civil War, 1862–65[9] ■ ■ ■ ■ ■ ■ ■ ■ ■ ■

The American Civil War was the bloodiest war America ever fought. Over 3 million people fought in this war, serving either the United States of America (USA) or the Confederate States of America (CSA). Some 700,000 soldiers died. USA president Lincoln originally called for 75,000 soldiers to serve for 90 days; CSA president Davis called for 50,000 soldiers to serve for 1 year. Once it became clear to both sides that the war would be protracted, replacement of the initial regular forces and state militias became of great concern. Both sides needed more soldiers. Both the USA and the CSA constitutions granted to their respective congresses the power to raise armies. This constitutional privilege was the basis for legislation on both sides to institute national conscription—the first such in U.S. history. The CSA Congress enacted its Conscription Act in 1862, just before the 1-year enlistments expired. The USA Congress enacted its Conscription Act in 1863, just prior to the pivotal victories at Vicksburg and Gettysburg.

The possibility of conscription put those eligible for service into a strategic quandary: should I volunteer or should I wait for the draft, which might or might not catch up with me? Since enlistment dates, ages, and other call-up criteria were sequential in nature, one person might have to make this decision earlier or later than another. The version of the game Conscription described here was played by literally millions of men. According to the census of 1860, at least 5 million men were eligible to serve on one side or the other. The age limits of 15 to 50 years were quite broad, and there were almost no exemptions. In the USA, you could be exempted if you were the sole supporter of your parents or if you had at least four brothers already serving. In the CSA, you could be exempted if your being drafted would reduce the ratio of white men to African-American slaves on a plantation below 1:25. That was pretty much it for exemptions.

In the version of Conscription presented here, there are only two men, although the same basic principle applies to the game played by millions. Again for simplicity, we consider the situation facing two men eligible for induction into the army of the USA. Similar incentives applied to men eligible for induction into the army of the CSA. The army needs one of these two for armed service. Player 1 has to move first. He can either volunteer, in which case

---

[9]Material has been drawn from Roy Gardner, "Resisting the Draft: A Perfect Equilibrium Approach," in *Game Equilibrium Models,* vol. 4, *Social and Political Interaction,* ed. Reinhard Selten (New York: Springer-Verlag, 1991), pp. 141–54.

the game ends, or he can wait for the draft. If player 1 volunteers, he gets the payoff $b - c$ and player 2 gets the payoff 0. The payoff parameter b represents the bonus for volunteering, which was substantial, about 1 year's wage for an average industrial worker.[10] The payoff parameter c represents the cost of serving, which is composed of two components: the expected loss of life and limb and the certain loss of civilian earnings. The payoff value 0 represents the civilian reference point. If player 1 waits for the draft, then player 2 faces the choice whether to volunteer or wait for the draft. If player 2 volunteers, the game ends and he gets the bonus for volunteering and serves in the army. If player 2 also waits for the draft, then the government conducts an equal-chance lottery to fill its draft quota. The catch is that a draftee serves, but does not get the bonus for volunteering. The only way to get the bonus, b, is to actually and truly volunteer. The extensive form of Conscription is shown in Figure 6.8a.

The subgame perfect equilibrium of Conscription depends very heavily on the size of the payoff parameters b (the bonus for volunteering) and c (the cost of serving). The values $b = \$300$ and $c = \$400$ (in 1863 dollars) are fairly realistic for this war. Let's find the subgame perfect equilibrium for these values (see Figure 6.8b). At the final chance subgame, reached if each player waits, the payoff vector is $(-c/2, -c/2) = (-200, -200)$. At the final subgame where he has a move, player 2 can volunteer, in which case he gets $-\$100$, or wait for the draft. If he waits for the draft, he has a 50% probability of losing $400, and a 50% probability of remaining civilian. Since this is an expected loss of $-\$200$, this player maximizes utility by volunteering for the draft. Any player who takes a sure loss rather than risking an even greater loss is called a **reluctant volunteer.** Player 2 in this case is a reluctant volunteer. He would rather volunteer and cut his losses than take a larger expected loss in the draft. We now work backward to player 1 at the start of the game. If player 1 volunteers, he gets $-\$100$, whereas if he waits, player 2 will do the volunteering for him and he gets $0. Player 1 can safely afford to wait. This is the subgame perfect equilibrium, (wait, volunteer). The player who moves last reluctantly volunteers.

The imperfect equilibrium here is just the opposite. Player 2, noncredibly, threatens to wait for the draft. Player 1, believing this threat, volunteers. At the imperfect equilibrium, it is the player who goes first who reluctantly volunteers. So both equilibria lead to the same behavioral conclusion: the draft quota is filled by reluctant volunteers.

What does all this have to do with America's bloody Civil War?[11] Just this. Of the 2.1 million soldiers who served in the Union army, only 50,000 were draftees. An astonishing 96% of all those who served were volunteers. Given the well-known costs of serving—over a quarter of these soldiers died—this number is truly remarkable. The volunteer rate for the Confederate army, at about half

[10]The bonus was $300 in 1863 dollars. The average wage for an industrial worker in the North at that time was about $25/month or $300/year.

[11]More soldiers died in 3 days at Gettysburg than in the heaviest *year* of fighting in Vietnam.

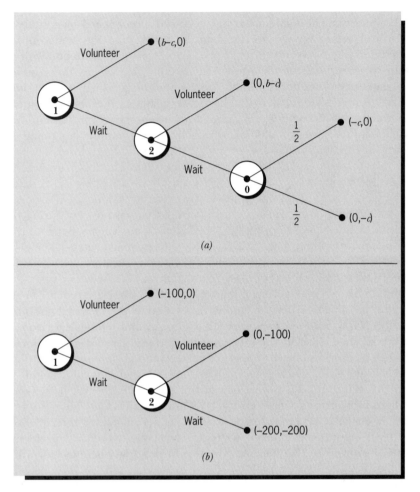

Figure 6.8. Conscription: (a) extensive form; (b) b = \$300, c = \$400.

the size of the Union army, was similar. This terrible war was fought by vast volunteer armies, many of whose members were reluctant volunteers.

6.5 Mutually Assured Destruction ■ ■ ■ ■ ■ ■ ■ ■ ■ ■ ■ ■ ■

Extensive form games with only two moves, one for each player, are by far the easiest to solve. All the games we have considered to this point could be represented by 2×2 matrices in normal form, since one of the moves by the first player terminated the game. This section examines a complicated game and finds increasingly complicated credibility issues as a result.

The game we consider is called **Mutually Assured Destruction** (MAD). MAD is played by two superpowers, country 1 and country 2. It will help to think back to the days when there were two superpowers, the United States and the Soviet

Union. An international incident has just occurred, precipitated by country 2. Country 1 can either ignore the incident, in which case the status quo is maintained and the game ends, or country 1 can escalate the situation with an ultimatum to country 2. In the event that country 1 escalates the conflict, country 2 can either back down from the confrontation, at a small loss of utility, or country 2 can escalate further. If country 2 escalates further, both countries are in a nuclear confrontation subgame. In this nuclear confrontation subgame, each country moves simultaneously. Each country gets one last chance to back down. Each country may also go nuclear, imposing large losses on both countries by an all-out attack, code-named Doomsday. The loss parameter L associated with Doomsday is a large negative number.[12] In either of the latter events, the game ends.[13] Figure 6.9a shows the extensive form of MAD.

MAD is a model of a nuclear weapons doctrine that was popular during the cold war. Each superpower kept massive stockpiles of nuclear weapons, so that in the event of serious escalation it had the wherewithal to impose massive assured destruction on its adversary. There was always controversy over whether the threat to use such weapons of mass destruction was credible. Let's see why, by computing the subgame perfect equilibria, of which there are two, for MAD.

The multiple subgame perfect equilibria arise from the fact that the final subgame has two equilibria, (back down, back down) and (Doomsday, Doomsday). Either of these could be the subgame equilibrium that starts the backward induction path. For instance, suppose that the equilibrium played on the subgame is (back down, back down). Then the backward induction begins by replacing this subgame with the payoffs of this equilibrium (−0.5,−0.5). Given that the final subgame is going to end in both countries backing down, country 2 prefers to escalate to reach this desirable conclusion, rather than to back down by itself beforehand. Since country 2 is escalating, country 1 prefers to ignore the provocation. This backward induction reasoning is reflected in the subgame perfect equilibrium path of Figure 6.9b, the path to final backing down. The equilibrium we have just found supports the payoffs (0,0). The strategies used by each country are as follows:

country 1:   ignore, then back down
country 2:   escalate, then back down

This is not the only subgame perfect equilibrium. Suppose that the equilibrium chosen in the final simultaneity subgame is (Doomsday, Doomsday). Then the backward induction begins by replacing this subgame with the payoffs of this equilibrium (−L,−L). Given that the final subgame is going to end in very large negative payoffs for both countries, country 2 prefers to back down early rather than to go nuclear. Since country 2 is backing down, country 1

[12]Saint Anselm would call it a number larger than which none can be imagined.

[13]According to some authorities, in the event of Doomsday, the world ends, too. See R. P. Turco et al., "Nuclear Winter: Global Consequences of Multiple Nuclear Explosions," *Science* 222 (23 Dec. 1983), 1283–1300.

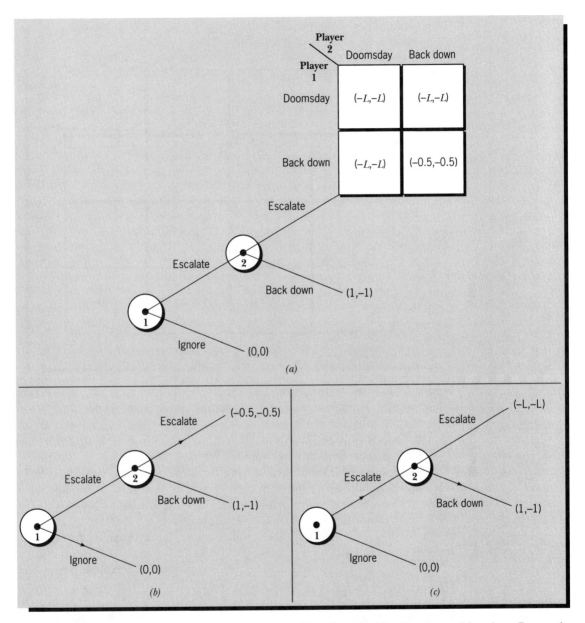

Figure 6.9. MAD, extensive form: (a) entire game; (b) path to final backing down; (c) path to Doomsday.

prefers to escalate. This backward induction reasoning is reflected in the subgame perfect equilibrium path of Figure 6.9c, the path to Doomsday. This second subgame perfect equilibrium supports the payoffs $(1,-1)$. The strategies used by each country are as follows:

	Country 2 e,D	e,b	b,D	b,b
Country 1 e,D	(−L,−L)	(−L,−L)	(1,−1) ⊙	(1,−1) *
e,b	(−L,−L)	(−0.5,−0.5)	(1,−1)	(1,−1)
i,D	(0,0) *	(0,0)	(0,0)	(0,0)
i,b	(0,0) *	(0,0) ⊙	(0,0)	(0,0)

Figure 6.10.   MAD, normal form: b = Back down; D = Doomsday; e = Escalate; i = Ignore; * = equilibrium; circled * = subgame perfect equilibrium.

country 1:   escalate, then Doomsday
country 2:   back down, then Doomsday

MAD was played at least once, during the Cuban missile crisis of 1962. The crisis was precipitated by the U.S. discovery of Soviet nuclear missiles on the island of Cuba. Instead of ignoring the incident, the United States escalated the crisis by quarantining Cuba, an act just short of war. At the brink, rather than going to all-out nuclear war, the USSR backed down, agreeing to remove its missiles from Cuba.[14] This is precisely the behavior that the inventors of the doctrine of mutually assured destruction had in mind. Each superpower had a credible threat to use its nuclear forces. Given that these threats were credible, a country that provoked a confrontation would not take the final escalatory step toward the nuclear showdown. Instead, that country would have to back down at the brink, thus losing the confrontation.

These are not the only equilibria of MAD. To make the other equilibria easier to see, Figure 6.10 shows the normal form of MAD. The normal form is 4 × 4, since each country has two choices to make at each of two information

[14]In a face-saving gesture for the USSR, the United States agreed to remove U.S. missiles that had been in Turkey for several years.

sets. As you look at these strategies, you immediately see a problem. If country 1 ignores the provocation at the start, then country 1 should never have a chance to back down later. So the complete plan of play (ignore, then back down) appears to be self-contradictory. Appearances are deceiving, however. The reason we require *complete* plans of play is to be ready for all contingencies, including the contingency that not everything goes according to plan. Of course, this raises the further question, why doesn't everything go according to plan? And if it doesn't, why isn't that included in the description of the game? These are tough questions, and they have vexed game theorists increasingly in recent years.[15]

As you can see from Figure 6.10, MAD has three pure strategy equilibria in addition to its two subgame perfect equilibria. Two of these—[(ignore, Doomsday), (escalate, Doomsday)] and [(ignore, back down), (escalate, Doomsday)]—have payoffs equivalent to those of the subgame perfect equilibrium where country 1 backs down. Their imperfection shows up later, in the parts of the game that should not be reached if everything goes according to plan. Their imperfection would be major, should country 1 escalate by mistake. This mistake would trigger Doomsday by country 2—just as in the movie *Dr. Strangelove*. The other pure strategy equilibrium—[escalate, Doomsday), (back down, back down)]—has payoffs equivalent to those of the subgame perfect equilibrium where country 1 escalates and country 2 backs down. This equilibrium again could have a Strangelovian ending. Suppose that country 2 escalates by mistake after country 1 has escalated. Then, according to the rest of the plan, country 1 goes Doomsday. This kind of nuclear nightmare, based on the possibility of mistakes, is the dark side of the MAD doctrine. A mistake by either side in this game could have disastrous consequences.

MAD has, in addition to the five pure strategy equilibria, an infinite number of mixed strategy equilibria. We will construct one of these now; the rest are left for the problem section. Suppose that country 2 uses the strategy (escalate, then Doomsday). Then country 1 can play the strategy (ignore, then back down) with probability .5 and the strategy (ignore, then Doomsday) with probability .5. This situation is tantamount to ignoring the provocation every time at the first move and then interchanging on backing down and Doomsday at the second move. Both strategies in this mixture pay zero. However, since these strategies put positive probability on a move with a credibility problem, Doomsday, they, too, are imperfect and so are not candidates for a solution.

The two subgame perfect equilibria meet the requirements for a solution for MAD. They represent equally credible doctrines of how to behave in the event of an international incident. The first equilibrium endorses brinkmanship, that is, both countries go to the very brink of destruction before both back down simultaneously. The second doctrine makes the escalatory ladder very short (a

---

[15]Chapter 8 studies a model in which mistakes happen by chance, with a small probability. If a mistake happens in the middle of a game that calls into question the very rationality of the other player, things get really complicated fast. See Philip Remy, "Rationality in Extensive Form Games," *Journal of Economic Perspectives* 6 (1992):103–18.

single escalation step), and has the perpetrator of the incident back down quickly. However, this quick resolution to the conflict relies on the mutual threat of destruction—credible in this case. If something should go wrong, in particular if player 2 should fail to back down as planned, then mutually assured destruction would be triggered. It might seem unsatisfactory for a game to have two solutions as different as these two. However, we might wonder whether one of these solutions should be excluded on other grounds.[16]

⚏ 6.6 Credible Quantity Competition: Cournot–Stackelberg Equilibrium ■ ■ ■ ■ ■ ■ ■ ■ ■ ■ ■ ■

We now turn to market games that have subgames. The first such games we will consider have quantity competition, hence, Cournot competition. In the original Cournot model, all firms move simultaneously, so there are no subgames. In the model we are about to study, one firm sends its quantity to market first. This sort of competition is named Stackelberg competition, after the economist who first studied it.[17] Putting the Cournot quantity element and the Stackelberg sequence element together results in Cournot–Stackelberg competition. This is the competition presented in this section.

Consider the market game in Section 5.1. Market price, P, satisfies

$$P = 130 - Q$$

where Q is market quantity, the sum of firm 1's and firm 2's quantities. Each firm has a constant average and marginal cost = $10. Firm 1 ships its quantity, x_1, to market first. Firm 2 sees how much firm 1 shipped and then ships its quantity, x_2, to market. The sum of quantities shipped equals quantity Q, which then determines price. The firms' profits are the market price times the quantity they shipped, minus their costs. Each firm has constant average and marginal cost $c = \$10$. We will now see that *the unique subgame perfect equilibrium of Cournot–Stackelberg competition is the* **Cournot–Stackelberg equilibrium.**

We start at the final subgame. Firm 2 has just observed firm 1's shipment, x_1. Firm 2 thus faces the following demand curve:

$$P = (130 - x_1) - x_2$$

where the intercept $(130 - x_1)$ reflects the fact that firm 2 only gets a residual demand, what is left after firm 1's goods are sold. Firm 2 now maximizes

---

[16]For a theory of how to select a unique equilibrium for a game such as that in Figure 6.10, see John Harsanyi and Reinhard Selten, *A General Theory of Equilibrium Selection in Games* (Cambridge: MIT Press, 1988).

[17]See Heinrich Freiherr von Stackelberg, *The Theory of the Market Economy* (London: William Hodges: 1952). Originally published in German in 1934.

profits,

$$\max \; u_2(\mathbf{x}) = x_2(130 - x_1 - x_2 - 10)$$

with respect to its own quantity, x_2. The first-order condition for profit maximization is that marginal profit equals zero. Differentiating with respect to firm 2's quantity, we get

$$0 = \frac{\partial u_2}{\partial x_2} = 120 - x_1 - 2x_2$$

Solving this marginal profit condition, we get firm 2's profit-maximizing shipments to market:

$$x_2 = g(x_1) = 60 - \frac{x_1}{2}$$

Notice that firm 2's strategy is a function of firm 1's shipments. For every possible shipment by firm 1 from 0 to 130, firm 2 has a response. The most general possible strategy for firm 2 would be an arbitrary function $x_2 = g(x_1)$. This is the first time, but not the last, that we will encounter a game where a player's strategy is an entire function. As we shall soon see, having a function for a strategy puts extreme demands on credibility.

Since firm 2 has maximized profits on its subgame, it has played the subgame equilibrium. We can now use backward induction to return to the start of the game and to firm 1's decision of how much to ship, x_1. Firm 1 faces the original demand, but also takes into account the profit-maximizing reaction by firm 2 contained in the function $g(x_1)$. Thus, firm 1 wants to maximize its profits, which are given by

$$u_1(\mathbf{x}) = [130 - x_1 - g(x_1) - 10]x_1$$

Firm 1 has induced firm 2's sales backward, using profit maximization as a guide. Since firm 2's profit-maximizing sales are a linear function of firm 1's shipments, we can substitute into firm 1's profit function to get

$$u_1(\mathbf{x}) = \left(120 - x_1 - 60 + \frac{x_1}{2}\right)x_1$$

At this point in the argument, firm 1's profits depend only on its own shipments, x_1. Taking the derivative of utility and setting it equal to zero yields

$$0 = 60 - x_1$$

This is the Cournot–Stackelberg equilibrium value of firm 1's shipments, $x_1^* = 60$.

Here is how the subgame perfect equilibrium path is played. Firm 1 ships 60 units. Firm 2, seeing these 60 units shipped, ships $60 - 60/2 = 30$ units. The total shipments are $Q = 60 + 30 = 90$, and the market equilibrium price is $P = 130 - 90 = \$40$. Compare this to the outcome of Cournot competition between the same firms (recall section 5.7). Since the firms' products are identical, Cournot competition where the firms ship to market simultaneously leads to a symmetrical situation ($x_1 = x_2 = 40$) and a market price of $50. Each firm has a one-half market share. However, when firm 1 gets to ship first and firm 2 responds by maximizing profits, then firm 1 gets a two-thirds market share as opposed to a one-third share for firm 2. Firm 1 enjoys a **first mover advantage** in Cournot–Stackelberg competition. Also, more units are shipped to market (60 + 30 = 90) and buyers enjoy a lower price ($130 – $90 = $40).

If we relax the assumption that c = $10 and allow for other values of c, we find that the firm that moves first will retain its first mover advantage and its market share as long as average variable costs are the same for both firms. It takes a substantial cost advantage for the firm that moves second to offset the advantage of the firm that moves first (see problem 6).

The solution we have just computed is the unique subgame perfect equilibrium to the Cournot–Stackelberg market game and so must be its solution. This does not mean that this is the only equilibrium to this extensive form market game. There are many other equilibria, but all of them have a credibility problem. For some of these, the credibility problem is enormous.

Here is just one example. If you follow this example, you should be able to come up with as many others as you want. We will construct an imperfect equilibrium that supports the Cournot outcome, where each firm sells 40 units. The idea is to create a noncredible threat on the part of firm 2, which, despite its lack of credibility, firm 1 believes. The trick that makes this easy is to have firm 2 do something really stupid—like flood the market with its product—if firm 1 ships anything other than 40 units. Here is a noncredible, market-flooding strategy for firm 2:

$$x_2 = 40 \text{ if } x_1 = 40$$
$$x_2 = 120 \text{ otherwise}$$

This strategy guarantees a price no greater than marginal cost unless firm 1 ships the quantity x_1 = 40. Note the credibility problem that pervades this strategy. If firm 1 shipped 42 units, firm 2 would make a lot of money by shipping 21 units. The resulting market price of $130 – $63 = $67/unit would lead to a profit margin of $67 – $10 = $57/unit, and so firm 2 would make 21($57) = $1197. However, since firm 1 did not ship 40 units, firm 2's strategy says it must ship 120 units instead. This floods the market, and these units have to be given away. Firm 2 loses a lot of money, (120 units)(–$10) = –$1200. This is a pretty high price to pay to keep a promise that isn't worth keeping in the first place. Try explaining this strategy to the stockholders at the next annual meeting.

To see whether you understand, see if you can construct an equilibrium like the preceding one, with firm 1 shipping 50 units instead of 40. Threats like that embodied in firm 2's function, which involve dire consequences (like market flooding) in the event that things don't go according to a player's plan, are called *dire threats* and the strategies that embody them, *dire strategies*. Dire strategies, which are triggered by deviation from what a player is aiming for, are also called *trigger strategies*. These are especially important in repeated games, presented in Chapter 7. If you know you are playing a market game against somebody rational, or somebody who has to answer to stockholders (which is roughly the same thing), you don't have to take dire threats seriously unless they are credible. And you can check for credibility by asking yourself whether carrying out this threat will pay your opponent when it comes time for the threat to be carried out.

⬛ 6.7 Credible Price Competition: Bertrand–Stackelberg Equilibrium ■ ■ ■ ■ ■ ■ ■ ■ ■ ■ ■

In Bertrand competition, price is the strategic variable. The Stackelberg element adds sequence to the moves. So in Bertrand–Stackelberg competition, firms use price as their strategic variable and one of the firms, say, firm 1, goes first. In the event of perfect substitutes, it is easy to see what the subgame perfect equilibrium of such competition is.

To keep things concrete, let's stick to the model of the last section. Demand is given by

$$P = 130 - Q$$

The two firms produce and sell perfect substitutes. Unit costs are constant at $10. All buyers are informed, so the lowest-priced firm gets all the customers. If prices tie, then the each firm gets half the customers.

To find a subgame perfect equilibrium, we start with the final subgames, where firm 2 is reacting to the price firm 1 has announced, p_1. Unless firm 2 matches or undercuts this price, it makes no sales and therefore makes no money. If firm 2 undercuts this price ever so slightly, say, by the minimum monetary unit, then it gets the entire market to itself, which is always better than splitting the market. Finally, firm 2 would like to monopolize the market if possible. This is a fairly realistic goal, since firm 2 only has to beat one price, p_1, and that price is already posted. Thus, if firm 1 charges a price above $70, the monopoly price, then firm 2 would want to go down to $70. Let $0.01 be the minimum monetary unit. Then firm 2's profit-maximizing response to firm 1's price is

$p_2 = \$70$, if p_1 is greater than $70

$p_2 = p_1 - \$0.01$, if p_1 is between $70 and $10.02

$p_2 = p_1$, if $p_1 = \$10.01$

$p_2 = \$10$ otherwise

Notice that once again firm 2's strategy is a function, $p_2 = g(p_1)$. Unlike the case of Cournot–Stackelberg competition, this function is not a straight line, but rather three straight-line segments spliced together.

Facing this pattern of profit-maximizing responses, firm 1 is in a real quandary. Any price it charges that is above $10.02 will get underbid. Firm 1's situation is not good. The best it can do is call out a price of $10.01. It makes almost no money at this price—the profit margin is only a penny. Firm 2 will match this price and both firms will make a pittance.

You can show that this solution can be generalized to the case in which firms have constant average costs c other than $10. You can also adapt this solution to cover cost asymmetries. These generalizations are left as end-of-chapter problems.

Besides the profit-maximizing function given here, which does not have a credibility problem, there are plenty of response functions that do. These are typically of the form, "I won't undercut you if you charge the price I want." A function for this would be

$$p_2 = g(p_1) = p_1 \text{ if } p_1 \geq p^*$$

or

$$= \text{average cost if } p_1 < p^*,$$

where p^* is the price that firm 2 wants.

The trouble is, such a promise is inherently not credible. The firm that moves last can undercut you any time it wants, if you move first. This is one reason that, in auctions, all the firms seal their bids or all the bids are taken out simultaneously. Having to make your final bid first is a serious disadvantage. And this disadvantage to moving first is just the opposite of getting to ship first in Cournot competition—this is the **second mover advantage.**

⚏ 6.8 Differentiated Products ■ ■ ■ ■ ■ ■ ■ ■ ■ ■ ■ ■ ■ ■ ■ ■ ■

Section 5.7 showed that differentiating the product mutes the differences between Cournot and Bertrand competitions. The same is true when these two types of competition have a Stackelberg component. Also, the extremely low prices characteristic of Bertrand–Stackelberg competition are not observed once firms differentiate their products.

Consider the following example (repeated from section 5.7). Firm 1 faces the demand

$$x_1 = 180 - p_1 - (p_1 - \text{average } p)$$

where average p is the market average price. Rearranging the demand equation, we get

$$x_1 = 180 - 1.5p_1 + 0.5p_2$$

Similarly, firm 2 faces the demand curve

$$x_2 = 180 + 0.5p_1 + 1.5p_2$$

Average costs are constant and equal $20. Firm 1 sets its price first. We will see that all profits are positive and substantial at the subgame perfect equilibrium.

We start, as always, with a final subgame. Firm 2 wants to maximize its profits, given the price firm 1 has set:

max $(p_2 - 20)(180 + 0.5p_1 - 1.5p_2)$

with respect to p_2. This maximum occurs where marginal profit vanishes:

$0 = 210 + 0.5p_1 - 3p_2$

Solving for the optimal price p_2^*, we get

$$p_2^* = g(p_1) = 70 + \frac{p_1}{6}$$

Notice that this is a nice, smooth pricing function, rather than the kinked function we saw with perfect substitutes. Since this pricing strategy maximizes profits, it is the subgame equilibrium for the final subgame played by firm 2 alone.

When firm 1 goes to set its price, it expects firm 2 to maximize its profits. This means replacing firm 2's price, p_2, by its pricing strategy, $g(p_1)$. Firm 1 then faces the task of maximizing the following profits, given the price firm 2 will set:

$$\max \ (p_1 - 20) \left[180 - 1.5p_1 + 0.5 \left(70 + \frac{p_1}{6} \right) \right]$$

with respect to p_1. The maximum occurs at

$$0 = 215 - \left(\frac{17}{12} \right) p_1 + (p_1 - 20) \left(-\frac{17}{12} \right)$$

The profit-maximizing price for the firm that goes first is

$$p_1^* = \frac{2920}{34}, \text{ or } \$85.88$$

Firm 2, which moves last, charges a slightly lower price than firm 1 does:

$$p_2^* = 70 + \frac{p_1^*}{6} = 70 + \$14.31 = \$84.31$$

The reason this is happening is that firm 1 has charged the best price it can to maximize profits. The price firm 1 charges allows firm 2 to undercut it advantageously. Notice that these Stackelberg–Bertrand prices are somewhat higher than $84, which is the Bertrand solution when both firms move simultaneously (see section 5.7). Firm 1 sells less than firm 2 does, $x_1^* = 93.34 < 96.48 = x_2^*$. This sales advantage translates into profits as well, as firm 2 makes more money:

$$u_2^* = (96.48)(84.31 - 20) = \$6204.63$$

whereas

$$u_1^* = (93.34)(85.88 - 20) = \$6149.24.$$

Since these firms have the same costs and equally competitive products, the sole reason for firm 2's higher profits is its second mover advantage.

You can show that Cournot–Stackelberg leads to practically the same result as Bertrand–Stackelberg in this market. You can also show that, in addition to these subgame perfect equilibria, there are many imperfect equilibria involving noncredible threats and promises. This work is left for the end-of-chapter problems.

♦ 6.9 This Offer Is Good for a Limited Time Only[18] ■ ■

How many times have you heard this phrase on advertisements on television? Should you believe it? The Nobel Prize–winning economist Ronald Coase gives us plenty of reason for doubt. When the good offered is durable, and has a long shelf life, then the offer has a serious credibility problem.

Here is an extreme case. A seller has 10 Civil War commemorative chess sets in stock, which can be stored at no cost for two periods. The seller can charge two prices in a period, either $100 or $20. There are 10 fully informed and interested buyers in the market, each of whom wants at most one Civil War commemorative chess set. Five of the buyers are willing to pay as much as $100 for a set, whereas the other five buyers are only willing to pay as much as $20 for a set. Buyers are indifferent as to whether they buy now or later.

The seller wants to make as much money as possible from selling these sets and prefers getting the money sooner rather than later. To get this result means charging a price of $100 in the first period, selling five sets, pocketing the $500 in revenue, and leaving the rest of the sets in the warehouse. This is much better than selling all the sets for $20 each in the first period, which only nets $200. If you watch television, you can imagine such a seller saying, "This offer is good for a limited time only." That limited time is period 1. The seller's complete plan of play is to post a price of $100/set. In the first period, five sets sell at this price; in the second period, no sets sell at this price. The limited time is exactly one period.

Suppose that the seller chose this plan and now we are in period 2. There are still five sets sitting in the warehouse, and there are still five buyers willing to pay $20 apiece for them. It is not credible for the seller at this point to say, "I refuse to sell these sets." The seller wants to sell these five sets for $20, pocketing an extra $100. The strategy to hold the price at $100 has lost its credibility. Those who would have bought in the first period, sensing the credibility problem, should wait until the second period, and so enjoy their 80% price reduction.

Extreme cases call for extreme measures. There is a solution to this seller's credibility problem: *destroy five of the Civil War commemorative chess sets!* This action definitely limits the offer to one period and prevents the first-period

---

[18]This material is inspired in part by Ronald Coase, "Durability and Monopoly," *Journal of Law and Economics* 15 (1972):143–49.

buyers from waiting for the price reduction in the second period. This situation illustrates in an especially graphic way the principle of **costly commitment,** which pervades economic life. Every time a business incurs a fixed cost, it incurs a costly commitment to some future action, which it may or may not take. A fixed cost represents the cost of a forgone opportunity, here the opportunity to sell Civil War commemorative chess sets in the second period.

Companies that sell things that last, **durable goods,** have to worry about the credibility of their offers. A number of durable goods industries have evolved rather ingenious techniques to make their claims credible. In textbook publishing, for example, the answer is called "the second edition." The first edition of a textbook is good for roughly 3 years, and this is the time limit during which the book is offered for sale. The second edition, if there is one, is waiting in the wings. So even if there are some copies of the first edition left in the warehouse when the 3 years are up, you won't see them in any bookstore. What you will see is the second edition instead. The model year in automobiles operates on the same principle, only with a shorter revision span. You should look for such patterns in other industries.

The next time you hear the words, "This offer is good for a limited time only," ask yourself whether there is a good reason to believe them before you run out to buy whatever is being offered. And if you are working for a company trying to sell its merchandise with these words, ask yourself whether your company has incurred any costly commitment that might give them weight.

◆ SUMMARY

1. A subgame is any part of a game that can be played by itself. Every game with perfect information has subgames.

2. A credibility problem is present if, at the moment when a threat (or promise) must actually be carried out, a player does not maximize utility by carrying it out. Players who make such threats or promises and then do not carry them out lose their credibility.

3. A strategy that is subgame perfect will always be credible. All strategies and equilibria that fail the test of subgame perfection are called imperfect; they have credibility problems.

4. The solution of a game in extensive form is subgame perfect. Subgame perfect equilibria are found by backward induction, solving a game starting with its final subgames.

5. Whether a threat or promise made by an opponent is credible or not depends on what type of payoffs that opponent has. If a threat or promise is not credible, a player will not have an incentive to carry it out when the time comes.

6. The doctrine of mutually assured destruction holds that nuclear deterrence is credible. This doctrine relies heavily on a particular subgame perfect equilibrium.

7. Cournot competition in a market game where one firm goes first is called Cournot–Stackelberg competition. The Cournot–Stackelberg equilibrium of such competition is its subgame perfect equilibrium. The first mover in such competition has an advantage.

8. Bertrand competition in a market game where one firm goes first is called Bertrand–Stackelberg competition. The Bertrand–Stackelberg equilibrium of such competition is its subgame perfect equilibrium. The second mover in such competition has an advantage.

9. Product differentiation mutes the differences between Cournot–Stackelberg and Bertrand–Stackelberg equilibria. However, the first or second mover advantages persist.

10. Credibility concerns help explain why publishers and durable goods manufacturers have instituted the second edition and the model year.

▞ KEY TERMS

subgame	Cournot–Stackelberg equilibrium
credibility problem	first mover advantage
subgame perfect equilibrium	Bertrand–Stackelberg equilibrium
type of opponent	second mover advantage
reluctant volunteer	costly commitment
Mutually Assured Destruction	durable good

▞ PROBLEMS

1. In the perfect information version of Telex versus IBM, suppose that IBM goes first. How does this affect the solution? Is there still a credibility problem with the strategy Smash?

2. Suppose that Centipede has three moves. If player 2 waits at his or her move, then the money on the table quadruples again and player 1 either takes it all or splits it. Draw the extensive form and solve. How would you play this game if you were player 1 and you thought player 2 was a nice opponent?

3. Solve the Conscription game when the bonus $b = \$500$ and the cost of serving $c = \$400$. How does this solution differ from that when $b = \$300$? Interpret your answer in terms of an all-volunteer army.

4. MAD has a lot of mixed strategy equilibria; you saw one in the text. Find two more. Why aren't these mixed strategy equilibria credible?

5. Suppose in MAD that at the endgame, if both players back down, the payoffs are -1.5 each. How does this affect the solution? Why is the solution so sensitive to the endgame payoffs?

6. In Cournot–Stackelberg competition, each firm faces the market demand $P = 90 - Q$. Each firm has unit cost $= \$30$ for each unit it ships to market.

Firm 1 moves first. Find the Cournot–Stackelberg equilibrium. Show that firm 1 has a big first mover advantage, evidenced by its profits.

7. In problem 6, suppose that firm 2, which moves second, has unit cost = c. What value must c be in order for firm 2 to have the same market share as firm 1 in the Cournot–Stackelberg equilibrium? This cost advantage is a measure of how big the first mover advantage is.

8. Find an imperfect equilibrium for the Cournot–Stackelberg model of section 6.6 with $x_1^* = 30$. (*Hint:* Try to mimic the dire strategy given in the text.)

9. In Bertrand–Stackelberg competition, each firm i faces the market demand

$$x_i = 90 - p_i - (p_i - \text{average } p)$$

Each firm has unit cost = \$10 for each unit it ships to market. Firm 1 moves first. Find the Bertrand–Stackelberg equilibrium. How does it compare to the equilibrium when both firms move simultaneously?

10. Solve for the Cournot–Stackelberg equilibrium of the market game given in section 6.8. It helps to write the demand system so that price is a function of quantity. You can find the necessary inverse demand system in Chapter 5.

11. Give three examples of industries or individual firms that have found a way to make This Offer Is Good for a Limited Time Only a credible strategy. Are there are industries for which this strategy is automatically credible?

▓ APPENDIX. ULTIMATUMS IN THE LABORATORY

Although games as complicated as MAD have not been played in the laboratory, simpler games with similar strategic content have. This appendix looks at one of these, called Ultimatum, shown in Figure 6.11. There are 2 players, 1 and 2, and \$3 on the table. Player 1, who moves first, offers either \$1 or \$2 to player 2. Player 2 hears the offer, and says either yes or no. If player 2 says yes, then player 2 keeps the money offered and player 1 gets what is left. Thus, if player 1 offers \$1 and player 2 accepts, the payoff is \$1 to player 2 and \$3 − \$1 = \$2 to player 1. All this is shown in the extensive form, Figure 6.11*a*.

The subgame perfect equilibrium of Ultimatum is easy to find. Player 2 says yes to whatever is offered (both \$2 and \$1 are better than 0), and player 1 offers \$1 (\$2 is better than \$1). However, this is not the only equilibrium. The easiest way to see this is by looking at the normal form of Ultimatum in Figure 6.11*b*. The matrix is 2 × 4, since player 2 has four pure strategies (two choices at each of two information sets). As you can see from the arrow diagram, there are three pure strategy equilibria. One of these, [offer \$1, (yes to \$2, yes to \$1)], is subgame perfect and is denoted by the circled *. The other two, [offer \$2, (no

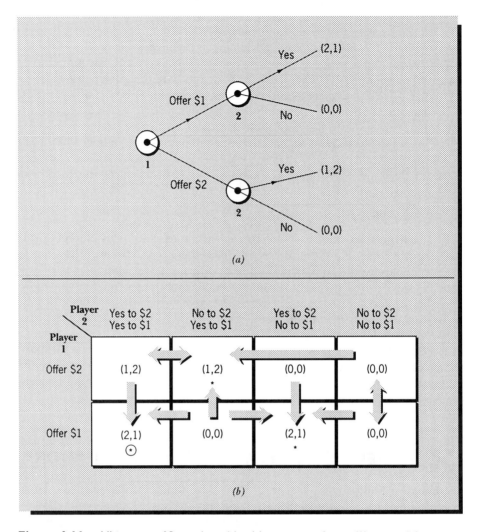

Figure 6.11.   Ultimatum, $3 on the table: (a) extensive form; (b) normal form.

to $1, yes to $2)] and [offer $1, (no to $2, yes to $1)], are imperfect. Their imperfection is manifest in the fact that they involve dominated strategies on the part of player 2. Either of the strategies

 yes to $2, no to $1

 no to $2, yes to $1

is dominated by the strategy

 yes to $2, yes to $1

The solution of Ultimatum in extensive form is its unique subgame perfect equilibrium; in normal form the solution is its unique undominated equilibrium.

An internationally renowned team of researchers recently ran a version of Ultimatum in the laboratory to see to what extent human subjects actually play the solution.[19] To defend against the criticism that the results might somehow be country specific, the experiments were run in four widely dispersed countries: the United States, Slovenia, Israel, and Japan. In the U.S. version of the experiment, instead of $3 on the table, $10 was on the table. Payoffs were calibrated by country to the same level of purchasing power and were made in the local currency. The minimum monetary unit was 5 cents. In this situation a lot of pure strategies are available to the players. For player 1, the set of pure strategies is {$0, $0.05, . . . ,$10}, that is, offer any amount between $0 and $10 that is divisible by 5 cents. There are 201 such strategies. For each of player 1's 201 pure strategies, player 2 says either yes or no, for a total of 2^{201} pure strategies. This is an immense number of strategies.

At a subgame perfect equilibrium, player 1 offers either $0.05 or $0 and player 2 accepts all offers. However, nothing like that happened in the laboratories of these four countries. Only about 1% of all offers observed were consistent with subgame perfection. Most offers were in the range of $4 to $5. For the United States and Slovenia, the modal offer was $5; for Japan and Israel, $4. Moreover, the observed frequency of acceptance was never 100%. In the United States, for example, an offer of $3 or less by player 1 was rejected almost 75% of the time. Even an offer of $5 was rejected 10% of the time. These data are not consistent with any equilibrium, much less the subgame perfect equilibrium. Human subjects find it more or less impossible to play an equilibrium of Ultimatum.[20]

Nevertheless, there appears to be a certain amount of rationality contained in this behavior. Suppose that player 1 knew the function relating the probability of acceptance to the size of the offer and maximized expected utility with respect to the offer accordingly. Then, for each of the four countries, player 1's maximum expected utility occurs at the mode of the actually observed offers for that country. What was observed in these experiments makes a certain amount of sense when we think of it as out-of-equilibrium behavior. We will return to the themes of bounded rationality and out-of-equilibrium behavior in Chapter 8.

[19]See Alvin E. Roth, Vesna Prasnikar, Masahiro Okuno-Fujiwara, and Shmuel Zamir, "Bargaining and Market Behavior in Jerusalem, Ljubljana, Pittsburgh, and Tokyo: An Experimental Study," *American Economic Review* 81 (1991):1068–95.

[20]Remember, any payoff vector of Ultimatum can be supported by some pure strategy equilibrium. For example, the payoff vector ($5,$5) is supported by the imperfect equilibrium (offer $5, reject any offer except $5).

CHAPTER 7

Repeated Games

Many, if not most, of the strategic interactions in our daily lives take place more than once. There is an enormous difference between a single date with someone, and dating that same person more than once. In many areas of business—durable goods, insurance, financial services, and meals and entertainment, to name just a few—repeat buyers are essential to profitability. This chapter examines *repeated games,* games where the same players meet to play a game more than once. Repeating a zero-sum game does not create anything new, strategically. For variable-sum games, however, repetition creates exciting new possibilities for new outcomes, some of which are far more attractive than the outcome of the game played once. Repeated games capture an important part of what enduring relationships are all about.

The chapter begins with strategies and payoffs for repeated games. One reason that repeated games possess such attractive possibilities is that they have so many more strategies than do games played once. Finite repetition of a Cournot market game is not enough for an industry to maximize profits, a fact well known to the members of OPEC. However, finite repetition of a variable-sum game with multiple equilibria creates many new payoff opportunities. A theorem about **finitely repeated games,** called the folk theorem for finitely repeated games, is introduced. The folk theorem describes subgame perfect equilibria of a repeated game and shows how even finite repetition can approach an efficient outcome. Discussion next turns to **infinitely repeated games,** which are fundamentally different from finitely repeated games. Infinitely repeated games are especially relevant to corporate interactions, where the corporation is viewed as having an infinite life ahead of it. An analogous folk theorem for infinitely repeated games is used to describe subgame perfect equilibria of infinitely repeated Cournot and Bertrand market games. The pricing pattern prevalent in the ready-to-eat cereals industry, called price leadership, illustrates some of the issues in industrial economics that surround these equilibria.

▓ 7.1 Strategies and Payoffs for Games Played Twice ■

Consider a generic 2×2 game in normal form, two players with two strategies each, the only difference being that this game is going to be played twice. Figure 7.1 depicts the situation schematically. There are four possible outcomes of the first play of the game. Each of these becomes a **possible history** leading up to the second play of the game. Each line from a cell of the initial matrix to the second matrix in Figure 7.1 represents a possible history. The game that is played each time is called the **one-shot game,** and the game that consists of all plays of the one-shot game is called the *repeated game.* In Figure 7.1, each of the five matrices is an instance of the one-shot game, whereas the entire figure represents the repeated game.

We can now define what a strategy, a complete plan of play, looks like for the game in Figure 7.1. Call the two strategies of the one-shot game Left (L) and Right (R). A strategy specifies what a player does at the first repetition, either L or R. Next, a strategy specifies what a player does at the second repetition, following each logically possible history leading to it. Since there are four possible histories and two choices for each possible history, there are 2^4 possible choices at this stage. Multiplying, we have $(2)(2^4) = 32$ strategies for the entire repeated game. These strategies are listed in Figure 7.2.

Some of these strategies are important enough to get special names. Strategy 1 plays left at the first repetition and plays left at the second repetition after any possible history. Such a strategy is an **unconditional strategy.** Strategy 32 is likewise unconditional, playing right. Strategy 16 is called a **rotation strategy.** It plays left at the first repetition, then plays right in the second repetition after any possible history. Strategy 17 is the reverse rotation. Strategy 6 is called a **trigger strategy.** This strategy plays left in the first repetition and plays left in the second repetition if and only if the opponent played left in the previous history. Trigger strategies are useful when you want your opponent to play only

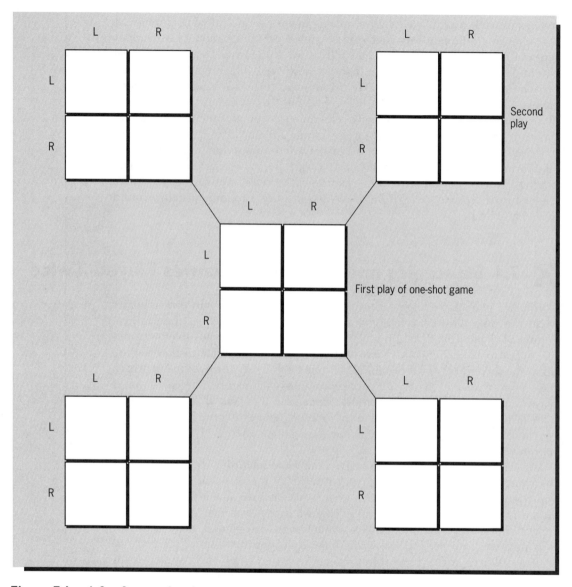

Figure 7.1.   A 2 × 2 game played twice.

one pure strategy in the one-shot game. Strategy 6 wants the opponent to play left. Strategy 27 is the trigger strategy for right.

To write down the normal form for a 2 × 2 game played twice, we would have to write down a 32 × 32 matrix. The matrices only get bigger with further repetition. There must be a better way to analyze repeated games, and there is—the extensive form. Repetition creates subgames. The 2 × 2 repeated game played twice has four final subgames. By exploiting the subgame structure

Strategy No.	Round 1	After (L,L)	After (L,R)	After (R,L)	After (R,R)
1	L	L	L	L	L
2	L	L	L	L	R
3	L	L	L	R	L
4	L	L	L	R	R
5	L	L	R	L	L
6	L	L	R	L	R
7	L	L	R	R	L
8	L	L	R	R	R
9	L	R	L	L	L
10	L	R	L	L	R
11	L	R	L	R	L
12	L	R	L	R	R
13	L	R	R	L	L
14	L	R	R	L	R
15	L	R	R	R	L
16	L	R	R	R	R
17	R	L	L	L	L
18	R	L	L	L	R
19	R	L	L	R	L
20	R	L	L	R	R
21	R	L	R	L	L
22	R	L	R	L	R
23	R	L	R	R	L
24	R	L	R	R	R
25	R	R	L	L	L
26	R	R	L	L	R
27	R	R	L	R	L
28	R	R	L	R	R
29	R	R	R	L	L
30	R	R	R	L	R
31	R	R	R	R	L
32	R	R	R	R	R

Figure 7.2. Strategies for Playing a 2 × 2 Game Twice.

inherent in repeated games, we can solve them without having to spend our lives writing down enormous matrices.

Payoffs for repeated games are reasonably straightforward. All we have to do is somehow add up the payoffs at each round. The most general way to do this is in terms of *present value,* the phenomenon according to which a dollar today is worth more than a dollar tomorrow. Let R be the discount factor, a number between 0 and 1. $R = 0$ means the future has no value; $R = 1$ means the future is just as important as the present. A payoff of \$1 T periods from now is worth \$1R^T now. Let $u_1(t)$ be player 1's payoff in repetition t. Then the present value for player 1 of a game played twice, u_1, is

$$u_1 = u_1(0) + Ru_1(1)$$

when the game starts now, at time $t = 0$. We define the present value for player 2 of a game played twice, u_2, similarly.

Here are two interpretations of the **discount factor.** One interpretation of R is as a discount factor purely for time. If r is the discount rate (often identified with the market interest rate), then the discount factor, R, satisfies

$$R = \frac{1}{(1 + r)}$$

An interest rate of 10% per period ($r = 0.1$) implies a discount factor of $1/1.1$ or $10/11$. At this discount factor, a dollar 10 periods from now is worth only $(10/11)^{10} = \$0.38$ today. A second interpretation of R is probabilistic. Under this interpretation, R is the **continuation probability,** the probability that the game will be played again. Suppose a player is uncertain whether a game will be continued or not. Then it makes sense to weight an uncertain future less than a certain present. A bird in the hand is better than two in the bush. Under either interpretation, we get exactly the same expression for u_1.

For all the finitely repeated games we study, we will set $R = 1$. Either the time between repetitions is very short, or the one-shot game is certain to be repeated. Also, we will normalize payoffs, so that payoffs from the repeated game have the same magnitude as the payoffs of the one-shot game. This is accomplished by dividing by the number of times the one-shot game is played, T. Thus, for a game played twice, we express the utility of player i in the one-shot game played twice, u_i, as

$$u_i = \left(\frac{1}{2}\right)[u_i(0) + u_i(1)]$$

Armed with payoffs and strategies, we are now ready to tackle some finitely repeated games. We turn to 2-person, zero-sum games first.

7.2 Two-person, Zero-sum Games Played More Than Once ■■■■■■■■■■■■■■■■■■■■■■■■

Solving a 2-person, zero-sum game played more than once is a cinch. Value isn't created when a zero-sum game is repeated. If the game is one in which both players break even when it is played once, then they continue to break even by playing their break-even strategy however many times the game is played. If the game is one in which player 1 can guarantee a positive payoff at player 2's expense, then player 1 can guarantee that positive payoff each and every time the game is played by using his or her winning strategy. Here are two examples.

Suppose that two firms are playing Competitive Advantage (Chapter 2) twice. The first time they play Competitive Advantage, the innovation is an MRI unit. The second time they play Competitive Advantage, the innovation is a positron emission tomography (PET) unit. Firm 1 has a dominant strategy to play Competitive Advantage played twice:

| first play: | firm 1 adopts the new technology |
| second play: | after any possible history, firm 1 adopts the new technology |

This is also a dominant strategy for firm 2 to play. An *equilibrium path* of a repeated game is what is observed each and every period when the players play a certain equilibrium. Along the equilibrium path of Competitive Advantage played twice, we observe that each firm adopts the new technology and gets a payoff of 0 each period. Just as in the equilibrium of the one-shot game, where $u_1 = u_2 = 0$, we get in the repeated game

$$u_1 = \frac{(0 + 0)}{2} = 0$$

and likewise for firm 2. If it is a dominant strategy to adopt the new technology next year, and it is a dominant strategy to adopt the new technology this year, then it is a dominant strategy to adopt the new technology both years.

Next, suppose that two television networks play Battle of the Networks (Chapter 2) twice. Since the networks run their programs every week, they actually play this game a lot more than twice—more like 52 times a year. Every week, network 1 enjoys a 4% viewer share advantage over network 2 if it plays its equilibrium strategy, Show a sitcom. Network 1 will, of course, stick with a winner, using the strategy

| first play: | show a sitcom |
| second play: | after any possible history, show a sitcom |

Firm 2 uses a similar strategy, only with "sitcom" replaced by "sports." The average viewer share advantage over 2 (or more) weeks is 4%, in favor of network 1. The equilibrium path of repeated Battle of the Networks is for network 1 to show a sitcom each period and for network 2 to show a sports show each period. This equilibrium is a subgame perfect equilibrium, since it programs an equilibrium on each of the four possible subgames that arise in the second play.

As you can see, nothing new happens when a 2-person, zero-sum game is repeated. You just get the same behavior and the same outcome over and over again. There really is nothing to correspond to a relationship in a 2-person, zero-sum game, no matter how often it is played. Things have the potential to be a lot more interesting when the game that is being repeated is variable sum. Even in that case, however, a lot depends on how many equilibria the one-shot game has.

7.3 Variable-Sum Games with a Single Equilibrium, Played Twice ■■■■■■■■■■■■■■■■■■■■■■■■■

Repeating a variable-sum game can give rise to a valuable relationship between the players. The major qualification to this concerns credibility. Since repeated

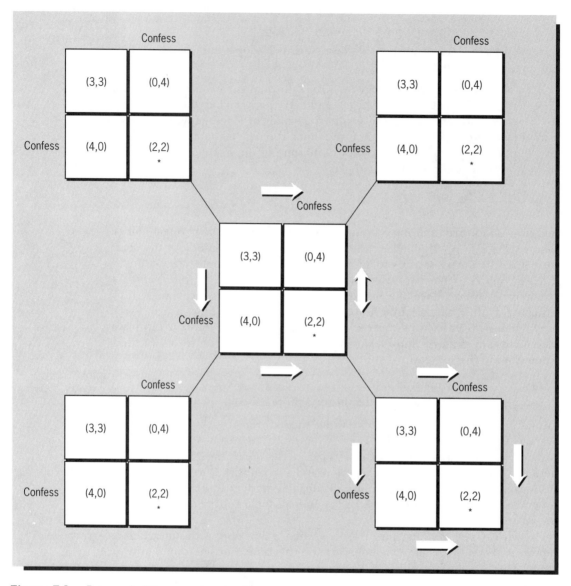

Figure 7.3. Prisoner's Dilemma, played twice.

games have a rich subgame structure, subgame perfection plays an especially prominent role in their solution. Whether repetition will create extra game value depends on how many equilibria the one-shot game has. If the one-shot game has a single equilibrium, then repetition is no more interesting than in a zero-sum game. The solution of a repeated game whose one-shot game has a unique equilibrium is that equilibrium played on every subgame.

We will prove this result for Prisoner's Dilemma played twice (see Figure

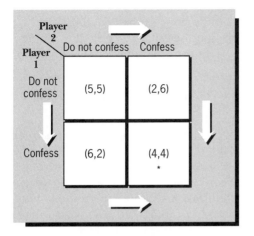

Figure 7.4. Prisoner's Dilemma, first play, after backward induction.

7.3). Prisoner's Dilemma played once has a unique equilibrium, where each player confesses. We can show, via backward induction, that the unique subgame perfect equilibrium of Prisoner's Dilemma played twice is for each player to confess on each subgame. As always with backward induction, we start with the final subgames. On each of the four final subgames, there is a unique equilibrium. Since a subgame perfect equilibrium must play an equilibrium on every subgame, and (confess, confess) is that subgame equilibrium, each player confesses on each subgame. This brings us back to the first play of the game, with the subgame equilibrium payoffs (2,2) added to each player's payoff. At the first play, there is again a unique equilibrium, with each player confessing (see Figure 7.4). The total payoff for the two plays of the game is 4 for each player, which gives an average payoff of $4/2 = 2$ per period. The complete plan of play for each player is the following unconditional strategy:

confess in the first period, and after every possible history

Credibility prevents the prisoners from reaching a better outcome than the one-shot equilibrium. A prisoner's promise not to confess in the second round, which is what it would take to get higher payoffs, just doesn't stand up to the scrutiny of credibility.

The result we have just shown for a 2×2 game with a unique equilibrium played twice is true for any game played finitely many times:

■ ■

Selten's Theorem. If a game with a unique equilibrium is played finitely many times, its solution is that equilibrium played each and every time.[1]

[1]Reinhard Selten, "A Simple Model of Imperfect Competition, Where 4 Are Few and 6 Are Many," *International Journal of Game Theory* 2 (1973):141–201, was the first to prove this in English.

Selten's theorem does not mean that there aren't other equilibria for such games. There always are other equilibria, but they all have credibility problems. Take Prisoner's Dilemma played twice. Here is a typical imperfect equilibrium:

first play: confess
second play: confess if at least one player confessed at the first play
                otherwise, do not confess

This strategy, when played by each player, has the same equilibrium path and payoffs as the subgame perfect equilibrium does. Its imperfection arises only on the subgame reached by the possible history (do not confess, do not confess) recorded in the first round. Since, according to the complete plan of each player, (confess, confess) is to be played in the first period, the possible history that activates the imperfection does not occur. If things did not go according to plan and both players unintentionally did not confess in the first period, each would face a serious credibility problem in the second period of this repeated game. Their strategy would tell them not to confess, but they could get a higher payoff by confessing.

The same principle that applies to finitely repeated Prisoner's Dilemma applies with equal force to finitely repeated Cournot or Bertrand market games when these have a unique Cournot or Bertrand equilibrium. The one-shot market game equilibrium, played each and every period, is the subgame perfect equilibrium path of the repeated market game (see problem 1 for details). The world market for oil, and especially the Organization of Petroleum Exporting Countries (OPEC) within that market, provides a good example of a repeated Cournot market game. To this market we now turn.

■■ 7.4 OPEC Drops Quotas[2] ■ ■ ■ ■ ■ ■ ■ ■ ■ ■ ■ ■ ■ ■ ■ ■ ■

The Organization of Petroleum Exporting Countries, **OPEC,** was founded in 1960. Led by Venezuela in the beginning, the oil-exporting countries who joined OPEC had as their goal raising world oil prices substantially above marginal cost. As long as the United States was an oil exporter, that is, until 1967, OPEC had no opportunity to realize this goal.

OPEC's magic moment came in 1973, in the wake of the Yom Kippur War. OPEC raised the price of a barrel of oil from $2 to $10, and the price increase stuck. This situation was helped by OPEC's embargo of oil to the United States—an embargo violated only by the then shah of Iran. OPEC repeated this success in 1979, driving prices up to a new record level, $30/barrel.

Like any cartel, OPEC was faced with the problem of maintaining the cartel price. Since price was substantially above marginal cost, each individual country had an incentive to produce and sell more oil and thereby make more money.

---

[2]This section draws on material from "OPEC Drops Its Quotas," *The Wall Street Journal,* January 19, 1993.

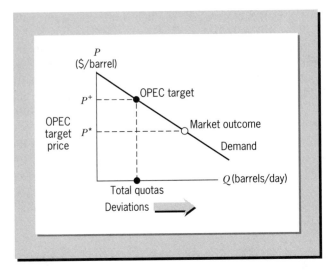

Figure 7.5. OPEC quotas.

This is just another reflection of the fact that a price near monopoly is not a one-shot game equilibrium.

OPEC decided to address the price maintenance problem by instituting a set of quotas, one for each of the 13 member countries. Saudi Arabia, the world's largest oil exporter, got the largest quota; Ecuador, the world's smallest oil exporter, the smallest. Bitter enemies, Iraq and Iran, got exactly the same quota. The total amount of the quotas led to a market quantity that would support the OPEC target price (see Figure 7.5). The OPEC target price was $30 (denoted P^+), corresponding to the total quotas supplied to buyers. The observed market price was $20 (denoted P^*), corresponding to the one-shot Cournot equilibrium.

The members of OPEC were aware of the unfortunate consequences to cartel profits of deviations by member countries. Nevertheless, each member continually exceeded its quota. Saudi Arabia, with a daily quota of 5 million barrels, was known at times to produce twice that (for instance, during the Gulf War).

One way, it would seem, for OPEC to escape this fate would be to exploit the efficiency-enhancing properties of repeated game equilibria. Unfortunately, for the cartel, two facts conspire to prevent this from occurring. One is that member countries are rapidly running out of oil. Both Venezuela and Indonesia expect to run out entirely by 2010. This makes the game finite in a hurry. Even if the countries act as if they are going to last forever, their oil is not. Second, given the structure of world demand for imported oil, there is a unique one-shot equilibrium involving the members of OPEC. Thus, Selten's theorem comes into play with a vengeance. The only subgame perfect, repeated game equilibrium is for all the members to cheat on their quotas each and every period—precisely what they did.

Even worse for OPEC, nonmember countries made major oil strikes in the 1970s and 1980s: the United Kingdom, Norway, and the Netherlands in the North Sea; Mexico, in the Gulf of Mexico; and the United States, on the north slope of Alaska. All these strikes made available vast new supplies of oil to the world market. OPEC saw the world market price in real terms steadily erode, until it returned to near 1973 levels.

Despite recurring pleas at OPEC oil ministers' meetings for discipline in the ranks, the countries continued to exceed their quotas by a hefty margin. At the beginning of 1993, OPEC quotas equaled 18 million barrels per day, whereas total OPEC daily sales were closer to 23 million barrels per day. The quotas had lost all force and all meaning by then. OPEC dropped them entirely on January 18, 1993, less than 20 years after its first great oil-price shock.

7.5 Variable-Sum Games with Multiple Equilibria, Played Finitely Many Times ■■■■■■■■■■■■■■■

As we have just seen, playing Prisoner's Dilemma or a Cournot market game a finite number of times doesn't do the players any more good, on average, than playing the game once. When a one-shot game has multiple equilibria, then repeated play opens up a lot of interesting new payoff possibilities. What's more, these new payoff possibilities are subgame perfect, so they pass the test of credibility.

To fix ideas, let's look at a new one-shot game, called Market Niches (note the plural). There are two players, firms 1 and 2, and two market niches, A and B. The one-shot game is shown in Figure 7.6. If both firms occupy market niche A, they get a payoff of 3 each. However, if either firm leaves market niche A for

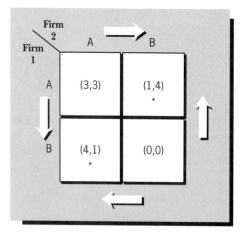

Figure 7.6.   Market Niches, the one-shot game.

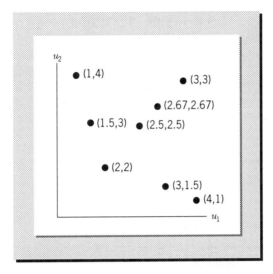

Figure 7.7. Market Niches, played two or three times, utility possibilities.

market niche B, it gets a higher payoff (4). Finally, there is only room at market niche B for one firm, so if both firms go there, both get payoff 0.

As you can see, the one-shot version of Market Niches has two very different pure strategy equilibria, (A,B) and (B,A), with payoff vectors (4,1) and (1,4). In addition to these pure strategy equilibria, there is a mixed strategy equilibrium. At this mixed strategy equilibrium, firm 1 goes to market niche A with probability 1/2 and to market niche B with the same probability. Firm 2 plays the same mixed strategy. Each firm has the expected value of 2 at this mixed strategy equilibrium. These one-shot game payoffs are recorded in the utility possibility diagram of Figure 7.7.

Each firm would rather have market niche B to itself. If Market Niches is played twice, then a rotation is possible. In particular, each firm can have the market niche B to itself once. Here is the subgame perfect equilibrium that sends firm 1 to market niche B in the first round, and then sends firm 2 to market niche B in the second round. Firm 1's complete plan is the following:

first play: go to B
second play: after every possible history, go to A

Firm 2's complete plan is the following:

first play: go to A
second play: after every possible history, go to B

These strategies are subgame perfect because they play an equilibrium on every subgame. The equilibrium path corresponding to these strategies is (B,A) first, followed by (A,B). This rotation yields the average payoffs in the repeated game of (5/2,5/2). By reversing roles, we can program the rotation in the reverse order, with firm 2 going to market niche B in round 1. That, too, is subgame perfect, and again yields the repeated game payoffs (5/2,5/2). This average utility of this rotation payoff is also shown in Figure 7.7.

We do not lose any feasible payoff vectors when the one-shot game is repeated. For instance, the payoff vector (4,1) corresponds to a subgame perfect equilibrium of Market Niches played twice. All we need is to play the same one-shot game equilibrium twice in a row. Firm 1's complete plan at the subgame perfect equilibrium that sends it to market niche B both periods is

first play: go to B
second play: after every possible history, go to B

Firm 2's complete plan at this equilibrium is

first play: go to A
second play: after every possible history, go to A

Notice that these strategies are unconditional. Using appropriate unconditional strategies, we can also get the equilibrium path (A,B) followed by (A,B), and the sequence of mixed strategy equilibria where each firm is equally likely each period to occupy either market niche. In addition, we could rotate between either of the pure strategies of the one-shot game and the mixed strategy equilibrium. These six possibilities are shown in Figure 7.7. Playing Market Niches twice already doubles the number of utility possibilities achieved by the subgame perfect equilibrium.

If we play Market Niches three times, we get a fundamentally new possibility in addition to unconditional repetition of a one-shot equilibrium and rotation among one-shot equilibria. The new subgame perfect equilibrium that arises when Market Niches is played three times is very attractive. Here is the equilibrium path. Both firms go to market niche A in period 1. In periods 2 and 3 they rotate on the market niches. What was not an equilibrium in the one-shot game, both firms going to market niche A, becomes part of an equilibrium in the repeated game. The average payoff vector

$$u_1 = u_2 = \frac{(3 + 1 + 4)}{3} = 2.67$$

that each firm gets from this equilibrium path dominates any other symmetrical equilibrium of Market Niches played three times. To support the equilibrium path (A,A) followed by (A,B) and then (B,A), the firms play the following strategies. For firm 1, the strategy is

first play: go to A
second play: go to A if the history is (A,A) or (B,B)
                and go to B in round 3 unconditionally;
                go to B if the history is (A,B) and go to B in round 3
                unconditionally;
                go to A if the history is (B,A) and go to A in round 3
                unconditionally

For firm 2, the strategy is

first play: go to A

second play: go to B if the history is (A,A) or (B,B) and go to A in
                round 3 unconditionally;
                go to A if the history is (A,B) and go to A in round 3
                unconditionally;
                go to B if the history is (B,A) and go to B in round 3
                unconditionally

Let's see how these strategies work. The equilibrium path is (A,A), followed by (A,B) and (B,A). Along the equilibrium path, firm 1 gets the average payoff

$$u_1 = \frac{(3 + 1 + 4)}{3} = 2.67$$

which firm 2 also gets:

$$u_2 = \frac{(3 + 4 + 1)}{3} = 2.67$$

Why doesn't one of the firms, say, firm 1, occupy niche B in the first period and thereby get a payoff 4 instead of 3? Notice what happens if firm 1 occupies niche B in the first period. Since firm 2 is sticking to its complete plan in this thought experiment, the possible history for the second round is (B,A). If (B,A) is the possible history, then in the second round firm 1 goes to A and firm 2 goes to B. This is a second round payoff vector (1,4), which is repeated in the third round. If firm 1 deviates from the strategy paying 2.67 by occupying market niche B at the first play, it gets the average payoff

$$u_1 = \frac{(4 + 1 + 1)}{3} = 2 < 2.67$$

It does not pay firm 1 to deviate, so this is indeed an equilibrium for firm 1. Moreover, since all subsequent play involves one-shot equilibria, we have shown that this pair of strategies is an equilibrium. Finally, since every threat that is carried out in the event that one of the firms deviates from the equilibrium involves one-shot game equilibria, this pair of strategies is subgame perfect. The payoff vector (2.67,2.67) can therefore be included in Figure 7.7.

   Now suppose that we play Market Niches not 3 times, but 101 times. Using strategies like the one just presented, we send each firm to market niche A for the first 99 periods, then rotate the final two periods. Again, using an argument similar to the previous one, we can show that this is a subgame perfect equilibrium path. Moreover, we can get very close to the average payoffs (3,3):

$$\frac{[99(3,3) + (4,1) + (1,4)]}{101} = (2.99, 2.99)$$

This is no accident, but rather a general result. Let w_i be the worst equilibrium payoff to player i in the one-shot game and let $\mathbf{w}$ be the vector of such payoffs.

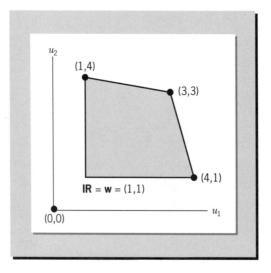

Figure 7.8. Folk theorem: Market Niches played finitely many times.

Say that a payoff has **individual rationality** if a player can guarantee that payoff to himself or herself regardless of what the opponents do. We are now ready to state the folk theorem for games that are played a large, but finite, number of times:[3]

■ ■

Folk Theorem for Finitely Repeated Two-Person Games. Suppose that a finitely repeated game has a one-shot equilibrium payoff vector that payoff dominates w. Then all individually rational and feasible payoffs are supported in the limit as average payoffs of subgame perfect equilibria.

This result is called the **folk theorem** because it was part of the folklore—what everybody in game theory knew and took for granted—years before anyone bothered to write down a proof and publish it.[4]

Figure 7.8 applies the folk theorem to Market Niches. Each firm can guarantee itself at least a payoff 1 by going to market niche A, so we get the reference vector for individual rationality, **IR:**

   IR = (1,1)

The worst one-shot equilibrium payoff to player 1 is achieved by the equilibrium (A,B) and equals 1; the worst one-shot equilibrium payoff to player 2 is achieved by equilibrium (B,A) and equals 1. Thus we have

   w = (1,1) = **IR**

[3]This theorem is stated and proved for the 2-player game by J. Benoit and V. Krishna, "Finitely Repeated Games," *Econometrica* 53(1985):905–22. A similar result is true for more than two players, but requires more conditions in the hypothesis.

[4]This explanation of the origin of the term *folk theorem* is due to Robert Aumann.

The mixed strategy equilibrium paying (2,2) payoff dominates **w.** Feasible payoffs include the matrix entries (1,4), (4,1), and (3,3). Also feasible are payoffs on the lines connecting these three points, as well as payoffs below those lines. Combining individual rationality and feasibility, we get the quadrilateral depicted in Figure 7.8. For example, with enough plays, we can get arbitrarily close to the vector (3,3) using subgame perfect equilibria.

Repetition creates new equilibria, and some of these new equilibria are very attractive. At the same time, repetition creates new problems. Consider the two firms competing in Market Niches. Thanks to the folk theorem, they face a plethora of equilibria. One of these is best for firm 1: play (B,A) every time. Another of these is best for firm 2: play (A,B) every time. The strategic problem facing the firms—namely, which firm gets market niche B—is merely pushed up to a higher level by repetition. Instead of fighting over which firm gets market niche B in a one-shot equilibrium, now the firms fight over which equilibrium to play in the repeated game. Game theory can exhibit the possible solutions in a case like this, but game theory alone cannot supply the answer.

♟ 7.6 Infinitely Repeated Games: Strategies and Payoffs ■ ■ ■ ■ ■ ■ ■ ■ ■ ■ ■ ■ ■ ■ ■ ■ ■ ■

We are about to study infinitely repeated games, and there's no avoiding the inevitable question, why? We are all going to die someday, and definitely a lot sooner than an infinitely repeated game will ever end, so what's the use of such games? Here are three reasons for this madness. First, even though you're going to die, with any kind of luck your company is going to survive you. Since a corporation is not a person, there is no reason a corporation cannot live— and therefore play—forever. The best examples of infinitely repeated games involve corporations. Second, even if you know you are going to die, it's unlikely that you will act as if death is around the corner. A lot of people act as if they are going to live forever. *And that is all it takes for an infinitely repeated game:* two or more players who act as if they will play the game forever. In this case "as if" is as good as "is." Finally, even though the folk theorem for finitely repeated games shows how repetition creates good equilibria for one-shot games with several equilibria, it doesn't do anything for one-shot games with a single equilibrium. For instance, it doesn't create new, credible equilibrium payoff possibilities for the Cournot or Bertrand market games we have studied. Only infinitely repeated games can do that.

A strategy for an infinitely repeated game must specify infinitely many choices for each play following each possible history. Such a strategy can easily become hopelessly complex. Suppose that two firms are locked in Cournot competition period after period, forever, and each can ship any quantity between 0 and 90 in any period. Here is an infinitely complex plan of play:

first play:	ship 3 units
second play:	ship 3.1 units after any possible history
third play:	ship 3.14 units after any possible history
fourth play:	ship 3.141 units after any possible history
fifth play:	ship 3.1415 units after any possible history

and so on. This firm's strategy is, unconditionally in period n, to ship the first n decimals of the number π. Even the world's largest computer can only play the first billion repetitions of this strategy—that is as far as the decimal expansion of π can be computed at this time. This strategy is infinitely complex.

The infinitely repeated games we study here can be solved by strategies that contain only a few program steps. An example of the simplest kind of strategy for the repeated Cournot game is

all plays: ship 16 units after any possible history

The unconditional strategy to do the same thing infinitely often is as simple as a strategy can get. A strategy like 16 can be programmed with a single program step. Rotations can be programmed also, with as many program steps as there are steps in the rotation. Suppose that a firm is rotating between shipping 16 units and shipping 20 units, starting with 16. Here is its strategy:

first play all odd-numbered plays thereafter: ship 16 units after any
   possible history
second play and all even-numbered plays thereafter: ship 20 units after any
   possible history

Trigger strategies are especially important for infinitely repeated games. Suppose that a firm wants to ship 16 units and wants every other firm to ship 16 units, too. Ninety units flood the market. A trigger strategy that wants to ship 16 units but is prepared to flood the market otherwise is

first play:	ship 16 units
Tth play:	ship 16 units after a history in which all firms shipped 16 units; otherwise, ship 90 units forever

for every $T > 1$. The threat in this strategy is triggered by some firm doing something other than shipping 16 units. The threat to flood the market is not credible. However, we will see how to construct really effective threats that are credible.

Evaluating payoffs for an infinitely repeated game presents more difficulties. A dollar a hundred years from now is not worth the same as a dollar right now—and an infinitely repeated game will be going on a hundred years from now. To handle the problem posed by time, future payoffs are discounted relative to the present. For mathematical reasons, the discount rate is set at

$R < 1$; otherwise, infinitely long streams of payoffs would not converge. We have to evaluate expressions of the form

$$u_1 = \Sigma \, R^t \, u_1(t)$$

where t goes from zero (now) to infinity (the distant future). Infinite sums can be a challenge to calculate, but as long as the terms in an infinite sum are constant, an exact answer can be found. This property is useful for finding equilibria for infinitely repeated games and also allows us to approximate series whose terms vary.

Suppose that player 1 gets the payoff 1 every time he or she plays a game, forever. Then, in the formula given, $u_1(t) = 1$ for all t. This player wants to find the value of the infinite series

$$u_1 = 1 + R + R^2 + R^3 + \cdots$$

For discount factors R between 0 and 1, $0 < R < 1$, the series sums to

$$u_1 = \frac{1}{(1 - R)} = 1 + R + R^2 + R^3 + \cdots$$

You can see why by multiplying both sides of the equation by $(1 - R)$ and collecting terms. Since R is less than 1, the denominator is less than 1, and we see that the present value of a dollar paid every period is greater than a dollar, but less than infinity. For example, let $R = .9$. Then

$$u_1 = \frac{1}{(1 - .9)} = \frac{1}{.1} = \$10$$

A dollar paid every period from now to infinity is the same as $10 paid now. This calculation is for a constant payoff of 1. To adjust for a constant payoff of k, simply multiply through:

$$u_1 = kR + kR^2 + kR^3 + \cdots$$
$$= k(1 + R + R^2 + R^3 + \cdots)$$
$$= \frac{k}{(1 - R)}$$

Finally, just as in finitely repeated games, we want to keep the payoffs associated with the infinitely repeated game on the same scale as those of the one-shot game. The way to do this is to multiply the infinite sum of utilities by $(1 - R)$. This is a linear transformation, so it does not affect any player's rankings of outcomes. To sum up, we record payoffs for player 1 in an infinitely repeated game by the infinite sum

$$u_1 = (1 - R) \, \Sigma \, R^t \, u_1(t)$$

and similarly for the other players. Armed with payoffs and strategies, we are now ready to tackle some infinitely repeated market games.

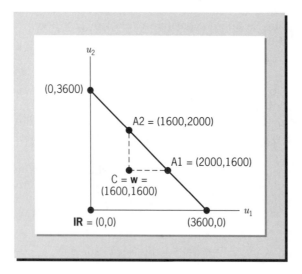

Figure 7.9. Folk theorem: Infinitely repeated Cournot market game.

7.7 Infinitely Repeated Cournot Market Games   ■ ■ ■

Each period, two firms, 1 and 2, bring quantities of their products, which are perfect substitutes for each other, to market. Each period, the market demand they face is

$$P = 130 - Q$$

where P is market price and Q is market quantity. Each firm produces its product at a constant average (and marginal) cost $c = \$10$. If these firms play this game once, the Cournot equilibrium is $x_1^* = x_2^* = 40$ (we played this as a one-shot game in section 5.2). The market price is $50, the profit margin for each firm is $40, and each firm makes $1600 in profits. This information is recorded as the point C (for one-shot Cournot) in the profit possibility diagram of Figure 7.9.

The one-shot monopoly solution is, of course, much more profitable. Monopoly would restrict output to 60 units, set the price at $70, enjoy a profit margin of $60, and make $3600 in profits. This possible profit is recorded as the line $u_1 + u_2 = 3600$ in Figure 7.9. If firms 1 and 2 could somehow play a better equilibrium in the infinitely repeated game, they could enjoy profits this high. The game has to be repeated infinitely often for there to be any chance of this situation occurring. Since this Cournot equilibrium is unique, it is the only solution of the market game finitely repeated.

We will now see that the one-shot Cournot equilibrium is an equilibrium of the infinitely repeated game—but that it is not the only one. Let's start with the unconditional strategy that plays Cournot infinitely often:

every play: ship 40 units after every possible history

Let both firms play this strategy. Each firm enjoys the profit stream of $1600 each period. The infinite sum of payoffs, normalized, to each firm is

$$\frac{(1 - R)\,1600}{(1 - R)} = \$1600$$

regardless of the discount factor.

Now, suppose that firm 1 tries to deviate to improve its profits. One promising deviation would be to ship one less unit to market each period. This strategy would have the advantage of driving the price up by $1. Let's see what this does to firm 1's profits. The market price rises from $50 to $51, while firm 1's shipments fall from 40 to 39. Firm 1's profits each period are now

$$u_1(t) = (51 - 10)\,39 = \$1599$$

Too bad, firm 1, this is $1 lower than at the Cournot equilibrium. If firm 1 were to do this forever, it would get

$$\frac{(1 - R)\,1599}{(1 - R)} = \$1599$$

again lower than 1600. The same conclusion holds true for firm 2. Reducing output does not raise profits. You can show (see the problems) that raising output also does not raise profits. Since neither raising nor lowering output increases profits, the one-shot Cournot strategy, played forever, is an infinitely repeated game equilibrium.

Notice that the size of the discount factor R played no role in the previous demonstration, because the strategies were unconditional and did exactly the same thing forever—played the one-shot Cournot equilibrium. To increase profits these firms are going to have to use some more imaginative strategies. In particular, they might as well go for the gold, and see if they can play strategies that get them the monopoly profits. If firms attach enough weight to future profits, that is, if R is close enough to 1, then monopoly profits can be earned at a noncooperative equilibrium of the infinitely repeated market game. In particular, there is a payoff-symmetrical equilibrium that yields this result and is subgame perfect. Now, let's find it.

It will take some doing to show all this. First, we need a strategy that will program monopoly, but still be an equilibrium. For this we use a trigger strategy. The trigger strategy has a stick and a carrot. The carrot is the stream of monopoly profits forever, which cannot fail to interest these firms. The stick is the punishment in the event that one of the firms deviates from the monopoly quantity recommendation. As we saw for coffee (Chapter 5) and oil (this chapter), firms have a temptation to ship more to market than is consistent with monopoly pricing. The stick has to be mean enough that firms do not want to do that. The stick also has to be credible—it can't be just another idle threat that no one would dream of carrying out. Here is a trigger strategy that will do everything we want a strategy to do:

first play: ship 30 units

*T*th play: ship 30 units after any history where both firms have-
shipped 30 units; otherwise, ship 40 units forever

where T counts the number of times the game has been played. The first part of this strategy is the carrot—it programs monopoly profits forever. A firm plays its part by shipping just enough to maintain monopoly profits. The second part of this strategy is the stick. Suppose that a firm does something it is not supposed to. Then all firms switch to playing the one-shot Cournot equilibrium from then on. This means lower profits for the firm that spoiled the monopoly, as well as for every other firm. *This is a stick that hurts.* A deviation from the monopoly pattern of behavior triggers punishment in the form of the stick. What is worse, this is a punishment that is eternal—it never ends.

We first have to show that this strategy is an equilibrium. This proof involves the discount factor. Then we show that it is credible. Credibility does not depend on the discount factor. Given the symmetry involved, we will consider firm 1 only. How could firm 1 do better than to play its role in the monopoly and ship 30 units? Well, just as an OPEC country, it could ship more than planned. However, it would have to hurry—it would only get one shipment of over 30 units before its opponent noticed and both entered the Cournot one-shot equilibrium phase for eternity. Next consideration—if firm 1 is going to ship more than 30 units, there is no better time than the present. With discounting, a dollar today is always worth more than a dollar tomorrow. So the most profitable deviation from shipping 30 units takes place today and amounts to a one-time-only bigger shipment. Still, firm 1 has to plan carefully just how big the shipment should be. If the shipment is too big, this move, too, will destroy the profit potential. To get the right-sized shipment, firm 1 must maximize one-period profits, given that its opponent will ship 30 units. Using the best-response function from section 5.3, we have

$$x_1 = f_1(x_2) = 60 - \frac{30}{2} = 45 \text{ units}$$

Firm 1 ships 45 units today instead of 30. The market price falls from $70 to $55, and firm 1's profit margin falls from $60 to $45. However, firm 1's short-term profits go up from $1600 to ($45)(45) = $2025. Right now, firm 1 earns a lot more money. But then the fun is over—it is Cournot play for eternity, at $1600 per period.

Now that we have found the most profitable way for firm 1 to break the monopoly agreement, we can check whether breaking the agreement pays or not. If it does pay, then the trigger strategy we are testing is not an equilibrium. If breaking the agreement in the most profitable way possible does not pay, then the trigger strategy is an equilibrium. Shipping 45 units for one period followed by an eternity of Cournot shipments pays the following:

$$\frac{u_1}{(1-R)} = 2025 + 1600(R + R^2 + R^3 + \cdots)$$

which is the profit from initially shipping 45 units, followed by one-shot Cournot profits forever. Rearranging, we have

$$\frac{u_1}{(1-R)} = 2025 - 1600 + 1600 + 1600(R + R^2 + R^3 + \cdots)$$

$$= 425 + \frac{1600}{(1-R)}$$

Multiplying by $(1-R)$ to normalize,

$$u_1 = 2025 - 425R$$

Breaking the monopoly pattern pays a premium today, but pays low forever after. As we have already seen, playing along the monopoly way pays $1800 each period, so after normalization this is simply $1800. We have now reached the crucial condition on the discount factor:

$$2025 - 425R < 1800$$

When the discount factor R satisfies this inequality, then deviating from monopoly pays less than playing one's part in a monopoly. Solving this inequality, we have

$$\frac{9}{17} < R$$

Any discount factor over $9/17$, or 53%, is enough to make firm 1 stick to the monopoly and not try to cheat.

This inequality captures precisely what is meant by "if the players' discount factors are sufficiently close to 1" and is very likely to be met in the real world. If the period of time were a year, it would take an annual interest rate of almost 100% to drive the discount factor down to near 50%. Instead, interest rates fall in the range of 5% to 20%. For these rates, the discount factor is never lower than 83%. We have just shown that the trigger strategy is an equilibrium. Even the best change of strategy imaginable does not pay.

Checking for credibility is a lot simpler. We have already verified that playing the one-shot Cournot equilibrium ($x_1 = 40$) every chance you get is an equilibrium. Hence, the threat to play this way if anyone ever breaks the monopoly pattern is credible. Of course, there are always worse threats available, such as to flood the market forever ($x_i = 120$). Any worse threat could be used to support the monopoly solution, too. However, any worse threat would also have a credibility problem.

This subgame perfect equilibrium for the infinitely repeated Cournot market game has exciting new payoff possibilities—in particular monopoly profits at the levels of $1800 for each firm. This outcome occurs in spite of the fact that the one-shot Cournot market game has a unique equilibrium. That this is possible is no accident. It follows immediately from the folk theorem for infinitely repeated games. As in the statement of the folk theorem for finitely repeated games, $\mathbf{w}_i$ represents the vector of lowest one-shot equilibrium payoffs.

■ ■

Folk Theorem for Infinitely Repeated Games. Suppose that an infinitely repeated game has a payoff vector that exceeds w_i for each player i. Then all individually rational and feasible payoffs that payoff dominate w are supported as payoffs of subgame perfect equilibria, as long as discount rates are sufficiently close to 1. In particular, efficient payoff vectors are supported as subgame perfect equilibria when discount rates are sufficiently close to 1.

To see how this theorem applies to the Cournot market game, notice that any firm can guarantee itself the payoff 0 by shipping no units and incurring no costs. This means that the individually rational reference vector, **IR**, is

$$\textbf{IR} = (0,0)$$

The only one-shot equilibrium yields **w**:

$$\textbf{w} = (1600,1600)$$

Then, according to the folk theorem for infinitely repeated games, any payoff vector in the triangle with vertices (1600,1600), (2000,1600), and (1600,3600) can be supported by a subgame perfect equilibrium—provided that firms are sufficiently patient. Figure 7.9 portrays the situation.

We have seen how to construct two such equilibria from infinitely many. Both of these equilibria were symmetrical. Let us now construct an asymmetrical equilibrium. Take the point with coordinates (1920, 1680). This equilibrium earns monopoly profits overall, but firm 2 gets only 46.7% of the market and of profits, while firm 1 gets the rest. Here is a pair of strategies that make this the outcome of a subgame perfect equilibrium. For firm 1, the strategy is

first play: ship 32 units

Tth play: ship 32 units after any history where total shipments have always been 60 units; otherwise, ship 40 units forever

where $T > 1$ counts the times the game has been played. For firm 2, the strategy is

first play: ship 28 units

Tth play: ship 28 units after any history where total shipments have always been 60 units; otherwise, ship 40 units forever

These are two different trigger strategies. Taken together during the initial phase, they monopolize the market, and the shipments generate the profit split (1920, 1680). If either firm ever deviates, then both go to the one-shot Cournot equilibrium, which is a credible threat. Again, as long as firms have discount factors sufficiently close to 1, they will not be tempted to deviate. Consider firm 2, which has the bigger temptation to deviate, since it gets the smaller market share. If it deviates at the outset, it should ship 44 units (the one-period best response to $x_1 = 32$; see Chapter 6.7). It makes a profit of 1936 that period, and

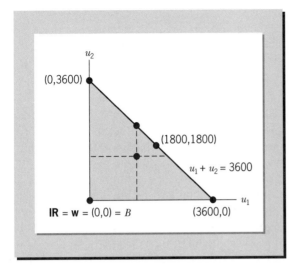

Figure 7.10. Payoff possibilities, infinitely repeated Bertrand market game.

1600 thereafter, compared to 1680 for all periods if it does not deviate. As long as $R > 256/336$, or 76.2%, firm 2 does better by not deviating. Similarly, firm 1 would not want to jeopardize this arrangement in an infinity of lifetimes, much less a single lifetime—unless its discount factor were extremely low. If firm 1 had a discount factor $R = 0$, that is, if today were the end of time, then firm 1 would cheat even on this terrific arrangement. People don't take the money and run unless they know the game is over.

To get the payoffs $(1680, 1920)$ as a repeated game equilibrium outcome, just reverse the roles of firm 1 and 2 in what we just did. Every consideration that applied to firm 1 now applies to firm 2, and vice versa. Firms in finitely repeated games face a difficult equilibrium selection problem. Here, the equilibrium selection problem is, if anything, even worse. There are an infinite number of subgame perfect equilibrium outcomes, some very good for one firm and not so good for the other. Indeed, we can think of the fight over quotas within OPEC in light of this result. If the members of OPEC think they will interact forever, then a fight over quotas is really a fight over which asymmetrical equilibrium to play. And there are infinitely many asymmetrical equilibria over which to fight.

The folk theorem for infinitely repeated games does not apply just to Cournot market games. It applies with even greater force to Bertrand competition. The only difference between Cournot and Bertrand competition shows up in the location of the one-shot game equilibrium in the profit possibilities diagram (see Figure 7.10). In Bertrand competition with perfect substitutes, the one-shot game equilibrium and the reference point for individual rationality coincide. The folk theorem gives an even bigger set of equilibria to fight over, the triangle with vertices $(3600,0)$, $(0,3600)$, and $(0,0)$. Here is how to program the infinitely repeated profits $(1800,1800)$:

first play: set price = $60

Tth play: set price = $60 as long as price = $60 has always been
              set otherwise, set price = marginal cost = $10 forever

You can show that this is an equilibrium for any discount factor greater than .5. This particular equilibrium is intuitively quite plausible under the probability of continuation interpretation if you are risk neutral. If the odds are greater than 50–50 that you will play this same game tomorrow, then half the market today and half the market tomorrow are better than all the market today and nothing forever after.

Corporations interacting on a daily basis for over a century approximate an infinitely repeated game. Any time the economic fundamentals change—demand shifts or costs change—the profit possibilities and the set of infinitely repeated game equilibria change, too. The problem of coordinating among infinitely many equilibria becomes overwhelming in such a case. We now look at how one industry, the ready-to-eat breakfast cereal industry, has adapted to the challenge posed by infinitely repeated games.

7.8 Price Leadership in the Ready-to-Eat Cereals Industry[5] ■■■■■■■■■■■■■■■■■■■■■■■■

Ready-to-eat cereal was invented by health-food advocates in the United States in the 1890s. Two of the inventors, Kellogg and Post, gave their names to the companies they founded. Two other companies, General Mills and Ralston-Purina, have also had important market shares in this industry. These four companies have been rivals throughout the twentieth century. Large corporations with strong earnings and bright futures, the big four in the ready-to-eat cereals industry have had every reason to think that they would interact in this market into the indefinite future. Thus they could act as if they were playing an infinitely repeated market game, one of whose equilibria is monopoly pricing.

There is one real-life constraint to the folk theorem for infinitely repeated games that hasn't been mentioned. Since 1890, U.S. federal statute (the Sherman Act and subsequent legislation) has forbidden "monopolizing, the attempt to monopolize, or the conspiracy to monopolize" a market. This antitrust legislation is enforced by two separate agencies of the executive branch, the Department of Justice and the Federal Trade Commission. Typically, the U.S. government does not prove that firms have monopolized a

[5]This material draws on Frederick M. Scherer, "The Breakfast Cereal Industry," in *The Structure of American Industry*, 6th ed., ed. W. Adams (New York: Macmillan, 1982), and John Sutton, *Sunk Costs and Market Structure: Price Competition, Advertising, and the Evolution of Concentration* (Cambridge: MIT Press, 1991), especially chapter 10. For readers already familiar with the story, problem 9 makes the same main point.

market—the evidentiary requirements for a conviction are too great. Instead, the government proves that firms have *conspired* to monopolize a market—smoke-filled rooms and paper trails indicating that companies have intentionally gotten together to fix prices at monopoly levels. The behavior underlying the folk theorem, which involves not even a whiff of conspiracy, hardly fills the bill for an antitrust violation. Nevertheless, companies with long horizons walk a thin line between antitrust legality and illegality.

Suppose that the major firms in an industry have reached the solution of an infinitely repeated game that supports monopoly profits. Their work has only begun. Every time an economic fundamental, such as cost or consumer preferences, changes, the equilibria to the infinitely repeated game change, too. The firms need some mechanism to move from the old equilibrium they were playing to a new one. Failing such a mechanism, they could wind up back at the one-shot equilibrium, with lower profits all around. The solution to this problem that has evolved in the ready-to-eat cereals industry, as well as in a number of other industries, is called **price leadership.** Under price leadership, one firm, the price leader, takes charge of the industry pricing policy. Every time a change in prices is called for by a change in economic fundamentals, the price leader makes that change. The members of the industry depend on the price leader to make the correct price changes, so that industry profits are as high as they can possibly be.

For most of this century, the price leader in the ready-to-eat cereals industry has been Kellogg's, which also happens to be number one in market share, consistently with more than 40% of all dollar sales. Considering the background inflation in the United States, especially since World War II, most of the price changes have involved price increases. In the period from 1950 to 1972, 99% of all price changes were price increases—and this figure controls for package size. A large fraction of all price increases, 80% in the period 1965–70, were led by Kellogg's. Other firms in the industry usually followed this lead promptly; occasionally they did not. Even when other firms did not follow, Kellogg's did not rescind its price increases. Instead, it advertised more intensely and waited for the rest of the industry to catch up to the price increase.

Price leadership helped the ready-to-eat cereals industry enjoy very high profit margins on their products and well-above-average rates of return on their assets. The Federal Trade Commission, ever alert to signs of conspiracy, brought suit against the firms in this industry. While admitting that it had no evidence of an outright conspiracy, the commission argued that, by their pattern of behavior, the cereals manufacturers were in effect a **shared monopoly,** and thus subject to antitrust remedies. The commission's notion of shared monopoly, if correct, confirms the view that the firms in this industry, following the price leadership of Kellogg's, have indeed found and maintained the profit-maximizing solution to their repeated game.

This case dragged on for several years in court, with all kinds of legal maneuvering over who would be the judge. The case also became heavily politicized. During the 1980 presidential campaign, candidate Reagan wrote to

Kellogg's, expressing concern for their legal plight. At the same time, organized labor, fearing the loss of thousands of jobs in Battle Creek, Michigan, and the surrounding area, leaned hard on President Carter to give Kellogg's a break. It became apparent to the commission that, even if it proved that a shared monopoly existed, it would still not prevail in court. The newly appointed judge in the case dismissed all charges against the ready-to-eat cereal companies in 1981. Kellogg's and its price followers continue to earn impressive rates of return to this day.

SUMMARY

1. A strategic interaction that takes place more than once is called a repeated game. Repeated games are more complicated than the one-shot game of which they are composed.

2. The strategy space of a game proliferates when the game is repeated. A 2×2 game, played twice, is 32×32 in normal form.

3. Repetition creates subgames. Subgame perfection is a powerful sufficient condition for a solution of a repeated game.

4. A trigger strategy is composed of two parts: an initial phase, usually desirable, and a punishment phase, which is dire.

5. A repeated zero-sum game is still zero sum. Its payoff possibilities are not enriched by repetition.

6. According to Selten's theorem, if a game with a unique equilibrium is played finitely many times, its solution is that equilibrium played each and every time.

7. Variable-sum games with multiple equilibria have large sets of subgame perfect equilibria. Payoffs in the repeated game are measured as the average per play of the game.

8. According to the folk theorem for finitely repeated games, if a one-shot game with multiple equilibria is repeated enough times, any individually rational and feasible payoff vector can be approximated as an average payoff of a subgame perfect equilibrium.

9. The members of OPEC appear to be playing a finitely repeated game in the world oil market.

10. Two or more players who act as if they will play a game forever constitute an infinitely repeated game. Payoffs in an infinitely repeated game are discounted either by time or by uncertainty.

11. The one-shot equilibrium of a Cournot market game repeated infinitely often is a subgame perfect equilibrium. This infinitely repeated game has infinitely many other equilibria. Some of these equilibria imply monopoly pricing.

12. U.S. corporations may run afoul of the antitrust law because of folk theorem considerations for infinitely repeated games, even when they have not conspired to monopolize the market.

⠏⠇ KEY WORDS

finitely/infinitely repeated game
possible history
one-shot game
unconditional strategy
rotation strategy
trigger strategy
discount factor

continuation probability
Selten's theorem
OPEC
individual rationality
folk theorem
price leadership
shared monopoly

⠏⠇ PROBLEMS

1. Show that the 2-person Cournot market game (Chapter 5), played twice, has a unique subgame perfect equilibrium. Also show that the 2-person Prisoner's Dilemma (Figure 7.3), played three times, has a unique subgame perfect equilibrium.

2. Find the average payoffs of subgame perfect equilibrium for Market Niche (Figure 3.2) played twice.

3. Find another strategy that achieves the average payoffs (2.5,2.5) for Market Niches played twice. How would a discount factor $R < 1$ affect how firms feel about rotations over the two market niches?

4. Find the average utility possibilities of subgame perfect equilibria for Market Niches played four times if the firms use only pure strategies. How close can you get to (3,3) with four repetitions?

5. Compare the strategic situation facing the coffee-producing countries to that facing the countries of OPEC. Which set of countries is more likely to be playing an infinitely repeated game? Does this in itself guarantee that the Coffee Agreement of 1993 will hold?

6. Show that in the infinitely repeated Cournot market game of section 7.6, it does not pay a firm to restrict output, if the firms are playing the one-shot Cournot equilibrium forever.

7. Find a subgame perfect equilibrium that supports monopoly payoffs for the Cournot market game of section 7.7 (both one-shot and infinitely repeated) if average cost = $30, a constant. Both firms have discount factors = .9. Market demand is $P = 130 - Q$.

8. Suppose in problem 7 that firm 1 has average cost = $10 and firm 2 has average cost = $30. Find the one-shot Cournot equilibrium. What are the profit possibilities of this game if it is repeated infinitely often?

9. Solve for the profit possibilities in problem 7 if the firms are in Bertrand competition. If firm 1 is the price leader, what price should it pick?

10. You are called as an expert witness by a corporate defendant in a case such as *United States* v. *Kellogg's et al.* Your job is to convince a jury that your client has done nothing wrong by acting as a price follower. Why would the corporation want your testimony on the witness stand? What would your testimony focus on?

CHAPTER 8

Evolutionary Stability and Bounded Rationality

We have taken for granted that the players of the games we have been studying were human—*Homo sapiens,* the smart hominid—with the exception of Fritz2, the Chess-playing computer from Chapter 1. In addition, we have assumed that these hominids were capable of unlimited acts of reasoning, such as are needed to play subgame perfect equilibria of infinitely repeated games. We have also relied on the players' being capable of rather exquisite inferences, such as those needed in Mutually Assured Destruction or in Market Niches played finitely many times. With such players, it is a foregone conclusion that they find the solution to a game at once and play that solution from then on. In the real world, however, even the best players are not this good. They don't always find a solution to a game right away; rather, they spend a lot of time learning to play the game. Also, they sometimes make mistakes. Players who have to learn how to play a game and who sometimes make mistakes are boundedly rational. This chapter studies the implications of **bounded rationality** for game theory.

The biggest implication of bounded rationality for a game is that, for much of the time that they are playing a game, the players are out of equilibrium.

When they are learning to play the game they are certainly out of equilibrium: they are groping for a solution. Even after they have learned how to play the game, whenever they make a mistake, they are once again out of equilibrium. This chapter begins by introducing a dynamic system to describe play when it is out of equilibrium. This dynamic system, called *replicator dynamics,* is widely used to describe the evolution of systems in chemistry and biology, and the same mathematical formulas apply to the evolution of players' behavior in games as well.[1] It is especially useful for describing the behavior of players who don't learn very fast. Replicator dynamics is first applied to symmetrical 2×2 games in normal form. Boundedly rational players obeying replicator dynamics eventually find an equilibrium, called an evolutionarily stable strategy. Thus, even dimwits will eventually satisfy the necessary condition for a solution to a game. This result leads to the example Frogs Call for Mates. The mating strategies of modern frogs—definitely boundedly rational players—have something to tell us about our own strategic behavior. The discussion then turns to asymmetrical 2×2 games in normal form. After extending replicator dynamics to handle asymmetry, this chapter shows that slow learners can still figure out Telex versus IBM. Some modifications of replicator dynamics for games with a finite number of players who are capable of fast learning are then considered. The chapter concludes by studying the rapidly evolving video game industry— an industry that has been out of equilibrium ever since Pong first showed up on a video screen. The appendix presents an example of the evolution of strategic behavior in a behavior laboratory.

8.1 How Boundedly Rational Players Play Games ■

Have you ever missed a question on an exam, or failed to understand something the first time you heard it? Did it take you more than an instant to learn how to play your first game? Then you are boundedly rational—just like me. Any limit to computing power or understanding, especially of the sort employed in game theory, imposes a bound on rationality. Boundedly rational players have to learn how to play a game, using some form of trial and error. This section builds a model of trial-and-error play called replicator dynamics and shows how that play eventually leads to the solution of Let's Make a Deal (see Figure 8.1).

Suppose there is a large population of players. At each point in time, one player is randomly paired with another to play Let's Make a Deal. Let x be the

---

[1]A good introduction to the mathematics and its applications is found in Josef Hofbauer and Karl Sigmund, *The Theory of Evolution and Dynamical Systems* (Cambridge: Cambridge University Press, 1988).

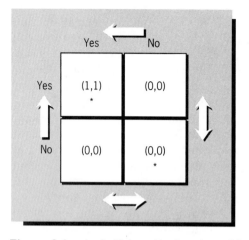

Figure 8.1.   Let's Make a Deal, stake = $2.

percentage of all players who choose yes and $1 - x$ be the percentage of all players who choose no. These are the *player types*. In a random matching, the probability of being matched with a Yes type is x and the probability of being matched with a No type is $1 - x$. On the basis of this random matching, we can compute expected payoffs for each of the two player types, Yes and No. We will use the notation $u(\text{yes})$ and $u(\text{no})$ to denote the expected payoffs of the corresponding player types. We have

$$u(\text{yes}) = (x)1 + (1 - x)0 = x$$
$$u(\text{no}) = (x)0 + (1 - x)0 = 0$$

Clearly, Yes player types get paid at least as much as No player types, regardless of how many of them are present in the population.

Replicator dynamics says that if a player type earns an above-average payoff, then its percentage in the population increases; if a player type earns a below-average payoff, then its percentage in the population decreases. The player types getting a below-average payoff will want to copy the player types getting an above-average return. Since they are slow learners, not all the below-average player types will switch all at once, but eventually all player types still present in the population will earn the average payoff. Any player type earning an average payoff in the population keeps its percentage of the population constant. These considerations apply in a straightforward way to business. No manager wants to be below average or to get below-average results. The job of a manager whose results are consistently below average is in real jeopardy. Being above average pays better. Replicator dynamics expresses precisely this logic mathematically.

The equation for replicator dynamics, the **replicator equation,** is the following:

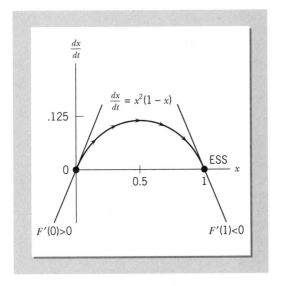

Figure 8.2. Let's Make a Deal, phase diagram.

$$\frac{dx}{dt} = x[u(\text{yes}) - \text{average } u]$$

In this equation, dx/dt is the rate of change of the percentage of Yes player types in the population, and average u is the average payoff in the population. Since Yes-type players cannot increase in the population unless they are already present, the rate of change of this player type, dx/dt, is taken proportional to its current percentage, x, of the population. The average payoff in the population is

$$\begin{aligned} \text{average } u &= (x)u(\text{yes}) + (1 - x)u(\text{no}) \\ &= (x)(x) + (1 - x)0 \\ &= x^2 \end{aligned}$$

An equivalent way to think of replicator dynamics is in terms of growth rates. Rewriting the replicator equation, we have

$$\frac{dx}{dt/x} = u(\text{yes}) - \text{average } u$$

The growth rate of Yes player types in the population equals the difference between their payoff and the average payoff, as long as this player type is present in the population.

We are now in a position to write down the replicator dynamics for Let's Make a Deal. Substituting for average u in the replicator equation, we get

$$\frac{dx}{dt} = x(x - x^2)$$
$$= x^2(1 - x)$$

This equation is plotted in Figure 8.2. Called a *phase diagram,* this figure plots the rate of change of x, dx/dt, against x itself. Such a diagram provides a way of seeing evolution take place. Suppose first that $x > 0$. We have $dx/dt > 0$, so x increases—just as replicator dynamics suggests. The proportion of players saying yes continues to increase in the population until it reaches $x = 1$. In the phase diagram, this direction to the dynamics is denoted by the arrows pointing to the right. We have just created a representation of the learning process. Players in this population are learning to play the strategy Yes. Eventually, all the players in the system learn to play the strategy Yes. At that point, represented by the value $x = 1$, learning ceases.

Even though learning has ceased, these boundedly rational players can and will still make **mistakes.** Next we see that the same learning process that brought them to the point $x = 1$ in the first place will keep them there, despite their mistakes. Suppose that, with probability ϵ, a player makes a mistake and switches from yes to no. Mistakes don't occur all that often, however, so ϵ is a number near zero. Then $1 - \epsilon$, the proportion of the population that still chooses yes, is a number close to 1. In the population with mistaken players, the strategy Yes pays

$$u(\text{yes}) = (1 - \epsilon)(1) + \epsilon(0)$$
$$= 1 - \epsilon$$

and the mistaken strategy No pays

$$u(\text{no}) = (1 - \epsilon)(0) + \epsilon(0)$$
$$= 0$$

Since $u(\text{yes}) = 1 - \epsilon > 0 = u(\text{no})$, the mistaken players are below average and will correct their mistakes.

An equilibrium is an **evolutionarily stable strategy,** or **ESS** for short, when two things happen: the replicator dynamics points toward this equilibrium, and low-probability mistakes do not destroy it.[2] The population $x^* = 1$, all of whom choose yes, is an ESS for Let's Make a Deal. Let's Make a Deal has another equilibrium, in which all players say no, represented by the population $x = 0$. *This equilibrium is not an ESS.* The replicator dynamics points away from this equilibrium. To see why, suppose that everyone in the population chooses no, when a small percentage of players mistakenly switch to yes. The players who have switched expect the payoff

---

[2] The exact definition of ESS and related concepts becomes more complicated in more complicated games. See P. Bomze, "Noncooperative 2-person Games in Biology," *International Journal of Game Theory* 15 (1991):31–58 for details.

$$u(\text{yes}) = (\epsilon)1 + (1 - \epsilon)0 = \epsilon$$

Whereas the rest of the players, all saying No, get

$$u(\text{no}) = \epsilon(0) + (1 - \epsilon)0 = 0$$

Even when they are rare, the Yes types do better than the No types. The learning process kicks in, as more and more players switch from no to yes. Hence, the game equilibrium at $x = 0$ is not an ESS.[3]

We have just seen that boundedly rational players can find the solution to Let's Make a Deal, even if they can't figure it out immediately. The next section shows to what extent this happy conclusion can be generalized.

8.2 ESS for 2 × 2 Symmetrical Games ■ ■ ■ ■ ■ ■ ■ ■ ■ ■

The replicator dynamics that solved Let's Make a Deal applies to any symmetrical game with two players and two strategies each. Every such game is a special case of the game in Figure 8.3. Let x be the percentage of the population playing strategy 1, and $1 - x$, the percentage of the population playing strategy 2. Compute the utility of the first strategy, u_1, the utility of the second strategy, u_2, and the average utility, according to

$$u_1 = xa + (1 - x)b$$
$$u_2 = xc + (1 - x)d$$
$$\text{average } u = xu_1 + (1 - x)u_2$$

Then set up the replicator equation

$$\frac{dx}{dt} = x(u_1 - \text{average } u)$$

Substituting for average u, we get

$$\frac{dx}{dt} = x[u_1 - xu_1 - (1 - x)u_2]$$

which simplifies to

$$\frac{dx}{dt} = x(1 - x)(u_1 - u_2)$$

Substituting once again, we get

---

[3]A special game theory concept applies just to the mistake part of ESS, and not to the learning part: perfect equilibrium. This concept is due to Reinhard Selten, "Reexamination of the Perfectness Concept for Equilibrium Points in Extensive Games," *International Journal of Game Theory* 4 (1975): 25–55. An ESS is always perfect, but not the converse.

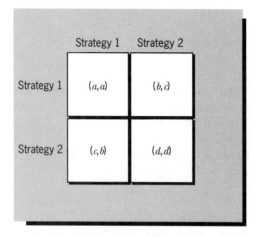

Figure 8.3.   2 × 2 symmetrical game.

$$\frac{dx}{dt} = x(1 - x)[x(a - c) + (1 - x)(b - d)]$$

which is solely a function of x.

For a population x^* to be an ESS, two things have to happen. First, x^* has to be a root of the replicator equation, so that $dx/dt = 0$ and the system is at rest. Also, the system has to be dynamically stable near x^*. That is, if there is a mistake of size ϵ that leads to either $x^* + \epsilon$ or $x^* - \epsilon$, the system will return to x^* on its own.

Replicator dynamics is a special case of the general differential equation

$$\frac{dx}{dt} = F(x)$$

For instance, in Let's Make a Deal, where $a = 1$ and $b = c = d = 0$,

$$\frac{dx}{dt} = x^2(1 - x)$$

There is a convenient test for when a root of the equation

$$\frac{dx}{dt} = F(x)$$

is dynamically stable. Suppose that $F(x^*) = 0$, so that x^* is a root of the function F. Now check the slope of F at x^*. If that slope is negative, then x^* is dynamically stable. This test is based on the following **Stability Theorem:**

■ ■

Stability Theorem. If $dx/dt = F(x^*) = 0$, and $dF(x^*)/dx < 0$, then x^* is dynamically stable.

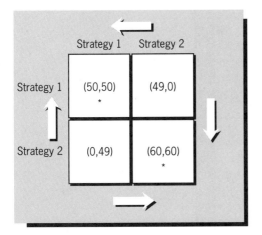

Figure 8.4. Coordination.

Graphically, the **stability theorem** says that if the replicator equation is downward sloping at a root x^* of the equation, then that root is an ESS.

Let's apply the stability theorem to Let's Make a Deal. Since $F(x) = x^2(1 - x)$, $dF(x)/dx = 2x - 3x^2$. Evaluating at the root $x^* = 1$, we get

$$\frac{dF(1)}{dx} = 2(1) - 3(1)^2 = -1 < 0$$

so the root $x^* = 1$ is an ESS. Notice by contrast that at the other root, $x = 0$, $dF(0)/dx = 0$ and the test is inconclusive. However, since for small positive ϵ, $dF(\epsilon)/dx = 2\epsilon - 3\epsilon^2 > 0$, we can see directly that once the system goes from $x = 0$ to $x = \epsilon$, it does not go back to $x = 0$. Thus the root $x^* = 0$ is not an ESS. You can see all this happening in the phase diagram of Figure 8.2. Let's Make a Deal has two equilibria, (yes,yes) and (no,no). One of these is an ESS; the other is not.

This example is quite optimistic: learning in a world of boundedly rational players leads to the best of all possible worlds, where total utility is maximized. In the nineteenth century, during the heyday of uncritical Darwinism, the doctrine of social Darwinism arose, alleging that evolution *always* leads to the best of all possible worlds. Unfortunately for this doctrine, replicator dynamics need not lead to an efficient outcome. If it did, we wouldn't be stuck with the keyboard configuration we now have, and we wouldn't divide the day into 24 hours, with each hour struck twice. These are just two examples of large-scale social coordination outcomes that could be improved on. However, inefficient coordination outcomes are rather to be expected according to replicator dynamics. Consider the game Coordination in Figure 8.4. It has pure strategy equilibria at (strategy 1, strategy 1) and (strategy 2, strategy 2), as well as a mixed strategy equilibrium. Let's first show that both pure strategy equilibria are ESS, whereas the mixed strategy equilibrium is not. To find the ESS,

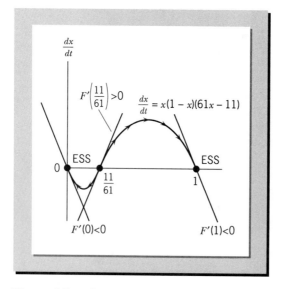

Figure 8.5.   Coordination, phase diagram.

substitute the values $a = 50$, $b = 49$, $c = 0$, and $d = 60$ into the replicator equation, which yields

$$\frac{dx}{dt} = x(1 - x)[50x + (49 - 60)(1 - x)]$$

$$= x(1 - x)(61x - 11)$$

The replicator dynamics for Coordination is plotted in Figure 8.5. The replicator equation has three roots, which can be found by setting each of the three factors equal to zero:

$$x = 0;\ 1 - x = 0;\ \text{and}\ 61x - 11 = 0$$

The slopes $dF(1)/dx$ and $dF(0)/dx$ are both negative, so the roots at 0 and 1 are both ESSs. The slope $dF(11/61)/dx$ is positive, so this root is not an ESS. The unstable root at $x = 11/61$ divides the interval $[0,1]$ into two zones. To the left of $x = 11/61$, learning heads toward $x^* = 0$. To the right of $x = 11/61$, learning heads toward $x^* = 1$. The arrows in Figure 8.5 portray these two directions of learning.

The two ESSs of the game are $x^* = 0$ (all players choose strategy 2) and $x^* = 1$ (all players choose strategy 1). Notice that the pure strategy equilibrium at (strategy 2, strategy 2) payoff dominates that at (strategy 1, strategy 1). In the event that learning converges to the equilibrium at $x^* = 1$, it leads to a less-than-best of all possible worlds. *Where learning winds up depends crucially in this case on where it starts.* If the initial proportion of type 1 players in the population is less than $11/61$ ($x < 11/61$), then the population heads toward the ESS where every player chooses strategy 2. Otherwise, the population heads

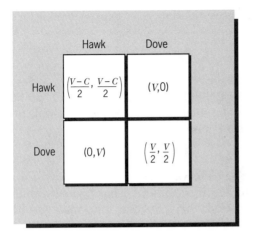

Figure 8.6. Hawk versus Dove.

toward the inefficient ESS. In particular, if any point on the unit interval is equally likely as a starting point for the learning process, then most of the time $(50/61 = 82\%)$, the population will learn the inefficient ESS.

The punchline of this discussion is hardly comforting for old-style social Darwinists and their modern descendants. Often enough in life, evolution leads to a world that is distinctly not the best possible. We have evolved some remarkable weapons of mass destruction, for example, but it is not clear that we are better off because we now have such weapons. We may merely have created the means of our own mass destruction.

This gloomy thought has occurred to biologists in the following terms.[4] Most animals are rather heavily armed, but they rarely use their armaments on each other. To take just one example, think of poisonous snakes. These snakes fight all the time with each other over territory, mating opportunities, prey, and the like. They could easily kill each other with one bite in a fight, but they almost never do. Instead of biting each other, they wrestle. They save their poison for use on members of other species.

The game called Hawk versus Dove explains why serious conflicts are rare, both among animals and also among boundedly rational humans. Hawk versus Dove is shown in Figure 8.6. The language originates from the Vietnam War era, when hawks wanted to escalate the fighting in Vietnam to the limits of conventional warfare[5] and doves wanted to deescalate the fighting to a cease-fire. There is a military value, V, at stake, and this value is being contested by two countries. There are two country types. Hawk is an aggressive type. When

---

[4]See the classic article by John Maynard Smith and George Price, "The Logic of Animal Conflicts," *Nature* 246(1973):15–18.

[5]Extreme hawks wanted to go nuclear, too.

two hawks meet, there is sure to be heavy fighting. The expected value of a fight is

$$\frac{1}{2}(V) + \frac{1}{2}(-C)$$

With probability 1/2, a combatant wins the fight and therefore V; with probability 1/2, a combatant loses the fight and incurs cost C.[6] In keeping with the assumption that the fighting is serious, we have

$$V < C$$

Dove is a nonaggressive player type. When a hawk meets a dove, the dove leaves the battlefield and the hawk takes the resource without a fight. Finally, when two doves meet, there is no fight. Instead, they partition the military value, getting 1/2 each. The doves reach a resolution by diplomatic means, without resorting to their weapons—just like the wrestling matches of poisonous snakes.

We now compute the payoffs of the two player types and the population average. Let x be the percentage of hawks in the population. Let hawk payoff be u_1 and dove payoff be u_2. Substituting the values $a = (V - C)/2$, $b = V$, $c = 0$, and $d = V/2$ into the replicator equation, we get

$$\frac{dx}{dt} = x(1 - x)\left[\frac{x(V - C)}{2} + \frac{(1 - x)(V)}{2}\right]$$

To get an idea of the dynamics involved, let $V = 2$ and $C = 12$. Cost greatly exceeds military value. Substituting, we get

$$\frac{dx}{dt} = x(1 - x)(1 - 6x)$$

This replicator equation is shown in Figure 8.7. It has roots at $x = 0$, $x = 1/6$, and $x = 1$. Notice that the only root of $F(x)$ where the slope of $F(x)$ is negative is at $x^* = 1/6$. Hence, the ESS implies a proportion 1/6 of hawks and 5/6 of doves. When two countries are matched in a potential conflict, the probability is only $(1/6)^2 = 1/36$ that a serious fight will actually occur. Almost all the time (35/36), potential conflicts are resolved by peaceful means—either by retreat of one of the two sides, or by a diplomatically arranged partition. You can show (end-of-chapter problem) that, as the cost of fighting goes up (as in an arms race), the probability of a fight becomes extremely small. The world can only support a small percentage of warlike states, and these states don't do any better at equilibrium than the peace-loving states do.

The three phase diagrams (Figures 8.2, 8.5, and 8.7) exhaust all the ESS possibilities for a 2 × 2 symmetrical game. Such a game has either one or two ESSs, and when it has two ESSs the outcome of the game depends crucially on

---

[6]You can think of V as already containing the cost of capturing it in war. The cost C is therefore the marginal cost of losing.

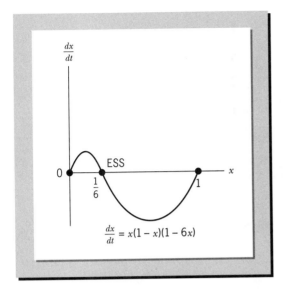

Figure 8.7. Hawk versus Dove, phase diagram.

the starting point. There is one other possibility, namely, that no ESS exists. Suppose that $a = b = c = d$. Both strategies pay exactly the same under all circumstances. Substituting into the replicator equation, we get

$$\frac{dx}{dt} = x(1 - x)(0) = 0$$

Every possible x is a solution to this system, but x is dynamically unstable. This example is extreme, but many interesting possibilities arise in more complicated games—including the emergence of chaos when no ESS exists. If you are interested in pursuing this subject further, it's worth studying differential equations, which are the ticket to advanced study. In the meantime, however, let's come back down to earth and take a look at some very boundedly rational beings, frogs.

8.3 Frogs Call for Mates[7] ■ ■ ■ ■ ■ ■ ■ ■ ■ ■ ■ ■ ■ ■ ■ ■ ■ ■ ■

Humans are not the only boundedly rational players on earth. Indeed, we are the least boundedly rational players. All other animals have much greater bounds on their rationality—and most of them are simply mindless. Nevertheless, animals manage to play many of the same games that people play, but the

---

[7]The material for this study is based on Roy Gardner, Molly Morris, and Craig Nelson, "Conditional Evolutionary Stable Strategies," *Animal Behavior* 35 (1987):141–55.

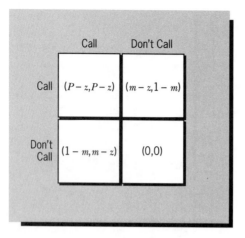

Figure 8.8.   Frogs Call for Mates.

mechanism by which they play them is very different. Animals don't solve games via necessary and sufficient conditions—that's what you're supposed to be doing. Rather, animals solve games by the process of natural selection. We will review just enough biology to see how this works.[8]

The *genome* of any creature contains all its genetic information—its DNA content. This information is arrayed along the chromosomes. A particular spot on a chromosome, called a *locus,* governs some aspect of a creature's form and behavior. In frogs, for instance, calling behavior is governed by their genetic code. Females do not call at all—the same genetic information that determines sex also shuts down the calling system. The code stored at a locus is called the *genotype,* and the possible factors that may be present in the code are called *alleles.* The information stored at the genetic level is expressed at the level of form and behavior. This is called the *phenotype* of the creature. In our context, the phenotype is the strategy chosen.

To see how this all works, consider the game in Figure 8.8. There are two strategies, Call and Don't call. The simplest genetic code for this behavior consists of a pair of alleles, A and B, at a single locus.[9] With sexual reproduction, there are three possible genotypes: AA, AB, and BB. The genotypes AA and AB produce the phenotype Call; the genotype BB produces the phenotype Don't call. We have to worry about payoffs as well as strategies. Instead of payoffs in dollars, frogs get payoffs in units of *fitness,* which can be measured by number of offspring. Fitness is just like utility—the more the better. The higher an animal's payoff, the more likely it is to transmit its genes to the next

[8]The following two paragraphs represent an enormous simplification of the relevant biology—rather like trying to compress all the information in this book in two paragraphs.

[9]Actually, the genetic code for frogs is much more complicated than this. However, the additional complexity does not affect the conclusions.

generation. The process by which genetic code is transmitted from one generation to the next is called natural selection. In *natural selection,* if a behavior has above-average fitness, then it increases as a percentage of the population as time goes on. This should sound familiar—it is exactly the same replicator dynamics we have used already. The limit of the process of natural selection, if such a limit exists, is an evolutionary equilibrium, where every surviving animal in a species has the same fitness. At the same time, this evolutionary equilibrium is a game equilibrium, where every strategy being played maximizes payoff.

There are many ways to test game theory, to see how well it predicts. We can run experiments in a laboratory, under controlled conditions, and see what happens. We can run experiments in the field, under less-controlled conditions, and see what happens. We can also watch what happens in the real world, completely beyond our control, and ask why it happened. Studying frogs combines elements of the last two kinds of science: making something happen that is not completely under our control, and watching something happen that is completely out of our control.

Some 300 million years ago, the ancestors of frogs did not have ears and did not make sounds. After a long period of evolution, all frogs have ears and the males make sounds—they call. The females do not have vocal chords and so they remain silent. Females do have excellent hearing, though: they can hear a male calling from a kilometer away. Enemies of frogs, especially snakes, also tune into the calls of males, the better to find and eat them. Male frogs are thus caught in this terrible dilemma. If they call, they can get eaten; if they don't call, they may never attract a female.

The species this section discusses in detail is *Hyla cinera,* the tree frog native to Indiana. The males of this species spend most of their time in trees, coming down to the ground to feed and to mate. The females are dispersed, and congregate with the males only during mating season, when females hear the calls of males and approach them. The game played by males, who are roughly the same size, is a 2-player symmetrical game. It is a 2-player game because in the overwhelming number of cases in the field (more than 95%), exactly two males are found in the same 4-meter radius of territory. The game is symmetrical because, as far as we can tell, females cannot tell the difference between one male frog and another.

An interesting experiment in this regard was conducted by Steve Perrill of Butler University. He placed two males in an arena with a 4-meter radius in a field at night. He then released a gravid female[10] on the edge of the arena. There were two treatments. In one treatment, both males were calling or both males were silent. In this treatment, the probability of the female mating with a given male was about 50%. In the second treatment, one male was calling and the other male was silent. In this treatment, the probability of the female

[10]That is, a female carrying unfertilized eggs.

mating with the male who called was 60%. At this short distance at night, the female was groping in the dark and basically mated with the first male she encountered.[11]

We can now set out some parameters to describe the game played by the male frogs. Let z be the cost of calling. This cost includes the danger of becoming prey as well as the danger of running out of energy. Calling takes a lot of energy, especially on a cold night. Becoming prey or running out of energy are equally fatal. Let m be the probability that a male who calls in a pair of males, the other of whom is not calling, gets a mate. For the Perrill data, we have

$$m = .6$$

Next, we normalize the attraction of females such that 1 male call = 1 female attracted, 0 male calls = 0 females attracted. Finally, frog calls display diminishing returns in the sense that two males calling attract P females each, with $0 < P < 1$. There is some interference between the frog calls, just as there is interference between competing advertisements for essentially the same product.

We can now write down the matrix for the game played by a pair of male frogs (see Figure 8.8). Each frog has two strategies, Call and Don't call. If both frogs call, each attracts P females and pays cost z. If only one frog calls, he attracts 1 female with probability m and 0 females with probability $1 - m$; in either event, he pays cost z. The frog that doesn't call attracts 1 female with probability $1 - m$ and 0 females with probability m; in either event, he pays cost 0. Finally, if both are silent, 0 females are attracted and no cost is paid. These are the payoffs shown in Figure 8.8.

There are three possible ESSs for this game, depending on the values of the payoff parameters (m,z,P). First, when $m < z$, it doesn't pay even a single male to call. Since $P < 1$, it also follows that $(P - z) < (1 - m)$. Thus we get an ESS at Don't call for each male—the area marked Don't call in Figure 8.9. Next, suppose that the cost of calling falls, so that $z > m$, but not too much, so that $(P - z) < (1 - m)$. Then we get a mixed strategy equilibrium, with some males calling and some males not calling. This is the zone marked Mix in Figure 8.9. Finally, suppose that the cost of calling drops even further, so that $(P - z) > (1 - m)$. The strategy Call is a strictly dominant strategy in this event and so Call is an ESS. This eventuality is shown by the zone Call in Figure 8.9.

Economic reasoning comes through loud and clear here: the cheaper it is to call, the more the frogs call. Not only can frogs play games, they can also obey the laws of economics, in this case the law of supply. When it costs too much to supply a call, they don't supply it.[12]

---

[11] Think if you can see any analogies between this scene and the typical bar scene among humans.

[12] Animals have been studied intensively in the laboratory to see if their behavior accords with the law of economics. See, for example, John Kagel, Raymond Battalio, Howard Rachlin, Leonard Green, Robert Bassman, and W. Klemm, "Experimental Studies of Consumer Behavior Using Laboratory Animals," *Economic Inquiry* 13 (1975):22–38.

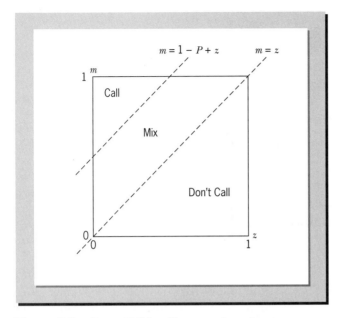

$$m = 1 - P + z \qquad m = z$$

Figure 8.9. Frogs Call for Mates, regime diagram.

Of these three possible ESSs, the one most likely under typical Indiana summer conditions is Mix. About 80% of the males on a typical night are calling, and 20% are not. At an ESS in mixed strategies, however, both Call and Don't call have the same payoff. On a really cold night, none of the frogs call, whereas on the warmest night of the year, they all call. ESS is the best way to organize all this data in a single explanation.

8.4 ESS for 2 × 2 Asymmetrical Games ■■■■■■■■

The ESS of a symmetrical game is itself symmetrical, a **symmetrical ESS.** In such games, all the boundedly rational players are essentially alike. However, boundedly rational players can also play asymmetrical games. In an asymmetrical game, the players are different and recognize the difference. The ESS of an asymmetrical game is called an **asymmetrical ESS,** and players at such an ESS may use different strategies. In such a case, you should think of ESS as standing for evolutionarily stable strategies, one for each player. We will study in detail how boundedly rational players play Telex versus IBM (recall Chapter 6), given in normal form in Figure 8.10.[13] The player in the role of Telex controls the

---

[13]This game is analyzed here in normal form. It could also be analyzed in extensive form, yielding similar results. See R. Selten, "Evolutionary Stability in Extensive Two-Person Games," *Mathematical Social Sciences* 5 (1983):269–363.

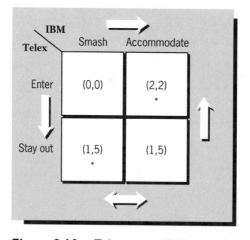

Figure 8.10.   Telex versus IBM, normal form.

rows of the matrix; the player in the role of IBM controls the columns. There are two Telex types, those who enter, called Entrants, and those who stay out, called Hesitators. There are also two IBM types, those who smash, called Smashers, and those who accommodate, called Accommodators. As you can see from Figure 8.10, this game has two equilibria: (stay out, smash) and (enter, accommodate). Only (enter, accommodate) is evolutionarily stable. The credibility problem that (stay out, smash) has in extensive form shows up as evolutionary instability. This makes a lot of sense. If you do something that is not credible, generations a long time from now will not believe it any more than the current generation does.

The asymmetry that shows up in Telex versus IBM is quite natural. All the ingredients necessary for a game like this are present whenever an upstart firm enters the turf of a large, established firm. Comparable asymmetries arise as cost advantages, first mover advantages (Cournot competition), second mover advantages (Bertrand competition), and information advantages—the subject of Part III of this book. Whatever the source of the asymmetry, it is clearly present in the minds of the players.

In an asymmetrical game, we apply replicator dynamics to each role separately. In Telex versus IBM, this means applying replicator dynamics to the Telex player types (Entrant and Hesitator) and to the IBM player types (Smasher and Accommodator) separately. We need two dimensions to represent these dynamics. Let x be the percentage of Entrants; $1 - x$, the percentage of Hesitators. Similarly, let y be the percentage of Smashers and $1 - y$ be the percentage of Accommodators.

We now compute for each role the expected payoff of each player type in that role. On the Telex side of the game, we have for Entrants

$$u(\text{enter}) = (y)\, 0 + 1(1 - y)\, 2 = 2(1 - y)$$

since the probability of being matched with a Smasher is y, and the probability of being matched with an Accommodator is $1 - y$. Again, for Hesitators, we have

$$u(\text{stay out}) = y\,1 + (1 - y)\,1 = 1$$

Staying out of the market yields a sure-thing payoff. On the IBM side of the game, we have for Smashers

$$u(\text{smash}) = x\,0 + (1 - x)\,5 = 5 - 5x$$

since they are matched with an Entrant with probability x (in which event they get 0) and with a Hesitator with probability $1 - x$ (in which case they get 5). By the same token, Accommodators can expect the payoffs

$$u(\text{accommodate}) = x\,2 + (1 - x)\,5 = 5 - 3x$$

Notice that $u(\text{accommodate}) = (5 - 3x) > (5 - 5x) = \text{u(smash)}$ unless $x = 0$, in which case they are equal. This result shows right away that accommodate dominates smash (which we saw in a different context in Chapter 6), although not strictly so.

An ESS for Telex versus IBM is a vector (x^*, y^*), where x^* is the equilibrium percentage of Entrants on the Telex side and y^* is the equilibrium percentage of Smashers on the IBM side. At an ESS, the behavior on each side of the game cannot be upset by mistakes. There is a replicator equation for each of the two roles. On the Telex side, we have

$$\frac{dx}{dt} = x[u(\text{enter}) - \text{average Telex}]$$

where $u(\text{enter})$ is the payoff to entry and average Telex is the average payoff to Telex player types. As we have just seen,

$$u(\text{enter}) = 2(1 - y) \text{ and}$$
$$u(\text{stay out}) = 1$$

The average Telex player gets

$$\text{average Telex} = xu(\text{enter}) + (1 - x)u(\text{stay out})$$
$$= x[2(1 - y)] + (1 - x)1$$

Substituting in the replicator equation for the Telex side of the game, we get

$$\frac{dx}{dt} = x(1 - x)[2(1 - y) - 1]$$
$$= x(1 - x)(1 - 2y)$$

Notice that the percentage of Entrants increases if

$$2(1 - y) - 1 > 0$$

Solving this inequality, we get

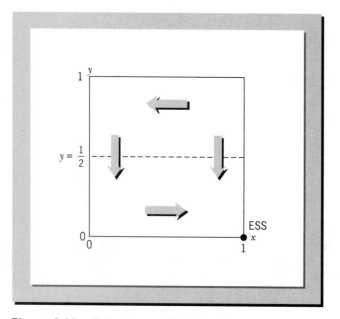

Figure 8.11.   Telex versus IBM, phase diagram.

$$y < 1/2$$

What this inequality means is that if the fraction of Smashers in the IBM population is less than $1/2$, it pays to enter. Figure 8.11 depicts the phase diagram for Telex versus IBM. The arrow below the line $y = 1/2$ pointing to the right shows that dx/dt is positive is this zone, and so x is increasing. The arrow above the line $y = 1/2$ pointing to the left shows that dx/dt is negative in this zone, and so x is decreasing.

Replicator dynamics is also at work on the IBM side. Here we have

$$\frac{dy}{dt} = y[u(\text{smash}) - \text{average IBM}]$$

where

$$u(\text{smash}) = 1 - x \text{ and}$$
$$\text{average IBM} = yu(\text{smash}) + (1 - y)u(\text{accommodate})$$
$$= (1 - x) + (1 - y)(1 + x)$$

Substituting into the replicator equation, we get

$$\frac{dy}{dt} = y(1 - y)(-2x)$$

Notice that dy/dt is always negative as long as there are any Entrants. This is reflected by the arrows pointing down in the phase diagram of Figure 8.11.

Telex versus IBM has two equilibria. One of these, (enter, accommodate), is played by a population with $x^* = 1$ and $y^* = 0$. All Telex player types are Entrants, and all IBM player types are Accommodators. This equilibrium is an ESS. Arrows point toward it from both directions. If an IBM player type were to make a mistake and smash, that player type would get a below-average return and be driven out of the population. Likewise, if a Telex player type made a mistake and stayed out, that player type would get a below-average return and be driven out of the Telex population.

The other equilibrium, (stay out, smash), is played by a population with $x = 0$ and $y = 1$. All Telex types are Hesitators, and all IBM player types are Smashers. This equilibrium is not an ESS. Replicator dynamics favors any IBM type who accommodates by mistake. Such a mistake yields a positive payoff instead of the zero from smash, and replicator dynamics is off and running, leaving the Smashers in the dust. The equilibrium with the credibility problem when played by rational players still has a problem when played by boundedly rational players—it's unstable.

For asymmetrical games, there is a very simple test for whether an equilibrium can possibly be an ESS. An equilibrium is a **strict equilibrium** if each player has a unique best response to the other player's strategy. In terms of an arrow diagram for the matrix game, this means that all arrows point in to an equilibrium, but no arrow points out (no two-headed arrows). Here is the test, called **Selten's test** after its discoverer:

■ ■

ESS for Asymmetrical Games. If (x^*, y^*) is an ESS, then (x^*, y^*) is a strict equilibrium.[14]

This test is very effective when applied to Telex versus IBM. The equilibrium (stay out, smash) is not strict, since accommodate is also a best response to stay out. Accordingly, (stay out, smash) played by the population $(x, y) = (0,1)$ cannot be an ESS. For 2 × 2 asymmetrical games, the converse is also true:

■ ■

ESS for 2 × 2 Asymmetrical Games. If (x^*, y^*) is a strict equilibrium, then (x^*, y^*) is an ESS.

Taken together, these two results give us an effective shortcut to finding all the ESS of a 2 × 2 asymmetrical game. We look for strict equilibria, and that's all. Since mixed strategy equilibria have multiple best responses (every strategy in the mixture pays the same), they can't possibly be strict and so they can't be ESSs of asymmetrical games.

---

[14]This result was first proved by R. Selten, "A Note on Evolutionarily Stable Strategies in Asymmetrical Animal Conflicts," *Journal of Theoretical Biology* 84 (1980):93–101. A short mathematical proof is given in Josef Hofbauer and Karl Sigmund, *The Theory of Evolution and Dynamical Systems* (Cambridge: Cambridge University Press, 1987), chap. 17.

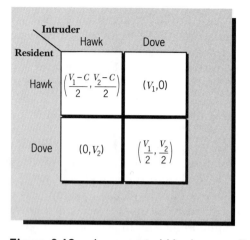

Figure 8.12.   Asymmetrical Hawk versus Dove.

Let's find the ESS of Hawk versus Dove when payoffs are asymmetrical. Military value of the contested item is V_1 to the row player, called the resident because he or she holds the territory at the beginning of the game. Military value of the contested item is V_2 to the column player, called the intruder because he or she does not hold the territory at the beginning of the game. We have

$$C > V_1 > V_2 > 0$$

The territory is worth more to the resident than to the intruder, but it is not worth the cost of a fight to either country. Asymmetrical Hawk versus Dove is shown in Figure 8.12. As you can see from the arrow diagram, there are two strict equilibria, (hawk, dove) and (dove, hawk). Each of these is an ESS. At the ESS (hawk, dove), the item goes to the country that attaches the higher military value to it. At the ESS (dove, hawk), the item goes to the country that attaches the lower military value to it. *No fighting is observed at an ESS.* The ESS we tend to see in international relations is (hawk, dove). If a parcel is extremely important to a country's security, that country tends to control it. It is when the same parcel is equally important to two countries, like the Golan Heights for Israel and Syria, that it becomes something the countries might go to war over. Asymmetrical Hawk versus Dove also has a third equilibrium, in mixed strategies. However, since a mixed strategy equilibrium is not strict, this cannot be an ESS.

There is a general principle underlying the ESS of Asymmetrical Hawk versus Dove. Although the boundaries we draw on maps are in some metaphysical sense arbitrary, once they are drawn they cannot be crossed without permission. The people who were there first have a right to stay there. Priority is a powerful asymmetry in international affairs. Entrants have to ask for permission to enter—otherwise, there could be trouble.[15]

As in the case of symmetrical games, where there may not be an ESS, in asymmetrical games there may also fail to be an ESS. Matching Pennies (Figure 3.1) offers the simplest example. This is an asymmetrical 2-person game. Its only equilibrium is in mixed strategies. Since mixed strategies cannot be strict, Matching Pennies has no ESS. Indeed, it is often difficult for boundedly rational players to learn a mixed strategy. The information-processing requirements exceed all but the highest rational capabilities.

⠏ 8.5 Fast Learning with a Finite Number of Players ■

This chapter has proceeded under two assumptions: the learning studied has been quite slow; only some of the players in a period adopt a higher-paying strategy. In addition, in order to use differential equations to describe the adjustment process, a large population of players has been assumed. In this section, both these assumptions are relaxed. We now allow players to adopt a higher-paying strategy immediately, and we allow for a finite number of players. In so doing, we achieve a certain sharpening of the results for symmetrical 2×2 games.

This section studies the game Coordination of Figure 8.4. Now, however, instead of a large number of players, there are only five players. Moreover, instead of being governed by replicator dynamics, the out-of-equilibrium behavior is described by **best-response dynamics.** That is, each player picks the strategy this period that maximizes payoff, given the experience of the previous period. Best-response dynamics allows for the fastest possible learning.[16]

Suppose that the players are arrayed on a circle, as in Figure 8.13a, and each player plays Coordination with the neighbors to the left and to the right each period. Thus player 1 plays each period with players 2 and 5; player 2, with players 1 and 3; and so on. The players against whom player i plays each period are his or her *neighbors*. A *state of the game* tells what each player did in the previous period (Figure 8.13b). There are $2^5 = 32$ possible states of this game. In this period, each player i picks a strategy to maximize utility, given the play of the neighbors in the previous period. Let $x_i(t)$ denote the number of player i's neighbors who played strategy 1 in period t; $2 - x_i(t)$, the number of player i's neighbors who played strategy 2 in period t. Then, in period $t + 1$, player i

---

[15]The same principle operates with patents. We can think of the evolution of the patent system as a way of making clear who is the resident and who is the intruder when a discovery is involved.

[16]A general model of this sort has been studied by S. K. Berninghaus and U. Schwalbe, "Evolution, Interaction, and Nash Equilibrium," working paper, University of Mannheim, 1993.

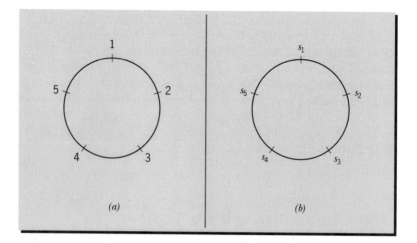

Figure 8.13. Player network: (*a*) five players; (*b*) state of the game.

picks a strategy to maximize utility, based on the state of the game in period *t*. Player *i* picks strategy 1 if

$$x_i(t)50 + [2 - x_i(t)]49 > x_i(t)0 + [2 - x_i(t)]60$$

Rearranging, we have

$$x_i(t) > \frac{22}{61}$$

Since $x_i(t)$ can only take on the values 0, 1, or 2, we have a simple rule for player *i* to follow:

Play strategy 1 this period if at least one neighbor played strategy 1 last period.

Finally, by symmetry, what is true of player *i* is true for any other player.

We will see that for all but one of the 32 possible states of the system, best-response dynamics leads to the ESS (strategy 1, strategy 1). To do this, we need to construct dynamics analogous to replicator dynamics. If every player in the game played strategy 2 at time *t*, then no player in the population has a neighbor who played strategy 1 at time *t*, so no player in the population plays strategy 1 in this period. Suppose that one player played strategy 1 at time *t*. Then two players this period have neighbors who played strategy 1 last period, and those two players will play strategy 1 this period, as shown in Figure 8.14*a*. Once at least one player plays strategy 1 in period *t*, the number of players playing strategy *i* in period *t* + 1 is greater than that in period *t*. This is what drives the players toward strategy 1.

In Figure 8.14*b* and *c* we see what happens when two players played strategy 1 in period *t*. We have to distinguish between two cases, depending on how many players have a neighbor who played strategy 1. If the two players who

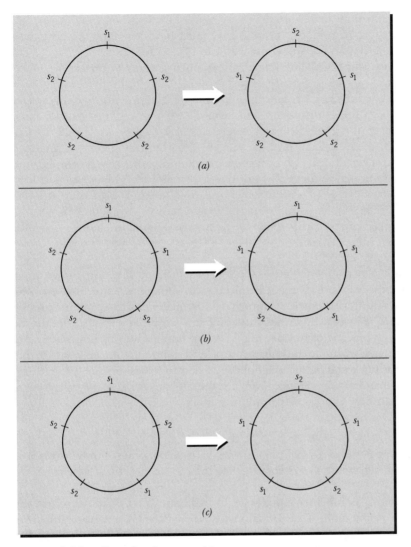

Figure 8.14. Coordination, transitions.

played strategy 1 are themselves neighbors (Figure 8.14*b*), then four players have a neighbor who played strategy 1 in period *t*, and these four players will play strategy 1 in period *t* + 1, a big increase. If the two players who played strategy 1 are not neighbors (Figure 8.14*c*), then three players have a neighbor who played strategy 1 in period *t*, and these three players will play strategy 1 in period *t* + 1, again an increase. Once three players are playing strategy 1 in period *t*, four or five of them have neighbors who played strategy 1, depending on how they are arrayed. That means either four or five players play strategy 1 in period *t* + 1, again an increase. Either the system has converged to its dynamic equilibrium, or it has come very close. Finally, when four players are playing strategy 1 in period *t*, every player must have a neighbor who played that strategy, and all players play strategy 1 in period *t* + 1.

This result verifies the claim made earlier: once strategy 1 appears, it quickly takes over. A player adopts strategy 1 just as soon as one of his or her neighbors does. In this way, strategy 1 comes to predominate in a process that never takes more than the number of players. The dynamics described here has two fixed points, corresponding to the cases where all players play strategy 2 and all players play strategy 1. Each of these was an ESS when the game was analyzed using replicator dynamics. In best-response dynamics, however, the equilibrium where all players play strategy 2 is no longer dynamically stable. Once at least one player plays strategy 1—even if by mistake—strategy 1 takes over. It is the only dynamically stable equilibrium in best-response dynamics. Strategy 1, which had the largest probability of being the outcome under replicator dynamics $(50/61)$,[17] is even more likely $(31/32)$ to be the outcome under best-response dynamics.

This result is not a coincidence. Rather, in 2×2 coordination games, most varieties of best-response dynamics converge for almost all initial states of the system to an equilibrium such as strategy 1.[18] To make this assertion precise, we need one new idea that describes strategy 1 in Coordination. First, define the *deviation loss* to player *i* of not playing a certain equilibrium by how much that player loses by switching to another strategy, and define the *deviation loss product* of an equilibrium to be the product of the deviation losses for each player. One equilibrium has **risk dominance** over another if its deviation loss product is larger. We can now express our result as follows:

■ ■

Theorem on Best-Response Dynamics. In 2×2 coordination games with best-response dynamics, learning almost always converges to the risk-dominant equilibrium.

To see how risk dominance applies to Coordination, let's walk through the steps of the calculation. The deviation loss to a player from switching from strategy 1 to strategy 2 is $50 - 0 = 50$. The deviation loss product for this equilibrium is $50^2 = 2500$. The deviation loss to a player from switching from strategy 2 to strategy 1 is $60 - 49 = 11$. The deviation loss product for this equilibrium is $11^2 = 121$. The equilibrium (strategy 1, strategy 1) risk dominates the equilibrium (strategy 2, strategy 2), since

$$2500 > 121$$

[17]That is, if every point in the unit interval is considered equally likely.

[18]A large number of recent papers have demonstrated this result. Two good examples are M. Kandori, G. J. Mailath, and R. Rob, "Learning, Mutation, and Long Run Equilibrium in Games," *Econometrica* 61 (1993):29–56; and H. Peyton Young, "The Evolution of Conventions," *Econometrica* 61 (1993):57–89.

The best-response dynamics converges to the ESS at strategy 1 in a finite number of periods, from all but one state of the system.[19]

Best-response dynamics speeds up learning and gives human players a shortcut to a game equilibrium. The same adjustment, according to replicator dynamics, might take aeons, if it occurred at all. Part of the reason that our species has taken over the earth from all other living things is our seemingly unlimited facility at exploiting this shortcut. Best-response dynamics is certainly important in rapidly evolving markets, such as that for video games, to which we now turn.

8.6 The Evolution of Video Games[20] ■ ■ ■ ■ ■ ■ ■ ■ ■ ■

In a perfectly coordinated world, any computer program could run on any computer. Unfortunately, this is not the world we live in. Ever since John von Neumann laid down the architectural principles for computers in 1945, computers have had difficulty coordinating with each other. In the industry we are about to consider, **video games,** the inability to coordinate has evolved as a standard part of the industry. Let's see how this happened.[21]

The first computer games were created in the early 1960s. You could only play these games if you had a computer. Nolan Bushnell, a computer engineer, created the first **video game,** Pong, in 1972. To play Pong, all you needed was a television monitor and the program that ran the game, housed in a microprocessor-based circuit board. Pong was a big hit, first in arcades and later (1974) in a home version, and launched Bushnell's newly created Atari Corporation. About 100,000 copies of Pong were produced in 1974, but only about 10,000 of these were made by Atari. Video games were simple to copy, and pirate versions flooded the market. Also flooding the market were entrants, well over a dozen by 1978.

One of those entrants was Nintendo. Nintendo was a large Japanese card and toy company. In 1975, Nintendo cut a deal with Magnavox, one of Atari's principal rivals, to market Pong-like video games in Japan. Nintendo introduced its own games for the first time 2 years later, beginning with Color TV Game 6. Color, better sound and graphics, and more interesting and challenging games soon became Nintendo hallmarks. Nintendo introduced its first big hit, Donkey Kong, in the United States in 1980. Sales quickly reached the $100 million mark. In a heated bidding contest, Coleco beat out Atari and Mattel for the exclusive rights to the home video version of Donkey Kong in 1982. Coleco ultimately sold over 6 million Donkey Kong cartridges. Despite its increased

---

[19]This conclusion continues to hold true if players make mistakes with a small probability.

[20]Material has been drawn from David Sheff, *Game Over* (New York: Random House, 1993).

[21]If you want to skip the story, go directly to problem 8, which gives the essential idea in an asymmetrical 2-player game with a unique ESS.

complexity, Donkey Kong also lost sales to counterfeit games—at least $100 million in sales, according to company figures. Nintendo pursued 35 counterfeiting cases in court, usually prevailing.

The year 1983 was a landmark year for the industry in the United States, especially if you consider cemeteries landmarks. Sales of video games fell from $3 billion in 1982 to about $100 million in 1983. Atari and Mattel nearly went under, and Coleco was barely hanging on. Nintendo, whose sales were still largely confined to Japan, where it had a dominant market share, saw the crash of the U.S. video game industry as a historic opportunity. Nintendo prepared to enter the U.S. market on its own in a big way. First, however, it had to make two strategic decisions. The first decision was how to introduce the rest of the games in its portfolio. Nintendo engineers developed a system, the Advanced Video System (or AVS, later known as the Nintendo Entertainment System, or NES) on which all the games could run. Second, Nintendo created an ingenious security system, called the *lockout system*. This system was basically nothing more than an electronic lock and key. The game-playing cartridge had to have a key to unlock the lock in the AVS player. The lockout system effectively put an end to counterfeiting. Its code wasn't broken for almost a decade, and then only by surreptitious access into the U.S. Patent Office, where it was on file.[22]

Nintendo brought its system to a nearly extinct U.S. market in 1984. Using the theme The evolution of a species is now complete, its marketing campaign featured pictures of Pong, color tennis, and a veiled video screen. Behind that screen, the buyer would uncover Donkey Kong, Super Mario Brothers, The Legend of Zelda—a panoply of great games. After a slow start, NES sales reached 7 million in 1988, with some 33 million game cartridges sold to go along with the system. The U.S. market recovered from the crash of 1983, with sales reaching the $5 billion level in 1992. In this U.S. market, Nintendo was the dominant firm.

Nintendo's lockout system had a very profitable, if unintended, aspect. Software producers could not create games to run on NES unless they had the key. They could only get the key by dealing with Nintendo. As a virtual monopoly, Nintendo could, and did, extract extremely favorable terms from software producers, who soon numbered more than 100. The same was true of toy retailers. Even giant chains, such as Toys 'R' Us, owed more than 20% of their profits to Nintendo sales. A further profitable feature was that the lockout system tended to lock players into the system. Once a player had acquired the system and a library of games, he or she (about 90% of all sales were to adolescent males) was much more likely to build a Nintendo library than to invest in another system.

One of Nintendo's biggest decisions came in 1990 and involved the 16-bit system that the company had developed, Super NES. Super NES could do

---

[22]Atari finally obtained a copy of the code by illegal means from the U.S. Bureau of Standards, where it had been registered for safekeeping.

everything better than NES. The only catch—and it was a big one—was that Super NES was not compatible with the NES. You couldn't run Super Mario Brothers 4 on NES, and you couldn't run Super Mario Brothers 3 on Super NES. With a price tag of $200 (the average annual expenditure on toys for a family of four) on Super NES, Nintendo was sure to encounter considerable buyer resistance. Nintendo was locked into its own success.

Despite all the negatives, Nintendo launched Super NES in the United States in 1991. In the 16-bit-system market, Nintendo and new rival Sega are running neck and neck. Nintendo's market dominance appears to be over, although a market in which all video games can be played on all systems still seems as elusive as ever.

From a historical perspective, the speed with which video games are evolving is truly astounding. It took millions of years for natural selection to evolve the calling behavior of tree frogs. It took 20 years to go from Pong to Super Mario Brothers 6. And it is still too early to say that a dynamic equilibrium has been reached.

▚ SUMMARY

1. Boundedly rational players make mistakes and learn slowly. When boundedly rational players play a game, they are usually out of equilibrium.

2. Replicator dynamics describes the out-of-equilibrium behavior of boundedly rational players. A strategy that does better than average is adopted by more players as time goes on. If a strategy is a stable equilibrium of the replicator dynamics, then it is a game equilibrium also. Such an equilibrium is called an evolutionarily stable strategy, or ESS for short.

3. An ESS is a game equilibrium to which replicator dynamics leads and that cannot be destroyed by small percentages of players making mistakes.

4. Let's Make a Deal has a unique ESS, which agrees with the rational solution.

5. Replicator dynamics has an obvious parallel in business, where it does not pay to be below average.

6. There are two main types of games that boundedly rational players play, symmetrical and asymmetrical. The properties of ESS for these two types of games are very different. In particular, the ESS of a symmetrical game must be in symmetrical strategies, and the ESS of an asymmetrical game cannot be in mixed strategies.

7. To test a 2×2 symmetrical game equilibrium for stability, we use the stability theorem, which tells us whether evolution is stable against mistakes in the vicinity of a game equilibrium or not.

8. Evolution need not lead to the best of all possible worlds. Coordination games have ESSs that are payoff dominated by other ESSs. This phenome-

non explains why certain computer operating systems, which might have been the best if universally adopted, have become extinct instead.

9. The ESS of a symmetrical game may be in mixed strategies, as in Hawk versus Dove. The ESS of an asymmetrical game must be in pure strategies. All ESSs of an asymmetrical game are strict equilibria, equilibria with a unique best response.

10. In 2×2 coordination games, best-response dynamics selects the ESS that is risk dominant. Best-response dynamics is particularly applicable to markets where the product is rapidly evolving and where firms adopt short-term profit-maximizing strategies.

▚ KEY TERMS

bounded rationality	symmetrical/asymmetrical ESS
evolutionarily stable strategy (ESS)	strict equilibrium
replication dynamics	Selten's test
replicator equation	best-response dynamics
stability theorem	risk dominance
mistakes	video games

▚ PROBLEMS

1. State the basic principle of replicator dynamics. Do you think the compensation of managers is based on this principle? Do you think it should be?

2. Find an ESS for Prisoner's Dilemma with payoffs $a = 3$, $c = 4$, $b = 0$, and $d = 2$, as in Figure 8.3. Is the ESS you found unique?

3. Find two ESSs for Coordination with $a = 3$, $b = c = 0$, and $d = 2$, as in Figure 8.3. Why isn't the mixed strategy equilibrium of this game an ESS? Why is a payoff dominated equilibrium evolutionarily stable?

4. Find the ESS for Hawk versus Dove (Figure 8.6) when $V = 2$ and $C = 100$. What are the odds of a fight occurring? What does this tell you about the probability of serious fights as cost gets large?

5. Set $m = .6$ and $P = .8$ in Frogs Call for Mates. Now find values of the cost of calling, z, such that each of the following happens: (a) Don't call is an ESS; (b) Mix is an ESS; and (c) Call is an ESS. Relate your answer to standard economic theory, in particular, the law of cost.

6. Suppose that there are two kinds of frogs in Frogs Call for Mates. Large frogs have a larger cost of calling (z_1) than do small frogs (z_2). Redraw the game matrix of Figure 8.8. What kinds of ESS are possible?

7. Assuming that $V_i < C_i$ for both i, construct a phase diagram for Asymmetrical Hawk versus Dove (Figure 8.12) like that for Telex versus IBM

Company XX \ Company xy	Open system	Lockout system
Open system	(6,4)	(5,5)
Lockout system	(9,1)	(10,0)

Figure 8.15. Video market game, two firms.

(Figure 8.11). This diagram will show in detail why this game has two ESSs.

8. Two boundedly rational video companies are playing the asymmetrical game in Figure 8.15. Company XX has to decide whether to have an open system or a lockout system. Company XY has to decide whether to create its own system or copy that of company XX. Find an ESS for this game. Interpret the Nintendo story on the basis of this ESS.
9. Apply the best-response dynamics to the Coordination game in problem 3. There are 4 players playing the game, arrayed on a circle, and each player makes the best response to the neighbors' strategies in the previous period. Which ESS is most likely to evolve? Why?
10. "A Cournot equilibrium is an ESS." Tell why this should be true in the Cournot game of Figure 5.1. The player types are the quantities that could be shipped by the manager of a firm.

APPENDIX. EVOLUTION IN THE LABORATORY[23]

The evolution of game behavior under controlled laboratory conditions has recently been the subject of intense investigation. This appendix considers one set of experiments that is especially instructive in this regard. Consider the games shown in Figure 8.16. The game in Figure 8.16*a* has a unique pure strategy equilibrium (that is also dominant), namely, (s_2,s_2). ESS theory has very

[23]This appendix is based on Russell W. Cooper, Douglas V. DeJong, Robert Forsythe, and Thomas W. Ross, "Selection Criteria in Coordination Games: Some Experimental Results," *American Economic Review* 80 (1991):218–33.

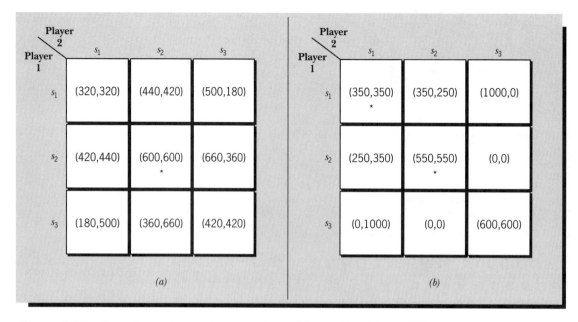

Figure 8.16. Experimental games in normal form: (a) one ESS; (b) two ESSs.

precise predictions for what happens if this game is played by boundedly rational players:

ESS Prediction 1. In the game in Figure 8.16a, play will evolve to the ESS at s_2.

The game in Figure 8.16b has two pure strategy equilibria, namely, (s_1,s_1) and (s_2,s_2). This game also has a mixed strategy equilibrium involving a probability distribution over strategies s_1 and s_2, with each player playing s_1 with probability .67. The phase diagram for this game would resemble that for Coordination (Figure 8.5), where the mixed strategy equilibrium is not an ESS but the two pure strategy equilibria are.

ESS Prediction 2. In the game in Figure 8.16b, play will evolve to either the ESS at s_1 or the ESS at s_2, depending on where play begins.

If the percentage of the population playing s_1 is sufficiently great (at least .67) at the outset, then the system will evolve to the ESS where all players choose s_1.

A team of four researchers from the University of Iowa and Carleton University conducted a series of experiments to study out-of-equilibrium behavior by boundedly rational players. The sample consisted of volunteers drawn from the ranks of upper division undergraduates and M.B.A. students at the University of Iowa. Subjects earned between $5 and $20 for participation in an experiment, depending on the strategies they and their opponents chose.

Subjects reviewed a set of instructions prior to play, after which the instructions were read out loud to them, all for the sake of making their choices as mistake free as possible. Each subject then played the game in Figure 8.16a for 10 periods, each period against a different opponent. This game, which is really easy to solve, served as a warm-up for the subjects. Each subject then played the game in Figure 8.16b for 21 periods, each time against a different opponent. This game was meant to be a bigger challenge for the subjects, and so it was.

The results of the experiment involving the games in Figure 8.16 are as follows. First, the data support for ESS prediction 1 is outstanding. Of 820 subject choices for the game in Figure 8.16a, 770 (94%) chose s_2. The vast majority went to this strategy almost immediately and stayed there. This phenomenon provides strong evidence for fast learning and also yields an estimate of the error rate of 6%, which is well within the range of error rates (5%–10%) observed in a wide variety of human behavior experiments. Second, the data support for ESS prediction 2 is also strong, although not as strong as that for prediction 1. The authors observed that the first 10 periods of play of this game basically involved learning. During this learning phase, play approached the ESS at s_1. The authors reported detailed data for the last 11 periods. During these 11 periods, of 110 subject choices, 83 (75%) chose s_1. During the last 5 periods, behavior came even closer to the ESS, with 42 of 50 subjects (84%) choosing s_1. By the end of a 2-hour laboratory session, with the play of an easy game followed by that of a more difficult game, behavior reminiscent of ESS had been observed twice.[24]

Although the results of this experiment are supportive of ESS theory, they reinforce a drawback of ESS already noted. The ESS at s_1 is payoff dominated by the ESS at s_2, yet a large majority of human subjects choose to play s_1. The evolution of behavior, whether it is slow according to the laws of natural selection, or fast according to the laws of cultural selection, is only guaranteed to find an ESS. It is not guaranteed to find an efficient ESS. It takes a lot more rationality than ESS provides for to get to better equilibria.

---

[24]Not all subjects played the game in Figure 8.16b; other games could be played in this stage.

PART THREE

Games with Imperfect Information

CHAPTER 9

▚▚▚▚▚

Signaling Games and Sequential Equilibrium

This chapter begins a new unit about games with imperfect information. Imperfect information has played a role in some of the games we have already studied. For instance, in Liar's Poker (section 3.3), player 1's gain was due entirely to the fact that player 1 knew what his or her card was and player 2 did not. A situation in which one player knows something that another player does not know is called an *information asymmetry*. Information asymmetries are pervasive in markets and in life. This and the following two chapters explore the implications of imperfect information and informational asymmetries for strategy.

This chapter considers signaling games. In a **signaling game,** one player knows more than another, and the player who knows more has to move first. For instance, the signaling game could be between you and a used-car dealer. The dealer knows a lot more about used cars than you do. The dealer also has to decide whether to put a given used car on the lot, and if so, what price tag to put on it, before you show up. Your decision is whether to buy a given used car or not. Signaling games go back to ancient times; the ancient Romans coined a phrase to apply to such games—*caveat emptor,* "let the buyer beware." Another signaling game, played for significantly higher stakes, arises when a privately held corporation goes public, offering its stock for sale to the public. The corporation knows a lot more about what it is worth than even the best-informed outside investor. Thus, signaling games are uniquely suited to the study of the phenomenon of *inside information.*

This chapter shows how to solve such games, beginning with a basic signaling game, where the informed player has two moves, one of which ends the game, and the uninformed player has two moves, either of which ends the game. The four kinds of market equilibria that can emerge from such a game are described. A new game equilibrium concept is presented, sequential equilibrium, which is invaluable to the study of signaling games. Markets have a hard time functioning properly in the presence of asymmetrical information. A particularly notorious example is called the market for lemons—a lemon is something of poor quality sold at too high a price. Repeated signaling games are studied next. In these games it is important for the uninformed player to learn what kind of player he or she is dealing with before entering into a long-term relationship. Bayesian updating is the technique used to make strategically sound decisions in such a case. Finally, the chapter looks at games where both sides are in the dark, but one side still has better information than the other. An outstanding example of this type of game was the leveraged buyout of RJR Nabisco in 1989. This was a signaling game replete with imperfect information on all sides.

9.1 Two-Player Signaling Games ■ ■ ■ ■ ■ ■ ■ ■ ■ ■ ■ ■

This section examines a game of imperfect information between two players, one of whom has the information (the **informed player**) and the other of whom doesn't have the information (the **uninformed player**). This game is called Caveat Emptor, after the ancient Roman saying that it embodies. Player 1, the seller, is informed and moves first. Player 2, the buyer, is uninformed and moves second. The game starts with a random move, the outcome of which is known only to the seller (see Figure 9.1). The item that the seller is selling is either good or bad. The seller knows whether the item is good or bad. All the buyer knows is that there is some probability p(good) that the item for sale is good, and some probability p(bad) that the item for sale is bad. After being informed about the quality of the good, the seller can either offer it for sale or withhold it from the market. If the seller withholds it from market, the game ends with the status quo payoffs of 0 each. If the seller offers the item for sale and it is good, it can be sold as is. If the seller offers the item for sale and it is bad, then it first needs to be cleaned up at cost c. After cleanup, a bad item looks just like a good item and the buyer can't tell the difference. In any event, the buyer does not see this cleanup operation. Moreover, the price for the

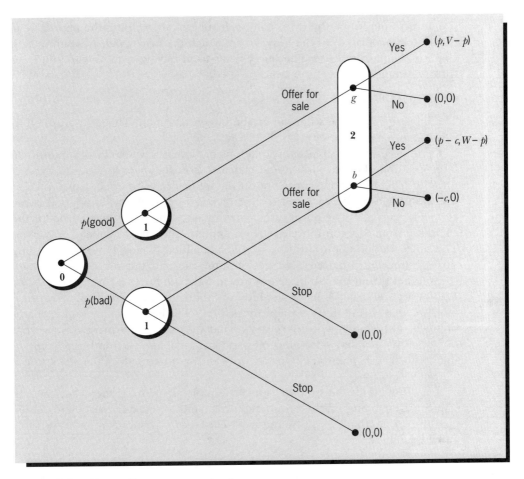

Figure 9.1. Caveat Emptor, extensive form.

item, p, is the same whether it is good or bad. Price can't give away the information, either.[1]

If the item is offered for sale, it is the buyer's turn to move. The buyer has two nodes in the information set: node g, corresponding to a good item being offered for sale, and node b, corresponding to a bad item being offered for sale. The buyer does not know which node the play has reached—both of them are in the information set. The buyer can say either yes or no to the item offered for sale. If the buyer says no, there is no deal. The buyer gets payoff 0, as does the good-type seller, but the bad-type seller gets the payoff $-c$. This seller cleaned up a bad item, only to see it go unsold. If the buyer says yes, there is a deal. The item sells for price p, which is the payoff to the good-type seller, and $p - c$ is the payoff to the bad-type seller. A good item is worth V to

[1]Later in this chapter the phenomenon whereby price does signal quality is studied.

the buyer, from which the price paid, p, is subtracted, yielding the payoff $V - p$. A bad item is worth W to the buyer, from which the price paid, p, is subtracted, yielding the payoff $W - p$. The buyer gains from buying a good type, but loses from buying a bad type:

$$V > p > W$$

The buyer gets burned when he or she buys a bad item. This, in a nutshell, is why the buyer must beware.

Here are three possible interpretations of Caveat Emptor. In the traditional interpretation, the seller is a used-car dealer and the buyer is about to visit the lot. The seller either puts a car out on the lot or not. The price, p, is posted in the windshield of the car. The cost, c, of making a used car look good is the cost of a paint job. The buyer either buys or not. The buyer gets burned if the car is a lemon. A second interpretation applies especially to college graduates. The seller is a job applicant, who is either qualified or not. However, by going through coaching that costs c, the job applicant can put on a good enough front to get through a job interview unscathed. The buyer is an employer. The employer gets burned if he or she hires an unqualified job applicant. The third interpretation is the most metaphorical. The seller is a company selling shares of stock. The company insiders know what the company's prospects are, but potential stockholders don't. By going to extra legal and accounting expense, c, the company can paint as rosy a picture as it wants. Buyers of the stock lose if the company is bad.

Even though Caveat Emptor is a very simple signaling game, a lot can still happen. Depending on the economic fundamentals represented by the parameters $p(\text{good})$, $p(\text{bad})$, p, V, W, and c, Caveat Emptor has four different possible game equilibria:

■ ■

Total Market Failure. All sellers, even the good-type sellers, fearing rejection by the buyers, withhold their goods from the market. The market ceases to function, even though gains from trade are available. An equilibrium where all informed players do the same thing is called a **pooling equilibrium.** Total market failure is an especially sinister pooling equilibrium.

Total Market Success. Only sellers with good items offer them for sale. Sellers with bad items withhold them from the market. Since all items offered for sale are good, buyers buy everything offered for sale. In this case, the market works perfectly. An equilibrium where the different types of informed players do different things is a **separating equilibrium.** In a separating equilibrium, *behavior reveals type.* The very act of offering the item for sale signals to the buyer that it is a good type. This signaling is the key to total market success.

Partial Market Success. All sellers offer their items for sale, good or bad. All buyers buy whatever is offered for sale. This is only a partial success: the market functions, but there are a lot of bad deals, which reduce market efficiency. This is another example of a pooling equilibrium. Unlike total market failure, however, this pooling equilibrium does generate some gains from trade.

Near Market Failure. Some, but not all, bad-type sellers offer their items for sale. Buyers buy what is offered for sale with a certain probability, but reject what is offered with some probability also. Thus, both buyers and bad-type sellers adopt a mixed strategy response to the imperfect information. In this market, total gains from trade are smaller than in complete market success or partial market success.

Each of these possibilities is a signaling game equilibrium for some payoff parameter values and some initial probabilities. Before exploring these equilibria further, we need a new equilibrium concept, which is indispensable for studying signaling games: sequential equilibrium.

▓ 9.2 Sequential Equilibrium: Pure Strategies ■

Caveat Emptor is the simplest possible signaling game there is. Still, it contains plenty of complexity. In particular, because of its imperfect information, this game has no subgames, which means subgame perfection can't be used as a solution device. This problem is endemic whenever information is imperfect and the informed player moves first. Intuitively, credibility has to be an important and appealing part of signaling—if you send a signal, you want the person who receives that signal to believe it. Otherwise, why would that person act on it?

The need for a sufficient condition that addresses credibility and applies more widely than subgame perfection is the inspiration for the concept of **sequential equilibrium.** A sequential equilibrium satisfies subgame perfection on subgames. On information sets like that of player 2 in Figure 9.1, which do not initiate subgames, sequential equilibrium requires that a player maximize expected utility—especially since the player may not know which node of the information set has been reached. To maximize expected utility presupposes a probability distribution over the nodes of the information set. A probability distribution over the nodes of player 2's information set {b,g} is a *belief*. Whenever possible, a belief should be based on hard evidence—the initial probabilities of the game, plus strategies of the other players. A sequential equilibrium for Caveat Emptor is a pair of strategies, one for each player, and a belief for player 2, which together satisfy backward induction on all information sets.[2]

---

[2]Strictly speaking, the definition just given is for perfect Bayes equilibrium. A sequential equilibrium puts a further condition, called consistency, on beliefs. However, for all the games studied in this book, these two concepts are identical, and so only the term *sequential equilibrium* is used. See D. M. Kreps and R. Wilson, "Sequential Equilibrium," *Econometrica* 50 (1982):863–94, for the original discussion. The authors prove an existence theorem for sequential equilibrium.

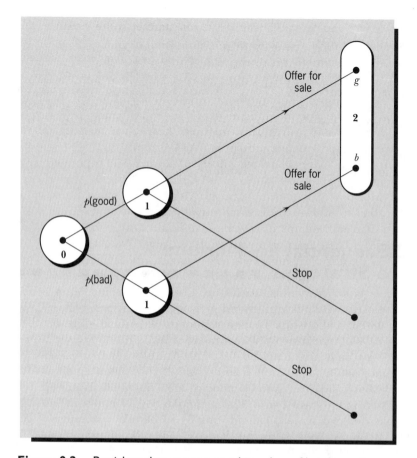

Figure 9.2. Partial market success, reaching player 2's information set.

Here is how to check whether an equilibrium is sequential, using an argument akin to backward induction on the signaling game. Suppose that the probability of a bad item is very small, so that the buyer knows that he or she is almost certain of buying a good item. Also suppose that the cleanup cost, c, is small relative to p. We can now show that the following is a sequential equilibrium:

> 1 offers the item for sale if it is good
> 1 offers the item for sale if it is bad
> 2 buys whatever is offered for sale
> p (node $g|$ offer) $= p$(good); p(node $b|$ offer) $= p$(bad)

Both types of sellers offer the item for sale, and the buyer says yes to all offers. First, note that the probability distribution over the nodes of the buyer's information set follows from the initial chance move and the strategy of the seller (see Figure 9.2). The node g of the buyer's information set is reached along the following path: chance picks good, and the seller offers the good item for sale. The probability that an item is good, given that it has been offered for sale, is given by the conditional probability

$$p(\text{good} \mid \text{offer}) = \frac{p(\text{good})p(\text{offer} \mid \text{good})}{p(\text{offer})}$$

where the probability of an offer, $p(\text{offer})$, is itself given by the conditional probability

$$p(\text{offer}) = p(\text{good})p(\text{offer} \mid \text{good}) + p(\text{bad})p(\text{offer} \mid \text{bad})$$

We have $p(\text{offer} \mid \text{good}) = 1$ and $p(\text{offer} \mid \text{bad}) = 1$, so that

$$p(\text{good} \mid \text{offer}) = p(\text{good})$$

This equation is often called **Bayes's rule** after its discoverer. What Bayes's rule does is take the information a player has at the beginning of the game and update it into information that a player can use during the game, or even later. Similarly, the probability that an item is bad, given that it has been offered for sale, is given by the conditional probability

$$p(\text{bad} \mid \text{offer}) = \frac{p(\text{bad})p(\text{offer} \mid \text{bad})}{p(\text{offer})}$$
$$= p(\text{bad})(1)$$

Given an offer, the probability that player 2 is at node g of the information set is

$$p(\text{node } g \mid \text{offer}) = \frac{p(\text{good} \mid \text{offer})}{p(\text{good} \mid \text{offer}) + p(\text{bad} \mid \text{offer})}$$
$$= \frac{p(\text{good})}{p(\text{good}) + p(\text{bad})}$$
$$= p(\text{good})$$

Likewise, the probability of being at node b of the information set, given an offer, is $p(\text{bad})$.

Now that we have a probability distribution over the nodes of player 2's information set, we can start a backward induction argument. If player 2 buys, he or she can expect the following utility:

$$Eu_2 = p(\text{node } g \mid \text{offer})(V - p) + p(\text{node } b \mid \text{offer})(W - p)$$
$$= p(\text{good})(V - p) + p(\text{bad})(W - p)$$

which for $p(\text{bad})$ small enough has to be positive. So the buyer maximizes utility by saving yes to any offer. Now, using backward induction, we can replace the information set of the buyer with its observable consequences (see Figure 9.3). The seller with a good item clearly maximizes utility by offering the item for sale, since

$$p > 0$$

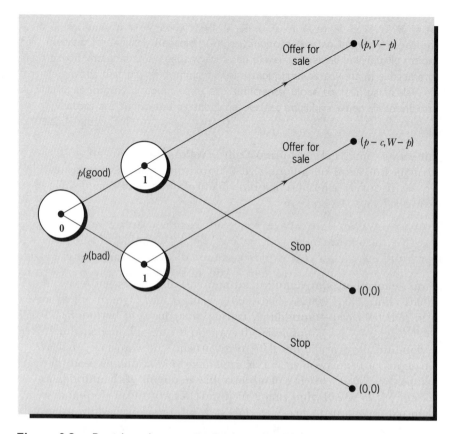

Figure 9.3.   Partial market success, backward induction, player 1's move.

At this point, this is an ordinary backward induction conclusion. Likewise, the seller with a bad item maximizes utility by offering that item for sale, since

$$p - c > 0$$

We have now backward induced all the way to the beginning of the game. Since we encountered no contradictions along the way, we have verified that the strategies and belief we started out with constitute a sequential equilibrium.

The sequential equilibrium we have found is a pooling equilibrium, partial market success. At a pooling equilibrium, a buyer gets no new information from seeing what the seller does. The buyer has the exact same information once his or her information set is reached that he or she had when the game began. The probability p(bad) of buying a bad item is small enough to ensure that the buyer's expected utility is positive. If anyone were to do otherwise, utility would go down. If a seller with a good item were to withdraw from the market, their seller's utility would drop from p to zero. If a seller with a bad item were to withdraw from the market, utility would drop from $p - c$ to zero. Finally, if a buyer were to refuse to buy, the expected utility would drop from positive to zero.

We have just found conditions that guarantee that partial market success is achieved by a sequential equilibrium of the signaling game. The conditions in which this happens are the following:

$p > c$ (this gives bad-type sellers an incentive to sell)

$p(\text{good})(W - p) + p(\text{bad})(V - p) > 0$

(this gives buyers an incentive to buy in a "buyer beware" world)

Under the right conditions, we can get a market to function under this informational handicap, although far from perfectly.

One slight change to a parameter value gives an entirely different sequential equilibrium—indeed, the best of all possible outcomes. Suppose that the cost of fixing up a bad item to make it presentable is prohibitive:

$c > p$

Even if you go to the trouble of fixing the item up and selling it, you still lose money. This is not an attractive proposition, considering that a seller can always withdraw from the market at no cost. Consider the following strategies and belief:

1 offers the item if it is good

1 stops if the item is bad

2 buys whatever is offered

prob(node g| offer) = 1; prob(node b| offer) = 0

We will now see that this is a sequential equilibrium.

First, note that the probability distribution over the nodes of the buyer's information set follows from the initial chance move and the strategy of the buyer (see Figure 9.4). The probability that an item is good, given that it has been offered, is the probability that chance picks a good item times the probability that a buyer offers the item for sale, given that it is good.

$$p(\text{good} \mid \text{offer}) = \frac{p(\text{good}) p(\text{offer} \mid \text{good})}{p(\text{offer})}$$

$$= \frac{p(\text{good})}{p(\text{offer})}$$

The probability of an offer is given by

$$p(\text{offer}) = p(\text{good}) p(\text{offer} \mid \text{good}) + p(\text{bad}) p(\text{offer} \mid \text{bad})$$
$$= p(\text{good})$$

Combining these two probabilities, we have

$$p(\text{good} \mid \text{offer}) = p(\text{node } g \mid \text{offer}) = \frac{p(\text{good})}{p(\text{good})} = 1$$

247

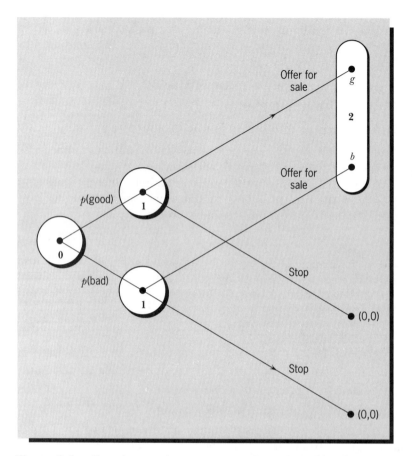

Figure 9.4.   Complete market success, reaching player 2's information set.

Likewise, the probability that play has reached the node b, given an offer, is 0.

Now that we have a probability distribution over the nodes of player 2's information set, we can start a backward induction argument. If player 2 buys, he or she can expect the following utility:

$$Eu_2 = p(\text{node } g \mid \text{offer})(V - p) + p(\text{node } b \mid \text{offer})(W - p)$$
$$= (1)(V - p) + 0(W - p) > 0$$

so player 2 maximizes utility by buying. Now, using backward induction, we can replace the information set of the buyer with its observable consequences (see Figure 9.5). The seller with a good item clearly maximizes utility by offering the item for sale, since

$$p > 0$$

At this point, this is an ordinary backward induction conclusion. Likewise, the seller with a bad item maximizes utility by not offering that item for sale, since

$$p - c < 0$$

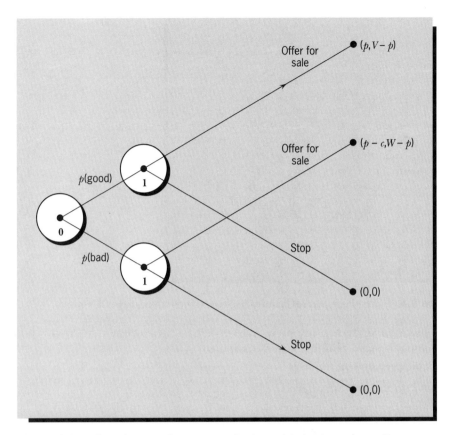

Figure 9.5. Complete market success, backward induction, player 1's move.

We have now backward induced all the way to the beginning of the game. Since we encountered no contradictions along the way, we have verified that the strategies and belief we started out with constitute a sequential equilibrium.

We have just found conditions that guarantee that complete market success is achieved by a sequential equilibrium of the signaling game. What we need is the following:

$p < c$ (this gives bad-type sellers an incentive not to sell)

This equation indicates that under the right conditions, we can get a market to function perfectly—to maximize gains from trade—even under this informational handicap. Complete market success is the first instance we have seen of an informative game equilibrium. The reason this sequential equilibrium is informative is that buyers, once they see an item offered for sale, know that it is good.

Both these sequential equilibria used probability distributions over the nodes of the buyer's information set based on given probabilities and strategies. It can happen that the belief in a sequential equilibrium is not based on data.

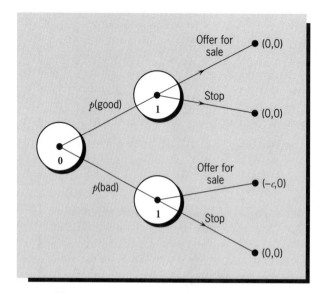

Figure 9.6.   Complete market failure, backward induction, player 1's move.

This situation underlies complete market failure. The sequential equilibrium for complete market failure is the following:

    1 stops whatever the item is

    2 says no to any item offered

    $p(\text{node } g | \text{offer}) = 0$; $p(\text{node } b | \text{offer}) = 1$

Notice that the buyer's information set is never reached by this pair of strategies, since the seller never offers the item for sale. Thus the probability distribution over the nodes of the buyer's information is not based on any data. The belief at this sequential equilibrium is the most pessimistic possible. It says that if the seller should, by mistake, offer an item for sale, that item must be bad. With beliefs this pessimistic, it is no wonder that the market breaks down.

    Now that we have a probability distribution over the nodes of player 2's information set, we can start a backward induction argument. If player 2 buys, he or she expects the following utility:

$$Eu_2 = p(\text{node } g | \text{offer})(V - p) + p(\text{node } b | \text{offer})(W - p)$$
$$= (0)(V - p) + 1(W - p) < 0$$

so player 2 maximizes utility by not buying. Now, using backward induction, we can replace the information set of the buyer with its observable consequences (see Figure 9.6). The seller with a good item is indifferent between offering the item for sale (where it is refused) or not offering it for sale:

    $0 = 0$

The seller with a bad item prefers not to offer it for sale:

$-c < 0$

We have now backward induced all the way to the beginning of the game. Since we encountered no contradictions along the way, we have verified that the strategies and belief we started out with constitute a sequential equilibrium.

At this sequential equilibrium, the market fails completely—nothing bought, nothing gained. We get an especially unfortunate type of pooling behavior on the part of sellers, as both withhold their products from the market. No gains from trade are realized, even though there is potential for such gains. Finally, this sequential equilibrium exists for all possible parameter constellations—a consequence of the fact that the belief crucial to it is not based on any data.[3]

We have just seen how partial market success, complete market success, and complete market failure can arise as pure strategy sequential equilibria of Caveat Emptor. The next section shows how near market failure can arise as a mixed strategy sequential equilibrium of Caveat Emptor.

⚏ 9.3 Sequential Equilibrium: Mixed Strategies ■

To show how near market failure can arise as a sequential equilibrium, two conditions have to be met. First, $p > c$, so that bad-type sellers have an incentive to offer their items for sale. Second, if buyers buy everything offered for sale, they lose:

$$Eu_2 = p(\text{good})(V - p) + p(\text{bad})(W - p) < 0$$

In this situation, buyers would refuse to buy. Then sellers with bad items would lose out. Mixed strategies provide the only way out of this situation.

The following example will help make clear what is going on. Suppose that this is a used-car market, and good and bad used cars are equally likely:

$$p(\text{good}) = p(\text{bad}) = .5$$

A good used car is worth $3000 to a buyer, whereas a bad used car is worthless to the buyer. The sticker price on all used cars is $2000:

$$\$3000 = V > p = \$2000 > 0 = W$$

It costs $1000 to clean up a bad used car. Notice that

$$c/p = 1000/2000 = 0.5$$

and that

---

[3]This sequential equilibrium ought to strike you as somehow bizarre. The strategy for player 1 (stop if good, stop if bad) is dominated by the strategy (offer for sale if good, stop if bad). Thus this sequential equilibrium fails the sufficient condition of undominated strategies.

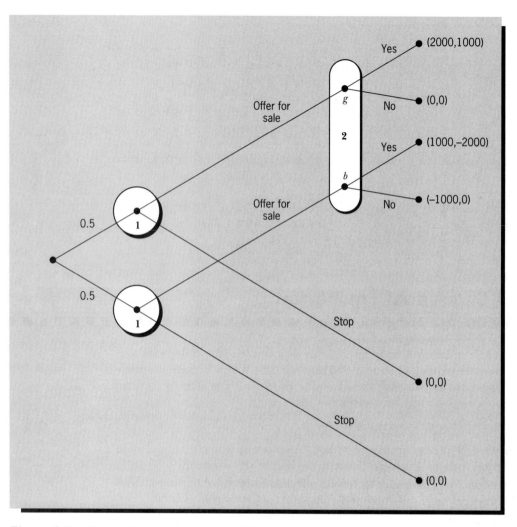

Figure 9.7.   Caveat Emptor, near market failure.

$$p(\text{good})(V - p) + p(\text{bad})(W - p) = .5(1000) + .5(-2000) < 0$$

so we satisfy the regime inequalities. The version of Caveat Emptor that results is shown in Figure 9.7.

The following is a sequential equilibrium for Caveat Emptor with these payoff parameters:

1 offers for sale if the used car is good

1 offers for sale with probability .5 if the used car is bad

2 buys the used car offered with probability .5

$$p(\text{node } g | \text{offer}) = \frac{2}{3}$$

$$p(\text{node } b | \text{offer}) = \frac{1}{3}$$

Note first that the probability distribution over the nodes of player 2's information set follows from the strategies and probabilities. With probability .5, an item is good and is offered for sale, so node g is reached with probability .5. With probability .5, an item is bad, and with probability .5 it is offered for sale, so node g is reached with probability .25. The resulting conditional probability distribution is this belief:

$$p(\text{node } g | \text{offer}) = \frac{.5}{(.5 + .25)} = \frac{2}{3}$$

$$p(\text{node } b | \text{offer}) = \frac{.25}{(.5 + .25)} = \frac{1}{3}$$

Now we check that the buyer is indifferent about buying or not buying. At these odds, the expected value of buying is

$$Eu_2(\text{buy} | \text{offer}) = p(\text{node } g | \text{offer})(1000) + p(\text{node } b | \text{offer})(-2000)$$

$$= \left(\frac{2}{3}\right)(1000) + \left(\frac{1}{3}\right)(-2000) = 0$$

the same payoff as for not buying. So the buyer passes the test for a mixed strategy equilibrium.

Next consider the seller with a good used car. If buyers buy with probability .5, then this seller expects

$$Eu_1(\text{offer} | \text{good}) = .5(2000) + .5(0) = 1000 > 0$$

The seller with a good used car maximizes utility by offering the car for sale. Finally, consider the seller with a bad used car. If this seller cleans up the used car and offers it for sale, he or she expects

$$Eu_1(\text{offer} | \text{bad}) = .5(1000) + .5(-1000) = 0$$

the same as not offering the used car for sale. Thus the seller of a bad used car also passes the test for a mixed strategy equilibrium.

We have just verified the sequential equilibrium for near market failure. This market is not functioning very well at all. Bad-type sellers and all buyers break even, and good-type sellers only sell half the time. Only complete market failure performs worse in terms of gains from trade than this mixed strategy sequential equilibrium. Imperfect information can really drive market performance down.

To sum up our discussion of Caveat Emptor, let's look at its complete solution in Figure 9.8, which is called a **regime diagram.** The crucial supply-side feature of the market, the cleanup cost, c, is plotted on the x-axis. On the y-axis

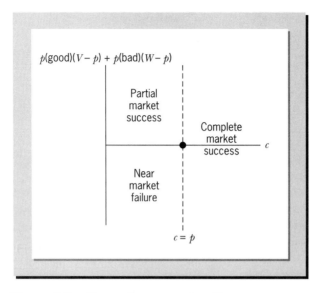

Figure 9.8. Caveat Emptor, regime diagram.

is plotted the crucial demand-side feature of the market, the expected value to the buyer if everything is offered and he or she buys: $p(\text{good})(V - p) + p(\text{bad})(W - p)$. There are three zones, or regimes, in the diagram. When $p < c$, we get complete market success. Only good types are offered for sale, and they are bought. This is the regime in which play is completely informative: you know exactly what type of good a seller has to sell the minute it is offered for sale (good) or withheld from the market (bad). When $p > c$ and the buyer's expected value is positive then we get partial market success. Everything, good or bad, is offered for sale and bought. This outcome is completely uninformative: the good and the bad are pooled together. Finally, when $c < p$ and the expected value of buying everything is negative, we get near market failure. Both buyers and bad-type sellers adopt mixed strategies in order to survive this "buyer beware" world.

Now that we have completely solved the basic signaling game, we are ready to take on the market for lemons. Lemons markets tell us the extent to which prices can signal quality when information is imperfect.

◼ 9.4 The Market for Lemons[4] ◼◼◼◼◼◼◼◼◼◼◼◼◼◼◼

The price of a good or service is often thought to convey information about its quality. In Caveat Emptor, everything sold at the same price and so price

---

[4]This material has been inspired by the classic article of George Akerlof, "The Market for Lemons: Quality Uncertainty and the Market Mechanism," *Quarterly Journal of Economics* 89 (1970):488–500.

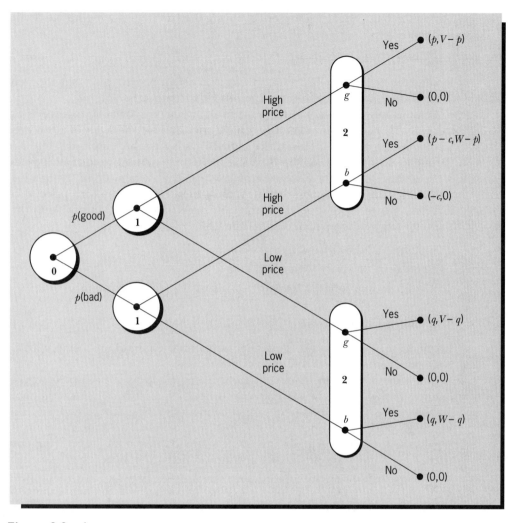

Figure 9.9. Lemons.

could not possibly convey information. Let's now relax this assumption and look for conditions under which price does reveal information about quality at a sequential equilibrium.

The game used to model this problem, called Lemons, is shown in Figure 9.9. There is a random move that determines the quality of the item in question (good or bad). Player 1, the seller, knows the quality and offers the items for sale, either at a high price, p, or at a low price, q. Player 2, the buyer, does not know the quality but does observe the price offered, high or low. The buyer says yes or no to the seller's offer. A good item (V) is worth more than a bad item (W) to the buyer. Even at a high price, buying the good item is better than buying the bad item at the low price; buying the bad item at a high price results in a loss:

$$V - q > V - p > W - q > 0 > W - p$$

Finally, the seller of a bad item must pay a cleanup cost, c, so that the item looks good. Otherwise, the seller can offer it for sale as is.

Lemons has the potential for price to signal quality. What is required is for the seller of a good item to charge a high price and for the seller of a bad item to charge a low price. Then price signals quality to the buyer: the buyer is getting exactly what he or she is paying for. The condition needed here is the same as that needed for Caveat Emptor: $c > p$. If it costs more to fix up a bad item and make it look good than its returns in sales, even at a high price, then it doesn't pay to clean it up at all. You can check (end-of-chapter problem) that the following is a sequential equilibrium when $c > p$:

1 charges a high price with a good item

1 charges a low price with a bad item

2 buys any item offered for sale

$p(\text{node } g | \text{high price}) = 1$

$p(\text{node } b | \text{low price}) = 1$

In this case, thanks to the separating sequential equilibrium, Lemons has a complete market success solution.

Unfortunately, under other conditions, Lemons can have a complete market failure solution. Take the extreme case, where $c = 0$. A bad item can mimic a good item for free. A good item cannot be identified by putting a high price on it: a high price can be put on a bad item just as well. This situation dooms a separating sequential equilibrium and its attendant market success. Suppose that all good items are priced at p and all bad items at q. Buyers buy every item offered. This is not an equilibrium. A seller of a bad item can put a high price on it and sell it at a bigger gain: $p > q$. What one seller of a bad item can do, so can another. Price no longer signals quality. Even worse, suppose that the buyer's expected value if sellers pool at either high prices or low prices is negative:

$$Eu_2 (\text{buy} | \text{high price}) = p(\text{good})(V - p) + p(\text{bad})(W - p) < 0$$

and

$$Eu_2(\text{buy} | \text{low price}) = p(\text{good})(V - q) + p(\text{bad})(W - q) < 0$$

In the very worst sequential equilibrium, the market breaks down completely:

1 charges a low price, good item or bad

2 does not buy at either price

$p(\text{node } g | \text{low price}) = p(\text{good})$

$p(\text{node } g | \text{high price}) = p(\text{good})$

The last belief, $p(\text{node } g | \text{high price}) = p(\text{good})$, is not pessimistic at all. The buyer believes that the probability of either type's sellers' asking a high price is the same as their frequency in the population. And at those odds, it doesn't pay to buy. Here is a reasonable sequential equilibrium where no sales take place, and the market ceases to function. This is dubbed, after Akerlof, the **lemons principle:** the bad drives everything out of the market.

In some markets that are especially information sensitive, the lemons principle is a major social problem. Take the market for health insurance for people over the age of 65. The player who goes first is the elderly person trying to buy health insurance, and that person usually knows whether he or she is healthy (good bet to insure) or unhealthy (bad bet to insure). Health insurance companies lose a lot of money when they insure unhealthy elderly people at rates comparable to those for healthy elderly people. The trouble is, the cosmetic cost, c, may be pretty close to zero here as well. Everything is in place in this market for the lemons principle to operate, and it does. The U.S. government introduced Medicare in 1965 in an attempt to correct an abundant market failure. The wave of health care reform proposals sweeping the country today suggests that this market failure has yet to be corrected.

9.5 Costly Commitment as a Signaling Device

A powerful device for signaling purposes is to commit oneself to a considerable cost at the beginning of a game. For example, a man wants to marry a woman and gives her an engagement ring. This is a costly commitment. If he should later decide to dump her, it's going to cost him the ring—which she is entitled to keep, or better still, liquidate, and enjoy the money. As another example, a couple wants to buy a house. They put down $5000 earnest money, which they forfeit if they do not go through with the transaction. This is a costly commitment—they will walk away from this deal only at great expense to themselves. The best kind of signal is a credible signal, and costly commitment is the best kind of credibility money can buy. This is called the principle of **costly commitment.**

Here is a game that illustrates how the principle of costly commitment works in a situation that would otherwise fall prey to the lemons principle. This game is called Money-Back Guarantee (see Figure 9.10). Money-Back Guarantee is just like Lemons with $c = 0$, so every seller would charge the high price. There is one difference to payoffs, though. Along with charging a high price, there is a standard money-back guarantee in this market. If a buyer does not get high quality (V) when he or she pays a high price (p), the seller will make up the difference. This is a very costly commitment if you are selling bad stuff. The guarantee assures the buyer of the payoff $V - p$ no matter what is bought. If

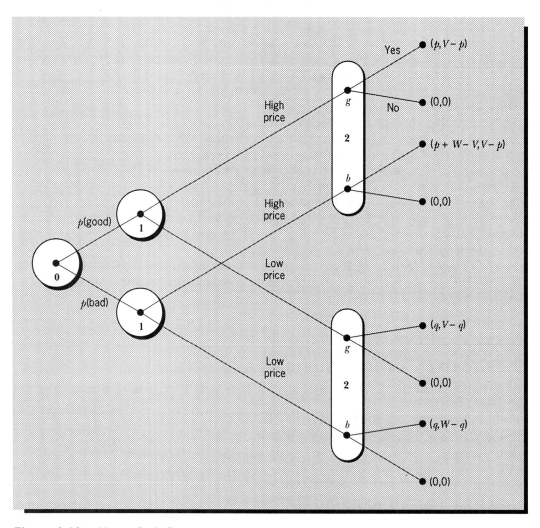

Figure 9.10. Money-Back Guarantee.

the buyer buys from a good source, that's fine. If the buyer buys from a bad source, the seller makes up the difference; The bad-type seller has to reimburse the unlucky buyer $V - W$. The money-back guarantee creates a sure-thing situation for the buyer.

If the money-back guarantee is costly enough, in particular, if

$$p + W - V < 0$$

then there is a sequential equilibrium leading to complete market success:

1 charges a high price with a good item

1 charges a low price with a bad item

2 says yes to a high price

2 says no to a low price

$p(\text{node } g | \text{high price}) = 1$

$p(\text{node } g | \text{low price}) = 0$

A seller with a good item has a dominant strategy to charge a high price, and the buyer has a dominant strategy to say yes to a high price. Once these two strategies are in place, the rest of the sequential equilibrium follows immediately. The discovery on the part of mass retailers in the United States in this century of the money-back guarantee revolutionized the entire retailing industry. Sellers of good items have nothing to fear from sellers of bad items: the money-back guarantee protects them (and buyers) from lemons.

Here is an outline of another example of costly commitment. You should be able to fill in the details. In Telex versus IBM, it makes a big difference to Telex whether IBM is mean or not. Suppose that the game begins with a random move that assigns a type to IBM. Although IBM does not get to set its price until the end of the game, it can send a costly signal after learning its type. In particular, IBM can create a large amount of capacity, incurring a large fixed cost—capacity it will need only in the event that it wants to smash Telex. Depending on the details of the game, you can construct sequential equilibria where mean IBM creates large capacity, whereas nice IBM does not. You can also construct sequential equilibria where both types of IBM create large capacity. In the latter case, nice IBM is bluffing, and gets away with it.

The principle of costly commitment also applies to international relations. During Operation Desert Storm, the United Nations put 500,000 men and women into Arabia to signal to Iraq that United Nations resolve should be believed. This commitment cost $50 billion. For reasons known only to Baghdad, this signal was not believed.

9.6 Repeated Signaling and Track Records ■■■■■■■■■■■■■■■■■■■■■■■■■■

Repeat buying is an important feature in many retail relationships, particularly for durable goods, such as automobiles and appliances. In a one-shot game where the type of the item sold can be clearly verified after purchase, the buyer will soon know whether to break off a retail relationship or not. If the item bought turns out to be a lemon, this indicates that the seller deals in bad items and should be avoided in the future. If the item bought turns out to be good, this indicates that the seller deals in good items and can be patronized in the future. With clear outcomes based on clear signals, then, the judgment whether to continue or terminate a business relationship is immediate. This is not the case, however, with noisy signals. A **noisy signal** contains information about the nature of the underlying type of business, but it also contains statistical noise, which confounds the attempt to determine the underlying type.

To make matters concrete, suppose that you are in charge of a law firm and have just hired a young lawyer named Kane. Lawyer Kane has yet to try a case, but you know from experience that two kinds of lawyers get through your screening process. A star performer wins 90% of cases. In terms of probabilities, the probability that a star will win a case, $p(\text{win}|\text{star})$, is .9. An ordinary performer wins 50% of cases. The probability that an ordinary performer will win a case, $p(\text{win}|\text{ordinary})$, is only .5. You never hire lawyers worse than this. A star performer stochastically dominates an ordinary performer, and you would like to sign nothing but stars to long-term contracts.[5] Based only on what you know before lawyer Kane tries a single case, you think it equally likely that this person is a star performer or an ordinary performer. In terms of probabilities, this means:

$$p(\text{star}) = p(\text{ordinary}) = .5$$

You are faced with a decision. Ultimately, you have to decide whether to make this person a partner in the firm or let Kane go. And you have to make this decision under conditions of imperfect information.

In order to turn this problem into a 1-player game, we need to attach payoffs to decisions. Suppose that making a lawyer a partner in the firm means that the lawyer will be trying cases forever, and that your discount factor is .95 (corresponding to a 5% interest rate). Normalize utility so that $u(\text{win}) = 1$, and $u(\text{loss}) = 0$. Then, if you make a star performer a partner, you expect the value

$$EV = \Sigma(.95)^t\,[.9(1) + .1(0)]$$
$$= \frac{.9}{(1 - .95)} = 18$$

using the formula for infinitely repeated games from Chapter 7. If, on the other hand, you make an ordinary performer a partner, you expect the value

$$EV = \Sigma(.95)^t\,[.5(1) + .5(0)]$$
$$= \frac{.5}{(1 - .95)} = 10$$

The lifetime consequence of making an ordinary performer a partner is a loss of almost 45% (8/18, to be exact), compared to making a star a partner.

You could make your decision on the basis of no data whatsoever—you could make someone a partner who has never tried a single case. That would be irresponsible, and no one with a sound mind would do that. What you do is give the new hire a *probationary period* instead. During the probationary period,

---

[5]This game assumes that the performance of a lawyer is determined solely by type, and not by effort. The next chapter looks at how to provide incentives for more effort through contractual clauses.

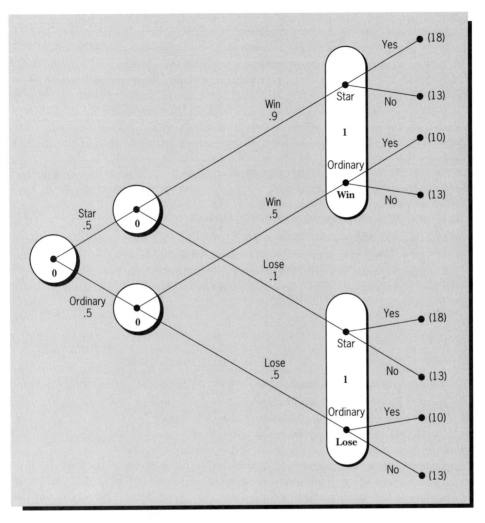

Figure 9.11. One-Period Probation.

the new hire builds a track record. The decision whether to make the person a partner or not depends on this track record.

During a probationary period, and afterward throughout a career, a person is judged on his or her track record. How many successes has the person had? What has the employee done for the company? This principle is called the **track record principle.** A sequential equilibrium judges people by their track records. The better the track record, the more likely a person is to be judged as a good type and hence to enter a long-term relationship.

The biggest decision from a game theory standpoint is how long the probationary period should be—how much time new employees should have to prove themselves. We first consider the shortest possible probationary period, one period long. The game One-Period Probation is shown in Figure 9.11. A random move at the beginning determines lawyer Kane's type; either type is equally likely. Lawyer Kane knows what the type is, but has no way to reveal this to you. (Why not? See end-of-chapter problem 8). A second random move determines the outcome of lawyer Kane's first trial. This trial constitutes Kane's probationary period. You, as player 1, observe the outcome of the trial, win or lose. Your decision is whether to make Kane a partner or let Kane go. Kane automatically accepts all offers. If you let Kane go, then you have a vacancy for one period (utility = 0), and then get the expected value of what the market has to offer $[.5(18 - 1) + .5(10 - 1)] = 13$.

You are going to make a decision based on what you see. Let's consider the four possible decisions, since here your strategy is the kind of decision you use:

I. *Yes no matter what.* This unconditional strategy has $EV = .5(18) + .5(10) = 14$.

II. *Yes if a win, No if a loss.* Evaluating this conditional strategy requires Bayes's rule again. What you want to know is the probability that you've hired a star, given that the case was won, $p(\text{star}|\text{win})$. From Bayes's rule, we have

$$p(\text{star}|\text{win}) = \frac{p(\text{star})\,p(\text{win}\,|\,\text{star})}{p(\text{win})}$$

where

$$p(\text{win}) = p(\text{star})\,p(\text{win}\,|\,\text{star}) + p(\text{ordinary})\,p(\text{win}\,|\,\text{ordinary})$$

Substituting into this formula $p(\text{win}\,|\,\text{star}) = .9$; $p(\text{win}\,|\,\text{ordinary}) = .5$; and $p(\text{star}) = p(\text{ordinary}) = .5$;

$$p(\text{star}|\text{win}) = \frac{.45}{.70} = \frac{9}{14}, \text{ or } 64.3\%$$

If you see a win, you upgrade the probability that Kane is a star from 50% to 64.3%. Kane's stock just went up in your eyes, as well it should. Bayesian updating is the mathematical foundation of the track record principle. On the other hand, the probability that you've hired an ordinary performer, who just happened to get lucky, $p(\text{ordinary}|\text{win})$, is given by

$$p(\text{ordinary}|\text{win}) = 1 - p(\text{star}|\text{win}) = 1 - \frac{9}{14} = \frac{5}{14} = 35.7\%$$

The probability that Kane is ordinary goes down when you observe a win, because stars produce wins much more often than ordinary performers do. This completes the calculations for what you do when you observe a win.

We next consider what you do when you observe a loss. Once again, we compute the probability that you are looking at a star who just got unlucky, $p(\text{star}|\text{loss})$. From Bayes's rule, we have

$$p(\text{star}|\text{loss}) = \frac{p(\text{star})\,p(\text{loss}\,|\,\text{star})}{p(\text{loss})}$$

where

$$p(\text{loss}) = p(\text{star})p(\text{loss}|\text{star}) + p(\text{ordinary})p(\text{loss}|\text{ordinary})$$

Substituting into Bayes's rule the information $p(\text{loss}|\text{star}) = .1$; $p(\text{loss}|\text{ordinary}) = .5$; and $p(\text{star}) = p(\text{ordinary}) = .5$;

$$p(\text{star}|\text{loss}) = \frac{.5(.1)}{(.05 + .25)} = \frac{1}{6}, \text{ or } 16.7\%$$

The odds that your loss was produced by a star are rather small, only 1 chance in 6. By the same token, the odds that your loss was produced by an ordinary performer, $p(\text{ordinary}|\text{loss})$, are

$$p(\text{ordinary}|\text{loss}) = 1 - p(\text{star}|\text{loss}) = 1 - \frac{1}{6} = \frac{5}{6}, \text{ or } 83.3\%$$

The odds are that the loss came from an ordinary performer.

Armed with all these probabilities, we can now compute the expected value of the strategy Yes if a win, No if a loss. A win occurs with probability .7. When a win occurs, the decision is yes. In the event of a win, the probability is 9/14 that Kane is a star and therefore worth 18; the probability is 5/14 that Kane is ordinary and therefore worth 10. A loss occurs with probability .3. When a loss occurs, the decision is no. Here the payoff is 13. Adding this all up, we get

$$EV = .7\left[\left(\frac{9}{14}\right)(18)+\left(\frac{5}{14}\right)(10)\right] + .3(13) = 14.5$$

Notice that Bayesian updating allows you to make a better decision than simply saying yes no matter what happens.

III. *No if a win, Yes if a loss.* This strategy sounds as bad as it is. Using the same probabilities as for strategy II, we get

$$EV = .7(13) + .3\left[\left(\frac{1}{6}\right)18 + \left(\frac{5}{6}\right)10\right] = 12.5$$

The strategy where you fire somebody the minute that person wins for you gets really low marks. You probably wouldn't want to spend your whole life working for such an outfit, anyway.

IV. *No, no matter what.* This unconditional strategy pays 13. If you fire everybody after the probation period, then you are always in the market for replacements and you can expect the replacement value.

We have clear rankings of the strategies: II beats I beats IV beats III. The best strategy if you are going to have one period of probation is to make Kane a partner with a win and let Kane go with a loss. This is the track record principle at work.

There is an obvious problem with probationary periods this short. The odds of making a mistake are still pretty high. There are two kinds of mistake you

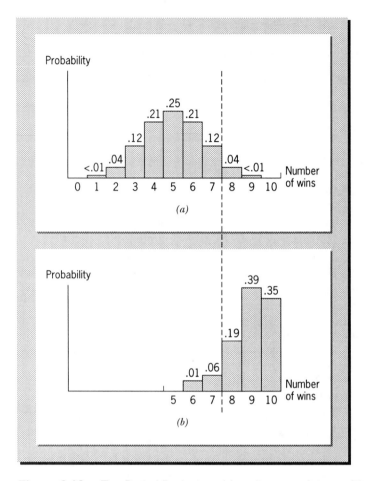

Figure 9.12. Ten-Period Probation; (*a*) ordinary performer; (*b*) star performer.

can make, even when you use the best strategy. One mistake is to make an ordinary performer a partner. If you use strategy II, you will make this mistake with probability (.7)(5/14). That is, 25% of the time you will make someone a partner just because he or she got lucky in court once. In the long run one-quarter of all your partners are going to be ordinary—hardly a star-studded law firm. Another mistake is to let a star performer go. If you use strategy II, you will make this mistake (.3)(1/6) of the time. That is, 8% of the time you will let someone go whom you should have kept because that person got really unlucky in court once.

In a world of imperfect information and noisy signals, mistakes are inevitable. The way to cut down on mistakes is to have a **repeated signaling** over a longer probationary period. Of course, this is expensive, too, especially when you are hanging on to someone who is clearly turning out to be ordinary. To see how a longer probationary period cuts down the odds of making these two kinds of mistakes, consider the implications of a probationary period 10 periods long for this same new lawyer Kane. Figure 9.1 shows the probability distributions of the number of wins for a star performer and for an ordinary performer.[6] A star performer can expect (probability of win)(number of chances) = (.9)(10) = 9 wins in this longer probationary period, with a little dispersion. An ordinary performer can expect (.5)(10) = 5 wins in this longer probationary period, again with some dispersion.

Now you have a longer track record to go on in evaluating the quality of this lawyer. One strategy along the lines of strategy II that would definitely reduce the probability of making either type of error is the following: if a lawyer has at least eight wins during the probationary period, make that person a partner; otherwise, let the lawyer go. A star performer will meet this standard more than 93% of the time; an ordinary performer, less than 5% of the time. The mistake of making an ordinary performer a partner only occurs 7% of the time the standard is met, instead of 5/14 = 38% of the time when probation is one period long. The other possible mistake is to let go someone who is a star but hasn't met the standard. A star performer will fail to meet the standard of at least eight wins with probability .07. An ordinary performer will fail to meet the standard with probability .95. The mistake of letting a star performer go occurs only 7% of the time the standard is not met, instead of 1/6 = 16% of the time when the probationary period is only one period long. Both kinds of mistakes have been substantially reduced.

Longer probationary periods and the track records that go with them cut down on mistakes. At the same time, costs mount with the length of the probationary period. The opportunity cost of hanging on to someone ordinary for 10 periods in the firm described is, on average, four wins. The benefits of better decisions and the costs of longer decision periods have to be, and are, weighed in various businesses. In law firms, for example, the standard probationary period is 7 years. Meeting the standard makes you a partner in the firm. For professors in the United States, the probationary period is normally 6 years. Meeting the standard there makes you a tenured professor. For football coaches in the Big 10, the probationary period is 5 years. Unless you have a winning team by the time 5 years has elapsed, your contract is unlikely to be renewed. The probationary period for Wall Street firms is somewhat shorter. The greater the pressure is to win, the shorter is the probationary period. On Wall Street, the cost of sticking with an ordinary performer is just too high to stay with one very long.

No matter how long the probationary period is, you will *never* be sure that you have made the right decision. In a world of imperfect information and noisy signals, mistakes are inevitable, no matter how hard you try and how much information you collect. You can cut down on mistakes by strategic use of your information, but you can't cut them out entirely. In a world of imperfect information, nobody is perfect.

---

[6]These distributions are based on the binomial distribution from discrete probability theory.

So far we have looked at situations in which one side to a transaction has had all the information it needed, even if the other side did not. It often happens that even the informed trader has received only a noisy signal, not a perfectly clear one. In such a case, the informed trader has better information than the uninformed trader, even though the information is not perfect. This topic is pursued in the next two chapters, but we already have enough experience with imperfect information to follow the action in the biggest business deal of the century, the leveraged buyout of RJR Nabisco.

⋮ 9.7 Barbarians at the Gate[7] ■ ■ ■ ■ ■ ■ ■ ■ ■ ■ ■ ■ ■ ■ ■

RJR Nabisco, the 19th largest company in the United States, was formed by the merger of Reynolds Tobacco (RJR, the tobacco company we've seen in Chapters 2, 3, and 4 already) and the National Biscuit Company (Nabisco, maker of Oreos and hundreds of other food products). In the fall of 1988, RJR Nabisco stock was trading in the low 50s. The top management of the company, led by CEO Ross Johnson, was thinking of taking the company private in a financial maneuver called a **leveraged buyout** (LBO). In an LBO, the management borrows a lot of money, enough to buy up all the shares of the company. It then breaks the company up and sells the pieces. If all goes well, the management makes a ton of money in the process. Of course, anyone else besides the management can try its own LBO. This is where the game comes in. In the words of Burrough and Helyar,

> In one way, an LBO is a lot like buying a used car. A target company's annual report and public filings can be compared to a classified ad. Like an advertisement, they contain useful information, although a savvy buyer knows that the numbers can convey anything a clever accountant needs them to.
>
> The car buyer wants to know more than just what's in the ad. He wants to talk to the owner, check under the hood, go for a ride around the block. For LBO buyers, a thorough inspection is equally crucial. More so than any takeover artist, the LBO buyer must know his prey. His success depends on determining exactly how much debt the target company can take on, and figuring precisely what budgets can be cut and what businesses sold to pay down that debit quickly. To take the used car analogy a step further, the LBO buyer must estimate, in precise detail, how many miles the car has left, how many spare parts he will need, and how much maintenance will be required. His margin of error is so thin that a worn

---

[7]This material was inspired by Bryan Burrough and John Helyar, *Barbarians at the Gate: The Fall of RJR Nabisco* (New York: Harper & Row, 1991).

[8]Ibid., p 301.

crank shaft or a blown gasket could prompt the bank to call his loan. Similarly, in an LBO, a wrong calculation or an inaccurate projectory can bring both buyer and seller down in an avalanche of debt.[8]

The RJR Nabisco management group commissioned a top secret report on the value of the firm. Entitled "Corporate Strategy Update" and dated September 29, 1988, the report estimated the value of RJR Nabisco stock at between $82/share and $111/share. This is an example of a noisy signal. Moreover, this signal was available to no one else at the time. We can convert share price into the value of the firm by multiplying it by the number of shares outstanding. RJR Nabisco had about 230 million shares outstanding. Thus, Johnson's own signal about the value of the firm put it in the range of $18.9 billion to $25.5 billion. Based on this signal, in mid-October Johnson offered to take the company private at $75/share, a $17 billion offer. At that moment, this was the biggest deal ever put on the table in human history. It was about to get bigger. At this price, the management group was confident they couldn't lose.

In addition to Johnson, three other groups were interested in a buyout of RJR Nabisco: Kohlberg Kravis Roberts (KKR), Forstmann Little, and First Boston. These groups did not have the inside information that the management group did; however, the law provides an opportunity for an LBO buyer to inspect the target company, called **due diligence.** The LBO buyer can make appointments with company insiders, question them, and examine their financial reports. This process, which usually lasts only a few days, generates a very noisy signal, especially when lawyers for the management group are present for most of the interviews (as they were in this case). Based on information gleaned from due diligence, Forstmann Little was comfortable bidding $85/share and KKR came in at $90/share. Meanwhile, the share price on the New York Stock Exchange started a big rally as the market started to believe that an LBO was really going to happen.

Bidding was scheduled to end at the end of November. The management group was not going to be outbid as long as the bidding was in its signal range. Johnson came in with a bid of $100 in mid-November. All these bids were delivered to the board of directors of RJR Nabisco, which kept them under tight wraps. Enough information leaked out, however, that the various LBO groups had some idea of where their bids stood. When Forstmann Little learned that bidding had reached $100/share, it dropped out. Meanwhile, KKR raised its bid to $94/share, apparently a lot lower than the bid of the management group.[9] With less than 2 days to go in the bidding, a new group entered the action, First Boston. It came in with a last-minute bid of $105/share. With no time to undertake due diligence, this bid was based mainly on an untried tax strategy and sheer guesswork.

---

[9]These bids are difficult to compare, because cash is a tiny component of them. Most of the bids were expressed in terms of junk bonds, warrants, and convertible preferred stock, making them a challenge to evaluate.

The RJR Nabisco board, perplexed by the three hard-to-compare bids, extended the bidding for another week, and then again for another day. The final bids were $112/share by the management group and $109/share by KKR, with First Boston a distant third. The RJR Nabisco board accepted the KKR bid, citing features that made it more favorable to stockholders than was the management group bid. The bidding had reached and finally exceeded the upper limit of $111/share set by the management group's own inside information.

At $109/share, this was a $25 billion deal for KKR. It is still not clear, almost 4 years later, whether they paid too much or not. What is abundantly clear is that they didn't pay too little. The jury is still out on whether the leveraged buyout of RJR Nabisco bought the world's biggest lemon or not.

❖ SUMMARY

1. In a signaling game of imperfect information, one player has a crucial piece of information that the other player does not have. The player with this crucial piece of information is called informed; the player without this crucial piece of information, uninformed.

2. When the informed player moves first, that play may convey information to the uninformed player. This possibility is called signaling.

3. There are four possible outcomes of the market signaling game Caveat Emptor. Complete market success is separating; complete market failure and partial market success are both pooling; and near market failure is a mixture of separating and pooling.

4. A sequential equilibrium extends the concept of subgame perfection to signaling games. It requires that players take decisions that maximize expected utility on all their information sets. Probability distributions over the nodes of information sets are based on the data and on the strategies of the other players.

5. When complete market success is the solution of a market signaling game, the market equilibrium informs all traders. When partial market success is the solution, the market equilibrium provides no new information. When mixed market success is the solution, the equilibrium provides some information.

6. In Caveat Emptor, as long as there is a cost to mimicking a good type, complete market failure is not the solution. The sequential equilibrium that supports it is in dominated strategies.

7. The lemons principle says that bad quality drives everything out of the market. This can happen as a sequential equilibrium of Lemons.

8. The principle of costly commitment says that signals gain in credibility when it costs the sender to make the signal. The money-back guarantee is an example of a costly commitment that alleviates the lemons problem.

9. In repeated signaling games, a track record provides information about a player's type. The longer the probationary period, the better the information. Sequential equilibrium uses Bayesian updating of information to implement the best decision strategy. There is a trade-off between the length of the probationary period and the probability of mistaken judgment.

10. The leveraged buyout of RJR Nabisco illustrates a signaling game in which one side has better information than the others, but even its information is imperfect.

 KEY TERMS

signaling game	costly commitment
informed/uninformed player	money-back guarantee
pooling equilibrium	repeated signaling
separating equilibrium	noisy signal
sequential equilibrium	track record principle
Bayes's rule	leveraged buyout
regime diagram	due diligence
lemons principle	

PROBLEMS

1. An art dealer has offered you a disputed Rembrandt. Art experts are evenly divided over whether this is an authentic Rembrandt (in which case it is worth $20 million) or the work of a student of Rembrandt's (in which case it is worth $1 million). Set this up as a signaling game and solve it. The price you are being asked is $5 million, and you are risk neutral. It costs $100,000 to get an art critic to authenticate the painting.

2. You are considering a leveraged buyout of Corporation X. The stock of X is worth either $1/share or $5/share. The management of the company knows what it is worth, and is asking $2/share for the 10 thousand shares outstanding. All you know is that the probability that the company is worth $5/share is 50%. Should you buy the company at this price? It costs the management $50 thousand to cook the books if it has to make the company look better than it really is.

3. Suppose in Caveat Emptor (Figure 9.1) that $p(\text{good}) = p(\text{bad}) = .5$. Give numerical examples of each of the following: complete market success; partial market success; and near market failure.

4. Suppose that in Caveat Emptor, the buyer goes first and has to say yes or no. Then it is up to the firm whether it wants to sell to the buyer or not. The seller of a bad type still has to incur the cleanup cost, c, or there is no

deal. Draw the extensive form, then find the sequential equilibrium. Show that there are three regimes.

5. Give three examples of costly commitments that effectively signal company type in business or daily life.

6. Show, using the numerical values $V = \$5000$, $W = \$1000$, $p = \$3000$, $q = \$500$, and a positive c of your choice, what the sequential equilibrium of Lemons (Figure 9.9) is. Is there a lemons problem associated with this equilibrium?

7. In One-Period Probation, find the rankings of the four strategies if the discount factor is .8. What conclusion do you draw from your result?

8. You often hear the advice, "Why not just ask the person?" when you are trying to determine whether someone is a star performer or an ordinary performer. What is wrong, strategically, with asking a person this question and forgetting all about this probationary period? (*Hint:* What does it cost to say the words, "I'm going to be a star"?)

9. In most criminal court cases, a defendant has the opportunity to post bail. If the defendant does not show up for court, then he or she forfeits the bail bond, and in addition is charged with a new felony, jumping bail. Explain this institution in terms of the principle of costly commitment.

10. You are one of the barbarians at the gate. Suppose you know that the true probability distribution of RJR Nabisco stock is the uniform distribution on [$82, $111]. Prepare your bid for the company. Estimate the expected value to a winning bidder who pays $109/share. Would you bid that high? Why or why not? What would you think if you saw somebody bid $112/share?

CHAPTER 10

Games between a Principal and an Agent

Every day in a mature market economy situations like the following arise. A person needs something done. Whether that person is capable of doing it or not, the cost is prohibitive. So, the person hires someone else to do this something. If information is reasonably complete, then the person hired can perform the task or service at a lower cost than can the person doing the hiring. This situation could be as simple as a person's going to the doctor or as complicated as a firm's stockholders' putting their stamp of approval on the management of the firm. This chapter studies such games, called games between a principal and an agent.

In legal language, a **principal** is any person or firm that hires another person or firm to perform services. An **agent** is any person or firm hired to perform services for a principal. This chapter looks first at situations where a principal has perfect information—the principal can monitor what the agent does at no cost. In this case, the principal can get exactly what he or she paid for at subgame perfect equilibrium. If the principal has imperfect information, then the principal has to offer the material incentives to the agent to get more work out of him or her. Otherwise, the agent might slack off. This chapter explores the details of these **incentive-based contracts** and works out a contract when all players are risk neutral. Next, a real-life game, Depositor versus S&L, is introduced. A person who puts money in a financial institution, such as a savings and loan (S&L), is a principal entrusting that money to an agent. The effect on incentive-based contracts of different attitudes toward risk is reviewed. Once we leave an all–risk-neutral world, significant inefficiencies can arise because of agency costs. The problem of heterogeneous agents is then addressed. The principal need not know at the outset of a relationship whether the agent is good or not. To solve this problem, certain kinds of repeated games, for instance, those involving a probationary period, can be played. Fairly simple compensation schedules, very much like those observed in real life, can be generated, recognizing the problems of long-term agency. Finally, corporate compensation is studied. Compensating corporate executives with incentives, such as stock options, rather than with straight salaries, is very much in the interest of the stockholders.

■■ 10.1 Principal versus Agent: Perfect Information ■

This section looks at the game played by a principal and an agent, called for reasons that will soon become clear, Principal versus Agent. We begin with the perfect information version, which provides a benchmark for what happens in the more realistic case when information is imperfect. Let player 1 be the principal; player 2, the agent. The principal moves first (see Figure 10.1) and has two choices. The principal can either offer a contract or not offer a contract. If the principal offers a contract, it must specify what wages will be paid if a **high effort** is observed and if a **low effort** is observed. If no contract is offered, then the game ends. If the principal offers a contract, then the agent has to decide whether to accept it or not. If the agent rejects the contract, then the game ends. If the agent accepts the contract, then the agent has to decide whether to put in a high effort or a low effort. If the agent puts in a high effort, the agent is paid the wage specified in the contract for high effort. If the agent puts in a low effort, the agent is paid the wage specified in the contract for low effort. In either case, the principal can verify what kind of effort the agent has put in and thus pay the agent accordingly.

Player 2, the agent, has the utility function

$$u_2(m_2, e_2) = m_2 - e_2$$

where m_2 is the money that player 2 receives, and $-e_2$ is the disutility that player 2 gets from putting in effort. The higher the effort the agent puts in, the lower that agent's utility. At the same time, the more money the agent makes, the

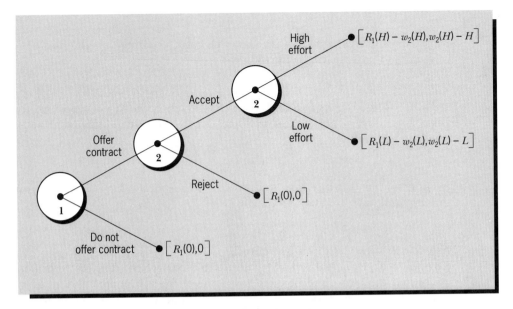

Figure 10.1. Principal versus Agent, perfect information.

higher that agent's utility. The agent gets money in the form of wages and salary from the principal:

$$m_2 = w_2(e_2)$$

There are two things to note about this setup. First, since the principal can observe effort, the contract makes the wage paid conditional on effort. Second, since the agent's utility is linear in money, the agent is risk neutral. These assumptions are substantive and will be relaxed later.

Player 1, the principal, has the utility function

$$u_1 = R_1(e_2) - w_2(e_2)$$

where R_1, the revenue the principal gets from the business, depends on how much effort the agent puts in, and the agent's wage is deducted as a cost. Since the principal's utility is linear in money, the principal is also risk neutral.

We can now spell out the payoffs for Principal versus Agent in Figure 10.1. First, suppose that no contract is offered or that a contract is offered and rejected. Then the agent puts in no effort, makes no money from the principal, and has utility $u_2 = 0$. We can think of this utility level, 0, as a baseline from which the agent measures the attractiveness of all contract offers. The principal gets no help from the agent and incurs no cost, so the utility to the principal is the revenue corresponding to having no agent, $u_1 = R_1(0)$. Next, suppose that a contract is offered and accepted. If the agent puts in a high effort ($e = H$), then the agent is paid on the basis of high effort, $w_2(H)$. Taking into account the disutility of labor, the agent comes out with the utility

$$u_2 = w_2(H) - H$$

The principal in this case enjoys the revenue corresponding to high effort from the agent and pays the high-effort wage:

$$u_1 = R_1(H) - w_2(H)$$

Finally, if the agent puts in a low effort ($e = L$), then the agent is paid on the basis of low effort, $w_2(L)$. Taking into account the disutility of labor, the agent comes out with utility

$$u_2 = w_2(L) - L$$

The principal in this case gets the revenue corresponding to low effort from the agent and pays the low-effort wage:

$$u_1 = R_1(L) - w_2(L)$$

These are the payoffs shown in Figure 10.1.

We will solve Principal versus Agent in the next section. First, however, let's define what the best of all possible worlds involving a principal and an agent would look like. Since both players are risk neutral, it makes sense to add utilities to get a measure of social welfare. Adding utilities, we get

$$u_1 + u_2 = R_1(e) - e$$

where effort, e, can take the value high (H) or low (L) if an agent is involved or 0 if no agent is involved. The best outcome possible would be one that maximized revenue net of effort: $e = H$, L, or 0. The wage paid corresponding to optimal effort would be a social device for dividing the gains accruing to the principal–agent relationship. In the event that the maximum sum of utilities occurred at zero effort, then no gains would be available to society from an agency relationship and no agent should be hired. Since one of the chief defenses of agency contracts and the legal system that enforces them is that such contracts enhance efficiency, it will be interesting to see to what extent solutions to Principal versus Agent reflect efficiency.

10.2 Principal versus Agent: Subgame Perfect Equilibrium ■

We will now solve the perfect information version of Principal versus Agent for its subgame perfect equilibrium. For the time being, we take the wages $w_2(H)$ and $w_2(L)$ as given. You can think of these wages as standard provisions in a contract. Later in this section, we will make the wage choice strategic also. At the final subgame of Principal versus Agent, the agent has to decide between putting forth a high effort or a low effort. Clearly, this decision depends on how much the agent is paid at each effort level and how much the effort costs. The agent will put in a high effort when

$$w_2(H) - H > w_2(L) - L$$

This inequality says that the wage net of the cost of effort for high effort exceeds that for low effort. Rewriting this inequality as

$$w_2(H) > w_2(L) + H - L$$

we see that if the agent chooses to put forth a lot of effort, then the agent has to be paid more than if he or she puts in a low effort. This kind of inequality is known as an **incentive compatibility constraint.** An incentive compatibility constraint makes precise what the incentives must be to get an agent to put forth a predetermined effort. Of course, the principal might want only a low effort. The incentive compatibility constraint in that case is

$$w_2(L) - L > w_2(H) - H$$

Just as it takes a high wage to induce a high effort, a low wage will suffice to induce a low effort. One solution to this inequality is always

$$w_2(L) = w_2(H)$$

since we then have, from the incentive compatibility constraint,

$$-L > -H$$

You can always be sure than an agent will put in a low effort if every effort level is rewarded the same. In such a situation, the agent maximizes utility by minimizing effort. This situation is precisely what occurs in dead-end, mini-mum-wage jobs.

Working our way back, the agent has another decision to make: whether to reject or accept the contract offered. Figure 10.2 focuses on this decision. In Figure 10.2a, the agent has chosen to put forth a high effort in response to the incentives provided by the principal. Now the agent must compare the result of putting forth a high effort to rejecting the contract altogether. The agent accepts the contract (and puts forth a high effort) when

$$w_2(H) - H > 0$$

where 0 is the utility of the outside option. This inequality is an example of a **participation constraint.** A participation constraint makes precise what the incentives must be to get an agent to participate in a certain contract with the principal. The agent rejects the contract when

$$w_2(H) - H < 0$$

When the high wages associated with high effort are still not high enough to compensate the agent, the agent will not sign on the dotted line.

Figure 10.2b shows the case where the agent has chosen to put forth a low effort in response to the incentives provided by the principal. Again, the agent compares this payoff to that from rejecting the contract outright. The agent accepts the contract when

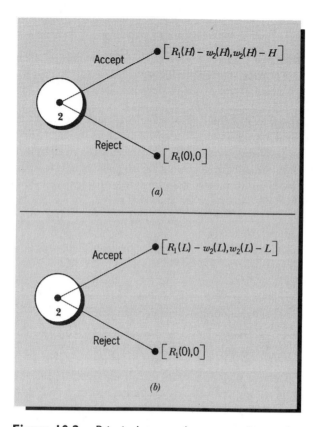

Figure 10.2.   Principal versus Agent, agent's participation decision: (*a*) high effort, final subgame; (*b*) low effort, final subgame.

$$w_2(L) - L > 0$$

This inequality also exemplifies a participation constraint. The low-effort wage is still high enough to get the agent to sign on. The agent rejects the contract when

$$w_2(L) - L < 0$$

At this low a wage, the agent is not interested in working for the principal.

We have now worked our way back to the beginning of Principal versus Agent, where it is the principal's turn to move. The principal faces the situation shown in Figure 10.3. If the agent's best move is to reject any contract, then it does not matter whether the principal offers a contract or not. In this case, there will be no relationship, either because the principal does not offer a contract or because the agent rejects any contract the principal offers. Only two cases are left to consider, corresponding to high or low effort on the part of the agent. Figure 10.3*a* shows the case where the agent accepts the contract and

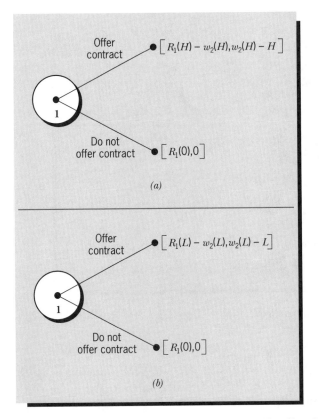

Figure 10.3. Principal versus Agent, principal's offer decision, agent accepts: (*a*) high effort; (*b*) low effort.

puts forth a high effort. The principal has to decide between offering a contract or not. The principal offers the contract when

$$R_1(H) - w_2(H) > R_1(0)$$

When the profits from hiring a high-effort agent are greater than those of doing the job himself or herself, the principal offers a contract with incentives for high effort. The principal offers no such contract when the inequality is reversed:

$$R_1(H) - w_2(H) < R_1(0)$$

The principal faces a similar decision when the agent accepts the contract and puts forth a low effort, as shown in Figure 10.3*b*.

Now that we have worked our way through Principal versus Agent, let's see how such a game plays out in practice. Suppose that the revenue function for the principal is quadratic in effort:

$$R(e) = 10e - e^2$$

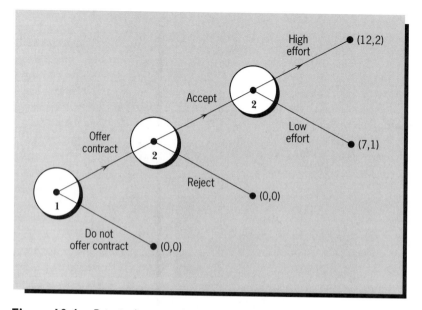

Figure 10.4. Principal versus Agent: $R(e) = 10e - e^2$; $L = 1$; $H = 2$; $w_2(L) = 2$; $w_2(H) = 4$.

Low effort $e = L = 1$; high effort $e = H = 2$. The wage for low effort is $w_2(L) = 2$; the wage for high effort, $w_2(H) = 4$. Substituting into the game tree of Figure 10.1, we get the same tree in Figure 10.4. At this high a wage, the agent has an incentive to put forth a high effort, since

$$w_2(H) - H = 4 - 2 = 2 > 2 - 1 = w_2(L) - L$$

Moreover, the agent has an incentive to accept the contract, since

$$w_2(H) - H = 4 - 2 = 2 > 0$$

Finally, the principal has an incentive to offer the contract, since

$$R_1(H) - w_2(H) = 10(2) - 2^2 - 4 = 12 > 0 = R_1(0)$$

This solution is shown by the arrows in Figure 10.4.

Notice that the outcome is indeed a social optimum. The sum of utilities, 14, that is achieved at the game equilibrium is the largest possible. To a large extent, this is a happy consequence of the wages that were fixed in advance. For instance, if the high-effort wage were fixed at the same level as the low-effort wage, $w_2(H) = 2$, then the agent would put in a low effort and the principal would still offer a contract (see Figure 10.5). Now, however, the game equilibrium implies a total payoff of 8 units, even though a payoff of 14 is still possible, via $u = (14,0)$.

Fixed prices cause lots of mischief in economics, and we have just seen an example. The social optimum prescribes what sort of wages are compatible with

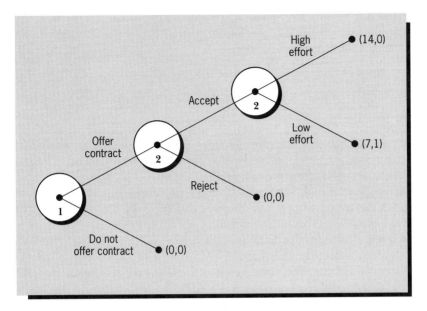

Figure 10.5. Principal versus Agent: $R(e) = 10e - e^2$; $L = 1$; $H = 2$; $w_2(L) = 2 = w_2(H)$.

it. If wages are fixed without regard to incentives, then game equilibrium need not embody a social optimum. Let's now relax the assumption that the wages are fixed in advance and allow the principal to set the wages stated in the contract he or she offers. We can show that, with perfect information, the principal can always arrange to accomplish two things simultaneously: maximize profits and achieve a social optimum. We get an **invisible hand outcome,** that is, a good outcome that was part of no individual's intention, even though the hands are very visible.

To see that when the principal sets the wages, the game equilibrium is an optimum, we will consider three possibilities in turn. First, suppose, as in the example just given, high effort on the part of the agent is the social optimum. The principal needs to propose a contract that the agent accepts (the participation constraint) and that provides incentives for the agent to put forth a high effort (the incentive compatibility constraint). In order to break ties, suppose that the minimum monetary unit is 1. Then the incentive compatibility constraint becomes

$$w_2(H) = w_2(L) + H - L + 1$$

where we have added 1 to the low-effort wage in order to break any possible tie. A high-effort wage this high will always get the agent to put in a high effort. The participation constraint becomes

$$w_2(H) - H > 0$$

The principal can be sure this constraint is satisfied by setting $w_2(L) = L$, that is, by making low-effort work a break-even proposition. Substituting into the incentive compatibility constraint, we get

$$w_2(H) = H + 1$$

or

$$w_2(H) - H = 1 > 0$$

satisfying the participation constraint. In this way, the principal can arrange for the social optimum to be supported by the game equilibrium (principal offers contract, agent accepts, agent puts forth a high effort).

Second, suppose that low effort on the part of the agent is the social optimum. Let the principal propose the wages $w_2(H) = w_2(L) = L + 1$. You can show that the game equilibrium (principal offers contract, agent accepts, agent puts forth a low effort) results. Finally, if zero effort is the social optimum, the principal need only propose the wages $w_2(H) = w_2(L) = 0$, saying, in essence, that the agent works for free. The agent will gladly say no—again the right answer. The details of these last two cases are left for end-of-chapter problems.

10.3 Principal versus Agent: Imperfect Information ■ ■ ■ ■ ■ ■ ■ ■ ■ ■ ■ ■ ■ ■ ■ ■

In Principal versus Agent with perfect information, the solution is determinate. If the principal has the power to set the terms of the contract, then the outcome that results is a social optimum.[1] In this section, we see to what extent this proposition remains true when information is imperfect. Two degrees of imperfection are considered. In both, the principal's revenue is a random function of the agent's effort. When the principal can still observe the agent's effort, this randomness in revenue is not so big a problem. When the principal can no longer observe the agent's effort, this randomness in revenue poses a much larger problem—a challenge to efficiency that cannot be entirely overcome.

To model randomness in revenue, we need a little extra notation. Suppose, as before, that there are two revenue levels, high revenue, $R(H)$, and low revenue, $R(L)$, with

$$R(H) > R(L)$$

When the agent puts forth a high effort, then high revenue is very likely. The probability of high revenue when the agent puts forth a high effort, written $p[R(H)|H]$, is a number close to 1. If your lawyer devotes a lot of effort to your

---

[1]The same would be true if the agent had the power to set the terms of the contract (see problem 3).

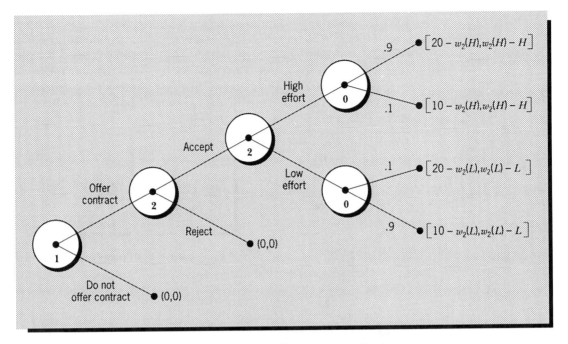

$$\begin{bmatrix} 20 - w_2(H), w_2(H) - H \end{bmatrix}$$

$$\begin{bmatrix} 10 - w_2(H), w_2(H) - H \end{bmatrix}$$

$$\begin{bmatrix} 20 - w_2(L), w_2(L) - L \end{bmatrix}$$

$$\begin{bmatrix} 10 - w_2(L), w_2(L) - L \end{bmatrix}$$

Figure 10.6. Principal versus Agent, imperfect information, monitoring.

case, you are likely to come out a winner. When the agent puts forth a low effort, then low revenue is very likely. The probability of low revenue when the agent puts forth a low effort, written $p[R(L)\,|\,L]$, is again the number close to 1. If your lawyer does not devote much time to your case, you are in big trouble. There is still a role for luck to play in all of this. First, you could be really unlucky. Your agent puts forth a high effort but there is little to show for it. Second, you could be really lucky. Your agent puts forth only a little effort but you hit the jackpot. Neither of these events is going to happen very much of the time—nobody's luck is always bad or always good—but they happen enough of the time to make things interesting.

Now, as long as the principal can see what effort the agent puts forth, randomness in revenue is a problem only for the principal. The agent continues to be paid according to effort rendered. If, in addition, the principal is risk neutral, then randomness in revenue is no problem for the principal, either. Here's an example to support this contention. Revenue can either be high, $R(H) = 20$, or low, $R(L) = 10$. A high effort produces high revenue 90% of the time, $p(20\,|\,H) = .9$; a high effort produces low revenue only 10% of the time, $p(10\,|\,H) = .1$. A low effort is a different matter. A low effort produces low revenue 90% of the time, $p(20\,|\,L) = .9$; a low effort produces high revenue only 10% of the time, $p(10\,|\,L) = .1$. If no agent is present, the principal gets revenue 0. All this is shown in Figure 10.6.

The final subgames are now random moves, but the principal can tell these two subgames apart. The principal knows when the probability distribution over his or her own revenue is based on high effort and when that probability distribution is based on low effort. The principal is able to **monitor** the agent. The principal keeps an eye on the agent, just as a professor monitoring an exam keeps an eye on the students. If the agent has chosen high effort, the principal can expect the revenue

$$EV_1(H) = .9[20 - w_2(H)] + .1[10 - w_2(H)]$$
$$= 19 - w_2(H)$$

when he or she observes high effort on the part of the agent. In this event, the agent gets the sure-thing payoff

$$w_2(H) - H$$

The principal can expect the revenue

$$EV_1(L) = .1[20 - w_2(L)] + .1[10 - w_2(L)]$$
$$= 11 - w_2(L)$$

when he or she observes low effort on the part of the agent. In this event, the agent gets the sure-thing payoff

$$w_2(L) - L$$

Notice that once we have replaced the final random-move endgames with their expected value to the principal and sure-thing value to the agent, we have essentially the same situation as in Principal versus Agent with perfect information. To see this result, suppose further that the principal's outside option $R_1(0) = 0$, high effort $H = 8$, and low effort $L = 2$. The principal offers the high-effort wage $w_2(8) = 9$ and the low-effort wage $w_2(2) = 2$. The game that results is shown in Figure 10.7. Replacing final subgames with their expected values, we see that high effort leads to the payoffs

$$EV_1(8) = .9(11) + .1(1) = 10$$

and

$$w_2(8) - 8 = 1$$

Low effort leads to the payoffs

$$EV_1(2) = .1(18) + .9(8) = 9$$

and

$$w_2(2) - 2 = 0$$

At the subgame perfect equilibrium, the principal offers this contract and the agent accepts and puts forth a high effort. The result is the social optimum, with maximum total payoff of 11. The additional uncertainty does not materi-

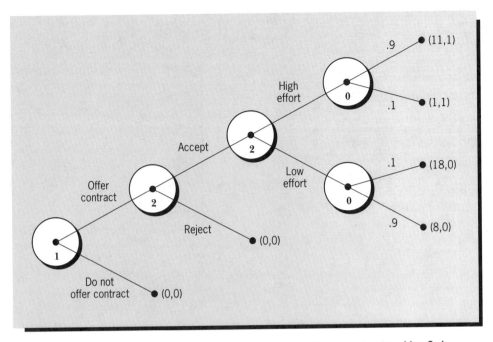

Figure 10.7. Principal versus Agent, imperfect information, monitoring: $H = 8$; $L = 2$; $w_2 (H) = 9$; $w_2 (L) = 2$.

ally affect the equilibrium outcome. As far as the game is concerned, this is entirely the same outcome as if the principal knew $R(8) = 19$ and $R(2) = 11$ with certainty.

Things get rather stickier when information is even more imperfect. Suppose that the principal can no longer observe effort. When high or low revenue occurs, the principal knows only what the probabilities are of the agent's having put in a high effort or a low effort, but not what the agent actually did. In such a case the principal cannot monitor the agent's effort. The agent could have been lucky (low effort, high revenue) or unlucky (high effort, low revenue). Thus the principal can no longer pay the agent according to effort. The only basis on which the principal can pay the agent is that of the revenue that actually occurs. When an agent is lucky, the agent is overpaid relative to effort; when the agent is unlucky, he or she is underpaid relative to effort.

The wage paid the agent when revenue is high is written $w_2[R(H)]$; the wage paid the agent when revenue is low, $w_2[R(L)]$. Figure 10.8 shows the game of Figure 10.6 when the principal cannot monitor the agent's effort. This difference is evident in the final information set of the game, which is still a random move, but now the principal does not know which node of this information set has been reached. The two wages are $w_2(20)$ and $w_2(10)$, depending on revenue, which is observable, and not depending on effort, which is not. The inability to monitor really complicates the principal's decision. This complica-

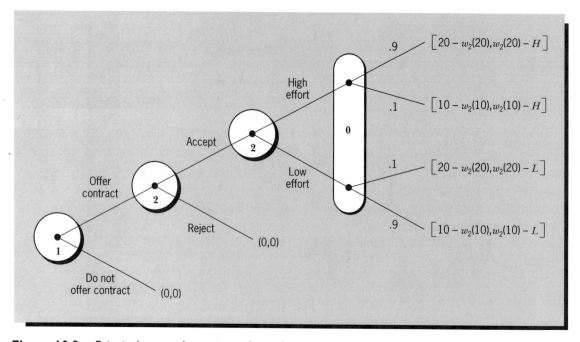

Figure 10.8. Principal versus Agent: imperfect information, no monitoring.

tion shows up in the agent's final decision, as expressed by the incentive compatibility constraint.

Suppose that the principal wants to provide an incentive for high effort— this makes sense, since high effort was the social optimum when the principal could monitor. When the agent puts forth a high effort, he or she expects to produce high revenue and get the high-revenue wage 90% of the time. The rest of the time the agent gets the low-revenue wage for high effort. The agent's expected value for high effort is

$$EV_2(H) = .9w_2(20) + .1w_2(10) - H$$

When the agent puts forth a low effort, then he or she expects to produce low revenue and get the low-revenue wage 90% of the time. The rest of the time the agent gets the high-revenue wage for low effort. The agent's expected value for low effort is

$$EV_2(L) = .1w_2(20) + .9w_2(10) - L$$

To induce high effort, the principal needs to make sure that high effort pays more than low effort:

$$EV_2(H) > EV_2(L)$$

Substituting the values $H = 8$ and $L = 2$ and solving the inequality, we get

$$.8w_2(20) > .8w_2(10) + H - L = .8w_2(10) + 6$$

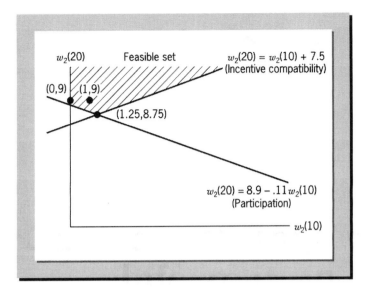

Figure 10.9. Principal versus Agent, no monitoring, incentive compatibility and participation constraints.

or

$$w_2(20) > w_2(10) + 7.5$$

The agent is paid more for producing more revenue—whether he or she worked hard or not.

Now we can work our way back toward a solution. Given that the agent has chosen to put forth a high effort, the principal wants to make sure that the contract offered is accepted—the participation constraint. The agent accepts the contract when the expected value from a high effort exceeds the outside option:

$$EV_2(H) > 0$$

Substituting the value $H = 8$ and solving the inequality, we get

$$.9w_2(20) + .1w_2(10) - 8 > 0$$

or

$$w_2(20) > 8.9 - .11w_2(10)$$

The inequalities corresponding to the incentive compatibility and participation constraints are plotted in Figure 10.9. The wages that satisfy both constraints have to lie above both lines in Figure 10.9. In addition, the minimum monetary unit is 1, so all wages must be in integers. The point (0,9) satisfies all these conditions and is less costly to the principal than is the point (1,9). Thus the principal would offer the contract $w_2(20) = 9$ and $w_2(10) = 0$. The agent is paid $9 if revenue is $20 and is paid nothing otherwise. This is a very different contract from what the agent was offered when monitoring was possible.

We can now check to make sure that the principal wants to offer this contract, and then compute its payoff implications. If the principal offers the contract $w_2(20) = 9$ and $w_2(10) = 0$, and the agent accepts and puts forth a high effort, then the principal can expect

$$EV_1 = 19 - .9(9) - .1(0) = 10.9 > 0$$

An agent who puts forth a high effort can expect the payoff

$$EV_2(H) = .9(9) - .1(0) - 8 = 0.1 > 0$$

Since the principal sets the price, the terms of the contract are especially favorable to the principal, who receives most of the gains from this relationship. Notice also that the total profit from the relationship, $10.9 + 0.1 = 11$, is exactly the same as when the principal could monitor the agent. We will see later that this is something of a fluke, since it is true only when both parties are risk neutral. Now, however, let's look at a principal–agent game that is played every time a depositor goes to the bank or savings and loan and that was especially prominent during the S&L crisis of the 1980s.

10.4 Depositor versus S&L[2] ■ ■ ■ ■ ■ ■ ■ ■ ■ ■ ■ ■ ■ ■ ■ ■

Every time you walk into a financial institution to deposit your money, you are playing a form of Principal versus Agent. You are the principal. You want the financial institution to take good care of your money, investing it wisely and paying back your principal plus interest when it is due. The financial institution is your agent. You cannot see behind the scenes, what the institution is doing with your money, but you might want to. During the 1980s, an entire industry of financial institutions, the **savings and loan,** or **S&L,** industry, performed very poorly as agents for their depositors. A version of Principal versus Agent shows why.

This game is called Depositor versus S&L. Player 1, the depositor, has $100,000 to invest, and moves first. The depositor can either deposit the money in the S&L or buy a 1-year U.S. government bond (G-bond). The G-bond is an absolutely sure thing—the government has never defaulted on its debt—and will repay the principal plus 3% interest, for a total of $103,000. If the depositor buys a G-bond, the game ends. If the depositor puts the money in an S&L, the game continues. The S&L is player 2. Since the S&L accepts all deposits, we do not have to model the accept/reject decision and there is no participation constraint. *The S&L always participates.* The S&L promises the depositor a rate of interest of 10% on an uninsured certificate of deposit (CD); however, this

---

[2]Material for this section was inspired by Kathleen Day, *S&L Hell* (New York: W.W. Norton, 1993).

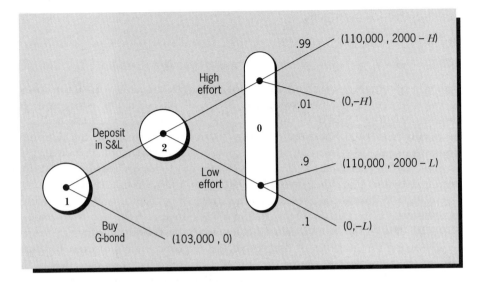

Figure 10.10. Depositor versus S&L.

promise is not ironclad. If the S&L loses all the money, it does not have to repay it—it simply goes bankrupt instead. In order to make any money, the S&L has to find an investment that pays more than 10% interest.

Assume, for simplicity, that there is a single type of investment opportunity available to the S&L, a junk bond.[3] A $100,000 junk bond is either good, and pays back principal plus 12% interest, or it is junk, worthless, with a payback of $0. If the S&L puts forth a high research effort, it can guarantee that the probability of a junk bond's being junk is only 1%. However, it costs money to conduct the required junk bond market research, as measured by H. If the S&L puts in a low research effort, it can guarantee that the probability of a junk bond's being junk is 10%. It costs less to perform this research, as measured by L. We now have the payoffs corresponding to the chance move at the end of Depositor versus S&L, which determines whether a junk bond is good or junk. Suppose that the S&L has put in a high effort. Then with probability .99, the junk bond is good. The depositor gets his or her money back with interest, $110,000. The S&L gets the junk bond back with interest, $112,000. After paying off the depositor and deducting research costs, the S&L is left with $2000 − H. With probability .01, the junk bond is junk. The depositor gets burned, losing all the money, and the S&L gets stuck with the research costs, −H. The same payoffs appear in the low-effort node—only the probabilities along the branches are different. This game is shown in Figure 10.10.

You can see what sort of jeopardy the depositor is in. Whether the S&L puts in a high effort or not depends on the following inequality:

[3]The official name for this sort of security is high-yield bond. The invention of high-yield bonds was Michael Milken's greatest contribution to American society.

$$.99(2000) - H > .9(2000) - L$$

or

$$180 > H - L$$

The cost of a high research effort cannot exceed by more than \$180 the cost of a low research effort. Otherwise, the S&L will put in a low effort and the depositor will be burned 10 times as often. If research costs are low, say, $L = 100 and $H = 200, then the S&L puts forth a high effort and the depositor comes out ahead. The depositor expects a repayment of principal plus interest of $(.99)(110,000) = $108,900$. Since the depositor is risk neutral, this result is better than the sure \$103,000 from the G-bond. However, just a few dollars difference in research costs (say, $H = 300), and the outcome is completely different. The S&L puts in a low effort, and the depositor expects $(.9)(110,000) = $99,000$, considerably less than the G-bond payoff.

The worst thing about all this is that the depositor may not even be aware that he or she is playing a game with the S&L. It is fairly certain that most of the depositors who bought \$100,000 uninsured CDs from Lincoln Federal, the infamous S&L run by Charles Keating, had no idea what game they were playing—until their money was gone.

▪ 10.5 Principal versus Agent When Attitudes toward Risk Differ ▪

Up to this point, principal and agent alike have been risk neutral, with the happy consequence that the solutions of the games between them have been socially optimal, even when the principal could not monitor the agent's behavior. Once the players in Principal versus Agent are not risk neutral, the social optimality of the interactions between principal and agent is no longer assured. In particular, when monitoring is no longer possible, a risk-averse agent will cost more to employ and the resulting game solution will be inefficient.

Recall the problem presented in section 10.3, with both players risk neutral (Figure 10.8). The social optimum was achieved when the agent put forth a high effort. Now suppose that the agent is very risk averse, with the utility function

$$u_2(e_2, m_2) = \log(m_2 - e_2)$$

where $\log(.)$ denotes the natural logarithm of a number.[4] Notice that the agent's indifference curves in (money, effort) space do not change. This is simply a monotonic transformation of utility, which does not change any

---

[4]This is quite a bit more risk averse than even the square root function.

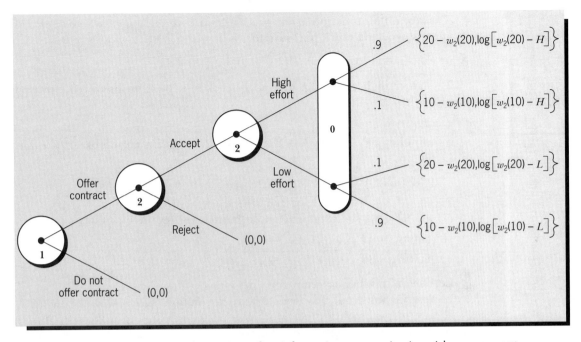

Figure 10.11. Principal versus Agent, imperfect information, no monitoring, risk-averse agent.

deterministic decision. However, since this is a nonlinear transformation of utility, it does affect decisions under uncertainty. The principal remains risk neutral. The social optimum, which produces the greatest gain from trade, is still equal to 11, and is still generated by a high effort on the part of the agent. Now, however, it will cost the principal more to provide the incentives necessary for high effort. The wage contract that the principal offered previously, $w(20) = 8$ and $w(10) = 0$, is no longer acceptable to this risk-averse agent. The zero wage in the event that low revenue is observed would mean the agent would get the utility $\log(0) = -\infty$, even if he or she put in zero effort! No agent would work for that kind of compensation—not when 0 utility is guaranteed just by saying no.

Let's work out the details of what it will take in this case for the principal to get the agent on board for a high effort. The game is shown in Figure 10.11. When the agent puts forth a high effort, he or she expects to produce high revenue and get the high-revenue wage 90% of the time. The rest of the time the agent gets the low-revenue wage for high effort. The agent's expected utility for high effort is

$$Eu_2(H) = .9 \log[w_2(20) - H] + .1 \log[w_2(10) - H]$$

Since the agent is now risk averse, all the wage payments net of effort get transformed accordingly. When the agent puts forth a low effort, he or she expects to produce low revenue and get the low-revenue wage 90% of the time.

The rest of the time the agent gets the high-revenue wage for low effort. The agent's expected utility for low effort is

$$Eu_2(L) = .1 \log[w_2(20) - L] + .9 \log[w_2(10) - L]$$

To induce high effort, the principal needs to make sure that high effort pays more than low effort:

$$Eu_2(H) > Eu_2(L)$$

Substituting the values $H = 8$ and $L = 2$, we get a nasty-looking nonlinear inequality:

$$.9 \log[w_2(20) - 8] - .1 \log[w_2(20) - 2] > .9 \log[w_2(10) - 2]$$
$$- .1 \log[w_2(20) - 2]$$

LF070Taking the exponent on both sides, we get the inequality

$$\frac{[w_2(20) - 8]^{.9}}{[w_2(20) - 2]^{.1}} > \frac{[w_2(10) - 2]^{.9}}{[w_2(10) - 8]^{.1}}$$

Let's leave this inequality for the time being.

Now we work our way back toward a solution. Given that the agent has chosen to put forth a high effort, the principal wants to make sure that the contract offered is accepted—the participation constraint. The agent accepts the contract when the payoff from a high effort exceeds the outside option:

$$Eu_2(H) > 0$$

Substituting the value $H = 8$ and solving the inequality, we get

$$.9 \log[w_2(20) - 8] + .1 \log[w_2(10)] - 2 > 0$$

Taking the exponent on both sides, this becomes

$$[w_2(20) - 8]^{.9} \, [w_2(10) - 8]^{.1} > 1$$

Fortunately, we don't need an exact solution of these two constraints to make our point. From the participation constraint it is clear that the low-effort wage $w_2(10)$ is going to have to exceed 8, so let's set $w_2(10) = 9$. Plugging this into the incentive compatibility constraint, we get

$$\frac{[w_2(20) - 8]^{.9}}{[w_2(20) - 2]^{.1}} > \frac{(9 - 2)^{.9}}{(9 - 8)^{.1}} = 5.76$$

Here's where you need your calculator. Starting with $w_2(20) = 10$ and working your way up, you will find that the smallest $w_2(20)$ that satisfies the inequality is $w_2(20) = 18$. The wages $w_2(20) = 18$ and $w_2(10) = 9$ provide a lower bound on the costs the principal can expect to face, ECost, if he or she hires the agent and provides incentives for high effort:

$$ECost = .9(18) + .1(9) = 17.7$$

Since the expected revenue is 19, the principal can still afford to hire this agent, only now at a considerably higher cost. When the agent was risk neutral, the expected cost of getting the agent to put in a high effort was only

$$ECost = .9(9) + .1(0) = 8.1$$

The cost has more than doubled. The cost increase is due solely to the agent's risk aversion—nothing else in the game has changed.

The intuition behind this result is the following. In any risky situation, efficiency dictates that the risk be borne by the party most willing to bear risk. In this case, that party is the risk-neutral principal. By bearing the risk, the principal is implicitly insuring the agent against bad outcomes. The low-re-venue wage has to be at least 9 to keep the agent's utility from getting nuked. Providing this insurance is costly to the principal and thus drives the cost of the agent up.

The contract the principal would have to offer to get high effort from the agent would result in an expected profit of 1.9. However, the principal isn't required to get high effort if it is very costly. The principal can switch to a low-effort contract, which is always cheaper. All that is required for low effort is for the principal to offer the same low wage regardless of outcome. The contract $w_2(10) = w_2(20) = 9$ will automatically satisfy the incentive compatibil-ity constraint. It will also satisfy the agent's participation constraint:

$$Eu_2 = .9 \log(9 - 2) + .1 \log(9 - 2) = .19 > 0$$

The agent accepts this contract. Moreover, the principal will now make more money, since

$$Eu_1 = 11 - 9 = 2 > 1.9$$

The **agency costs** have again gone up relative to the risk-neutral case. Now, however, a low effort is more attractive than a high effort. High effort costs so much to induce that it is priced out of the market. The principal adjusts to the increased costs of agency by switching from the expensive high effort to the less expensive low effort. The implication for society as a whole is that the economy shrinks as a result—the agency contract has not maximized gains from trade.

Following this same argument, you can show that it always costs more to hire a risk-averse agent than to hire a risk-neutral agent. Principals therefore have every incentive to deal with risk-neutral agents because they cost the least, and risk-averse agents will be at a disadvantage in the market because they come with a higher price tag. You should not expect to find a great deal of risk aversion in professions, such as medicine and law, whose practitioners are agents difficult to monitor.

▓ 10.6 Principal versus Agent with Two Types of Agents ■

In the situations we've reviewed so far, even if a principal could not monitor an agent, the principal did at least know what kind of agent he or she was dealing

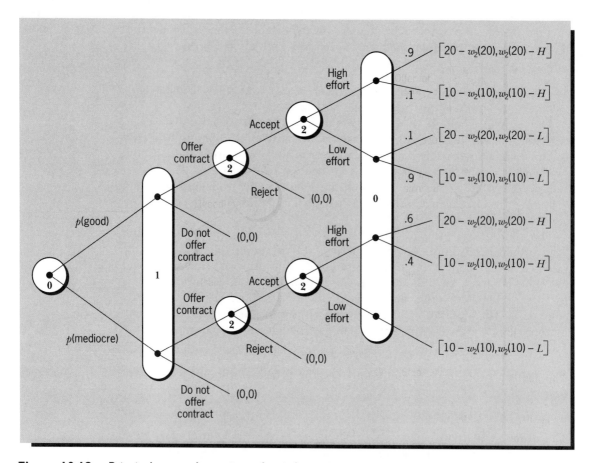

Figure 10.12.   Principal versus Agent, imperfect information, no monitoring, two types of agents.

with. This is a bold assumption. It is tantamount to saying that all lawyers or all doctors are equally good, which isn't always so. In this section this assumption is relaxed, so that there are two **agent types.** High effort on the part of a good lawyer means something different from high effort on the part of a mediocre lawyer. This section addresses this complication. To keep things as simple as possible, we will return to all risk-neutral players.

Figure 10.12 shows the sort of game that comes up with two types of agents. An initial random move determines whether the agent is good or mediocre. The agent sees the outcome of this move, but the principal does not. The principal then offers a contract or not. The same contract is offered to both types of agents, since the principal cannot tell the difference between them. Each type of agent can either accept or reject the contract. If either type of agent rejects the contract, then the game ends with the status quo payoffs (0,0). If an agent accepts the contract, then that agent can put in a high effort or a low effort. Let's assume that a good agent has the same characteristics as those of the agent in Figure 10.8: 90% of the time high effort leads to high revenue (20); 10% of the time high effort leads to low revenue (10); 90% of the time low effort leads to low revenue; and 10% of the time low effort leads to high revenue. With a mediocre agent, high effort only leads to high revenue 60% of the time, whereas low effort leads to low revenue for sure. There is a big statistical difference between good agents and mediocre agents, and a good agent is always a better deal than a mediocre agent given the same contract. Since the principal cannot monitor effort, either, all y of these endpoint possibilities come out of chance's final information set.

If the game is going to be played just once, the principal is not terribly interested in finding out whether the agent is good or mediocre. The principal just wants to make as much money as possible from hiring an agent. Nevertheless, the response to a contract offer may reveal an agent's type. For example when high effort $H = 8$ and low effort $L = 2$, offering the contract $[w_2(10), w_2(20)] = (0,9)$ to a good agent induces high effort—the subgame from Figure 10.8 that we already solved. Offering this same contract to a mediocre agent, we get for high effort

$$Eu_2(H) = .6(9) + .4(0) - 8 = -2.6$$

For low effort on the part of a mediocre agent, we get

$$Eu_2(L) = 0 - 2 = -2$$

Since $-2.6 < -2$, low effort is better than high effort for a mediocre agent. However, no effort is best of all. The mediocre agent rejects the contract altogether, since he or she can always get 0. Thus offering the contract $[w_2(10), w_2(20)] = (0,9)$ will actually serve two purposes. It induces a good agent to put forth a high effort, and it induces a mediocre agent to reveal his or her type when he or she rejects the contract, as a mediocre agent will.

Of course, in a one-shot game, getting the mediocre agent to reject the contract is not always the most desirable thing to do. If good agents are rare, that is, the probability of a good agent, $p(good)$, is small, then the principal may want to offer a contract that both types will accept and that will induce high effort on the part of a mediocre agent and low effort on the part of a good agent. In this case, it doesn't pay to cater to the incentives of a good agent. The principal is likely to be dealing with a mediocre agent, so it makes sense to cater to the incentives of a mediocre agent instead. You get to work out the details of this situation in problem 9.

If the principal–agent game is going to be played many times, a premium is put on dealing with a good agent rather than with a mediocre agent. In such a case it is worthwhile for the principal to explore contracts that mediocre agents would reject and good agents would accept. If the difference between a mediocre agent and a good agent is slight, such a contract may not exist mathematically, and the principal must use the probation period technique described in Chapter 9. The eventual establishment of a track record can determine, at least statistically, whether an agent in a repeated relationship is good or mediocre. An important example of repeated principal–agent games involves the stockholders and the CEO of a corporation. How CEOs are compensated is of great importance to stockholder interests, as we shall soon see.

❖ 10.7 Compensating Corporate Executives[5] ■ ■ ■ ■ ■ ■

The owners of a corporation are the owners of the corporation's stock. Taken as a whole, the stockholders are the principal in any game involving the corporation. All those working for the corporation are agents. In particular, the chief executive officer (CEO) and the other executives of a corporation act as agents of the stockholders. Designing compensation schemes for executives so that they have incentives to serve the stockholders' interests is a tricky and controversial area. Given the high levels of executive compensation prevalent in the United States, overpaying executives relative to their effort poses a serious problem for corporate performance. A CEO drawing a big salary and at the same time running the corporation into the ground is every stockholder's worst nightmare.

Information on executive compensation is available to stockholders from publicly held corporations and is contained in annual proxy statements. Kevin Murphy collected 18 years' worth of data (1964–81) from 73 firms that were on the 1981 Fortune 500 list. Executives were chairs, CEOs, presidents, and vice presidents. To be included in the study, an executive had to appear on the proxy statement during the first 6 years of the study (1964–70) and had to remain there for at least 5 years. These sample criteria were met by 461 executives, representing 4500 executive-years of experience. This is a large sample by almost any standard.

There are two major categories of executive compensation: salary and fringe benefits, which are not tied to firm performance; and **incentive payments,** which are tied to firm performance. Incentive payments include bonuses, deferred compensation (usually in the form of restricted shares of common stock), and stock options. All these forms of incentives have a strong tendency to rise in value when a corporation performs well. Bonuses are usually tied to annual profits. In a year when a corporation makes a lot of money, executives' bonuses are worth a lot. In addition, when a corporation makes a lot of money the price of its stock tends to go up, which directly raises the value of deferred compensation and indirectly raises the value of an option to buy the stock. **Total compensation** is the sum of salary and fringe benefits and incentives. The total compensation for an average executive in this sample in the year 1981 was

---

[5]Material for this study was drawn from Kevin J. Murphy, "Corporate Performance and Managerial Remuneration: An Empirical Analysis," *Journal of Accounting and Economics* 7 (1985):11–42.

$450,000,[6] divided roughly as follows:

salary and fringe benefits = $260,000

incentives = $190,000

More than 42% of total executive compensation was in the form of incentives.

Incentives are intended to increase in value when a corporation performs well. A good corporate performance is evidence that the executives are putting forth a high effort, which is showing up on the bottom line. (Of course, they could just be lucky, but the odds are against this.) The fact that nearly half of all compensation comes in the form of incentives makes corporate performance of considerable importance to the executives; the fact that they become owners (via deferred compensation and stock options) gives them a stake in the principal's side of the game as well as in the agent's side.

Whether the intention behind the incentives can actually be found in the data is a different issue. Although the data clearly indicate that total compensation rises with the size of the corporation, little hard evidence had been found previous to this study of a statistically significant link between corporate performance and total compensation. This study measured corporate performance by stockholders' annual rates of return, which is the sum of dividends and appreciation. All rates of return were adjusted for inflation and stock splits. The study found that when stockholders' rates of return went up (improved corporate performance), so did the total compensation of executives. For instance, for CEOs, a 20% increase in stockholders' rates of return led to a 3% increase in total compensation. If incentives constitute 42% of total compensation, this result indicates that incentive compensation rose more than 7% in response to a 20% increase in stockholders' rates of return. Effects of a similar magnitude were found for the other three categories of corporate officers.

Compensation in the form of incentives is an important part of the total compensation of corporate executives; these executives stand to gain a lot when the corporation performs well. It is nearly impossible for stockholders to monitor corporate executives, much less design schemes to weed out the good from the mediocre. Stockholders have a lot at stake in keeping agency costs down. Compensation in the form of bonuses, deferred compensation, and stock options appears to point corporate executives in the right direction, making their payoff go up with that of the stockholders.

▚ SUMMARY

1. A principal is any person or firm that hires another person or firm to perform services. An agent is any person or firm so hired. Principal versus Agent is the game played between the two.

[6]All figures reported are in constant-value 1983 dollars. To convert these figures to current dollars, multiply by 1.42.

2. In Principal versus Agent, the principal offers or does not offer a contract to the agent. The agent either accepts or rejects the contract (the participation decision). If the agent accepts the contract, the agent can either put forth a high effort or a low effort (the incentive compatibility decision).

3. When there is perfect information and both the principal and the agent are risk neutral, the solution of Principal versus Agent is a social optimum. This outcome is an example of the invisible hand at work.

4. When information is imperfect but the principal can monitor the agent, the solution of Principal versus Agent is a social optimum. This result holds true even if the principal cannot monitor the agent, as long as both are risk neutral.

5. When a depositor puts money into a financial institution, he or she is playing a form of Principal versus Agent with the depositor as the principal. Such games played with some S&Ls as agents in the 1980s led to considerable losses on the part of depositors.

6. When the agent is risk averse, agency costs rise, because the principal must implicitly insure the agent against unlucky outcomes. The game solution in this case does not maximize gains from trade.

7. When there is more than one type of agent and the principal cannot detect types, then the principal is constrained to offer the same contract to all types of agents, thus incurring an additional agency cost.

8. In a repeated-game setting, the principal has an added incentive to learn the agent's type before committing to a long-term relationship. When the two types of agents are sufficiently different, this determination can sometimes be made with a contract that one type accepts and the other type refuses.

9. A major form of Principal versus Agent is played in a mature market economy between the stockholders of a corporation (the principal) and its top executives (the agents).

10. A little less than half the total compensation of top corporate executives derives from incentive payments, which include deferred compensation, bonuses, and stock options. At least one study has found a positive and significant relationship between corporate performance and incentives.

✦ KEY TERMS

principal	monitoring
agent	savings and loan (S&L)
incentive-based contracts	agency costs
high effort/low effort	agent types
incentive compatibility constraint	incentive payments
participation constraint	total compensation
invisible hand outcome	

⊞ PROBLEMS

1. Give three examples of principal–agent games that you or a company you have worked for have played. For each example, estimate how serious the agency problem was or might have been.

2. The principal has the revenue function $R(e) = 20e - e^2$, where e is effort on the part of the agent. The agent has the utility function $u_2 = m_2 - 2e_2$. Effort can be either high ($e = H = 4$) or low ($e = L = 0.5$). The wages are fixed in advance at $w_2(H) = 10$ and $w_2(L) = 4$. The principal can observe effort. Write down the principal–agent game in extensive form and solve it. How does your solution compare to the social optimum?

3. Use the data from problem 2, except that now the principal gets to set the wages. Is the outcome a social optimum? Why or why not? Is the outcome different? Why or why not?

4. Solve the game in problem 2 when the agent gets to set the wages. Is the outcome different from that in problem 3? Explain.

5. A principal is considering hiring a lawyer to represent him or her in a lawsuit. The principal gets $250,000 if the suit is won and $0 otherwise. If the agent works hard (100 hours), there is a 50% chance that the principal will win the suit. If the agent does not work hard (10 hours), there is a 15% chance that the principal will win the suit. Without a lawyer, the principal is sure to lose the suit. The principal can monitor the agent, and both parties are risk neutral. The agent's utility function is $m - 50e$, where m is money in dollars and e is effort in hours. The agent's fee for this case is $100 per hour, and the outside opportunity is worth $500. Write down the game in extensive form and solve it.

6. The data are the same as in problem 5, except that the principal cannot monitor the agent. The principal offers the agent a contingency contract. Instead of billing by the hour, the agent is paid one-third of whatever is won. Write down the game in extensive form and solve it. How does your solution compare to that in problem 5? What principal, if any, is operating here?

7. In Depositor versus S&L, suppose that the S&L can invest $100,000 in a junk bond with the following rates of return: with high effort, the probability is .98 that the rate of return is 15% and .02 that the money vanishes; with low effort, the probability is .92 that the rate of return is 15% and .08 that the money vanishes. The rate of return on government bonds is 4%. Draw the extensive form and solve. Where should the depositor put the money? (*Hint:* Use Figure 10.10 as a guide.)

8. In the example of section 10.6, suppose that the risk-average agent has the utility function $[r\,(m_2 - e_2)$. Write down the game in extensive form. Show that agency costs go up relative to the risk-averse game solution. Do they go up as much as they do when the risk-averse agent has logarithmic utility? What does the principal do?

9. In Figure 10.12, suppose that the probability of getting a mediocre agent is 95%. Show that a contract that induces high effort from the good agent is not the best possible for the principal.

10. The CEO of a large corporation, citing the need to hold the line on costs, has suggested converting all the existing incentive programs into straight salaries on a dollar for dollar basis. The CEO argues that incentive programs are getting too expensive. As a stockholder, how would you vote on this proposal at the next proxy meeting? Why?

CHAPTER 11

Auctions

Auctions are the most pervasive instance of Bertrand competition in our economy. Every day, contractors bid to sell their services to the public and private sectors and investors bid to buy goods, services, and financial assets. This chapter studies auctions as normal form games. The text consistently refers to auctions to buy; the theory for auctions to buy is easily adapted to auctions to sell, and the adaptors are supplied as needed.

The chapter begins with auctions with complete information, where each bidder knows what the item on the auction block is worth to each of the other bidders. These are the easiest auctions to understand, and they highlight principles that apply to all auctions. Two basic kinds of auctions are distinguished: first-price auctions, where honesty is not the best policy, and second-price auctions, where honesty is the best policy. Next, the assumption of complete information is relaxed, so that each bidder knows only what the item on the auction block is worth to him or her. Such auctions are called individual private value auctions. The less information a bidder has, the more complicated smart bidding gets. The best strategy for individual private value first-price auctions is to consistently underbid. With this background, the chapter turns to the cleanup of the biggest financial disaster in U.S. history, failed thrifts on the auction block. The Resolution Trust Corporation is currently conducting a multibillion dollar individual private value auction to liquidate the assets of savings and loan associations that went bankrupt in the 1980s—an auction with macroeconomic implications. Finally, the chapter addresses the most complicated auctions, where a bidder does not even know what the item on the block is worth to him or her, because no one can know the item's value. Such auctions are called common-value auctions. Bidding for offshore oil provides an important example of this type of auction. The result of bidding for oil anywhere is inherently uncertain, and especially so for offshore oil. Oil companies bid millions of dollars for drilling rights with no way of knowing exactly what lies under the floor of the continental shelf. Several oil companies have lost substantial sums of money in these auctions. Strategic bidding could have avoided, or at least curtailed, the losses.

11.1 Sealed-Bid Auctions with Complete Information ■■■■■■■■■■■■■■■■■■■■■

Consider an auction to buy with two bidders, numbered 1 and 2. The item on the auction block is worth z_1 to bidder 1 and z_2 to bidder 2. These individual values are positive. Both bidders know both these values—an unrealistic assumption that will be relaxed shortly. Each bidder can make any bid, so a bid b_i, for bidder i is any number. Bidders make their bids simultaneously and put them in sealed envelopes—a **sealed-bid auction.** So much for the mechanics of bidding.

Let $\mathbf{b} = (b_1, b_2)$ be a vector of bids. In any auction, the winning bidder has bid the highest. Let $b(\max)$ equal the largest bid in the bid vector $\mathbf{b}$. We assume that ties are broken by an even-chance lottery among the tied bidders. The question is, what price does the winning bidder pay? Let's consider two possibilities. First, the winning bidder could pay a price P equal to the winning bid: $P = b(\max)$. This type of auction is a **first-price auction** and is the most common auction. Second, the winning bidder could pay a price P equal to the second-highest bid. This type of auction, called a **second-price auction,** is fairly rare, but it has some interesting features and deserves to be used more often.

We will now set up a first-price auction as a game. Assume that bidders are risk neutral. Bidder i's utility function, $u_i(b_1, b_2)$, can be written

$$u_i = z_i - b_i \qquad \text{if } b_i = b(\max)$$
$$0 \qquad \text{otherwise}$$

If you bid less than the object on the auction block is worth to you and you win the auction, you pocket the difference. This is buyer's surplus in its purest form. If you bid more than the object is worth to you and you win the auction, you lose money. Suppose that the item is worth \$1000 to you, you bid \$2000, and your bid wins. You have just lost (\$1000 – \$2000) = –\$1000. Way to go! Bidding $b_i > z_i$ is called **overbidding**. Overbidding may win you auctions, but it costs you money. By contrast, if you bid zero, you cannot lose. It is a common mistake in auctions, and potentially a very expensive mistake, to overbid. This observation is summarized by the following principle of bidding:

■ ■

Bidding Principle 1. Never overbid. As a strategy, overbidding is dominated by bidding zero.

To see that bidding zero dominates overbidding, consider the following two cases. You overbid and you win the auction, but you lose money—in this case bidding zero would have saved you a lot of money. Or, you overbid and you lose the auction—in this case bidding zero would have led to the same result. Since bidding zero never pays less than overbidding and sometimes pays more, it dominates overbidding as a strategy.

Given that you shouldn't overbid, maybe you should bid true value. Suppose that $z_1 \geq z_2$. If players bid their true value in a first-price auction, the resulting bid vector $\mathbf{b} = (z_1, z_2)$ is not an equilibrium. To show that $\mathbf{b}$ is not an equilibrium, consider player 1. Suppose that instead of bidding true value, this player bids a number z between z_1 and z_2. The utility to player 1 at the vector of honest bids, $\mathbf{b}$, is

$$u_1(\mathbf{b}) = 0$$

since $z_1 - b(\max) = z_1 - z_1 = 0$. The utility to player 1 at the vector (z, b_2) is

$$u_1(z, b_2) = z_1 - z > 0$$

and player 1 still wins the auction. Player 1 does better by underbidding. This examples shows that bidding true value does not pay. The same would hold true for player 2, if player 2 had the high valuation. Bidding below true value is called **bid shaving**, a term inspired by language from the construction industry. This discussion leads to our second bidding principle:

■ ■

Bidding Principle 2. If you know you are the high bidder in a first-price auction, you should always shave your bid.

The question is, how much should you shave your bid if you place the top value on the item being auctioned? To find the answer, we will proceed inductively. Consider the game in Figure 11.1, where $z_1 = \$2$, $z_2 = \$1$, and all bids must be multiples of \$1. Given that players do not overbid, we only need to consider a 3 × 2 game, where players are at or below their true values using allowable bids. This game has three equilibria: (1,1), (1,0), and (0,0). All these equilibria

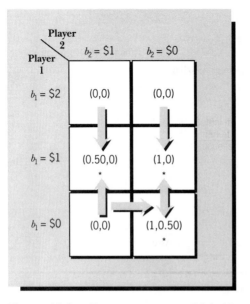

Figure 11.1.   First-price auction, $1 bidding interval.

involve underbidding by the high-value player. Notice that player 1 has a dominant strategy at $b_1 = \$1$, the closest allowable bid below true value. This amount is what the high-value player should bid when all bids must be multiples of $1. Whether the low-value player bids true value or not, the low-value player comes out of the auction the same as he or she went in, even.

We will now see what happens as the bidding interval, the minimum difference between bids, gets smaller. Consider Figure 11.2, where the bidding interval has shrunk to $0.50. Player 1 contemplates bidding $1 or the two adjacent strategies, $1.50 and $0.50. Player 2 contemplates bidding $1, $0.50, and $0. Again, there are three equilibria, at (1.5,1), (1,1), and (1,0.5). The high-value player always underbids. The strategy $b_1 = z_2 = \$1$ (bid the next highest player value) is dominant in this range. Again, the low-value player gets payoff 0 at every equilibrium.

Now we take the limit. Let $z_1 \geq z_2$, let the bidding limit be ϵ, an arbitrarily small positive number, and consider the set of strategies for player i, $[0,v_i]$. Figure 11.3 focuses on the neighborhood of the bid vector $\mathbf{b} = (z_2,z_2)$, where previous equilibria have been located. There are two pure strategy equilibria, at $(z_2 + \epsilon, z_2)$ and at $(z_2, z_2 - \epsilon)$. There is also a mixed strategy equilibrium, with player 2 mixing on bidding true value and ϵ below true value. This equilibrium satisfies:

$$z_1 - z_2 - \epsilon = \frac{p_2(z_2)\,(z_1 - z_2)}{2} + p_2(z_2 - \epsilon)(z_1 - z_2)$$

where $p_2(z_2)$ is the probability that player 2 bids true value z_2, and $p_2(z_2 - \epsilon)$ is the probability that player 2 bids just below true value. As ϵ approaches zero, all

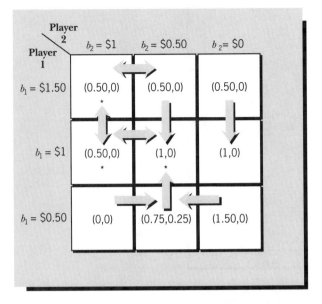

Figure 11.2. First-price auction, $0.50 bidding interval.

these equilibria get arbitrarily close to one another. Player 1 is bidding as close as possible to player 2's true value, and player 2 bids true value or just below it. Player 2, who breaks even at all these equilibria, is bidding so as to keep player 1 at least somewhat honest. The limiting solution, as bids become perfectly divisible, is for the high-value bidder to win the auction and pay a price

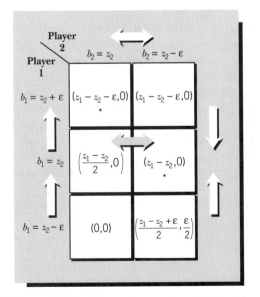

Figure 11.3. First-price auction, bidding interval ϵ.

303

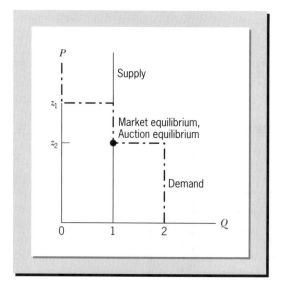

Figure 11.4. First-price auction as a market.

approximately equal to the second-highest valuation. This discussion leads to our third bidding principle:

■ ■

Bidding Principle 3. If you have the high valuation in a first-price auction, you should bid as close to the second-highest valuation as the bidding interval allows.

This auction equilibrium makes sense from the standpoint of the theory of perfect competition. Figure 11.4 shows the market demand and supply curves, under the assumption that supply is inelastic at one unit (the unit on the auction block) and bidders bid true value. Bidding true value yields the step-shaped market demand. Demand equals supply at any price P on the interval $(z_1, z_2]$. Since the high-value player has no incentive to bid true value, the market equilibrium that results from a first-price auction is one unit traded at a price just above z_2. This result should come as no surprise. It is simply the analogue of the result in Chapter 5: Bertrand competition among two competitors (here, buyers; there, sellers) with complete information suffices for perfect competition.

It is easy to generalize this result to n bidders. Simply rank the valuations from high to low:

$$z_1 > z_2 > \cdots > z_n$$

Then you can show that all strategic action involves the two high-value players, and the rest of the players just watch (for instance, by bidding true value or bidding zero). This is exactly how a market would work, too. All the buyers who put a value on the item less than z_2 are priced out of the market.

It is not quite as easy to generalize from a sealed-bid to an **English auction,** where bidders call out their bids and the last person bidding when the bidding stops wins the auction. However, once you abstract from the complexities of the extensive form, the action in an English auction once again boils down to the two highest-valuation players. Between them, once the bidding reaches the second-highest valuation, the auction has but one round of bidding to go. So the result for an English auction is again the same as for a sealed-bid auction.

⬛ 11.2 Second-Price Auctions ■ ■ ■ ■ ■ ■ ■ ■ ■ ■ ■ ■ ■ ■ ■ ■

In first-price auctions, the highest bidder wins and pays a price equal to the winning bid. There is another kind of auction, rare in practice but with interesting incentives, called a *second-price auction*. In a second-price auction, the highest bidder wins and pays a price equal to the second-highest bid.[1] This situation might make little or no sense if you are a seller—until you realize that the high bidder in a first-price auction is going to be bidding as close as possible to the second-highest value anyway. At this point, second-price auctions start to make sense.

To see how a second-price auction works, look at Figure 11.5, which has the same individual valuations ($2 and $1) and bidding interval ($1) as Figure 11.1. Overbids for both players are included to show that overbidding doesn't pay here, either. Take the outcome where both players overbid, each bidding $3. The second-highest price is $3, because of the tie. The random mechanism for tiebreakers awards the item to bidder 1 with probability .5 and to bidder 2 with probability .5. Bidder 1's expected value from this pair of bids is

$$EV_1 = .5(2 - 3) \quad \text{(bidder 1 wins the auction)}$$
$$+.5(0) \quad \text{(bidder 1 loses the auction)}$$
$$= -0.5$$

Things are even worse for bidder 2, whose expected value from this pair of bids is

$$EV_2 = .5(1 - 3) \quad \text{(bidder 2 wins the auction)}$$
$$+.5(0) \quad \text{(bidder 2 loses the auction)}$$
$$= -1$$

These are the entries corresponding to the bid vector $\mathbf{b} = (3,3)$. The other entries in the matrix are computed similarly.

---

[1]You can also define third-, fourth-, fifth-, and nth-price auctions by putting the corresponding adjective in place of "second." Although such auctions have no appeal from the point of view of the seller of a single item, they make a lot more sense when you are auctioning off a lot of items all at once.

Player 2 / Player 1	$b_2 = \$3$	$b_2 = \$2$	$b_2 = \$1$	$b_2 = \$0$
$b_1 = \$3$	(−0.5,−1)	(0,0)	(1,0) *	(2,0) *
$b_1 = \$2$	(0,−1)	(0,−0.5)	(1,0) *	(2,0) *
$b_1 = \$1$	(0,0) *	(0,0)	(0.5,0)	(2,0)
$b_1 = \$0$	(0,1) *	(0,1)	(0,1)	(1,0.5)

Figure 11.5.   Second-price auction, $1 bidding interval.

As you can see, there are plenty of pure strategy equilibria, six in all: (3,1), (3,0), (2,1), (2,0), (1,3), and (0,3). However, only one of these withstands the sufficient condition of dominated strategies. For bidder 1, bidding the true value of $2 is a dominant strategy: it dominates bidding 0, 1, or 3. Likewise, for bidder 2, bidding the true value of $1 is a dominant strategy: it dominates bidding 0, 2, or 3. So, of the six equilibria, only (2,1) satisfies undominated strategies. The solution to this second-price auction is for each bidder to bid true value. Notice also that the equilibrium of a second-price auction is consistent with perfect competition. The bids in a second-price auction reveal the true demand curve, the resulting price clears the market, and the item is allocated to its highest-value use—precisely what should happen in an efficient market.

The result we have just seen holds for any number of strategies, not just four. In a second-price auction, bidding true value is always a dominant strategy. The argument is the same as for the matrix. First, let's compare bidding true value to overbidding. As long as your rival does not overbid, these two strategies pay the same. However, if your rival does overbid, in particular if your rival bids more than your true value, and you win the auction by overbidding, then you lose money. In this case, it would be better to bid true value and break even. Second, let's compare bidding true value to underbidding. Most of the time, these two strategies pay the same. The only time underbidding makes a difference is if doing so makes you lose an auction that you would have otherwise won. In this case, bidding true value is again a better strategy. This insight is enshrined as a principle for second-price auctions:

■ ■

Bidding Principle 4. In a second-price auction, always bid true value.

This principle holds true regardless of the number of bidders. As in a first-price auction, the auction will come down to the top two valuations, at which point the results we just obtained provide the solution. Moreover, this principle does not depend on knowing your rival's valuation. It is just as true if you don't know your opponent's true value. Even in that case, paying the second-highest price means you can't lose when you bid true value. And you still can't do better by underbidding—you can only do worse.

Perfectly competitive markets work efficiently. For a market to be perfectly competitive, it needs perfect information. In particular, in order for the market demand curve to be correct, the individual buyers have to reveal their true demand curves. In terms of an auction market, each buyer has to reveal his or her underlying true value in the market. The only auction in which all buyers have an incentive to reveal their underlying true value is a second-price auction. In any other auction, the market will operate based on biased information, and the efficiency of market outcomes will thereby be jeopardized.

✖ 11.3 Individual Private Value Auctions ■ ■ ■ ■ ■ ■ ■ ■ ■ ■

From now on we will consider only first-price auctions, which are by far the most common (second-price auctions are a rarity, despite their attractive economic properties). However, we will drop the assumption that each bidder knows everyone's valuation. In an **individual private value auction,** you know only your own valuation of the item on the auction block. You have some information about where the valuations of your bidding rivals come from, but you don't know what those valuations are. In particular, you know the probability distribution from which the valuations of your bidding rivals are drawn—and that is all. Such a situation is called **complete information.**[2] The information situation is symmetrical, in the sense that your rivals know the probability distribution from which your valuation is drawn. All valuations are drawn from the same probability distribution—this is the final link in informational symmetry.

From an informational standpoint, an individual private value auction is just like Poker. You see your own hand and know its value, but this knowledge is private information because no one else sees your hand. All you know about

---

[2]If bidders do not know the distribution from which valuations are drawn, the situation is one of incomplete information, and is vastly more complicated.

the other hands (values) is what probability distribution they came from—but you don't actually see the other hands before you have to bid.

The problem, as always in a first-price auction, is to determine how much to shave your bid. If you are bidder 1, you base your bid, b_1, on your individual private value, z_1. When you bid, you don't know whether you will win or not, so your utility is now an expected utility. For now we will assume risk neutrality, so that expected utility is expected value. Let $p_1(\text{win})$ denote the probability that player 1 wins the auction; $p_1(\text{lose})$, the probability that player 1 loses the auction. We can write expected value EV_1 as

$$EV_1 = p_1(\text{win})(z_1 - b_1) + p_1(\text{lose})(0)$$

If player 1 wins the auction, player 1 gets the individual value less the winning bid; if player 1 loses the auction, player 1 gets zero. This boils down to

$$EV_1 = p_1(\text{win})(z_1 - b_1)$$

As soon as we figure out the probability of winning, we can figure out the right way to bid.

The probability of winning is going to depend on how high your bid is, which in turn depends on the probability distribution your rival's valuation is drawn from. Suppose, just to keep things simple, that your rival's valuation is drawn from the uniform distribution on [0,100]. With a continuous distribution, the probability of drawing the exact same two valuations is zero, so we don't have to worry about ties. If you bid zero, you can't win the auction, and if you bid 100, you can't lose the auction: these are the two extremes of the probability distribution. What you want to bid is some amount in between, which depends on your individual value, z_1. Your task is to find an entire **bidding function,** $b_1(z_1)$, that tells you what to bid given whatever valuation z_1 you have drawn from this uniform distribution.

Finding an entire function is always a complicated proposition. Here, a big hint will help. Let's assume (which turns out to be true) that the higher an individual value is, the higher the player bids. In mathematical language, the bidding function is *monotonic.* Figure 11.6 shows three monotonic bidding functions, two of them linear and one nonlinear. The bidding function $b_1(z_1) = z_1$ always bids true value. The expected value of this bidding function is zero—the same as the bidding function $b_1(z_1) = 0$ (which is not in the figure because it isn't monotonic). You ought to be able to do better than zero in expected value terms. Two other monotonic bidding functions, $z_1/2$ and $\sqrt{z_1}$ are also drawn. Notice that if both you and your rival use a monotonic bidding function and the probability distribution is uniform, your probability of winning is proportional to your bid. You are twice as likely to win an auction with a bid based on an individual value of 80 as you are with a bid based on an individual value of 40. And all we need is something proportional to $p_1(\text{win})$ to find the strategically right bidding function.

Write the probability of winning as $p_1(\text{win}) = kb_1$, where k is a proportionality constant. Substituting into player 1's expected value, we have

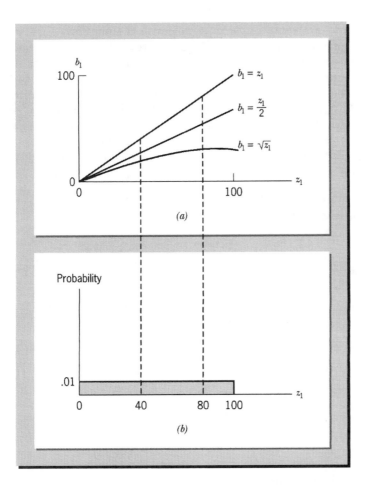

Figure 11.6. (*a*) Three monotonic bidding functions. (*b*) Uniform distribution of valuations.

$$EV_1 = kb_1(z_1 - b_1)$$

which player 1 wants to maximize by choosing the best bidding function. The maximum occurs at the first-order condition

$$0 = kb_1(-1) + k(z_1 - b_1)$$

Solving, we get the bidding function

$$b_1(z_1) = z_1/2$$

In an individual private value auction, bidding against a single rival, you should bid half your individual private value. This bidding function is shown in Figure 11.6. Thus, if the item is worth the maximum value to you, $100, then you should bid only $50, and so on. If your rival is risk neutral also, then the game is symmetrical (same strategies available, same form of utility function, and same kind of information), and we are entitled to invoke the sufficient condition of payoff symmetry to show that this bidding function actually solves the individual private value auction with two players bidding.[3]

This result can be extended to auctions with many players bidding. All we have to do is adjust the probability of winning the auction when you are bidding against more than one rival. If player 1 is bidding against two rivals, player 1 must beat them both. Since each rival draws a valuation independently from the same probability distribution, the probability of beating both is the probability of beating one of them times the probability of beating the other:

$p(1$ wins against two rivals$) = p(1$ wins against first rival$)$
$\times\, p(1$ wins against second rival$)$
$= p_1(\text{win})^2 = (kb_1)^2$

using the earlier result. The probability of winning an auction with n players is

$p(\text{win against } n - 1 \text{ rivals}) = (kb_1)^{n-1}$

Using this probability of winning, we can recompute the bidding function.
Substituting into player 1's utility, we have

$$EV_1 = (kb_1)^{n-1}(z_1 - b_1)$$

which player 1 wants to maximize by choosing the best bidding function. The maximum occurs at the first-order condition

$$0 = (n - 1)(kb_1)^{n-2}(z_1 - b_1) + (kb_1)^{n-1}(-1)$$

Simplifying, we get

$$0 = (n - 1)z_1 - (n)b_1$$

Solving, we get the bidding function

$$b_1(z_1) = (n - 1)z_1/n$$

This checks with our known result for $n = 2$ players, when a player is bidding against one rival. As the bidding competition among symmetrical bidders intensifies, each player has to bid closer and closer to true value. Indeed, as the number of players, n, gets large, we get perfect competition as a limiting result. As n goes to infinity, all players bid true value and the market allocates the item efficiently—and this despite the informational handicap inherent in first-price auctions. In this sense, the intensity of competition among bidders creates a substitute for complete information.

So far we have assumed that all players are risk neutral. Attitude toward risk has a big impact on bids, which is worth our attention. We go back to the

---

[3]For more complicated probability distributions, the bidding function that solves the game gets more complicated. Solving asymmetrical auctions gets complicated fast, too.

2-player auction, only now each player is risk averse. Each player has the utility function $\sqrt{(\text{money})}$. Hence, player 1 wants to maximize

$$Eu_1 = (kb_1)\sqrt{(z_1 - b_1)}$$

The bidding function that maximizes utility for this risk-averse player satisfies the first-order condition

$$0 = (kb_1)(.5)(z_1 - b_1)^{-0.5}(-1) + k\sqrt{(z_1 - b_1)}$$

Solving, we get

$$b_1(z_1) = 2z_1/3$$

Instead of bidding half true value, as would a risk-neutral agent, this risk-averse agent bids two-thirds of true value, a whole lot more. The explanation for this action is that a risk-averse bidder is afraid of losing an auction by bidding too low and so raises the bid substantially to lessen that risk. You can show (end-of-chapter problem) that the more risk averse a bidder is, the closer that bidder's bidding function is to true value.

As is usually the case, risk-seeking players and risk-averse players go in opposite directions. Suppose that player 1 is a risk seeker with utility function $(\text{money})^2$. This player wants to maximize

$$Eu_1 = (kb_1)(z_1 - b_1)^2$$

The bidding function that maximizes utility for this risk seeker satisfies

$$0 = (kb_1)2(z_1 - b_1)(-1) + k(z_1 - b_1)^2$$

Solving, we get

$$b_1(z_1) = z_1/3$$

A risk seeker bids substantially less than does a risk-neutral agent because a risk seeker likes to run the risk of losing an auction and so bids really low. You can show (end-of-chapter problem) that the more risk seeking a bidder is, the closer that player's bidding function is to zero.

We have spent a lot of time on the game theory of auctions. It's time to look at how a real-life auction works, in particular, the auction to clean up the S&L industry.

◼ 11.4 Auctioning Off Failed Thrifts[4] ◼ ◼ ◼ ◼ ◼ ◼ ◼ ◼ ◼ ◼ ◼

Congress passed the Financial Institutions Reform, Recovery, and Enforcement Act of 1989 to clean up the savings and loan (S&L) industry, which was by then

---

[4]Some of this material was drawn from Roger Stover and Roy Gardner, "RTC Auctions: Learning the Bid Strategy" (1994, mimeographed). For a very readable introduction to the entire S&L story, see Kathleen Day, *S&L Hell.*

in the throes of financial crisis. One of the major provisions of that law was the establishment of the **Resolution Trust Corporation** (RTC), a federal agency whose job it was to resolve (in most cases, this means auction off) failed S&Ls that had been seized by federal regulators during the 1980s. The RTC has been conducting first-price, sealed-bid auctions of failed thrifts ever since.

Of course, in some cases, there isn't much left of a failed thrift for the RTC to auction off. For instance, at Charles Keating's notorious Lincoln Savings and Loan, over 90% of all loans were in default.[5] Most of these loans were later declared uncollectible. Resolving this single S&L cost the U.S. Treasury (and therefore the taxpayers) about $2.5 billion. Since the basic criterion for S&L failure is for its deposit liabilities to greatly exceed its loan assets, large default rates on loans are typical of the failed thrifts on the RTC auction block. This situation leads to one of the unique features of RTC auctions: negative bids are allowed. Indeed, if the winning bid is negative in an RTC auction, then the winning bidder gets the failed thrift and in addition is paid by the RTC to accept the failed thrift. For instance, suppose that the winning bid is –$500,000. Then the RTC pays the winning bidder $500,000 to take over the failed thrift.

Prior to the auction of a failed thrift, the RTC holds a bidders' conference. Every bidder who has met the requirements (basically, a minimum capital and no felony convictions) to bid is entitled to attend this conference. At the bidders' conference, the RTC informs the bidders of the exact condition of the failed thrift—its assets and liabilities as of that moment. In addition to attending the bidders' conference, the bidders can take advantage of the due diligence procedure to determine exactly what the failed thrift is worth to them. Since many winning bids come from financial intermediaries located in the same region, locational and marketing considerations are built into a bidder's appraisal of the failed thrift. Finally, the rules provide for a winning bidder to withdraw a bid, for instance if the bidder has made a computational error in arriving at the bid. Since "computational error" can be interpreted extremely broadly, this provision practically guarantees that a winning bidder does not overbid. These three features—the bidders' conference, due diligence, and the provision for withdrawal—make RTC auctions individual private value auctions. In the period August 1989 to March 1992, for which data are available, the RTC handled 640 separate resolutions.[6] Resolutions fall into three categories. In purchase and assumption transactions, the most frequent resolutions (395), deposits, certain other liabilities, and a portion of assets are sold to the winning bidder. The buyer is purchasing assets and assuming liabilities, hence the name for these transactions. Of special importance to buyers are core deposits. The RTC defines core deposits as all nonbrokered deposits under $80,000. The incentive for any buyer of these deposits is the ability to lend them to make money the old-fashioned, financial intermediary way, by charging more interest

---

[5]Keating is currently serving a 10-year sentence in the federal penitentiary for bank fraud.

[6]Data on all these auctions were obtained from the Freedom of Information Office of the RTC and supplemented with discussions with RTC officials and bidders at RTC auctions.

on loans than is paid on deposits.[7] In insured deposit transfers, the next most frequent resolutions (157), the buyer serves as paying agent for the RTC and establishes accounts for the failed S&L's depositors. In insured deposit payouts, the least frequent resolutions (88), the RTC directly pays depositors their insured amount and retains all assets.

Since the RTC computes core deposits down to the last dollar for the benefit of prospective bidders, the main task for bidders is performing due diligence of the assets. Determining whether loans are performing or not, or can reasonably be expected to perform in the future, becomes a due diligence nightmare—besides clogging up the cleanup. The RTC, facing a large backlog of auctions, changed the rules in April 1991 so that earning assets were stripped out and handled separately. Since that time, bidders have been able to treat all remaining assets as junk unworthy of due diligence attention.

We have seen that strategic bidding in an individual private value auction depends on the number of bidders. The more bidders, the higher the bid you should make based on your individual value. In a statistical analysis of RTC auction data, there is a strong positive correlation between the winning bid and the number of bidders. This analysis is based on 201 winning bids in purchase and assumption transactions for which the entire failed thrift was on the auction block.[8] This result makes sense, since the number of bidders at the bidders' conference is a good signal of how many bidders there will actually be. The strongest explanatory variable by far for the winning bid is core deposits. This makes sense, too, since core deposits are the best possible signal of what the S&L is worth to a winning bidder. Both these empirical regularities are in accord with the theory of individual private value auctions.[9]

The RTC's stated goal is to obtain "the highest total premium to the RTC." By giving bidders access to the best possible information, and by holding bidders' conferences that make the bidders aware of the competition prior to bidding, it appears to have done just that. In the 4 years of its existence, the RTC has collected billions of dollars in winning bids, helping to lessen the impact of the S&L crisis on the U.S. taxpayer.

---

[7]The conditions "nonbrokered" and "under $80,000" guaranteed that such deposits would continue to be insured by an agency of the federal government, even after the demise of the Federal Savings and Loan Insurance Corporation (FSLIC) in 1989. Prior to its demise, the FSLIC had insured such deposits; after its demise, such deposits were insured by the Federal Deposit Insurance Corporation.

[8]The excluded purchase and assumption transactions all have the feature that the RTC was auctioning off the failed thrift in pieces, a typical piece being a branch office.

[9]The regression equation for the bidding function based on this sample of bids is the following:

$$\text{bid} = -89980 + 8397\ \text{core} + 977n - 320\ \text{repo} + 5841\ \text{put},$$

where core represents core deposits, n is the number of bidders, repo is the ratio of repossessed assets to total assets (another measure of financial condition), and put represents the rule change of April 1991. All t-values exceed 3.6, and the adjusted R^2 is 0.24.

⚙ 11.5 Common-Value Auctions ■■■■■■■■■■■■■■■■

This section looks at the first-price auction with the least information, and therefore with the most complex bidding, the **common-value auctions.** In a common-value auction, a bidder does not know what the item on the auction block is worth to him or her or to anybody else. All the bidder receives is a noisy signal about the value of that item. Each bidder knows that his or her own noisy signal, as well as that of every other bidder, is drawn from the same probability distribution. The bidder also knows what this probability distribution is. Still, this is not very much information to go on.

As with individual private value auctions, let's assume that the signals about the value of the item on the block are drawn from a uniform distribution. The bidders know this distribution. Unfortunately, they have no way of determining when they are overbidding. A bidder may have gotten a low signal when true value was high or vice versa. We can be sure, however, that if the bidder receiving the highest signal bids anywhere near that signal, that bidder stands to lose a lot of money.

We can illustrate the basic problem in terms of tossing dice. Each of the six faces on a die is equally likely, and if you toss the dice a lot of times, the expected value of a toss is

$$EV = (1 + 2 + \cdots + 6)/6 = 3.5$$

Now imagine that the common value of an item at auction is generated by tossing a pair of dice. The first die is shown to bidder 1; the second die, to bidder 2. That is their private information about underlying value. The underlying true value is the average of the two signals, but all the bidder sees is his or her own noisy signal. If bidder 1 receives the signal $z_1 = 5$, the underlying value could be anywhere between $(1 + 5)/2 = 3$ and $(6 + 5)/2 = 5.5$. Bidder 1 is still pretty much in the dark. The same is true for bidder 2, whose piece of information is drawn independently of bidder 1. Figure 11.7 shows the 36 equally likely outcomes of two dice being tossed simultaneously. For each possible outcome, the *maximum* of the two tosses is recorded in the cell corresponding to the noisy signals received by each player.

Now suppose that each player bids exactly the noisy signal received. The average maximum bid, which is found by totaling the entries in each cell and dividing by 36, is 4.56. If the bidder receiving the highest signal bids that signal, that bidder can expect to lose. The difference between expected value of the item and expected high bid is 3.5 − 4.56 = −1.06. In percentage terms, the expected loss from bidding the noisy signal and winning the auction is a whopping −30% (−1.06/3.5). A projected loss this big calls for some serious bid shaving. The phenomenon where bidding signal value in a common-value auction leads to an expected value loss is called the **winner's curse.** The winner of a common-value auction who has not shaved the bid appropriately can expect to be cursed.

Bidder 2 signal	$z_2 = 1$	$z_2 = 2$	$z_2 = 3$	$z_2 = 4$	$z_2 = 5$	$z_2 = 6$
Bidder 1 signal						
$z_1 = 1$	1	2	3	4	5	6
$z_1 = 2$	2	2	3	4	5	6
$z_1 = 3$	3	3	3	4	5	6
$z_1 = 4$	4	4	4	4	5	6
$z_1 = 5$	5	5	5	5	5	6
$z_1 = 6$	6	6	6	6	6	6

Figure 11.7. Generating a noisy signal, table of maximum values.

Suppose every bidder bids their signal value, and bidder 1 wins. That means that bidder 1's signal value was highest, and hence that the true value of the item being auctioned is less than z_1. Thus, bidder 1 has just lost money by winning the auction. For example, suppose $\mathbf{z} = (2,1)$. Bidder 1 has the highest signal, and bids \$2, winning the auction. The item is only worth $(1 + 2)/2 =$ \$1.50, so bidder 1 has just lost \$.50. What a bidder in a common value auction has to do is bid substantially less than their signal value, in order to avoid losing money by winning the auction. The strategic question is how much to bid below signal value.

We will consider a simple version of Figure 11.7, where each bidder i can receive either the signal $z_1 = 1$ or the signal $z_1 = 2$ with probability ½, and the true (but unknown to the bidders) value v of the item at auction is

$$v = (z_1 + z_2)/2$$

A bidder knows his or her signal value before they bid. Therefore, a strategy for bidder 1 is a function $b_1(z_1)$, which tells this bidder what to bid based on the signal value he or she receives. The bidding interval is assumed to be \$.10, so all bids are multiples of ten cents. This assumption reduces the number of possible strategies, but does not otherwise affect the results. Bidders bid simultaneously (for instance, by putting their bids in sealed envelopes and handing them to an auctioneer). Since the bidders have the same strategy sets, have access to the same kind of information, and move simultaneously, the game is symmetric. We will compute a symmetric equilibrium, although as you will see, the game has asymmetric equilibria as well.

The following observation is crucial to the solution of any common value auction. If bidder 1 has received a higher signal than bidder 2, then in equilibrium, bidder 1 outbids bidder 2:

$$b_1(z_1)^* > b_2(z_2)^* \text{ when } z_1 > z_2$$

The reason for this is that if bidder 1 bid the same or lower than bidder 2, then bidder 1 would lose or tie an auction that he or she could profitably win. (Remember, bidder 2 does not want to bid above signal value z_2). Beating bidder 2's bid, although not by too much, will raise bidder 1's expected payoff. This observation allows us to solve a common value auction by working our way up from the lowest possible signal.

To begin with, suppose that bidder 1 has received the signal $z_1 = 1$. How should bidder 1 bid if this were the highest signal anyone received? In that case, it must also be true that bidder 2 received the signal $z_2 = 1$, so that the bidders have tied evaluations. Also, the true value of the item in this event is \$1. Thus, if bidder has received the signal $z_1 = 1$, and it is the highest signal, this bidder is playing the first price auction depicted in Figure 11.8. The figure focuses on where the equilibria can be found. For instance, if bidder 1 bids \$1, then he or she automatically breaks even, regardless of what bidder 2 bids. Bids higher than \$1 are sure to lose, while bids lower than \$.80 are too low to win in equilibrium. There are two equilibria, one at $\mathbf{b}(1)^* = (b_1(1)^*, b_2(1)^*) = (.80, .80)$ and another at $\mathbf{b}(1)^* = (.90, .90)$. A bidder bids at least 10% and as much as 20% below their signal value, if he or she knows that their signal value $z_1 = 1$ is high.

Now take the high signal value, $z_1 = 2$. Suppose bidder 1 has received this signal. How should bidder 1 bid in this case? Bidder 1 knows that this signal value cannot be beaten. The probability is 50% that bidder 2 received the signal $z_2 = 1$, in which case the item is worth \$1.50; and 50% that bidder 2 received the signal $z_2 = 2$, in which case the item is worth \$2. Thus, if bidder 1

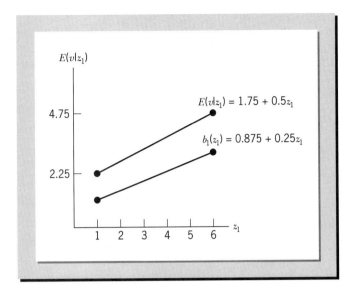

Figure 11.8. Common-value auction, two bidders.

Solving, we get

$$b_1(z_1) = 0.875 + 0.25z_1$$

This bidding function is also plotted in Figure 11.8. Notice that the bidding function is monotonic in the signal and that it is always below the conditional expected value of the item. This is the analogue in the common-value auction of shaving the bid in previous auctions. For really low signals in the vicinity of $z_1 = 1$, the bidder actually bids above the signal. However, for any signal above $z_1 = 2$, bids are below the signal. In particular, for signals that are very likely to lead to winning bids, bid are substantially below the signal value. For instance, at $z_1 = 6$, the bid is only 2.375.

As in individual private value auctions, in a common-value auction a risk-averse bidder will bid more than a risk-neutral bidder, who will in turn bid more than a risk-seeking bidder (see the end-of-chapter problems). Also, as the number of bidders gets large, the winning bid approaches the expected underlying true value. Let's outline the argument for three bidders. The biggest hurdle is to compute the conditional expected value $E(v|z_1)$. Suppose that bidder 1 receives the signal $z_1 = 1$. The underlying value is the average of all three signals received, $(z_1 + z_2 + z_3)/3$. To compute the conditional expected value, take all 36 possible combinations of two signals, as in Figure 11.7, and add. This represents the unknown signal to the other two bidders. Now add bidder 1's signal, $z_1 = 1$, and divide the result by 3 to get the underlying value, v. Finally, divide by 36, the number of possible signals to the two other bidders.

Figure 11.9. Common-Value Auction, $z_1 = 2$ is a maximum signal.

Player 1 \\ Player 2	$b_2(2) = \$1.70$	$b_2(2) = \$1.60$	$b_2(2) = \$1.50$
$b_1(2) = \$1.70$	$(-.025, -.025)$	$(.05, 0)$ *	$(.05, 0)$
$b_1(2) = \$1.60$	$(0, .05)$ *	$(.05, .05)$ *	$(.15, 0)$
$b_1(2) = \$1.50$	$(0, .05)$	$(0, .15)$	$(.125, .125)$

symmetric: $\mathbf{b(2)^*} = (1.60, 1.60)$. Each bidder i bids \$1.60 when he or she receives the signal $z_1 = 2$, and each bidder expects to gain \$.05 in this case. At this equilibrium, each bidder is bidding 20% below signal value. The other equilibria are asymmetric: $\mathbf{b(2)^*} = (1.70, 1.60)$ and $(1.60, 1.70)$. One bidder bids 15% below signal value; the other, 20% below signal value. This concludes our coverage of the two possible high signals.

We can now assemble an equilibrium for the overall auction by putting together its strategic pieces in the above two cases. There are six such equilibria, of the form

$$\mathbf{b^*} = (b_1(z_1)^*, b_2(z_2)^*),$$

where $b_1(z_1)^*$ and $b_2(z_2)^*$ are equilibrium bidding functions for the two bidders. The simplest of these equilibria to describe has the following bidding functions:

$$b_1(z_1)^* = .8z_1$$

for each player i. At this bidding equilibrium, each bidder bids 20% below signal value, for whatever signal value is received. You get this equilibrium by choosing $\mathbf{b(1)^*} = (.80, .80)$ and $\mathbf{b(2)^*} = (1.60, 1.60)$. By varying the choices of $\mathbf{b(1)^*}$ and $\mathbf{b(2)^*}$, you can generate the other 5 equilibria as well. The important thing to note is that all of these equilibria involve substantial underbidding relative to signal value. Every bid is at least 10% below signal value. This is how bidders protect themselves from the winner's curse in a common value auction. The above analysis works for more than two possible signals. You can show for instance (end-of-chapter problem) that bidding 20% below signal value continues to be an equilibrium when the possible signals are $z_1 = 1, 2,$ or 3, each with probability one-third. It is also possible to analyze common value auctions with more than two bidders. Here, unlike the case with individual private value auctions, bids do not always increase with the number of bidders. For signals at the low end, it remains true that the increased number of bidders increases competition, and so the bid approaches the signal value from below. However, for signals at the high end, the opposite is true. The more bidders there are, the more likely it is that a high end signal, if it is the highest of all, exceeds by far the value of the item. This winner's curse effect outweighs the competition effect, and so the bid for a high end signal is reduced. Demonstrating this gets complicated in a hurry, so we will not pursue it here.[10] Instead, we turn to an instance of real-life common value auctions.

▨ 11.6 Bidding for Offshore Oil[11] ■ ■ ■ ■ ■ ■ ■ ■ ■ ■ ■ ■ ■ ■

The U.S. government has been leasing rights to drill for offshore oil since 1954. The government uses first-price, sealed-bid auctions to award the **offshore oil leases.** Almost 20% of all oil produced in the United States comes from offshore wells, so the outcome of these auctions is important to the entire economy. The government typically provides no information beyond a legal description of the location of the area being leased, called a tract. Prior to these auctions, the oil companies are responsible for gathering whatever information they can about the oil-bearing potential of the tracts being offered. A typical tract covers about 5000 acres of ocean floor. Since the same geologic and seismological science and technology are available to all the oil companies, this information setup closely matches that of a common-value auction. This situation raises the possibility that oil companies might fall prey to the winner's curse in bidding for offshore oil.

Recently, three economists did an exhaustive study of these auctions for the period 1954–69. During this period, the government auctioned off 1200 tracts. All the major oil companies bid, as well as a large number of independent wildcatters. The total number of bids submitted on all tracts was 4050, meaning that a typical auction had three bidders. Winning an auction to drill for oil

---

[10]For readers interested in pursuing this subject further, the best place to start is the excellent survey by Robert Wilson, "Strategic Analysis of Auctions," in *Handbook of Game Theory,* vol. 1, eds. R. J. Aumann and S. Hart (New York: Elsevier, 1992) pp 227–79.

[11]Material for this study was drawn from Kenneth Hendricks, Robert H. Porter, and Bryan Boudreau, "Information, Returns, and Bidding Behavior in OCS Auctions: 1954–1969," *Journal of Industrial Economics* 35(1987):517–42.

does not oblige the winning company to actually drill for oil. Of the 1200 tracts leased, the winner drilled on 872 of them, about 73%. In the other 27% of cases, the oil company, on further review, decided that the tract was not promising enough to be worth exploring. This is a sure sign of a noisy signal. If the signal had been clear, then every winning bidder would have drilled for oil. Everybody knows that the oil business is risky. Already, 27% of all tracts have shown up as losers. And just because a company drills for oil, doesn't mean it's going to find any. Of the 872 wells that were actually drilled, 472 struck oil. So the conditional probability of striking oil, given that a company has decided to drill, is 54%—a little better than 50–50. This probability is even stronger evidence of a noisy signal about tract value. To sum up, of 1200 winning bids, 472 struck oil, or 39%. Winning the bidding for an offshore oil lease is no guarantee of finding oil.

It doesn't matter if a company only strikes oil 39% of the time it wins the auction, as long as its winning bid isn't too high. The industry as a whole came out very well in these 1200 auctions. The average winning bid was $2.26 million/tract, and industry profits net of bids and exploration costs were about $2 million/tract. Overall, bids were low enough to absorb all the dry holes and all the above-average signals and still make money. There were some notable exceptions, however. Texaco, Phillips, and Sunoco all lost substantial amounts of money; Texaco was the biggest loser of all.

Now, you might be tempted to chalk this up to bad luck—the oil industry is certainly an environment replete with risk. Texaco's hit rate (13/38 = 34%) was below the industry average, whereas its drilling rate (38/44 = 86%) was above average. However, overall gross profits (that is, profits before deducting the winning bid) were positive on Texaco's 38 tracts. This situation provides some evidence that Texaco was overbidding. To look further into the question whether Texaco was a winner cursed or not, the study used 20–20 hindsight. The economists asked, if Texaco had won every auction it bid on, what would it have made per tract? The answer was a whopping –$1.18 million/tract. Texaco could complain about its bad luck if it wanted to—but Texaco was really lucky. Had the company won all 128 tracts it bid on, it would have lost $151 million.

The U.S. government continues to auction off drilling rights for offshore oil. Stockholders of Texaco will be pleased to hear that Texaco's bidding performance has improved lately, compared to 1954–69. There is a lot of money at stake in these auctions, and woe to the winning bidder who has bid too much.

SUMMARY

1. Auctions are the most pervasive instance of Bertrand competition in our economy. Auctions can be to buy or to sell a good, a service, or an asset.
2. Any auction in which the bidders simultaneously submit their bids is called a sealed-bid auction. Such auctions are modeled as normal form games.

3. There are three types of information conditions in an auction. Complete information means each bidder knows the valuation of every bidder. Individual private value means each bidder knows only his or her own valuation. Common value means each bidder has only a noisy signal of underlying valuation.

4. In any auction for a single item, the highest bidder wins. In a first-price auction, the winning bidder pays a price equal to the winning bid. In a second-price auction, the winning bidder pays a price equal to the second-highest bid.

5. In a first-price auction, regardless of the information condition, the bidder with the highest valuation or highest signal of valuation should underbid. The precise way in which to underbid depends on the information condition.

6. In a second-price auction where the bidder knows his or her own valuation, bidding that valuation is a dominant strategy.

7. The solutions of both first-price and second-price auctions with complete information are consistent with perfect competition. The same is true of individual private value and common-value auctions as the number of bidders becomes large.

8. The Resolution Trust Corporation is conducting a series of individual private value auctions to clean up the savings and loan crisis.

9. The winner's curse refers to a winning bidder in a common-value auction who had bid too close to the signal of underlying value. Such a bidder can expect to lose money.

10. The U.S. government has been conducting common-value auctions for rights to drill offshore since 1954. The oil industry has profited from these auctions, with the notable exception of companies that overbid.

KEY TERMS

sealed-bid auction
first-price auction
second-price auction
overbidding
bid shaving
English auction
complete information

individual private value auction
bidding function
Resolution Trust Corporation
common-value auction
winner's curse
conditional expected value
offshore oil leases

PROBLEMS

1. Suppose that there is complete information that valuations are $z_1 = \$5$ and $z_2 = \$4$. All bids must be multiples of $2. Draw the normal form for the first-price auction and solve.

2. Using the data in problem 1, solve the second-price auction.

3. In a first-price auction to sell, the low bidder wins and receives a price equal to the low bid. In an auction to sell, z_i, represents the cost of providing the good or service, if sold. The utility function for a bidder i, u_i, is

$$u_i(\mathbf{b}) = b_i - z_i \qquad \text{if } b_i = \min(\mathbf{b})$$
$$0 \qquad \text{otherwise}$$

Show that the three principles of bidding in first-price auctions apply to auctions to sell when you replace "overbid" with "underbid."

4. Suppose that the individual private value auction in section 11.3 is on the interval [0,50] instead of [0,100]. How does the solution change, if at all? Interpret your result.

5. When utility is a function of money, according to the function $(money)_a$ the parameter a measures attitude toward risk. Risk seekers have $a > 1$, risk-neutral players have $a = 1$, and risk-averse players have $a < 1$. Show that in an individual private value auction with two bidders, the more risk averse an agent is, the more that agent bids.

6. Use the same setup as in problem 5, but show that the more risk seeking an agent is, the less that agent bids.

7. You are contemplating bidding on a failed thrift. What information would you want before submitting your bid? Would this information be enough to form an individual private value?

8. The common value in a common-value auction is being determined by a coin toss. One coin toss provides a signal to bidder 1; a second coin toss provides a signal to bidder 2. Heads = 3; tails = 1. Find an equilibrium for the common value auction, and show that it involves substantial underbidding.

9. In Section 11.5, we solved a common-value auction where there were 2 signals. Suppose that in that common-value auction there are three signals, $z_1 = 1, 2$ or 3, each with probability one-third. The true value v is still the average of the signals to each player. Show that $b_1 = 0.8z_1$ is an equilibrium bidding function for this more complicated auction. (Hint: first redo figures 11.8 and 11.9 for the new probabilities. Then consider the case where $z_1 = 3$ is the high signal.)

10. You are a large stockholder in Underwater Oil Company, which specializes in drilling for oil offshore. Underwater's earnings have been consistently negative, despite very strong earnings industrywide. In its annual reports, the management attributes its earnings to bad luck. You have the microphone for 2 minutes at the annual stockholders' meeting. What do you say?

[12]John H. Kagel, "Auctions: A Survey of Experimental Research," in *Handbook of Experimental Economics* eds. John H. Kagel and Alvin E. Roth (New York: North Holland, 1994).

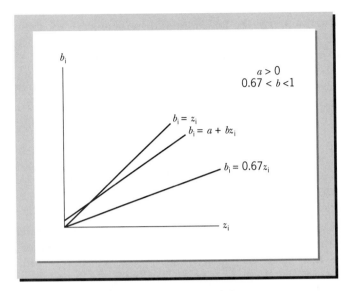

$a > 0$
$0.67 < b < 1$

$b_i = z_i$
$b_i = a + bz_i$
$b_i = 0.67 z_i$

Figure 11.10. Bidding function of a typical subject.

APPENDIX. AUCTIONS IN THE LABORATORY

No subject has received more attention in economics behavior laboratories than auctions. Kagel's admirable survey contains more than 115 references, and it is by no means exhaustive.[12] This appendix reviews two notable examples from the survey, one an individual private value auction and the other a common value auction.

Experimental procedures for auctions are fairly standard. Subjects are volunteers recruited from the student population of the experimenter's university. Subjects are paid $3 to $5 for showing up. After signing a consent form required by federal regulations, they work through a set of instructions concerning the auction they will be in. The instructions are couched in language as neutral as possible. Usually the subjects have to pass a quiz or practical exercise before they begin to play for real money. If there is a strong possibility that the subjects will lose money (not allowed by federal regulations), then they are given an initial capital stake. The idea is that the initial capital will keep them from going broke while they learn how to play the game correctly.

The first auction we look at here is an individual private value auction.[13] In this auction, subjects were told how many people they were bidding against,

[13]James C. Cox, Vernon L. Smith, and James M. Walker, "Theory and Individual Behavior of First-Price Auctions," *Journal of Risk and Uncertainty* 1(1988):61–99.

what their own individual value for the item was, and the uniform probability distribution from which individual values (their own and their rivals') would be drawn. Subjects then proceeded through a sequence of between 10 and 30 auctions. A typical subject's behavior is shown in Figure 11.10. This subject was in a 3-person auction for 20 periods. Each period the subject was given a new individual private value and opportunity to bid. Individual private value is shown on the x-axis; the agent's bid, on the y-axis. The three straight lines shown are as follows:

$$b_i(z_i) = 0.67z_i \qquad \text{(the solution for risk-neutral players)}$$
$$b_i(z_i) = a + bz_i \qquad \text{(the line that best fits the data: } a > 0, 0.67 < b < 1)$$
$$b_i(z_i) = z_i \qquad \text{(break-even bidding}$$

Almost all bids lie between the break-even line and the solution for risk-neutral players. This regularity appears in the data of several hundred subjects. Since the slope of the best-fitting line is greater than the slope for risk-neutral players, the authors concluded that the typical subject was risk averse. However, this does not explain the positive intercept.

The next auction we look at is a common-value auction.[14] The subjects in this experiment were mostly M.B.A. students at the University of Houston. This experiment studied both first-price and second-price auctions. The major finding in both types of auctions was that subjects overbid. Inexperienced subjects were especially prone to overbidding. In first-price auctions, subjects bid on average more than $2.50 above conditional expected value. As a consequence, more than 40% of the subjects went bankrupt: they ran out of money and were sent away from the experiment. In second-price auctions, the overbidding was less severe ($1 more than conditional expected value). This experiment provided very clear evidence of the winner's curse. With experience, about 70% of the subjects who didn't go bankrupt eventually did learn to avoid the winner's curse. These subjects bid at or below conditional expected value. But even the subjects who survived barely broke even.

These results raise a question. Considering that oil companies and others in real-world common-value auctions seem to do pretty well on average, why are laboratory rates of return so poor? In an effort to answer this question, Kagel and Levin ran further experiments with special subjects—bidding executives from Texas oil companies. Interestingly enough, the bidding behavior of the professionals in this experiment was statistically no different from that of the M.B.A. students. The experimenters did raise the stakes substantially to keep the executives interested. Kagel and Levin conjecture that there are features of real-world common-value auctions—known only to insiders—that lend a strong component of individual private value to these auctions. Such features give bidders a benchmark from which to gauge overbidding—a benchmark more accessible than conditional expected value.

[14]John H. Kagel, Ronald M. Harstad, and Dan Levin, "Information Impact and Allocation Rules in Auctions with Affiliated Private Values: A Laboratory Study," *Econometrica* 55(1987):1275–1304.

PART FOUR

Games Involving Bargaining

CHAPTER 12

Two-Person Bargains

This chapter begins a new unit, games with substantial gains from and opportunities for cooperation. The simplest such games involve two players, and the coalition function form, first mentioned in Chapter 1, is often a useful way of describing and involving them. The coalition function form can be considered a shortcut to a solution—especially when the same answer can be derived from normal or extensive form versions of the game.

The real-world context in which opportunities for cooperation are paramount is bargaining. All games in this chapter are interpreted as bargaining games. The paradigm bargaining game, Let's Make a Deal (Chapter 2), is described in considerable detail and studied in some depth. Two classic solutions to bargaining problems are introduced, called the Nash bargaining solution and the Kalai–Smorodinsky bargaining solution after their discoverers. The properties of these solutions, and in particular how they handle various attitudes toward risk, are examined. Then a recent example of bargaining, the deal struck between MCI and British Telecommunications, is reviewed. Next, the chapter turns to sequential bargaining, with its sequence of offers and counteroffers and the classic solution of Stahl and Rubinstein. Of particular importance are bargaining problems with imperfect information, in which offers, rejections of offers, and counteroffers may reveal private information. Both sequential and imperfect information aspects surround the ongoing trade talks between the world's two largest economies, the United States and Japan.

12.1 Bargaining Games ■■■■■■■■■■■■■■■■■■■■

Chapter 2 looked at a normal form game called Let's Make a Deal. This section takes another look at this game and the general class of games to which it belongs, called **bargaining games.** Suppose there is a sum of money M on the table. There are two sides with an interest in the money, called player 1 and player 2. The players could be individuals, for example, the buyer and the seller of a house; one could be an individual and the other a corporation, such as a baseball player and the ball club; both sides could be corporations, such as MCI and British Telephone; or both sides could be countries, for example, the United States and Japan. The description of the bargaining game between the two sides is the same, regardless of the exact nature of those sides.

In Let's Make a Deal, M was $15 million and a strategy for each side was to say either yes or no to a proposed even split of the money. *Disagreement* occurs when both sides are unable to say yes to a proposal to divide the money at stake. We denote disagreement by the vector $\mathbf{d} = (d_1, d_2)$, called the **disagreement point.** For now, we will assume that disagreement means that the money on the table vanishes, so that $\mathbf{d} = (0,0)$. For instance, in the case of a house buyer and seller, disagreement means that there is no trade and hence no gain from trade available to these two parties. Similarly, in the case of the basketball player and the team, if they can't agree on a contract, the player doesn't play for the team. Again, neither side gains from the relationship. The same holds for larger entities, such as corporations and nations—if they can't reach an agreement on a deal, there is no deal and no gain to either side that might have been realized from the deal.

Rather than having a proposal already on the table, we now allow each side to make a proposal. In particular, a strategy for player i is to ask for an amount of money a_i. We assume that a_i lies between zero and M. If you ask for more than M, then this implies a negative payoff to the other side. Since the other side can get zero by saying no, such an offer will not be accepted at equilibrium. By the same token, if you ask for less than zero, you are making a big mistake. Such a proposal, if accepted, will cost you, whereas you can get zero by refusing to agree to anything. An **efficient division** of the money satisfies the following equation:

$$a_1 + a_2 = M$$

When the asks add up to all the money on the table, then all the gains to agreement are captured by the two sides and no money is left on the table. Nothing is wasted—and no waste here means efficiency.

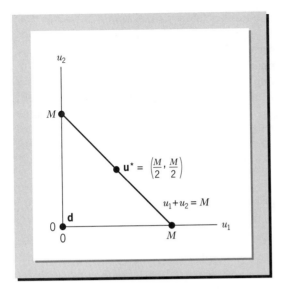

Figure 12.1. Bargaining game, coalition function form.

Next, suppose that each player is risk neutral, so that utility equals money for each player:

$$u_1 = a_1;\ u_2 = a_2$$

if the asks are actually accepted. Substituting these utility functions into the efficient division line, we get

$$u_1 + u_2 = M$$

The disagreement point **d** and the efficient division line together constitute the **coalition function form** of the bargaining game. The coalition function form presents information solely on payoffs, without going into any of the strategic detail underlying those payoffs. The coalition function form of the bargaining game between risk-neutral players is shown in Figure 12.1.

If we want, we can supply the strategic detail by looking at a normal form game that underlies the coalition form. Each player i simultaneously asks for an amount of money a_i. If the sum of the two asks does not exceed the money on the table, then the players have an agreement and both get exactly what they asked for. If the sum of the two asks exceeds the money on the table, then there is no deal and they get the disagreement payoffs. This situation is represented by the payoff functions:

$$u_1(a_1,a_2) = a_1 \text{ if } a_1 + a_2 \leq M$$
$$\qquad\qquad = 0 \text{ otherwise}$$
$$u_2(a_1,a_2) = a_2 \text{ if } a_1 + a_2 \leq M$$
$$\qquad\qquad = 0 \text{ otherwise}$$

This normal form game has several equilibria. Any pair of asks $a = (a_1, a_2)$ that satisfies $a_i \geq 0$ and $a_1 + a_2 = M$ is an equilibrium. If the sum of the asks exceeds M, then both players are getting zero and at least one player could reduce the ask and get a positive payoff. Similarly, if the sum of the asks is less than M, then money is being left on the table and one of the players could increase the ask and get a bigger payoff. Finally, if either player is getting a negative payoff, that player could raise utility to zero by disagreeing instead of agreeing. Since the payoff functions are symmetrical and each player has the same set of strategies, the game is symmetrical. Therefore, its solution, in light of payoff symmetry, is the one symmetrical equilibrium in all these possibilities:

$$a_1 = a_2 = M/2$$

The solution to the symmetrical bargaining problem among risk neutrals is to split the money on the table evenly. Reaching an agreement by splitting the difference between the two parties is a time-honored and widely accepted principle of bargaining, and we have just shown why, from a strategic standpoint.

We just solved the bargaining game in normal form. We get the same solution, only faster, by applying the following two principles to the coalition function form. The first, **bargaining symmetry,** merely restates symmetry:

■ ■

Bargaining Symmetry. The solution of a symmetrical bargaining game is symmetrical.

For a symmetrical bargaining game like that shown in Figure 12.1, any feasible point on the line $u_1 = u_2$ satisfies symmetry. The second principle replaces the necessary condition of being an equilibrium:

■ ■

Bargaining Efficiency. The solution of a bargaining game is efficient.

Bargaining efficiency means that the solution must lie on the efficient bargaining line. The symmetry line and the efficiency line cross at exactly one point, the equal division point, and this is the solution of the bargaining game, obtained via the shortcut of the coalition form. Rather than going through the necessary and sufficient conditions for a solution in normal form, we simply write down the coalition function form and apply the principles of bargaining symmetry and bargaining efficiency. The solution is the same, but the route is shorter.

These two principles suffice to solve any symmetrical bargaining games, but many interesting bargaining games are not symmetrical. How asymmetries arise and two competing concepts of how asymmetrical bargaining games should be solved are the subjects of the next section.

12.2 Asymmetries and the Nash Bargaining Solution ▪ ▪ ▪ ▪ ▪ ▪ ▪ ▪ ▪ ▪ ▪ ▪ ▪ ▪ ▪ ▪ ▪

This section looks at four types of asymmetries that can have an impact on bargaining games. All these asymmetries change the look of the bargaining game in Figure 12.1. The four asymmetries are the medium of payment of the money on the table, attitude toward risk, outside options, and legal limits on asks.

The first possible asymmetry is that the players are paid in different currencies. For instance, player 1 may be paid in dollars, and player 2 in German marks. Suppose that the exchange rate is 1.5 German marks = $1. Player 2, in addition to being paid in marks, also makes asks in marks. Thus both asks and utility have to be converted to dollars in order to make them comparable with those of player 1. If there is $10,000 on the table, then the efficient division line is

$$a_1 + \frac{a_2}{1.5} = 10{,}000$$

Substituting utility for cash, we get

$$u_1 + \frac{u_2}{1.5} = 10{,}000$$

The disagreement point is still at (0,0), since $0 = 0 marks. Figure 12.2 shows the coalition function that results from the medium-of-payment asymmetry. If we apply symmetry to this asymmetrical game, we get $u_1 = u_2 = 6000$. The odd thing here is that player 1 is getting paid $6000, whereas player 2 is getting paid 6000 marks, or $4000, so the outcome is not really symmetrical at all. This is just not the same as each player getting $5000.

Most people don't believe that this asymmetry in a bargaining problem should matter. They believe that you should get paid the same, whether you are paid in one currency or another. The following principle contains the antidote to this asymmetry. It makes sure that players get paid the same, no matter what the currency:

▪ ▪

Bargaining Linear Invariance. Suppose that $u^* = (u_1^*, u_2^*)$ is the solution to the bargaining game with efficient division line $u_1 + u_2 = M$. Then the solution to the bargaining game with efficient division line $u_1/k_1 + u_2/k_2 = M$ is $(k_1 u_1^*, k_2 u_2^*)$.

What **linear invariance** does is convert the payoff to player 2 into dollars by multiplying by the exchange rate ($k_2 = 1.5$), thus keeping the dollar payoffs to the two players the same. The solution that satisfies linear invariance is shown by the vector $\mathbf{u}^* = (5000, 7500)$ in Figure 12.2. When both exchange rates are

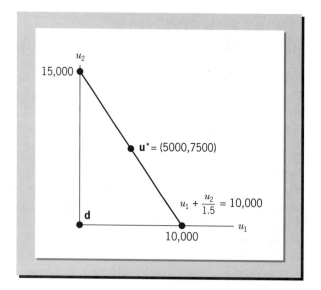

Figure 12.2. Medium-of-payment asymmetry.

different from 1, then both players are being paid in a third currency; for example, the amount of money on the table might be denominated in French francs, player 1 might be paid in British pounds, and player 2 might be paid in marks. The bargaining solutions studied in this chapter satisfy linear invariance.

The three remaining asymmetries are ones that most people do think should matter in a bargaining game. Attitude toward risk has an especially pronounced effect on the shape of a bargaining game. Suppose that player 1 is still risk neutral but that player 2 is now risk averse, with $u_2 = (a_2)^b$, where $b < 1$. Substituting this utility function into the efficient division line, we get a curve, the efficient division curve:

$$u_1 + (u_2)^{1/b} = M$$

This curve is shown in Figure 12.3 for $b = 0.5$ and $M = 100$. Intuitively we expect that the more risk averse a player is, the more that player would be afraid of disagreement, and so the more he or she would be willing to come down from an even split of the money.

We can make this intuition rather more precise by appealing to risk dominance (recall section 8.5). The risk dominant equilibrium maximizes the product of players' utilities, given that the alternative to equilibrium is a zero payoff. The maximum of the function $u_1 u_2$ on the curve $u_1 + (u_2)^{1/b} = M$ can be found as follows. Substitute the equation of the curve into the objective, yielding:

$$\max u_1 (M - u_1)^b$$

The maximum of this product occurs when

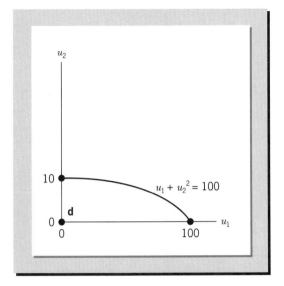

Figure 12.3. Bargaining game, risk attitude asymmetry.

$$0 = (M - u_1)^b + u^1 b (M - u_1)^{b-1}(-1)$$

Multiplying both sides by $(M - u_1)^{1-b}$ and simplifying, we get

$$M - u_1 = bu_1$$

Solving, the risk dominant payoff to player 1, who is risk neutral is

$$u_1 = M/(1 + b)$$

The money that is left, $M - u_1 = bM/(1 + b)$, is the money that goes to player 2. For instance, if $b = 0.5$ and $M = 100$, then risk-neutral player 1 gets two-thirds of the money (\$66.67), and risk-averse player 2 gets half as much (\$33.33). You can show that the more risk averse a player is (the closer b is to 0), the closer that player's share of the money is to 0. According to risk dominance, an extremely risk-averse player can be bargained almost all the way down to zero.

The bargaining solution based on risk dominance that we have just computed was first introduced by John Nash in 1950 and is called the **Nash bargaining solution** in his honor.[1] When the disagreement point is $(0,0)$, this solution maximizes the product of players' utilities, a calculation you can perform without having to attend to the equilibria of the underlying game in normal form. This is the shortcut once again. You can show that the Nash bargaining solution satisfies symmetry, efficiency, and linear invariance. Next, we will see one more condition that it satisfies.

[1]See John F. Nash, "The Bargaining Problem," *Econometrica* 18 (1950):155–62.

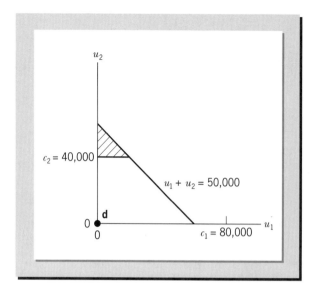

Figure 12.4.   Bargaining game, Bankruptcy.

The next asymmetry we consider involves restrictions on what a player can ask. Such restrictions arise in bankruptcy. Suppose that players 1 and 2 have claims against the assets of a bankrupt company. By law, neither player can ask for more from the bankrupt company than that player is owed by the company. If the two players are owed different amounts, there is an asymmetry. We are only looking at one source of asymmetry at a time, so we let both players be risk neutral. Suppose that the bankrupt company owes $80,000 to player 1 and $40,000 to player 2. Suppose further that the bankrupt firm has $50,000 in assets that can be paid out to the creditors if they can reach an agreement. Otherwise, the creditors are paid nothing. The efficient agreement line is

$$u_1 + u_2 = 50,000$$

where $a_1 = u_1$ cannot exceed $80,000, and $a_2 = u_2$ cannot exceed $40,000. The coalition function form is shown in Figure 12.4. Notice that the game is not symmetrical—the left-hand corner of the payoff triangle with vertices at $(0,0)$, $(0, 50,000)$, and $(50,000, 0)$ is unavailable to player 1. For reasons discussed in the next section, the Nash bargaining solution ignores this asymmetry—it divides the $50,000 equally between the two creditors.

The final asymmetry we will study results from differences in the outside option. This asymmetry shows up as a nonzero disagreement point. Suppose there is $50,000 at stake in negotiations between player 1 and player 2. In the event that negotiations break down between the two, player 1 has a firm offer worth $15,000 from a third party, whereas player 2 gets $0. The disagreement point is then $\mathbf{d} = (15,000,0)$ instead of $(0,0)$. Everyone agrees that this asymmetry is really important. The money on the table represents gains, and

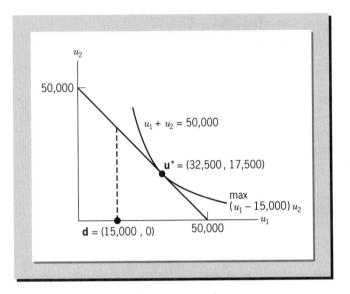

Figure 12.5. Bargaining game, $d \neq 0$.

not money that players already have in their pockets from another source. We need another form of linear invariance to take this circumstance into account:

■ ■

Invariance with Respect to the Disagreement Point. Suppose that u^* is the solution to the bargaining problem with M at stake and disagreement point $(0,0)$. Then $u^* + d$ is the solution to the bargaining problem with disagreement point d and $M + d_1 + d_2$ at stake.

To see how this works, consider the bargaining problem between risk neutrals with \$35,000 at stake. At the solution $\mathbf{u}^*$, the players divide this money equally, $\mathbf{u}^* = (17{,}500,\ 17{,}500)$. Now suppose there is \$50,000 at stake, but player 1 has an outside option worth \$15,000. Then player 1 gets half the \$35,000 plus the outside option (\$15,000), for a grand total of \$32,500. In equation format,

$$\mathbf{u}^* + \mathbf{d} = (17{,}500,\ 17{,}500) + (15{,}000,\ 0) = (32{,}500,\ 17{,}500)$$

The upshot is that the player with the better outside option comes out of the bargaining better. This is a very intuitive result. You know you have the upper hand when you can walk away from a deal and walk into another one nearly as good, and your bargaining partner has nothing to fall back on.

The Nash bargaining solution satisfies invariance with respect to the disagreement point by maximizing $(u_1 - d_1)(u_2 - d_2)$ when the disagreement point is not equal to zero. In the bargaining game of Figure 12.5, the maximum of $(u_1 - \$15{,}000)(u_2)$ on the line $u_1 + u_2 = 50{,}000$ occurs at $u_1 = 32{,}500$.

✖ 12.3 Bankruptcy I: Independence of Irrelevant Alternatives and the Nash Bargaining Solution ■ ■ ■ ■ ■ ■ ■ ■ ■ ■ ■ ■ ■ ■ ■ ■ ■

In the last section the Nash bargaining solution gave a puzzling answer to a **bankruptcy game.** With $50,000 of assets to divide between two risk-neutral creditors, one of whom was owed $40,000 and the other of whom was owed $80,000, the Nash bargaining solution gave each creditor $25,000. This section looks at the bankruptcy game in more detail to see why the Nash solution gives so much money to the smaller claimant. Once again, we need some more notation.

Let A denote the assets of the bankrupt firm. We won't even bother to identify this firm—once in bankruptcy, it plays no role in the game. There are two claimants to the assets of the bankrupt firm, claimant 1 and claimant 2.[2] Claimant i has a claim C_i on the bankrupt firm. Each claim represents a legal liability on the part of the bankrupt firm. We first assume that both claimants are of equal seniority. In a bankruptcy game, claims exceed assets:

$$A < \Sigma C_i$$

This inequality of assets and liabilities is what creates the problem for the creditors; there is not enough left to pay them all off. We further assume that both claimants have the same outside option, 0, in the event that negotiations break down and no assets of the bankrupt firm are claimed. Finally, both claimants are risk neutral. With these assumptions, the only possible asymmetry lies with the claims. When $C_1 = C_2$, the game is symmetrical: equal seniority claims of equal value to the assets. The efficient division of assets line is $a_1 + a_2 = A$, and the disagreement point $\mathbf{d} = (0,0)$. Given risk neutrality, the efficient division of assets line is also the efficient division of utility line:

$$u_1 + u_2 = A$$

In the case of a symmetrical bankruptcy game, the Nash bargaining solution divides the assets equally:

$$u_1^* = u_2^* = A/2$$

Notice that once the claims are equal, they play no further role. When the claims are unequal, then the bankruptcy game is asymmetrical. In this case the claims play a bigger, but still limited, role. It turns out to be handy to rank the claims in order of their size:

$$C_1 < C_2$$

---

[2]The problem can be generalized to any number of claimants. Large bankruptcy cases, such as those involving bad debt of foreign countries, may have hundreds of claimants, chief among them U.S. banks. See Chapter 14.

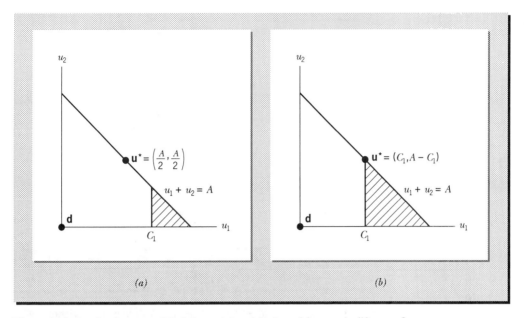

Figure 12.6. Bankruptcy, Nash bargaining solution: (a) case 1; (b) case 2.

There are two cases to consider, depending on how much is left of assets relative to claims. These two cases are shown in Figure 12.6. To see why there are two cases, notice what happens when the assets are less than the smaller claim. In such a case, the Nash bargaining solution treats both claimants as if they were the same, because neither of them can feasibly ask for all the money back. The Nash bargaining solution continues to divide the money up equally as long as assets are not too much bigger than the smaller claim.

Case 1. $A/2 < C_1$. This case is shown in Figure 12.6a. The maximum product of utility occurs at the equal asset division.

Case 2. $A/2 > C_1$. This case is shown in Figure 12.6b. The maximum product of utility occurs at the corner where $u_2^* = A - C_1$, and $u_1^* = C_1$. In this case, the smaller claimant is fully compensated, whereas the larger claimant gets what is left after paying off the smaller claimant.

This solution may strike you as sort of weird. It is clearly not the way we usually settle bankruptcy cases among equally senior claimants. Indeed, it is as if the Nash bargaining solution is creating seniority where none exists. The smaller claim is treated as though it is senior once assets are double that claim. Prior to that point, both claims are treated the same.[3]

---

[3]In a strict seniority system, senior debt is fully paid off before a cent is paid to junior debt. If claimant 2 were truly senior in this case, then the seniority solution would also have two cases: $u_2 = A$ when $A < C_2$, and $u_2 = C_2$, when $A > C_2$.

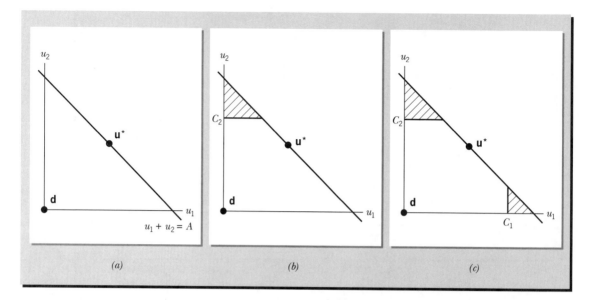

Figure 12.7. Independence of irrelevant alternatives: (*a*) generic game; (*b*) with player 2's claim; (*c*) with player 2's claim and player 1's claim.

There is a special property, peculiar to the Nash bargaining solution, that is responsible for the way it solves bankruptcy games. This property is called the **independence of irrelevant alternatives,** and it works as follows. Suppose you know the solution $\mathbf{u}^*$ to a bargaining game. Then you get rid of some of the possibilities available in that bargaining game, but not $\mathbf{u}^*$. Then $\mathbf{u}^*$ is the solution of the game with fewer possibilities. The missing alternatives are irrelevant after all.

Figure 12.7 shows how this works. Figure 12.7*a* is a standard bargaining game over an amount of money A. Efficiency and symmetry imply an even split of A. Now add player 2's claims to the game (see Figure 12.7*b*). Since claimant 2 cannot ask for more than he or she is owed, the claim C_2 eliminates alternatives. However, since none of these alternatives was the solution, they are irrelevant and can be disposed of without further ado. Next, add player 1's claim to player 2's claim (see Figure 12.7*c*). Since claimant 1 cannot ask for more than he or she is owed, the claim C_1 eliminates alternatives. Again, none of these alternatives was the solution. They, too, are irrelevant and can be disposed of without further ado. The result is the Nash bargaining solution to the bankruptcy game in case 1 (Figure 12.6*a*).

If we go through this same argument for case 2, then the smaller claimant's claim eliminates a relevant alternative, the old solution. In fact, the *only* relevant alternative is the old solution. Once the equal-split solution is irrelevant, the Nash bargaining solution gives all the money it can to the smaller claimant.

You can prove that the Nash bargaining solution is the only bargaining solution that satisfies symmetry, efficiency, linear invariance, and independence of irrelevant alternatives. Every bargaining solution worthy of serious attention satisfies the first three of these conditions. The independence condition is used to address asymmetries, and controversy is bound to arise when asymmetries are present. Still, it seems that what one is owed is always relevant to what one gets back in a bankruptcy proceeding.

12.4 Bankruptcy II: Monotonicity and the Kalai–Smorodinsky Solution ■■■■■■■■■■■■■

Given the controversial way in which the Nash bargaining solution handles bankruptcy games, there has been considerable interest in proposing other solutions to bargaining games in general and to bankruptcy games in particular. The main idea behind such attempts has been to replace the independence of irrelevant alternatives with some other condition. Perhaps the most successful of these proposals is that of Kalai and Smorodinsky.[4] They proposed the following property for bargaining solutions, called **monotonicity.** Suppose that the efficient payoff curve shifts out in player 1's direction. Then player 1's bargaining solution payoff does not go down. The same holds true for player 2, if there is a shift outward in player 2's direction. The spirit behind monotonicity is the old saying, A high tide raises all the boats.

In general, the Nash bargaining solution does not satisfy monotonicity. Figure 12.8 provides a simple counterexample. Start with the bargaining game in Figure 12.8a, whose Nash bargaining solution $\mathbf{u}^* = (0.6, 0.6)$. Now shift utility possibilities out, as in Figure 12.8b, by adding a new possibility, $(0.5, 0.8)$, to the efficient curve. This new possibility becomes the new Nash bargaining solution $\mathbf{u}^*$. Player 1's payoff has gone down, even though player 2's has gone up. This violates monotonicity for player 1.

You might wonder if it is possible for a bargaining solution to satisfy monotonicity in every possible case. After all, this is a very strong condition. Kalai and Smorodinsky have shown that there is a unique bargaining solution satisfying efficiency, symmetry, linear invariance, and monotonicity.

The **Kalai–Smorodinsky bargaining solution** is easy to describe and does not require calculus to compute. Consider all the utilities available to the players that are at least as good as disagreement. Let U_1 be the highest such utility available to player 1 from bargaining. Let U_2 be the highest such utility available to player 2. Write $\mathbf{U} = (U_1, U_2)$ for the vector of these maximum utilities. Now draw the line between the disagreement point $\mathbf{d}$ and the point $\mathbf{U}$.

[4]See Ehud Kalai and Meir Smorodinsky, "Other Solutions to Nash's Bargaining Problem," *Econometrica* 43 (1975):513–18.

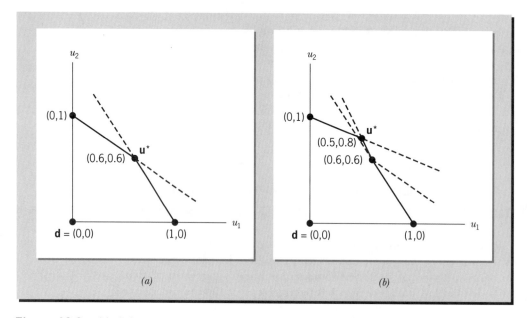

Figure 12.8.   Nash bargaining solution violates monotonicity.

The Kalai–Smorodinsky solution is where this line crosses the efficient payoff curve.

To see how the Kalai–Smorodinsky bargaining solution works, consider again the game given in Figure 12.8, now reproduced in Figure 12.9. The disagreement point $\mathbf{d} = (0,0)$, and the point of maximal asks $\mathbf{U} = (1,1)$. In Figure 12.9a, the Kalai–Smorodinsky solution agrees with the Nash solution, $\mathbf{u}^* = (0.6,0.6)$, as it must, since both solutions satisfy symmetry and efficiency. In Figure 12.9b, the Kalai–Smorodinsky solution sticks to the (still efficient) solution $\mathbf{u}^* = (0.6,0.6)$, despite the outward shift. This solution *will not make one player better off unless it can make both players better off.* That is how the Kalai–Smorodinsky solution satisfies monotonicity.

To take another example, consider the bankruptcy game with $C_1 = \$50{,}000$, $C_2 = \$100{,}000$, and $A = \$120{,}000$. We have $\mathbf{d} = (0,0)$ and $\mathbf{U} = (50{,}000, 100{,}000)$. The line between them is given by the equation

$$u_2 = 2u_1$$

and the efficient payoff line is given by the equation

$$u_1 + u_2 = 120{,}000$$

These two lines cross at the point $(u_1, u_2) = (40{,}000, 80{,}000)$, which is the Kalai–Smorodinsky bargaining solution. Compared to the Nash solution of $(50{,}000, 70{,}000)$, the Kalai–Smorodinsky solution does not pay off claimant 1 in full. No claimant is paid off in full unless all claimants are paid off in full.

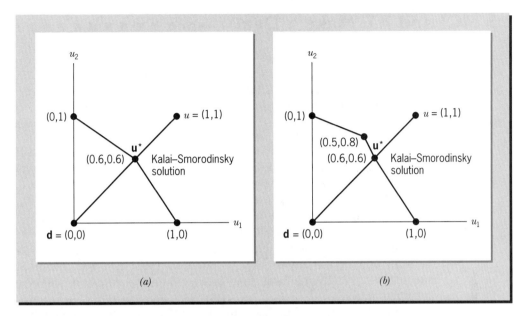

Figure 12.9. Kalai–Smorodinsky bargaining solution satisfies monotonicity.

As with the Nash bargaining solution, the Kalai–Smorodinsky bargaining solution pays less to risk-averse bargainers than to risk-neutral bargainers. Here is a quick example. Suppose that player 1 in the bankruptcy game just given is risk averse, with $u_1 = (a_2)^{0.5}$. Claimant 1's claim in utility terms is $(50,000)^{0.5} = 223.6$. The efficient payoff curve is given by

$$u_2 + (u_1)^2 = 120,000$$

The disagreement point **d** is still (0,0); the point **U** is now (223.6, 100,000). The line between **d** and **U** has the equation

$$u_2 = \left(\frac{1}{0.002236}\right) u_1$$

Substituting this line into the efficient payoff curve and solving the resulting quadratic equation, we get $u_1 = 188.8$. This result implies that $u_2 = 84,400$. The cash paid out to risk-averse claimant 1 is $(188.8)^2 = \$35,600$, less than the $40,000 that would be paid to this claimant if he or she were risk neutral. In their attitude toward risk aversion, the Nash and the Kalai–Smorodinsky solutions act in the same direction, even if not with the exact same values.

Often, the way in which bargainers represent the bargaining game they face has a major impact on the agreement they reach, if any. This factor is at work in a recent instance of 2-player bargaining, the deal between MCI and British Telecommunications.

▞ 12.5 MCI and BT Make a Deal[5]   ■ ■ ■ ■ ■ ■ ■ ■ ■ ■ ■ ■ ■

On June 2, 1993, MCI and British Telecommunications (BT) announced a major deal, bringing the world's fourth and sixth largest communications carriers into a global alliance.[6] Although MCI and BT had first talked 3 years earlier, and intermittently since then, talks had never progressed very far. In early May 1993, the chairs of the two corporations agreed that both corporations stood to gain from making a deal.

For MCI, the new alliance allows them to compete more effectively with AT&T, the industry giant, in international services, where BT is already a major player. The alliance also allows MCI to compete more effectively on domestic services, such as data network management services and data transmission services, the so-called outsourcing services, which are a hot item in telecommunications nowadays. For BT, the alliance allows them to penetrate further the world's largest market, the United States. It gives them an attractive profit stream from one of the largest U.S. corporation (MCI had $8.4 billion in revenue in 1991). Finally, it affords them access to one of the savviest marketers in the United States.

The financial structure of the agreement was a cash-for-stock arrangement. BT agreed to pay $4.3 billion in cash for 20% of MCI stock outstanding, at a negotiated price of $64/share. The market price of MCI stock was $52.75/share immediately prior to the announcement. The MCI share price rose to $54.375 on news of the agreement; however, investors in London sent BT shares down 5 pence per share (down to 421.5 pence/share) on late trading. The premium paid on shares over the market price gives an estimate of how much money the two companies thought was on the table. Multiplying the $11.25 premium/share times roughly 100 million shares purchased yields about $1.1 billion on the table. MCI gets the cash, and BT gets the shares, hence the future profits from those shares. The present value of these future profits constitutes BT's gain from the agreement.

We can say something about the disagreement point for this bargaining game. AT&T had announced a plan to offer global telecommunications services to multinational corporations 1 week prior to the MCI–BT agreement. Moreover, AT&T was in the market for a European partner. Had the MCI deal fallen through, it is extremely likely that AT&T and BT would have begun negotiations in earnest. MCI's outside option is not nearly so clear, since two other large European possibilities, Deutsche Telekom and France Telecom, had already set up their own joint venture. MCI would probably have gone to Cable&Wireless as its outside option. Neither outside option could be characterized as firm. As it turns out, AT&T will probably go after an agreement with

---

[5]Material was drawn from John H. Keller, "Clear Message: MCI-BT Tie Is Likely to Set Off Major Battle in Global Telecommunications Market," *The Wall Street Journal,* June 3, 1993.

[6]The top six carriers in order are AT&T, Deutsche Telekom, France Telecom, BT, Cable & Wireless (a U.K. corporation), and MCI.

Cable&Wireless—as signaled by the 5% rise in Cable&Wireless's share price in London the day of the MCI–BT announcement.

Although it is difficult to know exactly how these gains are divided, there are two obvious benchmarks for a split. One is an even division of the gains, which would be in accord with symmetrical bargaining. If the companies view each other as equals in the agreement, then an even split makes sense. Another obvious benchmark is a division of the gains proportional to the size of the companies. Since BT is roughly three times the size of MCI, this would imply a 3-to-1 split of the gains. Whether the companies view themselves as asymmetrical partners in the agreement or not is crucial to which of these divisions actually takes place. Some evidence for a 3-to-1 split is contained in a side agreement to the main deal. MCI and BT are committed to invest more than $1 billion in a new joint-venture company to provide outsourcing to multinational corporations. Although BT will have an ownership share of about 75%, MCI spokespersons hasten to add that their corporation will act as an equal partner in this new venture.

Speculation continues to surround this deal. In particular, MCI, now flush with cash, is rumored to be in the market for a cable TV company, as well as in the market for advanced software companies. MCI confirms that it has been talking to TCI, the cable TV giant, about buying a possible stake. AT&T is not likely to sit idly by while all these deals are taking place. "This is AT&T's worst nightmare," says one industry analyst. The bargaining games will continue in the telecommunications industry.[7]

❖ 12.6 Sequential Bargaining with Perfect Information ■

We have been modeling bargaining games in normal form, where each party to the bargain makes an offer and there is a deal or there isn't. This simple model of bargaining takes us a long way. Sometimes, however, we need to go to the extensive form to explain certain real-world phenomena. Of special interest is the behavior known as holding out for a better deal. A **holdout** is someone who refuses to reach an agreement until better terms are offered. This section shows that in sequential bargaining with complete information, holding out does not take place along the subgame perfect equilibrium path. In the next section, where information is incomplete, holding out may indeed take place along that path—if it is the only way to make private information credible.

---

[7]In August 1993, AT&T announced that it was buying 33% of Cellular One, the largest cellular telephone company in the United States, for $3.73 billion. AT&T also purchased, for an additional $600 million, an option to buy a controlling interest in Cellular One at any time during the next 7 years. See *Mannheimer Morgen*, August 18, 1993, p. 7.

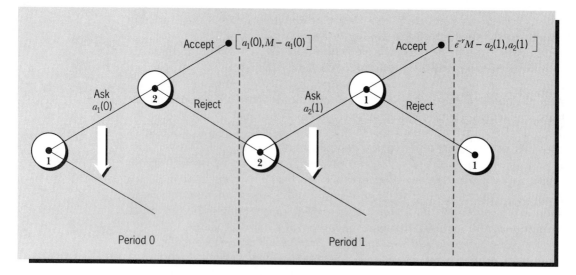

Figure 12.10.   Sequential bargaining, first two periods.

Bargaining in extensive form is modeled as a sequence of offers and counter-offers, **sequential bargaining.** Suppose there is a sum of money of size M on the table. Let $a_i(t)$ represent the amount that player 1 asks for at time t. Player 1 is the first to move at time $t = 0$. Player 1 asks for an amount $a_1(0)$ of the money, with the rest of the money, $M - a_1(0)$, going to player 2 if player 2 accepts at once. If player 2 rejects player 1's proposal, then after one period of time has elapsed, player 2 gets to make a counterproposal, $a_2(1)$. It is then player 1's turn to accept or reject. The game can go on indefinitely, with player 1 making proposals during even-numbered periods and player 2 making proposals during odd-numbered periods. This situation is shown schematically in Figure 12.10.

Players do not have an incentive to stall in their bargaining. Time is money, as the saying goes, and there is a considerable opportunity cost attached to having the money M tied up on the table. This opportunity cost is the interest forgone because a split of the money has not been agreed on. Suppose the interest rate per period of time is r, and interest is compounded continuously. Then the value of the money on the table after T periods have passed is only Me^{-rT}. If the two players never agree, then the money on the table eventually becomes worthless. This is the meaning of disagreement in sequential bargaining. There is a reason for modeling bargaining in extensive form as a game that could go on forever. If there is a finite time limit, then we tend to get very extreme solutions to the game. For instance, suppose that the time limit is 0—that is, player 2 must take or leave the offer made by player 1 and the game ends. This is ultimatum bargaining, as described in the appendix to Chapter 6. At subgame perfect equilibrium, player 1 gets all or almost all the money. If the game can last another period, allowing player 2 to make a counterproposal, then player 1 can no longer get away with almost all the money.

Since the amount of money on the table is shrinking fast, player 1 would like to make an offer enticing enough that player 2 accepts immediately. Suppose that player 1 has asked for $a_1(0)$, and so is offering player 2 the remainder, $M - a_1(0)$. When should player 2 accept? One guide to our thinking is the following principle, which embodies subgame perfection in the case of bargaining that can go on forever:

■ ■

Bargaining Consistency. You should never ask for something that you have previously rejected.

If you are consistent in bargaining, at least you won't look stupid. You would look really stupid if you were to reject an offer of $1 million early on in the negotiations, and then later on ask for $500,000. Bargaining consistency says, a bird in the hand now is better than a bird in the hand later—the time cost breaks the tie.

We now construct a subgame perfect equilibrium outcome for sequential bargaining. Suppose that player 1 asks $a_1(0)$ initially, thus leaving $M - a_1(0)$ for player 2. If player 2 rejects this amount, then player 2 should ask for at least as much when it is his or her turn to propose. Since player 2 has to wait one time period before making a proposal, player 2 should ask at least $a_2(1)$, satisfying

$$a_2(1) = [M - a_1(0)]e^{-r}$$

where e^{-r} represents the one-period discount factor, and r is the one-period interest rate. If the one-period interest rate is 10%, then getting $40 right now is the same as getting $44.21 one period from now. The subgame that begins with player 2 making an offer at time $t = 1$ with amount M on the table looks exactly like the subgame that begins with player 1 making an offer at time $t = 0$ with amount M on the table. Suppose player 1 makes an acceptable ask $a_1(0)$ right now. Then player 2's ask one period hence is also acceptable, provided that

$$a_1(0) = a_2(1)$$

Putting these two equations together, we get

$$a_1(0)* = \frac{M}{(1 + e^{-r})} = a_2(1)*$$

A subgame perfect equilibrium outcome is for player 1 to ask for $a_1(0)*$, leaving player 2 the amount $M - a_1(0)* = Me^{-r}/(1 + e^{-r})$, which he or she immediately accepts. Holding out doesn't pay here. Since the terms are never going to get better, it is best to accept them now. This solution, first noted by

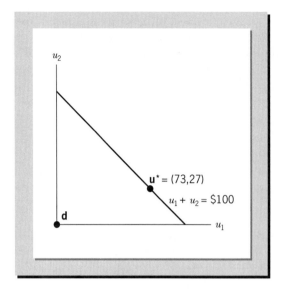

Figure 12.11. Sequential bargaining, coalition function form, $r = 25\%$.

Stahl in 1971, was rediscovered by Rubinstein a dozen years later.[8] This solution is now called the **Stahl–Rubinstein bargaining solution** in their honor.

Figure 12.11 shows the Stahl–Rubinstein solution for $M = \$100$ and $r = 25\%$. At a loan-shark rate of interest like this, there is a big first mover advantage. The player who moves first gets 73% of the money on the table, as opposed to the player who moves second, who gets 27%. As the rate of interest falls—thereby reducing the time cost of holding out—the first mover advantage shrinks. At $r = 5\%$, the player who moves first gets just 51% of the money on the table. You can show that in the limit as the rate of interest goes to zero, the first mover advantage disappears. The interpretation of this result is that the time required between rejecting one proposal and making a counterproposal shrinks to zero.

12.7 Sequential Bargaining with Imperfect Information[9] ■ ■ ■ ■ ■ ■ ■ ■ ■ ■ ■ ■ ■ ■ ■ ■ ■ ■ ■

---

[8]The relevant sources are Ingolf Stahl, *Bargaining Theory* (Stockholm: Stockholm School of Economics, 1972) and Ariel Rubinstein, "Perfect Equilibrium in a Bargaining Model," *Econometrica* 50 (1982):97–109. Rubinstein also proved that this was the unique subgame perfect equilibrium when money is infinitely divisible.

[9]For readers interested in going more deeply into this topic, I heartily recommend the survey by John Kennan and Robert Wilson, "Bargaining with Private Information," *Journal of Economic Literature* 31(1993);45–104.

The Stahl–Rubinstein solution depends crucially on the fact that both players know exactly how much money there is on the table at the outset. Holding out does not pay if both sides know exactly how much money is at stake. If information is imperfect and one of the players does not know how much money is at stake, then holding out might pay. In such a situation, the rejection of a proposal and the subsequent counterproposal by an informed player can signal the other side what the true amount of the money on the table is.

Here is an example of **sequential bargaining with imperfect information.** Player 1 is a novelist, who is about to offer a novel to a motion picture company as the basis for a movie. The novelist makes the first move. However, the novelist has only a vague idea of what the novel is worth as a movie property. This vague idea takes the form of a probability distribution. The probability is 90% that this novel is an okay movie property, in which case it is worth $100,000; the probability is 10% that this is a blockbuster property, in which case it is worth $1,000,000. This is a fairly optimistic assumption. Even Michael Crichton, who has written a lot of good books, has only written one *Jurassic Park*. Player 2, the movie company, actually knows what the novel is worth—but for obvious reasons is not telling.[10] Everyone involved is risk neutral. The parties have agreed in advance that they will split any money on the table evenly, once an agreement has been reached.[11]

Given the even split provision, the best thing the novelist can do at the outset is ask for $500,000, half the value of the novel if it is a blockbuster. If the novel is a blockbuster movie property, then the movie company knows this, and should accept at once. The same reasoning that underlies perfectly informed sequential bargaining applies to the movie company in this situation. If the novel is an okay movie property, then the movie company knows this and rejects the novelist's proposal. Now the movie company waits before coming back with a counterproposal. This is the **holdout phase.** The movie company has to wait to make its information—the novel is merely an okay movie property—credible. If the movie company rejects the $500,000 proposal and immediately turns around and says, "We'll give you $50,000 instead," the novelist should reject the offer, because it could just as well be a $450,000 lie. However, if the movie company holds out long enough, then the signal does become credible. In fact, the movie company has to hold out long enough for the profit from a $450,000 lie to completely vanish. If the movie company lies and rejects a sure gain of $500,000, it is looking at $(950,000)e^{-rt}$ during the holdout phase. This $950,000 is the movie company's $500,000 gain from

---

[10]Yes, this is a heroic assumption, given the number of dud movies made every year. The point of the example still goes through if the movie company has a better signal of underlying value than does the novelist.

[11]Either they are using a symmetrical and efficient shortcut such as the Nash bargaining solution, or they are using an efficient solution, such as Stahl–Rubinstein, with an infinitesimal time interval between negotiation rounds.

getting hold of a blockbuster plus the $450,000 lie. The movie company's possible lie has lost all its value when

$$\$500,000 = (\$950,000)\,e^{-rt}$$

Solving for t, we get

$$t = \frac{-\log(0.526)}{r} = \frac{0.64}{r}$$

The lower the rate of interest, the longer the movie company has to wait before getting back to the novelist with the $50,000 counteroffer. Take an extreme value, $r = 100\%$/year. Then the holdout phase lasts 0.64 years, that is, about 7 months. If the interest rate is only 10%, then the holdout phase last 6.4 years. This is one of the reasons that Hollywood negotiations can be so protracted. If you think you have any chance at all of having a hot property, it may take years for someone to convince you otherwise. We now turn to a real-world instance of protracted negotiations under incomplete information. Note the sequence of proposal and counterproposal in these events.

12.8 United States–Japan Trade Negotiations ■■■■■■■■■■■■■■■■■■■■■■■

The United States and Japan are the two largest economies in the world, and trade between them results in large gains to both sides. Exports sold by a nation make its economy bigger, whereas imports makes its economy smaller. When trade is balanced, and exports equal imports, then the gains from trade are fairly evenly divided between two countries.

Under current arrangements, Japan gets a larger share of the gains from trade than does the United States. This disparity in gains shows up in the $50 billion trade surplus that Japan enjoys annually with the United States. The data for January and February 1993 were $3.90 billion and $4.13 billion, respectively. At these monthly levels, Japan accounts for 73% of the total U.S. trade deficit. The gains from trade would be shared a lot more equally if this trade deficit were reduced to near zero, as it is with other large trading partners of the United States.

In a perfectly competitive world, trade deficits of this sort would not persist. Prices—here, exchange rates—would adjust until the deficit disappeared. The yen has fallen from 140 yen = $1 to about 100 yen = $1 recently, but the trade deficit has yet to disappear. Thus, the primary explanation for the trade deficit is imperfections in competition. The Clinton administration began bargaining for trade concessions from Japan as soon as Clinton took office. President Clinton and then-Prime Minister Miyazawa met on April 18, 1993, to announce a new framework for United States–Japan trade.[12] At a news conference following a day of meetings, the president said that he was "deeply concerned about the inadequate access for American firms, products and investors in Japan." For his part, Prime Minister Miyazawa said that improvements could not "be realized with managed trade nor under the threat of unilateralism." The sense of these meetings was that it would take months or even years of bargaining before the trade deficit issue could be fully resolved. The two leaders did agree to set up an agenda for talks on the new framework at the G-7 summit in July.

A week later in Tokyo, Secretary of the Treasury Ron Brown said, "It is a little disingenuous for the Japanese to complain about managed trade. I mean, after all, they have been some of the most successful and obvious managers of trade over many years."[13] The secretary's remarks provoked a sharp response from the Japanese. One high-ranking Japanese official spoke of Japanese retaliation, for instance, by reducing its investments in the United States. Secretary Brown countered by saying that he had been quoted out of context. In any event, Secretary Brown is urging Japan to agree to "measurable results" in a number of trade areas. "Our goal is not better rules, it is demonstrably open markets," he said. The administration's position is that Japanese restrictions on imports from the United States are primarily responsible for the trade imbalance—a position captured in the metaphor unlevel playing field. The United States' push for a level playing field is an effort to share the gains from trade more evenly.

The official Japanese response to Secretary Brown's remarks and other initiatives by the Clinton administration has been sure and swift. On May 11, 1993, Japan issued a report accusing the United States of unfair trade practices and calling the United States the worst offender among the large economies.[14] According to the Japanese report, the United States breaks the General Agreement on Tariffs and Trade (GATT) rules in 9 of 12 major sectors. Furthermore, the Japanese government announced in late May that the new framework must include an agreement on underlying principles. One of these underlying principles is bilateralism: "if either side evokes unilateral measures, the other will reserve the right to suspend those talks."[15]

Just prior to the G-7 meetings in Tokyo, Japan made a major concession on the issue of measurable results. Japan said that it would be willing to consider "illustrative examples" of numbers in certain product areas—numbers that

[12]Bob Davis, "U.S., Japan Endorse Trade Framework, But Outlook Is for Continued Haggling," *The Wall Street Journal*, April 19, 1993.

[13]Jacob M. Schlesinger and Quentin Hardy, "War of Words between U.S. and Japan over Trade, Exchange Rates Heats Up," *The Wall Street Journal*, April 26, 1993.

[14]Jacob M. Schlesinger, "Japan Accuses U.S. of Unfair Trade Policies," *The Wall Street Journal*, May 12, 1993.

[15]Jacob M. Schlesinger, "Japanese Say They'll Impose Conditions in Trade Talks Contrary to U.S. Views," *The Wall Street Journal*, May 28, 1993.

would not be binding, but would serve as dimensions along which to measure agreement.

After the G-7 summit, Clinton and Miyazawa agreed on a framework for trade. In this agreement, called the framework agreement, each side made two major commitments. Japan agreed to open its markets to more imports, making the rules and regulations more transparent to foreign companies. Japan also agreed to reduce its trade surplus with the rest of the world, not just with the United States, a surplus that reached $120 billion in 1992. For its part, the United States agreed to reduce its government deficit considerably and to raise the competitiveness of its manufacturers. The framework agreement was supposed to be finalized and agreed to in writing at a summit meeting between the two leaders in Washington, D.C., February 11, 1994. The threat of a trade war ensuing from disagreement on trade issues appeared to have been averted.

⠏ SUMMARY

1. In a bargaining game, two players stand to gain if they can come to an agreement. The coalition form of a game is useful for describing and solving bargaining games.

2. A bargaining game is described by its disagreement point and its efficient division curve. The disagreement point tells what happens if negotiations break down. The efficient division curve tells how the bargainers get the most from their opportunity to agree.

3. The principle of bargaining symmetry says that the solution of a symmetrical bargaining game is symmetrical. The principle of efficient bargaining says that the solution of a bargaining game is efficient. Together, these two principles select a unique solution to symmetrical bargaining games.

4. Even when bargainers have all necessary information, four asymmetries can affect the outcome of a bargaining game: the medium of payment, attitudes toward risk, outside options, and legal limits on asks. The concept of linear invariance says that the medium of payment really shouldn't matter to the outcome of bargaining.

5. The Nash bargaining solution is the only bargaining solution that satisfies symmetry, efficiency, linear invariance, and independence of irrelevant alternatives. This bargaining solution embodies the notion of risk dominance in bargaining games.

6. The Kalai–Smorodinsky bargaining solution is the only bargaining solution that satisfies symmetry, efficiency, linear invariance, and monotonicity. It gives more appealing solutions to bankruptcy games than does the Nash bargaining solution.

7. Bargaining games in the corporate sector are often played for billion dollar stakes. The outcomes of such games are a complicated mixture of bargaining solution principles.

8. In sequential bargaining with perfect information, the player who goes first has an advantage. The Stahl–Rubinstein bargaining solution solves such games.

9. In sequential bargaining with imperfect information, the informed player has an informational advantage. However, the informed player may have to hold out in such a game in order to make private information credible to the other side.

10. In bargaining between nations, business goes on as usual, which reduces the time cost of bargaining and the pressure to reach an agreement. The recent agreement between the United States and Japan may take years to implement.

✣ KEY TERMS

bargaining games	Nash bargaining solution
disagreement point	bankruptcy game
efficient division	monotonicity
coalition function form	Kalai–Smorodinsky bargaining solution
bargaining symmetry	holdout
bargaining efficiency	sequential bargaining
linear invariance	Stahl–Rubinstein bargaining solution
independence of irrelevant alternatives	sequential bargaining with imperfect information

✣ PROBLEMS

1. Two risk-neutral bargainers have $500 on the table. If they disagree, player 1 gets nothing, whereas player 2 has an outside option worth $100. Find the Nash and Kalai–Smorodinsky bargaining solutions. Do they agree or disagree?

2. Same data as in problem 1. Find the Kalai–Smorodinsky bargaining solution. Compare this solution to the Nash bargaining solution in problem 1.

3. In problem 1, player 1 is risk neutral and player 2 is risk averse, with utility function $u_2 = (\text{cash})^{0.5}$. Find the Nash and Kalai–Smorodinsky bargaining solutions. Do they still agree?

4. Same data as in problem 3. Find the Kalai–Smorodinsky bargaining solution. Compare this solution to the Nash bargaining solution in problem 3.

5. Players 1 and 2 are claimants in a bankruptcy game. Player 1 has a claim worth $1 million; player 2 has a claim worth $5 million. Both are risk neutral. Work out the Nash and Kalai–Smorodinsky bargaining solutions

when the assets at stake are $1 million, $3 million, and $5 million. How do the two solutions compare?

6. You are called to testify in a bankruptcy case as an expert witness for a small claimant. You will be asked in court why the Nash bargaining solution should be used in this case. Prepare your testimony—you will be well paid.

7. There is $1 trillion on the table in United States–Japan Trade. Trade talks are sequential, there is perfect information, and the interest rate is 10%. All trade is suspended for the duration of the talks. The United States gets to make the first offer. What should it offer Japan? What should Japan do with this offer?

8. Show that when the interest rate $r = 0$, the Stahl–Rubinstein solution divides the money on the table equally.

9. In the novelist–movie company negotiations, suppose that an okay novel is worth $400,000 as a movie property and the rate of interest is 20%. Describe the solution to the bargaining. How long does the movie company hold out? Would it be right to say that the novelist is making the movie company hold out?

10. You represent Japan at upcoming trade talks with the United States. Describe your negotiating position—what you would hope to get out of the talks, what you would be willing to do in case of disagreement, what sort of counterproposals you would bring. What rule does a deadline play in negotiations?

▚ APPENDIX. BARGAINING IN THE LABORATORY[16]

A wide variety of experiments on bargaining behavior have been run in the laboratory.[17] One of the veterans of this activity is Alvin E. Roth, the George W. Mellon Professor of Economics at the University of Pittsburgh. This appendix reports on some of what Roth and his coworkers have found.

The basic setup for a bargaining experiment is as follows. There are two players, recruited from the student population as subjects. Each subject is told that both a large prize and a small prize are available. If the subject does not win the large prize, the small prize is automatically awarded. The large prize is awarded by a lottery at the end of the experiment. The large prize goes to the player holding the winning number. At the start of bargaining, there are 100

---

[16]Material in this section was drawn from Alvin E. Roth, "Bargaining Phenomena and Bargaining Theory," in *Laboratory Experiments in Economics*, ed. Alvin E. Roth (Cambridge: Cambridge University Press, 1987), 14–41.

[17]For a good survey of the activity in this field, the interested reader should consult Alvin E. Roth, "Bargaining Experiments," in *Handbook of Experimental Economics* (John H. Kogel and Alvin E. Roth, editors) New York: North Holland, 1994.

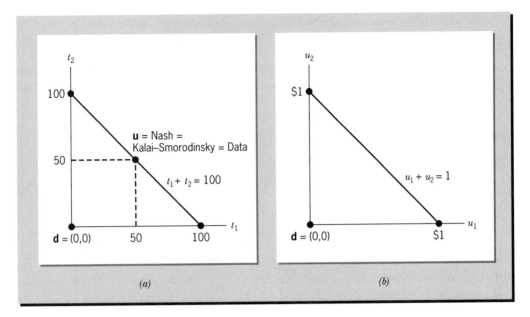

Figure 12.12. Bargaining in the laboratory, Divide a Dollar: (*a*) ticket possibilities; (*b*) utility possibilities.

lottery tickets on the table, numbered 1 to 100. The more lottery tickets a subject obtains by bargaining, the greater that subject's chance of winning the large prize. The winning number is drawn by chance from the uniform distribution, so that each number is equally good. The lottery tickets on the table represent money on the table. Subjects bargain over how many of the tickets each will get. In the event of disagreement, there is no lottery for the large prize, and each subject gets his or her small prize.

Figure 12.12*a* shows the ticket possibilities with this setup. If player 1 gets all the tickets, player 1 is sure to win the large prize; if player 2 gets all the tickets, player 2 will win the large prize. In the event of disagreement, neither player gets any tickets. We can convert tickets into utilities by the following transformation:

$$u_i = t_i A_i + (1 - t_i) a_i$$

where t_i is the number of tickets player i holds, A_i is player i's grand prize, and a_i is player i's small prize. In the simplest experiments, the large prize $A_i = \$1$ for both players and the small prize $a_i = \$0$ for both players. The utility possibilities that result are shown in Figure 12.12*b*. This figure represents one particular set of rules for playing Divide a Dollar. When human subjects played the game in Figure 12.12*b*, every single pair (11 in all) picked the 50–50 ticket distribution, just as predicted by the bargaining solutions discussed in this chapter.

Now suppose that player 2 is allowed to receive at most 60 tickets. According

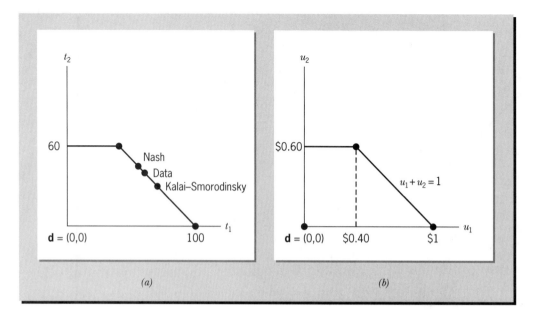

Figure 12.13. Bargaining in the laboratory, independence of irrelevant alternatives: (*a*) ticket possibilities; (*b*) utility possibilities.

to the independence of irrelevant alternatives, this restriction should not matter. Figure 12.13 shows the ticket possibilities and the utility possibilities that result. Many pairs of subjects played this game, and the results were somewhat different from the results of the other version. On average over all pairs, player 2 got 1.9 fewer tickets than player 1, whereas the Nash bargaining solution says that there should be no difference. Note that the large standard deviation of the ticket difference, 12.2, suggests that it is not statistically significant. The Kalai–Smorodinsky solution says that the restriction should make a difference, and in player 1's favor. However, according to the Kalai–Smorodinsky solution, the tickets should be split in the ratio 5:3, so that player 1 gets 25 more tickets, rather than just 2 more. The upper bound on player 2's tickets injected a great deal of noise into the data, and subjects had a difficult time dealing with the bargaining problem they faced. The observed data are not terribly supportive of either bargaining solution.

At this point, the experimenters varied the sizes of the large prizes (the small prizes were still worth $0 to each player). The large prize was worth $1.25 to player 1, but $3.75 to player 2. There were no limits on how many tickets player 2 could get. The utility possibilities that result from this setup are shown in Figure 12.14. According to the Nash bargaining solution, the players split the money in the ratio 1:3, with player 1 getting $0.625 and player 2, $1.875. This result follows from linear invariance applied to the game Divide a Dollar. This division of the money implies a 50–50 ticket split. Notice that since the Kalai–Smorodinsky bargaining solution satisfies linear invariance, it agrees with

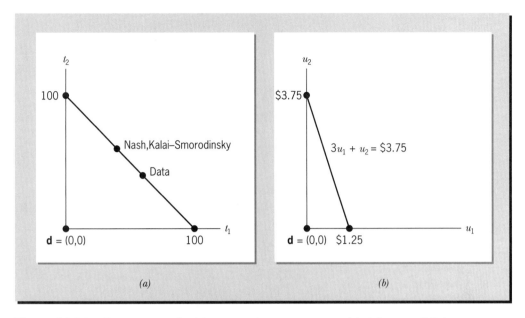

Figure 12.14. Bargaining in the laboratory, linear invariance: (*a*) ticket possibilities; (*b*) utility possibilities.

the Nash bargaining solution in this case. When this game was played in the laboratory, something remarkable happened. Instead of splitting the tickets evenly, player 1 got on average 34.6 more tickets than player 2,[18] an observed ratio of more than 2:1. This is certainly not what either bargaining theory would predict. What happened was that ticket agreements tended to cluster between the 50–50 ticket split predicted by the bargaining solutions and the 75–25 split that led players to get the same expected payoff. The average of these two types of agreements led to the observation in between, namely, a ticket difference between 0 and 50.

As a final treatment, the sizes of the prizes were kept the same as in this last setup, but player 2 could ask for at most 60 tickets. The joint treatment of linear invariance and independence of irrelevant alternatives is shown in Figure 12.15. The Nash bargaining solution continues to predict that the tickets will be split evenly. The Kalai–Smorodinsky solution says that utility will be split in the ratio 5:9, which implies a ticket split of 61 for player 1 and 39 for player 2. When 11 pairs reached agreements in this bargaining game, the average ticket difference was 21.6 tickets in favor of player 1.[19] This outcome is remarkably close to the Kalai–Smorodinsky prediction of 22 more tickets to player 1, and quite different from the Nash prediction of no ticket difference.

[18]The standard deviation of this difference was quite high, 19.3.
[19]With a standard deviation of 22.5.

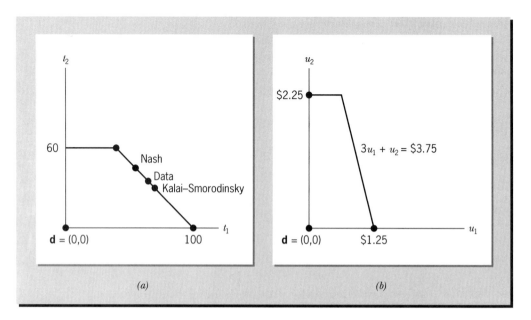

Figure 12.15. Bargaining in the laboratory, both conditions: (*a*) ticket possibilities; (*b*) utility possibilities.

The conclusions from this series of experiments are mixed; each bargaining solution gets some support, but also some disconfirmation. Data from the real world—and laboratories are part of the real world—are never as clean and clear-cut as game theory would like. In addition to the mixture of results reported here, some other things happen in bargaining experiments that are even more puzzling. First, we have been speaking only about agreements. In roughly 20% of all pairs in bargaining experiments, no agreement is reached. Disagreement should never happen according to the efficiency condition, but, unfortunately, it does. It would seem that one or both players are holding out for a better deal when time runs out. (There are time limits on all bargaining sessions, typically on the order of 6 minutes.) Second, and apparently related, there is a pronounced deadline effect. More agreements are reached in the last 30 seconds of bargaining than in the rest of the time combined, with a peak number of agreements in the last 5 seconds. You can expect future bargaining experiments to address these issues of efficiency and timing.

CHAPTER 13

■■■■■

Arbitration

In all the bargaining games of Chapter 12, if the players could not agree, they went to the disagreement point and the game was over. In certain well-defined situations, however, failure to reach agreement means that players can go to arbitration and the arbitrator will supply an agreement for them. Arbitration is available in the United States for disagreements between management and labor (labor arbitration) or between companies (commercial arbitration). In international law, going to arbitration is available to nations as an alternative to going to war.[1]

The decisions whether to go to arbitration and what sort of demand to share with the arbitrator are full of strategic content. In all cases considered here, the decision of the arbitrator is final. If decision can be overruled, the process is

---

[1]A recent example comes from the Middle East. When Egypt and Israel signed their peace treaty in 1977, the status of the small island of Taba, off the coast of the Sinai Peninsula, was left undecided. After more than a decade of contention, the two countries opted for international arbitration rather than fighting further over the island. The international arbitrator in this case decided in favor of Egypt.

called mediation instead. A mediator tries to get the two sides talking to each other, but lacks the power to impose an agreement. Conventional arbitration, where the two sides make offers to the arbitrator, who then comes back with a settlement based on the two offers, is studied first. Split the difference is a form of conventional arbitration. What the two sides know about the arbitrator makes a great deal of difference to what they demand. The chapter then considers conventional interest arbitration, where there is a sum of money at stake if the two sides can reach an agreement, followed by conventional grievance arbitration, where there is a contract in force that one of the sides thinks may have been breached. Interest arbitration is especially evident in negotiations over a new contract, where the contract terms are so important. The equilibria of both these forms of conventional arbitration are computed. An interview with a professional arbitrator who has over 40 years' experience in labor arbitration is then presented. The chapter concludes with final offer arbitration. In this type of arbitration, each side makes an offer, its final offer. The arbitrator must pick one of the two offers as the settlement. Final offer arbitration prevents the arbitrator from splitting the difference, and that is one of its chief justifications among arbitrators. This type of arbitration leads to some complicated strategic arguments as the two sides try to outsmart each other as well as the arbitrator. Final offer arbitration is used to resolve some salary disputes in Major League Professional Baseball, where there can be more than a million dollars on the table.

✖ 13.1 Conventional Arbitration ■ ■ ■ ■ ■ ■ ■ ■ ■ ■ ■ ■ ■ ■ ■

If bargainers have complete information and never make a mistake, then bargaining should lead to an efficient outcome. There should be an agreement, and it should capture all the gains available to the two sides of the agreement. If bargainers fail to use their information, if one or both are particularly intransigent, or if one continues to hold out for a better deal, negotiations may break down. In the model of the last chapter, a breakdown in negotiations meant going to the disagreement point, and the game was over. However, in certain clearly defined situations, the players may opt for binding **arbitration** instead.

It helps to visualize the physical process by which arbitration takes place. Each side agrees in advance on the identity of the arbitrator.[2] Each side also prepares its case to present to the arbitrator. The arbitrator schedules a hearing, at which each side has the opportunity to present its case orally. Each side also gives the arbitrator a written presentation. At the hearing, the arbitra-

---

[2]This agreement is required in the United States for reasons involving the Fourth Amendment of the Constitution.

tor is both judge and jury. As jury, the arbitrator can ask questions. As judge, the arbitrator can decide what evidence counts and what evidence does not count. Finally, as jury, the arbitrator renders a decision that is binding on both parties. The arbitrator is supposed to base the decision on the evidence presented, and the arbitrator is bound by federal and state law. This process is often called *binding arbitration*, since the decision of the arbitrator is binding on the two sides. U.S. law provides for arbitration in disputes involving organized labor, as an alternative to a strike or walkout. Arbitration is also available for commercial disputes, as an alternative to suing and going to court.

Arbitration is different from **mediation.** In mediation, the mediator attempts to get the two sides to resume talking, in the hope that they will get off the disagreement point and head toward an agreement. A mediator can, and usually does, make suggestions to the two sides and put proposals on the table for them to consider. However, a mediator cannot make a decision that is binding on the two sides. The mediator is at best a facilitator, not a decision maker. Right now, there are mediators at work in Bosnia, trying to put together a peace agreement or at least an effective cease-fire, but these mediators do not have the power to stop the fighting. An arbitrator would have the power, if the warring parties were to agree to international arbitration to settle their conflict.

The airline industry provides an example of successful mediation. In the week before Thanksgiving 1993, the flight attendants' union went on strike against American Airlines. The strike cost the company $25 million a day, and if it had lasted much longer, it might have cost the flight attendants their jobs. President Clinton, acting as mediator, got both sides to agree to go to arbitration with their dispute. The arbitrator (who won't be President Clinton) will conduct a hearing and render a decision in 1994.

This section studies **conventional arbitration.** In conventional arbitration, the two sides make a proposal to the arbitrator, who is then free to make any decision he or she wants. To be credible, however, the arbitrator's decision ought to be based on the evidence brought by the two sides on their behalf. Otherwise, the arbitrator would appear to be completely arbitrary. We can model the arbitrator as part of the outcome function. Rather than being a player in the conventional sense, the arbitrator takes the claims of the two sides and turns them into an outcome. The arbitrator is the physical manifestation of an outcome function. To start, we will restrict attention to **interest arbitration,** where the dispute is over the terms of a contract still to be agreed on. Later we will look at grievance arbitration, where the dispute is over whether an existing contract has been breached or not.

Let M dollars be on the table for the two sides to split. This is the value of an agreement to the two sides when they came to arbitration. Each player i has a strategy a_i, which is a number from the interval $[0,M]$. A player can ask for some or all of the money on the table and can bring evidence to bear to support any such claim. The arbitrator is represented by the payoff function

$$\mathbf{f}(\mathbf{a}) = [f_1(\mathbf{a}), f_2(\mathbf{a})]$$

where $\mathbf{a} = (a_1, a_2)$ is a vector of asks and $f_i(\mathbf{a})$ is the amount the arbitrator awards to player i based on the vector of asks.

Certain conditions on the arbitrator's function are desirable. It is absolutely essential that the arbitrator's decision be feasible:

$$f_1(\mathbf{a}) + f_2(\mathbf{a}) \leq M$$

The only reason the two sides are in arbitration is that what they are asking for is not feasible:

$$a_1 + a_2 > M$$

Otherwise, they would already have an agreement. The arbitrator fixes that. The situation is even better if the arbitrator is efficient:

$$f_1(\mathbf{a}) + f_2(\mathbf{a}) = M$$

The arbitrator's decision, if efficient, wastes nothing. It is important that arbitrators be perceived as fair. The condition representing fairness is symmetry:

$$f_1(a_1, a_2) = f_2(a_2, a_1)$$

Finally, the arbitrator ought to respect the claims of the two sides in the event that they actually constitute an agreement:

$$\mathbf{f}(\mathbf{a}) = \mathbf{a} \text{ when } a_1 + a_2 = M$$

This condition is called *nonimposition*. There are many functions f that satisfy these four requirements.

We will now add a requirement that, in the presence of the four requirements just given, only one function $\mathbf{f}$ can satisfy. This requirement is linearity. Suppose that when there is M on the table and the vector of asks is $\mathbf{a}$, the arbitrator decides $\mathbf{f}(\mathbf{a})$; when there is M' on the table and the vector of asks is $\mathbf{a}'$, the arbitrator decides $\mathbf{f}(\mathbf{a}')$. Next suppose that there is $M + M'$ on the table and the vector of asks is $\mathbf{a} + \mathbf{a}'$. The arbitrator's function $\mathbf{f}$ satisfies linearity if $\mathbf{f}(\mathbf{a} + \mathbf{a}') = \mathbf{f}(\mathbf{a}) + \mathbf{f}(\mathbf{a}')$. Although the concept of linearity is rather abstract, it embodies a well-known economic principle, the *principle of equal sacrifice*. When what the two sides are asking for exceeds what is available, then equal sacrifice says that each side gives up the same dollar amount in order to reach an agreement.

Here is an example of the link between linearity and equal sacrifice. Suppose that $\mathbf{a} = (60, 60)$ and $M = 10$. Efficiency and symmetry require that $\mathbf{f}(\mathbf{a}) = (5, 5)$. Next suppose that $\mathbf{a}' = (70, 50)$ and $M = 120$. Nonimposition requires that $\mathbf{f}(\mathbf{a}') = (70, 50)$. Now add up, to get $\mathbf{a} + \mathbf{a}' = (130, 110)$ and $M + M' = 130$. Linearity says that $\mathbf{f}(\mathbf{a} + \mathbf{a}') = (5, 5) + (70, 50) = (75, 55)$. Notice in this last case that the two sides' demands exceed the money on the table by $240 - 130 = 110$. This is the total sacrifice called for. Then equal sacrifice means that each side gives up half of 110, or 55 units, from what it is asking for. Player 1 gets $130 - 55 = 75$; player 2, $110 - 55 = 55$.

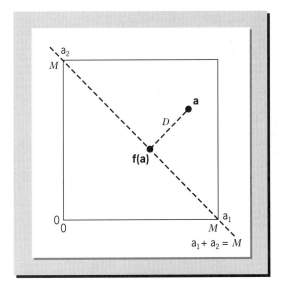

Figure 13.1. Split-the-difference arbitration.

This discussion can be summarized as follows. There is a unique arbitration function **f** satisfying efficiency, symmetry, nonimposition, and linearity. This function requires equal sacrifice on the part of the two sides to reach an agreement. In the language of arbitration, we say that **f** *splits the difference*. Define the difference, *D*, as

$$D = a_1 + a_2 - M$$

Then the arbitration function f that splits the difference takes the form

$$f_1(\mathbf{a}) = a_1 - D/2$$
$$f_2(\mathbf{a}) = a_2 - D/2$$

The action of **split-the-difference arbitration** is shown in Figure 13.1.

All we need to complete the specification of the arbitration game are utility functions for the two players. Since the arbitrator awards amounts of money, the utility function for player i is given by

$$u_i[f_i(\mathbf{a})]$$

where u_i is an increasing function. Figure 13.2 shows the normal form of split-the-difference arbitration when each side can ask for either half the money on the table or all the money on the table and each side is risk neutral. Notice that there is a unique equilibrium, with each player asking for all the money on the table: $\mathbf{a}^* = (M,M)$. Moreover, asking for all the money on the table is a dominant strategy. You can show that these two features are true in general.

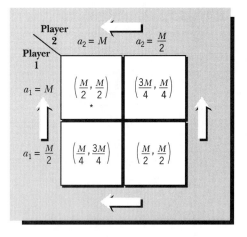

Figure 13.2.   Split-the-difference arbitration, 2 × 2 case.

Both follow from the fact that a player's utility is always increasing in the amount the player asks for:

$$0 < \frac{\partial u_i}{\partial a_i} = \frac{\partial f_i}{\partial a_i} = \frac{1}{2}$$

Hence the only equilibrium for a player is at the corner $a_i = M$, and a higher ask can always dominate a lower ask.

Even though split-the-difference arbitration satisfies many appealing properties, it has one large drawback. It provides incentives for each side to make extreme demands, the most extreme possible. Arbitrators have long complained about having to settle cases where the two sides are so far apart. The next section considers a form of arbitration that attempts to avoid extreme demands by the use of probability.

13.2 A Random, but Not Arbitrary, Arbitrator ■

In the last section, the arbitrator in conventional arbitration split the difference between the two sides. This section studies a rather different kind of arbitrator, the **random arbitrator.** Suppose that the evidence on both sides for their positions is equally convincing to an outside observer. Then there is no fair way to break the tie short of a random mechanism. In this model, the arbitrator is a probability distribution over asks, with each side getting what it asks for with probability .5.

We can formalize this situation as follows. The arbitrator function **f(a)** for random arbitration satisfies:

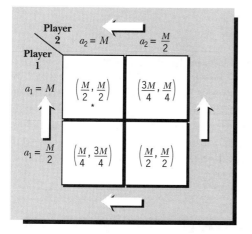

Figure 13.3. Random arbitration.

$$\mathbf{f(a)} = (a_1, M - a_1) \qquad \text{with probability .5}$$
$$(M - a_2, a_2) \qquad \text{with probability .5}$$

Figure 13.3 shows the normal form for random arbitration for the case of two risk-neutral agents restricted to asking for either half the money or all the money. To get the payoffs in the cell $(M, M/2)$, it suffices to compute

$$\mathbf{f}\left(M, \frac{M}{2}\right) = (M, 0) \qquad \text{with probability .5 (1 wins at arbitration)}$$
$$= \left(\frac{M}{2}, \frac{M}{2}\right) \qquad \text{with probability .5 (2 wins at arbitration)}$$

Computing expected values, we get

$$\mathbf{f}\left(M, \frac{M}{2}\right) = \left(\frac{3M}{4}, \frac{M}{4}\right)$$

The other entries in the normal form follow similarly.

Notice that the unique equilibrium is for each player to ask for all the money. Again, this is a dominant strategy. The matrix in Figure 13.3 is exactly like that in Figure 13.2. When both players are risk neutral, random arbitration is equivalent to split-the-difference arbitration. Once players are not risk neutral, random arbitration leads to a different payoff matrix, but not to different incentives. Each player will still want to make the largest possible demand.

To see this result, consider the expected utility of player 1, $Eu_1(\mathbf{a})$, given by

$$Eu_1(\mathbf{a}) = .5u_1(a_1) + .5u_1(M - a_2)$$

If player 1 wins at arbitration, player 1 gets what he or she asked for; if player 1 loses, he or she gets what player 2 leaves. Player 1's marginal utility is

$$\frac{\partial Eu_1}{\partial a_1} = \frac{.5\partial u_1}{\partial a_1} > 0$$

since the only time player 1's utility depends on his or her own strategy is when player 1 wins. Player 1 wants to ask for as much as possible in the event of a win, which in this case means asking for all the money on the table. Just as in split-the-difference arbitration, random arbitration provides incentives for each side to make maximal demands.[3] Later in this chapter, we will study an increasingly popular form of interest arbitration that does not provide such incentives. Before we do that, however, let's turn to the other major category of conventional arbitration, grievance arbitration.

13.3 Conventional Grievance Arbitration ■ ■ ■ ■ ■ ■ ■ ■

In **grievance arbitration,** as opposed to interest arbitration, what is at stake is a principle rather than a sum of money. If money is involved, it is a secondary issue. The principle might be a work rule, a contract provision, or a customary practice that the grievant believes has been violated. The other side of such arbitration believes that there is no such work rule, contract provision, or customary practice or that, if there is, it has not been violated. If negotiation over the grievance breaks down, then the two sides may go to arbitration. The alternatives to going to arbitration in such cases are going out on strike, which is costly to both sides, or going to court, which is, again, costly to both sides.

Here is an example of grievance arbitration that involved player 1 (a worker) and player 2 (a company).[4] The worker had worked for the company for 19 years when he was involved in a serious accident and required hospitalization. After 117 days in the hospital and four operations, the worker died. The company carried life insurance on all employees, which included provisions for accidental death and dismemberment in addition to ordinary life coverage. To be eligible for the accidental death benefit under this policy, an employee had to die as a direct result of the accident within 90 days of the date of the accident. The company paid the ordinary life benefit, but refused to pay the accidental death benefit, arguing that the 90-day limit had expired while the worker was hospitalized. The union to which the worker belonged went to grievance arbitration on behalf of the worker's widow. The union's position was that the worker had died, for all practical intents and purposes, within the

---

[3]Another way to think of this result is that asking for more stochastically dominates asking for less. Thus, the result is true for a much broader class of players than those who maximize expected utility.

[4]This example was drawn from Arthur A. Sloane and Fred Witney, *Labor Relations,* 7th ed. (Englewood Cliffs, N.J.: Prentice Hall, 1991) 347–54. In keeping with freedom of information considerations as they apply to arbitration cases, the identities of the worker and the company are withheld.

90-day period. The attending physician testified that the worker was kept alive solely by life support systems the last 35 days of his life. Therefore, except for this artificial extension, his life had effectively ended 82 days after the accident, hence within the 90-day period.

The arbitrator in this case held for the union, interpreting "life" to mean more than maintenance on life support in a terminal vegetative state. However, the arbitrator was quick to add that, had the worker not been attached to life support until after 90 days had elapsed from the date of the accident, he would have ruled for the company. The arbitrator had no intention of overturning a clause of long standing in this union–company relationship. The union therefore won as far as the principle involved, narrowly construed, was concerned. As a secondary matter, the widow of the worker was paid the accidental death benefit.

As you can see, the issues in grievance arbitration can get very tricky, and what the arbitrator decides depends crucially on the evidence the two sides bring to the case. Inspired by this case, let's model such arbitration as a game of imperfect information. There are two players, 1 and 2. Player 1 has a grievance. Player 1 has to decide whether to file a grievance or not. Prior to making a decision, player 1 gets a signal, z_1. The way to think of this signal is that it represents evidence available to player 1 (and only to player 1), that player 1 can bring to the arbitration hearing. Evidence can be strong or weak. A value of the signal $z_1 = 1$ says to player 1, "You have a strong case." A value of the signal $z_1 = 0$ says to player 1, "You have a weak case." Player 1 observes one signal or the other; all player 2 knows about player 1's signal is that $z_1 = 1$ and $z_1 = 0$ are equally likely.

If, based on the signal, player 1 decides not to file a grievance, then the game ends and the status quo payoffs (0,0) result. If, based on the signal, player 1 goes ahead and files a grievance, then player 2 gets a signal, z_2. A value of the signal $z_2 = 1$ says to player 2, "The grievant has a strong case." A value of the signal $z_2 = 0$ says to player 2, "The grievant has a weak case." Player 2 observes one signal or the other; all player 1 knows about player 2's signal is that $z_2 = 1$ and $z_2 = 0$ are equally likely. Based on the signal and on the fact that player 1 has filed a grievance, player 2 has to decide whether to contest the grievance or not. The sequence of actions is shown in Figure 13.4.

If player 2 decides not to contest the grievance, then player 1 wins and player 2 loses. This situation is represented by the payoff vector $\mathbf{u} = (w, l)$, where

$$w > 0 > l$$

Winning a grievance is better than the status quo (0), and the status quo is better than losing a grievance. If player 1 files a grievance and player 2 contests the grievance, then the two sides go to arbitration. It costs each side an amount C to prepare a case for the arbitration hearing. At the arbitration hearing, the arbitrator receives the entire signal vector $\mathbf{z} = (z_1, z_2)$. The arbitrator averages the evidence into a single signal, $z(A)$, which is given by

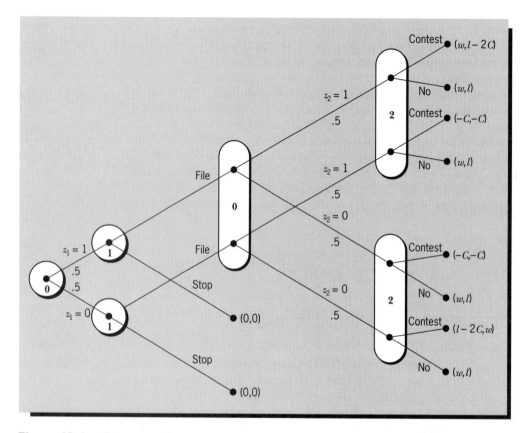

Figure 13.4.   Grievance arbitration.

$$z(A) = \frac{(z_1 + z_2)}{2}$$

The calculation of the arbitrator's signal is shown in Figure 13.5a. The arbitrator bases the decision solely on $z(A)$. If the evidence on both sides favors the grievant, $z(A) = 1$, then the arbitrator decides in favor of player 1. Player 1 wins at arbitration and player 2 loses. In this event, the losing player bears the entire cost of arbitration. This outcome, where player 1 wins in arbitration and player 2 loses, is given by the payoff vector

$$\mathbf{u} = (w,\, l - 2C)$$

If the evidence is mixed, $z(A) = 0.5$, then neither side wins at arbitration. The outcome is just the status quo, except that both sides have paid their own cost of going to arbitration:

$$\mathbf{u} = (-C,\, -C)$$

Finally, if the evidence on both sides is against the grievant, $z(A) = 0$, the

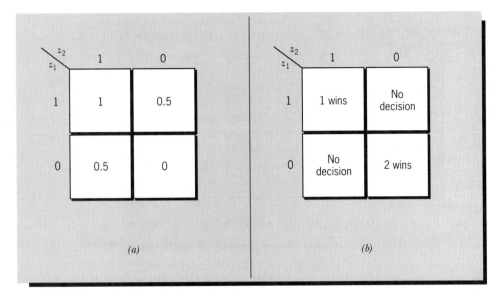

Figure 13.5. The arbitrator in grievance arbitration: (*a*) arbitrator's signal;
(*b*) arbitrator's action.

arbitrator decides against the grievant. In this event, player 1 bears the entire cost of arbitration. This outcome, where player 1 loses at arbitration and player 2 wins, is given by the payoff vector

$$\mathbf{u} = (l - 2C, w)$$

These payoffs are shown in Figure 13.5*b*. This completes the specification of the grievance arbitration game.

Each player in grievance arbitration has two information sets with two moves at each information set, for a total of four pure strategies. Player 1 decides whether to file a grievance or not, based on two possible signals. Player 2 decides whether to contest a grievance or not, based on two possible signals and on the knowledge that player 1 has filed a grievance. Rather than work out the complete 4×4 matrix, let's look at the types of sequential equilibria, depending on how much it costs to file a grievance.

Case 1. $-l/3 < C < -l = w.$[5] In this case, play is informative. Player 1 files a grievance only on receipt of the signal $z_1 = 1$. Otherwise, player 1 doesn't file. Player 2 contests a filing only on receipt of the signal $z_2 = 0$. Otherwise, player 2 doesn't contest a grievance that has been filed. At this equilibrium, each side has a strong case, and the arbitrator is always faced with extremely tough calls.

Let's show that the behavior

---

[5]From this point on, let us assume that $w + l = 0$, merely for convenience. There is no essential change to the regime analysis when the zero-sum assumption is relaxed.

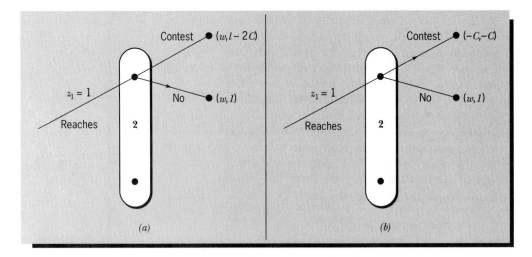

Figure 13.6. Backward induction, case 1, player 2: (a) $z_2 = 1$; (b) $z_2 = 0$.

> 1 files only if $z_1 = 1$
>
> 2 contests only if $z_2 = 0$

is a sequential equilibrium, using backward induction (see Figure 13.6). Consider player 2 at the information set $z_2 = 1$. According to the given pair of strategies, the node of this information set corresponding to $z_1 = 1$ must have been reached (player 1 does not file unless $z_1 = 1$). Player 2 is sure to lose if he or she contests the grievance. Since it is even more costly to contest and lose than to admit the grievance, player 2 does not contest:

$$l > l - 2C$$

This situation is shown in Figure 13.6a. Next, consider player 2 at the information set $z_2 = 0$. Again, the node of this information set corresponding to $z_1 = 1$ must have been reached. Player 2 gets a draw if he or she contests; otherwise, player 2 loses. In this regime,

$$-C > l$$

so player 2 contests the grievance. It is even more costly not to contest, as seen in Figure 13.6b.

We are now back to player 1's move. Suppose that player 1 has received the signal $z_1 = 1$. Given that player 2 only contests if he or she receives the signal $z_2 = 0$, player 1 faces the situation shown in Figure 13.7a. If player 1 files a grievance, then with probability .5 player 2 gets the signal $z_2 = 0$ and there is a contest ($u_1 = -C$); with probability .5 player 2 gets the signal $z_2 = 1$ and there is no contest ($u_1 = w$). We have

$$0 < .5(-C) + .5(w)$$

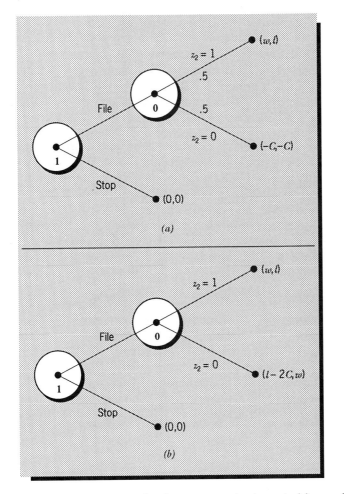

Figure 13.7. Backward induction, case I, player I: (*a*) $z_1 = 1$; (*b*) $z_1 = 0$.

in this regime, so this player 1 files a grievance. On the other hand, suppose that player 1 has received the signal $z_1 = 0$. Player 1 faces the situation shown in Figure 13.7*b*. If player 1 files a grievance, then with probability .5 player 2 gets a winning signal and there is a contest ($u_1 = l - 2C$); with probability .5 player 2 gets the signal $z_2 = 1$ and there is no contest ($u_1 = w$). We have

$$.5(l - 2C) + .5w < 0$$

in this regime, so this player 1 does not file a grievance.

We have just verified the sequential equilibrium of case 1. When arbitration costs are not too high, in particular when it costs less to go to arbitration than to take a certain loss in a grievance case, then the institution of arbitration functions well. Strategic play reveals all the relevant information, and only worthwhile cases are filed and contested. At this equilibrium, the arbitrator is always up against really tough cases. If a case weren't tough, it wouldn't be brought to arbitration. In a clear-cut situation, such as $z_1 = z_2 = 0$, player 1 files a grievance and player 2 settles without going to arbitration.

This sort of behavior is intuitively appealing. You file a grievance only if you have a strong case; you contest a grievance only if you have a strong case. If people acted this way in civil court—only filing suit if they had a strong case—the courts would be a lot less clogged than they are.

Case 2. $C > -3l$. The cost of arbitration is very high. Even with a strong signal, player 2 will not contest a grievance. Thus player 1 will always file, regardless of the signal received. In this case, the sequential equilibrium is uninformative. Those who feel aggrieved always file a grievance, and the other party never contests. The arbitrator never gets called in this case.

The outcome in this case is terribly one-sided. The player getting hit with all the grievances cannot afford to use arbitration as a defense, because arbitration costs are too high. Situations like this are tailor-made for the civil court system. Arbitration cannot solve all disputes. Sometimes you really do have to go to court.

Case 3. $-l < C < -3l$. The cost of arbitration is between the two earlier extremes. As in case 1, player 1 with the signal $z_1 = 1$ files a grievance, and player 2 with the signal $z_2 = 0$ does not contest a grievance. Now, however, not all players 2 with a strong signal $z_2 = 1$ will contest a grievance. This situation provides an incentive for some players 1 with the signal $z_1 = 0$ to file a grievance. The result is a sequential equilibrium in mixed strategies. You can check in this case that the conditional strategies

$$p_1(\text{file} \,|\, z_1 = 0) = \frac{(-2l + C)}{w}$$

and

$$p_2(\text{contest} \,|\, z_2 = 1) = \frac{C}{(-l)}$$

are the required mixing probabilities. Player 1 with a weak case gets the status quo payoff 0, whether player 1 files a grievance or not. Player 2 with a strong case gets the payoff $-l$, whether player 2 contests a grievance or takes a sure loss. In terms of the frequency with which arbitration occurs, this case is intermediate between the other two.

The detailed arguments for these last two cases of grievance arbitration are saved for the problems. The key is to show that player 1 with a strong signal has a dominant strategy to file a grievance. Then backward induction, plus the hints contained in the text, should do the rest.

In all these models of arbitration, we have modeled the arbitrator as the payoff function. We ought not lose sight of the fact that arbitrators are real people, too. It's time to meet one.

13.4 Fred Witney, Professional Arbitrator[6]

Fred Witney arbitrated his first case in 1953, and has arbitrated over a thousand cases since. Fred, who is Emeritus Professor of Economics at Indiana University, is somewhat atypical of the arbitration profession. Some 60% of all arbitrators are lawyers, which Fred isn't. Another 30% are professors, among them labor economists and industrial relations specialists, which Fred is. The remaining 10% are drawn from all walks of life. No license is required to be an arbitrator, but you do have to demonstrate experience to join one of the arbitrators' two major national associations. This is a kind of catch-22, since it's hard to get experience as an arbitrator unless you already are one. The two major national associations are the American Arbitrators Association (AAA), a private body, and the Federal Mediation and Conciliation Service (FMCS), which is public. The members of the AAA pay voluntary dues, which support the association's activities. The FMCS is federally funded and levies no dues. The FMCS was created as part of the body of national labor relations law, to help prevent or settle strikes and generally improve labor–management relations. In certain situations, such as strikes by hospital workers, the two sides are obliged to use the FMCS to help settle the strike. Each of these two associations has about 3000 members, who are for the most part the same people. Demographically, some 20% of the membership is women and 5% is minority. Arbitration remains a bastion of older white males, although this situation is slowly changing. In addition to these two national associations, there is a third body, the National Academy of Arbitration (NAA). The 600 members of the NAA, all of whom are elected, represent the crème de la crème of arbitrators. You need a national reputation as an arbitrator even to get on the ballot. Fred Witney belongs to all three of these organizations.

Fred Witney specializes in labor arbitration cases. There are an estimated 35,000 cases nationwide each year. There is an even larger number of commercial arbitration cases annually. These are all cases that are kept out of the court system by arbitration. The AAA and the FMCS function primarily as referral services. The two sides to a dispute contact one of these national associations, which then provides them with a list of five to nine nominees who may serve as arbitrator. Both sides to a dispute have to agree to the arbitrator. The average compensation for arbitrating a case is $500 per day plus travel expenses. It is customary for the arbitrator to travel to the site of the negotiations to conduct the hearing.

Fred says, "Three things make an arbitration case tough: contradictory features in the contract, ambiguous contractual language, and technical

---

[6]This material is based on a personal interview, conducted on June 3, 1993, in Professor Witney's office.

language. Technical language is especially a problem when doctors are involved." An arbitrator gets a thick packet of documentation from both sides before the hearing. At the hearing, the arbitrator is both judge and jury. The two sides present their cases, but the arbitrator is in charge. The rules of evidence are not those of a courtroom, but those of the arbitrator. The arbitrator cross-examines the witnesses and interrogates the lawyers who are usually present at the hearing. "The most important thing for an arbitrator is their reputation for fairness," according to Fred. Both sides have to feel they have received a fair hearing, even if they lose. Any party who thinks he or she didn't get a fair hearing can fire the arbitrator—that is, refuse to approve the arbitrator another time. Arbitrators whose performance is acceptable to both sides can be signed to long-term contracts and hear cases repeatedly as they come up. For instance, an arbitrator may be hired for the duration of a labor contract—this is called **permanent arbitration.**

Of the thousand cases Fred has arbitrated, most have involved job evaluation, time and motion disputes (such as disputes over breaks or restroom use), and incentive clauses in contracts. All these are fertile areas for ambiguous contractual language and contradictory contractual features. These cases tend toward mind-boggling complexity. Some arbitrators get so burned out on time and motion disputes in particular that they refuse to arbitrate them any more. Fred says that the best guide to such cases is past practice. Support for one side more than the other in past practice can be the pivotal point in deciding the case. Arbitrators don't have the luxury of second-guessing themselves. An arbitrator's decision is final, a principle upheld by the United States Supreme Court. Moreover, an arbitrator is paid to be decisive and is expected to render a judgment, usually within 30 days of the hearing. So the arbitrator is constantly poring through the evidence of the two sides, looking for something that will turn the case one way or the other.

Many of Fred's interest arbitration cases have involved rather small sums, on the order of a few thousand dollars. Both sides in such cases have a marked tendency to complain about the cost of arbitration—although it should be noted that arbitration is a whole lot cheaper than taking such cases to court. The biggest case Fred has handled involved $60,000 on the table. The *Chicago Daily Racing Form* had converted its operations from typesetting to computerized printing. This move led to a major labor dispute because working conditions no longer conformed to the language of the contract. In particular, workers were not being transferred within the operation according to the rules previously in force. A recent large case involved $35,000. In this case, the question was whether the employer was required to pay $35,000 for supplemental medical insurance or not. In both these cases, the local union took the matter to arbitration.

Fred has also handled many grievance arbitration cases. Most of these cases involved questions surrounding seniority and discharge and proved quite thorny to decide. We have seen how important arbitration costs are to grievance arbitration. A noteworthy point in this regard is that if a national union files a grievance, the national union pays for arbitration. However, if the local chapter of a union files the grievance, the local must pay. The one exception is grievances involving the U.S. Postal Service. In these cases the national union always pays for arbitration; however, the national union must approve before a local can file a grievance.

Arbitration between private parties in the United States was put on its current sound footing by three Supreme Court decisions in 1960, the so-called **Trilogy cases.** In *Warrior & Gulf Navigation,* the Court said it would not rule out arbitration unless there was a prior agreement between the parties that expressly forbade arbitration. In *American Manufacturing,* the Court reversed a lower court that had found a grievance "frivolous." The Court ruled that courts could only rule on whether a matter could be sent to arbitration, and not on the merits of the matter itself. Finally, in *Enterprise Wheel & Car Corporation,* the Court upheld a lower court ruling that an arbitrator's decision is "final and binding." Without this provision, the loser at arbitration would be continually tempted to go to court to get a ruling overturned. The one legal constraint that the Court has recognized since 1960 involves Title VII. If an employee loses a grievance in arbitration and can subsequently show that the grievance involved racial discrimination, then the employee can pursue that aspect of the case further.

Arbitrators need the wisdom of Solomon and the patience of Job. They perform a major service to our economy, for which they get very little recognition. An arbitrator like Fred Witney is a true and valuable economic resource.

▚ 13.5 Final Offer Arbitration ■■■■■■■■■■■■■■■■

We have seen that conventional interest arbitration gives both sides an incentive to ask for all the money on the table. This pattern of behavior became sufficiently pervasive and obnoxious in the 1950s that a new kind of interest arbitration, **final offer arbitration,** was introduced. Final interest arbitration is very different from conventional arbitration. Each side presents a final offer (or ask). The arbitrator must pick one of the two proposals. Since the arbitrator is restricted to these two offers, there is no possibility of splitting the difference, or of imposing a third option. The intention behind this innovative form of arbitration was to discourage extreme offers (they would be unlikely to be accepted). We shall see that, depending on attitudes toward risk, this intention is usually fulfilled.

The general setup for final offer arbitration is as follows. The amount on the table is M dollars. Each player i simultaneously asks for a_i dollars, thereby offering $M - a_i$ to the other side. An ask cannot exceed the money on the table. The arbitrator forms a probability distribution $\mathbf{p}(\mathbf{a}) = [p_1(\mathbf{a}), p_2(\mathbf{a})]$ based on the asks received. Let $p_1(\mathbf{a})$ be the probability that the arbitrator decides in favor of player 1 and therefore gives a_1 to player 1 and the rest to player 2. Let

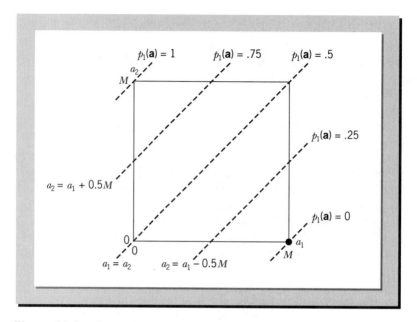

Figure 13.8.   Final offer arbitration, linear probability.

$p_2(\mathbf{a})$ be the probability that the arbitrator decides in favor of player 2, and therefore gives a_2 to player 2 and the rest of the money to player 1. We will consider first risk-neutral players in arbitration. The utility function for risk-neutral player 1 is

$$u_1(\mathbf{a}) = p_1(\mathbf{a})a_1 + [1 - p_1(\mathbf{a})](M - a_2)$$

With probability $p_1(\mathbf{a})$, the arbitrator decides in favor of player 1 and player 1 gets what he or she asked for. In the opposite case, player 1 gets what is left. The utility function for risk-neutral player 2 is similar:

$$u_2(\mathbf{a}) = p_2(\mathbf{a})a_2 + [1 - p_2(\mathbf{a})](M - a_1)$$

This completes the description of the arbitration game between the two sides.

In final offer arbitration, an arbitrator is defined by the probability distribution $\mathbf{p}(\mathbf{a})$. We can think of the random arbitrator of Section 13.2 as a special case of final offer arbitration, where $\mathbf{p}(\mathbf{a})$ does not depend on $\mathbf{a}$:

$$p_1(\mathbf{a}) = .5 = p_2(\mathbf{a})$$

for all $\mathbf{a}$. As we have already seen, such arbitration leads to extreme demands on both sides.

If the whole purpose of final offer arbitration is to make offers less extreme, then the arbitrator cannot simply pick one of the two offers at random. The probability distribution $\mathbf{p}(\mathbf{a})$ has to be somehow sensitive to what the two sides ask for. Figure 13.8 shows a particularly appealing kind of arbitrator for the problem at hand. If player 1 asks for everything and player 2 asks for nothing, then the probability that player 1 wins, $p_1(\mathbf{a})$, is 0. This player is obviously too greedy. If player 1 and player 2 asks for the same amount, then the probability that player 1 wins is .5. The arbitrator does not discriminate between equal asks. Finally, if player 1 asks for nothing and player 2 asks for everything, then the probability that player 1 wins is 1. The less greedy a player appears, the more likely the player is to win. The formula for this kind of arbitrator, called a **linear probability arbitrator,** is

$$p_1(\mathbf{a}) = \frac{(M - a_1 + a_2)}{2M}$$

$$p_2(\mathbf{a}) = \frac{(M + a_1 - a_2)}{2M}$$

The probability of getting the nod from the arbitrator is linear and decreasing in your ask. The more you ask for, the less likely you are to win. At the same time, the more you ask for, the more you win when you do win. These two factors trade off against each other in the formulation of a player's ask.

Since the utility functions are differentiable, we begin our search for a solution by taking first derivatives. Player 1 maximizes utility by asking a_1 such that

$$\frac{\partial u_1}{\partial a_1} = 0 = a_1 \frac{\partial p_1}{\partial a_1} + p_1 - \frac{\partial p_1}{\partial a_1}(M - a_2)$$

using the rule for the derivative of a product. Associating terms, we have

$$0 = (a_2 + a_1 - M)\frac{\partial p_1}{\partial a_1} + p_1$$

Since the derivative of p_1, player 1's probability of winning, is

$$\frac{\partial p_1}{\partial a_1} = -\frac{1}{2M}$$

we can substitute to get

$$0 = (a_2 + a_1 - M)\left(\frac{-1}{2M}\right) + \frac{(M - a_1 + a_2)}{2M}$$

After a little algebra, we get

$$a_1^* = M$$

Player 1's best strategy is to ask for all the money. A similar calculation shows that player 2's best strategy is

$$a_2^* = M$$

At the unique equilibrium of final offer arbitration with risk-neutral players and a linear probability arbitrator, each player asks for all the money on the table. The arbitrator has to choose between two final offers that are as far apart as they possibly could be.

This result is a little disappointing, since the whole point of introducing final offer arbitration was to make equilibrium asks less extreme. However, if players are risk averse, then in final offer arbitration, they do reduce their asks somewhat. Suppose that both players are risk averse, with utility functions

$$u_1[f_1(\mathbf{a})] = a_1^{0.5}$$

Substituting into the utility function, we get

$$u_1(\mathbf{a}) = p_1(\mathbf{a}) a_1^{0.5} + [1 - p_1(\mathbf{a})](M - a_2)^{0.5}$$

and similarly for player 2.

Player 1 maximizes utility by choosing the ask a_1 so that

$$\frac{\partial u_1}{\partial a_1} = 0 =$$

$$a_1^{0.5} \frac{\partial p_1}{\partial a_1} + 0.5 \, a_1^{-0.5} \, p_1 - \frac{\partial p_1}{\partial a_1} (M - a_2)^{0.5}$$

again using the rule for the derivative of a product. Unlike the earlier case, we now have to solve a nonlinear equation to get player 1's optimal ask. We would have a similar nonlinear equation to solve for player 2. We can make life simpler by imposing symmetry at this point. Associating terms, we get

$$0 = [a_1^{0.5} - (M - a_2)^{0.5}] \frac{\partial p_1}{\partial a_1} + p_1$$

Now we make three substitutions, one each for player 1's probability of winning, the derivative of that probability, and player 2's best ask. After a little algebra, this leads to

$$0 = a_1 - \sqrt{(M - a_1^2)} - \frac{M}{2}$$

After rearranging and squaring both sides, we get the quadratic equation

$$0 = 2a_1^2 - a_1 M + \left(\frac{M^2}{4 - M}\right)$$

Solving this equation, we get

$$a_1^* = \frac{(2 + \sqrt{2})M}{4}$$

By symmetry, this is also player 2's best ask. When both players are risk averse to the same degree, each asks for less than all the money on the table. In particular, in this case they each ask for only 85% of the money on the table. This outcome makes a lot of sense if you are risk averse. You would rather ask for less money and be more certain of getting it, then ask for everything in sight, only to lose in arbitration. You can show (end-of-chapter problem) that the more risk averse both players are, the less they ask for in final offer arbitration.

So far we have only considered cases where both players have exactly the same attitude toward risk. When one player is risk neutral and the other is risk averse, then the risk-neutral player asks for more money than does the risk-averse player. The risk-averse player's fear of losing at arbitration results in a somewhat shaved ask. To see this result, note first that the risk-neutral player's optimal ask, just derived, did not depend on the opponent's attitude toward risk. All you have to do is substitute the risk-neutral player's optimal ask into the first-order condition for the risk-averse player and solve. The details are left for an end-of-chapter problem. Let's now turn to an industry in which final offer arbitration gets a lot of publicity and involves millions of dollars: Major League Professional Baseball.

▚ 13.6 Final Offer Arbitration in Major League Professional Baseball[7] ■ ■ ■ ■ ■ ■ ■ ■ ■ ■ ■ ■ ■ ■ ■ ■ ■ ■

Since 1974 the agreement between **Major League Professional Baseball** and the Player's Association has provided for arbitration of salary disputes for any player with 3 years' or more experience. At the end of the 1992 season, 100 players filed for arbitration. The number of players who file each year varies; for instance, 162 players filed in 1989, whereas only 80 filed in 1993. Of the 100 cases filed in 1992, all but 18 were settled prior to arbitration. This is typical. The vast majority of filings never reach an arbitrator, but are settled by the two sides beforehand. The mere threat of final offer arbitration appears to have a marked effect on the players' and the owners' propensity to reach agreements. Of the 18 cases that went to arbitration, the players won 6 and the owners won 12.

Baseball arbitration cases are handled like any other arbitration cases, despite the large sums of money on the table. The arbitrator conducts a hearing at which both sides are present—usually the player and the player's agent and the owner or general manager and counsel. O'Hare Airport in Chicago is a favorite hearing site. The arbitrator hears all the evidence and decides in favor of one of the two offers, usually within 72 hours. The evidence is both broad ("I had a good year") and narrow ("He batted .222 with men on third base"). Comparative worth arguments are often used. In these arguments, a player compares himself to a player at the same position who is highly paid, whereas the owner compares the player to one at that position who is not highly paid. Even if there is a million dollars on the table, the arbitrator gets paid about $500 per day plus expenses for making this million-dollar decision.

The mechanics of baseball arbitration are as follows. Each side brings to the hearing a contract with the space where the player's salary goes filled in. Each

---

[7]Material for this study was drawn from Ben Walker, "McDowell Seeks $6.5 Million," *Bloomington Herald-Times*, January 19, 1994.

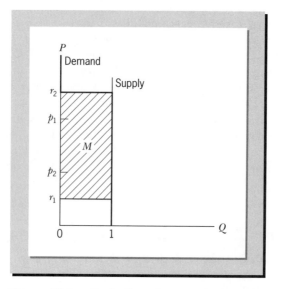

Figure 13.9.   Final offer arbitration in baseball.

side signs its contract and hands it to the arbitrator. The arbitrator, after hearing all the evidence, destroys one of the contracts. The contract that remains is the contract that will be in force for the coming year.

Figure 13.9 illustrates the market logic behind arbitration in baseball. The baseball player is player 1; the team is player 2. The reservation price for the baseball player, r_1, is the lowest price at which he is willing to play for the team. The player asks for a price p_1 that is higher than his reservation price. The reservation price for the team, r_2, is the highest price the team is willing to pay to have the player on the team. The team offers a price p_2 that is lower than its reservation price. Since the two sides cannot agree on a price, $p_1 > p_2$. The amount of money on the table is the potential gain from trade,

$$M = r_2 - r_1$$

As outside observer we are not privy to the individual reservation prices, but the baseball player and the team are. In particular, we have

$$M \geq r_2 - p_2 \qquad \text{(the team does not try for more than } M\text{)}$$

and

$$M \geq p_1 - r_1 \qquad \text{(the player does not ask for more than } M\text{)}$$

Combining these inequalities, we see that

$$M = r_2 - r_1 \geq p_1 - p_2$$

Thus the difference between what the player asks for and what the team offers is a lower bound on the actual amount of money on the table. If each side is demanding all the gains from trade, then the difference between their announced prices is M.

The difference between the two announced prices can be substantial. The largest difference between announced prices after the 1993 season was $1.9 million. The Texas Rangers were offering their star slugger (and American League home run champion), Juan Gonzalez, $3 million, and he was asking for $4.9 million. From the difference between these prices, we can infer that there was at least $1.9 million on the table.

If the owner is more risk averse than the player, and particularly if the owner is risk averse and the player is risk neutral, then the player will tend toward a more extreme demand. To put Gonzalez's number into perspective, it is a lot less than the $6 million that Ron Gant of the Atlanta Braves was asking for, even though Gonzalez hit 10 more home runs. Typical evidence at the arbitration hearings involves comparable worth, and these two ball players, both outfielders, are quite comparable. At any rate, it is clear that if Gonzalez wins at arbitration, he will get the lion's share of the gains. The largest amount asked for in arbitration was Jack McDowell's $6.5 million. McDowell, Cy Young Award–winning pitcher for the Chicago White Sox, was offered $5.3 million by the team. Pitchers, since they do not play every day, on average earn less than everyday players, such as outfielders.

The owners won twice as often as the players in 1992, but 18 cases is too small a sample for testing a statistical hypothesis. However, if we use the entire data set for the period 1974–92, we get a pretty large sample. Of the 358 cases that went to arbitration during these years, the owners won 198, or 55.3%. If both sides were risk neutral in linear probability arbitration, we would expect the owners to win 50% of the cases. With a sample this large, the difference between 50% and 55.3% is statistically significant. There is no evidence to suggest that the arbitrators are unfair (using an asymmetrical probability function). One explanation is that the players who go to arbitration are less risk averse than are the owners. In most cases, the teams are offering the players big raises anyway. Of the 100 players who filed after the 1993 season, 98 were being offered raises by their teams. According to this explanation, the players are willing to ask for somewhat larger salaries, even if it means the odds are somewhat against them.

Jack McDowell lost his arbitration hearing in February 1994. He will be paid only $5.3 million for the 1994 season. Ironically, McDowell won at arbitration the previous season, earning $4 million for 1993. He will have to settle for his 32.5% raise for 1994. In baseball arbitration, sometimes you win and sometimes you lose.

▚ SUMMARY

1. In certain well-defined situations, failure to reach agreement means that players can go to arbitration. The arbitrator supplies an agreement for them.

2. In conventional arbitration, the two sides make offers to the arbitrator, who then comes back with a settlement based on the two offers. For instance, the arbitrator can split the difference between the two offers.

3. Interest arbitration involves a sum of money on the table in the event a contract is agreed on. In grievance arbitration, there is an existing contract and the question is whether it has been breached or not.

4. In split-the-difference arbitration, each side has a dominant strategy to ask for all the money on the table.

5. In grievance arbitration, the arbitrator averages the evidence brought to the hearing by the two sides.

6. Grievance arbitration has three kinds of sequential equilibrium, depending on the costs of arbitration. When arbitration costs are low, then only strong cases are filed and contested. When arbitration costs are high, all cases are filed and none are contested.

7. Although modeled as payoff functions, arbitrators are real people. The typical arbitrator in the United States is a lawyer with many years' experience. Arbitrators earn about $500 per day per case, even if there is a million dollars at stake.

8. In final offer arbitration, each side makes a single offer, and the arbitrator picks one of the two offers.

9. A linear probability arbitrator in final offer arbitration penalizes extreme offers with a small chance of winning. The equilibrium asks of such arbitration are lower, the more risk-averse players are.

10. Major League Professional Baseball uses final offer arbitration. The owners win about 55% of the time, suggesting that players who reach arbitration are less risk averse than the owners are.

KEY TERMS

arbitration	grievance arbitration
mediation	permanent arbitration
conventional arbitration	Trilogy cases
interest arbitration	final offer arbitration
split-the-difference arbitration	linear probability arbitrator
random arbitrator	Major League Professional Baseball

PROBLEMS

1. Show that split-the-difference arbitration satisfies efficiency, linearity, non-imposition, and symmetry.

2. Suppose that player 1 in the game of Figure 13.2 is risk averse, with $u_1(m_1) = \sqrt{m_1}$. Solve the game. Does strategic behavior change? Why or why not?

3. Suppose that in the game of Figure 13.3, player 1 is risk averse, as in problem 2. Redo the normal form and solve. Does strategic behavior change? Why or why not?

4. Here is an amended form of split-the-difference arbitration to punish extreme demands. The arbitrator announces that if any player asks for more than 75% of the money on the table, the other player will automatically be awarded what he or she asks for. If both players ask for more than 75% of the money on the table, the arbitrator pays $M/2$ each. Otherwise, the arbitrator splits the difference. What is the equilibrium of this form of arbitration?

5. Fill in the details in the arguments for cases 2 and 3 of sequential equilibrium in conventional grievance arbitration. Do all three cases of equilibrium reveal some of the information held privately by the two sides?

6. What is permanent arbitration? Explain why two sides to a long-term labor contract might opt for permanent arbitration. Use the theory of repeated games (if it applies) in your answer.

7. In final offer arbitration with $1 million on the table and a linear probability arbitrator, player 1 is risk neutral and player 2 is risk averse, with $u_2(\text{cash}) = (\text{cash})^{0.6}$. Find the equilibrium. What are the probabilities that each will win?

8. In final offer arbitration with $1 million on the table and a linear probability arbitrator, both players are risk averse and both have the exact same attitude toward risk: $u_i(a_i) = a_i^{0.5}$. Find the best ask for each player and show that this ask is closer to $500,000 than the asks for the players in problem 7 would be.

9. What would you expect to happen in final offer arbitration if one side is risk averse and the other side is risk seeking? Give an example to support your contention.

10. Suppose that in Major League Professional Baseball arbitration, you observe the players win 100 cases and the owners win 200 cases. What would you conclude? (There may be more than one explanation here.)

CHAPTER 14

n-Person Bargaining and the Core

The bargaining and arbitration games studied so far have had exactly two sides, the two players. This is fairly restrictive. In many real-world cases, there are more than two sides in a bargaining game. For instance, there may be hundreds of creditors involved in a bankruptcy game. In the G-7 talks among the United States and its allies, seven sides are represented. This chapter looks at bargaining when more than two sides are involved.

First, the basic model of a bargaining game is extended to accommodate three or more players. Each of the players in an *n*-person bargaining game has a *veto*, that is, any player can kill any proposed agreement by refusing to agree. A function, called the coalition function, is introduced to represent such a game. The Nash bargaining solution and the Kalai–Smorodinsky bargaining solution for *n*-player bargaining games are studied next. These two solution concepts are applied to *n*-player bankruptcy games, and the differences are highlighted. The biggest single bankruptcy case in history, that of the Bank of

Credit and Commerce International (BCCI), is described. This ongoing case involves 73 countries and a million depositors in a bankruptcy game. If some or all of the players lack a veto, then bargaining becomes much more complicated. In particular, coalitions with fewer than all players may still be able to reach valuable agreements on the side. The bargaining game solution concept that captures this notion is the *core*. A bargain is in the core if no coalition can create a better deal for itself relying only on its own strategies. The core may be empty. A sufficient condition for the core to exist in a 3-person game is given. The core is very useful in studying issues of defense economics, especially alliance formation and burden sharing within an alliance. These ideas are illustrated with a study of peace plans for the latest Balkan war, Bosnian Peace Plans.

14.1 *n*-Person Bargaining Games

In the bargaining and arbitration games of the last two chapters, there were exactly two sides, two players. This chapter studies what happens if there are more than two sides, more than two players. The set of players is $N = \{1, 2, \ldots, n\}$, which contains n players in all. Just as in 2-person bargaining, in **n-person bargaining** there is a sum of money, M, at stake and each player i can ask for part of the money, a_i. Let $\mathbf{a} = (a_1, a_2, \ldots, a_n)$ be a vector of asks, and suppose for now that all players are risk neutral. If the sum of all the asks does not exceed the money on the table, then each player gets what he or she asked for; otherwise, no one gets anything. The payoff function for a typical player i, $u_i(\mathbf{a})$, is

$$u_i(\mathbf{a}) = a_i \qquad \text{if } \Sigma a_i \leq M$$
$$0 \qquad \text{if } \Sigma a_i > M$$

The efficient division line for the *n*-person bargaining game is

$$\Sigma a_i = M$$

Any vector of asks that exhausts the money on the table is efficient. Substituting the utility functions into the efficient division line gives us the efficient payoff line:

$$\Sigma u_i = M$$

A payoff is efficient if it exhausts all the money on the table.

Equilibria for the *n*-person bargaining game have precisely the same nature as those for the 2-person bargaining game. First, there are efficient equilibria of the form

$$\Sigma a_i^* = M$$

which also satisfy the boundary condition $a_i^* \geq 0$. In a bargaining game, it is a strategic mistake to ask for less than zero—you very well might get exactly what you asked for. Such a strategy is dominated by asking for zero, $a_i^* = 0$. There are also inefficient equilibria, where everyone gets zero. To construct an inefficient equilibrium, you only need two players, each of whom asks for all the money. Then, no matter what the other $n - 2$ players ask for, there is no agreement and everyone gets the payoff 0. Even if one of the greedy players were to reduce the demand all the way to zero, it would not raise the payoff. These two classes of equilibria come together at the vectors $\mathbf{a} = (M,0,\ldots,0)$, $\mathbf{a} = (0,M,\ldots,0)$, and so on, where the equilibrium is efficient but one greedy player gets all the money on the table.

This *n*-person bargaining game, like the 2-person bargaining game with all risk-neutral players, is symmetrical. Thus its solution is symmetrical. In this case, risk dominance requires that the product of utilities be maximal. Since the maximum product of utilities occurs along the efficient payoff line, the solution of the game is efficient. Symmetry and efficiency together imply that the solution of the bargaining game occurs when each player asks for an equal share of the money on the table:

$$a_i^* = \frac{M}{n} = u_i$$

In a symmetrical bargaining game, an efficient agreement is reached and every player comes out the same.

There is a special interpretation of this result when $M = 1$, which deserves our attention. Interpret $M = 1$ as the amount of political power to be shared among the n players. Next, suppose that every player has **veto power,** that is, the ability to derail any proposal by simply voting against it. Then the bargaining game solution represents *power-sharing*—each player in the power game has $1/n$ of the political power available. An example of such a polity is the European Union (EU). On very serious matters, like the Treaty of Maastricht, each of the 12 member countries has a veto. This is a 12-player bargaining game, where each of the players is a member country. Denmark alone could stop the treaty, simply by voting no—which, until the referendum of May 1993, is exactly what it did. In this game, Denmark, with 8 million inhabitants, has the same power as Germany, with 80 million. Polities where every player has a veto are heavily weighted toward the status quo—you have to build the biggest possible tent to get *everyone* in it.

The bargaining game solution just given is a special case of the Nash bargaining solution for *n*-person games. This solution and the Kalai–Smorodinsky bargaining solutions are reviewed in the next section.

14.2 Solutions for *n*-Person Bargaining Games in Coalition Function Form ■■■■■■■■■■■■■■■■■■

Let's begin with the bargaining game where n risk-neutral players are bargaining over M dollars. In the event of disagreement, the outcome of the game is

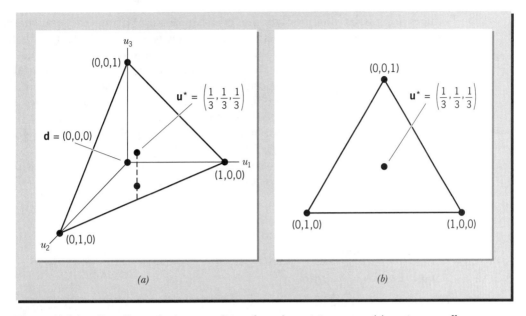

Figure 14.1. Payoff tetrahedron, coalition form bargaining game: (*a*) entire payoff set; (*b*) efficient set.

the disagreement point

$$\mathbf{d} = (d_1, d_2, \ldots, d_n)$$

Since the players are risk neutral, the efficient division line is

$$\Sigma u_i = M$$

The efficient division line and the disagreement point constitute the representation of the game in coalition form.

The Nash bargaining solution for 2 players generalizes to *n* players in an obvious way. Define the **Nash product** as the product of utility gains over disagreement:

$$\text{Nash product} = \Pi \ (u_i - d_i)$$

Nash bargaining solution **u*** is the outcome that maximizes the Nash product over all available bargains. Since the Nash product is increasing in each of its arguments, the maximum occurs on the efficient division plane.

We can gain insight into the *n*-person Nash bargaining solution by looking at the case of three bargainers, which can be studied graphically. Suppose that $M = 1$ and $\mathbf{d}$ = the vector of zeroes. Figure 14.1 shows the payoff tetrahedron representing this bargaining game. This tetrahedron has vertices at the disagreement point $\mathbf{d} = (0,0,0)$, as well as at the best agreements for each of the parties, $(1,0,0)$, $(0,1,0)$, and $(0,0,1)$, respectively. This coalition function form is shown in Figure 14.1*a*. Since the Nash bargaining solution is efficient, it suffices to restrict attention to the efficient division plane, the equilateral triangle atop the coalition function form, which is enlarged in Figure 14.1*b*. The vectors on the boundary of this triangle have at least one component equal to zero, so that the Nash product on the boundary is zero. In the interior of the triangle, the Nash product is positive. Given that the disagreement point is positive, the maximum Nash product occurs at the median of the triangle, the vector $(1/3,1/3,1/3)$, with the Nash product $= (1/3)^3 = 1/27$. Figure 14.1 also shows the indifference curve for the Nash product equal to 0.03, which goes through the vector $(5/12,2/12,5/12)$, among others.

We can always find the Nash bargaining solution using calculus. When the disagreement point is the zero vector, we maximize

$$\max \Pi \ u_i$$

subject to $\Sigma u_i = M$. One way to solve a calculus problem like this is to use Lagrange's multiplier. Form the Lagrange function L, given by

$$L = \Pi \ u_i + \lambda \ (\Sigma u_i - M)$$

The Lagrange function depends on the vector of utilities **u** as well as on the multiplier λ, $L(\mathbf{u},\lambda)$. The maximum Nash product occurs where the first derivatives of the Lagrange function all vanish:

$$0 = \frac{\partial L}{\partial u_i} = u_1 u_2 \ldots u_{i-1} u_{i+1} \ldots u_n + \lambda \quad \text{for each } i$$

$$0 = \frac{\partial L}{\partial \lambda} = \Sigma u_i - M$$

The last equation simply requires that the Nash bargaining solution be efficient. We can solve the n first-order condition involving products of utility as follows. First note that each product of $n - 1$ utilities equals the negative Lagrange multiplier

$$-\lambda = u_1 u_2 \ldots u_{i-1} u_{i+1} \ldots u_n \quad \text{for each player } i$$

Taking two adjacent players, such as player 1 and player 2, this condition implies that:

$$u_2 u_3 \ldots u_n = u_1 u_3 \ldots u_n$$

Since none of the utilities can be zero if we are at a maximum, we get

$$u_2 = u_1$$

Players 1 and 2 get the same payoff. Repeating the argument for any pair of players i and j, we get

$$u_i = u_j$$

Now call this common utility u_i^* and substitute into the efficient division plane. The result is

$$0 = nu_i^* - M$$

or

$$u_i^* = \frac{M}{n}$$

This result is the same as that for this bargaining game in normal form, and it checks with the result for $n = 2$ players in Chapter 12. The Nash bargaining solution of the bargaining game in coalition form splits the gains equally, and it embodies the sufficient condition of risk dominance.

The Nash bargaining condition for n players satisfies bargaining efficiency, bargaining symmetry, linear invariance, and independence of irrelevant alternatives, just as it does for two players. We have just seen how it satisfies bargaining efficiency and symmetry. The following two examples illustrate how it satisfies linear invariance. First, suppose that M is given in dollars, $M = \$1$ million. The players split this amount equally. If there are 10 players, each gets $\$1$ million/10 = \$100,000. Now suppose that $M = 1.6$ million DM (German marks), an equivalent amount of money. The players split this amount equally, each getting 1.6 million DM/10 = 160,000 DM = \$100,000. This is linear invariance. We would get the same outcome if some players were paid in German marks and others were paid in dollars. As a second example of linear invariance, this time with respect to the disagreement point, suppose that $M = \$1$ million and disagreement means $\$0$ to every player except player 1, who gets $\$100,000$. We subtract this $\$100,000$ from the money on the table, since it really isn't money on the table. Player 1 does not walk away from this bargaining game with nothing. That leaves $\$900,000$ for the players to split evenly. If there are still 10 players, that leaves $\$900,000/10 = \$90,000$ for each player. Player 1 gets the $\$90,000$ gain plus the outside option of $\$100,000$, for a total of $\$190,000$. Notice that the resulting sum of $\$190,000 + 9(\$90,000) = \$1$ million exhausts the money on the table. This is precisely the answer you get if you maximize

$$\max \Pi \ (u_i - d_i) \qquad \text{for all } i$$
$$= \max \ (u_1 - 100{,}000) \Pi \ u_i \qquad \text{for all } i > 1$$

which you can check, using the Lagrange multiplier technique.

The Nash bargaining solution for n players also satisfies independence of irrelevant alternatives. The easiest way to see this is by an example. Figure 14.2 shows the efficient payoff triangle, together with the restriction that player 1's utility u_1 must be at least 0.25. This restriction cuts off a large chunk of the triangle, including the vertices $(0,0,1)$ and $(0,1,0)$. However, since it doesn't disturb the previous Nash bargaining solution at the median, that is still the solution. The Nash bargaining solution considers this lower bound of player 1's payoff irrelevant—although player 1 might consider it very relevant indeed.

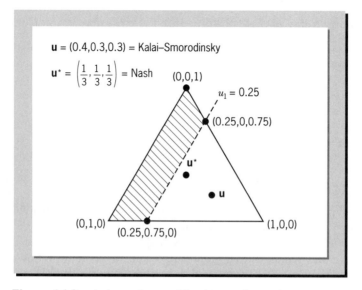

Figure 14.2.   Independence of irrelevant alternatives.

The next section shows how such restrictions can arise in the context of bankruptcy games.

We can just as easily extend the Kalai–Smorodinsky bargaining solution to *n* players. Suppose that the disagreement vector is **d,** each player *i* is risk neutral, and each player *i* has the right to ask for all the money on the table, $a_i = M_i = M$. Here M_i represents the largest payoff that player *i* could conceivably get from a bargain. Now draw the line from the disagreement point *d* to the **vector of maximal asks,** $(U_1, U_2, \ldots, U_n)$. The Kalai–Smorodinsky solution occurs where this line crosses the efficient payoff plane.

The Kalai–Smorodinsky solution doesn't require calculus to find, just geometry. When the disagreement point **d** is $(0,0, \ldots, 0)$, the amount on the table is *M* dollars, and each player has the right to ask for all the money, then the line between disagreement and maximal asks crosses the efficient payoff plane at the point $(M/3, M/3, M/3)$. This result occurs because the line between $(0,0,0)$ and (M,M,M) can be written parametrically as (s,s,s), where *s* is between 0 and *M*. The point (s,s,s) crosses the efficient payoff plane when $s + s + s = M$, or $s = M/3$. Hence this process yields the Kalai–Smorodinsky bargaining solution.

The Kalai–Smorodinsky bargaining solution satisfies bargaining symmetry and bargaining efficiency, as this result illustrates. The Kalai–Smorodinsky bargaining solution also satisfies linear invariance. Suppose that player *n* is paid in German marks and the other players are paid an equivalent amount in dollars. Now convert disagreement and maximum ask for player *n* into German marks:

$$d_n = 0 \qquad (\$0 = 0 \text{ in German marks})$$
$$M_n = 1.6M \qquad (\$M = 1.6M \text{ in German marks})$$

The line between $(0,0,0)$ and $(M,M,1.6M)$ is written parametrically as $(s,s,1.6s)$, where s is between 0 and M. The point $(s,s,1.6s)$ crosses the efficient payoff plane:

$$u_1 + u_2 + \frac{u_3}{1.6} = M$$

at the point $u_1 = u_2 = u_3 = M/3$, just as before.

The Kalai–Smorodinsky bargaining solution also satisfies monotonicity. If the efficient payoff plane moves out in a player's direction, that player cannot lose as a result. At worst, the payoff will remain the same because the shift did not affect where the line between disagreement and the maximal ask vector hit the efficient payoff plane. In every other case, the payoff will go up.

However, the Kalai–Smorodinsky bargaining solution continues to violate independence of irrelevant alternatives—just as the Nash bargaining solution continues to violate monotonicity. Consider the game in Figure 14.2 from the standpoint of the Kalai–Smorodinsky bargaining solution. Players 2 and 3 can ask at most 0.75, since player 1 is guaranteed at least 0.25. Player 1 can still ask for all the money on the table. The vector of maximal asks is $(0.75,0.75,1)$. Disagreement is $(0,0,0)$. We can write the line between these two points parametrically as $(s,0.75s,0.75s)$, where s is between 0 and 1. This line crosses the efficient payoff plane at

$$s + 0.75s + 0.75s = 1$$

or $s = .4$. The Kalai–Smorodinsky bargaining solution is $(0.4,0.3,0.3)$. This solution considers the lower bound on player 1's payoff to be quite relevant to the outcome. The Kalai–Smorodinsky bargaining solution violates independence of irrelevant alternatives—the even split is still available, but it is no longer the solution.

To get a Nash bargaining solution violation of monotonicity, start with the payoff plane $\Sigma u_i = 1$, whose Nash solution is $(1/3,1/3,1/3)$. Now take the vector $\mathbf{u} = (1/2,1/2,1/4)$ and add it to the feasible set. The Nash product of $(1/2,1/2,1/4)$ is $1/16$, which is greater than the Nash product of $(1/3,1/3,1/3) = 1/27$, the old solution. Thus, we now have a Nash solution of $(1/2,1/2,1/4)$. This solution violates monotonicity. We have added utility possibilities, but player 3's payoff has gone down.

The differences between these two bargaining solutions are quite pronounced when dealing with *n*-person bankruptcy games.

14.3 *n*-Person Bankruptcy Games ■■■■■■■■■■■■

This section focuses on *n*-person bankruptcy games for two reasons. First, bankruptcy occurs all the time in a modern capitalist economy and most bankruptcies involve many creditors. Second, bankruptcy games highlight the differences between the two major solution concepts for bargaining games.

Consider a set of n creditors, with claims on the bankrupt firm that can be ranked as follows:

$$C_1 < C_2 < \cdots < C_n$$

Claimant 1 has the smallest claim on the bankrupt firm; claimant n has the largest. The bankrupt firm has assets, A, which fall short of total claims:

$$A < \Sigma C_i$$

If the claimants can reach an agreement, they can divvy up all or part of the assets of the bankrupt firm. Otherwise, each claimant walks away from the proceedings empty-handed. Thus the disagreement point $\mathbf{d} = (0,0,\ldots,0)$.

As in the case of two players, the Nash bargaining solution creates a seniority system among the n creditors—even though all of them have equal seniority. Indeed, if one of the creditors, say, creditor 1, were truly senior to the rest, then that creditor would be paid off in full before any of the other creditors got so much as a penny out of the assets. In such a case, the coalition form of the game would consist of all the junior claimants, with the money on the table equal to what is left after the senior claim is paid off. This endogenous Nash bargaining solution seniority system directly generalizes the solution when there are two claimants.

We will work out the Nash bargaining solution to the bankruptcy game with three claimants in detail, leaving the more general cases as problems. As with two claimants, the solution is sensitive to how many assets A are at stake. There are three cases to consider, one case per claimant.

Case 1. There are very few assets relative to even the smallest creditor, $A < 3C_1$. The Nash bargaining solution treats all claimants equally. Each is paid the same, $A/3$.

Case 2. A exceeds this threshold, $3C_1 < A$, but not by too much: $A < C_1 + 2C_2$. The Nash bargaining solution treats the smallest claimant as senior and pays that claimant off in full. The remaining two claimants are paid equally from what is left. The solution is $\mathbf{u}^* = [C_1, (A - C_1)/2, (A - C_1)/2]$. This case is shown in Figure 14.3*a*.

Case 3. $C_1 + 2C_2 < A$. Once A exceeds this threshold, the Nash bargaining solution treats the two smallest claimants as senior and pays them off in full. The largest claimant gets what is left after the other claimants are paid off. The solution is $\mathbf{u}^* = (C_1, C_2, A - C_1 - C_2)$. This case is shown in Figure 14.3*b*.

The Nash solution easily generalizes to n claimants, using the following algorithm. See if you can pay all the claimants equally (case 1). If you cannot, because you are paying one or more of them too much, then pay off the smallest claimants in full. Divide the remainder of the proceeds equally among

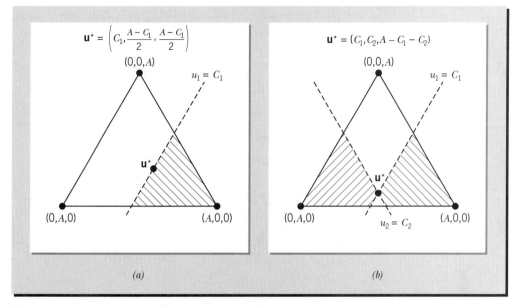

Figure 14.3. Bankruptcy, Nash bargaining solution, $n = 3$: (*a*) claimant 1 is senior; (*b*) claimants 1 and 2 are senior.

the remaining claimants. If no one is being paid more than the claim, stop. If at least one claimant is being paid more than the claim, pay that claimant off in full and divide the remainder among the remaining claimants. Complete this process until all assets have been exhausted.

This process of creating senior claims where none really exist is quite elegant, but it might strike the large claimants as rather arbitrary. After all, it means they are getting stuck with large losses whereas the small claimants get all their money back. Such is not the case with the Kalai–Smorodinsky solution. Every claimant is treated as equally senior in this solution. Nevertheless, we have to treat $n + 1$ cases—one more case than the number of players—because, if a player's claim is larger than the assets available, the most that player can ask for is all the assets. Let us consider the solution for $n = 3$ in detail.

Case 1. $A < C_1$. In this case, the vector of maximal asks is (A,A,A). The line between the disagreement point and (A,A,A) is given by (s,s,s), where s is between 0 and A. This line crosses the efficient payoff line when $s + s + s = A$, or $s = A/3$. The solution in this case is to pay all the claimants equally—since there is almost nothing left anyway.

Case 2. $C_1 < A < C_2$. In this case, claimant 1 is constrained to claim only what he or she is owed, and the other claimants are constrained by the available assets. The vector of maximal asks is (C_1,A,A). The line between the disagreement point and (C_1,A,A) is parameterized by $[(C_1/A)s,s,s]$, where s is between 0 and A. This line crosses the efficient payoff line when

$$\left(\frac{C_1}{A}\right)s + s + s = A$$

Solving, we get $s = A^2/(C_1 + 2A)$. The resulting solution is

$$\mathbf{u}^* = \left(\frac{C_1 A}{(C_1 + 2A)}, \frac{A^2}{(C_1 + 2A)}, \frac{A^2}{(C_1 + 2A)}\right)$$

The smallest claimant gets rationed according to the claim.

Case 3. $C_2 < A < C_3$. In this case, both claimant 1 and claimant 2 are constrained to claim only what is owed them, and the remaining claimant is constrained by the available assets. The vector of maximal asks is (C_1,C_2,A). The line between the disagreement point and the vector of maximal asks is parameterized by $[(C_1/A)s,(C_2/A)s,s]$. This line crosses the efficient payoff line when

$$\left(\frac{C_1}{A}\right)s + \left(\frac{C_2}{A}\right)s + s = A$$

Solving, we get $s = A^2/(C_1 + C_2 + A)$ The resulting solution is

$$\mathbf{u}^* = \left[\frac{C_1 A}{(C_1 + C_2 + A)}, \frac{C_2 A}{(C_1 + C_2 + A)}, \frac{A^2}{(C_1 + C_2 + A)}\right]$$

The smallest two claimants get rationed according to their claims.

Case 4. $C_3 < A$. In this case, all claimants are constrained to claim only what is owed them. The vector of maximal asks is simply the vector of claims (C_1, C_2, C_3). The line between the disagreement point and the vector of maximal asks is parameterized by $[(C_1/A)s,(C_2/A)s,(C_3/A)s]$, where s is between 0 and A. This line crosses the efficient payoff line when

$$\left(\frac{C_1}{A}\right)s + \left(\frac{C_2}{A}\right)s + \left(\frac{C_3}{A}\right)s = A$$

Solving, we get $s = A^2/(C_1 + C_2 + C_3)$. The resulting solution is

$$\mathbf{u}^* = \left[\frac{C_1 A}{(C_1 + C_2 + C_3)}, \frac{C_2 A}{(C_1 + C_2 + C_3)}, \frac{C_3 A}{(C_1 + C_2 + C_3)}\right]$$

All three claimants get rationed according to their claim. This particular formula is often used by courts to apportion claims of equal seniority.

The Kalai–Smorodinsky solution to the bankruptcy game readily generalizes to n claimants. The only thing you need to keep track of is the relationship of assets to the sizes of the various claims. Once assets exceed even the largest claim, then the proportional rationing formula, where each claimant i gets a share of the assets proportional to the share of total claims $(C_i/\Sigma C_i)$ yields the

Kalai–Smorodinsky solution. We now turn to the largest bankruptcy case in history, unfolding right before our very eyes, and involving thousands of players.

▪▪ 14.4 The Bank of Credit and Commerce International Goes Bust[1] ▪▪▪▪▪▪▪▪▪▪▪▪▪▪▪▪▪

In 1972, a Pakistani banker, Agha Hasan Abedi, founded the Bank of Credit and Commerce International (**BCCI**) in Abu Dhabi, a part of the United Arab Emirates. The principal investors in the new bank were the billionaire ruler of Abu Dhabi, Sheikh Zayed, and the Bank of America, then the largest bank in the United States. The next year, BCCI opened its first branch office in London. Although incorporated in Luxembourg, the London office served as BCCI's headquarters in the ensuing decades. By the end of 1973, BCCI had assets totaling $200 million and had launched an aggressive program of international expansion and joint ventures. Four years later the bank had assets exceeding $2.2 billion and was regarded as the fastest growing bank in the United Kingdom. The expansion and growth continued unabated until, at the height of its power at the end of 1988, BCCI had branches in 73 countries and assets in excess of $20 billion. This made it one of the world's largest privately held banks.

One of the bank's principal objectives from the outset was to penetrate the U.S. market. Foreign banks operating inside the United States must meet a wide array of state and federal rules and regulations, including scrutiny by the Federal Reserve Board. Already in 1975, New York state banking officials had denied BCCI permission to acquire Chelsea National Bank in New York City. Soon thereafter, Bank of America, troubled by BCCI's operations, suspended all further investment in the bank and began liquidating its entire holdings in the bank, a process completed in 1980. BCCI next tried to acquire the National Bank of Georgia, closely associated with Bert Lance, director of the Office of Management and Budget in the Carter administration. This transaction ran afoul of a Securities and Exchange Commission lawsuit and was canceled in 1978. BCCI was represented in this case (which was settled out of court) by Clark Clifford, one of Washington's premier lawyers and secretary of defense during the Vietnam War. Thus began a long association between BCCI and its agents, Lance and Clifford.

Finally, in 1981, a group of Arab investors received government permission to acquire Financial General Bankshares (FGB), with the proviso that BCCI would have no involvement whatsoever in the affairs of FGB. The fact that the

[1]Material for this study was drawn from Peter Truell and Larry Gurwin, *False Profits: The Inside Story of BCCI, the World's Most Corrupt Financial Empire* (Boston and New York: Houghton Mifflin, 1992).

Arab investors were heavily involved in BCCI was not reported to regulators. FGB changed its name to First American Bankshares, with Clifford as its chairman and Clifford's law partner, Robert Altman, as a member of the board. BCCI eventually acquired the National Bank of Georgia and opened branches around the country.

BCCI was never run on what could be called conventional banking principles. Although Abedi spoke of the bank as an institution committed to investing in the development of the poor countries of the world, the bank did not invest in Third World development. Instead, it invested in political support in the host countries (roughly $8 million was donated to ex-President Carter's favorite charities during the 1980s, for instance). The list of world leaders and tyrants who banked with BCCI, led by Manual Noriega and Saddam Hussein, is impressive. Often BCCI proffered loans to political figures without any intention of ever collecting on them. BCCI met its interest payments to existing depositors with the proceeds of new deposits—the classic Ponzi scheme of banking.

BCCI's unconventional banking practices did not go unnoticed by regulators and auditors. As early as 1978, the comptroller of the currency of the United States reported serious irregularities that could pose grave dangers to the financial health of the bank. These irregularities did not improve with time. In 1987, as part of a federal investigation of drug-money laundering, an undercover U.S. customs agent began banking at BCCI's Tampa branch. Indictments came down a few months later, and convictions were returned in the summer of 1990. However, any profits BCCI made from its drug-money laundering operations weren't showing up on the bottom line. BCCI reported losses of around $500 million for 1989, followed by layoffs of 30% of its employees worldwide. In an attempt to keep the bank afloat, Sheikh Zayed injected new capital into the bank, bringing his ownership position to 77%. The bank was unwilling to allow British authorities to inspect its books, preferring instead to move its headquarters from London to the United Arab Emirates in 1990. Depositors, sensing trouble, began to withdraw their deposits from the bank.

On July 5, 1991, regulators in the United States, the United Kingdom, and several other countries shut down BCCI operations in their countries. Three days later, Luxembourg determined that BCCI had lost more than its entire net worth in 1990 alone, which is what precipitated the infusion of new capital by Sheikh Zayed. Indictments were handed down later that month in both federal district court and New York state court, charging violations of federal and state banking law—in particular, illegal acquisition of banks in the United States. So far, however, no one has been convicted in federal or state court of any wrongdoing.

When BCCI was shut down, about half its depositors had already retrieved their money. Almost $10 billion in deposits remains to be covered. Of the $10 billion in assets needed to satisfy these claims, approximately $9.5 billion is missing, which leaves about $0.5 billion to cover the claims. If there were an international arena in which to play the ensuing bankruptcy game, then the 73 countries in which BCCI operated might bargain over what is left and then distribute the resulting proceeds among their depositors. As it turns out, there is no such international arena (the United Nations and the World Court don't handle such cases), so each individual country must proceed on its own. The depositors in an individual country are the claimants for whatever BCCI assets can be seized in that country.

Citizens of the United States are fortunate, to the extent that BCCI did not conduct commercial banking operations here. Where it did, such as in the United Kingdom, depositors stand to lose most, if not all, of their money. Even in the United States, though, the indirect costs of BCCI are substantial. For instance, one of the biggest failures in the S&L scandal, CenTrust Savings Bank, was a big customer of BCCI. For those unlucky enough to have put their money in BCCI and not have taken it out, the future looks grim indeed. Five cents on the dollar (or a little more) is what these depositors are looking at when the books finally close on BCCI.

▚ 14.5 The Coalition Function When Intermediate Coalitions Have Power ■■■■■■■■■■■■■■■■■■■■

One hallmark of bargaining games, whether they have two players or n players, is that any player can stop any deal. Every player has a veto. The minute that some or all players lack a veto, then groups of players, called coalitions, may be able to walk away from the bargaining table with money, even in the absence of an agreement. A **coalition** is any group of players. An **intermediate coalition** in an n-person game has from 2 to $n - 1$ players. A coalition with a single player is called a **singleton.** A coalition consisting of all n players is called a **grand coalition.** This section studies games where intermediate coalitions can negotiate their own side agreements if they choose.

First we need a bit of set notation. Coalitions are sets of players. Let S represent a coalition in an n-player game. The grand coalition in this game is $N = \{1, 2, \ldots, n\}$. A singleton is denoted $S = \{1\}$ if player 1 is alone, $\{2\}$ if player 2 is alone, and so on. $S = \{1, 2\}$ is an intermediate coalition, consisting of players 1 and 2. As a real-world example, NATO is a coalition consisting of 13 countries. Let $N =$ NATO. Within NATO, there are various groupings. For instance, the set $S = \{$Belgium, Netherlands, Luxembourg$\}$ represents the coalition of the low countries. The set $S = \{$United States, Canada$\}$ represents the NATO countries in North America. For any given S, the set $N - S$ represents the members of N who do not belong to S. For $S = \{$United States, Canada$\}$, the set $N - S$ is the set of 11 NATO countries that are in Europe.

In the rest of the chapter, it is assumed that all players are risk neutral. The *coalition function* then shows how much money the members of a given coalition can guarantee themselves if they walk away from the bargaining table. The coalition function, written $v(S)$, associates to every coalition S the guaranteed value of its side agreement.

The coalition function of a bargaining game with M dollars on the table and disagreement point $\mathbf{d}$ = the zero vector is easy to write down. First, the only coalition that can walk away from the table with any guaranteed money is the grand coalition, so we have

$$v(N) = M$$

If any other coalition walks away from the table, it does so empty-handed:

$$v(S) = 0, \text{ for } S \neq N$$

What $v(N) = M$ means is that the members of N can divide up the M dollars on the table any way they choose:

$$M = v(N) = \Sigma u_i, \text{ where } i \text{ is in } N$$

Thus, $v(N)$ is shorthand for the efficient payoff line. Similarly, $v(S) = 0$ means that the members of N can divide up \$0 on the table any way they choose:

$$0 = v(S) = \Sigma u_i, \text{ where } i \text{ is in } S$$

Thus, $v(S)$ is shorthand for the disagreement point as it applies to each coalition S not equal to the grand coalition.

Now suppose that the disagreement point $\mathbf{d}$ is not the zero vector, but some other vector. In this event, intermediate coalitions can walk away from the table with their disagreement values. If player 1 walks away from the table, he or she gets $v(\{1\}) = d_1$. If players 1 and 2 walk away from the table together, they get $v(\{1,2\}) = d_1 + d_2$. In general, a coalition S walking away from the table will get

$$v(S) = \Sigma d_i, \text{ where } i \text{ is in } S$$

We can convert a bargaining game with a nonzero disagreement point into a bargaining game with a zero disagreement point via the following trick. Transform every player's utility in the following way:

$$u_i' = u_i - d_i$$

Simply subtract every player's disagreement value from that player's utility. In the new utility coordinates,

$$v'(S) = \Sigma u_i' = \Sigma(u_i - d_i) = 0, \text{ where } i \text{ is in } S$$
$$v'(N) = \Sigma u_i' = \Sigma(u_i - d_i) = M - \Sigma d_i, \text{ where } i \text{ is in } N$$

The players take their disagreement values from the money on the table and bargain over what is left. So, in any bargaining game, intermediate coalitions still play no role.[2]

In the game **Majority Rule,** intermediate coalitions play a manifest role. There are three players, $N = \{1,2,3\}$; $v(N) = 1$, meaning that the grand

---

[2]This conclusion remains true if players have attitudes toward risk different from risk neutrality.

coalition can achieve 100% political power (this is one way of expressing the notion of popular sovereignty, if N is equal to the people, or Rousseau's notion of the general will); $v(\{i\}) = 0$; any singleton is powerless; and $v(S) = 1$, if S has two members. In a 3-player polity a coalition with two members is a majority, and under majority rule a majority can take 100% of the power. Majority Rule can be played with any number of players n. In the general case, its coalition function is

$v(S) = 0$, if S is not a majority, but is a minority or exactly $\frac{1}{2} N$

$v(S) = 1$, if S is a majority

Of course, what is used to measure size is important. Under the principle of one person, one vote, each player counts the same. Under the principle of one share, one vote, each share of voting stock counts the same.

A second example of a game in which intermediate coalitions matter is drawn straight from the market. Suppose that players 1, 2, and 3 are firms in the telecommunications industry. Any firm going it alone earns a normal rate of return ($u_i = 0$). If firms 1 and 2 form a joint venture, they earn an above-normal rate of return, $v(\{1,2\}) = 0.15$. Similar opportunities await firms 1 and 3 ($v(\{1,3\}) = 0.10$) and firms 2 and 3 $v(\{2,3\}) = 0.05$. If all three firms form a joint venture, the earnings are again above normal, $v(\{1,2,3\}) = 0.15$. Any time you see a joint venture consisting of exactly two firms—like MCI and BT in Chapter 12—you are seeing a game in which intermediate coalitions matter.

We can adapt the triangle diagram for bargaining games to this game, as in Figure 14.4. The corners of the triangle represent maximum utility for each of the three firms in the game. The line $v(\{1,2\}) = 0.15$ shows the various ways in which firms 1 and 2 can divide up their above-normal profits should they form a joint venture. Similarly, $v(\{1,3\}) = 0.10$ and $v(\{2,3\}) = 0.05$ show the same thing for those coalitions. Once the number of firms exceeds three, it is hard to depict the coalition function—but we can still study such games using systems of inequalities.

Once intermediate coalitions have value, solving a game becomes much more difficult. There are so many more aspects to take into consideration. How will this or that coalition react to a proposal? Can some coalition upset an agreement? Which coalitions are likely to form, and which are unlikely to form? We will now turn to a solution concept that tackles such questions.

14.6 The Core of a Game in Coalition Function Form ■

A bargain has to have something to offer to everybody at the table. Suppose that some individual or group S is contemplating walking away from the

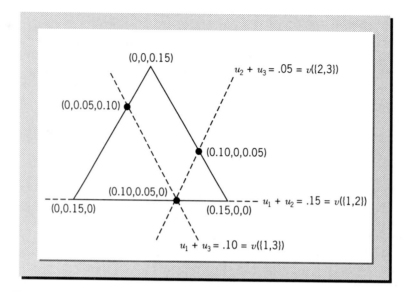

Figure 14.4.   Joint venture, coalition function form.

bargaining table. If the players walk away from the table and make their own side agreement, it is worth $v(S)$ to them. If the proposal on the table is worth at least that much to them, then they don't gain by walking out. Such a proposal should appeal to them—it definitely has something to offer them. A proposal is in the **core** of a game in coalition function form when it has something to offer every possible coalition.

Let $\mathbf{u} = (u_1, u_2, \ldots, u_n)$ be a proposal on the table. In order to have something to offer every coalition, this proposal must satisfy $2^n - 1$ inequalities of the following sort:

$v(S) \leq \Sigma u_i$, where i is in S

There are $2^n - 1$ inequalities because that is how many different coalitions can be formed from a group of n members. One of these inequalities is actually an equality:

$v(N) = \Sigma u_i$, where i is in N

With at most M dollars on the table, everybody involved can get no more than M dollars if they all walk away from the table.

This system of inequalities may or may not have a solution. There is an existence problem for the core, just as there is an existence problem for equilibrium. We will see what large classes of games in coalition function form, including market games, matching games, and bankruptcy games, have solutions in the core. The game Joint Ventures has a unique solution in the core. There are $2^3 - 1 = 7$ inequalities that have to be satisfied:

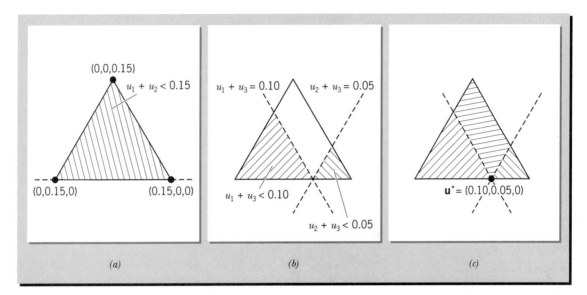

Figure 14.5. Joint Venture, core: (a) coalition ({1,2}); (b) coalitions ({1,3}) and ({2,3}); (c) core.

$$v(\{1\}) = 0 \leq u_1$$
$$v(\{2\}) = 0 \leq u_2$$
$$v(\{3\}) = 0 \leq u_3$$
$$v(\{1,2\}) = 0.15 \leq u_1 + u_2$$
$$v(\{1,3\}) = 0.10 \leq u_1 + u_2$$
$$v(\{2,3\}) = 0.05 \leq u_2 + u_3$$
$$v(\{1,2,3\}) = 0.15 = u_1 + u_2 + u_3$$

Solving a large system of linear inequalities usually involves a machine. Fortunately, in this case we can see the solution graphically. Figure 14.5 reproduces Figure 14.4 with some new information. Note first of all that if a vector **u** lies in the triangle, it satisfies both the requirement that the individual payoffs be nonnegative and the requirement that the individual payoffs sum to .15. This leaves three inequalities to solve for. Take the inequality for the joint venture of firms 1 and 2, $v(\{1,2\}) = 0.15 \leq u_1 + u_2$. All the points on the base of the triangle have $u_1 + u_2 = 0.15$. Since firms 1 and 2 should not settle for less, this inequality eliminates all points in the triangle except along the base (Figure 14.5a). This elimination is reflected by the cross-hatching. The other two inequalities, involving the joint venture between firms 1 and 3 and the joint venture between firms 2 and 3, cross at the point of the triangle **u** = (0.10,0.05,0) (Figure 14.5b). Since this point is on the base of the triangle, it satisfies firms 1 and 2. Thus it satisfies all the inequalities. The proposal **u** = (0.10,0.05,0) is in the core of the game Joint Ventures (Figure 14.5c).

This proposal is the only one in the core. Since firms 1 and 2 together have to get a rate of return of .15, the situation between them is constant sum.

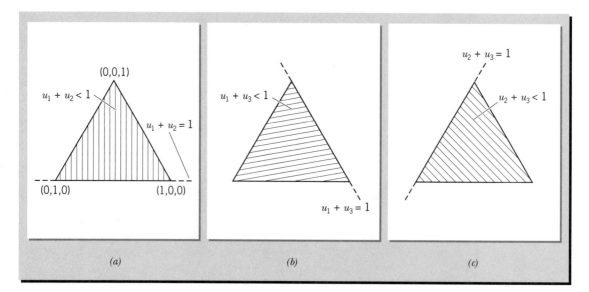

Figure 14.6. Majority Rule, empty core: (a) v ({2,2}); (b) v ({1,3}); (c) v ({2,3}).

Suppose that firm 1 got more than a 10% return, say, an 11% return. Firm 2 is only getting 4%. Then firm 2 could propose a joint venture with firm 3, offering firm 3 a 0.5% return and itself a 4.5% return. At this point, firms 2 and 3 could walk away from the table and be better off. So firm 1 can't get more than 10%. Similar reasoning shows that firm 1 can't get less than 10% either, since then it could walk away from the table with firm 3.

Majority Rule is an example of a game whose core is empty. Any proposal in the core of Majority Rule would have to satisfy the following inequalities:

$$v(\{1\}) = 0 \le u_1$$
$$v(\{2\}) = 0 \le u_2$$
$$v(\{3\}) = 0 \le u_3$$
$$v(\{1,2\}) = 1 \le u_1 + u_2$$
$$v(\{1,3\}) = 1 \le u_1 + u_2$$
$$v(\{2,3\}) = 1 \le u_2 + u_3$$
$$v(\{1,2,3\}) = 1 = u_1 + u_2 + u_3$$

These inequalities have no solution, as illustrated by Figure 14.6. Each of the inequalities for the 2-player coalitions require that the payoff lie on one side of the triangle. However, there is no point on the triangle that lies simultaneously on all three sides. Hence, Majority Rule does not have a core.

Games that lack cores can be quite turbulent. In Majority Rule, any proposal to share power can be upset by another proposal. If player 1 offers to share power equally with player 2, player 3 can upset this relationship by offering player 2 a larger share of the power, and so on. Some real-world polities using majority rule, such as Italy, exhibit just such instability. The instability can be avoided, or at least lessened, if certain coalitions cannot form for ideological reasons. For instance, suppose that player 1 represents the Left; player 2, the Center; and player 3, the Right of the political spectrum. Further, suppose (which is the case in Italy) that players at the opposite ends of the spectrum refuse to have anything to do with one another. Then the only coalitions that will share power in practice are {Left, Center} or {Center, Right}. The player at the Center will anchor each and every possible government, thereby providing stability.

There is an easy sufficient condition for a core in a 3-person game. Suppose that the disagreement point is zero and that the amount on the table is M dollars. We have the system of inequalities:

$$v(\{1\}) = 0 \le u_1$$
$$v(\{2\}) = 0 \le u_2$$
$$v(\{3\}) = 0 \le u_3$$
$$v(\{1,2\}) \le u_1 + u_2$$
$$v(\{1,3\}) \le u_1 + u_2$$
$$v(\{2,3\}) \le u_2 + u_3$$
$$v(\{1,2,3\}) = M = u_1 + u_2 + u_3$$

As we have just seen, the inequalities for individuals and the equality for the grand coalition are satisfied by the efficient payoff triangle. The three inequalities for the intermediate coalitions are crucial. Adding these three inequalities, we get

$$v(\{1,2\}) + v(\{1,3\}) + v(\{2,3\}) \le 2(u_1 + u_2 + u_3)$$

At the same time, the sum of all utilities must equal M. Substituting, we get

$$v(\{1,2\}) + v(\{1,3\}) + v(\{2,3\}) \le 2M$$

Basically, what this condition says is that if the intermediate coalitions do not have claims too large against the money on the table, then there is an outcome in the core.[3]

▚ 14.7 Sharing Defense Burdens ■ ■ ■ ■ ■ ■ ■ ■ ■ ■ ■ ■ ■ ■ ■

Chapter 15 studies the cores of market games and matching games. This section presents a game that arises in a nonmarket setting, in particular, among

---

[3]There is an elegant generalization of this condition for a nonempty core when there are n players. See Herbert Scarf, *The Computation of Economic Equilibria* (New Haven, Conn.: Yale University Press, 1973), for details.

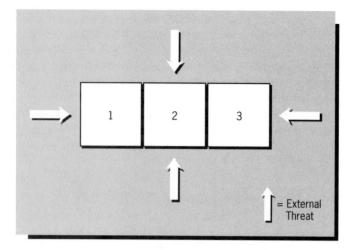

Figure 14.7.   Mutual Defense, physical situation.

the members of an international alliance. The game, called **Mutual Defense,** involves alliance formation against an external threat. Suppose that players 1, 2, and 3 are three countries situated as in Figure 14.7. Each country is one unit square, arrayed in a line with the others, and surrounded by external threats against which each wishes to defend. The cost of defending a country against a surrounding external threat is proportional to the perimeter of the area being defended. According to NATO doctrine, for instance, it takes one armored division to defend a front 20 miles long against hostile attack.

In Mutual Defense, a coalition is an alliance, and the coalition function $v(S)$ represents the cost of defending that alliance. If an alliance walks away from the bargaining table, it will have to defend itself. Suppose that it costs one unit to defend one side of a country. Then $v(\{1\}) = -4$, the cost of defending country 1 when it is by itself, and so on. The coalition function for the entire game is

$$v(\{1\}) = -4 \le u_1$$
$$v(\{2\}) = -4 \le u_2$$
$$v(\{3\}) = -4 \le u_3$$
$$v(\{1,2\}) = -6 \le u_1 + u_2$$
$$v(\{1,3\}) = -8 \le u_1 + u_2$$
$$v(\{2,3\}) = -6 \le u_2 + u_3$$
$$v(\{1,2,3\}) = -8 = u_1 + u_2 + u_3$$

The alliances {1,2}, {2,3}, and {1,2,3} all involve cost savings because they all involve adjacent states. When countries 1 and 2 form an alliance, neither of them has to defend against their common boundary. The United States–Canada alliance has saved an enormous amount in defense costs for both countries.

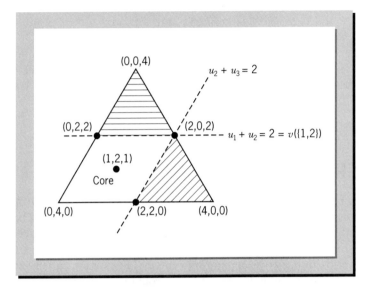

Figure 14.8. Mutual Defense, transformed payoffs, core.

For graphic purposes, it is convenient to transform the payoffs so that the disagreement point is zero. This can be accomplished by the transformation $u'_i = u_i + 4$. The coalition function that results is

$$v(\{1\}) = 0 \leq u'_1$$
$$v(\{2\}) = 0 \leq u'_2$$
$$v(\{3\}) = 0 \leq u'_3$$
$$v(\{1,2\}) = 2 \leq u'_1 + u'_2$$
$$v(\{1,3\}) = 0 \leq u'_1 + u'_2$$
$$v(\{2,3\}) = 2 \leq u'_2 + u'_3$$
$$v(\{1,2,3\}) = 4 = u'_1 + u'_2 + u'_3$$

The transformed coalition function values represent the cost savings available to the countries in a given alliance. For instance, if all three countries form an alliance, then they save four units of defense.

Mutual Defense always has proposals in the core, and usually many such proposals. Figure 14.8 shows the core of this version of Mutual Defense. Countries 1 and 2 can walk away from any proposal, such as (0,0,4), that does not offer them two units of cost savings. Countries 2 and 3 can likewise walk away from any proposal, such as (4,0,0), that does not offer them two units of cost savings. The remaining rhombus of proposals is the core. This is a lot of proposals, an entire convex set. Thus, the average of any two proposals in the core is itself a proposal in the core. In particular, the center of gravity of this rhombus $\mathbf{u} = (1,2,1)$ would strike many people as very appealing. It gives country 2 a bigger share of the cost savings, and without country 2 in the alliance, there aren't any costs to save.

Like any model of real life, Mutual Defense leaves out many of the complexities surrounding negotiations among members of an alliance or a projected alliance. Nevertheless, it gives us some insight into the latest Balkan war, 1991 to the present.

⊞ 14.8 Bosnian Peace Plans[4]   ■■■■■■■■■■■■■■■■

The area comprising present-day Bosnia has been a fault line through Europe for millennia. During the time of the Roman Empire, the language line separating the Latin-speaking empire to the west and the Greek-speaking empire to the east ran through this area. After Slavic-speaking peoples entered the area in the seventh century, the separation ceased. The current inhabitants of Bosnia all speak the same language, Serbo-Croation. However, the old language line survives in two forms. Croatian is written in the Latin alphabet and Croatia is predominantly Roman Catholic; Serbian is written in the Cyrillic alphabet and Serbia is predominantly Orthodox. When the Turks invaded Europe in the fifteenth century, their conquests included Byzantium in 1453, Serbia in 1489, and Bosnia soon thereafter.

For the next four centuries, Bosnia was part of the Ottoman Empire. During this period, a large minority of the population converted to Islam. As part of the rollback of the Turks from Europe, at the Congress of Berlin (1878) Serbia regained its independence and Bosnia was attached to the Austro-Hungarian Empire. It was in the capital of Bosnia, Sarajevo, that a Serbian nationalist assassinated the heir to the throne of Austria-Hungary, precipitating World War I. Bosnia became part of the southern Slavic confederation, Yugoslavia, after the war. That confederation began to crumble in 1991, with the secession of Slovenia and Croatia. This is a lot of history in a rather small place.

On the verge of its declaration of independence in 1992, Bosnia was a mosaic of three religions. Muslims were in the areas surrounding Sarajevo, which itself was ethnically mixed, as well as in the Bihac region. Croatians were centered around Mostar. Serbs were scattered in pockets around the rest of the country. Bosnia declared independence in the summer of 1992, and hostilities immediately broke out. Sarajevo is the military headquarters of the Muslims; Mostar, of the Croats; Pele, of the Serbs. The Bosnian Serbs, with military assistance from what remains of Yugoslavia (Serbia and Montenegro), made enormous gains in the ensuing fighting. At the outset of the fighting, Serbs controlled 45% of the territory; Muslims, 35%; Croats, 20%. At present, Serbs

---

[4]This material was informed in part by the trenchant analysis of John J. Mearsheimer and Robert A. Pope, "The Answer," *The New Republic,* June 14, 1993, pp 22–28.

Figure 14.9. Vance–Owen peace plan. (*Source:* from *The Wall Street Journal,* May 17, 1993, 12.)

control 64% of the territory; Croats, 25%, Muslims, 11%. The ferocity of the fighting rivals that of World War II. More than 130,000 people have died, and another 2 million have been displaced in this Balkan war.

In an effort to stop the fighting, representatives of the United States (Vance) and the United Kingdom (Owen) have proposed a **Bosnian peace plan** under the aegis of the UN (see Figure 14.9). The Vance–Owen plan would create a Bosnian confederation along ethnic lines, retaining the percentage of territory held by the combatants before the war. This plan has been accepted by the Croats (who break even, so to speak) and by the Muslims (who are losing the war badly). The Serbians have rejected the plan. Even if they weren't winning the war, accepting the plan would hand them an entity in three separate pieces, very costly to defend. Vance–Owen gives the Muslims a territory in two pieces, almost as costly to defend. Only the Croats come out of this plan with connected territory.

A peace plan is in the core only if it has something to offer everybody. A peace plan not in the core has no chance of acceptance: at least one of the parties will walk away from it. In addition, it is desirable for a peace plan to create viable entities. Otherwise, war may break out again before the ink on the plan is dry. A two-piece Muslim state in the midst of various Serbian territories hardly sounds like a recipe for lasting peace. As things now stand, however, there appears to be no peace plan that could possibly be in the core. The reasoning is as follows. Measure utility in terms of percentage of the country held. If the Serbs and Croats form a coalition, they can take over the country:

$$v(\{\text{Serb, Croat}\}) = 1$$

If the Croats and Muslims form a coalition, they can hold 35% of the country:

$$v(\{\text{Croat, Muslim}\}) = .35$$

If the Serbs and Muslims form a coalition, they can hold 90% of the country:[5]

$$v(\{\text{Serb, Muslim}\}) = .9$$

It should be noted that, at one or another time during the fighting, each of these alliances has existed, at least briefly. Finally, all three sides can hold 100% of the country:

$$v(\{\text{Serb, Croat, Muslim}\}) = v(N) = 1$$

The set of inequalities defining the core has no solution, since:

$$v(\{\text{Serb,Croat}\}) + v(\{\text{Croat,Muslim}\}) + v(\{\text{Serb,Muslim}\})$$
$$= 1 + .36 + .9 = 2.26 > 2v(N) = 2$$

There is no alternative in the core as things now stand. Meanwhile, both the peace talks and the war drag on. If game theory sometimes presents us with a grim calculus, this reflects the fact that sometimes the world we live in is a grim place.

◈ SUMMARY

1. In *n*-person bargaining there is a sum of money M at stake and each player i can ask for part of the money. Every player has to agree to a proposal before it is a deal. Any player can veto a deal. In the event of a veto, each player gets the disagreement payoff.

2. There are two kinds of equilibria, efficient and inefficient, for *n*-person bargaining games in normal form. The solution of such games is efficient. If the game is also symmetrical, then so is the solution.

---

[5]These numbers are based on battlefield capabilities, given that the current sanctions against former Yugoslovia and Bosnia remain in place and no great power intervenes.

3. There is a special interpretation for the bargaining game with one unit of value on the table. This unit can be interpreted as political power; the object of negotiations is then to share that power. When every player has a veto, power is shared equally.

4. The Nash and Kalai–Smorodinsky bargaining solutions generalize to n players. Even with n players, they retain their distinctive properties.

5. In the n-person bankruptcy game, the Nash bargaining solution creates senior rights, with the smallest creditor the most senior. In contrast, the Kalai–Smorodinsky bargaining solution treats all creditors proportionally.

6. BCCI, once the world's fastest-growing bank, is now the world's largest bankruptcy case. Depositors in 73 countries face the loss of almost 95% of their money in ongoing bankruptcy negotiations.

7. An intermediate coalition in an n-person game has from 2 to $n - 1$ players. A coalition with a single player is called a singleton. A coalition consisting of all n players is called a grand coalition.

8. When intermediate coalitions have value, bargaining is much more complicated. The coalition function expresses the value of intermediate coalitions.

9. A proposal is in the core when no coalition can do better by walking away from the bargaining table than by accepting the agreement. Being in the core means satisfying a set of linear inequalities. Not all games have nonempty cores.

10. The game Mutual Defense has a large core. This game is a model of savings in defense costs available to alliance partners.

11. The Vance–Owen peace plan is not in the core of the war game involving the Serbs, Croats, and Muslims of Bosnia. No peace plan is in the core under current conditions.

▚ KEY TERMS

n-person bargaining	singleton
veto power	grand coalition
Nash product	Majority Rule
vector of maximal asks	core
BCCI	Mutual Defense
coalition	Bosnian peace plan
intermediate coalition	

▚ PROBLEMS

1. There are three bargainers and $100 on the table. Bargainers 1 and 2 are risk neutral, whereas bargainer 3 is risk averse, with utility function $u_3 =$

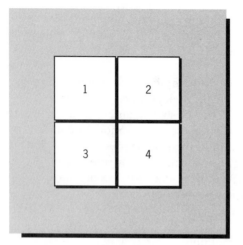

Figure 14.10.   Mutual Defense, four countries.

$\sqrt{a_3}$. Find the efficient payoff curve. Find the Nash bargaining solution. Show that the risk-averse bargainer gets less than do the risk-neutral bargainers.

2. Find the Kalai–Smorodinsky bargaining solution for problem 1. Show that the risk-averse bargainer gets less than do the risk-neutral bargainers.

3. Suppose that there are three players in a bargaining game. Give an example of a Nash bargaining solution that violates monotonicity and of a Kalai–Smorodinsky bargaining solution that violates independence of irrelevant alternatives.

4. In a bankruptcy game, claimant 1 can claim $1 million; claimant 2, $2 million; claimant 3, $3 million; claimant 4, $4 million. All claimants are risk neutral. There is $5 million in assets available. Find the Nash and the Kalai–Smorodinsky bargaining solutions and compare them.

5. Solve problem 4 if there is only $2.5 million in assets available.

6. Give three examples of signals in the saga of BCCI that could have indicated to depositors to withdraw their deposits before it was too late. If you had $100,000 in BCCI on July 5, 1991, how much would this deposit be worth today?

7. In the game Joint Ventures, we claimed that firm 1 will walk away from the table if offered a return of less than 10%. Prove this in detail.

8. Suppose that, in Mutual Defense, the intermediate coalitions are not allowed to form and so have coalition value 0. Find the Nash and Kalai–Smorodinsky bargaining solutions and show that they are in the core.

9. Find the coalition function for the 4-country version of Mutual Defense in Figure 14.10. Each country is a unit square. Then find a proposal in the core.

10. New proposals for peace in Bosnia offer to lift the sanctions against Yugoslovia and Bosnia in exchange for their accepting a peace plan. Show how such a proposal might create an alternative in the core. (*Hint:* Utility now consists of both territory held and economic value from the foreign trade.)

PART FIVE

Games, Markets, and Politics

CHAPTER 15

Two-sided Markets and Matching Games

In the market games in Chapter 4 the strategies were chosen by the sellers, and the buyers were passive players represented by a determinate demand function. In the auctions in Chapter 11 bids were chosen by the buyers, and the seller was a passive player willing to take any winning bid. These were **one-sided market games.** A market game is *one-sided* when one side of the market or the other has all the strategies. Chapters 12 and 13 looked at economic bargains struck through negotiations or arbitration. These situations were two-sided: both sides to the transaction got to choose strategies to influence the outcome. However, with only one buyer and one seller, the market involved was quite thin.

This chapter studies **two-sided market games** in coalition function form, where all players are risk neutral. It provides an algorithm for computing market equilibria of two-sided games, based on market fundamentals, and then uses those market fundamentals to construct the coalition function for a two-sided market game. The coalition function for such games, suitably normalized, measures **gains from trade,** which is the motive for all market transactions. A famous and important result, the core equivalence theorem, is proved. Core equivalence says that every market equilibrium is in the core of the market game and that every bargain in the core of the market game is a market equilibrium. This is a major strategic reason for the amazing stability of market outcomes—they have something to offer to everyone who trades. Core equivalence is then considered in light of various imperfections of information. The RJR Nabisco takeover is revisited to see what light the core sheds on it; the outcome lies in the core of the market game for this company. A game can be two-sided even if no money is at stake. Matching processes, such as those that match dates for the prom or pledges to fraternities and sororities, are a case in point. These two-sided matching games have a lot in common with two-sided market games. They also satisfy a version of core equivalence. Sorority rush—which some of you may have gone through—is an interesting real-life matching game, matching recruits to sororities on college campuses.

15.1 Two-sided Markets: The Fundamentals ■ ■ ■ ■ ■

This section models markets where each buyer is interested in buying one unit of an indivisible commodity and each seller is interested in selling one unit of that same commodity. The markets for houses and cars conform to this pattern pretty closely. For a given commodity in question, there is a set $N(\text{buy})$ of buyers, and a set $N(\text{sell})$ of sellers. We will denote the buyers with odd numbers, $N(\text{buy}) = \{1, 3, \ldots, 2n - 1\}$ and the sellers with even numbers, $N(\text{sell}) = \{2, 4, \ldots, 2n\}$. As we shall see in a moment, we lose no generality by assuming that the number of buyers and the number of sellers are the same, n. Let's turn first to the demand side of the market.

Each buyer i has a utility function, u_i, of the form

$$u_i(M, p) = M_i + b_i - P \qquad \text{if the item is bought}$$
$$= M_i \qquad\qquad \text{if the item is not bought}$$

The parameter b_i represents the marginal utility of the item to buyer i. It is also the highest price that buyer i can pay for the item without losing utility overall. The expression $(b_i - P)$ measures buyer i's gain from trade at the price P. Use of the same notation used in Chapter 11 for bidding behavior is deliberate. In a complete information framework, there is no reason not to bid what an item is worth to you, since everyone knows what it is worth to you anyway. Later we will distinguish between bids (which are publicly observable) and private information (which is not). Since utility is assumed linear in money M_i, the buyers are risk neutral. This assumption will also be relaxed later. It will prove useful to have the buyers ranked by bid, high bid first:

$$b_1 \geq b_3 \geq \ldots \geq b_{2n-1} \geq 0$$

Most of the time, these inequalities are strict. One exception is a *dummy* buyer i, for whom the item is worthless: $b_i = 0$. We can include as many dummies as we

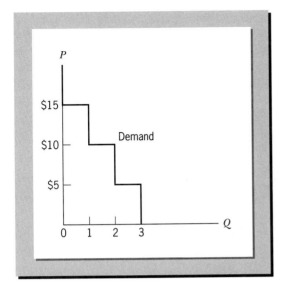

Figure 15.1. Two-sided market, demand side, $n = 3$.

need on the demand side of the market to make the two sides formally equal. Figure 15.1 shows the demand function that results when there are three buyers, with $b_1 = \$15$, $b_3 = \$10$, and $b_5 = \$5$. At a price above \$15, there is no willing buyer. At a price below \$5, there are three willing buyers. Notice that demand in a market like this must obey the law of demand.

We can model the supply side of the market in a similar fashion. Each seller j has a utility function, u_j, of the form

$$u_j(M,p) = M_j + P - a_j \qquad \text{if the item is sold}$$
$$= M_j \qquad \text{if the item is not sold}$$

The parameter a_j represents the marginal cost of the item to seller j. It is also the lowest price that seller j can receive for the item without losing utility overall. The expression $(P - a_j)$ measures seller j's gain from trade at the price p. Again, use of the same notation used in Chapters 12 and 14 for bargaining behavior is deliberate. In a complete information framework, there is no reason not to ask what an item costs you to sell, since everyone knows this already anyway. Later we will distinguish between asks (which are publicly observable) and private information (which is not). Since utility is assumed linear in money M_j, the sellers, like the buyers, are risk neutral. This assumption will also be relaxed later. It will prove useful in a minute to have the sellers ranked by ask, low ask first:

$$0 \le a_2 \le a_4 \le \cdots \le a_n \le \infty$$

Most of the time, these inequalities are strict. One exception is a *dummy* seller u, for whom the item is infinitely costly: $a_j = \infty$. We can include as many

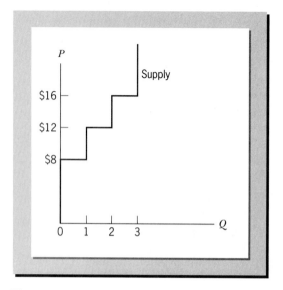

Figure 15.2. Two-sided market, supply side, *n* = 3.

dummies as we need on the supply side of the market to make the two sides formally equal. Figure 15.2 shows the supply schedule that results when there are three sellers, with $a_2 = \$8$, $a_4 = \$12$, and $a_6 = \$16$. At a price above \$16, there are three willing sellers. At a price below \$8, there are no willing sellers. Notice that supply in a market like this must obey the law of supply.

A market is in equilibrium at a price P^* when demand equals supply. Figure 15.3 shows the equilibrium that results when the demand of Figure 15.1 meets the supply of Figure 15.2. There is one unit transacted. The lowest-cost seller, seller 2, sells this unit to the highest bidder, buyer 1, at a price P^*, between \$10 and \$12. If the price were lower than \$10, demand would exceed supply, $2 > 1$. The excess demand would drive the price up, a strategic process that will be made precise in the next section. If the price were higher than \$12, supply would exceed demand, $2 > 1$. The excess supply would drive the price down, a strategic process that will be made precise in the next section as well. Notice that, although the equilibrium quantity is unique, there is an entire interval, [\$10,\$12] of equilibrium prices. The lowest price in this interval maximizes gain for the buyers; the highest price in this interval maximizes gain for the sellers.

There is a simple algorithm, developed by the Austrian economist Eugen von Boehm-Bawerk, for finding an equilibrium in a two-sided market.[1] His method is called the **method of marginal pairs.** It works like this. Start with the

[1]Eugen von Boehm-Bawerk, *Positive Theory of Capital* (New York: G. E. Stechert, 1923). (Originally published in German in 1891.) Boehm-Bawerk is the only economist currently appearing on a national currency—the Austrian 100-shilling note.

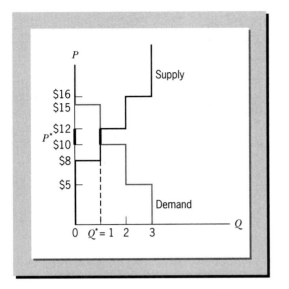

Figure 15.3. Two-sided market, equilibrium, $n = 3$.

first pair of traders, buyer 1 and seller 2. If $b_1 \geq a_2$, then have these two traders trade and go on to the next pair. If $b_1 < a_2$, stop. There are no gains from trade available in this market if the lowest-cost seller cannot make money by selling to the highest bidder. The next two traders are buyer 3 and seller 4. If $b_3 \geq a_4$, then have these two traders trade and go on to the next pair. If $b_3 < a_4$, stop. All gains from trade have been exhausted. Continue the algorithm until reaching the nth pair of traders, or stop, whichever comes first. The last pair of traders before stopping is called the *marginal pair*. The equilibrium price lies between the individual bid and ask of the marginal pair. Often, an equilibrium price can lie anywhere in this entire interval. In this example, however, the equilibrium prices lie in an even narrower band, given by the individual bid and ask of the pair next in line after the marginal pair.

In the market of Figure 15.3, the method of marginal pairs starts with buyer 1 and seller 2. Since $b_1 = \$15 > \$8 = a_2$, these two trade and we go to the pair consisting of buyer 3 and seller 4. Since $b_3 = \$10 < \$12 = a_4$, we stop at this point. One unit is sold at equilibrium. The marginal pair is {1,2}, and the equilibrium price is between \$10 and \$12. The next section shows that the reason the method of marginal pairs works is that it mimics, or reproduces, the reasoning that underlies the core of the market game.

15.2 The Coalition Function of a Two-sided Market Game ■■■■■■■■■■■■■■■■

This section derives the coalition function $v(S)$ of a market game, where S is a set of buyers and sellers trading only among themselves. We begin with singleton coalitions. Take buyer i. This buyer can't create a gain from trade all alone, and so $v(\{i\}) = M_i$, the amount of money buyer i starts with. The same is true for seller j: $v(\{j\}) = M_j$. Only coalitions with two or more traders can effect gains from trade. Even then, however, two conditions must be met. First, both buyers and sellers must be present in the coalition. A coalition composed of all buyers or all sellers has nothing to trade among its members. If the coalition S consists of all buyers, then

$$v(S) = \Sigma M_i, \; i \text{ in } S, \; i \text{ in } N(\text{buy})$$

Similarly, if the coalition S consists of all sellers, then

$$v(S) = \Sigma M_j, \; j \text{ in } S, \; j \text{ in } N(\text{sell})$$

Second, at least one pair in the coalition must gain from trade, that is, there must be one pair $\{i,j\}$ such that $b_i > a_j$. A coalition builds up value by matching up such pairs and having them trade. Suppose that $\{i,j\}$ is just such a pair. Then $v(\{i,j\})$ is realized when buyer i buys from seller j:

$$
\begin{aligned}
v(\{i,j\}) &= u_i(M_i,P) + u_j(M_j,P) \\
&= M_i + b_i - P + M_j + P - a_j \\
&= M_i + M_j + b_i - a_j
\end{aligned}
$$

Notice that the coalition value of $\{i,j\}$ exceeds the no-trade outcome, $M_i + M_j$, only when trade is mutually beneficial between buyer i and seller j. This formula holds for any buyer–seller pair that enjoys gains from trade.

Now is a good time to introduce an extremely useful normalization. You have probably noticed that the amount of money each player starts the game with, for buyer i, M_i, shows up in every formula. The problem does not change at all—it is merely a linear transformation of the data to subtract this term from every coalition where player i appears. In the new coordinate system, we have

$$
\begin{aligned}
v(\{i\}) &= v(\{j\}) = 0 \\
v(\{S\}) &= 0 \text{ if } S \text{ is a subset of } N(\text{buy}) \text{ or } N(\text{sell}) \\
v(\{i,j\}) &= b_i - a_j \text{ if } b_i > a_j \\
&= 0 \text{ otherwise}
\end{aligned}
$$

In this new coordinate system, $v(S)$ represents the gains to trade accruing to coalition S if its members should happen to trade among themselves in an optimal fashion.

Now consider a coalition with three members, two buyers (players 1 and 3) and one seller (player 2). If both {1,2} and {2,3} enjoy gains from trade, then from what we have just seen

$$v(\{1,3\}) = 0$$
$$v(\{1,2\}) = b_1 - a_2$$
$$v(\{3,2\}) = b_3 - a_2$$

From this foundation, we can find $v(\{1,2,3\})$. Seller 2 can only sell to one buyer, either buyer 1 or buyer 3. Buyer 1 values the item as least as much as does buyer 3. Therefore, we have

$$v(\{1,3\}) = b_1 - a_2 \geq b_3 - a_2 = v(\{2,3\})$$

The best the coalition $(\{1,2,3\})$ can do is to have buyer 1 buy from seller 2:

$$v(\{1,2,3\}) = v(\{1,3\}) = b_1 - a_2$$

Notice that we could have gotten the same answer by applying the method of marginal pairs within the coalition {1,2,3}: identify the highest gains-from-trade pair and match them; then go on to the next pair; and so on until all gains from trade have been exhausted. The resulting outcome will maximize gains from trade for the coalition S.

We can now write down the coalition function for the 6-player, two-sided market game, with $N(\text{buy}) = \{1,3,5\}$, $N(\text{sell}) = \{2,4,6\}$, bid vector $\mathbf{b} = (\$15,\$10,\$5)$, and ask vector $\mathbf{a} = (\$8,\$12,\$16)$. All 2-player coalition values are zero except for the following:

$$v(\{1,2\}) = 15 - 8 = 7$$
$$v(\{1,4\}) = 15 - 12 = 3$$
$$v(\{3,2\}) = 10 - 8 = 2$$

We can build up the value of larger coalitions based on the 2-player coalition values, since all gains from trade are realized in bilateral exchange. For instance, for three players we get

$$7 = v(\{1,2,3\}) = v(\{1,2,4\}) = v(\{1,2,5\}) = v(\{1,2,6\})$$
$$3 = v(\{1,4,3\}) = v(\{1,4,5\}) = v(\{1,4,6\})$$
$$2 = v(\{2,3,5\}) = v(\{2,3,4\}) = v(\{2,3,6\})$$

The other 3-player coalitions have zero value. If a 4-player coalition contains {1,2}, it has value 7; if it contains {1,4} but not {1,2}, it has value 3; if it contains {3,2} but not {1,4} and not {1,2}, it has value 2; otherwise, it has value zero. Each 5-player coalition must have a positive value:

$$v(\{1,2,3,4,5\}) = 7 \quad (1 \text{ and } 2 \text{ trade})$$
$$v(\{1,2,3,4,6\}) = 7 \quad (1 \text{ and } 2 \text{ trade})$$
$$v(\{1,2,3,5,6\}) = 7 \quad (1 \text{ and } 2 \text{ trade})$$
$$v(\{1,2,4,5,6\}) = 7 \quad (1 \text{ and } 2 \text{ trade})$$

$$v(\{1,3,4,5,6\}) = 3 \qquad \text{(1 and 4 trade)}$$
$$v(\{2,3,4,5,6\}) = 2 \qquad \text{(2 and 3 trade)}$$

Finally, for the grand coalition N consisting of all buyers and all sellers, we have

$$v(N) = 7 \qquad \text{(1 and 2 trade)}$$

The grand coalition cannot do any better than the coalition consisting of buyer 1 and seller 2.

Even for as few as six players, the coalition function is complicated. It has to specify $2^6 - 1 = 63$ different values. As we have just seen, in a two-sided market game, depending on how many pairs can create value, the specification of the coalition function is somewhat less complicated. For instance, when only three pairs can create value, as in the example given, then the coalition function has a lot of zero values.

15.3 The Core of a Two-sided Market Game ■ ■ ■ ■ ■

We are now in position to find the core of the two-sided market game. We can save a lot of time with the following observation. A player i in a game is a *dummy* if every time that player joins a coalition S, zero value is added to the coalition's value $v(S)$:

$$v(S \text{ and } i) - v(S) = 0 \qquad \text{for every coalition } S$$

This usage corresponds to that for markets. A buyer who doesn't want to bid more than zero for something is a dummy; and a seller who wants to ask infinitely many dollars for something is a dummy. Such a buyer or seller is not going to bring any gains from trade when he or she joins a coalition.

In the market game whose coalition function we derived earlier, buyer 5 and seller 6 are dummies. Buyer 5 is a dummy because the bid (\$5) is below the ask of any seller—buyer 5 can't create gains from trade with anybody else in the market. Similarly, seller 6 is a dummy because the ask (\$16) is above the bid of any buyer—seller 6 can't create gains from trade with anybody else in the market, either. A coalition can't count on any help from any of its dummy members when it is pondering whether to walk away from the negotiating table or walk out of the market. The core of a two-sided market game reflects this situation in the dummy principle:

■ ■

Dummy Principle. If player i is a dummy player, or player j a dummy seller, in a market game, then $u_i = u_j = 0$ in any outcome in the core of the game.

According to the dummy principle, we will find the core when we have solved the following system of inequalities:

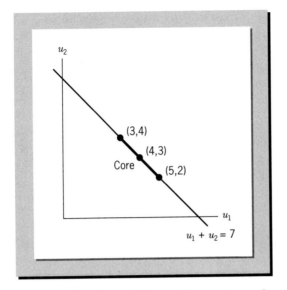

Figure 15.4. Core of the market game, $n = 3$.

$$u_1 + u_2 \geq 7 = v(\{1,2\})$$
$$u_3 + u_2 \geq 3 = v(\{2,3\})$$
$$u_1 + u_4 \geq 2 = v(\{1,4\})$$
$$u_1 + u_2 + u_3 \geq 7 = v(\{1,2,3\})$$
$$u_1 + u_2 + u_4 \geq 7 = v(\{1,2,4\})$$
$$u_1 + u_3 + u_4 \geq 3 = v(\{1,4,3\})$$
$$u_2 + u_3 + u_4 \geq 2 = v(\{2,3,4\})$$
$$\Sigma u_k = 7 = v(N)$$

We have already set $u_5 = u_6 = 0$, since buyer 5 and seller 6 are dummies.

Figure 15.4 shows solutions to this set of inequalities. One solution has $u_1 = 5$, $u_2 = 2$, $u_3 = u_4 = 0$. Another solution has $u_1 = 3$, $u_2 = 4$, $u_3 = u_4 = 0$. It is easy to see that these two vectors are in the core. Take the first of them. Substituting into the system of inequalities, we get

$$u_1 + u_2 = 5 + 2 = v(\{1,2\})$$
$$u_3 + u_2 = 0 + 3 = 3 = v(\{2,3\})$$
$$u_1 + u_4 = 5 + 0 \geq 2 = v(\{1,4\})$$
$$u_1 + u_2 + u_3 = 5 + 2 + 0 = 7 = v(\{1,2,3\})$$
$$u_1 + u_2 + u_4 = 5 + 2 + 0 = 7 = v(\{1,2,4\})$$
$$u_1 + u_3 + u_4 = 5 + 0 + 0 \geq 3 = v(\{1,4,3\})$$
$$u_2 + u_3 + u_4 = 2 + 0 + 0 = 2 = v(\{2,3,4\})$$
$$\Sigma u_k = 5 + 2 + 0 + 0 = 7 = v(N)$$

You can check that the other solution is in the core. You can also show that any point on the line between these two solutions is in the core, for instance, the point $u_1 = 4$, $u_2 = 3$, $u_3 = u_4 = 0$. Moreover, the outcome in Figure 15.4 must be all the outcomes in the core, since traders 1 and 2 have to get all the gains from trade in the grand coalition, $v(\{1,2\}) = v(N)$.

Let's now squeeze some intuition out of what we have just seen. The core says that buyer 1 and seller 2 get all the gains from trade, but there are limits on what each can get. Buyer 1 has to get at least a $3 gain, but can get no more than a $5 gain. Here is why. Suppose that buyer 1 was getting only a $2 gain. This means that buyer 1 would be paying a price of $13. At a price of $13, buyer 1 would not have to buy only from seller 2. Buyer 1 could switch to seller 4, who would also be willing to sell at a price of $13. Indeed, seller 4 would be interested in selling at any price above the reservation price of $12. This potential excess supply on the part of the next most costly seller puts an upper bound on the price seller 2 can get, and therefore a lower bound on the gain buyer 1 can get, in the two-sided market game.

Next, consider what happens if buyer 1 gets more than a $5 gain, say, $6. In this case buyer 1 would be paying a price of only $9. At a price of $9, seller 2 would not have only buyer 1 to sell to. Seller 2 could switch to buyer 3, who would also be willing to buy at a price of $9. Indeed, buyer 3 would be interested in buying at any price below the reservation price of $10. This potential excess demand on the part of the next highest bidder puts a lower bound on the price buyer 1 can pay, and therefore an upper bound on the gain seller 2 can get, in the two-sided market game.

Now compare the gains from trade corresponding to the market equilibrium in Figure 15.5 with the core of the market game in Figure 15.4. Market equilibria gains from trade are parameterized by the equilibrium price P^*:

$$u_1 = 15 - P^* \qquad \text{(buyer's gain)}$$
$$u_2 = P^* - 8 \qquad \text{(seller's gain)}$$

where $10 \leq P^* \leq 12$. Take the market equilibrium $P^* = 10$. This is the lowest possible equilibrium price, which is best for the buyer. This price corresponds to $u_1 = 5$, $u_2 = 2$, which is at one end of the core. Take the other extreme market equilibrium price, $P^* = 12$. This is the highest possible equilibrium price, which is best for the seller. This price corresponds to $u_1 = 3$, $u_2 = 4$, which is at the other end of the core. All the market equilibrium prices in between these two extremes line up, one to one, with points in the core. For instance, the price $P^* = 11$ corresponds to the core outcome $u_1 = 4$, $u_2 = 3$.

The phenomenon whereby market equilibria correspond to outcomes in the core, and vice versa, is known as the **core equivalence theorem.** You can show

---

[2]The easiest proofs require linear programming, which is beyond the mathematical scope of this book. For a particularly insightful treatment, see Lloyd S. Shapley and Martin Shubik, "The Assignment Game I: The Core," *International Journal of Game Theory* 1 (1972):111–30.

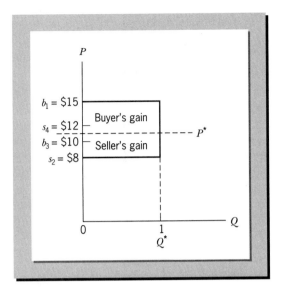

Figure 15.5. Gains from trade, market equilibrium.

that for any two-sided market game with a finite number of players, the market equilibria and the core outcomes are equivalent.[2] When goods are perfectly divisible, the situation becomes much more complicated. For instance, the existence of a market equilibrium or of outcomes in the core is no longer guaranteed, but requires more structure. In such situations, if there are infinitely many players, none of whom is risk seeking, then core equivalence holds.

Core equivalence explains why market outcomes hold up so well to criticism. If any group could do better by not being in the market, it is free to get out of the market and do its own thing. However, if the market is in equilibrium, then there is no such group. All participants in the market are doing at least as well as they would on their own. The market has something to offer everyone who is active in equilibrium.

⚃ 15.4 Limitations on Core Equivalence ■■■■■■■■■■

In settings where markets are likely to fail, core equivalence is likely to fail also. The link between competitive markets, where price is set by supply = demand, and the core of an associated game, may be tenuous indeed, or may even disappear. There are two obvious places to look for market failure. One involves the formation of conspiracies on the buyers' or sellers' side to fix the price in their favor. Another, which may exploit imperfect information, involves shaving asks and bids to move the price in one's favor. We will consider these phenomena in turn.

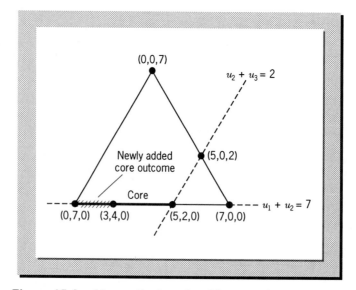

Figure 15.6.   Monopolized market. The core does not equal perfectly competitive equilibrium.

First let's look at attempts to monopolize the market. Suppose that all the sellers in a market merge to form a single player, a merger that we will call player 2. This single entity, which still has the same costs of production of its individual members, henceforth will act as the only seller in the market. The impact of this merger will be to extend the core beyond the set of market equilibria and in a direction favorable to the monopoly.

Here's how monopoly works in a two-sided market game. Take the bid and ask data from the market game of the previous section, only now seller 2 can sell as many as three units. There are still independent buyers, 1, 3, and 5. Using the coalition function we have already derived, we have

$$v(\{1,2\}) = 7$$
$$v(\{3,2\}) = 2$$
$$v(\{1,3,2\}) = 7 = v(N)$$

and all other coalitions have value zero. We have already set $u_5 = 0$, since buyer 5 continues to be a dummy player. An outcome in the core must satisfy the following set of inequalities:

$$u_1 + u_2 \geq 7 = v(\{1,2\})$$
$$u_3 + u_2 \geq 2 = v(\{3,2\})$$
$$u_1 + u_2 + u_3 = 7$$

The solution to these inequalities is shown in Figure 15.6. The core consists of the line segment between (5,2,0) and (0,7,0) on the bottom edge of the gains from trade triangle. In particular, the monopoly player can get as much as $u_2 = 7$ at a core outcome. Prior to the merger, the maximum gain to the sellers in the core was only 5. All the points from $(3,4,0)$ to $(0,7,0)$ have been added to the core, thanks to monopolization. The core is now larger than the set of perfectly competitive market equilibria, and all the new points in the core are better for sellers who have monopolized the market.

What the monopoly has done is repeal the effect of excess supply on market price. In order to achieve a gain of 7, the sellers have to get a price of \$15 for one unit sold. At this price, there would ordinarily be two units for sale, not one. The monopoly prevents the second unit from being sold. Moreover, from the total gain of 7 units, the monopoly can distribute *side payments* to its participating members:

$$7 = u_2 + u_4 + u_6$$

The monopoly can parcel out the gains to make everybody in the merger better off, for instance by paying \$5.50 to (premerger) seller 2, \$1 to seller 4, and \$0.50 to seller 6. Compare this to the best possible premerger core outcome, where the payoffs were \$5, \$0, and \$0. Premerger seller 2 could justify the side payment to seller 4 as a reward for not spoiling the fun by offering a unit for sale at the price of \$15, and the side payment to seller 6 as a reward for keeping quiet about the whole business. What we have just described is a conspiracy to fix prices. Since such conspiracies are a felony in the United States, it behooves the participants to keep things quiet.

Sellers aren't the only ones who can monopolize a market. Buyers can, too—witness the recent conviction of the owners of Major League Professional Baseball for fixing the prices of free agents below market levels in the late 1980s. You can show that when buyers form a monopoly,[3] the core expands in a direction favorable to them (see problem 4).

We have just seen core equivalence fail when one side or the other of the market is monopolized. In this case, the set of outcomes in the core expands, and the set of market equilibria stays the same. Another route by which core equivalence may fail is when bids or asks are made strategically. To adapt our notation to this possibility, let z_i be the underlying value of the item for buyer i; z_j, the cost of producing the item for seller j. These underlying values are known to all players. This crucial assumption means that the coalition function and the inequalities defining the core do not change. Buyer i *bids honestly* when $b_i = z_i$; seller j *asks honestly* when $a_j = z_j$. The market demand and supply schedules, such as in Figures 15.1 and 15.2, presuppose that all buyers bid honestly and all sellers ask honestly. Unfortunately, the market participants usually have an incentive to act otherwise.

---

[3]The official jargon for a monopoly formed by buyers is a *monopsony*.

[4]Such an auction is often called an English auction. It is the kind of auction most encountered in the United States.

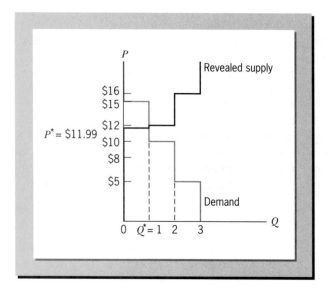

Figure 15.7. Strategic asks in the market. The core does not equal perfectly competitive equilibrium.

Suppose that the market is run by an ascending auction, in which the auctioneer raises the price until demand equals supply.[4] The auction will stop at the lowest competitive equilibrium price. Suppose that k knits have been sold, so that the marginal pair at equilibrium consisted of buyer $2k - 1$ and seller $2k$. Then this auction rule sets $P^* = a_{2k}$. From a game equilibrium standpoint, seller $2k$ would like to raise the ask. By doing so, seller $2k$ raises the gains from trade. This seller can afford to raise the ask until it is just below the cost of the next seller in the cost ranking:

$$a_{2k} = z_{2(k+1)} - e$$

where e is the minimum monetary unit. The reasoning here is just like the reasoning for the equilibrium behavior in a complete information first-price auction; the only difference is that now there are many units on the auction block instead of just one.

Let's apply this conclusion to the market data of Figure 15.3 (see Figure 15.7). If sellers are bidding strategically, then seller 1 asks $11.99, not $8. The supply schedule that is revealed to the market is not the true supply schedule, but a supply schedule shifted upward in the vicinity of the market equilibrium quantity. The sellers who aren't active do not have an incentive to misreveal their costs, but the marginal seller (here, seller 1) certainly does. The outcome corresponding to $P = \$10$, which is still in the core, is no longer a market equilibrium outcome.

You can show that dishonest bidding can occur also in an auction among buyers. Suppose that the market is run by a descending auction, in which the auctioneer lowers the price until demand equals supply.[5] The auction will stop at the highest competitive equilibrium price. Suppose that k units have been sold, so that the marginal pair at equilibrium consisted of buyer $2k - 1$ and seller $2k$. Then this auction rule sets $P^* = b_{2k-1}$. From a game equilibrium standpoint, buyer $2k - 1$ would like to lower the bid. By doing so, this buyer raises the gains from trade. Buyer $2k - 1$ can afford to lower the bid until it is just above the underlying value of the next buyer in the value ranking:

$$b_{2k-1} = z_{2k} + e$$

where e is the minimum monetary unit. The reasoning here is again just like that for the equilibrium behavior in a complete information first-price auction. Now the outcome corresponding to $P = \$12$, which is still in the core, is no longer a market outcome. The details are left for an end-of-chapter problem.

Recall from Chapter 11 that there is an institution to combat the problem of **dishonest asks** and **dishonest bids** when there is one item on the auction block: the second-price auction. We can adapt this institution to the present situation, where there are k units being transacted at equilibrium. In a *$k + 1$ price auction* among buyers, all bids greater than the $k + 1$ highest bid win and pay a price equal to the $k + 1$ highest bid. In a $k + 1$ price auction among sellers, all asks less than the $k + 1$ highest ask win and receive a price equal to the $k + 1$ highest ask. If $k = 4$, there are four items being transacted at equilibrium, and these would be fifth-price auctions. A $k + 1$ auction among buyers gives each buyer an incentive to bid honestly. Indeed, this is a dominant strategy, just as it was in second-price auctions, and for exactly the same reasons. Your bid, if it wins, does not affect the price you pay, but if you underbid, you may lose an auction you should otherwise win. A $k + 1$ auction among sellers gives each seller an incentive to ask honestly. Unfortunately, there is no way to provide incentives to ask and bid honestly to both sides of the market at the same time.[6] Thus there is a second major limitation to core equivalence, resulting from strategic bidding behavior. Such behavior played a major role in the bidding for RJR Nabisco during the takeover episode of 1989.

15.5 Barbarians at the Gate II: The Core[7] ■ ■ ■ ■ ■ ■ ■

When we last looked at the leveraged buyout of RJR Nabisco in Chapter 9, we were interested mainly in what it had to tell us about signaling. Let's take a

[5]Such an auction is often called an Dutch auction and is sometimes encountered in the United States.

[6]This result is known as the Hurwicz Impossibility Theorem after its discoverer, Leonid Hurwicz. See his "On Informationally Decentralized Systems," in *Decisions and Organization*, ed. B. McGuire and R. Radner (Amsterdam: North Holland, 1972).

[7]Material for this analysis was derived from Bryan Burrough and John Helyar, *Barbarians at the Gate: The Fall of RJR Nabisco* (New York: Harper & Row, 1990).

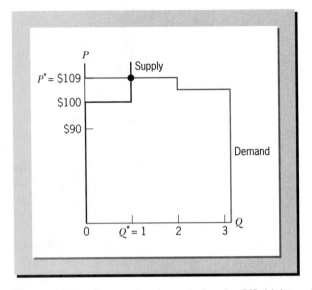

Figure 15.8. Demand and supply for the RJR Nabisco LBO.

second look. This time, we will emphasize the two-sided market aspect of this event.

We take up the story at the point in the bidding where there were three buyers left: the management group, led by CEO Ross Johnson (player 1); Kohlberg Kravis Roberts (KKR), led by Henry Kravis (player 3); and First Boston, led by Jim Maher (player 5). The single seller is the board of directors of RJR Nabisco (player 2). Bidding had reached $100/share, which the board was already inclined to accept, as this represented a whopping $45/share premium over current stock market value. The board's oft-stated goal throughout the proceedings was to maximize shareholder value, which here meant maximum gains from trade for the seller.

Figure 15.8 shows the market demand and supply schedules for RJR Nabisco. Since the company has to be bought lock, stock, and barrel, there is one indivisible unit of company for sale. The board has already shown its willingness to accept $100/share, hence the supply schedule with the company for sale at any price above that. Based on inside information (buyer 1), due diligence (buyer 3), and sheer guts (buyer 5), there are three willing buyers at any price up to $106/share, and two willing buyers at any price up to $109/share.[8] The market equilibrium, where demand equals supply, occurs at a unique price, $109/share, with either buyer 1 or buyer 3 getting the company.

As we have seen, the winning bidder has an incentive not to bid that high

---

[8]The management group actually bid $112/share at the end. After reading the fine print and evaluating the heavy load of junk bonds in this bid, the board of directors ruled that it was equivalent to the KKR bid of $109/share.

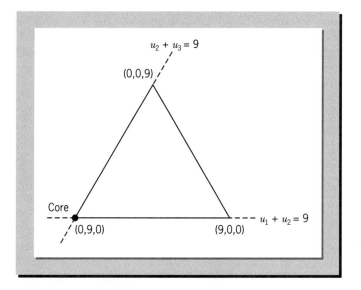

Figure 15.9. Core of Barbarians at the Gate.

and would much prefer to get the company for a lower price. Thus, when the first bidding deadline occurred (end of October 1988), none of the bids was that close to underlying value. The management group had bid $100/share and KKR, $94/share. First Boston had come closest to its underlying valuation, at $101/share.

At this point, the seller did something quite unusual. The board asked each of the buyers for a new bid. The implication of this move was clear: the seller suspected the buyers of holding out and expected the new bids to be higher than the old ones. Indeed, the new bids were higher: the management group went up $1/share, KKR went up $12/share, and First Boston went up $5/share. This strategy worked so well the first time that the board tried it one more time. This time, the board asked each bidder for a final bid. The final bids reached market equilibrium levels, with First Boston no longer an active part of the equilibrium.

The inequalities that describe the core of this game are as follows:

$$u_1 + u_2 \geq 9 = v(\{1,2\})$$
$$u_3 + u_2 \geq 9 = v(\{3,2\})$$
$$u_5 + u_2 \geq 6 = v(\{5,2\}$$
$$\Sigma u_k = 9 = v(N)$$

The gains from trade are the $9/share available to split between the seller and either buyer 1 or buyer 3, or the $6/share between the seller and buyer 5 (see Figure 15.8). Even though buyer 5 is not a strategic dummy, this buyer still gets shut out at any core outcome: $u_5 = 0$. Figure 15.9 shows the core of this two-sided market game. The core is the single outcome (0,9,0)—the seller gets all the gains from trade. This is equivalent to the market equilibrium price—a share price of $109. This is core equivalence with a vengeance—but it took a really clever move on the part of the seller to get this price.

15.6 Two-sided Matching Games ■ ■ ■ ■ ■ ■ ■ ■ ■ ■ ■ ■

In every market, there are two sides, the buyers and the sellers, and gains from trade at stake. In nonmarket situations, there may still be two sides, but something different from money at stake. Consider what happens prior to a high school **prom**. There are two sides, boys and girls. Individuals from the two sides get matched somehow, and form dates to the prom. Each person who goes to the prom would like to be matched with his or her preferred date. Although it may not look like it, this, too, is a game, a **two-sided matching game**. And even though there is no money at stake, it has strategic properties very reminiscent of those of two-sided markets. This stands to reason, since markets also perform a matching function, namely, matching buyers to sellers. In particular, its core will prove to be just as important as that of a two-sided market game.

To fix notation, let the odd numbers represent one side of the matching game, $N(\mathrm{I}) = \{1,3,\ldots,2n-1\}$ and let the even numbers represent the other side of the matching game, $N(\mathrm{II}) = \{2,4,\ldots,2n\}$. The grand coalition N is simply the union of these two sides, $N(\mathrm{I})$ and $N(\mathrm{II})$. A player i on side I of the market has a ranking of the players on the other side in terms of preference as a date. A player also has the option of not going to the prom at all. Suppose that $n = 3$. Then player i could have preferences of this sort:

> i: 4,6,NO,2

Player i's preferred date is player 4, followed by player 6. Player i would rather not go to the prom than go with player 2. Similarly, a player j on side II of the market has a ranking of the players on the other side in terms of preference as a date. This player also has the option of not going to the prom at all. Player j might have preferences of the sort:

> j: 1,3,5,NO

Player j's preferred date is player 1, followed by player 3, followed by player 5. The absolute worst for this player is not to go to the prom at all.

To motivate the idea of equilibrium for the prom, we will study a small prom with $n = 3$. The preferences are as follows. On side I, we have

> 1: 2,4,6,NO
>
> 3: 2,6,NO,4
>
> 5: 2,NO,4,6

All the players on this side rate player 2 first. This is obviously a very popular player. On side II we have

2: 1,5,NO,3

4: 5,3,1,NO

6: 3,1,NO,5

There is no clear favorite on side II for a date to the prom.

The definition of an **equilibrium matching** is a bit abstract.[9] It contains two parts. First, suppose that players i and j are matched up. Then it must not be the case that either or both of them can find a more preferred date, either among those already matched or among those not yet matched. If either one of them could still get a better date, then that player would break this date—a clear sign of disequilibrium. Both have the best date they are going to get. Second, suppose that player i or player j is not yet matched. Then the unmatched player prefers not going to the prom to going with any of the dates still available. If an acceptable person were still available, player i or player j could ask that person to the prom—another clear sign of disequilibrium.

Although there is no simple graphic for describing an equilibrium matching, there is a simple algorithm for arriving at one. A variant of this algorithm is enshrined in the custom, "The boy asks the girl to the prom." We will call this the boy-asks-girl algorithm, and it goes like this. Each of the boys asks his favorite date to the prom. Each of the girls says yes to the best offer she gets, or says no to all of them if she ranks not going to the prom higher. All boys who get accepted stand pat. The boys who have not yet heard "yes" next ask out the girl they rank highest who is still available. The girls compare offers they have just received to dates they already have, breaking any date in favor of a better one. This process continues until all the dating possibilities are exhausted.

Let's apply the boy-asks-girl algorithm to the 6-player prom data given. At the first step, each boy invites his favorite date, player 2, to the prom. Player 2 accepts her favorite among these, player 1. She says no to the other two boys. So after the first step, we have a match {1,2}. Boys 3 and 5 are left at step two. Boy 3 asks girl 6, and boy 5 says no to the whole process. If boy 5 can't go with girl 2, he's not going at all. Girl 6 ranks boy 3 first, and is thrilled to say yes. We have a second match, {3,6}. Since boy 5 has hit NO in his rankings, this completes the algorithm.

Now let's check that the matching {1,2}, {3,6}, and 4 and 5 stay home is an equilibrium. Since players 1, 2, and 6 get their first choice, they have to be in equilibrium. Likewise player 5, who prefers not going to the prom to going with anyone other than player 2. Player 3 gets his second choice, but player 3's first choice is getting her first choice, so there is nothing player 3 can do about it.

---

[9]The term *stable matching* is often used as well. See Alvin E. Roth and Marilda A. Oliveira Sotomayor, *Two-sided Matching: A Study in Game-Theoretic Modeling and Analysis* (Cambridge: Cambridge University Press, 1990) for an admirable treatment of this entire subject.

Player 4 would like to go to the prom, but all her choices are either taken or unwilling to go with her.

The boy-asks-girl algorithm always leads to an equilibrium matching. You can turn the process completely around in the form of a girl-asks-boy algorithm. This algorithm, too, will always lead to an equilibrium matching, although not necessarily the same matching as when boys ask girls (see problem 8). We now turn to the coalition form of a matching game and show that an equilibrium matching is equivalent to being a core outcome.

15.7 Matching Games in Coalition Function Form ■ ■

The first task in constructing a coalition function is to find a way to represent preferences. It will suffice for our purposes to use an **ordinal utility.** Suppose there are n possible dates to the prom, plus the option NO. Then attach $n + 1$ utility points to the highest-ranked option, n utility points to the next-highest-ranked option, and so on down to 1 utility point to the lowest-ranked option. This process yields an ordinal scale that expresses preferences numerically.

Armed with a numerical utility, we can now find the coalition function. First, take a singleton i. The only thing that a player in a matching game acting alone can guarantee is the outcome NO. It takes two players, one from each side of the game, before gains from going to the prom together can be realized. This gives the coalition function value

$$v(\{i\}) = u_i(\text{NO})$$

The only dates you should consider are ones that are better than staying home from the prom. Now consider a doubleton $\{i,j\}$, one from each side of the market. Here, one of two things can happen. First, each member of this pair may prefer going to the prom with the other to staying home. In this case, their coalition value is the vector of utilities they achieve by going to the prom together:

$$v(\{i,j\}) = [u_i(j), u_j(i)]$$

Second, at least one member of this pair may prefer staying home to going to the prom with the other member. In this case, the best this pair can do is stay home:

$$v(\{i,j\}) = [u_i(\text{NO}), u_j(\text{NO})]$$

Clearly, such a coalition will never form.

The remarkable thing about two-sided matching games is that all the information in the coalition function is contained in the values for singletons and doubletons. There are two reasons for this phenomenon. First, there isn't any money on the table to divide: you either go to the prom with someone or you don't. Second, to go to the prom, all you need is one other person. If you were in a coalition with a lot of other people, you would still break down into pairs for prom night. This should become clearer when we write down the coalition function for the prom we just studied.

First, we check out the singletons. On the boys' side, $N(\mathrm{I})$, we have

$v(\{1\}) = u_1(\mathrm{NO}) = 1$ (1 ranks NO fourth)
$v(\{3\}) = u_3(\mathrm{NO}) = 2$ (3 ranks NO third)
$v(\{5\}) = u_5(\mathrm{NO}) = 3$ (5 ranks NO second)

On the girls' side, $N(\mathrm{II})$, we have

$v(\{2\}) = u_2(\mathrm{NO}) = 2$ (2 ranks NO third)
$v(\{4\}) = u_4(\mathrm{NO}) = 1$ (4 ranks NO fourth)
$v(\{6\}) = u_6(\mathrm{NO}) = 2$ (6 ranks NO third)

Next, we check out the pairs. There are nine possible pairs with one member from each of the two sides of the game. Of these, five lead to possible dates:

$v(\{1,2\}) = [u_1(2), u_2(1)] = (4,4)$
$v(\{1,4\}) = [u_1(4), u_4(1)] = (3,2)$
$v(\{1,6\}) = [u_1(6), u_6(1)] = (2,3)$
$v(\{3,6\}) = [u_3(6), u_6(3)] = (3,4)$
$v(\{5,2\}) = [u_5(2), u_2(5)] = (4,3)$

With the other four possible pairs, $\{3,2\}$, $\{3,4\}$, $\{5,4\}$, and $\{5,6\}$, one or the other member of the pair would rather stay home. As far as the core is concerned, we only have to satisfy the demands of the five pairs who could conceivably date.

Now consider a coalition with three members, say, $\{1,2,4\}$. This coalition can do one of two things: send $\{1,2\}$ to the prom or send $\{1,4\}$ to the prom. The former achieves $v(\{1,2\})$; the latter, $v(\{1,4\})$. So $v(\{1,2,4\})$ is simply $v(\{1,2\})$ or $v(\{1,4\})$, the set union of these two payoff vectors. Larger coalitions break up into couples as far as their coalition value is concerned.

A vector $\mathbf{u} = (u_1, \ldots, u_6)$ is in the core of the matching game if it satisfies the following inequalities:

$u_1 \geq v(\{1\}) = 1$
$u_3 \geq v(\{3\}) = 2$
$u_5 \geq v(\{5\}) = 3$
$u_2 \geq v(\{2\}) = 2$
$u_4 \geq v(\{4\}) = 1$
$u_6 \geq v(\{6\}) = 2$
$(u_1, u_2) \geq v(\{1,2\}) = (4,4)$
$(u_1, u_4) \geq v(\{1,4\}) = (3,2)$
$(u_1, u_6) \geq v(\{1,6\}) = (2,3)$
$(u_3, u_6) \geq v(\{3,6\}) = (3,4)$
$(u_5, u_2) \geq v(\{5,2\}) = (4,3)$

This is a tough list of requirements to satisfy. Let's show first that the equilibrium matching we found earlier—{1,2}, {3,6}, and 4 and 5 stay home—is in the core. This matching generates the utility vector

$$\mathbf{u} = (4,4,3,1,3,4)$$

Since {4,5} can't even contemplate going out, they cannot do better than take their stay-home payoffs. The pair {1,2} is getting top payoffs (4,4), so they aren't about to walk away from this proposal. Finally, the pair {3,4} are getting next-to-top and top payoffs, respectively, so this coalition doesn't have anywhere better to go, either. The vector $\mathbf{u}$ is in the core.

This is true in general: an equilibrium matching is in the **core of the matching game.** Even more remarkable, the converse is true. If an alternative is in the core of the matching game, then it is an equilibrium matching. Since the prom has a unique equilibrium matching, there is a unique solution to this set of inequalities. Just as in a two-sided market game, in a two-sided matching game the set of equilibria is equivalent to the core. We can get some intuition into this result by observing the following. The way a coalition gets its coalition value is by making a date. The coalition {1,2} can walk away from any matching that gives them payoffs less than what they can get by making a date, namely the payoffs (4,4). That no individual or pair can gain by walking away from a proposed matching defines equilibrium. At the same time, it is the test that outcomes in the core must pass as well.

This chapter closes with a real-life example of a matching game, sorority rush on U.S. college campuses.

15.8 Sorority Rush[10] ■

Each year brings a familiar sight on campuses—female students all dressed up and lined up in front of a sorority they hope to join. This ritual is part of the **sorority rush.** Rush is the recruitment process of the sorority system as a whole. It is supervised by the Panhellenic Council (Panhel), a nationwide organization with local chapters, one per campus. The point of rush is to match sororities with recruits, **rushees,** taking into account the preferences of both.

Rush begins with a series of parties. The first parties are called open houses. These parties allow the rushees to inform themselves, and so form preferences, about the various sororities. The parties also allow the sororities to inform themselves about the rushees. Later parties are called preference parties. A rushee may attend at most three preference parties. Panhel urges sororities to invite to preference parties only rushees in whom they are interested.

When the parties are over, the matching process begins in earnest. Each rushee fills out a preference card. On this card, she is supposed to list in order,

[10]Some material for this study came from Susan Mongell and Alvin E. Roth, "Sorority Rush as a Two-sided Matching Mechanism," *American Economic Review* 81(1991):441–64.

from top on down, all the sororities she is interested in joining. If a rushee does not list a sorority on her preference card, she cannot be matched. If a rushee lists only one sorority, she is said to have "suicided." If that sorority doesn't want her, she cannot be matched, and she must wait a year before the next rush to try to get in to a sorority. Panhel explicitly urges rushees not to **suicide.** While rushees are filling out preference cards, the sororities are filling out something analogous, called *bid lists*. On its bid list, each sorority lists all the rushees it is willing to accept. Each sorority has a quota to fill—this is the number of names it can put on its bid list.[11]

Panhel has its own matching algorithm, called the preferential-bidding-system (PBS) algorithm, which it has used since 1928. The PBS algorithm works as follows. The rushees' preference cards are put in alphabetical order. The first choice on each preference card is called out. If that choice is on the bid list of the sorority named, this is a match. That person is removed from the pile, and the sorority's quota is reduced by one. If that choice is not on the bid list of the sorority named, and this person has not suicided, she is put into the hold pile. If this person has suicided, her card is discarded.[12] When all the first choices have been matched or not, then all the cards in the pile are read for the second choices. This process continues until no further matches are possible, either because all the sororities are full, or because no sorority wants any of the rushees left in the pile.

The matching process surrounding sorority rush is a lot like the matching process surrounding the prom. The only real difference is that each sorority can recruit more than one rushee, whereas each rushee can only be matched to one sorority. The PBS algorithm does not have all the properties of the boy-asks-girl or girl-asks-boy algorithms for the prom. In particular, it may lead to matches that are not equilibria, and therefore not in the core. In practice, however, most rushees appear to get their top choices, and so have no incentive to walk away from the matching.

Two economists, Susan Mongell and Alvin E. Roth, have studied sorority rush at four campuses in the northeastern United States for several years.[13] The data from 1987 are typical. On one campus, 56 of 68 rushees got their first choice, and 59 of 68 were matched overall. On another campus, 93 of 125 rushees got their first choice, and 105 of 125 were matched overall. On a third campus, 91 of 119 rushees got their first choice, and 105 of 119 were matched overall. Averaging over all three campuses, 77% of rushees got their first

---

[11]The exact procedures vary across campuses. At one large midwestern university, rushees are allowed to put only names of sororities to whose preference parties they have been invited on their preference cards. At this same university, the Panhel algorithm is worked from the other side, with sorority bid lists read first, and the algorithm is run on a computer.

[12]Panhel officials may, if they wish, contact the rushee and ask if she wants to reconsider before they discard her card.

[13]Panhel is very reluctant to divulge information about rush. The researchers were able to use data from these four universities only on condition of anonymity.

choice, and 86% got matched. It is interesting to note that 184 of the 312 rushees suicided, even though they were told not to. Of these 184, 149 (or 81%) got their first and only choice. A rushee had a slightly better chance of getting her first choice if she suicided than if she didn't. With suicide rates this high, the possibility that the PBS will lead to an outcome outside the core is remote.

SUMMARY

1. A market is one-sided if only one side of the market has strategies. A market is two-sided if both sides have strategies.
2. Two-sided markets where each buyer buys at most one unit of an indivisible good and each seller sells at most one unit of that good always obey the law of supply and the law of demand.
3. Equilibria of a two-sided market can be found using the method of marginal pairs. There are usually many equilibria in a two-sided market; there is always at least one.
4. The coalition function of a two-sided market game measures gains from trade. When all buyers and sellers are risk neutral, the coalition function value is a dollar number.
5. The core of a two-sided market game is a proposal from which no coalition can profitably walk away. Every market equilibrium is in the core of a two-sided market. The converse is also true, a result known as the core equivalence theorem.
6. The fact that market equilibria are in the core of a market game accounts for their considerable stability.
7. The core equivalence theorem breaks down when competition is imperfect or when agents on one side of the market bid strategically.
8. A two-sided matching game differs from a two-sided market game in that no money is at stake on the table. Otherwise, the two kinds of games are quite similar. In particular, they both exhibit core equivalence.
9. Two-sided matching games are analyzed using ordinal preferences. The coalition function value for a doubleton in such a game is a single vector.
10. Sorority rush on campus is a two-sided matching game. In practice, most rushees get their first choice of sororities.

KEY TERMS

one-sided market games	prom
two-sided market games	two-sided matching game
gains from trade	equilibrium matching
method of marginal pairs	ordinal utility
core equivalence theorem	core of the matching game
merger	sorority rush
dishonest asks	rushees
dishonest bids	suicide

PROBLEMS

1. Suppose that buyers have bids $b_1 = \$100$ and $b_3 = \$50$ and that sellers have asks $a_2 = \$25$ and $a_4 = \$40$. Plot the market demand and supply schedules. Find the market equilibria. Find an outcome in the core of the market game.

2. Two new traders, one buyer and one seller, have entered the market in problem 1. The buyer has bid $b_5 = \$40$; the seller has ask $a_6 = \$50$. Find the market equilibria. Find two outcomes in the core of this market game. What, if anything, has changed?

3. We have considered only risk-neutral buyers and sellers in this chapter. Suppose that $b_1 = \$10$ and $a_2 = \$0$. Buyer 1 is risk averse with utility function $\sqrt{M_1}$, while buyer 2 is risk neutral. Show that the core equivalence theorem still holds for this market.

4. The sellers in problem 2 merge to monopolize the market. Find an outcome in the core that is not a perfectly competitive equilibrium.

5. Suppose that in a two-sided market, there are three buyers and three sellers on each side. Two units are transacted at equilibrium. Define a third-price auction for buyers. Show that in this third-price auction, honest bidding is a dominant strategy for the buyers.

6. Suppose that in a market with two buyers and one seller, a second-price auction is used to sell the item. However, if the second price is lower that what the seller is asking, the seller's ask becomes the sale price. Give a numerical example where the seller has an incentive to overstate the costs of production.

7. Suppose that in Barbarians at the Gate II, First Boston had an underlying value for RJR Nabisco of $\$115$/share. What would the outcome of the game have been? Derive the core while you are at it. Is the outcome you predicted in the core?

8. Consider a prom matching algorithm that is just like boy-asks-girl, except that the girls ask the boys instead. Work out the details of this algorithm, then apply it to the prom problem in section 15.6. Do you get a different answer from the one derived using the boy-asks-girl algorithm? Can you explain why or why not?

9. In the prom problem of section 15.6, suppose that player 5 has the rankings:

    5: 2,4,6,NO

   Nothing else has changed. Derive the coalition function. Find all outcomes in the core.

10. There are 2 sororities and 10 rushees participating in rush. Rushees are identified by the odd numbers 1 through 19. Sorority Alpha Alpha Alpha finds rushees 1 through 9 acceptable and so notes on its bid sheet." Sorority Zeta Zeta Zeta finds all rushees whose numbers are prime (i.e.,

1,2,3,5,7,11,13,17,19) acceptable and so notes on its bid sheet. Each soroity has a quota of 10. Rushees numbered 10 and below prefer Alpha Alpha Alpha to Zeta Zeta Zeta; rushees numbered 11 and above prefer just the opposite. Every rushee wants to get into a sorority. Work out the result of the PBS algorithm, on the assumption that every rushee suicides (the sororities go in Greek alphabetical order). Is the outcome you get a matching equilibrium? Why or why not?

CHAPTER 16

Voting Games

Voting is a major part of business and economic life. As Thoreau wrote in his essay "On Civil Disobedience," "All voting is a sort of gaming, like checkers or backgammon, with a slight moral tinge to it, a playing with right and wrong, with moral questions; and betting naturally accompanies it." Proxy fights, votes to oust a CEO, and an industry lobbying for votes on Capitol Hill are just three business examples. This chapter looks at some of the strategic aspects of voting games.

The first section sets up voting games in extensive form, where candidates move first and voters move second. Subgame perfection is used to solve the voting game. When voters are distributed symmetrically on a discrete issue spectrum, then each candidate has a dominant strategy to move to the center. This result is generalized as the median voter theorem. The chapter then turns to 3-candidate elections and voting rules proposed for them. Plurality rule, which is most often used in the United States, is examined first. Three-candidate elections make possible strategic voting, where voters vote in a way that differs from their true preferences in order to get a better outcome. The only way to avoid strategic voting is by dictatorial elections. These complications show up in a major way in the three-way presidential elections that have occurred, albeit infrequently, in U.S. history. Three-way elections pose special difficulties for voters who want to maximize their utility, rather than simply send a message to the politicians. The Borda voting rule is used in elections such as those for Most Valuable Player (MVP) or for the National Champion of college football. Strategic voting is rampant in such elections. Finally, voting games in coalition function form are reviewed. Such games are especially suited to the study of party formation and coalition governments. An index of voting power is developed for voting games in coalition function form. This index is used extensively to explore the power implications of expanding the United Nations Security Council to include Japan and Germany, the world's second and third largest economies.

16.1 Two-Candidate Voting Games with a Discrete Issue Spectrum ■■■■■■■■■■■■■■■■■

This section studies voting games with two candidates, named 1 and 2. Each candidate adopts a position along an **issue spectrum.** Figure 16.1 shows two kinds of issue spectra, discrete and continuous. In a discrete spectrum (Figure 16.1*a*), each candidate can pick a position on the Left (L), in the Center (C), or on the Right (R). In a continuous spectrum (Figure 16.1*b*), each candidate can pick a position anywhere between the far left (0) and the far right (1). The

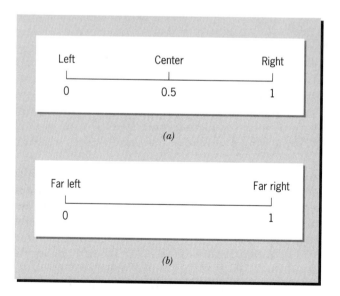

Figure 16.1.   Issue spectra: (*a*) discrete spectrum; (*b*) continuous spectrum.

basic difference between discrete and continuous spectra lies in their ability to distinguish among various political positions. For simplicity, the issue spectrum is couched in terms of the political spectrum, from Left to Right. Other interpretations are also possible. For instance, the candidates can be vying for CEO of a corporation, and the points on the spectrum can represent various corporate strategies, from conservative (risk averse) to liberal (risk seeking), which lie on the risk–return frontier. A more conservative strategy accepts less risk and gets less return. A third interpretation could be in terms of a proxy fight, involving various strategies for managing a corporation, again aligned on a spectrum.

In the voting game, the candidates move first. Each candidate i chooses simultaneously a position s_i on the spectrum. The voters move second. Each voter rates candidates based on how close they are to what the voter wants most. Suppose that each voter j has a favorite position on the spectrum, v_j. Then voter j's utility, u_j, from a candidate taking position s_i is measured in terms of distance from the voter's favorite position:

$$u_j = - d(v_j, s_i)$$

The minus sign reflects the fact that the further away a candidate is from the voter's preferred position, the lower the voter's utility from that candidate. A voter maximizes utility by voting for the candidate closest to the favored position. In the event that two candidates are equally distant from the position, the voter plays a mixed strategy, tossing a coin and voting for each with probability .5.

Candidates' utility is measured by how many votes they receive. Suppose there are 4 million voters, distributed on the discrete issue spectrum as follows:

on the Left, 1 million

in the Center, 2 million

on the Right, 1 million

As we will see later, the optimal strategies for the candidates depend on how the voters are distributed. In this case, the voters are distributed *symmetrically* on the issue spectrum. Since the candidates move before the voters do, they do not necessarily know how the voters will vote. However, an appeal to subgame perfection will remove any doubt. For instance, suppose that candidate 1 chooses Left and candidate 2 chooses Center. Then candidate 1 will get all the votes on the Left, 1 million, since candidate 1 is closest to these voters, at distance 0. Candidate 2 will get all the rest of the 3 million votes. This candidate is right on top of the Center with its 2 million votes, and a lot closer to the Right, with its 1 million votes, than candidate 1 is. Using subgame perfection in this way generates the 3×3 normal form matrix game between the two candidates in the first stage of the voting game (see Figure 16.2). The result is recorded in the cell (L,C). Note that whenever both candidates occupy the same position, they split the total votes.

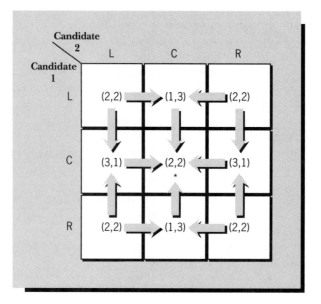

Figure 16.2. Voting game, discrete issue spectrum, symmetrical distribution; vote totals in millions.

As is clear from Figure 16.2, the voting game has a unique subgame perfect equilibrium. Each candidate adopts a position at the Center. Indeed, this is a dominant strategy for each candidate. The voters then respond by voting for each candidate in equal numbers. The candidates split the total votes, with 2 million each. This result, when both candidates in a 2-candidate election move to the middle of the political spectrum, is called the median voter theorem.[1] If the average, or median, voter is in the middle of the political spectrum, that is also where the candidates want to be. This theorem explains the persistent tendency for candidates for national office in the United States to establish positions in the middle. Woe unto candidates who get stuck on the far left or far right—they will pay a big price in lost votes on election day. We will establish this result in a fairly general form in the next section.

Before doing so, however, it is useful to solve a voting game where the candidates do not seek out the Center. Suppose that the distribution of voters is heavily stacked toward the Right:

    on the Left, 1 million voters

    in the Center, 0.5 million voters

    on the Right, 2.5 million voters

---

[1]This result is sometimes called Black's theorem, in honor of the British mathematician Duncan Black, who first proved it. See Duncan Black, *The Theory of Committees and Elections* (Cambridge: Cambridge University Press, 1958).

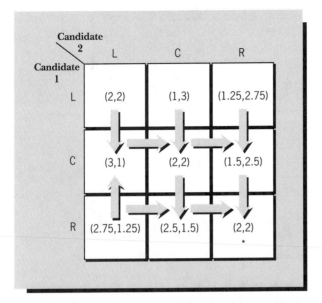

Figure 16.3. Voting game, discrete issue spectrum, asymmetrical distribution; vote totals in millions.

The median voter isn't in the middle anymore, but on the Right. Proceeding as before, and using subgame perfection, we get the first-round matrix game in Figure 16.3. Taking a position on the Left is dominated twice, by taking a position in the Center or on the Right. The unique equilibrium has both candidates taking positions on the Right, again splitting the total vote. Both candidates being in the Center is not an equilibrium. A candidate can move to the Right and pick up an extra 500,000 votes. The political calculation is straightforward. At the Center, the candidate was getting the Left and the Center for 1.5 million votes. By moving to the Right, the candidate gives up half the Left (0.5 million votes) and half the Center (0.25 million votes), but gets half the Right (1.25 million). The total is a half-million more votes. In a voting equilibrium, the median voter gets exactly what he or she wants, whether that is a centrist outcome or an extremist outcome.

♟ 16.2 Two-Candidate Voting Games with a Continuous Issue Spectrum ■■■■■■■■■■■■■■

This section studies voting games on a continuous spectrum and extends the results of the previous section. This extension is a famous result in political science. The **median voter theorem,** introduced in the previous section, can be formally stated as follows:

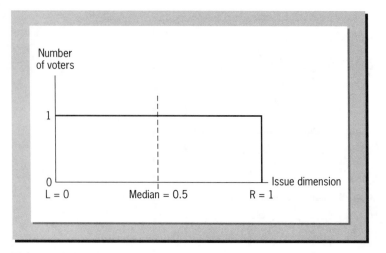

Figure 16.4. Continuous issue spectrum, uniformly distributed voters.

■ ■

Median Voter Theorem. Suppose that there are two candidates and voters are arrayed in a continuous distribution on the issue spectrum [0,1]. Let s^* be the median of the voter distribution. Then the candidate position vector (s^*, s^*) solves the voting game.

We will establish this result when voters are distributed uniformly on the issue spectrum [0,1] (see Figure 16.4). In order for voters to be distributed in a continuous fashion, there must be infinitely many of them. This is one way to model mass elections involving millions of voters.

As before, candidates move first. Each candidate i picks a point s_i on the issue spectrum. At the end of the candidate stage, the voters are faced with a vector $\mathbf{s} = (s_1, s_2)$ of candidate positions. Each voter ranks candidates according to how close the candidate's position is to his or her own position. A voter j whose ideal position is located at point v_j would maximize utility as follows:

$$u_j(s) = -d(v_j, s_1) \qquad \text{if } d(v_j, s_1) \leq d(v_j, s_2)$$
$$= -d(v_j, s_2) \qquad \text{if } d(v_j, s_2) \leq d(v_j, s_1)$$

where $d(\ )$ is the distance function from the appendix in Chapter 5. For instance, suppose that $\mathbf{s} = (0.4, 0.8)$ and $v_j = 0.5$. Then the distance from voter j to candidate 1 is 0.1, and the distance from voter j to candidate 2 is 0.3. Since candidate 1 is closer, voter j votes for this candidate.

Using subgame perfection in this way, we can establish vote totals for the two candidates at the voting stage, based on the vector of positions they have taken, **s**. These vote totals establish a utility function in the first stage for the candidates. Solving this first stage game will lead to a solution for the entire voting game. The biggest challenge is establishing the vote totals. We make our task a lot simpler by noticing that, for the candidates, the voting game is symmetrical. Both candidates have the same strategy set, [0,1]. If both candidates pick the

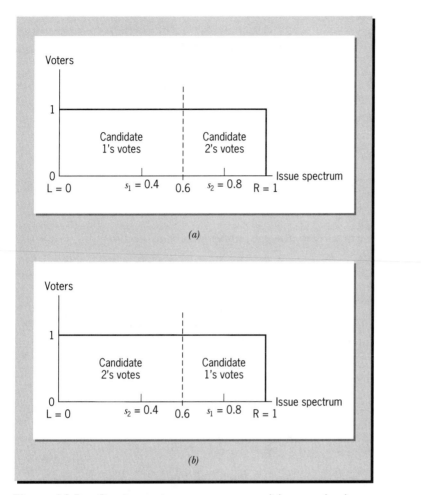

Figure 16.5. Continuous issue spectrum, candidates trade places.

same strategy, they split the vote. Finally, if candidates trade places, they trade vote totals, as illustrated by Figure 16.5. In Figure 16.5a, the candidate position vector $\mathbf{s} = (0.4, 0.8)$. Candidate 1 gets all the votes to the left of the position 0.6, which amounts to 60% of all votes. Candidate 2 gets all the votes to the right of position 0.6, which amounts to 40% of all votes. In figure 16.5b, the candidates trade places, with the position vector $\mathbf{s} = (0.8, 0.4)$. Now candidate 1 gets 40% of the votes, and candidate 2 gets 60% of the votes. Trading places means trading vote totals. In terms of candidate utilities, we have

$$u_1(s_1, s_2) = u_2(s_2, s_1)$$

We have just verified all that we need for symmetry.

We are now ready to write down a general utility function for the two candidates in the first stage of the game. By symmetry, it is enough to write down the utility function for candidate 1, $u_1(\mathbf{s})$. There are three cases to consider, depending on the relationship between the two candidates' strategies:

Case 1. $s_1 < s_2$. This is the case illustrated in Figure 16.5a. Candidate 1 gets all the voters from 0 up to the boundary value $(s_1 + s_2)/2$. Since the distribution of voters is uniform, we get

$$u_1(s) = \frac{s_1 + s_2}{2}$$

Notice that candidate 1's utility is increasing in the candidate's own strategy in this case.

Case 2. $s_1 = s_2$. In this case, the candidates split the vote

$$u_1(s) = 0.5$$

Case 3. $s_1 > s_2$. This is the case illustrated in Figure 16.5b. Candidate 1 gets all the voters from the boundary value $(s_1 + s_2)/2$ up to 1. Since the distribution of voters is uniform, we get

$$u_1(s) = 1 - \frac{s_1 + s_2}{2}$$

Notice that candidate 1's utility is decreasing in the candidate's own strategy in this case.

This exhausts the possible relationships between the two candidates' positions and therefore completes the derivation of candidate 1's utility function. Since the total vote percentage is 100% = 1, the game is one sum, so candidate 2's utility function is

$$u_2(\mathbf{s}) = 1 - u_1(\mathbf{s})$$

The indifference lines for candidate 1's utility function are shown in Figure 16.6. Notice that there is a big discontinuity in candidate 1's utility in the vicinity of the line $s_1 = s_2$. For instance, at $\mathbf{s} = (0.24, 0.26)$, $u_1 = 0.25$, whereas at $\mathbf{s} = (0.26, 0.24)$, $u_1 = 0.75$. In between, at $\mathbf{s} = (0.25, 0.25)$, $u_1 = 0.5$. This discontinuity prevents us from using calculus to find an equilibrium.

We can find an equilibrium by other means, however. By symmetry, we know that an equilibrium must lie on the line where $s_1 = s_2$ and where $u_1 = u_2 = 0.5$. Since the game is constant sum, the solution theorem applies. Candidate 2 can guarantee that candidate 1's utility is never greater than 0.5 by setting $s_2 = 0.5$. As you can see from Figure 16.6, this choice of s_2 puts u_1 in the interval [0.25, 0.5]. Since u_1 has to equal 0.5 at equilibrium, this means that $s_2^* = .5$ supports the equilibrium. Then by symmetry, we have as the equilibrium $\mathbf{s}^* = (0.5, 0.5)$. The solution of the game has each candidate staking out a position in

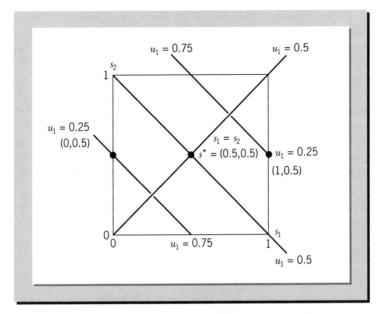

Figure 16.6. Indifference lines, candidate 1, continuous issue spectrum.

the middle of the issue spectrum, precisely where the median voter is. This establishes the median voter theorem for the uniform **distribution of voters' favorite points.**

The median voter theorem holds for any symmetrical distribution of voters' favorite points, not just for the uniform distribution. The median for any symmetrical distribution on [0,1] is at $s^* = 0.5$. Although the indifference curves for u_1 will look different, the argument just given still holds, and the median voter will be where candidates locate. If the distribution of voters' favorite points is asymmetrical, then the median need not be in the middle, but candidates will still locate at the median voter. Finally, if the distribution of voters' favorite points contains gaps, there may be two median voters. In this case, there may be a candidate at each of two medians (see problems 2 through 4 for details).

✖ 16.3 Multicandidate Voting Games ■ ■ ■ ■ ■ ■ ■ ■ ■ ■ ■ ■

The voting games considered so far have had exactly two candidates. It turns out to be an important restriction. Once there are three or more candidates, the strategic considerations increase enormously. In particular, voter preferences may be quite a bit more complicated, and voters may do well to vote strategically, rather than according to their preferences. The very notion of majority rule becomes somewhat ambiguous when there are three or more candidates. This section takes up these issues. To keep the complexity manageable, we will assume throughout that *candidates have already adopted positions.* One explanation for this situation is that they are bound by party platforms or by other credible commitment devices. This assumption puts all the complexity on the side of the voters.

Consider an election with three candidates, represented by the vector of candidate positions $\mathbf{s} = (s_1, s_2, s_3)$. In the United States an election with three candidates is conducted by **plurality rule.** Each voter receives a ballot with all three candidates' names on it and a box beside each name. The voter may mark one candidate's box. The candidate with the most marks wins. Since the winning candidate will have more marks than any other candidate, this candidate will have a plurality.

To see how plurality rule works, suppose that there are three types of voters. Voters rank the candidates, from top to bottom, as follows:

voter type 1: $s_1 > s_2 > s_3$
voter type 2: $s_2 > s_3 > s_1$
voter type 3: $s_3 > s_1 > s_2$

Furthermore, there are 20 voters of type 1, and 15 voters each of types 2 and 3. Voters vote *honestly* when they fill out the ballot exactly in accordance with their ranking of candidates. In this case, honest voting leads to the election of candidate 1. The type 1 voters vote for candidate 1; the type 2 voters, for candidate 2; the type 3 voters, for candidate 3. The vote totals are candidate 1, 20; candidate 2, 15; and candidate 3, 15. Candidate 1 wins.

Several problems with plurality voting are readily apparent from this example. First, a minority candidate can be and often is elected. Candidate 1 wins with $20/50 = 40\%$ of the votes in this election. Second, the winning candidates may actually have a majority opposed to his or her election. For instance, in the election here, all type 2 and 3 voters rank candidate 3 above winning candidate 1. In this example $30/50 = 60\%$ of the voters favor candidate 3, a loser, over candidate 1, the winner. This is a majority in opposition. Third, any time there is a majority in opposition, there is a strong incentive to vote *strategically*. *Strategic voting* is any voting not in accordance with the voter's true preferences. When it succeeds, strategic voting leads to an outcome that the voter prefers to the outcome that results from voting honestly. Suppose that type 2 and 3 voters all vote for candidate 3. This is honest voting for type 3, but strategic voting for type 2. Candidate 3 is elected, by a 60% to 40% margin, over candidate 1. The election of candidate 3 is preferred by the type 2 voters to the election of candidate 1. Strategic voting by the type 2 voters has succeeded.

Given all the problems inherent in plurality voting, there have been many attempts to find a better way of conducting elections with three or more candidates. A short list of commonly accepted desiderata for an election would include at least **efficiency, decisiveness, truthfulness** and **neutrality:**

■ ■

Efficiency. The winner of the election is efficient. This means that there is no candidate whom every voter ranks higher than the winner. The need for this condition is pretty self-evident. Every voter would clamor for electoral reform if a three-way election chose a candidate that every voter ranked last.

Decisiveness. The electoral process leads to a unique winner each time. The whole point of an election is to reach a decision, which is not accomplished by a tied election. Tie-breaking mechanisms are therefore needed. In the United States, these mechanisms include the extraordinary vote of the vice president when the Senate is tied (Al Gore broke two 50–50 ties in 1993), recounts of ballots, and, as a last resort, runoff elections.

Truthfulness. No voter ever has an incentive to vote strategically. In a truthful election, every voter would get his or her best possible outcome by voting honestly.

Neutrality. The winner does not depend on the names of the candidates or on the way in which the names are arrayed on the ballot. There are many ways to steal an election that is not neutral. The presidential election held in South Vietnam in 1971 was definitely not neutral. The number 9 is very important in Vietnamese culture, and the incumbent president Thieu made sure that he was listed as candidate number 9 on the ballot.

Unfortunately, if there are at least three voters and three candidates, there is only one voting rule that satisfies efficiency, decisiveness, truthfulness, and neutrality. This voting rule has a very familiar name: *dictatorship.* In a dictatorship, only one voter's preferences matter, those of the dictator. This is one-man, or one-woman, rule. It is easy to check that dictatorship satisfies the four desiderata. First, a dictator is efficient. A dictator picks what he or she wants most. There can be no alternative that everyone, including the dictator, likes better. Second, a dictator is decisive. As long as the dictator has a unique favorite, the dictator picks that favorite and the election is over. A dictator who has multiple favorites can decide among them by tossing a coin or by some even more whimsical procedure. Third, a dictator is truthful. Since the dictator gets what he or she wants anyway, lying on the ballot isn't necessary. The same holds true for the other voters, since in a dictatorship the outcome is whatever the dictator wants, regardless of how the other ballots are filled out. Fourth, a dictator is neutral. It doesn't matter what the ballot looks like or how the candidates are named—the dictator's first choice always wins. Despite these appealing features, however, dictatorship is inconsistent with democratic principles. The immense concentration of power in the hands of a Hitler or a Stalin can lead to disastrous consequences for human rights and world peace.[2]

The reason dictatorship shows up here is a fundamental result in economics

---

[2]The list of dictators or near dictators who were good guys is very short. One nominee would be George Washington, who, as commander in chief of the Continental army, was in a position to become king of America. Instead, he gave up his army command to run for president.

called Arrow's impossibility theorem.[3] This theorem shows that, under conditions similar to those given, the only possible social welfare function is dictatorship. You can show, although the proof is involved, that the four desiderata imply the existence of an Arrow social welfare function, and hence imply dictatorship.[4]

An appealing voting scheme that comes close to satisfying the four desiderata without being dictatorial was derived by the Marquis de Condorcet. Condorcet was one of the major figures of the Enlightenment and the French Revolution. His contributions to economic science include the invention of national income accounting and the voting proposal that bears his name.[5] Condorcet proposed that the winner in a 3-candidate election should have a majority against every other candidate in two-way comparisons. When such a winner exists, then every voter has a dominant strategy to vote honestly. Here's an example in which Condorcet's proposal works fine. There are three types, with the rankings

$$\text{voter type 1: } s_1 > s_2 > s_3$$
$$\text{voter type 2: } s_2 > s_3 > s_1$$
$$\text{voter type 3: } s_3 > s_2 > s_1$$

Suppose that there is one voter of each type. Candidate 2 has a 2-to-1 majority over candidate 1 and a 2-to-1 majority over candidate 3. Therefore, candidate 2 is the winner. Note that plurality voting would lead to a three-way tie instead of a clear-cut winner. Moreover, strategic voting would lead to a worse outcome for the voter. For instance, suppose that voter type 1, in an attempt to manipulate the outcome, voted for candidate 3 instead of candidate 2 in the contest between candidates 3 and 2. Then candidate 3 would win a majority against both candidate 2 and candidate 1 and would be elected. This outcome, however, would be the worst possible for voter 1, who would be getting the bottom candidate instead of the middle candidate.

Condorcet's proposal satisfies neutrality, efficiency, and truthfulness. If we model the previous election as a game in coalition function form, then the election of candidate 2 is the unique outcome in the core of the voting game.

---

[3]See K. J. Arrow, *Social Choice and Individual Values*, 2nd ed. (New York: John Wiley & Sons, Inc., 1963).

[4]See Alan Gibbard, "Manipulation of Voting Schemes: A General Result," *Econometrica* 41 (1973):587–601. Also see Mark Satterthwaite, "Strategy-Proofness and Arrow's Conditions: Existence and Correspondence Theorems for Voting Procedures and Social Welfare Functions," *Journal of Economic Theory* 10 (1975):187–217. One way to prove this theorem is to show that the conditions imply the existence of a social welfare function satisfying Arrow's conditions, which then runs afoul of the Arrow impossibility theorem.

[5]Condorcet was a fervent believer in human progress, which he thought unstoppable. The economist Malthus wrote his gloomy *Essay on Population* in direct opposition to Condorcet's position. In a final irony, Condorcet was one of the 30,000 victims sentenced to the guillotine during the French Revolution.

Unfortunately, however, Condorcet's voting scheme is not decisive. Suppose that we replace the earlier rankings for voter type 3 with the following rankings:

voter type 3: $s_3 > s_1 > s_2$

Candidate 2 has a 2-to-1 advantage over candidate 3, candidate 3 has a 2-to-1 advantage over candidate 1, and candidate 1 has a 2-to-1 advantage over candidate 2. No candidate has a majority against every other. Hence no decision is reached. What is worse, Condorcet's voting scheme is forced to be decisive. By picking a minority outcome in this case, an opportunity for strategic voting is created.

Suppose that, for the sake of decisiveness, a minority decision is forced and that decision elects candidate 2. This creates a golden opportunity for voter type 3 to vote strategically. If voter type 3 switches sides on the contest between candidates 1 and 3, in effect revealing the rankings

$$s_1 > s_3 > s_2$$

then candidate 1 has a majority against both candidates 2 and 3. The voting scheme has just become untruthful.

In a way, the fact that we are caught on the horns of a dilemma between dictatorship and untruthfulness is not so surprising. It is yet another indication that strategy matters. Thoreau may not have approved of the way things are in this respect, but this is the price we must pay if we want a democracy. Given all the problems that arise with multicandidate elections, it should come as no surprise that these have proved very troublesome in U.S. presidential politics, as we shall now see.

16.4 Multicandidate Presidential Elections, 1824–1992

The members of the Constitutional Convention were familiar with the problems surrounding plurality voting, and so created an institution, the electoral college, to limit its role. This system has nevertheless worked remarkably like plurality voting in 2-candidate races. In all but two such races, the candidate with the most popular votes was also the candidate with the most electoral votes, and so was elected president. The exceptions were Rutherford Hayes versus Samuel Tilden in 1876, and Benjamin Harrison versus Grover Cleveland in 1888, both of which were extremely close in the popular vote.

With **multicandidate elections,** however, the results have been much more volatile and have left great scope for strategic voting, as might be expected. In the first multicandidate race,[6] in 1824, four candidates received votes in the electoral college. Andrew Jackson received a plurality of both the popular and the electoral college votes, but not a majority of the latter. Thus the election went to the House of Representatives. Meanwhile, the second-place candidate, John Quincy Adams, was busy assembling a winning coalition. He promised (and delivered) the office of secretary of state to Henry Clay of Tennessee in exchange for Clay's support in the House vote. This move gave the Adams bloc the votes to win in the House. Jackson and his supporters screamed they had been robbed by a crooked bargain, conveniently forgetting that they could have made the same deal with fellow southerner Clay, and perhaps at a lower price.

The next multicandidate race was in 1860. The incumbent Democrats were favored to win the election, until they split into Northern and Southern factions, led by Stephen Douglas and John Breckenridge, respectively. This split in their ranks opened the door for Abraham Lincoln's Republicans, who ran only in the North and were therefore in no danger of splitting along North–South lines. Lincoln won the ensuing election, with less than 40% of the popular vote but with a majority of the electoral vote. This was an outcome that neither Northern nor Southern Democrats wanted. Had the Democrats been able to preserve their party, or at least to vote strategically, they might have been able to preserve the Union without a Civil War.

Lincoln's repeat victories in 1860 and 1864, and the Union victory in the Civil War, led to a Republican dynasty that lasted half a century.[7] Republican presidential dominance only ceased in 1912, thanks to a split in the Republican ranks between incumbent president Howard Taft and former president Theodore Roosevelt. The Republican split allowed a Democrat, Woodrow Wilson, to capture the White House with only a minority of the votes—once again, an outcome that strategic voting could have prevented. Wilson's victory ushered in a period of Democratic dominance that lasted for 40 years.[8]

One of the most intriguing multicandidate races of all time occurred in 1968. This race pitted Republican Richard Nixon against Democrat Hubert Humphrey in a battle of vice presidents and pitted both against Alabama governor George Wallace, a southern Democrat. In hindsight, it appears that Wallace was playing the role of the spoiler (see Chapter 4), making certain that

---

[6]Multicandidate race refers to a race in which at least three candidates receive 10% or more of the popular vote. Every presidential election includes a wide assortment of crank, protest, or otherwise minor candidates, whose presence has no effect on the outcome or the strategies employed. There were over 4000 officially registered candidates for president in 1992. All races since the constitutional reform of 1804 are considered here. Prior to 1804, there was no distinction between candidates for president and candidates for vice president. The candidate with the most electoral votes was named president; the candidate with the next most electoral votes was named vice president.

[7]Cleveland's victories in 1884 and 1892 were the only Democratic victories between 1860 and 1912.

[8]Between 1912 and 1952, the only Republican victories were those of Harding in 1920, Coolidge in 1924, and Hoover in 1928.

Humphrey, a political enemy of the southern Democrats since 1948, was denied the White House. Nixon won handily in the electoral college, even though he had but 43% of the popular vote. The Democratic split handed the White House to the Republicans, and they held on to it for all but one election (Carter, 1976) until 1992.

The most recent multicandidate race occurred in 1992. This race pitted incumbent Republican president George Bush against Democratic challenger Bill Clinton and third-party candidate Ross Perot. Perot dropped out of the race suddenly in midsummer, when he was leading in the polls. He reentered the race in September, in a move widely regarded as playing the spoiler. Perot split the political Right and thus helped hand the election to the left-of-center Democratic governor of Arkansas. Democrat Clinton, in a by-now-familiar pattern, won the election with 43% of the popular vote and a large majority of the electoral vote.

In every case of multicandidate elections since 1824—1860, 1912, 1968, and 1992—the losers had an opportunity to vote strategically, an opportunity that, once lost, meant they faced a very bad outcome. Even a modified form of plurality voting, as in the form of the electoral college, exhibits all the drawbacks that game theory leads us to expect from plurality voting.

■■ 16.5 Positional Voting Rules ■■■■■■■■■■■■■■■

In the period of Enlightenment before the French Revolution, another Frenchman, the Count de Borda, proposed an improvement on plurality voting. His system is based on attaching point values to various positions in the rankings, with the final ranking based on total point values. Such systems are now called **positional voting rules.** The **Borda voting rule** belongs to this class and is used today in contexts such as voting for the Most Valuable Player and the Cy Young Award in baseball and for the national collegiate championship in football.

Borda's original example considered a 3-candidate election. He proposed a 3-line ballot. On the first line, the voter would put the highest ranked candidate, and this candidate would be awarded 3 points. On the second line, the voter would put the second highest ranked candidate, and this candidate would be awarded 2 points. On the bottom line, the voter would put the lowest ranked candidate, and this candidate would be awarded 1 point. All the points would be added for each candidate. The final ranking of the candidates would be according to their total point counts.

To see how Borda's voting rule works in practice, consider again the 3-candidate election we studied earlier. There are three voter types, as follows:

voter type 1: $s_1 > s_2 > s_3$
voter type 2: $s_2 > s_3 > s_1$
voter type 3: $s_3 > s_1 > s_2$

There are 20 type 1 voters, and 15 voters each of the other two types. Suppose that all voters vote sincerely. Then candidate 1 gets 20 first-place rankings worth 60 points, 15 second-place rankings worth 30 points, and 15 third-place rankings worth 15 points, for a total of 105 points. Candidate 2 gets 15 first-place rankings worth 45 points, 20 second-place rankings worth 40 points, and 15 third-place rankings worth 15 points, for a total of 100 points. Candidate 3 gets 15 first-place rankings worth 45 points, 15 second-place rankings worth 30 points, and 20 third-place rankings worth 20 points, for a total of 95 points. The outcome is

1. Candidate 1, 105 points
2. Candidate 2, 100 points
3. Candidate 3, 95 points

In this case the winner is the same under both Borda and plurality voting. However, just like plurality voting, Borda voting is very susceptible to strategic voting.

Type 2 and 3 voters have every incentive to try to get candidate 3, currently in last place, elected instead of candidate 1. Moreover, they have the votes to do this. What they have to do is fill out their ballots as follows:

voter type 2: $s_3 > s_2 > s_1$
voter type 3: $s_3 > s_2 > s_1$

Candidate 1 now gets 20 first-place votes and 30 third-place votes for a total vote of 90, substantially less than before. Candidate 3 now gets 30 first-place votes worth 90 points, and 20 third-place votes worth 20 points, for 110 points, much more than before. Candidate 2 gets 50 second-place rankings, worth 100 points, the same as before, for a total of 100. The outcome of this fine piece of strategic voting is

1. Candidate 3, 110 points
2. Candidate 2, 100 points
3. Candidate 1, 90 points

The former winner is now ranked last. The key to this result was having all voter types 2 and 3 rank candidate 1 last.

This example is by no means unusual. Strategic voting can be rampant in positional voting rules. For instance, let's look at the form of positional voting used for the national collegiate championship in football. Each voter fills out a ballot with 25 places. The top place on the ballot gets 25 points, and so on down to the 25th team, which gets 1 point. All teams not ranked (there are roughly 100 teams eligible for the Division I title) get 0 points. Suppose that there are two undefeated teams after the bowl games, one from the Pac 10 and one from the ACC. Suppose further that a voter has a distinct preference for a team from the Pac 10 to win the championship. What this voter can do is leave the team from the ACC off the ballot completely, giving it 0 points. Meanwhile, the voter ranks his or her favorite team first, for 25 points. Although this may not seem like sporting conduct, it is perfectly legal—it is nothing more than strategic behavior responding to very clear incentives. Nevertheless, the result of such behavior can be very far from the goal of the NCAA—to name the best football team in the country the national champion.[9]

16.6 Voting Games in Coalition Function Form ■

In a voting game, the more the voters are organized as a bloc, the more likely they are to get what they want. This is the reason for the existence of political parties, coalition governments, international alliances, and cliques within a board of directors. The easiest way to study the phenomenon of voting coalitions is with games in coalition function form.

Let N be the set of voters, $N = \{1, 2, \ldots, n\}$. A coalition S, which is a subset of N, can either be *winning* or *not winning*. A **winning coalition** can take control of the political process to achieve its ends. Any coalition that is not winning cannot take control of the political process to achieve its ends. In terms of the coalition function, we have

$$v(S) = 1 \qquad \text{if } S \text{ is a winning coalition}$$
$$v(S) = 0 \qquad \text{if } S \text{ is not a winning coalition}$$

In this representation, the coalition value 1 means 100% control of the political process. We have encountered an example of such a coalition function before, in our study of n-player bargaining games in Chapter 14. The coalition function corresponding to a bargaining game is

$$v(S) = 1 \qquad \text{if } S = N$$
$$v(S) = 0 \qquad \text{otherwise}$$

In a bargaining game, the only coalition that controls things is the grand coalition. Any other coalition that walks away from the table is powerless to affect outcomes.

Any game in coalition function form that is limited to the values 0 or 1 is called a **simple game.** Some restrictions on simple games are necessary to avoid contradiction. For instance, two winning coalitions cannot coexist, since only one coalition at a time can be in charge. This contradiction would occur if there were disjoint coalitions S and T, both with $v(S) = v(T) = 1$. This situation is avoided by the exclusivity condition:

---

[9]The same phenomenon appears in MVP or Cy Young voting in baseball, when top contenders are left off sportswriters' ballots.

■ ■

Exclusivity. If *S* is winning, then *N* − *S* is not winning. In equation form, $v(S) = 1$ implies $v(N - S) = 0$.

Exclusivity says that if a coalition *S* is winning, then the countercoalition, *N* − *S*, consisting of all players in *N* not in *S*, is not winning. Another contradiction would occur if a coalition *S* was winning, but a larger coalition *T* that included *S* was not. This contradiction is avoided by the monotonicity condition:

■ ■

Monotonicity. If *S* is winning, and *T* includes *S*, then *T* is winning. In equation form, if $v(S) = 1$ and *T* includes *S*, then $v(T) = 1$.

A final regularity condition is that at least one coalition, the grand coalition, is winning. This condition is called nonnullity:

■ ■

Nonnullity. The grand coalition *N* is winning, $v(N) = 1$.

In the case of bargaining games, only the grand coalition is winning. All the voting games worth studying satisfy exclusivity, monotonicity, and nonnullity.

Here are two examples of how winning coalitions are generated in real life. First, consider the process by which a bill becomes law in the United States. The set of players in the voting game by which a bill becomes law consists of the president, the Senate, and the House of Representatives. There are two recipes for a winning coalition. A bill becomes law if it gets a majority (218 votes of 435 seats) in the House of Representatives, a majority in the Senate (51 votes of 100 seats), and the signature of the president.[10] This kind of winning coalition—the win is the bill being passed into law—needs the president, at least 218 representatives, and at least 51 senators—270 people in all, in just the right numbers. A bill can also become law if Congress overrides the president's veto, his or her refusal to sign the bill. An override requires a 2/3 majority in both the Senate and the House. This kind of winning coalition—the kind without the president—needs at least 290 representatives (exactly double the remaining 145) and at least 67 senators (more than double the remaining 33). The U.S. Constitution makes it difficult, but not impossible, to form winning coalitions. The voting game that results satisfies exclusivity, monotonicity, and nonnullity.

Corporate voting is another good example of how winning coalitions are formed. Here the set *N* of voters consists of all stockholders with voting stock in a corporation. Let *i* be a stockholder and $w(i)$ be, the number of his or her shares. The total shares in the corporation are $\Sigma w(i)$. Each share is worth one

---

[10]As we have seen, if the vice president can be trusted to vote with the president, then 50 senators and the vice president suffice to win in the Senate.

vote. A winning coalition has to have a majority of the shares in the corporation:

$$v(S) = 1 \text{ if } \Sigma w(i), \, i \text{ in } S > \left(\frac{1}{2}\right) \Sigma w(i), \, i \text{ in } N$$

Needless to say, a winning coalition can be very small as long as it includes some big owners. Proxy fights and other struggles for corporate control center on getting 51% of outstanding shares because this is the magic number for a winning coalition.

16.7 Measuring Power ■■■■■■■■■■■■■■■■■■■■■■

Now that we have a representation of political structure in a voting game, let's solve such games. As we saw in Chapter 15, the core will not be of much help, since it is empty in the game Majority Rule—and, as it turns out, in most other simple games. Thus we need a different concept for solving simple games. The concept presented here, the **Shapley value**,[11] is based on the idea that power consists in the ability of a player to turn a coalition that is not winning into a coalition that is winning.

Recall the definition of player i's **marginal product** to the coalition S, MP(i,S):

$$MP(i,S) = v(S \text{ and } i) - v(S)$$

In a simple game, a player's marginal product can take only two values, 0 or 1. For instance, suppose that coalition S is winning before player i joins. By monotonicity, {S,i} is still winning, so player i's marginal product is

$$MP(i,S) = 1 - 1 = 0$$

Next, suppose that coalition S is losing before player i joins and is still losing after player i joins. We have

$$MP(i,S) = 0 - 0 = 0$$

In both these cases, player i's marginal product to the coalition is 0. This player adds nothing. There is exactly one way for a player's marginal product to be positive—when coalition S is not winning before player i joins and is winning afterwards. We have

$$MP(i,S) = 1 - 0 = 1$$

---

[11]The index of voting power was first introduced in Lloyd Shapley and Martin Shubik, "A Method for Evaluating the Distribution of Power in a Committee System," *American Political Science Review* 48 (1954):787–92. This index is a special case of a more general concept, the Shapley value. See Lloyd S. Shapley, "A Value for *n*-Person Games," in *Contributions to the Theory of Games,* vol 2, (ed. Harold W. Kuhn and A. W. Tucker) (Princeton, N.J.: Princeton University Press, 1953), 307–17

In this case, player i is **pivotal** to the coalition's winning.

The Shapley value says that a player's political power is the likelihood that that player will be pivotal. If a player will never, under any circumstances, be pivotal, then that player is powerless. No one would ever need such a player's vote. As before, such a player is called a **dummy.** On the other hand, if a player is always, under all possible circumstances, pivotal, then that player is all-powerful. Such a player—there can be at most one, by exclusivity—is called a **dictator.** These are the two extremes between which most players are found.

In order to compute the likelihood that a player will be pivotal, we need a mechanism for generating probabilities. Of the many stories for such a mechanism, we will adopt that of the *veil of ignorance.*[12] Imagine that players have not yet been assigned their identities in the game. It is as if they are waiting backstage to play various parts in a play, but the curtain, or veil, hasn't risen yet and they don't know which part they will play. All they know is that each of them has the same probability of playing a given role. Imagine further that the parts are going to be assigned at random. What the Shapley value does is identify a player's role with that player's position in a random ordering of all players. When each random ordering is equally likely, then each player is equally likely to be in first place, second place, . . . , last place. For instance, if there are 2 players, then there are $2! = (2)(1) = 2$ random orderings:

    1,2   (player 1 is first)

    2,1   (player 2 is first)

Each of these random orderings occurs with probability $1/2$ when the veil of ignorance is lifted.

The Shapley value of player i, written Shap(i), is the expected value of that player's marginal product in a random ordering of all the players:

$$\begin{aligned}
\text{Shap}(i) &= EV\,MP(i,S) \\
&= (\text{probability of being pivotal})\,(1) \\
&\quad + (\text{probability of not being pivotal})\,(0) \\
&= \text{probability of being pivotal}
\end{aligned}$$

A player's marginal product is equal to 0 or 1, so the expected value of this marginal product is positive only when a player is pivotal. When a player is pivotal, his or her marginal product is 1. The probability with which a player is pivotal is precisely that player's Shapley value.[13]

---

[12]This notion comes from the renowned game theorist John C. Harsanyi, "Cardinal Welfare, Individualistic Ethics, and Interpersonal Comparisons of Utility," *Journal of Political Economy* 63(1955):309–21. Although Harsanyi uses the veil of ignorance to argue for utilitarianism, Rawls's theory of justice uses the veil of ignorance to argue just the opposite.

[13]There are other ways to measure power in addition to this one. One such alternative is the power index of John F. Banzhaf III, "Weighted Voting Doesn't Work: A Mathematical Analysis," *Rutgers Law Review* 19(1965):317–43.

Figure 16.7. Majority Rule, Shapley Value, **n** = 3.

Random Ordering	MP (1,S)	MP (2,S)	MP (3,S)
1 2 3	0	1	0
1 3 2	0	0	1
2 1 3	1	0	0
2 3 1	0	0	1
3 1 2	1	0	0
3 2 1	0	1	0
	2/6	2/6	2/6
Shap (i)	i = 1	i = 2	i = 3

This is all rather abstract. Let's look at some sample calculations. Take 3-player Majority Rule. Figure 16.7 spells out the required computations. Since there are three players, there are 3! = 6 possible random orderings of players: 123, 132, 213, 231, 312, 321. Each of these random orderings is equally likely, hence probability 1/6. In the first row, the random ordering is 123. Player 1's marginal product in this random ordering is 0, since neither the coalition with 0 members nor the coalition {1} is winning. Player 2's marginal product in this random ordering is 1, since the coalition {1} is not winning but the coalition {1,2} is winning. Player 2 has been pivotal in creating a winning coalition. Player 3's marginal product in this random ordering is 0, since coalition {1,2} is winning and so is coalition {1,2,3}. This reasoning underlies the marginal product calculations in the figure. Finally, since each random ordering is equally likely, each of a player's marginal products is multiplied by 1/6, yielding the bottom-line Shapley value. For instance, for player 1,

$$\text{Shap}(1) = \left(\frac{1}{6}\right)(0 + 0 + 1 + 0 + 1 + 0) = \frac{2}{6}$$

Figure 16.7 shows that in one-person, one-vote Majority Rule, each player has the same power, 1/3.

When all the players have the same impact on the vote, as in a bargaining game or in one-person, one-vote Majority Rule, the Shapley value says that power is equally divided. When the players have differential impact, the Shapley value picks that up, too. Here is an extreme case. There are three players. Any coalition that includes player 1 is winning; and only coalitions that include player 1 are winning. Figure 16.8 contains the relevant calculation for the Shapley value. As you can see, player 1 is always pivotal and gets a Shapley value of 1. Player 1 is a dictator. Players 2 and 3 are never pivotal. These players, with 0 Shapley value each, are powerless.

Sometimes a player can be a dummy in a voting game, even though the player apparently has influence. Suppose in the example just given that player 1 has 51% of the voting stock in a corporation; player 2 has 25%; and player 3 has 24%. Player 1 alone can win any vote. Players 2 and 3, despite all their

Figure 16.8. Dictatorship, Shapley Value, **n = 3**.

Random Ordering	MP (1,S)	MP (2,S)	MP (3,S)
1 2 3	1	0	0
1 3 2	1	0	0
2 1 3	1	0	0
2 3 1	1	0	0
3 1 2	1	0	0
3 2 1	1	0	0
Shap (i)	6/6 i = 1	0/6 i = 2	0/6 i = 3

stock, cannot win a vote without player 1. Such a situation is exactly what is intended in a 51%–49% takeover, where corporate ownership–player 1 owns 51%—is much less extensive than corporate control—Shap (1) = 100%.

Player i has a *veto that cannot be overridden* if no coalition can win unless player i is a member. Such a player is called a **veto player.** The president of the United States is not a veto player, since his or her veto can be overridden. However, there are numerous examples of veto powers that cannot be overridden. For instance, if the commissioner of baseball vetoes a player deal, the teams involved must annul it.[14] If an arbitrator rules in a certain way, the parties involved cannot appeal the decision. If one of the permanent members of the United Nations Security Council vetoes a Security Council resolution, the resolution is dead. We will next study the power structure of the Security Council in considerable detail, and especially the implications of adding Japan and Germany to the Council.

16.8 Expanding the United Nations Security Council[15] ■■■■■■■■■■■■■■■■■■■■■■

The United Nations was founded by the victorious powers of World War II in 1945. Their purpose was to ensure world security in the aftermath of the world's greatest conflagration and to prevent further world war. To this end, the United Nations included a Security Council, to deal with matters of world security, and in particular to sanction the use of force by the members of the United Nations in disputes threatening world peace and order. The five great

[14]This may be why the owners have been slow to name a new commissioner since they sacked Fay Vincent.

[15]This material was drawn from Julia Preson, "U.S. Seeks to Expand U.N. Security Council," *Washington Post,* June 10, 1993, and "Morgen oder Ubermorgen" (Tomorrow or the day after), *Der Spiegel,* July 12, 1993, pp. 77–82.

powers that won World War II—the United States, the USSR, France, the United Kingdom, and China—had permanent seats on the **United Nations Security Council.** Seven (later 10) other seats were held on a rotating basis by other United Nations member states.

The Security Council uses three-fifths majority rule for its decisions. Under its current configuration, this means a winning coalition needs 9 of the 15 members. However, each of the five permanent members has a veto over any proposal. This veto cannot be overridden: its exercise kills a proposal. In 1950, the USSR could have vetoed the proposal to send United Nations forces to defend South Korea against the attack by North Korea, a Soviet ally. For reasons still unexplained, the Soviet ambassador to the United Nations was not present at the Security Council deliberations and did not veto the United Nations initiative in South Korea. Thus, not only does a winning coalition need to have nine members, but it also needs to have every country with a veto. Currently, the five members with a veto are the United States, Russia (inheriting the USSR's veto), France, the United Kingdom, and the People's Republic of China (inheriting the Republic of China's veto).

In June 1993, the United States proposed enlarging the Security Council with the addition of the world's second- and third-largest economies, who coincidentally were the big losers in World War II—Japan and Germany. This proposal has been vigorously opposed by two current Security Council members, the United Kingdom and France. The Shapley value will help explain their opposition.

To compute the Shapley value for a political system with 15 players, like the current Security Council, requires the examination of 15! ($= 15 \times 14 \times \cdots \times 1$) random orderings, more than 1.3 trillion in all. This entire book could not contain the calculation. Obviously, we are going to need some cunning to pull this off. The best way in science is to start with a simple model and work your way up. That's what we've done before in this book, and that's exactly what we will do here. Let's start with a model security council, like the current one, only divided by 5—one country, 1, with veto power, and two countries, 2 and 3, without veto power. Figure 16.9 contains the relevant computation. With three countries, we only have to worry about 3! = 6 random orderings.

There are several useful things to note about this computation. First, the only time a country without a veto is pivotal is when it is in second place preceded in the random ordering by the country with a veto. So, in the random ordering 123, country 2 is pivotal; in the random ordering 132, country 3 is pivotal. It is easy to see why this is so. If the country with a veto is not already present in the random ordering, then adding a nonveto country cannot make the coalition a winning one. If all the countries with vetoes are already present in the random ordering, then adding a nonveto country is pivotal only when the coalition is one country short of a majority. This reasoning explains why the nonveto country has to be in second place to be pivotal. Second, each nonveto country has the same Shapley value, 1/6. This makes sense, since each is a perfect substitute for the other; that is, every time country 2 is pivotal, so is

Figure 16.9.   Security Council, Shapley Value, **n** = 3.

Random Ordering	MP (1,S)	MP (2,S)	MP (3,S)
1 2 3	0	1	0
1 3 2	0	0	1
2 1 3	1	0	0
2 3 1	1	0	0
3 1 2	1	0	0
3 2 1	1	0	0
	4/6	1/6	1/6
Shap (i)	i = 1	i = 2	i = 3

country 3, and vice versa. Finally, note that each country is in second place in a random ordering 1/3 of the time.

Based on these three observations, we will use the following shortcut to obtain the Shapley value for this mini security council. We need to compute the probability that a given nonveto country is pivotal. Once that is done, everything else will follow. To compute the probability that country 2 is pivotal, the argument is as follows. Country 2 will be in second place in a random ordering 1/3 of the time. We need to compute the probability that country 1 is ahead of country 2 in this ordering. To do so, we need to know how many different combinations could precede 2 in the random ordering and how many of these combinations contain country 1. This is a problem in combinatorics, for which the combinations function $C(n,m)$—choose m items of n available—is essential. The value of $C(n,m)$ is given by

$$C(n,m) = \frac{n!}{[m!(n-m)!]}$$

There are two countries available for first place in the random ordering, one with a veto and the other without. Clearly, the probability of choosing the one with the veto power from these two is 1/2. Here is how to get this probability, using the combinations function. Start with

$C(1,1)$ = the number of ways of choosing one country with a veto
            from the set containing one country with a veto

$C(1,0)$ = the number of ways of choosing 0 countries without a veto
            from the set containing 1 country without a veto

$C(2,1)$ = the number of ways of choosing 1 country from the set
            containing 2 countries

Then the probability of choosing one country with a veto from the set containing two countries is

$$\frac{[C(1,1)][C(1,0)]}{C(2,1)} = \frac{(1)(1)}{(2)} = \frac{1}{2}$$

the same as before. This more complicated method is the one used for bigger security councils.

Next, the probability is 1/3 that country 2 is in second place. Multiplying these two probabilities, we get

$$\text{Shap}(2) = \frac{1}{3}\left(\frac{1}{2}\right) = \frac{1}{6}$$

as before. Now apply symmetry to get

$$\text{Shap}(2) = \text{Shap}(3) = \frac{1}{6}$$

Finally, to account for all the power, we have

$$\text{Shap}(1) = 1 - \text{Shap}(2) - \text{Shap}(3) = \frac{4}{6}$$

These answers check with our previous ones, and we didn't have to go through all the random orderings to get them.

Now we are ready to tackle the Security Council as it currently stands. A nonveto country has to be in ninth place in a random ordering to be pivotal. The probability of this is 1/15. Moreover, all five veto countries have to be in the random ordering already in order for this nonveto country to be pivotal. The probability of a nonveto country being preceded by all five veto countries and three nonveto countries is given by

$$\frac{[C(5,5)][C(9,3)]}{C(14,8)} = \frac{1}{33}$$

Multiplying these two probabilities leads to the Shapley value for a nonveto country,

$$\text{Shap}(\text{nonveto country}) = \left(\frac{1}{15}\right)\left(\frac{1}{33}\right) = \frac{1}{495}$$

or about 0.2%, a very small number. A nonveto country as things now stand has minimal power in the Security Council. Even the 10 nonveto countries taken together only have about 2% of the power. This leaves 98% of the power to be divided up evenly among the five countries with veto power. Each of these has 98%/5 = 19.6% of the available power.

There are two scenarios under which Germany and Japan could join the Security Council. In the first of these, they become permanent members, but without a veto, and the Security Council remains at size 15. Under this scenario, Germany and Japan would each have 0.2% of the power, up from their current 0%, and France and the United Kingdom would retain their current power of 19.6% each. This scenario would only have an affect on nonpermanent members. The United Nations has 183 member states. Right now, 178 of these are not permanent members of the Security Council, and these countries have an equal chance of getting one of the $15 - 5 = 10$ seats not held by the veto powers. Thus, each of these countries has a $10/178 = 5.6\%$ chance of being on the Security Council. If two more countries get permanent seats on the Security Council, then this probability drops to $8/176$, or 4.7%. The countries of the Third World are the big losers in the first scenario. Under the second scenario, Germany and Japan become permanent members, but with a veto, and the Security Council grows to size 17. To see the implications of this situation, we need to perform some more Shapley value calculations. Intuitively, it seems this would have a big impact on the power of every current veto player. As we shall see, not only do the veto countries become less powerful, but there is also a marked negative impact on the power of nonveto countries.

Consider a Security Council with 7 veto countries and 10 nonveto countries. Under three-fifths majority rule, it would take 11 countries, including all 7 veto countries, to form a winning coalition. A nonveto country would have to be in 11th place in a random ordering to be pivotal. The probability of being in 11th place in a random ordering of 17 players is $1/17$. Moreover, all 7 veto countries would have to be present already in the random ordering in order for this nonveto country to be pivotal. The probability of this event is given by

$$\frac{[(C(7,7)][C(9,3)]}{C(16,10)} = \frac{3}{286}$$

Multiplying these two probabilities, we get

$$\text{Shap(nonveto country)} = \left(\frac{1}{17}\right)\left(\frac{3}{286}\right) = \frac{3}{4862}$$

or about 0.06%. Each nonveto country loses about one-third of its power, which wasn't that big to start with. All nonveto countries taken together have 0.6% of the power. This leaves 99.4% of the power to be divided up among the 7 veto countries. Each of them would get $99.4\%/7 = 14.2\%$ of the available power. For a current veto power, such as France or the United Kingdom, this represents a drop of almost 20%—a bitter pill to swallow. Under this second scenario, both Third World countries and current veto-power members are losers.

To change the Security Council requires a two-thirds approval among the 183 member states. Hence, 122 member states must approve. Next, these member states must get the approval of their national legislatures. Finally, every veto-power state must refrain from vetoing the proposal. This is a tough set of requirements to meet. It is estimated that it will take at least a decade before Germany and Japan are in any position to take seats on the United Nations Security Council, whatever the scenario.

⣎ SUMMARY

1. Voting is a major part of business and economic life. Proxy fights, votes to oust a CEO, and lobbying to affect economic policy are all examples.

2. The median voter theorem gives conditions under which, in a 2-candidate election, the candidates will appeal to the voter in the middle of the distribution of voters' favorite points. When the distribution of voters' favorite points is symmetrical, the candidates position themselves in the middle of the political spectrum.

3. When there are more than three candidates, the median voter theorem no longer holds. Many voting rules try to extend majority rule to this case, including plurality rule and Condorcet's rule.

4. Plurality rule has several defects, among them that it may elect a minority candidate. This result has happened several times in U.S. elections for president.

5. Strategic voting occurs when a voter fills out the ballot other than in accord with personal preferences and thereby gets a better outcome. A voting rule is truthful if no voter ever has an incentive to vote strategically. Plurality voting is not truthful.

6. In a multicandidate election, if a voting rule is efficient, decisive, truthful, and neutral, then it must be dictatorial. Conversely, dictatorship is efficient, decisive, truthful, and neutral—but not very appealing, given its massive concentration of power.

7. Positional voting rules are used in many sports elections, for instance, for national collegiate football champion. Strategic voting is rampant in such voting rules.

8. The coalition function for a voting game focuses on whether a coalition is winning or not. A winning coalition can take control of the voting process to achieve its ends.

9. A voter is pivotal when adding that voter to a coalition turns it into a winning coalition. The Shapley value of a player in a voting game is the probability that the player is pivotal. The Shapley value provides a measure of voting power.

10. The U.S. proposal to add Germany and Japan to the UN Security Council as permanent members with veto power would decrease the Shapley value of existing Security Council members by about 20% each.

■ KEY WORDS

issue spectrum
median voter theorem
distribution of voters' favorite points
plurality rule
strategic voting
decisiveness
truthfulness
neutrality
multicandidate elections
positional voting rules

Borda voting rule
simple game
winning coalition
Shapley value
marginal product
pivotal
dummy
dictator
veto player
United Nations Security Council

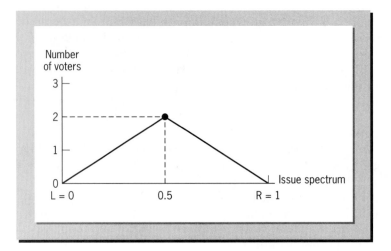

Figure 16.10.   Triangular distribution of voters' favorite points.

◼️ PROBLEMS

1.   In a discrete issue spectrum, there are 2.5 million voters on the Left, 1 million voters in the Center, and 0.5 million voters on the Right. Draw the normal form of the 2-candidate election and find the solution.

2.   Suppose that the distribution of voters' favorite points is triangular and symmetrical, as shown in Figure 16.10. Prove the median voter theorem in this case. A diagram of candidate utility, such as Figure 16.6, may help.

3.   Suppose that the distribution of voters' favorite points is asymmetrical, as shown in Figure 16.11. Find the median voter. Prove the median voter theorem in this case.

4.   In a discrete issue spectrum, half the voters are on the Left, and half are on the Right. Find an equilibrium where the candidates stake out different positions. Does this kind of situation deserve to be called polarized?

5.   Define the core of a voting game. (*Hint:* Compare this to the core of a matching game.) Show that the Condorcet winner in section 16.3 is in the core of the voting game.

6.   Suppose that there are three candidates for MVP and that Borda's rule is being used. Show that a coalition with more than 4/7 of all the voters can guarantee any outcome it wants.

7.   Which of the following conditions does Borda's rule satisfy: efficiency, decisiveness, truthfulness, or neutrality? Which does it fail?

8.   Show that the provisions of the U.S. Constitution for making a bill law satisfy nonnullity, monotonicity, and exclusivity. What would happen if the Constitution did not satisfy these provisions?

9.   Consider the following mini security council. There are four members,

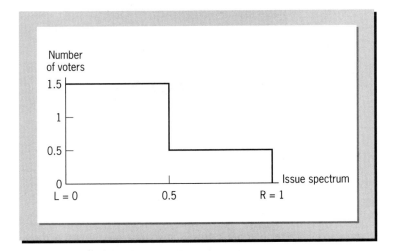

Figure 16.11. Asymmetrical distribution of voters' favorite points.

one of whom has a veto. Compute the Shapley value. Describe the effect on countries' power when a nonveto country is added.

10. It is hard to explain why the United States is pushing to get Japan on the United Nations Security Council in view of the effect this change would have on the power of current members. Try to explain this action in light of the trade negotiations between the United States and Japan (see Chapter 12). Could this be part of a larger bargain between the world's two largest economies?

Suggestions for Further Reading

You have reached the end of a fairly long book. If you have come this far and want to go further, there are many excellent sources for you to consult, some of which have already been cited in the text. These sources can be broken down into four categories: advanced textbooks, surveys, special topics, and journals.

First, many higher-level textbooks are available. Here are five that I have found especially valuable:

Ken Binmore, *Fun and Games: A Text on Game Theory,* Heath, Lexington, Mass., 1992. This book is especially strong on questions of rationality and knowledge.

James W. Friedman, *Game Theory with Applications to Economics,* Oxford University Press, Oxford, 1990. This book is valuable for its balanced coverage, and it comes with all the necessary proofs.

Drew Fudenberg and Jean Tirole, *Game Theory,* MIT Press, Cambridge, 1991. This book covers only noncooperative games, but it covers them extremely well.

David M. Kreps, *A Course in Microeconomic Theory,* Princeton University Press, Princeton, N.J., 1990. The last half of this book is devoted to game theory and includes excellent applications to economics.

Roger B. Myerson, *Game Theory: Analysis of Conflict,* Harvard University Press, Cambridge, 1991. This book is especially strong on questions of mechanism design and incomplete information.

Second, six (soon to be eight) really useful surveys are available. The nice thing about a good survey is that it can take you through the important results of the last 10 or 20 years and bring you right up to the research frontier. These surveys are:

Robert J. Aumann and Sergio Hart, eds., *Handbook of Game Theory,* vol. 1, North-Holland, Amsterdam, 1993. This book represents the state of the art in game theory; it contains 19 survey articles, ranging in topics from Chess to auctions to matching games. Two more volumes of the *Handbook* are in production. If you want to see what has been done in a particular topic in the last 10 years, you can find it in this source.

John Eatwell, Murray Milgate, and Peter Newman, eds., *The New Palgrave Game Theory,* W.W. Norton, New York, 1989. This book, for those with a taste for encyclopedia articles, contains articles on all the key terms in game theory.

John H. Kagel and Alvin E. Roth, eds., *Handbook of Experimental Economics,* Princeton University Press, Princeton, 1995. This handbook contains survey articles on all the major aspects of games that have been studied in the behavior laboratory. The articles provide a detailed follow-up to the experiments presented in the appendixes on externalities (Chapter 4), bargaining (Chapters 6 and 12), learning (Chapter 8), and auctions (Chapter 11).

Martin Shubik, *Game Theory in the Social Sciences: Concepts and Solutions,* MIT Press, Cambridge, 1982, and *A Game-Theoretic Approach to Political Economy,* MIT Press, Cambridge, 1984. These two surveys are unrivaled in their coverage of game theory from its beginnings to the early 1980s.

H. Peyton Young, ed., *Negotiation Analysis,* University of Michigan Press, Ann Arbor, 1991. This book provides very readable survey articles on bargaining and arbitration.

The third category of further reading consists of special topics. Again, many of these have already been cited in the text.

Matthew B. Canzoneri and Dale Henderson, *Monetary Policy in Interdependent Economics: A Game-Theoretic Approach,* MIT Press, Cambridge, 1991. This book studies central issues in monetary economics and macroeconomics using 2- and 3-player games.

John Harsanyi and Reinhard Selten, *A General Theory of Equilibrium Selection in Games,* MIT Press, Cambridge, 1988. This book develops a theory that finds a unique solution for any finite game in normal form.

John McMillan, *Game Theory in International Economics,* Harwood, London, 1986. This book shows the many ways in which game theory applies to questions in international trade and finance.

Martin J. Osborne and Ariel Rubinstein, *Bargaining and Markets,* Academic Press, San Diego, 1990. This book applies Stahl–Rubinstein bargaining theory to a wide range of market contexts, as well as to negotiations.

Elinor Ostrom, Roy Gardner, and James Walker, *Rules, Games, and Common-Pool Resources,* University of Michigan Press, Ann Arbor, 1994. This book shows how game theory applies to a wide variety of problems in resource economics and global environmental change.

Alvin E. Roth and Marilda A. Oliveira Sotomayor, *Two-Sided Matching: A Study in Game-Theoretic Modeling and Analysis,* Cambridge University Press: Cambridge, 1990. This is the classic study of the material on matching games presented in Chapter 15.

Herbert Scarf, *The Computation of Economic Equilibria,* Yale University Press, New Haven, 1973. This book studies core equivalence in great detail and exhibits a machine algorithm for computing points in the core when many inequalities are involved.

Reinhard Selten, ed., *Game Equilibrium Models,* vol. 1, *Evolution and Game Dynamics,* Springer-Verlag, Berlin, 1991. This book contains articles on evolutionary stability and bounded rationality (Chapter 8), as well as other applications. Volumes 2 through 4 in this series contain articles on experimental games, voting games, and bargaining games.

Finally, the fourth category of sources is scholarly journals. These journals represent the edge of the research frontier. Two journals are devoted entirely to game theory, *Games and Economic Behavior* and the *International Journal of Game Theory.* Most scholarly journals in business and economics publish at least some articles applying game theory to their subject area, among them the *Journal of Finance,* the *Journal of Economic Management and Strategy,* the *Journal of Economic Theory,* and *Econometrica.*

Games List

The following games are explored in this book:

Asymmetrical Hawk versus Dove
Asymmetrical Market Niche
Bankruptcy
Barbarians at the Gate
Battle of the Networks
Blackjack
Caveat Emptor
Centipede
Chess
Cigarette Television Advertising
Competitive Advantage
Conscription in the Civil War
Coordination
Depositor versus S & L
Divide a Dollar
Escape and Evasion
Everyday low pricing
Frogs Call for Mates
Hawk versus Dove
Lemons
Let's Make a Deal
Liar's Poker
Mutually Assured Destruction (MAD)

Majority Rule
Market Niche
Market Niches (repeated Market Niche)
Matching Pennies
Money-Back Guarantee
Mutual Defense
Pick the Largest Number
Poker
Pot of Gold
Principal versus Agent
Prisoner's Dilemma
Small Business
Solitaire
Speed Chess
Subsidized Small Business
Telex versus IBM
Ten
This Offer is Good for a Limited Time Only
Tic-Tac-Toe
Tragedy of the Commons
Ultimatum
Video System Coordination

To locate these games, check the Index.

Index

*n entries refer to footnotes.

471